SHARON

SHARON

ISRAEL'S WARRIOR-POLITICIAN

Anita Miller, Jordan Miller
& Sigalit Zetouni

Academy Chicago Publishers
&
Olive Publishing

Published in 2002 by
Academy Chicago Publishers & Olive Publishing
363 West Erie Street
Chicago, Illinois 60610

Cover Photo by Michael Kramer
Maps by Marc Miller
Photos provided by Israel Government Press Office and The Library of Congress

Front end-sheet: Joshua Neustein, *Totem of Middle East, 1992*
Back end-sheet: Joshua Neustein, *Map of Israel Inverted* (detail), *1993*

Printed in the U.S.A.

Library of Congress Cataloging-in-Publication Data

Miller, Anita.
 Sharon: Israel's warrior-politician / Anita Miller, Jordan Miller & Sigalit
 Zetouni.
  p. cm.
 ISBN 0-89733-496-5
 1. Sharon, Ariel. 2. Prime ministers—Israel—Biography. 3. Generals—
 Israel—Biography. 4. Israel—Politics and government. I. Miller, Jordan. II.
 Zetouni, Sigalit. III. Title.
 DS126.6.S42 Z48 2002
 956.9405'4'092—dc21
 [B]   2001053485

CONTENTS

Photographs between pages 216–217 and 472–473.

EARLY YEARS

—————

ARIEL SHARON WAS BORN on February 27, 1928, son of Samuil and Dvora Scheinerman, in Kfar Malal, a small agricultural community, or *moshav*, in central Palestine, some fifteen miles northeast of Tel Aviv on the coastal Plain of Sharon.

Samuil's father, Mordechai, a Hebrew teacher in Brest Litovsk, was a dedicated Zionist who had been a delegate to the World Zionist Congress in Basel, Switzerland, in 1897, and had spent two years in Palestine from 1910 to 1912, teaching school in Rehovot. But he found life there too difficult for his wife and children and returned to Russia, intending some day to go back and settle permanently in Palestine. This was an ambition that did eventually materialize; he settled with his family in Tel Aviv just a few years before he died.

Mordechai Scheinerman indoctrinated his son Samuil with his own fervent Zionism, teaching him Hebrew and Bible studies at home, in addition to the classical education the boy received in Russian schools. When he was graduated from secondary school, Samuil, preparing for life as a farmer, entered the school of agriculture at the University of Tiflis near Baku where the family had moved to escape the fighting in the first World War. It was at Tiflis that Samuil met Dvora Schneirov, a medical student at the university, one of eight children, whose father was a timber merchant in a small Belorussian village.

Four years after the 1917 Russian Revolution, the Red Army was moving toward Baku and Tiflis. Samuil had finished his studies, but Dvora needed two more years to earn her medical degree, which she desperately wanted. However, because Samuil was a known Zionist, the Communists would certainly have arrested, and, most likely, executed him. Up to that time, he had been teaching Hebrew at the Zionist Club in Tiflis. On a day when he happened to be late to class, Communist activists raided the club and all the members were arrested and eventually sent to Siberia. After the raid, in February, 1922, Samuil and Dvora, who were recently married, fled to Palestine.

Dvora had hoped to continue her studies in their new home, but she found herself in a wilderness. This was very difficult for her: she knew only Russian and had never intended to become a farmer. She had to give up her dream of becoming a doctor, and this sacrifice was to haunt her for the rest of her life. And while she worked hard and was a dedicated helpmate to her husband, she did not entirely share his views. Years later, she said that her husband "had converted her to Zionism by force."[1]

In 1921, Palestine was in turmoil. Bloody battles were raging between the Jews and Arabs and, in addition, there were internal conflicts amongst the Jewish pioneers themselves over security and land cultivation. It was against this background that in 1922 Dvora and Samuil settled in Kfar Malal on land purchased by the Jewish National Fund, an agency of the World Zionist Organization. Samuil chose this *moshav* over a *kibbutz*, a collective where everything was owned in common. Samuil was not interested in socialism, to put it mildly; he was a strong individualist who wanted to own his own land, and in a moshav, although farmers lived together in a community, each family owned its own house on its own property while the main farming and marketing operations were pooled.

Kfar Malal is now a fully developed, lushly landscaped village. But when the Scheinermans first moved there the settlement lacked water and electricity and the couple had to live in a tent while they built their own cabin. It was dangerous, too: the village had been destroyed by Arabs the year before, and was being rebuilt by the moshavniks. Land acquired by the early settlers was not always in arable condition, but was often a wilderness of stones, sand dunes and marshes.

The British Mandate Authority considered the growing Jewish settlements as yet another irritant in an already volatile Palestine. In 1929, a wave of anti-Jewish riots broke out to protest Jewish immigration and the practice of Jewish prayer at the Western Wall. In less than a week, 133 Jews were killed and 340 wounded and many more inhabitants of Hebron were later slaughtered.[2] This violence led the settlers—without permission from the British authorities—to reorganize their defenses, creating a new militia called the *Haganah*.

Sharon grew up during the time when the *Yishuv* (as the Palestine Jewish community was called prior to the establishment of the State of Israel) was literally fighting for its survival. It is probably not possible to exaggerate the traumatic effect of this violence and social ferment on the young Sharon's consciousness. Since Kfar Malal had been destroyed by Arabs once before, the settlers could never feel safe. Samuil carried a pistol, and Dvora too knew how to use it. Samuil was ambushed twice, once coming back from an orchard and once by a sniper when he was examining a sabotaged irrigation line. Both times he escaped unscathed. From the time of his bar mitzvah, Sharon shared night guard duty, holding a knotted club, scanning the fields for marauders who could come silently in the dark to threaten the settlers' lives.[3]

In reflecting on his early life, Sharon credits his parents' "strength, determination and stubbornness" for their success as pioneers and for the influence these qualities had on his own life and perspective. They worked hard, but were obviously not given to demonstrations of open affection. "They did not wear their hearts on their sleeves,"[4]

Sharon recalls, perhaps rather wistfully. The Scheinermans differed from their fellow moshavniks not only temperamentally, but also politically. Although Samuil was certainly an ardent Zionist, he stood out in the isolated agricultural communal world of the moshav as a militant individualist and this added to the difficulties of the Scheinermans' already hard life in Kfar Malal. There was more than simply political disagreement; Sharon speaks of a festering hostility that had a corrosive effect on the community. For one thing, Samuil wanted to be addressed by the title "Agronomist Scheinerman"— which the other farmers refused to do, resenting what they understandably considered a display of arrogance and self-importance.

Furthermore, Samuil built a fence with a locked gate around his orchard and even planted a grove of trees as a sort of buffer between his land and the road. The fact that his was the only fenced property in the settlement further alienated him and his family from other moshav members. He and his wife had little or no dedication to community, something which was important to settlers at that time. One incident which exemplifies their attitude toward their neighbors occurred when Ariel was only three years old: he badly cut his chin in a fall, and instead of consulting the doctor in their own community, Dvora ran to the office of a Russian doctor more than two miles away with the child in her arms.[5] There were objections also to Samuil's radical agricultural innovations, although he was a trained agronomist, and ultimately his new methods of farming were to be adopted by many other Jewish settlements.

But according to Sharon himself, arguments about crops or agricultural techniques were far less traumatic than the bitterness that followed the murder in 1933 of Chaim Arlozoroff, a Zionist socialist leader. Sharon's parents were outraged by the fact that other Jews were being accused of killing him, a crime allegedly perpetrated by the followers of Zeev Jabotinsky, a militant Revisionist. Although Samuil was, like his neighbors, a member of David Ben-Gurion's Mapai (Zionist Labor Party) his anger at the charges was so intense that it caused a serious rift between himself and the other moshavniks who were equally bitter on the other side. Feelings ran so high that the Scheinermans were barred from visiting the local clinic and synagogue and from using the moshav's cooperative truck, which meant that they could neither get deliveries from it nor use it to collect their produce.[6] As a measure of the hatred that existed between them, in his will Samuil specified that no one from Kfar Malal speak at his funeral and that the aforementioned truck not be used to transport his body to the cemetery.[7]

Dvora supported her husband in all his work. But, as we have seen, she lacked her husband's zealous dedication to Zionism. She frequently thumbed through her old Russian medical books, reliving the student days that had meant so much to her. Nonetheless, she worked barefoot in their citrus groves and fields and tended the goats and cows. She scrimped and saved every way possible for her children's education, even depriving herself of personal necessities. Both Dvora and Samuil—unlike most other moshavniks—were intent on their children having a high school education that included liberal arts.

According to some moshavniks who remember them, Dvora was very friendly. It was Samuil who was arrogant and remote. But Dvora did have a strong personality; it was she who made sure that both Ariel and Yehudit—Sharon's sister, two years older than he—took violin lessons and put particular pressure on her daughter to excel on the instrument. Sharon quit taking lessons fairly soon, but to this day one of his greatest pleasures is listening to classical music.

Years later, neighbors reminisced about the family. Rahel Gaffney, a classmate of Sharon's in grade school, said, "There was plenty of intelligence in that house. It was poor—I remember the jug under the leaking roof—but you felt that you entered into a world of intellect. They weren't any less Zionist than the others, but they were more interested in cultural pursuits than we were. The father had his own opinions, but the children were like the rest of us. We all played in the sandy road together."[8] Yosef Margalit, who was in the same class with Yehudit said that "no one called them Yehudit and Ariel. They were Dita and Arik."[9]

Rahel Gaffney mentioned a time in the fourth or fifth grade when the class became angry at one of the teachers. "We decided to boycott the school, but Arik disagreed. He said, 'I came to school to learn and if there is a problem with the teacher we ought to sit and talk.' We didn't go to school for three days and at the end we were punished. But Arik held to his opinion that we should have continued to go to class. I don't remember him ever lying. Sometimes people didn't like what he said, but he always said what he really thought. Arik always knew where he was headed. His mother always told him that it was important to be educated and to have a goal. He never sat quietly. Very ambitious."[10]

Sharon joined the Labor Youth Movement and his group counselor, Yosef Gilboa, remembered that young Scheinerman sometimes helped him to discipline disobedient children, and that even then he disliked disorder.[11]

In 1941, when Sharon was thirteen, he started high school in Tel Aviv, a long bus ride and an hour's walk from the moshav. He greatly enjoyed the new world that opened up to him in the city, made many friends, and was an eager student. His experience at school was a welcome relief from the rigors of his father's demanding discipline, although the boy did not question his parents' isolation from their neighbors.

The turmoil in the Middle East accelerated during the Second World War, and Allied troops moved back and forth across Palestine, responding to the Axis threats to Egypt and the Suez Canal. The Jewish Agency, headed by David Ben-Gurion, was agitating for a Jewish Army, a brigade that was destined to come into existence within three years. In the meantime, the Haganah, a poorly armed and partially undercover militia, was recruiting Jewish youth. Sharon joined when he was fourteen, and received training on Saturdays and one night a week. Soon he was transferred into the "Signallers," an elite force that also received training from the Jewish Settlement Police, established nationwide by the British to protect both the Jewish settlements and British installations.

Later he joined the Gadna, an acronym for "Youth Battalions," where he got one of his first tastes of concentrated military training in Ruchama, a remote kibbutz in the Negev desert. Sharon thus received military training from the British as well as from the Haganah—this despite the fact that the British were doing everything they could to prevent Jewish refugees from entering Palestine, causing frustration and rage to build in the Jewish community.[12]

As early as 1907, Zionists had established a tradition of guarding Jewish settlements with a secret organization called *Ha-shomer*; Ben-Gurion had joined it when he first arrived in Palestine. These men, Martin van Creveld says, "were the first to take the military road not merely as a means to a military end, but with the explicit goal of shedding the supposed characteristics of the Wandering Jew, replacing him with a new, hardy, and courageous type who would take up arms in defense of himself, his settlement, and his country."[13] When Ha-shomer was disbanded in 1920, it was replaced by Haganah, which, though illegal, was more or less tolerated by the British. The Haganah was later associated with the *Histadrut*,[14] or National Labor Foundation, until an Arab uprising in 1929 demonstrated the importance of a strong militia, and control passed to Ben-Gurion, as head of the Jewish Agency. Gradually Haganah was strengthened by intensive training and an inflow of armaments with support from international Jewish communities. In addition, in the early thirties, Jewish immigration to Palestine increased markedly, spurred by the rise of the Nazis in Europe and the closing of admission to the United States.

In May, 1936, the Supreme Arab Committee called a general strike that lasted for almost six months and gave rise to innumerable terrorist attacks against both Jews and the British.[15] After a violent battle between the British Army and Arab guerrillas in March, 1938, a reasonable calm was restored. Although sporadic attacks were still occurring when World War II began in September, 1939, the British and the Haganah—the latter profiting from the excellent training of British Captain Orde Wingate—held this unrest to a minimum. However, the situation was not improved when in May, 1939, the British issued the White Paper, refusing to honor the Balfour Declaration, a promise made in 1917 to the Zionists, led by Dr Chaim Weizmann, to establish a national home for the Jewish people in Palestine. (The Arabs, for their part, were enraged by this promise, which they considered a betrayal of British promises made to *them* in 1916 and 1917 when they rebelled against the Ottoman Empire.) The White Paper limited Jewish purchase of land and immigration and promised Arab independence in the country in ten years. The reaction of the Yishuv to this news can be imagined. Hope that the Zionists could work with the British was abandoned, although there was certainly awareness that the Axis powers presented an imminent danger.[16]

There were other small military organizations besides the Haganah in the late thirties: the *Irgun Tsvai Leumi* (National Military Organization) had engaged in guerrilla activities against Arabs and British, but at the outbreak of war had announced it would cooperate with the British against the Axis. However in December, 1941, the *Struma,* a decrepit cattle boat holding 769 Jewish refugees, was turned away from the Constantinople harbor after a wait of two months while the Turks and British negotiated; in the end, the Turks refused to allow the passengers entry to Palestine. The ship sank as soon as it went to sea, and both crew and passengers—including 250 women and 70 children—perished with the exception of a single survivor.[17] The Irgun split over this catastrophe and an extremist faction, led by Abraham (Yair) Stern, broke away to resume actions independently against the British. They were known as the Stern Gang.

While the Jewish Agency counseled patience and cooperation, Haganah organized "special" units which engaged in covert activities like smuggling and assassinations, against both the British and the Arabs. Nevertheless, the British frequently were forced to call on the Haganah special companies for support in times of great danger. Haganah wanted a Jewish regiment to fight in the war and to this end built the *Palmach*—specially trained "shock companies"—with British permission. But when in 1943 the tide of the war turned and it was obvious that the Allies were going to win, the British turned against the Haganah.

By late 1943, both the Stern Gang and the Irgun, now led by Menachem Begin—who was later to become prime minister—were carrying on terrorist activities against the British. There were now three separate Jewish military groups: the Haganah, the Irgun and the Stern Gang. By the end of the war, they were all intent on ridding the country of the British, but they could not work together. In fact, they hated and even raided one another. Haganah was the only one with some legal status—the British reluctantly ceded them the right to protect remote settlements—and in order to avoid British retaliation for the assassination of Lord Moyne, the British ambassador in Cairo, Haganah tracked down Irgun and Stern members and turned them over to the British.

The high school students were divided between these two radical factions. Sharon himself sympathized with the extremists and hated what the Haganah was doing. He did not object to their stopping terrorist activity, but he did not believe they should turn these people over to the British. In 1945, when he was graduated from high school, World War II had ended, but he knew that the struggle for control was just beginning. Despite his reservations, he entered a secret Haganah squad leader training group in a remote kibbutz on the edge of the Negev Desert. After two months, he had failed to achieve the corporal rank he wanted, becoming only private first class. He went back to Kfar Malal, planning to join the Palmach, the "shock force" which had been organized in 1941 by the Haganah and which had become an elite force of three thousand. It seemed the logical place to learn to handle weapons, get tactical field training and become familiar with the country's rugged landscape, an important step for anyone with military ambitions. But the Palmach, as a division of the Haganah, had worked for the British in monitoring the activities of the growing number of Jewish extremists— and had, in fact, turned some of them over to the British, enraging many settlers, including Samuil Scheinerman.

Sharon recalls that, one day as they were working together in the orange groves, his father told him that he was free to follow whatever course in life he wished, but that he wanted him to swear that he would "never, never participate in turning Jews over to non-Jews."[18] Samuil did not mention the Palmach by name, but his meaning was clear to Sharon, who honored his father's request. At this time, the Stern Gang and the Irgun were bombing police stations and army outposts and blowing up bridges, railroad lines and coast guard stations. A number of perpetrators were caught and hanged. Sharon's heart was with these extremists: he admired what he considered their heroic dedication and self-sacrifice. But at the same time he seems to have felt ambivalent about what they were doing. He says he was going through his own "internal struggle," because he did not believe that people should just "go off and do whatever they wanted to do" even if what they did required a great deal of courage.[19]

In any case, he gave up the idea of joining the Palmach and instead enrolled in the British-sponsored Jewish Settlement Police; this provided cover for his connection with the Haganah, since the British police commanders showed up only for inspections. While he served in the police, Sharon continued to live at home and help his father, who was showing signs of the heart trouble that was eventually to kill him. It was at this time that Sharon met Margalit

Zimmerman, called "Gali," a sixteen-year-old girl who had recently arrived from Rumania, and who lived on a neighboring farm. Sharon had to cut a hole in his father's fence so that he and Gali could meet.[20]

But the political situation did not leave much time for courtship. Relations between the Arabs and the Jews were worsening day by day, and Sharon had to be called up frequently to patrol the terrain at night to hunt down Arab raiders. It was then that he began to develop the facility for memorizing landmarks and rock formations. The first operation that Sharon led was one intended to confiscate the prized car of a local sheik to discourage him from participating in undercover activities. Sharon led a group of ten youths to a spot on a narrow dirt road, which they blocked with a long table used for crating oranges. The car came down the road and careened to a stop. The driver, who was the sheik's son, leapt out and ran off, but took the car keys with him. Sharon chased him for half a mile before giving up. The car had to be hidden before a British patrol turned up, but engines were a mystery to most of the farmers who made up the squad. Finally, one of the men was able to start the motor, and after what seemed like an eternity, they drove the car into the barn of a nearby sympathizer.[21]

By the fall of 1945, the Haganah had joined with the Irgun and the Sternists in the anti-British struggle, Haganah concentrating on smuggling in immigrants, building illegal settlements and organizing demonstrations, while the two smaller groups, now virtually working as one, indulged in assassinations, ambushes and bombings. Efforts were made to avoid targeting civilians.

Incident was piled on incident; the British lost the public relations war when they interned Holocaust survivors behind barbed wire in camps in Palestine and Cyprus. Things got even worse when the British renegades—in retaliation for the Irgunist bombing of British police headquarters in the King David Hotel in Jerusalem on

July 22, 1946, killing ninety-one people, including civilians—blew up military vehicles on Ben Yehuda Street in the same city, destroying two apartment buildings, also killing and wounding fifty-two Jews.[22]

Finally, in February, 1947, when Sharon was nineteen, the British, having failed in several attempts to negotiate a compromise between the factions, exhausted and frustrated by their appearance as Goliath in a struggle with David, gave up and dumped the problem in the lap of the United Nations, where it was decided by the end of the summer that partition was the only answer. On November 29, 1947, this decision was put to a UN vote. Sharon and his family listened to the tally on the radio, as everyone in Palestine was doing. The vote was thirty-three in favor, thirteen against and ten abstentions. There were celebrations in Kfar Malal: there was now officially a State of Israel. But everyone knew that the Arabs would not accept it. In six months, the British Mandate would end, and then the surrounding Arab states had made clear their avowed intention to attack and wipe the new country off the face of the earth.[23]

On December 12, Sharon was mobilized into what was now a legal, full-time army. All of Israel's military units were now combined into an army which ultimately became the Israeli Defense Forces (IDF). The Grand Mufti of Jerusalem had returned to the Middle East from Nazi Germany and declared a *jihad*, a holy war, against the Jews. Arab forces—organized into what was called the Army of Salvation—were operating around Jerusalem and south of Tel Aviv. In the winter of 1947–48, the British pulled out, and the Arabs took control of the country's roads and bridges in order to cut off Jewish towns and settlements from each other, so that each could be dealt with separately. Not surprisingly, Kfar Malal and its surrounding villages were targets of this military tactic. There was not enough Jewish manpower to take over the roads, so ten-man squads and larger platoons concentrated on raids and ambushes to distract the enemy and keep them on the defensive.

Gradually, Sharon became a leader of these actions, which involved travelling in the dark of night through unmarked fields and streams, or *wadis*, so that the men could be in place to strike before dawn. These were basically small guerrilla activities. In the winter of 1948, Sharon was chosen to lead an attack against Bir Addas, a fortified Arab village used as a base by Iraqi irregulars near Kfar Malal and neighboring settlements. This was his group's first experience of this kind: it was not a small guerrilla action, but a sustained attack that called for coordination and careful planning.

The operation was not a success: Sharon was chagrined by the order to retreat issued from field headquarters. He was upset by the casualties his group had taken and considered the attack a waste, even though the next day the Iraqis pulled out of Bir Addas.[24] The good news for him was that he was promoted to platoon commander. He was going to lead young men he had grown up with in Kfar Malal, whose families had quarrelled incessantly with the Scheinermans. But now all that was forgotten by the moshavniks in a burst of good feeling toward Sharon and his entire platoon, which was part of what was called the Alexandroni Brigade.

Throughout the winter of 1947–48, there were daily skirmishes and battles and many casualties. On May 14, 1948, at 4:30 in the afternoon, at a special session of the Jewish National Council of Palestine—held in Tel Aviv because Jerusalem was besieged—David Ben-Gurion declared that the State of Israel would come into being at midnight when the British Mandate expired. To Sharon, who had been overwhelmed with joy at the United Nations decision, this announcement meant basically that the Syrians, Lebanese and Egyptians, together with the Jordanian and Iraqi Arab Legion led by British officers, would swarm across the borders intent on mass destruction. What ensued was called the War of Independence by the Israelis.

When the British evacuated Jerusalem on May 14 and 15, it had already been cut off from the rest of Jewish Palestine for several weeks. The Old City was being pounded by artillery and there was constant fighting over the highway between Tel Aviv and Jerusalem, which was the only conduit for supplies to the besieged city. The Jews could only sporadically open the approaches before they were driven off or departed to defend some other endangered area. Meanwhile in Jerusalem, food and water had virtually run out and the situation was desperate.

A key point on the Tel Aviv–Jerusalem highway was the village of Latrun. In late May 1948, Ben-Gurion and the General Staff of the Haganah decided that it was crucial to take Latrun so that supplies could be convoyed to the Old City. Although their manpower resources were stretched beyond the breaking point, they created the Seventh Brigade, largely with immigrants who had just been released from British detention camps in Cyprus, but with a battalion from the Alexandroni Brigade serving as the core of the new group.

As he watched the new recruits arrive, Sharon wrote to his parents:

> It's a very hot day and my platoon and I are relaxing in the shade of an olive grove, thinking about the impending battle. We feel as though we're part of the land, that these are our roots, that we belong here, have a right to be here.
>
> Suddenly, a convoy of trucks stops and disgorges a bunch of new recruits. They look very foreign and rather pale. They wear sleeveless sweaters, striped shirts and gray pants and speak many languages. I hear them calling to each other: names like Hershel, Yajik, Yahn and Meiteik and they seem somehow out of place among the olive trees, the rocks, the golden wheat.
>
> They come from European death camps, having crossed forbidden borders. I watch them as they take off their civilian clothes and try to fit into their new military uniforms, struggling with gear belts, asking for help from their new commanders. They are very pale and quiet, as if trying to come to terms with their strange new lives. None of them cries, and their taut

faces don't even seem to say: "Give us some breathing room after all the horrors we have suffered." And yet it is as if they really know that they are now part of yet one last battle on the long and painful road to Jewish fulfillment.[25]

The brigade wound its circuitous way in a convoy of buses to its staging area at Kibbutz Hulda, where the men rested while the immigrants received hasty training: they had entered the country only to be involved in a deadly battle for which they were completely unprepared. Sharon was uneasy about the situation in general, not only because of these raw recruits. His assignment was to drive the Jordanians from their position in the village of Latrun, which sat on a hill overlooking the Jerusalem road, then to capture first a Trappist monastery and then a Jordanian-held former British police fort, both farther down the hill. He believed he could accomplish all this, but he felt out of his element in this rocky terrain, away from his familiar orange groves.

Because of what appeared to be a last-minute argument amongst the unit's officers, Sharon's group arrived at their objective five hours behind schedule, with dawn threatening to break soon. Through a dark fog, from their protected elevated position, the Jordanians rained machine-gun and rifle fire, mortars and artillery onto the attackers, who were pinned down in an open field without any drinking water. When the fog suddenly lifted, Sharon's men found themselves exposed in bright daylight. They had no choice but to hunker down in a gully and wait for help or for nightfall to protect their retreat. After about two hours, Sharon saw to his horror that the enemy was advancing toward them in preparation for a frontal attack. The Arab soldiers advanced and retreated repeatedly, driven off by gunfire only to return again, while two enemy planes dropped bombs on the field.

Around noon, Sharon was wounded in the lower abdomen and groin. The battle continued for another two hours until the firing stopped and Sharon realized that the Israeli units had retreated and he and his men were alone. Armed Arab villagers were making their way down the hillside, pausing to deal with the dead and wounded Israeli soldiers who littered their path. The only hope was to get out of there as rapidly as possible. All the survivors were wounded, but they managed to stumble, leaning on one another, often crawling over rocks, for miles through the smoke and haze until they came upon Israeli half-tracks searching for survivors. Sharon's entire platoon had been destroyed. The Latrun station was not taken and remained an Arab bastion of defense against Israeli attack for many years afterward.

Sharon's wounds were serious: the bullet had gone through his abdomen and come out the upper part of his thigh, and he had lost a lot of blood, but his life was not in danger. As he lay in the hospital, he brooded over the defeat. He said many years later that he

was eaten up by despair and the shame of the defeat. I even thought about quitting the army. For like many others, I had enlisted in order to end the war as soon as possible and go home. I had planned to study agriculture, like my father, and work on the farm. But that awful feeling of helplessness was too terrible to forget. I had time in the hospital to analyze what had happened. Of course, I had no access to the military details, but I had learned that what we lacked most of all was 'the spirit of battle.' We had gone into the fight, but I had the feeling at the time that we hadn't tried hard enough to win. You know, somehow we were motivated more by the desire to return home safely than feeling the absolute necessity of winning the battle.

Not everyone felt that way, but most of the men did. If only we had been more intense, had a stronger will to win, we would have won.[26]

While Sharon was recovering from his wounds, the UN-sponsored truce took effect. Jerusalem was still isolated and the Egyptians were

twenty miles from Tel Aviv and had cut off settlements around
Ruhama. After a month of relative peace, the United Nations Security Council suggested that the truce continue, but the Arabs rejected this proposal; they did not want the Israeli state to develop
more credibility as time went on. The Israelis had used the time of
the truce to stockpile arms—there had not been enough rifles for
everyone—and to work to turn the fighting force into a real army
since fighting around the country had started again.

By mid-July, Sharon was well enough to rejoin his battalion,
where he noticed the welcome increase in available armaments. He
was still in pain and still upset by the memory of the defeat at Latrun. His condition was not helped when, a few weeks after his
return, he broke some ribs and injured his spine in a jeep accident.
While he was recuperating from this accident, a second truce was
declared, but was in a shambles by the middle of October. Fighting
broke out in the Negev, in Galilee and around Jerusalem, but the
siege there had been lifted. The tide in general had turned: the Lebanese had been pushed back in Galilee and the Arab Liberation Army
was decimated. Commander Yigal Allon had defeated the Egyptians at Beersheba and opened the Negev.

Sharon was appointed reconnaissance officer for his battalion
in the Alexandroni Brigade and engaged in clashes against first the
Iraqis and then against 40,000 Egyptians under the command of
Said Taha Bey, a Sudanese professional soldier trained in the British
army. Taha Bey's men were trapped in a pocket between Faluja and
Iraq el Manshiyeh, but Taha Bey, whose determination Sharon admired, refused to surrender. Fighting went on till the end of October. On December 27, a final attack was launched, but it was a
failure, on a par with the defeat at Latrun. Taha Bey finally took his
men home after a negotiated settlement.

This fiasco did not have a lasting effect on the outcome of the
war. On February 27, 1949, the Egyptians signed a final cease-fire
and by the beginning of March, the fighting had dwindled into fron-

tier skirmishes with the Egyptians, Lebanese and Jordanians. Israel was now a nation. But Sharon was plagued by nightmares and was still brooding over the deaths of his friends and the carnage and defeats in which he had been involved. It was September before he recovered his spirits. He was appointed commander of the reconnaissance company of the Golani Brigade when the Alexandroni Brigade was relegated to reserve status. Sharon was now responsible for training recruits to patrol borders, to gather intelligence and to fight at night. It was a job he relished, and did so well that in 1950 he was promoted to captain, and then to intelligence officer for the Central Command. While he was serving in this capacity, the Central Command engaged for the first time in war games against the Southern Command, headed by Moshe Dayan.[27]

Sharon was not impressed by Dayan either as a man or as a commander. When the Central Command had difficulties in a maneuver during the war games against Dayan's unit, Sharon took command of the brigade, leading it into a kibbutz near Beersheba. He believed that he had held Dayan to a standoff in the games; Dayan, however, claimed victory. Sharon was told a few days later that his job was not to lead the brigade, but to keep the commander supplied with up-to-date intelligence.[28] Sharon did not consider this a reprimand, but he resented what he perceived to be a lack of appreciation for his actions in a difficult maneuver.

About this time he contracted recurrent malaria and took a two-month leave of absence during which he went abroad for the first time, visiting relatives in Paris and friends in England. But the high point of his holiday was the time he spent in the US, staying for a while with an aunt in New York and then traveling through the South. He returned to Israel apparently cured of his malaria and feeling like a cosmopolitan, a sophisticated man of the world. He was appointed chief of intelligence for the Northern Command shortly before Moshe Dayan became commander of that group. The relationship between these two men was destined to become a complicated one.

In the fall of 1952, Sharon, now twenty-four years old, was making plans to marry Gali, who was twenty and a psychiatric nurse in a suburban Jerusalem hospital. He was not sure that he wanted to pursue a career in the army. Both his parents, but his mother in particular, wanted him to go to university; she still mourned her aborted studies. He considered studying agriculture as his father had, but he wanted to develop an understanding of Arab culture and society, so he enrolled in a Middle Eastern history program at the Hebrew University in Jerusalem, and he and Gali were married on March 29, 1953, in a simple ceremony in an army rabbi's office. He was enjoying both married life and his studies in a tiny apartment in the city, and he would have continued in school if a new wave of violence had not engulfed the country.

Moshe Dayan wrote twenty years later that it was

practically impossible to describe the tense atmosphere of the two-year-old Israeli nation. By the end of the War of Independence on March 1, 1949, the 650,000 Jewish inhabitants were in the midst of a wide-scale immigration absorption campaign.

On the other side of the border, hundreds of Arab refugees . . . [waited] for the day they could go back into what were now Jewish cities. In the meantime, they lived in tents in the big refugee camps from which they had a clear view of the homes they had fled. Their hatred of the Jews had now become a personal one.

During the first four years following the establishment of the State of Israel, the main security problem was that of infiltration—from Jordan and Egypt. At first the aims of infiltration were theft or an attempt to take over and cultivate no-man's land. Israel was in danger of reverting to a state in which ownership was established by actual possession of the land and not in accordance with a signed document. In effect, the cease-fire borders were not final ones, despite their having been agreed upon and entered onto maps. Any lapse in the rigid watch kept upon the countryside would result in a mass reoccupation of the fields and villages by the Arab refugees. This was of course dangerous, since it opened up a possibility of penetration of Arab spies along with the farmers.

As the infiltration grew . . . it began to be accompanied by violence . . . on the part of the refugees, and armed attempts to prevent these crimes on the part of the Jews. During the fifteen months after the War of Independence, 134 Jews were killed by infiltrators and 104 were wounded. Travel along the roads became dangerous; no one would leave the cities at night un-armed, and people avoided a nocturnal journey to Beersheba at all costs. Eilat was reached only by caravans, with special permission of, and surveillance by, the army.

Jews living in the border settlements would lock themselves in after dark, afraid to stir. Any unexpected suspicious noise from the stable or the cowshed would cause a serious dilemma—should one go out and check that the single cow was tied up, despite the possibility that Arab thieves were prowling about?

These first years (1949–1953) were years of insecurity. A continual effort was made to block Arab infiltration and to defend the country against military attacks from the other side of the border, and at the same time try to organize and train the Israeli army.

Zahal [the Israeli Defense Forces] tried to activate its forces against the terrorists, and a number of retaliatory raids were carried out in the Jordanian villages of Nahlin, Palma and Idna. But Zahal was not sufficiently trained for night raids, nor was it adequately equipped. The attacking units were forced to re-treat.[29]

Under these circumstances, it became increasingly difficult for Sharon to concentrate on his studies. He was deeply disturbed and disappointed by the army's failures. He knew very well that it was not a question of conscious negligence, but that the soldiers were untrained, knew neither the language nor the country, were afraid of war and wanted only to finish their service as quickly as possible, stay alive and go home. As recent immigrants, they had other problems as well: they had not yet adapted to life in a young, poor and struggling state. They had suffered through untold traumas and were worried about employment and integration into this strange new society.

The IDF could not tackle the enormous security problems facing the country in those troubled years. It could not prevent infiltration simply by hermetically sealing the borders. It could not defend itself against minor armed attacks, or retaliate effectively on a small scale, and any large-scale military activity might well lead to even larger-scale battles with serious international complications.

Many others besides Sharon* were frustrated by the IDF's inability to cope—some had served with it, some had not, but they were all deeply concerned about this lack of readiness because, obviously, Israel's survival depended on a well-trained and well-equipped military force. And they knew that these skirmishes revealed Israel's military flaws to the enemy: weakness would encourage the Arabs to renew the war, and could lead to a final defeat. In addition, lack of efficiency was damaging the army's image and making recruitment difficult.[30]

---

* When he was a young officer, he changed his name from Scheinerman to Sharon, after the valley in which he grew up. This was a common practice amongst Israelis with non-Hebraic names after the War of Independence in 1948.

2

THE FORMATION OF UNIT 101

———

IN MID-JULY, 1953, SHARON was preparing for a history exam when he was summoned to the office of Colonel Michael Shacham, chief of the Jerusalem Brigade of which Sharon was a reserve battalion commander. Colonel Shacham wanted Sharon's help in eradicating an Arab gang that had just killed two watchmen. The leader of this band was well-known: he was Mustafa Samueli, who lived in the village of Nebi Samuel, located north of Jerusalem, on the crest of a hill behind Jordanian lines. Samueli made almost nightly forays into Jewish territory, did his mischief and slipped back over the border into Jordan. He had sworn to avenge the death of his brother in the 1948 war by killing one hundred Jews, and he marked each killing with a notch on the butt of his rifle. Jewish complaints to the UN were ineffectual; Samueli was a hero to his people.

Shacham asked Sharon if he would be willing to pull together a crew who would carry out a raid in Nebi Samuel to "terrorize" Samueli into giving up his nocturnal activities. To Sharon, this request was further proof that the IDF was not really a professional army; only the few thousand members of the Palmach had had real military training. Moreover, Ben-Gurion had integrated the Palmach into the army, removing its separate command structure, and then, after the war, had further downgraded this crack force into a reserve unit so that most of the officers had resigned and gone home.

According to the statistics, in 1951, 137 Israelis, most of them civilians, were killed by extremists; in 1952 the death toll was 162 and in 1953 there were 3000 incidents, 160 of them ending in death. Retaliation raids had accomplished nothing: frequently the men could not find their way in the dark, and if they did arrive at their targets they would simply exchange gunfire with Arab watchmen and withdraw, very often with casualties of their own.

Shacham, completely frustrated by this situation, had decided to employ unorthodox methods to combat it. He told Sharon that he would have a free hand and could choose any soldiers or veterans he would like to carry out this mission. Sharon replied that he thought he could do it with seven or eight men and sufficient supplies.

When he got home, Sharon contacted eight friends he had served with in the army, all of whom had, like Sharon himself, left the military and a few of whom were also university students. They gathered in Sharon's suburban apartment on a Friday night to study maps and plot their action, which was to cross the Jordanian border after dark, locate Samueli's house, demolish the entrance and take the inhabitants by surprise. The next night they were briefed by Shacham's security people and then set out, loaded with explosives and ammunition, for Nebi Samuel. They remembered that in 1948 the Palmach had tried and failed to take Nebi Samuel and had suffered heavy casualties in the attempt.

They climbed high up into the northwestern hills surrounding Jerusalem and then carefully picked their way through the dry riverbed of the Shorek toward the village. What they did not know was that Samueli had already left his house. The column walked through fields, climbed the mountain and finally reached the village on the peak. They successfully evaded Jordanian patrols and local guards, locating Samueli's house near the mosque where the prophet Samuel was supposedly buried—thus giving the village its name. The three-man demolition squad unpacked their explosives and sprinted for the house while the other five waited. They set the charge against the door, and ran for cover, but there was no explosion, only a fizzle setting off a small fire that did not seriously damage the door.

But even this roused the village and there was a great deal of shouting and confusion. One of Sharon's men tore the shutters from a barred window, firing a burst from his machine gun while his companion lobbed two grenades through the bars. There was no response from the empty house, but shots were echoing all around them. They set off another charge at a nearby house, and this time there was an explosion that provided enough cover for them to beat a hasty retreat down the mountain. It was not yet dawn when they crossed the border, exhausted and depressed.

Sharon informed Colonel Shacham that the raid had not been a success, probably because the raiders—despite their earlier army experience—were not sufficiently professional. What was needed, he said, was a properly trained, adequately equipped elite force, a small, effective commando unit. Then he returned to his studies, unaware that Colonel Shacham had contacted Major General Mordechai Makleff, commander-in-chief of the IDF, to propose the formation of a special commando force for the express purpose of retaliatory raids.[1] The proposal was presented to Moshe Dayan, who liked it, especially since he had formed a somewhat similar patrol unit when he was Southern Commander. Dayan later said,

> We were in need of a man of daring, a man with a great deal of personal ambition, a skilled leader who would be flexible and original enough to adapt literal orders according to the situation he found himself in.
>
> This force could not be allowed to disobey orders or change the goals that had been decreed from above. On the other hand, this was a new and special unit, a force that would have to establish and carry out novel methods of warfare. Therefore the commander of this new force had to be superior in his ability to think and perceive clearly and coolheadedly. Arik Sharon seemed to fill all these requirements.[2]

Thus, at the end of July, a few weeks after the Nebi Samuel fiasco, Sharon was called to General Headquarters and told by Major General Makleff that the commando unit he had proposed was going to be organized, and would be called Commando Unit 101, and that he, Sharon, was the army's choice to lead it. Sharon's response to this was mixed: he agreed to accept the post, but he regretted having to leave his studies for what appeared to be an open-ended assignment, and he knew that Gali and his parents would worry about him. However, he also felt strongly that this new attack unit could hold Arab actions at bay, calming the fears of the population and bolstering the IDF's morale.

He left the university and devoted himself to forming this new unit, a task that was difficult because the army was so demoralized that there were few volunteers for dangerous missions. Sharon had no hesitation in looking outside the regular army for people whom he remembered had distinguished themselves in the War of Independence. As word about his search circulated, many soldiers responded, especially having heard that members of this unit would not wear uniforms and would not receive their orders from General Headquarters. People who had served with Sharon, veterans of the Palmach and crack brigades like the paratroopers, began to inquire about this new unit and to volunteer. Many had had experience scouting and fighting at night.

By early September, Sharon had twenty volunteers; he wanted no more than forty-five, and had signed up that many by October. Among the first to volunteer were Shlomo Baum, who had been one of the group at Nebi Samuel; Shimon Kahaner, nicknamed "Kacha"; Yitzhak Gibli, who had joined the Palmach as a teenager; two farmers, Zevele Amit and Yossele Regev; and Meir Har-Zion, who was to become a national hero. During the five months that it existed it had a dramatic impact on Israel's war against Arab infiltration.

Camp 101—no one knew why the unit had been given this number—was set up in a remote spot on a mountain not far from Jerusalem.

It was not a traditional army camp: the rules governing it were not ordinary army regulations or boot camp standards, but were designed to create small, rigidly disciplined light combat units where physical fitness and expert marksmanship were essential. Each soldier had to be in perfect physical condition to be able to walk thirty miles in one night, loaded down with equipment; to throw grenades accurately from various distances in a variety of situations; to operate in the dark as easily as in daylight; to slip soundlessly by enemy guards; to freeze under fire and to hold his fire.

Each had to know how to handle a knife and to kill with it, to fight hand-to-hand, to learn the topographical details of every terrain, to be aware of his surroundings at all times so that he would not stray or lose his way—a supremely dangerous undertaking in Arab territory. These soldiers practiced lobbing more grenades than any other unit in the IDF; they shot thousands of rounds of ammunition at bottles and cans; they went out on nocturnal marches that became successively longer and harder. When they returned at dawn, they were ordered out for daytime training exercises. Their main training ground was a deserted Arab village, complete with houses, yards, groves and orchards, where they could study its architecture, terrain, wells, caves—every detail of its environment.

In this camp, standard rules of military discipline and formality were not observed; they were not considered necessary to mold specially trained fighters. This was not unusual in Israeli military circles. The Palmach fighters had dispensed with salutes and insignia of rank, along with uniforms: they wore home-knitted hats, open shirts, very short khaki shorts and long hair, and called their officers by nicknames. Although Ben-Gurion disliked this—he had always admired the British hierarchical military system—this style suited the Israeli spirit better than the British emphasis on uniforms, rank and rigid military rules. In Sharon's field operation, rank did not count as much as ability: thus, on occasion, officers might take orders from a sergeant. Many volunteers enlisted in this new unit, underwent training for a week or two, and then washed out, unable to meet the rigorous standards. Those who passed the tests and became part of the unit knew that they were members of what was to become a military elite, a special force in every sense of the word. And although the unit had an egalitarian character, there was an insistence on military standards for such things as condition of weapons, comradeship in battle and respect for life.[3]

These efforts to raise the bar of physical fitness higher and higher paid dividends. These men were very fit and well-trained for night raids. They crossed the border, usually in groups of three, and frequently came in contact with the enemy. They kept changing and perfecting their methods of infiltration, demolition and ambush. Shimon Kahaner recalled that on his very first day he was sent on a two-hour-long march up and down steep mountain terrain at a breathtaking pace, and ordered not to stumble or slow down. And on that same night, he joined three other men on a patrol across the border. Before they set out, Meir Har-Zion, his close friend who had brought him into the unit, said to him, "Listen, Kacha, my boy, forget all you've learned in the army so far, and we'll start all over again."[4]

Commando Dan Margalit wrote, "To a great extent, 101 was an experimental course, a sort of primary military laboratory where new methods of warfare were formalized and put to the test. . . . Everyone involved learned from their mistakes, studying the results of our campaigns. And Arik, the tactician, was learning too."[5]

Sharon was not unaware that the formation of such a superior cadre of fighters might also have its negative side: such intensive training might conceivably cause some of the men to use force too freely on the other side of the border. They could become bloodthirsty adventurers, all too eager to use their knives and guns. Sharon tried to obviate this possibility with some special psychological training, by focusing attention on specific tasks rather than on a general desire for revenge. To this end, he would conduct a sort of tactical focus group at the end of a meal: "A Jew was murdered in a moshav near Jerusalem. He had heard a suspicious noise and gone out to check. He was shot and killed. The killers have been traced to an enemy village across the border. We've been asked to retaliate. I'm open to suggestions."

Someone suggested penetrating the village and blowing up a house. Someone else asked what good that would do. The answer: "So they can't do whatever comes into their heads."

"But," a third person would say, "if there's a family in that house—what then?" The reply to that was that the moshavnik was killed for no reason either. Then the question was whether that was right. The answer was that it was not right, prompting a further question: "Do you want to be like them?" And the answer to that was yet another question: "What then? Should we sit still and do nothing?"

"No," Sharon would say, "we must retaliate, but in a different way. Because the Arab villager doesn't necessarily know that someone killed a moshavnik across the border. But when he wakes up in the morning and sees the debris and the bodies of the innocent, he'll seek revenge and he'll bless those who slaughter Jews. So what will we have gained?"

"What," someone would ask, "if we leave leaflets there, saying something like, 'A man from your village has murdered a Jew. We deserve peaceful nights just as you do. If you stop the infiltration into our territory, we won't harm you.' That way they'll try to stop the terrorists."

"If only that were the case," Sharon would say. "But you know it isn't. First of all, they'll deny that the murderer came from their village. They'll tell the press that the murderer might have passed through their village, but why should they be blamed for that? Anyway, what are we asking them to do? Is the safety of Jews their responsibility? And if they stopped someone from committing a terrorist act, wouldn't they be accused of doing the IDF's work and of collaborating with Israel, with traitors, with the thieves who conquered their lands and destroyed their homes? Who would have the courage to stop terrorists under those circumstances?"

Then would come the inevitable question: "So what do you suggest?" And the only answer: "We've got to think this through."

Obviously, it was an insoluble problem.

Sharon tested the men by sending them into enemy territory every night for practice. He told them again and again to go in, reach their target and leave silently, without attracting notice, without firing a single shot, without leaving any sign of having been there.

These silent forays across the border had at some point to turn into real action. There were 100,000 Arab refugees in the Gaza Strip, apart from permanent residents, and it had become a center for the Arab *fedayeen*—militants, whose accelerated actions were being sponsored by Egyptian intelligence. Sharon decided to carry out a raid on the refugee camp in Gaza. He divided his men into three small units, two of which would attack the Egyptian advisors in the center of the enormous camp; the third would move on to what was assumed to be the headquarters of the fedayeen outside the camp. But before they left, one of the commandos, Samuel Nissim, known as Falach, flatly refused to participate. This was unprecedented. After all those months of training for this very purpose, one of the unit's best men was refusing to go. He explained that he would not participate in the murder of innocent people. "I doubt," he said, "that we'll be able to single out the very ones who attacked us. And killing those who aren't responsible doesn't solve our problem; in fact, it perpetuates it."

The other commandos understood his point of view, but sharply disagreed with him. A heated argument ensued; they tried to convince him that their raid would teach the Arabs a lesson, that this was the consequence of their own infiltration into Israeli territory, where they struck at innocent men, women and children. But Falach stood firm. "I volunteered for this unit," he said, "and I have never given up my right to my private opinion. I refuse to go. You can court-martial me for refusing to obey a command, if you like. You can throw me in jail. I'm not going."

Sharon did not seem upset by this. "Okay, Falach," he said. "You go with the third squad instead." Falach agreed, since the third squad was going to attack fedayeen headquarters outside the refugee camp itself.

That night the refugee camp was brightly lit; the sounds of children crying, dogs barking and Arab music in cafes drifted through the air. Near the camp, the squads encountered an Egyptian guard; after a brief fight, the Israelis rushed into the camp and took up their assigned positions. The camp became a battlefield. Refugees, armed with automatic machine guns, surrounded two of the Israeli squads, which somehow succeeded in struggling through the melee and escaping.

At the same time, the third squad made its way through the wadi, toward the fedayeen headquarters, which was surrounded by a stone wall. The three members of the squad crawled rapidly to the wall. The gate was locked, and had to be blown up by the sapper, while the other two ran in, throwing grenades and shooting through the doors and windows of the house. They set it aflame and withdrew in a barrage of enemy fire. After they had covered a good distance, the sapper told them he had been wounded. They did what they could for him as quickly as possible, rushed on to escape their pursuers and reached their home base.

Sharon was not happy with their performance, but felt confident that they would improve. He recognized that they were trying hard, but they needed to do better and eventually they began to be more successful in small actions against bands operating from Jordanian villages.[6]

But sometimes the unit's actions caused controversy, as in the case of the attack on the village of Kibeyeh.

3

THE ATTACK ON KIBEYEH

———

ONE EVENING IN OCTOBER, 1953, at approximately the same time that the men of Unit 101 were having dinner in their mess, two Arabs sat in a café in Kfar Kibeyeh on the Israeli border. Outwardly, they seemed no different from hundreds of their brethren who had left their fields and set out for home after their day's work. The only clue to their singular identity was hidden from view: the two knapsacks beside them were packed with hand grenades, machine guns and explosives. When night fell, they set out, stopping to buy cigarettes. The few villagers who noticed them saw that they were strangers and, like the café owner who sold them the cigarettes, knew that they had come to the village on their way to Israeli territory. Kibeyeh had become a sort of halfway house for Arab infiltrators. A wadi, well-camouflaged by trees and shrubs, led from Kibeyeh to Israel making the village a natural way station.

No one will ever know their exact mission, or even if they had one. But it is known that as they entered the slumbering Israeli village of Yahud, they were attracted by the light of a lantern in one of the houses. Silently, they crept up to the lighted window, and saw a woman and her two children, one and three years old, asleep inside. After they carefully examined the area and decided on an escape route, one of them took a grenade from his knapsack, pulled the safety pin and lobbed the explosive into the room.

Seconds later, an explosion shattered the quiet night; neighbors rushed to the house and found the inhabitants dead. People crowded into the room, shocked and angry. Someone ran out to the road to flag down a car, while someone else raced to the administrative building to phone for help. In the confusion, the infiltrators slipped away, crossing the road to be swallowed up by the deserted plantations as they made their way back to Kibeyeh.

Police trackers arrived in Yahud the next day, leading dogs on leashes; UN observers and reporters came with cameras, filling the streets of the stunned village. The evening papers carried headlines demanding retribution. Even the most politically moderate Israelis believed that the country had to retaliate if there were to be any security at all.

Sharon was summoned the next day to Central Command headquarters in Ramle where he found not only the Central Command staff and people from General Headquarters, but also the deputy commander of the nation's paratroop battalion. The walls of the meeting room were covered with huge detailed maps of the area. A decision had been made to retaliate against Kibeyeh, to penetrate the center of the town and leave it in ruins. The paratroopers would attack the village while Unit 101 would divert the Jordanian troops in the vicinity and put up roadblocks to keep them away.

To everyone's surprise, the paratroop commander said that he did not think his paratroopers were prepared to carry out such an action. Sharon found this incredible, and broke in on the ensuing discussion, volunteering to take command of the paratroopers as well as Unit 101. His offer was accepted and two paratroop platoons were to be assigned to his commando unit. The combined forces were to convene the next day, October 14, for a last-minute briefing.

Sharon returned to his camp to begin preparations for the raid. The next day, he knew, all the weeks of ceaseless training, of nocturnal patrols and minor infiltrations of enemy land, would be put to the test at last. He hoped that this raid would put an end to Israeli military failures and signal a new era for the country's defensive capabilities.

The attack on Kibeyeh was indeed historic, but not in the way he or anyone else foresaw. By nightfall all plans were in place. Meir Har-Zion was to lead a small force to Shukeibah, an Arab village about three miles to the east of Kibeyeh, where they would create a diversion to distract attention from the real target. They were to leave before the other groups, because Shukeibah was a good distance from the border. They had to move quietly since the element of surprise was crucial.

Half an hour later the main force under Sharon started toward Kibeyeh; halfway there, the force split in two. One group, headed by Ariel Schlein, went south to the village of Nahlin to lure enemy reinforcements there. The old eastern part of Kibeyeh would be attacked and the houses blown up by Shlomo Baum, Sharon's second in command, while a second force headed by Aharon Davidi, assistant commander of the paratroop battalion, would attack and take over the Arab legion stronghold in the western part of the village. An additional squad of explosives experts would remain hidden in the valley to await Sharon's orders.

Unfortunately, this elaborate plan was never carried out.

Meir Har-Zion's squad were creeping through the moon-dappled olive groves bordering Shukeibah when a sudden cry from an Arab guard pierced the silence.

"*Min hada?* (Who's there?)"

The Israelis froze instantly, trying to distinguish human figures from the distorted olive trunks. Nobody moved.

"*Min hada?*"

The Israelis remained immobilized. Finally they could see two Arab guards carefully searching the grove. When they came closer, Har-Zion gave an order and the two guards were quickly disarmed and tied up. Rags were stuffed into their mouths and they were told to march silently with the force. The men moved forward quickly to make up for the time lost, but the two captives slowed them down. Shimon Kahaner saw the younger of the two trying to free his hands and warned Har-Zion. But it was too late: before anyone could stop him, the young Arab broke free, rushed up to Har-Zion, struck him and fled. In the ensuing furor, the second guard also ran off. Pulling themselves together, the Israelis fired at the fleeing guards, killing one instantly. The second guard was hit, but continued to run, crying out in pain.

The shots of course destroyed the element of surprise. Ever since the killings in Yahud, the Jordanians had been expecting Israeli retaliation. The Jordanian government had actually issued an appeal to Israel, pleading for time to capture the killers themselves in order to forestall any action. However, the Israelis did not want Jordanian intervention; they felt that would damage the IDF's self-respect and its image as an efficient, independent force.

But the two shots had spoiled their plan, and the villagers of Kibeyeh were alerted.

This was not the only part of the plan that went awry that night. Ariel Schlein's secondary unit unexpectedly encountered a three-man Jordanian patrol hidden in the hills. Once again the cry *"Min hada?"* shattered the silence. After the initial shock, the unit circled the patrol and tossed a grenade, hitting two of the three men, destroying the ambush, but the element of surpise was lost yet again.

Meanwhile, the main force under Sharon and Aharon Davidi, the hundred-man paratroop battalion, was moving slowly toward Kibeyeh. They were heavily burdened, each man carrying more than twenty pounds of TNT in addition to weapons and ammunition. Inevitably the men made noise—rifles clanking, a dislodged rock clattering down a hill. In a moment, Arab guards appeared on the ridge of the hill above and began to fire down in the dark. But the shots went wild because the guards could not see their targets; they simply shot at noises, while the Israelis held their fire and continued to climb.

When they seemed to be close enough to the village, the men dropped their packs and began the attack. Most of the Arab guards were killed, and shortly afterward the forces entered the village itself. The streets were deserted; Sharon received radio reports that hundreds of villagers were observed rushing past roadblocks in a frantic effort to escape the fighting and he recalled many years later that "an eerie silence hung over the place, broken only by the strains of Arab music coming from a radio that had been left playing in an empty café."

At midnight the Israelis began to blow up the stone village houses. Sharon later insisted that the soldiers had searched each building to make sure it was empty before the charges were detonated, that they had rescued a boy and a girl in two separate houses—the girl being taken from a house where the fuses had already been lit—and that these were the only living souls found by the Israelis in Kibeyeh.

The demolition went on for several hours, explosions punctuated by shots from the diversionary forces some miles away. Toward dawn, Sharon ordered a retreat. He reported to Central Command that forty-two buildings had been blown up, no Israelis had been lost, and the enemy had suffered ten or twelve casualties.[1]

But early the next morning, Jordanian radio announced that sixty-nine civilians had been killed in the raid, most of them women and children. This was very bad news indeed, and Sharon tried to offer a rational explanation for it. For years, he said, Israelis in reprisal had blown up only a few buildings on the outskirts of Jordanian villages; as a result, he conjectured, some of the Kibeyeh families may have decided to hide in cellars or remote rooms of their large houses, keeping quiet when the soldiers called out their warnings, on the assumption that they would soon withdraw.

Whatever did in fact happen, this large loss of life cast a pall over the reputation of the IDF; people around the world were shocked, as was the Israeli public. But Sharon, while calling the civilian deaths a tragedy, believed that the raid on Kibeyeh marked a turning point for Israel. For the first time, the army had demonstrated its competence and its ability to strike deep into Arab territory. But a number of inquiries and investigations followed this attack, as a result of which new military guidelines were issued, the most important being a requirement that all enemy structures marked for demolition be thoroughly inspected to make sure that all civilians had been evacuated.

Sharon continued to believe that the Kibeyeh raid had had a strong, positive effect on army morale, and on the morale of the citizens who before 1953 had felt completely defenseless against extremist attacks in population centers like Lod and suburban Tel Aviv as well as in more remote areas. "The Jordanian and Egyptian governments could see that if Israel was vulnerable, so were they," Sharon said. Ben-Gurion himself sent for Sharon and told him that international opinion in this case did not matter. What mattered was opinion at home, that the Jews could go on living in their country because they had forced their enemies to think twice before they acted. For Sharon and Ben-Gurion, the action was justified.[2]

4

UNIT 101 & THE PARATROOPERS

———

ON DECEMBER 6, 1953, Moshe Dayan was named chief of the General Staff. He had originally objected to the formation of Unit 101, saying that the whole army should be trained in commando tactics, and special units were not needed. But by the time he took over command of the army, he had changed his mind. He knew by then that Unit 101 had been largely responsible for changing the army's fighting methods and that this small contingent had managed to bring about peace with the Bedouin tribes that had been terrorizing the Nitsanah area. Dayan decided to merge Unit 101 with the paratroop battalion and to appoint Sharon to head the new combined force.

But the men of 101 were not at all pleased with the unit's sudden expansion. They liked their camp near Jerusalem, the camaraderie of their small group and the feeling of uniqueness. They were used to relying on friends under enemy fire on those cold, dark nights of battle. And, not least of all, they preferred the informal dress of the commando to the standard military uniform of the conscripted soldier, and enjoyed Unit 101's notorious lack of discipline. Now all that was about to change: they would have to become soldiers like any others, to spruce up their appearance, to display rank, to wear military caps.

Sharon urged his men to cooperate, telling them that they had not enlisted permanently to be an army within an army. "We were the vanguard. We were lucky enough to formulate a new kind of

military warfare; a new reality. And we did this in only four months."
Now, he told them, the time had come for them to train the entire
army in the same unique way, beginning with paratroopers who
were something more than ordinary infantry. "We didn't make the
effort just for our personal gratification; we wanted to make the
army better. Now we have to become instructors so that our army
as a whole can become as fine a fighting machine as our unit has
become."[1]

Sharon actually had better luck with his men than Dayan had
with the paratroopers, who considered themselves something of an
elite too, with close comradeship and strong athletic training. But it
was because their performance was no better than that of the ordinary army that Dayan decided to merge them with 101 under Sharon's
command. According to Sharon, Dayan was not very tactful in telling Judah Harari, the paratrooper chief, that he would now be subordinate to Sharon. The paratroopers themselves rebelled, actually
jeering at Sharon on the parade ground when he came to take over.
Harari publicly invited any officers to join him who wanted to leave.

Stunned by the strong reaction against him, Sharon divided the
companies, sending each of them to separate locations outside the
camp to cut off communication between them. Then he arranged
for all the Harari loyalists to be swiftly transferred out of the paratroopers. Even so, he was able to retain nearly half of the officers,
including the assistant commander, Aharon Davidi, whom he named
his second in command.[2]

He had his nucleus of forty 101 men and he began to send out
patrols of five—two 101 members and three paratroopers—on long
missions over the border to build up their stamina. At first the paratroopers had difficulty keeping up, but Sharon recalled that within
a month the atmosphere lightened as the paratroopers' resentment
evaporated when they saw an improvement in their abilities and
began to appreciate their new experiences.

After the traumatic attack on Kibeyeh, terrorist activities subsided somewhat, but only briefly. Soon the wave of infiltrations, ambushes and sabotage began again, though somewhat less frequently because of the cold and snowy weather and overflowing rivers. When spring arrived, Arab saboteurs arrived with it. Incidents reached a peak when a bus was attacked near Maale-Haakrabim on its way north. Eleven passengers were killed and all the others were wounded. At the beginning of April, 1954, Sharon planned a reprisal. The mission involved an attack on Arab Legionnaires and National Guardsmen and the blowing up of some houses in the village of Nahlin, near Bethlehem, about three miles from the Israeli border.

For most of them, this would be the first crossing of the border to penetrate enemy lines. No one knew whether the feelings of cooperation and comradeship of 101 could be infused into this new integrated unit. Sharon believed that a soldier could be tested only under fire; that the men who survived that night's attack would be transformed into members of a unified group. He was also worried that the mission might become a reenactment of the Kibeyeh disaster. He warned the men that a court-martial awaited any of them who did not take pains to make sure that women and children were not harmed.

The men clambered onto trucks and were driven to a kibbutz near the border; from there they approached the outskirts of the village of Nahlin, where they could hear dogs barking. Two subdivisions took up assigned positions while the main force entered the village, taking the inhabitants by surprise; resistance was minimal. From his command point, Sharon heard the Arabic-speaking Israelis order people out of their houses. Most of them came quietly, afraid for their lives. Sniper fire began, but none of the paratroopers was hit; they threw smoke bombs into the houses to make sure that they were empty. When the smoke cleared, they entered the houses, searched them and planted explosives. When one family refused to leave their home, one of the paratroopers, a sergeant, burst into the house and was killed on the spot. The house was then summarily blown up, along with its occupants. When Legionnaire reinforcements encountered the restraint force, their way was blocked by a new explosive device invented by Simon Tal, a demolition expert who headed the restraint unit.

When the demolition was over, the men reassembled, collected the one dead and two wounded troopers and were crossing back into Israel, when suddenly they were attacked by a Jordanian ambush force. Sharon, hearing the first shots, was worried about whether the men would be able to fight their way out. They had been told time after time that if they were ambushed they could either retreat or rush the enemy, but if they retreated they would be vulnerable and would probably be mowed down by enemy fire. Sharon told them that in case of a sudden attack like this, they had to return fire instantly and attack the enemy lying in wait.

Fortunately, the paratroopers acted according to instructions and returned to base exhilarated that they had won their battle. They had confronted the enemy and realized that the rigorous exercises they had been forced to undergo had actually saved their lives.

As the paratroopers were being tested, Sharon ordered his core of 101 fighters to become competent parachutists, to overcome their natural fear of jumping from a moving plane into the abyss; as Sharon put it, "to overcome logic and the will to live." In 1954, Dayan issued an order that every able senior officer be required to pass a parachute course. He also ordered every combat soldier to wear a red felt patch on his beret to indicate that he had encountered enemy fire. The paratroopers wore both their parachutists wings and this red symbol of combat duty and were awarded a special status in the army.[3]

5

THE GIBLI AFFAIR

———

IN JUNE, 1954, A RESIDENT of Raanana was killed by Jordanians, and still another retaliation raid was planned. But in order to avoid another Kibeyeh, the unit was ordered to concentrate on military targets. Sharon and Davidi decided to send a small section of the reconnaissance unit into one of the Arab Legion camps to do as much damage and create as much commotion as possible. They chose a camp in an area opposite the Sharon Valley, where the Israeli citizen had been killed.

Sharon was acting on the assumption that the Jordanians would not attack the IDF's own bases—an extremely risky assumption, since in 1954 many people in Israel feared that deliberate provocation of the Arab Legion, considered the strongest Arab army, would push the Arabs into starting a new war. But Sharon was determined to continue his policy of deterrence. He believed that the history of Arab warfare demonstrated that it had been based primarily on the actions of courageous individuals rather than on the concept of organized military campaigns.

On the night of June 25, a six-man squad, headed by Major Davidi and Meir Har-Zion, was driven to the outskirts of Kfar Saba, near the border. Davidi, Sharon's second in command, had been sent more as an observer than a commander, so that decisions about general tactical plans could be made on the basis of this action. The third man in the squad, Yitzhak Gibli, an explosives expert, or sapper, had been added to the team at the last minute, when he arrived just before they set out. He had come from his father's death bed, begging to be allowed to participate in the action, and he could not be refused.

When the six men started on their mission, Sharon remained behind at the border: as battalion commander, he was required to oversee the battle from the rear. As soon as they crossed the border, they ran into a Jordanian patrol that shot at them and called up reinforcements. The squad decided to continue anyway, creeping past other ambushes. Once they discovered an ambush a moment before it had spotted them.

They advanced quickly and arrived at the camp, which was already astir; obviously no one had gone to sleep because they had been alerted by the first patrol. The men divided the tents between them and prepared to fire. Gibli was assigned a lighted tent in the center of the camp where four Legionnaires were sitting. The Israelis crawled over to the watchman and killed him. Then they attacked and the enemy came after them from all sides. Gibli had burst into the tent and fired an entire magazine. He stepped back to recharge his tommy gun and suddenly found himself on the ground. He tried to get up, but he couldn't. He called out, "I've been wounded in the leg!" and went on firing.

Davidi rushed up to him and told him that they would finish up and then take care of him. A little while later, Har-Zion hoisted him over his shoulder and ran, while the others covered them. Hurrying away under mortar fire, Har-Zion fell under Gibli's weight. When Har-Zion picked him up, Gibli whispered that he thought he had been hit again, in the neck. Har-Zion looked at the wound and found that a bullet had apparently entered Gibli's back and had come out through his cheek.

Dawn was two hours away. Gibli was upset because he could hear his companions' heavy breathing as they labored under his weight and he knew he was delaying them. He began to insist that they leave him there. They told him to shut up, but he kicked Har-

Zion in the ribs and yelled, "Leave me here or else we'll all be killed!" Reluctantly, they realized that he was right. If the Arabs caught one man, it might not be a disaster, but if they took six prisoners it would be a great propaganda victory for them. Gibli was left behind.

Sharon became obsessed with the incident and when he heard a few days later that Gibli was alive and in prison. He forced the General Staff and the Foreign Office to pressure the UN and the Red Cross into trying to arrange Gibli's release. But the Jordanians were not easily influenced. It wasn't every day that an Israeli commando fell into their hands alive. Sharon sought a way to speed the process up and believed he had found it when two settlers from a moshav in the Jerusalem mountains were murdered, and a soldier was killed by Jordanians who penetrated an Israeli observation stronghold near Latrun.

Sharon planned a reprisal in the Latrun area. He told his officers that he was not interested only in retaliation; he wanted his men to capture some Legionnaires to use as bargaining chips for Gibli's release. The action this time would be somewhat complicated: three explosives would have to be planted, of which two were intended only to bring Legionnaires out into the open.

The force set out at nightfall for the village of Beit Likiya. From radio contact, Sharon learned that a successful road block had been set up and that everything was going as planned. Suddenly there was a burst of Jordanian machine-gun fire. The men had stumbled unexpectedly against a tall barbed wire fence, making a terrific racket. Major Moshe Yanuka reported that the Israeli soldiers were behaving badly, hitting the ground under machine-gun fire from one Legionnaire and ignoring the officers' orders. Yanuka, another commander and a small group of soldiers tried to save the situation by using a flamethrower to break through the fence and firing in all directions while the other commanders reassembled the force and started to evacuate the wounded.

Sharon was horrified as he received these reports. From his position, he could hear the shots and see the fire. He roared into the radio, "Make more noise! I want the whole Legion to come out!" But it was obvious that a retreat was in order. Yanuka later described this retreat as a debacle:

"For a moment, it seemed that there was going to be a mass escape rather than an organized retreat," he wrote. "Some of the soldiers were shocked, terrified and did nothing to help with the evacuation of the wounded. We had failed. The men whom we had thought were well-trained and disciplined soldiers, turned out to be irresponsible and inefficient. As we started back, carrying the dead and wounded on our shoulders, I was told that two stretchers had been left behind, that there was no one to carry them."[1]

Sharon was furious. He couldn't believe what had happened. He pulled himself together to shout an order over the radio to Mordechai "Motta" Gur, recently appointed a paratroop commander, to send half his men to block off the way to Latrun, and the other half to help Davidi's men carry the wounded. Motta Gur's men, who were mostly new recruits themselves, soon connected with the column of miserable, defeated soldiers.

Sharon said he considered this defeat a personal failure, but at the same time he blamed the IDF, saying that their general mediocrity had infected his paratroopers. A few days after this Beit Likiya fiasco, he reorganized the battalion, changing the rules, demanding that the men obey standard military regulations on appearance and dress. Practice became much more exacting, maneuvers more complicated. The paratroopers underwent special training in evacuation of the wounded, with and without stretchers. The pressure on the men was intense; some thought it tantamount to torture. In fact, some broke under the strain and left the unit.[2]

The agitation to free Yitzhak Gibli went on. Sharon said later that the commotion caused the chief UN observer, a Canadian general, to say that he "had never seen a country that could become so angry over one sergeant."

Finally, the paratroopers captured seven Legionnaires to hold as hostages, and these seven were exchanged for Gibli, who, after four months in captivity, was given a royal reception. He was cited for bravery and his release was celebrated across the country with ceremonies and bonfires.[3]

6

THE GAZA RAID

———

IN THE EARLY SPRING and summer of 1954, Sharon expended all his energies on the combined paratroop and commando unit, now called Unit 202. His aim was to bring the paratroopers up to the training level of the old Unit 101. He was convinced that, as exemplars, Unit 202 could raise the IDF to a higher level of performance. Not everyone agreed. Some thought that no army could consist primarily of commandos; no army ever had. Others feared that Israeli society would become militaristic, even fascistic, if all the country's resources were to be devoted to the war effort, to the neglect of social and economic development. Even many of Sharon's friends were upset. They argued that he was on the wrong track, that he should remember he was dealing with a regular army and not a special underground defense force.[1]

And indeed, it seemed obvious that Sharon's raids had not accomplished his goal of deterrence. In 1954, there were three times as many border incidents as there had been in 1953: thefts, bombings, ambushes, the killing of farmers and attacks on patrols and buses. Israeli settlers organized their own patrols against Arabs. But Sharon remained adamant. He granted that every Israeli soldier could not be a commando *per se* and that it was not his intention to turn the whole army into a commando corps. Nevertheless, he insisted that the IDF had to have special training to make up for its size: it was a small army doing battle with three or four large, highly equipped forces.

The turning point for Sharon was the decision, mentioned earlier, to stop attacks on civilians and concentrate instead on military targets. Early in 1954, instructions to men going out on raids always included the phrase, "women and children are not to be hit under any circumstances."[2] Although this made raids more complicated, it raised morale; some of Sharon's men had been upset by the harshness of many of their actions. As a result of this tactical change, even unsympathetic Israeli and Arab commentators acknowledged that villages were no longer being targeted. The commandos developed a new sense of pride: they could display captured weapons to international visitors and bask in the praise their accomplishments generated.

Martin van Creveld quotes Shimon Peres on the subject of their popularity: "Children want to emulate them, mothers pray for their safety, rural settlers admire their achievements, and youth regard them as the embodiment of all its own virtues."[3] The paratrooper units received special equipment: comfortable red rubber-soled combat boots as opposed to the army's standard heavy black hobnailed variety; new Uzi submachine guns instead of antiquated bolt-action rifles.

Thus equipped, they thirsted for action. In February, 1955, an opportunity to test their mettle presented itself in the Gaza Strip, which lies along the Mediterranean coast about forty miles south of Tel Aviv, and, under Egyptian control, was filled with refugee camps from which desperate fedayeen launched bombings and ambushes. On February 27, when an Israeli worker was murdered in an orange grove near the Weizmann Institute, the government ordered the paratroopers to attack the main Egyptian base in Gaza.[4]

Sharon found this the most difficult assignment his unit had ever been given. The strip was an armed camp: the Egyptians had fortified an escarpment on the eastern border overlooking Israeli settlements. The headquarters camp would have to be isolated, and the men would have to maneuver between dense orange groves and cactus hedges, and to move quickly so that they could get out before their escape route to the border was cut off by enemy reinforcements. Sharon was worried too about UN observers who patrolled the borders and who were on the alert for Israeli retaliation for the death of the orange grove worker. If the UN observers reported an incipient raid, the Egyptians would inevitably hear about it and take extra precautions.

The morning of the raid, Sharon held a briefing for his officers in his bedroom, spreading out maps of the terrain, with which some of the men were familiar because they had participated in the demolition of the Gaza waterworks a few months earlier. This was to be the most complex action in the paratroopers' experience. Sharon pointed out the new objectives: the military camp, the waterworks again and the railway station. According to intelligence reports, the camp was lit up along its fences. Nearby were the waterworks and to the south was the railway station.

The raid was considered so important that Major General Dayan came to the camp to wish the unit luck. As darkness fell, they set off; there was no fence, nothing official to mark the border as they crossed it. Leading the company was the scout party commanded by Saadyah Alkayam, "Supapo," one of the unit's most respected fighters. He was followed by Sharon and his liaison officers. Two members of the General Staff had come along as observers: Major Michael Kartan and Lieutenant Colonel David Elazar, who was later to become chief of the General Staff.

This Staff group was followed by the company commanded by Motta Gur, who was later to become, like Elazar, IDF chief; one of the platoons was to stay behind as a reserve unit covering the orchard through which the men would begin their retreat. They had hardly begun to move when a shout in Arabic rang out, followed by bursts of gunfire. Sharon's group hurried forward to find that Supapo's scouts had killed four Egyptian soldiers who had set up an ambush to close the gap between two Egyptian positions.

Leaving Moshe Yanuka's force at the rear to cover the final retreat route through hostile, well-fortified territory, Sharon's group
entered dense orange groves near where he was to set up headquarters in a deserted house. On either side of the road—about a quarter
mile to the south—were the two Egyptian camps, one on the left
and the larger headquarters farther down the road on the right.
Sharon's plan was to circle around and attack both camps from the
rear: his reserve unit would go after the smaller one while Supapo's
men destroyed the headquarters and Motta Gur engaged the Egyptians at the railway station, another quarter mile west of the main
camp.

Soon the silence was broken by the explosive sounds of Supapo's
attack. But there had been a miscalculation: Supapo had hit the
smaller camp instead of the headquarters. When he realized his mistake, he hurriedly led his column down the highway to break through
the gate of the main camp. This was a dangerous move because the
Egyptians had now positioned themselves close to the road and were
pouring heavy fire into the darkness. Supapo was killed, along with
several of his men.

One of his officers, Uzi Trachtenberg, cut through the wire fence
at the side of the camp and led Supapo's group inside. After a brief,
fierce exchange, the Egyptians abandoned the field. Sharon's reserve
unit attacked the smaller camp and Motta Gur, as planned, moved
against the railway station. They had done everything they had set
out to do, but they had sustained many casualties. They needed to
blow up the buildings, gather their wounded, and retreat. While
Sharon watched, the casualties were carried to the trucks, and, horrified, he recognized Supapo among the dead.

Sharon left the trucks behind to block attacks. Then the column
set out on foot, carrying fourteen wounded and six dead, on stretchers and on their backs, sandwiched between scouts and a rear guard.
They met up with Yanuka's platoon which was securing their route
back. About a mile from the border, they suddenly found them-

selves encountering heavy fire from Egyptians who were blocking the road. The fire was coming in bursts, and after they sensed the rhythm of the volleys, the commanders began to send the men across the road a few at a time, doubled over, still carrying the stretchers or with the dead slung over their shoulders. Two more men were killed in this attack; their bodies were dragged across by the others. The firing went on behind them as they moved toward the border.[5]

The paratroopers had performed well, but one would have not guessed it from their appearance. Exhausted, tired, they were particularly shocked at the loss of their comrades, including Supapo, the first paratroop officer to die in a retaliation raid.[6]

7

KUNTILLA

———

THE EGYPTIAN GOVERNMENT, HEADED by Gamal Abdel Nasser, reacted strongly to the Gaza raid which had demonstrated the vulnerability of the Egyptian military in the region, but which only reinforced Nasser's determination to carry on the battle. There were repeated Egyptian attacks and repeated commando reprisals. Dayan supported all the reprisal actions, many of which exceeded instructions from headquarters in the number of enemy troops killed and the amount of damage done, actions which distressed the dovish Moshe Sharet, who had replaced Ben-Gurion as prime minister. Ben-Gurion stood foursquare behind Dayan and Sharon.

The Egyptian forces were, in fact, no match for Sharon's forces, which added tanks, field guns and patrol planes to their attack units. The morale of the Egyptian troops was low, their equipment was outdated, and there was no budget for new materiel—which mattered little, inasmuch as the British and Americans refused to sell munitions to them, as well as to the Israelis.

In September, 1955, Nasser announced that in exchange for cotton and rice, Czechoslovakia would provide Soviet-made jet fighters, light bombers, tanks, field and anti-aircraft guns, minesweepers, destroyers, torpedo boats and even submarines. This brought the Cold War into the Middle East and devastated the Israelis, who saw themselves at a huge disadvantage if this deal actually went through.[1]

In early November, these Soviet arms began to trickle into Egypt. Ben-Gurion, now prime minister once again, and Dayan, head of the IDF, began to mull over the possibility of a preventive war.

In the middle of all this ferment, Sharon was extremely exasperated to find himself in court accused of actions unbecoming an officer. The charges were based on a 1954 incident in which Sharon had slapped a quartermaster who had refused imprisonment for absence without leave. The man had been thrown into the stockade, had escaped and, when captured, had been handcuffed and thrown in the stockade again. He had complained to the military police about the slap and the handcuffs, and, as a result, Sharon had to interrupt his taxing schedule to sit in court to defend himself before a three-judge military panel. To make matters worse, the courtroom was one reserved for trials of captured terrorists. Furthermore, the complainant was dead, having accidentally shot himself some months earlier.

The trial dragged on for more than two months. Sharon was planning a raid on Kuntilla, an isolated Egyptian outpost eight miles inside the Sinai desert. The trial was driving him to distraction, and when he heard that two military policemen had come to his office in paratroop headquarters with a warrant to search his desk, he exploded and rushed to Tel Aviv to appeal first to Assaf Simchoni, the deputy chief of operations, and then he planned to go on to ask Dayan for relief. Simchoni told him it would be better if he, Simchoni, talked to Dayan himself. Sharon said that either the trial should be postponed or someone else should take over his responsibilities while he sat in court. Simchoni did not get back to him, but a few days later the hearings were postponed, and ultimately the charges were dropped.[2]

Sharon went ahead with his plans for the Kuntilla raid. He intended to rendezvous at two in the afternoon and drive across the stony plain that led to the border, then leave all the cars and proceed on foot to surprise the Egyptian garrison situated on a craggy promontory and estimated to be manned by about forty soldiers. The plan was for the unit to be back across the border before dawn. But the going was slower than he had anticipated, and at six o'clock night had fallen. They were still several miles from the border and Har-Zion said he thought it would be better to avoid the stony plain and drive instead through the sandy riverbed that led directly to the Kuntilla crag.

So at seven o'clock they entered the wadi, still in Israel, and began to drive across the soft sand. But they could not get traction with their convoy of heavy vehicles; the engines were struggling and their fuel supply was low. At ten o'clock, still ten miles from the target, Sharon decided to abandon the vehicles and go on foot. They trudged on in two columns, with Sharon in the lead, through the cold desert night, hoping to reach Kuntilla by one in the morning so they could get back across the border before dawn made them an easy target for Egyptian planes. When he stopped to give the men a five-minute rest, they fell asleep immediately; their obvious exhaustion caused Sharon to question the wisdom of attempting this raid altogether. But they had already come a long way, and their purpose was to capture as many of the enemy as possible, so they would have bargaining chips for the release of captured Israelis. In this case, there were two soldiers being held by the enemy. The men had been instructed to try taking prisoners first, rather than shoot.

Half an hour after their few minutes of rest, the commandos lay in the sand beneath their craggy goal. There was unusual activity above them in the Kuntilla fortress; new troops had arrived within the hour, doubling the number of Egyptians in the garrison to about eighty. The camp was thus in a state of confusion and, undetected, the Israelis had the vital element of surprise. The battle was a short one, and when it ended, the commandos had taken twenty-nine prisoners, most of them newly arrived troops, who seemed disoriented. One of them, Sharon says, protested, "We aren't involved in this. We just got here." The base commander surrendered personally to Sharon.

Weapons and other equipment found at Kuntilla were piled into two Egyptian trucks and sent back to the border, while the other trucks were dumped over the cliff. There was so much military equipment that the commandos assumed this was the result of the purchase agreement with the Soviets, but they learned later that the materiel had actually come from Spain. As the sun came up, the troop and its prisoners crossed the border after a four-hour march, during which two wounded Israelis died. In their attempt to take prisoners without gunfire, one had been shot and the other stabbed. The Egyptian and Israeli wounded had been sent back in one of the captured trucks.

Years later, Sharon told a journalist that when his troops arrived back in Israel, completely exhausted, "No one was there to greet us, to see how we were, to offer us water." He added, possibly to mitigate his anger, "It just wasn't done at that time, and we didn't expect it." Nevertheless the memory that it was not done had stayed with him.[3]

There was a question in the Israeli public mind about these raids—even though Dayan supported them. Was the price paid in human life worth it? To capture the enemy simply for prisoner exchange, when often more soldiers died in such raids than were sitting in Arab jails? Sharon had no problem with this; he continued to organize and supervise raids—seventy altogether, he says, from 1954 to 1956. In December, 1955, in response to Syrian attacks on Israeli fishermen in the Sea of Galilee, the paratroopers, deployed along twelve miles of Syrian territory, destroyed a series of well-fortified outposts at one blow. From a barge on Lake Kinneret, Sharon directed the actions in which thirty prisoners were taken. The death toll was fifty-four Syrians, including six civilians, and six Israelis. Fourteen paratroopers were wounded. Martin van Creveld comments that at this time "the IDF was not a tame instrument in the government's hands. . . . At a minimum, lower-level commanders such as Sharon . . . systematically exceeded their instructions."[4]

And indeed, although Dayan supported this attack, Ben-Gurion was upset by it, and he sent for both Dayan and Sharon to tell them so. When Sharon responded that he believed the raid was successful, Ben-Gurion said, "Too successful!" One of Sharon's most trusted lieutenants had been killed by a hand grenade, and another seriously wounded. By the end of 1955, Israel had sustained 268 dead and wounded.

Sharon's mindset at that time is interesting in the light of the policies he implemented when he later became prime minister. Looking back in the late 1980s, he wrote that he believed the Arabs were excellent fighters and "the key to beating them was to keep them off balance. The trick, the necessity, was not to let them fight their battle but always to do the unexpected." The purpose of the raids, he came to believe, was "not simply . . . retaliation or even deterrence in the usual sense. It was to create in the Arabs a psychology of defeat . . . to beat them so decisively that they would develop the conviction that they could never win."

By the same token, he objected to limited strikes: "I came to believe that whenever we were forced to strike, we should do so with the aim of inflicting heavy losses on enemy troops . . . to neutralize the Arabs' desire to make war on us . . . to convince the Arabs that war was futile, that aggression would bring them nothing but humiliation and destruction."[5]

8

QALQUILYA

———

In 1956, THE PACE of incursions, attacks, retaliations and raids by both sides accelerated. The threat of Soviet support for Egypt was of grave concern to the Israeli General Staff. It was obvious to the military that war with Egypt was inevitable; that it would take six to eight months for Egypt to arm. Consequently, they expected an attack before autumn. Many in the IDF wanted to start a preventive war, but they did not have the support of the Israeli public, who thought primarily in terms of defense, not offense, and would not condone their country taking what they considered an aggressive posture. There was a good deal of pressure on the government to develop defensive mechanisms like forts, trenches and mines, instead of relying on military interdictions.

The defense budget was greatly increased and the government turned to the US for purchases of heavy armaments. But because of the Czech part of the equation, the State Department—under John Foster Dulles—rejected the Israeli request, partly out of fear that sales of arms to Israel would drive the Arabs further into the Soviet orbit. By and large, the British position was the same, except that they did at least agree to supply six night-fighter planes. The situation was finally alleviated when the French, after a round of secret negotiations in Paris led by Shimon Peres, then general director of the Ministry of Defense, agreed to supply the desperately needed tanks, missiles, trucks and planes.[1]

War was imminent. But Sharon clung to his policy of deterrence through retaliation. He believed, as we have seen, that if it had not been for the incessant commando retaliatory raids, the frightened Israeli immigrant populations would have fled to the center of the country, vacating the border settlements and putting the entire country at risk. On the other hand, he was well aware that the policy of retaliation had not in fact created the deterrence for which it was designed. Questions about this policy came to a head with Sharon's raid—October 10 and 11—on the Jordanian police headquarters in Qalquilya, a densely populated Arab town. This was in response to King Hussein's release from prison of a band of smugglers identified by Israeli Intelligence as responsible for eight murders in Israel, including the killing and mutilation of two workers in an orange grove near Kfar Malal.

The paratroopers crossed the border around nine o'clock in the evening and a violent battle ensued against the Arab Legion that did not end until half past eleven. The police fort and its environs were, in Dayan's words, "stormed, subdued, combed and cleared and the fort blown up." A second unit deep inside Jordan blocked Legion reinforcements moving toward Qalquilya, but was trapped on the way back and, outnumbered under heavy fire, had to be saved by a special rescue unit that brought them back as dawn was breaking.

In this massive raid, eighteen Israeli soldiers were killed and sixty wounded, while the Jordanian death toll was one hundred, with twice as many wounded. This heavy loss of life caused a reconsideration of the retaliation policy, while the raid itself created a rift between Sharon and Moshe Dayan, who had unexpectedly issued orders for changes of plan, limiting the scope of action just as the paratroopers were starting out. Sharon made it clear that he was enraged with the General Staff's interference with his plans: he continued to argue with Dayan, who was also on the scene, even during the battle itself, and in the aftermath he held the General Staff responsible for the heavy casualties. Sharon and his battalion commanders were summoned by Dayan to General Headquarters where there was an unpleasant scene with a good deal of shouting and recrimination.[2]

What Sharon did not know, or did not take into consideration at the time, was that Ben-Gurion and Dayan were planning the Sinai campaign with the British and the French. Since Jordan had a defense treaty with Britain, the General Staff wanted to limit Sharon's action so that Jordan would not be driven to invoke that treaty, an eventuality that would have caused embarrassing complications.

In his diary, Dayan summed up the situation facing the General Staff:

> In all the discussions that took place that week—in the Parliamentary Committee on Security and Foreign Affairs, in the General Staff, in the defense minister's office—one question was asked: 'How and where shall we go on?' I expressed my opinion that we could not continue in this situation—neither war nor peace; that we must force our Arab neighbors to choose between ceasing to infiltrate Israel and entering a war against us . . .
>
> Nowhere was anything specific decided upon concerning the future, but we all realized that we had reached the end of the chapter of nocturnal reprisals.[3]

9

THE SINAI CAMPAIGN: MITLA PASS

———

"THE ISRAELI RAID ON GAZA brought to a definitive end whatever remained of the possibility for a rapprochement between Nasser's government and leaders of the Jewish state."[1]

On July 26, 1956, Nasser announced that Egypt was nationalizing the Suez Canal. The IDF chief of staff, General Meir Amit, was approached by the French about the possibility of a joint action against Egypt. There was no question about Israeli support for this. British Prime Minister Anthony Eden hesitated to join the action openly because of political problems at home, to say nothing of British doubts about the effectiveness of the IDF. But a plan was worked out in late October: the Israelis would invade Egypt and the British and French would then enter the fray on the pretext of defending the canal against both the Egyptians and Israelis. This was the only basis on which the British would move, and the French would not move without the British.[2]

The Israelis agreed reluctantly to go along with this scenario, which cast them as the sole aggressors; what they wanted to do was to occupy the Gaza Strip and open the Straits of Tiran, which had been closed to Israeli shipping since 1949. The Egyptians had withdrawn half their forces from the Sinai because they were mobilizing against an expected attack from the British and French.

Dayan had agreed to begin hostilities with a parachute drop on Mitla Pass, some twenty miles from the canal. "So remote was the area selected . . . Nasser exclaimed that the Israelis were 'attacking sand.'"[3] This plan would involve Israel's fighting alone until the British and French used the Israeli invasion to enter the fighting themselves. The Israeli government distrusted the British because of their behavior in Palestine during World War II and in their 1948 evacuation when they turned arms and forts over to the Arabs. Ben-Gurion feared air attacks on Tel Aviv and Haifa, and no one wanted Sharon to find himself fighting alone in the Sinai. It was decided that they would accept the Anglo-French plan, but would cloak their attack as a series of raids rather than as the beginning of a full-scale war, despite the fact that the British wanted the appearance of a full-scale IDF invasion to support their own military actions.

Since the Egyptian enclaves at Thamad and Nakhl in the middle of the Sinai were small, as opposed to the heavy concentration of military force in the northern Sinai with its capitol city of El Arish, it was reasonable to suppose that the Egyptians would not see this action as an all-out attempt to conquer the Sinai. And if the English and French backed off, Israel would not be left in an invidious and vulnerable position, but could rapidly retreat back through Thamad and Nakhl.

The plan was for the Israelis to start their action on Monday, October 29, at five in the afternoon, and for the British and French to attack at dawn on Wednesday, two days later. Dayan was told that the British forbade Israel to attack Jordan, but could retaliate if Jordan attacked first, and that there was no Anglo-French objection to Israeli capture of the Straits of Tiran and the Gaza Strip. Mobilization went forward with the enthusiastic support of the population; in order to avoid alerting the Egyptians, the pretense was that this action was directed against Jordan.

In late afternoon, a 395-man paratrooper battalion commanded by Raful Eytan, was dropped more than 120 miles inside Egyptian territory, east of Mitla Pass, their objective. The area was so remote that there were no Egyptian troops there. Meanwhile, Sharon planned to move nonstop across the Sinai. Unit 202 overran

Kuntilla—not a difficult feat since the garrison had decamped. After that, the paratroopers took heavily fortified Thamad, with fifty Egyptian and four Israeli casualties and moved on to Nakhl, where they defeated two Egyptian companies. Their next move was westward, toward Mitla Pass. The desert presented a difficult obstacle, wrecking ten or eleven of their thirteen tanks: trucks bogged down in the sand; no one had thought to bring proper tools to get them moving again. On October 30, after thirty hours, the exhausted unit linked up with Eytan's isolated paratroopers, who had been under Egyptian air bombardment.

The British and French did not start their campaign until late in the afternoon on October 31, having left the Israelis on their own for forty-eight hours. But by the fourth day the Israelis had, in Martin van Creveld's words, "effectively broken the Egyptian army in the Sinai."[4] At dawn on October 31, Sharon, on the brink of moving into Mitla Pass, received a cable from headquarters telling him that plans had changed and that he should remain where he was. Shortly afterward, he received word from Israeli aircraft, which had swooped in overhead and driven off Egyptian jet fighters, that an Egyptian armored brigade was now forty miles away.

Sharon found this news alarming, since he was far behind the Egyptian lines with no relief to rely on. He asked for permission to move into the pass—a narrow passage between steep cliffs—but permission was refused. However, when the Southern Command chief of staff, Rehavam Zeevi, arrived in a light plane, Sharon appealed to him and received permission to send a patrol into the pass, provided that it did not engage in heavy combat.

Sharon immediately sent in what Moshe Dayan later described as "a full combat team . . . of two infantry companies on half-tracks, a detachment of three tanks, the brigade reconaissance unit on trucks and a troop of heavy mortars in support." Motta Gur was in command. Sharon said that his goal was to move twenty miles to the western end of the pass and dig in there to hold off the Egyptians and that he expected no fighting to occur inside the pass. But he had not sent out scouts to explore the surrounding hills, and had made no attempt to secure that rocky terrain, which certainly presented the danger of entrapment.

As soon as the convoy entered the narrow defile, about twelve-thirty or one o'clock in the afternoon, it was hit by fire from both sides of the cliff wall. This was actually coming from an entire Egyptian Brigade—five infantry companies—that had not retreated, as Sharon had mistakenly believed, but was entrenched in caves and fissures of the cliffs on either side of the pass, hidden from the Israeli pilots who had surveyed the area. At dawn the day before, the Egyptians had come through the western end of the pass and ensconced themselves in the cliffs, heavily armed with anti-tank and machine guns and recoilless rifles, and with the expectation of air support from ten fighter planes. Gur, wrongly assuming that the initial salvo was coming from a small ambush, did not retreat, but continued to advance into the pass, where the attack on the convoy intensified. The fuel truck was the first to go up in flames, followed by an ammunition truck, four half-tracks, a tank, a jeep and an ambulance.

Motta Gur was pinned down on the floor of the pass until late in the afternoon when the brigade second in command provided cover for him to get out. Reconnaissance units climbed the cliff on one side, hoping to attack the enemy from above; when they received fire they assumed that it was coming from below them, though it was actually coming from crevices in the cliff opposite them. Confused, they rushed down the steep hillside; many plunged to their deaths and others were felled by gunfire from below and opposite them.

After dark, two small units were dispatched, one to each cliffside. The result was hand-to-hand combat, a fierce, bloody battle that lasted for two hours, until eight o'clock that night. The Israelis were victorious, but at considerable cost: thirty-eight paratroopers killed and 120 wounded. The number of Egyptian dead was estimated by Sharon at 260, and by Dayan at 150. In any case, Sharon abandoned Mitla Pass after he captured it and there was no further action anywhere in the area: the Egyptians had withdrawn because of the threat of an attack by the British and the French. This was a completely unnecessary battle and also unfortunately the bloodiest encounter of the war.

Moshe Dayan and the General Staff instituted an inquiry into Sharon's actions at Mitla Pass; Motta Gur also questioned these actions. Clearly, Sharon had not obeyed the orders he received to send in only a patrol and specifically to avoid heavy combat. He defended himself heatedly, saying that it was necessary to pick up the wounded and that he needed to organize a defense against what he thought was an imminent Egyptian attack from the north. Dayan was privately extremely critical of Sharon, but his public comments were relatively mild. He was most upset, he said, because he believed that the paratroop commander had attempted to mask a heavy combat unit as a "patrol" and had not been honest with the General Staff. The action might have been necessary, he said, if the unit had been instructed to breach the defenses of the Suez Canal, but in fact the intention was to go south to Sharm al-Sheikh. In any event, the inquiry came to no resolution, but Sharon's reputation had been tarnished.

An ultimatum had been issued by the Anglo-French, who followed it with the bombardment of Egyptian airfields. But all three aggressors—the British, the French and the Israelis—were condemned by the United States, Russia and the UN: John Foster Dulles exerted strong pressure for the abandonment of the action, as did Soviet Premier Nikolai Bulganin, who threatened retaliation against the three countries, reserving his strongest language for denunciation of Israel and eventually going so far as to break off Russian-Israeli diplomatic relations. Since, in addition, Anthony Eden had little support for the action in Britain, it was obvious that it was going to have to be aborted. Before that could happen, the IDF wanted to move quickly to end the Egyptian blockade by capturing Sharm al-Sheikh, and thus opening the Straits of Tiran to shipping and air flights.

On the morning of November 2, the Ninth Brigade, under Avraham Yoffe, was ordered to advance from Ras en Nakb, on the coast of the Gulf of Aqaba just south of Eilat, against Sharm al-Sheikh, which was being held by two Egyptian battalions. At the same time, two paratrooper companies were dropped at A Tur on the southwest coast of the Gulf of Suez where they were joined by Raful Eytan's combined troop of infantry and paratroopers travelling overland. Yoffe came almost dead south and Eytan moved southeast; Yoffe's Ninth Brigade arrived first and, with air support, opened the attack. Then Eytan joined him and in twelve hours of fighting—November 4 and 5—Sharm al-Sheikh was captured.

In four days, the Israelis, despite various bungles and missteps—from many of which Sharon could not be exonerated—had succeeded in breaking the Egyptian army in the Sinai. They withdrew to their borders, but they had opened the Straits of Tiran, and demilitarized the Sinai, where a UN peacekeeping force was established. The UN took control from Egypt of Sharm al-Sheikh. Until they were pressured to withdraw from it, the Israelis held the Gaza Strip, filled with Arab refugee camps and hence a base for fedayeen incursions into Israel. But apart from that, the Sinai campaign gave the Israelis a much-needed boost in morale and demonstrated to their hostile neighbors that they were a force to be reckoned with.[5] "Having defeated its enemy, the IDF, riding sky-high, felt it could face its future with confidence."[6]

10

CHANGE OF PACE

———

WHEN IT WAS OFFICIAL that a parachute jump at Sharm al-Sheikh had been rendered unnecessary, Sharon went home for a visit to a new house in a military suburb of Tel Aviv to be with Gali, then seven months pregnant. On the way he stopped at Kfar Malal to see his father, who was extremely ill and upset that Sharon had no intention of moving back and taking up life in the moshav orchards. In late December, Gali gave birth to a boy, Gur Shmuel, and three days later, on December 31, 1956, Samuil Scheinerman died. Sharon was twenty-eight years old, and because of his military involvement, had hardly seen his father since 1947. He was of course overjoyed at the birth of his son—an event that he and Gali had hoped for for years—but he felt he had neglected his father.[1]

For two months, before the UN multinational force took over the Sinai, Sharon's Unit 202 spread out everywhere over that territory, making maps and charts, learning the terrain, because Sharon was not only enraged that Israel was forced to withdraw from the Sinai, but was convinced that the UN occupation was not going to provide a permanent solution to the problems of the area. He also found it difficult to accept—or even to understand—the withdrawal, under international pressure, from the Gaza Strip, where Ben-Gurion had established a settlement. "Our overriding goal," he wrote later about the Sinai war, "had been to find a way of forcing Egypt to accept responsibility and put an end to [the relentless terror from the strip]. And now the Egyptians would be coming back. It was as if we had not solved anything at all."[2]

He remained as paratroop commander until the fall of 1957, when Dayan sent him for a year to a British army staff college in Surrey. He stayed the week days in officers' quarters at the college and spent the weekends in London with Gali and the baby. This was a broadening experience for Sharon, who enjoyed not only the cultural advantages of London, but also his studies, as well as his introduction to life as a British army officer—which included the personal services of a batman, a kind of valet. He liked and respected the British tradition: the ceremonies and protocol. Nothing could have been more of a contrast to his years as an Israeli paratrooper commander.

When he returned from England, he received a promotion from lieutenant colonel to colonel, but had to accept a post as commander of infantry training, a position that he hated but in which he served for four years. He tried to vary his routine by studying law at night at a branch of the Hebrew University in Tel Aviv—he was to receive his degree in 1966—but he was restless and resented his assignment. Suddenly, these problems dwindled in importance when Gali, who had been working as a supervisory psychiatric nurse at the Ministry of Health in Jerusalem, was killed in an automobile accident on her way to work.

Sharon was left with his five-year-old son Gur, who became despondent, lost his appetite and apparently his interest in life, despite all Sharon's efforts to comfort him. But things improved when Gali's younger sister Lily came to take care of him. Gradually the child recovered, putting on weight and becoming once more the boy he had been before his mother's death.[3] Sharon too was comforted by Lily's presence and eventually they became more to each other than brother- and sister-in-law. In August, 1963, they married.[4]

In 1963, Yitzhak Rabin had become commander-in-chief and appointed Sharon chief of staff for the Northern Command under his old friend Avraham Yoffe. The Northern Command was trying to cope with fallout resulting from a weak Lebanese government, and minor attacks by the Syrians on a few hundred Israeli farms near the Golan Heights. But the most dangerous controversy arose over water, what has been called the Battle of Water, which Sharon maintains was the actual seed of the 1967 war.

On January 13, 1964, at a first Arab summit in Cairo—attended by thirteen Arab leaders—a decision was announced to build a canal to divert water into Jordan from two rivers that flowed into the River Jordan. Martin van Creveld says that this was in response to Israel's beginning a major project in the late fifties to divert water from the Sea of Galilee into the Negev. In any case, Sharon points out that before 1967, a third of Israel's entire water supply came from the Jordan River. The prospect of a dramatic reduction of that supply could hardly be taken lightly by the Israelis, who determined to prevent the completion of work on the canal. The result, by November, was shooting, shelling and even bombing along the Israeli-Syrian border. In late winter and early spring of 1967, Van Creveld says, there were major border incidents, even though by that time the Syrians had given up their water diversion project.

At this same water summit meeting, the thirteen Arab heads of state who attended also began preliminary discussions about the formation of a Palestine Liberation Organization (PLO). At a later summit in May of that year in east Jerusalem, the organization took formal shape. Its founding principle was to "attain the objective of liquidating Israel."[5]

While all this was going on, Sharon moved to an apartment in a farmhouse in Nahalal, the oldest moshav in the country, and in August of 1964 greeted the birth of a second son, Omri.[6] His enjoyment of farm life was interrupted when Avraham Yoffe retired and was replaced by General David Elazar. Sharon did not welcome this change. Perceiving an unpleasant new atmosphere in the Northern Command, he decided to go on a five-week trip through Africa with

Yoffe. Getting to Africa was a tricky business at the time, since the Egyptians had once more taken over the Sinai and Israelis were hemmed in. But Sharon and Yoffe succeeded and had some interesting adventures in Uganda, Ethiopia and Eritrea.

When he returned, he found that another chief of staff had been appointed to share the Northern Command with him. Bickering and intrigue, he says, were the order of the day. In October of 1965, he expected another promotion but was sure he would not get it when Rabin called him into his office and gave him a severe dressing-down, listing his many mistakes and his personal shortcomings, including his attitude toward General Elazar. But after he finished berating him, Rabin, to Sharon's great surprise, promoted him to major general and appointed him director of military training and commander of a reserve unit.

In order to be close to his new offices, Sharon and Lily moved from the moshav to their previous house in Zahala where in six months a third son, Gilad Yehuda, was born.[7]

THE SIX-DAY WAR

———

ON MAY 14, 1967, a Sunday, Sharon was in Jerusalem watching Israel's nineteenth annual Independence Day celebrations, when word came that the Egyptians were moving troops across the Suez Canal into the Sinai. Things had been relatively quiet along the Sinai and Gaza Strip border: United Nations Emergency Forces had been stationed there since the 1956 war. For five years, Nasser had been preoccupied with fighting in Yemen, where Egypt was supporting a leftist revolution. There had been, however, a good deal of hostile activity on the Syrian and Jordanian borders: the Syrians pounded Israeli settlements in the Jordan and Hulah valleys from their fortifications on the Golan Heights, and there were innumerable border clashes and reprisals. In response to heavy shelling, the Israeli Air Force had bombed the Golan Heights and gone so far as to shoot down Syrian planes over Damascus.

On May 17, Nasser called for the withdrawal of UN forces from the Sinai and the Gaza Strip; two days later Secretary General U Thant agreed. The Palestine Liberation Organization took over the UN emplacements in Gaza, and 80,000–100,000 Egyptian troops, with 800–1000 tanks, poured into the Sinai. On May 22, Nasser declared the closing of the Straits of Tiran to all ships bound to or from Israel. This was an open act of war. On May 26, Nasser announced his intention to destroy Israel. He had, he said, allowed the UN to remain only while he was building up his military.

On May 30, King Hussein put his Jordanian army under the Egyptians, who also controlled not only Iraqi forces but also units from Kuwait and Algeria. Hussein might have preferred to stay out of this action, but in a sense he was forced to cooperate: he did not want to be on bad terms with Nasser and ostracized by all other Arab countries. He also had his own border problems with the Israelis. In any case, by the first week in June, Israel was surrounded on all sides by Arab armies, and appeared to be outnumbered and outgunned in every way, with fewer troops, tanks, artillery and planes than their enemies.

To Sharon, this was not really as terrifying a prospect as it may have appeared. He felt that Israel was in a much better situation than in 1956. He was quoted as saying that Israel was "no longer an isolated, fragile people whose survival was open to doubt," but an experienced nation with international contacts, he wanted to strike quickly, to win before the US and Russia demanded a cease-fire, as they had in 1956. But Prime Minister Levi Eshkol and most of his General Staff did not see it that way. They felt trapped, in real danger of extinction and tried to think of the best way to survive. They decided to appeal to the international community, or at least to the Big Four nations, to get the blockade lifted and the Arab troops withdrawn. But their appeals were not successful.

According to Moshe Dayan, the Soviets urged Nasser on by spreading false rumors that Israel was massing troops on the Syrian border in preparation for an invasion. Abba Eban, Eshkol's foreign minister, asked Britain, the United States and France to honor their 1957 pledge to keep the Straits of Tiran open. The French response was certainly not encouraging: General DeGaulle held up delivery to Israel of arms already paid for; his motive, he said, was to prevent Israel from starting a war. He advised the Israelis to agree to the blockade and all Arab demands, including the return of refugees to the country. Dayan believed that another motive for DeGaulle was the cementing of good Arab-French relations. Italy and Spain too did not want to upset the Egyptians.

Harold Wilson's foreign minister, George Brown, flew to Moscow on May 24, to try to get the Russians to support mandating the return of the UN troops and to press Egypt to evacuate Sharm al-Sheikh. These requests were summarily rejected by Aleksei Kosygin. Brown suggested a combined British-US naval task force to keep peace in the region, but this did not happen, although President Johnson declared that the US was opposed to the blockade and to the UN evacuation. The United States, Johnson said, was committed to the security of Israel. He suggested looking for a compromise to avoid war, and sent Robert Anderson as special emissary to Cairo. Nasser's reply was that he would postpone the blockade for two weeks of discussion if Israel agreed not to send shipping through the straits during that time. In effect, he would postpone the blockade if Israel agreed to a blockade. Since Anderson had told him that Johnson did not intend to join in sending an international force through the straits, Nasser felt justified in believing that the Big Four would do nothing to stop war, but would demand an immediate halt to it if it broke out.

The Israelis were thus convinced that they were on the brink of annihilation. Sharon was disgusted with Eshkol and the General Staff. They did not seem to know what to do; they hesitated over plans. Some thought it would be a good idea to move in phases: to begin by taking over the Gaza Strip and using it to negotiate with Nasser. They would offer to return the strip if he would open the straits. Sharon was strongly against this idea of phases. If they didn't move quickly, he said, the US and Russia would demand a cease-fire; in addition, if they took Gaza and then stopped to talk, Nasser would use the time to build his forces and orient them to the desert.

The Southern Front divisional commanders—Sharon, Israel Tal and Avraham Yoffe, called out of retirement—were summoned to

Tel Aviv to meet with Eshkol, Chief of Staff Yitzhak Rabin, and Minister of Labor Yigal Allon. Eshkol and his people more or less gave up the Gaza Strip idea, but they still were considering fighting in "stages": one division first, then the other two twelve hours later. Sharon was not alone in arguing for a direct attack everywhere at once: Moshe Dayan had stated his belief that it was important in every psychological way for Israel to prove that she could stand up to the Arabs and not look weak and frightened by trying to negotiate her way out of war. But confusion seemed to reign; opinions were divided. Units were removed, then restored.

On May 28, two weeks after Egypt had begun moving large forces across the canal, Eshkol made an eagerly awaited radio address to the nation. The speech was a complete fiasco, filled with stammering and hesitation, a performance that could only reinforce the conviction that the prime minister was not up to the job. On May 30, King Hussein flew to Cairo and signed a defense pact with Nasser. This pact was to be extended to include Iraq: armies were thus poised to attack Israel from the north, the east and the south. On June 1, Moshe Dayan was appointed minister of defense. On June 2, Sharon, Tal and Yoffe were called back to Tel Aviv to discuss military plans with Dayan and Rabin.[1]

On the evening of June 3, the final decision was made to go to war. Van Creveld says that during a visit from the head of Mossad, US Secretary of Defense Robert McNamara had given the clear impression that the US would not object if "Nasser's bones were broken."[2] The decision was for war. Two days later—on June 5—air raid sirens sounded throughout the country, the signal that war had been declared. Earlier, 188 Israeli planes had taken off at dawn, flying low and maintaining radio silence to avoid radar detection. In less than three hours, wave after wave of airplanes hit nineteen Egyptian airfields, and nearly three hundred aircraft—sitting targets—were destroyed on their runways.

Sharon had developed a lightning plan of attack. The northern half of the Sinai held all major Egyptian bases and fortifications, and five of seven Egyptian divisions. The most significant were at Rafah and El Arish in the northern Sinai and Abu Agheila and Um Katef. Kusseima, twenty miles to the south, was also a prime defense area for the Egyptians, as was Kuntilla, south of Kusseima.

These areas, probable jumping-off points for Egyptian attacks, held infantry, tank and artillery units. Behind them were two Egyptian strike forces, and two other Egyptian divisions near Kuntilla in the south. Three Israeli divisions faced them: one led by Tal, one by Yoffe and one by Sharon. The road from Beersheba to Ismailia in Egypt had to be opened, and this entailed the taking of Abu Agheila and Kusseima, held by the Egyptian Second Division. The road to Ismailia went right through Abu Agheila. If Abu Agheila fell, the Israelis would control all the roads behind Kusseima, and the Egyptians in Kusseima would be cut off.

On the morning of June 5, while the Israeli air force was bombing the Egyptian air fields, Tal broke through the fortifications of Rafah in the northern sector, capturing a divisional headquarters and reaching the outskirts of El Arish on the Mediterranean before dark. El Arish fell the next day; motorized units moved quickly from there toward the canal.

Um Katef, crossing the Ismailia road fifteen miles from the Israeli border, was a long swell of sand set between swampy sand dunes on the north and jagged cliffs on the south. The Egyptians had constructed an elaborate defense network there; three parallel trench systems crossed the road to Ismailia, each protected by a line of gun positions, storage depots and communications centers, behind minefields manned by a full infantry brigade. A mile or so behind the trenches was a mobile reserve of more than eighty tanks; just south of this reserve was a nest of artillery with a greater range than those of the Israelis. This formidable concentration of forces was screened by perimeter outposts to the east and, most strongly, to the north, where its flank was guarded by a fortified batallion of infantry and tanks.

Sharon launched his attack on Um Katef at 11 pm on June 5. Paratroopers landed behind Egyptian lines and wiped out artillery batteries which were shelling the approaches to Um Katef and Abu Agheila. The infantry brigade crossed the dunes, bursting into the Um Katef trenches and taking them under heavy fire and in hand-to-hand combat. At the same time, Sharon's armored unit engaged the tanks in Um Katef while another tank batallion moved west and then swung around to attack Abu Agheila from the rear. Yoffe's armored brigade moved through Sharon's lines and pressed westward to catch up with Tal's tank brigade. By the morning of June 6, the battle was over.

The breakthrough had been completed in just two days. When it was learned that Cairo had ordered a retreat, Israeli paratroopers were dispatched by helicopter to take Sharm al-Sheikh. They landed there at 1 pm, June 7, to find, to their amazement, two Israeli torpedo boats tied up at the quay. The naval force had reached the port at 11:30 that morning, found it deserted and sent two detachments ashore. The blockade had been lifted.

On the evening of June 7, the General Staff was informed that the UN Security Council was about to hold an emergency session and would undoubtedly impose a cease-fire. At one o'clock the next morning, Tal moved within ten miles of the Suez Canal, followed by paratroopers. At 7:30 am on June 9, he reached Ismailia. Seven hours later, the Egyptian retreat route had been cut off. Yoffe blocked the entrance to Mitla Pass with nine tanks; those enemy forces already inside the pass were strafed by the IAF. Sharon hurried south after retreating Egyptian armored divisions, ambushed enemy tanks at Nakhl and advanced to join Yoffe at Mitla Pass. It was Friday evening, June 9. Sharon called the scene "indescribable. The entire pass was choked with the wreckage of the Egyptian army. Tanks, artillery, half-tracks—countless hundreds of vehicles smoked and burned, sending up a black haze that hung like dirty gauze in the clear desert sky. It was impossible to look at that feast of death and not know that the remnants of the Egyptian Sinai force had met their fate right here."[3]

On June 7, the Security Council had demanded a cease-fire. On June 8, Nasser accepted the cease-fire, just minutes after the Soviets had submitted a draft resolution calling for Israel to withdraw to its 1949 borders.

The conquest of the Sinai was completed on the evening of Saturday, June 10. The entire campaign had taken ninety-six hours. Sharon, hailed as a hero, gave many press interviews. In one, he was quoted as saying, "I must admit that looking at our soldiers in perspective, they seem like an unruly herd. They're wonderful soldiers, they've got excellent officers, but they weren't properly dressed and their vehicles were mostly milk trucks. I thought of what the captured Egyptians would say when they saw us. But our soldiers are fantastic. In our army, the word 'Forward!' practically doesn't exist—officers yell 'Follow me!' It's our secret weapon, the secret of our success, not the tanks and artillery."[4]

With the fighting over, Sharon remained in the Sinai for several days. He had to round up thousands of Egyptian soldiers who were wandering around in the hot desert sands, exposed to attacks by nomads who wanted their weapons. At first, Sharon planned to take them as prisoners of war, but, eventually, after holding more than 6000 and facing the difficulty of supply, he was ordered by Rabin to keep only the officers. Although there was no formal agreement about the repatriation of prisoners of war, thousands of Egyptian soldiers were taken to Kantara, on the east bank of the canal, where they boarded ferries to take them home. The officers, however, were transported to POW camps to be used in exchange for captured Israeli soldiers.

In six days, Israel had defeated Jordan, Egypt and Syria.

A NEW REALITY

———

BACK IN THE BOSOM of his family, Sharon was euphoric. He took Lily and Gur to see the Old City. East Jerusalem was a festive place then, filled with Jews who had finally been allowed to enter freely after twenty years of being banned under Jordanian rule. There were also thousands of tourists who came to see holy places like the Western Wall, believed to be a remnant of the ancient Temple. Sharon—readily recognizable—was besieged with well-wishers.

Israel now controlled land three times its pre-war size and thus needed to draw new lines of defense, particularly along the Suez Canal. Rabin said: "We had never before thought of distance in terms of hundreds of miles. We had to overcome the resultant logistics and transport difficulties with limited manpower, since tens of thousands of reservists had returned to their fields and factories, schools and offices."[1] As Israel had in fact become an occupying power, much of this internal debate revolved around how the West Bank and Gaza Strip should be ruled.

Moshe Dayan appointed Chaim Herzog governor of the West Bank, an area then populated by some 800,000 Palestinians. He told Herzog: "Let the Arabs rule themselves under our control. I want an Arab to be born, raised and live in the West Bank and never to see an Israeli official. It's bad enough that we have to suffer from our bureaucracy. Why should they?"[2] The Palestinian Arabs, newly freed from Jordanian and Egyptian rule, could hardly be expected to celebrate yet another occupation. After having lived under the poor conditions and discrimination of the Hashemite Kingdom, Palestinians felt that self-rule was long overdue.

Both Chaim Herzog and Yigal Allon, deputy prime minister and minister of immigration absorption, favored the idea of an independent Palestine under Israeli sovereignty. Dayan, however, rejected the idea of Palestine self-rule, fearing that it would be ruled by Ahmed Shukeiry, the PLO commander who was inciting violence against Israel in the West Bank. It was not until twenty-five years later that David Kimche, an Israeli diplomat, told the story of how a group of Palestinian activists—headed by attorney Aziz Shehada—tried in good faith to negotiate an agreement with Israel to implement their goal of an independent Palestine in the West Bank and Gaza. According to Kimche, forty Palestinian leaders had planned to convene in Jericho to craft a peace agreement that would ultimately lead to some form of Palestinian self-rule. But when leaders of the PLO heard about the plan, they became alarmed and Yassir Arafat sternly reproached Shehada, accusing him and the other activists of betrayal. He warned them that their attempts to negotiate a small Palestinian state to co-exist with a Jewish state would endanger Palestinian liberation and put an end to the Palestinian cause. As a result, Shehada's plan was scrapped.[3]

There was also opposition to Palestinian independence from Jordan's King Hussein, who had just lost control of the West Bank. He proclaimed that there was only "one Jordan" east and west of the river and warned Palestinians of the perils of "separatism." Jordanian radio announced that disloyalty to the king and cooperation with the Jews would be considered treason, punishable by death.

Elul, 1967—the end of the summer—the twelfth month of the Jewish year, looked promising for Sharon. He was enjoying his home and family life and, back at GHQ, none of his duties as director of military training involved any of the tension he had felt in earlier months. Sharon recalled that he "was able to enjoy the luxury of being at home. Omri, our second child, was three; Gilad, our third, was approaching his first birthday. I felt I was making up for lost time, and with Lily and Gur too. I began to relax. Memories of my friends who had died were still fresh. But, painful as they were, when you know you have achieved something crucial you feel even terrible losses differently, they taste less bitter." He was immensely proud of his son Gur, now almost twelve years old, to whom he was growing even closer. Gur was good-looking and talented. "It seemed to me that a precious gift had been inexplicably bestowed on me," Sharon said.[4]

At GHQ, Sharon had a new assignment which dovetailed with his defense strategy as well as his ideas for development of the territory. He made detailed plans to move various military schools from their old Israeli bases to the West Bank and instructed one commander of an infantry school to move from its base in Netanya to the captured Jordanian army base near Nablus, a notorious hotbed, even then, of Palestinian nationalism. Within a few months, Sharon was able to move infantry, engineering, paratrooper and artillery schools. He wanted to build a complete infrastructure to establish a military presence. His aim was to "establish Jewish footholds as fast as possible. . . . This area was an integral part of the country that had been captured by the Arab armies in 1948. Now we had come back."[5]

He tried to convince Moshe Dayan to start housing construction for the growing number of officers stationed at West Bank bases, and was annoyed when Dayan refused. Sharon believed that Israel needed to settle the West Bank to guard against the possibility that "in a moment of weakness" Israel might offer to give up the terrritory. He felt this was much less likely if there were established, well-populated Jewish centers in the territory. "I knew from our previous experience that the only way to permanently secure the most strategic terrain in our hands was to live on it."[6]

In 1967, the evening of Rosh Hashonah, the Jewish New Year, fell on October 4. That morning, Sharon was home with the children and Lily was out in the city for some last-minute holiday shopping. While he was on the phone, he heard the sound of a gunshot in front of his house and rushed outside: to his horror, he found Gur stretched out on the grass, his face covered with blood. Next to him lay an antique shotgun. Evidently, one of his playmates had filled it with powder, playfully pointed it at Gur—and it had gone off. Sharon rushed him to the hospital, but it was useless. The child died.

Gur was buried next to his mother, Margalit. Shlomo Goren, the chief military rabbi, conducted the burial service. Looking at the grave he said: "She took him back to her."[7] Sharon could not stop weeping. He and Lily were devastated and for months could find no relief. "There seemed to be no single moment when it was not present. Nothing could soothe it, nothing could lay it to rest."[8]

After that, says Uzi Benziman, Sharon always kept a rake and a shovel in the trunk of his car. "Periodically, he would drive to the cemetery to weed the plots and water the flowers. Alone he would stand next to the graves with tears in his eyes."[9]

13

THE WAR OF ATTRITION

———

A WEEK AFTER THE Six-Day War, Israel made peace overtures. The main condition attached to their proposal was that the areas in question become demilitarized. "By June 19," said Chaim Herzog, "the Israeli government had agreed in principle to return Sinai to Egypt and to return the Golan Heights to Syria in exchange for peace and demilitarization. . . . Appropriate arrangements were prepared separately for Jordan." These proposals were approved by the Americans and King Hussein was ready to discuss them in detail, but Nasser warned him, Herzog says, to wait until the Arab summit conference in Khartoum.[1] But on September 1, a resolution emerged from that summit which put paid to further discussion: "No peace. No negotiation. No recognition."[2]

Soon after losing the Six-Day War, Nasser appeared on television to announce his resignation. He accused "the imperialist powers"—Britain and the United States—of supplying the Jewish state with arms, but finally accepted personal responsibility for the Egyptian defeat. "I have decided to give up completely and finally every official post and every political role and return to the ranks of the public as any other citizen."[3]

Within minutes of his announcement, the streets of Cairo were jammed with people protesting Nasser's resignation and demanding his return to power. As a result, he relented and resumed the presidency and—urged on by the Soviets—released a new military plan against Israel. "What was taken by force," he declared, "must be restored by force."[4] The result was the War of Attrition, which began shortly after the Six-Day War and by the end of 1969 had evolved into a serious conflict. Nasser announced his goal: "We shall weaken Israel and damage its ability to withstand our push to regain our captured territory. We will kill soldiers and civilians alike wherever our glorious fedayeen find them. Israel's morale will suffer and it will not be able to continue. And when that time comes, we shall strike to the heart of the enemy territory, unleash our superior forces of war and the battle shall be won."[5]

On July 1, 1967, Egyptian commandos ambushed an Israeli patrol on the eastern bank of the Suez Canal, killing Major Uriel Menuhin, the first Israeli casualty of the war. Ten days later, in a fierce firefight, nine Israeli soldiers were killed. These quick, decisive actions were designed to keep the IDF from establishing a foothold in Port Fuad where they could readily navigate the canal. In October, the Egyptians fired a Styx missile from Port Said, sinking the *Eilat*, an Israeli destroyer, with the loss of forty-seven sailors. Israel retaliated by pounding refineries and oil depots in Suez and Ismailia, causing enormous property damage and the flight of some 700,000 civilians.[6]

As a result, a period of relative calm followed, during which the Soviets helped the Egyptians in a massive build-up of their army: supplying new equipment and working to develop their military command. Brezhnev sent thousands of Russian advisors to Egypt and, by early 1968, Egypt had a radar and surface-to-air (SAM) missile system in place as well as 300 newly trained pilots. And in February, 1968, Levi Eshkol had met in Texas with President Johnson and convinced him to sell American Phantom jets to Israel. For the superpowers, it was beginning to take on the shape of an adjunct Cold War.[7]

Meanwhile, General Chaim Bar-Lev, who succeeded Yitzhak Rabin as IDF chief of staff, devised a plan to defend Israeli soldiers from attack along the Suez Canal and prevent Egyptian recapture of the canal's east bank. The proposal, which involved the establishment of a chain of forts on the water line, became the subject of lively debate at GHQ and there were times when strong differences of opinion led to bitter argument.

Sharon harshly criticized the Bar-Lev plan. He believed that the Sinai should be defended by mobile armored units and he felt strongly that Bar-Lev's plan would be a disaster because it would make the IDF an inflexible, immobile force: "We would be making fixed targets of ourselves three hundred yards from the Egyptian lines. Our positions and movements would be under constant surveillance. Our procedures would become common knowledge. Our patrols and supply convoys would be vulnerable to ambushes, mining."[8]

Sharon believed passionately that in the 175 miles of desert the IDF should develop an intricate and mobile defensive strategy, rather than a rigid one. Specifically, he proposed that the IDF draw a line of defense along the hills and dunes that run parallel to the canal and extend five to eight miles east. A second natural line of defense would be offered by the mountains fifteen to twenty miles from the canal where the Mitla and Gidi passes cut toward the interior. Finally, between the first line of defense and the canal, Sharon suggested patrols be constantly on the move, so that in the event of an Egyptian crossing, the Israelis would be in a position to launch the kind of free-flowing, fast-moving attack they were best at.

At the end of August, 1968, Egypt began artillery shelling and infiltration to mine roads on the east bank of the canal. In early September, they opened fire in the northern sector of the canal, killing ten Israeli soldiers and wounding eighteen. Two weeks later, Egyptian artillery pounded Israeli positions along the canal, killing fifteen Israeli soldiers and wounding thirty-four. In retaliation, helicopter-borne IDF commando units struck the Nile valley inside Egyptian territory, destroying bridges and power stations. Shaken, the Egyptians called for a cease-fire.

As casualties grew, so did the rift between Sharon and Bar-Lev. Sharon's relationship with Bar-Lev's supporters—IDF generals—was also strained. Some of them were convinced that Sharon was leaking stories about their dispute to the press. As the debate became more heated, Sharon found his support dwindling. There was an especially unpleasant GHQ meeting with Moshe Dayan present in which General Elazar and other IDF generals accused Sharon of unfairly and relentlessly attacking his colleagues. Their tone became personal and eventually Sharon stood up and said, "I thought we were here to discuss the advantages and disadvantages of the Bar-Lev line. That's the reason for this meeting and that's what I'm willing to participate in, so I can tell you again what a dangerous and stupid idea it is. But if you think for a moment that I am going to sit here and be tried by a *mishpat chaverim* (in moshavs and kibbutzim, a trial by one's friends) you're dead wrong."[8]

Bar-Lev was furious and determined to force Sharon out of the IDF altogether. Since Sharon's contract was up for renewal, Bar-Lev took the opportunity to turn down his application for re-enlistment. Sharon, enraged, sought help from Dayan, who declined to intervene. Sharon then turned to Golda Meir, who had become prime minister following Eshkol's death in February, 1969. He told her he was appalled by what Bar-Lev had done and that there seemed to be no appeal from his decision. Mrs Meir told him that while she sympathized with his predicament, it was a matter which could be resolved only by Moshe Dayan. At the age of forty-one, Sharon was facing the end of his military career.

But he was not the sort of man who would go gently into that good night. He began to think about a political career and the more he thought about it, the more appealing it became. Although he had been a member of the Labor Party, his views—not surprisingly—did not always conform to the party line. Thus, he began to consider what possibilities there might be amongst opposition parties. He contacted his friend, Joseph Sapir, whom he had known since childhood, and who for years had urged him to think about entering politics. Sapir was head of the Liberal Party and his ally was Menachem Begin, head of Herut, a right wing party. Sapir suggested that the three get together and they set up a meeting at the King David Hotel in Jerusalem, where they discussed the possibility of forming a Liberal-Herut bloc for the coming 1969 elections.

Sharon was somewhat intimidated by Begin, a man who had an extraordinarily powerful presence. It was an uncomfortable and somewhat rare sensation for the self-confident Sharon. Compared to the seasoned politicians, Begin and Sapir, he was a novice. But he did not let his feelings of intimidation deter him and the three toasted their new alliance with a bottle of brandy. "But even as we raised our glasssses," Sharon said, "I felt that I was locked in with someone about whom I had inexplicable feelings of apprehension." That night, at home, he told Lily that he felt he was not ready for a political campaign with Menachem Begin.

But the following morning, newspapers reported: "Sharon Joins Herut-Liberals," causing a good deal of concern amongst Labor Party leaders. Finance Minister Pinchas Sapir (no relation to Joseph Sapir) called Bar-Lev and told him that by forcing Sharon out of the IDF, he was making it more difficult for the Labor Party to win the election. Bar-Lev grasped the finance minister's point and arranged a meeting at which Sharon apologized to Bar-Lev for walking out of the staff meeting and promised to be less contentious. Then, at last, Bar-Lev approved Sharon's re-enlistment and assigned him special duty, lecturing at universities, army bases and schools all over the world. Sharon's political ambitions were postponed. As for the Bar-Lev military plan, it finally did prevail; the fortifications at the Suez Canal became the largest engineering project ever undertaken by

Israel. It was nearly completed by March, 1969, when Egypt intensified the war.[10]

In March, as fighting in the War of Attrition increased, Israeli mortars crashed into an Egyptian bunker in the northern sector of the canal, killing their chief of staff, General Abdul Munim Riad and several other high-ranking officers. Cairo Radio said: "With the death of Riad, we have lost a saint who served his homeland loyally." But despite this grievous loss, Egypt continued to press its offensive, to which Israel responded with attacks on more emplacements in the Nile Valley and the western shore of the Gulf of Suez.[11] The Israeli press—reflecting the public's restless mood—expressed reservations about the war as fighting continued unabated. Protest groups began to gather and high school graduates who were about to be drafted into the army demanded that the government pursue every possible avenue to peace. A popular play attacked the Israeli defense establishment, a scant three years after its exploits had won international acclaim.[12] The Egyptians monitored these Israeli protests with interest. During a meeting with Western journalists, Nasser, who announced that sixty percent of the Bar-Lev line had been destroyed, said that a country which publishes the previous day's casualties in the newspapers could not win a long-range war of attrition.[13]

In December, 1969, Sharon replaced Yeshayahu Gavish—who moved to the General Staff—as head of Southern Command. The war was of course Sharon's greatest concern, but there were others as well: troubles in the the Arava region—situated between the Dead Sea and Eilat, on the Straits of Tiran—where there was heavy PLO infiltration over the long Jordanian border; and the Gaza Strip, where the PLO was becoming increasingly powerful.[14]

Despite his intense opposition to the Bar-Lev line, Sharon followed his colleague's instructions to the letter and, in just a few days, he was able to show impressive progress in fortifying a series of thirty-two *maozim*, strong points or mini-fortresses, against trajectory fire. Sharon supervised hundreds of workers in the building of a system of control over the water supply: they built underground bunkers, high sand walls, patrol roads, and laid water lines. As a result of all this, the relationship between the two commanders improved markedly, as did the morale of the General Staff.[15]

On January 5, an Egyptian unit crossed the Suez and fired on an Israeli post. The Israelis' return fire destroyed the entire unit; they then started a massive bombing attack on Egypt proper while the IAF stepped up the frequency and intensity of their sorties along the borders. In addition, the IAF hit terrorist bases in Lebanon and Jordan, as well as bases on Mount Hermon in Syria. The aim of the air onslaught was to forestall the Egyptian movement of SAM launchers closer to the canal. Sharon proposed that the Israelis cross the canal near Kantara to destroy all SAM sites even before the Egyptians had a chance to move them, and then quickly withdraw. He also recommended keeping a limited bridgehead on the Egyptian side of the canal, and, although GHQ rejected this idea, it became an important prospective tactic for the IDF.

The war continued through the spring of 1970, and, on May 30, Egyptian commandos ambushed an Israeli patrol, killing eighteen soldiers. That was Israel's worst day of the war. In July, Soviet-piloted jets joined the battle, and on July 30, Israeli pilots downed five of these MIGs. Fearing an endless escalation of hostilities, Joseph Sisco, the American diplomat who had been working on a Middle East peace since April, promised Nasser that a cease-fire would be based on Secretary of State William Rogers' plan calling for a complete Israeli withdrawal from the Sinai.[16]

Both sides agreed and in August, 1970, a cease-fire was signed. According to Benny Morris, 367 Israelis died in the war on the Egyptian front, 260 of whom were killed "between March, 1969, and August, 1970."[17] Considering Israel's small population, these were enormous casualty figures.

FIGHTING TERROR

———

A PERPETUAL PROBLEM THAT became more pronounced after the '67 war was the infiltration from Jordan of PLO fighters who came down from the mountains in the night, hid during the daylight hours and in the evening descended on the Arava Wadi, or dry rift, to set ambushes, plant mines and lob mortars at refineries and the small agricultural settlements. Through the Arava for about a hundred miles ran an isolated highway, a main road connecting the industrial north with Eilat on the Red Sea. The Dead Sea potash and bromide works and an important oil pipeline were within mortar range of the border, which ran down the middle of the wadi and was no more than half a mile at its farthest point from the highway, where cars were attacked and passengers frequently murdered. It was an intolerable situation, and since this area was a Southern Command front, it was Sharon's responsibility to cope with it.

He set out to hunt the hunters, so to speak, to try to limit their access to the border, and if they did cross it, to cut off their return to the safety of the Jordanian mountains. This could only work, he decided, by taking the offensive; he sent long-range night patrols across the border into the mountains to set up listening posts and ambushes. The result was a loss of confidence for the infiltrators; they could no longer rely on their secret routes and they could never be sure when they themselves would be tracked down and attacked. As a consequence, infiltrations dropped sharply.

Sharon, however, was not satisfied with frustrating these sporadic raids; he wanted a long-term solution, a way to put a stop to those border infiltrations. Certainly the Jordanians showed little inclination to seal the border, and neither did the Saudi brigade which patrolled the mountains near the Dead Sea. In his autobiography, Sharon notes dryly that the world press often referred to the Saudis as "moderates," but the Israelis did not think of them that way: the Saudis had fought alongside the Egyptians in 1948, on the Jordanian front in 1967, and under Syria in 1973.[1] In any case, Sharon determined to convince the enemy that, as he put it, "any attempt to launch operations in this region would be suicidal."[2] What was needed, he believed, was a consistent Israeli presence. When the PLO hit the Dead Sea potash works with mortars from a base in Sufi, a deserted Jordanian village, he saw his opportunity.

Sufi was a good base for the PLO, with plenty of available drinking water and a Saudi camp nearby. Shortly after the mortar attack on the potash works, Sharon sent his units to attack Sufi. The battle with the PLO and the Saudis was over quickly, and the Israelis occupied the village. The next morning they began to construct a road from Sufi to the Dead Sea works; this was completed in three days, providing a vital communication link. Sharon's unit stayed in Sufi for three months. From that strategic vantage point, he built up his patrols and pushed the infiltrators farther and farther from the border, so that if they crossed over, they ran the very real risk of being caught in Israeli territory in daylight. He also worked on enhancing the barrier zone: setting up barbed wire fences, mine fields and a ten-yard-wide soft sand belt designed especially to show footprints.

The method he devised to track footprints in the wadi region was unusual. In the Negev, he found several hundred Bedouin who enthusiastically volunteered to act as trackers, riding their camels across the sands. Later the camels were trained to ride on platforms in large open Jeep command cars, so that if footprints were discovered thirty or forty miles from the nearest camel unit, the camels could be driven quickly to the spot and then unloaded. The Bedouin were excellent trackers. By the fall of 1970, most of the infiltrators had been killed or captured, and the Arava border was quiet. In an agreement with King Hussein, the Israelis pulled out of the village. When they were gone, the Jordanians, to Sharon's amusement, attacked the empty village with tank fire and announced that they had driven the Israelis out.

In Jordan itself, terror was full blown as thousands of armed Palestine Liberation Organization fighters attempted to assassinate the king and take over the country. Yassir Arafat, who had fled to Jordan from the West Bank in 1968, had become chairman of the PLO in 1969 when it was absorbed by his Fatah group, which he had helped to found ten years earlier. The PLO charter declared that "armed struggle is the only way to liberate Palestine." In 1970 the Popular Front for the Liberation of Palestine, under George Habash, came under the PLO umbrella. It was indeed Black September as the rebellion against Hussein was punctuated with acts of international terrorism. On September 6, 1970, terrorists simultaneously hijacked four commercial planes over Europe: Swissair, Pan American, TWA and El Al. The attempt on El Al did not succeed: one of the two hijackers was killed, and the other, a woman named Lyla Khaled, was turned over to British police when the plane landed at Heathrow. But the passengers and crew of the other three planes were not as fortunate. The Pan Am Boeing 747, too big to land in the desert, was diverted to Cairo and summarily blown up after the passengers and crew were evacuated. The other two planes, Swissair and TWA, were forcibly landed in a remote area of Jordan where the passengers and crew were held hostage.

Responsibility for these hijackings was claimed by the PFLP, which issued demands to the Swiss, West German, British, US and Israeli governments for the release of terrorists held in those countries. They wanted the British to release Lyla Khaled, who, in addition to her recent El Al exploit, had taken part in 1969 in the hijacking of a TWA plane flying from Rome to Lod. From the Americans the PFLP demanded the release of Sirhan Bishara Sirhan, who had been convicted of the murder of Robert Kennedy. If these demands were not met, or if the Jordanian army tried to interfere with them, the terrorists threatened to blow up the two planes along with the hostages. They had planted sticks of dynamite at various places inside the two aircraft. For three days, these planes sat on the Jordanian airstrip in the baking desert sun with the air conditioning turned off. Later they were joined by a third, a British Overseas Airways plane which had been hijacked on its way from Bahrein to London. The PFLP announced that this last hijacking was intended to emphasize to the British the necessity for Lyla Khaled's quick release.

Swiss, German and British representatives met with Secretary of State William Rogers and an Israeli deputy, and it was agreed that the terrorists in custody would be released only if all the hostages were freed, including Israeli and Jewish passengers. The Red Cross delivered food and medicine to the hostages while the UN Security Council issued a call for their release. Eventually the passengers were released to go to hotels in Amman, with the exception of sixty Jewish women and children who were kept aboard. Even the Iraqi government appealed to the PFLP to release them, but to no avail.

Finally, at 3 pm on September 12, after six agonizing days, the terrorists evacuated the remaining passengers and blew up all three planes. Forty hostages were held and taken to a refugee camp, where they were freed only when Jordanian soldiers attacked and took over the camp.[3]

The PLO repeatedly attacked Israeli civilians in Israel and around the world. Benny Morris says that between 1968 and 1977 Palestinians hijacked or attempted to hijack twenty-nine aircraft. On December 26, 1968, PFLP activists in Athens attacked an El Al plane on the ground, killing one passenger and wounding a stewardess. In February, 1970, forty-seven people, including thirteen Israelis, were killed when their Swissair plane en route from Zurich to Israel was blown up by a bomb planted by a PFLP breakaway group. That same day seven Jews were murdered in a home for the elderly in Munich. It was in Munich, too, in 1972, that terrorists were to kill eleven Israeli athletes competing in the Olympics.[4] In August, 1970, Yassir Arafat declared, "Our basic aim is to liberate the land from the Mediterranean Sea to the Jordan River. We are not concerned with what took place in June 1967 or in eliminating the consequences of the June war. The Palestinian Revolution's basic concern is the uprooting of the Zionist entity from our land and liberating it."[5]

Oddly enough, at that time Sharon hoped the PLO would win in Jordan, where Palestinians made up more than seventy percent of the population. He believed that if Arafat replaced the king and established a Palestinian state there, the issue of Palestinian self-determination would be resolved, thus ending the conflict with Israel. However, King Hussein responded to the hijackings and the rebellion with savage efficiency: he ordered artillery and tanks into the refugee camps, killing 2000 PLO fighters, as well as several thousand Palestinian civilians.[6] The back of the revolt was broken; the surviving Palestinians fled across the Jordan River into, as Martin van Creveld puts it, "the arms of the IDF."[7] In 1996, Chaim Herzog said that Arafat and Hussein still hated each other, "but they must get along. And so they do, the strangest of bedfellows. In a way, it's a matter of survival."[8]

In 1968, the PLO and the PFLP began to increase their activity in the Gaza Strip, establishing a web of local command headquarters from which recruits were sent out to involve Arab populations in missions against Israel. Supplies of weapons and explosives were delivered by boat from headquarters in Syria, Lebanon and Jordan. Initially PLO and PFLP commanders put tremendous pressure on Arab civilians, many of whom, despite their resentment of the Israeli occupation, were taking advantage of new economic opportunities in the Israeli marketplace. Buses, cars and taxis carrying Arabs to work in Israel were bombed, families were blackmailed and

suspected informants for Israeli Intelligence were tortured and brutally murdered. Sharon commented that "mutilated and tortured
bodies . . . turned up almost every day. It was as if all the stops of
cruelty had been drawn."[9]

Moshe Dayan, then minister of defense, saw this as an Arab-on-
Arab problem and was at first reluctant to intervene. Sharon argued
that if this terror was not stopped, "today's murdered Arabs would
become tomorrow's murdered Jews."[10] And, in fact, several subsequent incidents of violence against Jews convinced Dayan to change
his mind. In January of 1971, a hand grenade attack on the Ar-
royos, an English immigrant family visiting Gaza caused public outrage; two children were killed and their mother severely wounded.
A few days later, Dayan and Chief of Staff Chaim Bar-Lev gave
Sharon the green light, instructing him to "take care" of Gaza.[11]

Sharon spent the next two months carefully studying the region. Every day he packed his lunch and a canteen of water and
walked through orange groves and refugee camps. He noted that
the density of the orange groves would provide good cover for terrorists and would be difficult for military squads to penetrate. The
towns and refugee camps were overcrowded; obviously one could
not easily spot terrorists among the people. The situation was complicated and confusing. But gradually Sharon devised a plan of action, deciding to fight terror with terror, calling it "anti-terrorist
guerilla warfare."[12]

He drew a map of the area, dividing it into small segments, each
representing approximately a square mile. He assigned each square
a number and a squad of soldiers, making each squad responsible
for rooting out and killing terrorists in its own area. He met personally with each and every squad, bypassing the chain of command
and lecturing the soldiers on their assignment. They had to know,
he told them, how terrorists think. They too had to think like terrorists, always be on the move, avoid rigid patterns of behavior

and, above all, be creative: "Create a new situation for every terrorist every day."[13]

For seven months, from July, 1971, to February, 1972, Sharon worked with these soldiers. Day and night, he joined them in surveillance, searching and brainstorming. His tactics disoriented the terrorists and their leadership, confronting them on the ground in their own territory. It was said that Sharon carried with him a "wanted" list of PLO and PFLP terrorists and that he crossed out the names of those captured and killed. In November, 1971, the head of the PFLP, Ziad al-Husseini, committed suicide in his hiding place in the cellar of the mayor of Gaza, Rashid Shawa. Al-Husseini left two letters, one addressed to the mayor, thanking him for hiding him, looking after him and helping him to stay in contact with his terrorist group. The second letter, marked "Will," bitterly attacked the mayor. "I was deceived," Husseini wrote, "by the man called Haj Rashid Sa'id al-Shawa from Gaza, who is the greatest traitor, a Zionist agent. . . and Manzur, son of the filthy Rashid al-Shawa, who was once a noble man, but the son of the duck swam like the duck himself, and was a traitor . . ."

Shawa, considerably shaken, came to see Dayan and told him that Ziad al-Husseini had come to his house to ask for help in leaving the country for fear of Sharon's men. He had tried and failed to flee to Lebanon. Early in November, the mayor had asked Dayan to let al-Husseini and his group leave the country quietly. When Dayan refused, al-Husseini had shot himself. Faced with the necessity to make a decision about Shawa himself, Dayan decided to let him stay in office and to overlook his cooperation with the enemy, in the hope of improving relations with the Arabs. He understood that the mistrust and division among the Palestinian leadership was frightening the civilians who were caught between their would-be liberators and the Israeli forces.[14]

Sharon vigorously continued his Gaza operation into the winter. He not only hit terrorists, but innocent civilians as well. At times he used excessive force and was unnecessarily rough. He put refugee camps under a twenty-four-hour curfew, and his soldiers conducted house-to-house searches after gathering the male inhabitants in the main square for questioning. Many of these men were forced to stand waist-deep in the Mediterranean for hours during searches. When Palestinian children began to stone Israeli soldiers, Sharon met with the parents and warned them that they would be held responsible for their children. He told them that stoning was unacceptable, just as the beating of students by soldiers would be unacceptable. "The parents were told that if a child was caught stoning a soldier, that child's father or elder brother would be given a jar of water, a loaf of bread, a head covering, some Jordanian money and a white flag. We would then transport him to the Jordanian border, point out the direction of the nearest Jordanian town, and send him on his way."[15]

By February of 1972, after seven months of this crackdown, 104 terrorists had been eliminated, compared to 179 over the previous four years. Thus, Sharon was able to halt terror in Gaza for the next ten years. The region was made safer for Jews and Arabs, although Palestinian radicals continued to mount scattered attacks against Arab collaborators. Moshe Dayan was pleased and publicly praised Sharon, but at the same time he had to deal with friction among the other Israeli commanders.

Yitzhak Pundek, the military governor of Gaza, believed that if Israel extended economic and humanitarian aid to the impoverished population of Gaza, the terrorists would lose public support and eventually be forced to decrease their activities. Pundek was opposed to Sharon's policy of deterrence by instilling fear in civilians. Instead, Pundek wanted to rebuild the local economy, to bring in social welfare services and youth programs, to improve the living conditions of the residents. And many professional army officers agreed with Pundek. For example, Yitzhak Abadi, a senior field commander who had served under Sharon as a paratrooper and who admired his leadership, determination and superb organizational skill, submitted his resignation. Dayan sent for Abadi and asked him why he had decided to leave. Abadi replied that although he admired Sharon, he could no longer put up with his harsh policy toward Arab civilians. Abadi said that he preferred Pundek's approach and he suggested that Dayan intervene. Dayan promised that he would.

A few days later Sharon called Abadi into his office and asked him to recount his conversation with Dayan. Abadi told him that he supported Pundek's approach, and this led to a long discussion of the issue of obedience and freedom of opinion in the military. Abadi reminisced about their years together in the paratroop units and told Sharon that he had learned a lot from him. Emotions ran high and tears were shed.[16]

Shortly afterward, Dayan ordered the jurisdiction of Gaza transferred from the Southern to the Central Command. Sharon said later that he was not surprised. "I knew what it was, this message from Moshe. You have done a good job, he was telling me. Be happy about it. You have succeeded in destroying the terrorists and giving these people the chance to live normal lives. But from this point on, we'll let somebody else handle it."[17]

15

WHOOP'D OUT

———

Months after the cease-fire, Sharon noted that the Egyptian army was increasing the pace of its activities, focusing on the building of fortifications and on surveillance: soldiers were rehearsing canal-crossings south of Kantara, where the canal splits into two branches. He was alarmed because he sensed that the Egyptian units seemed somehow different—transformed, better prepared to take on military maneuvers. Anwar Sadat—one of the officers who had participated in deposing King Farouk in 1952—succeeded to the presidency after Nasser died in September, 1970, and announced to his nation: "Next year I will be addressing you from the Sinai." Nevertheless, the Israelis were feeling self-confident. Moshe Dayan believed that the Arabs were incapable of defeating the IDF and Golda Meir exuded optimism at Israeli cabinet meetings, proclaiming to her colleagues that "the mere thought of the Egyptian army crossing the canal is an insult to (the) intelligence."[1]

In January, 1972, Major General David Elazar replaced Chaim Bar-Lev as commander-in-chief of the IDF. The two were close friends who believed in traditional military tactics, unlike Sharon who was something of a maverick. Elazar, a veteran of the Palmach, had headed Israel's Northern Command. A few months after he became commander-in-chief, Elazar told Sharon that it was time for him to retire from the IDF. Sharon, who had long aspired to become commander-in-chief himself, realized that this was now impossible and once again began to seriously consider a career in politics. The more he thought about it, the more he felt this might be the way for him to make a difference in the development of the country, now nearly twenty-five years old.

He also had an emotional connection with farming; he wanted his own land. He and Lily began to search the countryside for a suitable place and became instantly attracted to a large, rundown farm in the wilderness of northern Negev. It was owned by an Australian Zionist who had dreamed of developing a sheep farm, but had been discouraged by the wave of terrorism in Gaza in the 1950s. "But I found the primitiveness of the place an attraction," Sharon said. "In fact, the moment I saw this land I experienced a surge of emotion, for it was just down the road from Kibbutz Ruhama, where twenty-seven years earlier I started my career as a soldier . . . I felt that it was this place and this place alone that I had to have." The price of the farm was beyond his means and he began to look around for a loan. Meshulam Riklis, a wealthy American businessman originally from Israel, had donated funds for a paratroopers' recreational facility. When Sharon told him that he was leaving the IDF to become a farmer, Riklis offered him an interest-free loan of $200,000. Samuel Sax, a principal in the Exchange National Bank of Chicago and an ardent supporter of Israel, lent him an additional $400,000. This loan was for a sixteen-year period at six percent interest, calculated in US dollars with an additional two percent interest calculated in Israeli currency. Sharon looked forward with enthusiasm to his new career on Sycamore Farm.[2]

But in May, 1973, the Egyptians put their army on high alert. David Elazar immediately mobilized some Israeli reserves while Sharon brought Southern Command to a state of readiness. He also made detailed plans for an Israeli crossing at Kantara—if the Egyptians had something similar in mind, he would surprise them by acting first. Israeli intelligence discovered that when the Egyptians got wind of what the Israelis were up to, they put off their own plan until October. Unfortunately, neither Dayan nor Golda Meir would acknowledge the imminence of the threat and even criticized Elazar for causing unnecessary panic.

Alarmed by their attitude, Sharon tried to have his retirement delayed for a year, but Elazar refused. The 1969 scenario was repeated. Sharon then went back to Dayan who, again, would not take a stand and suggested that Sharon talk to Golda Meir, but she said, as she had in 1969, that she she didn't want to interfere in what she considered to be Dayan's jurisdiction.

On July 15, a few hours before handing over Southern Command to General Shmuel Gonen, Sharon said frankly to Dayan: "If we have a war here, and we might have one, Gonen does not have the experience to handle it." But Dayan shrugged off Sharon's concern: "Arik, we are not going to have a war this year. Maybe Gonen is not too experienced. But he will have plenty of time to learn."[3] Sharon returned home, got into his work clothes and sandals and as he was leaving to look over his herd of sheep, he told a few reporters who had gathered outside his house: "This is it. Now it is time to raise sheep, lambs and horses on my farm. I served in the military for twenty-eight years, but at the end of the day I am essentially a farmer."[4]

Several days later, Sharon was given a going-away party to which he invited all Southern Command officers as well as many of the region's mayors and even some Bedouin with whom he had developed a close relationship during his years in the south. That evening he addressed the crowd: "As it happens, I have been forced to leave the military, and I want to say emphatically that this was not my choice. I feel I need to explain this because a lot of people have asked me to stay. But at least I'm happy to leave while I'm still young and I'm happy to have had this memorable career. There has not been a war in which I have not participated and it's been a great privilege for me to have been part of our crucial twenty-five year history.

"I have felt the thrill of victory, the horror of fear and the anguish at the loss of friends and relatives. For me it's been an era of both joy and sorrow: the joy of victory, the feeling of love and warmth shared with colleagues and friends as well as the sorrow and pain which come from loss. Perhaps more than anyone else I have felt all these contradictory emotions. If there is one thing I am exceedingly proud of it is the fact that in the last three years I have been able to function on my own, avoiding cliques.

"I have always said that my only clique is my family: my wife, Lily, my mother and my sons, Omri and Gilad. I adhere to the principle that a person must express his opinions and fight for them; they act in the national interest and so do I. In fact, I have been dealing with matters of national interest for thirty years. And these interests will always matter: settlements, borders, the availability of water, etc etc. It's only natural for me to continue the struggle for national interests."[5]

The guests were visibly taken aback by Sharon's bitter comments. It was supposed to have been an evening of fun and nostalgia, with plenty of food and drink—and even entertainment by a popular Israeli singer. He obviously felt he had been ill-treated by the High Command. He was like Coriolanus, who had been "whoop'd out" of Rome.

Nineteen-seventy-three was an election year and Sharon felt it was an opportune time to challenge the Labor Party which had ruled the Israeli government continuously since the country's inception. He felt that "Labor hegemony," as it was called, had outgrown its Socialist vision and had become a heavy burden on the country's economic and social infrastructure. So not long after his retirement, Sharon crossed party lines, joined the Liberal Party and tried to form a coalition of right-wing parties which he hoped would eventually change the Knesset's balance of power. He hoped to capitalize on the resentment of the European Jewish establishment felt by the Sephardic Jews, Jewish immigrants from Arab countries, and to marshal the support of these disaffected groups.

Sharon contacted the heads of the Liberal, Free Center and RAFI parties as well as the Land of Israel Movement and Herut's Menachem Begin, the most influential member of the opposition and a key figure in any coalition-building plan. Begin was one of a generation of Zionists who cared little for material things, living austerely in a sparsely furnished apartment. Because of his own experience with Irgun, he profoundly admired freedom fighters for their dedication. "For Begin, as for Ben-Gurion," Sharon said, "Jewish fighting men were something special . . . [they] spoke to something deep in their psyches." Sharon, on the other hand, lived much more expansively, both as a military officer and as the proprietor of a large farm.

Sharon and Begin discussed ways to achieve a united front; they realized that their beliefs and attitudes about Israel's future were similar. They both believed that the territories won by Israel should be retained. They also discovered a surprising connection in their family histories: in 1904, after Zionist leader Theodore Herzl's death, the rabbi of Brest Litovsk locked the gates of his synagogue to prevent a memorial service in Herzl's honor—a man ultra-Orthodox Jews considered a disgrace. But Begin's father and Sharon's grandfather—along with a third ardent Zionist—broke into the synagogue and performed a memorial service despite the rabbi's objection. Sharon was delighted to discover also that his grandmother, Bluma Scheinerman, was the midwife who had delivered Menachem Begin.[6]

In the process of trying to unite the various parties, Sharon got a crash course in political maneuvering. The negotiations were difficult and there were constant disagreements about exactly who would get seats, what places on the list of candidates would go to whom and what issues would get top priority in the platform that eventually evolved. Sharon was astonished by the differences between military and political pursuits. ". . . at the beginning," he said, "you experience a kind of shock when you understand that in the political arena nothing you have done in your previous life makes any difference. You may be arguing with someone who has never served in the army . . . and when it comes to a decision his vote is worth exactly what yours is . . . and it just made no difference that I had jumped into trenches or been wounded or managed complex battles. None of this counted in the least. I was in a new game in a new arena."[7]

On September 14, an agreement was reached and a coalition party called Likud (Unity) was formed. Its goals were "Peace, security, return of Jews from all countries, absorption of immigrants, a social policy based on liberty and justice, the elimination of poverty, development of a national economy, a fair standard of living for all, improvements to the environment, making local laws more equitable and in general offering a democratic alternative to the Labor Party."[8]

On this newly forged political platform, Sharon stood as campaign manager for the upcoming November election.

16

THE YOM KIPPUR WAR

———

ON SEPTEMBER 28, 1970, six weeks after the end of the War of Attrition, and the day after he signed a peace agreement with King Hussein of Jordan, Gamal Abdel Nasser suffered a heart attack and died. His successor, Anwar Sadat, was considered a buffoon both in Egypt and Israel, an opinion that was reinforced when he dispensed with the services of his Soviet military advisors. Israeli self-confidence, already high, was buoyed by this because it was widely believed that the Egyptians were incapable of handling complicated Russian equipment. The Ministry of Defense felt so confident, in fact, that it began to consider cutting required military service from three to two-and-a-half years.

What the Israelis did not know was that Sadat was preparing to wage a limited war—one carefully calculated not to provoke the Israelis into using nuclear weapons, which the Egyptians tended to think they had, although the Israelis had not admitted it. Sadat's intention was to move forward several miles to liberate the Sinai. The Egyptians set to work constructing a high wall of earth along the canal, behind which they mustered a force of 200,000 men— 110,000 in the north and 90,000 in the south, sandwiched between infantry and mechanized divisions. The plan was that the infantry, backed by more than 1000 tanks, would cross the canal first in rubber boats, protected by air strikes and heavy artillery cover. Water cannon mounted on rafts would destroy the walls on the Israeli side and mechanized divisions would follow across pontoon bridges.

In Syria, Hafez Assad had seized power through a coup in October, 1970. Like Sadat, he dispensed with Soviet advisors, and began a military buildup in coordination with the Egyptians and with some help from the king of Morocco. The Syrians planned a sudden attack, probably intended to liberate the Golan Heights.

The Israelis were of course aware of these build-ups, but Military Intelligence tended to minimize their significance. As late as the summer of 1973, the IDF was expressing confidence that they could make short work of any invasion. The press, not wishing to alarm the public, did not challenge this assessment. However, by late September of 1973, Dayan and IDF chief David Elazar were uneasy enough to reinforce the Golan Heights and bring in more men and tanks.

On Friday morning, October 5, 1973, Israelis were preparing to observe Yom Kippur, the "Sabbath of all Sabbaths," the most sacred day in the Jewish calendar, which would begin at sundown. The newspapers that morning carried mainly good news: in an interview in *Haaretz*, Moshe Dayan was quoted as saying that the Egyptians did not present an immediate threat because they were not prepared for war; the Arabs, he said, would try to damage Israel through a series of political moves in the international arena. Golda Meir told *Davar* that Israel's comfortable position was not threatened and none of the opposition party's dark prophesies had come true.[1]

But the public were not told that, the day before, Mrs Meir had met—and that very morning was meeting again—with General Eliyahu Zeira, the chief of Military Intelligence, Moshe Dayan, General Elazar and members of the cabinet to discuss mobilization and the possibility of launching a preemptive strike against the enemy's airfields and antiaircraft. Mrs Meir ruled out such a strike because of the political ramifications and the effect on Israel's relations with the United States. Elazar said that there was evidence that an offensive was in the offing and that the situation called for an intensive

IDF mobilization. The question arose, at the October 5 meeting, about how and when the mobilization should be announced, to minimize panic just before the Yom Kippur holiday. Mrs Meir decided, on Elazar's advice, to mobilize all four divisions of the reserves, rather than only two, as Dayan had suggested. As he left the meeting, Shimon Peres said, "It seems to me there is going to be a war." But later that same day, General Elazar announced that in his opinion the Arabs were not going to start a war, and certainly not in the next twenty-four hours.[2]

That afternoon Sharon received a phone call from Southern Command. A few months earlier, when he retired from the IDF, he had asked Dayan to assign him to one of the reserve armored divisions. Since then, as we have said, he had decided to enter politics and had begun working with the Liberal party, part of the opposition coalition. Now he left campaign headquarters to go home and meet with Yehoshua Saguy, who had served as chief of intelligence when Sharon was Southern Commander. Saguy showed him air photographs and other evidence that the Egyptians had marshalled a massive force along the canal. This left no doubt in Sharon's mind that war was imminent.

At eight in the morning on Yom Kippur, a pair of Phantom fighters zoomed in the air over Israel, breaking the Sabbath silence and sending a signal to the population that something extremely unusual was afoot. Since radio broadcasting had been shut down for Yom Kippur, soldiers had to go house to house through the empty streets to call up the reserves who were all to be found at home because of the holiday. But at two in the afternoon, before the IDF could completely mobilize, the Arabs made surprise full-scale simultaneous attacks on two fronts.

The Egyptians began by swiftly striking by air and on the ground with a massive artillery barrage. Fifteen minutes later, 8000 Egyptian assault troops, protected by a missile umbrella, crossed the canal on pontoon bridges and rubber boats. Some simply swam across.

The Egyptian infantry numbered 100,000; the Israeli army, 8500. Equipped with highly effective anti-tank weapons and carrying Soviet-made personal anti-aircraft missiles, the Egyptians successfully moved personnel and materiel. They broke through the Bar-Lev Line fortifications and spread eastward into the Sinai, the hundred miles of desert separating Israel from the canal. The IDF was caught unprepared, with only three tanks and one brigade to defend the Egyptian's crossing points. In the first eight hours of fighting it was clear that the Southern Command had suffered a heavy blow.

While the Egyptians were crossing the canal, the Syrians attacked the Golan Heights in the north. Their initial onslaught was rapid, with 600 T-54 and T-55 Soviet-built tanks backed by 690 field guns, against 177 Israeli tanks backed by only forty-four field guns. The Syrian force, with a Moroccan brigade, broke through the Israeli border and advanced almost halfway across the Golan, which spans only fifteen miles at its widest point. If the Syrians were able to reach the descent to the Jordan River, Israel would have been in extreme peril.

Many of the Israeli tanks were hit hard and their crews killed. In one desperate attempt to survive, an Israeli lieutenant, Tzvika Gringold, gathered together four tanks (known as Force Tzvika) and advanced toward the Syrians, fighting them all night and destroying many of their tanks. He was able to create the impression that he led a large force and thus hold back the enemy advance for several critical hours. He did not stop their advance, but he did break their momentum and give the IDF a chance to bring up reinforcements. After midnight, the Syrians deployed an additional 300 tanks and, on the following morning, they advanced into the Israeli camp at Nafekh, southwest of Kuneitra, just six miles from a bridge across the Jordan leading to northern Galilee.

At nine o'clock on the night of October 6, Moshe Dayan announced on Israeli television that the Arab attack was "the start of all-out war again," and that Israel was not in a state of readiness, but he reassured the public that the enemy's advantage of surprise would not last when Israeli army reserves reached both fronts. Dayan was in fact very disturbed about the situation: Israeli infantry was outnumbered ten to one and the enemy were equipped, as they had not been in the past, with sophisticated Soviet anti-tank and anti-aircraft weapons. In addition, Egypt and Syria together had nearly 1000 warplanes.[3]

To add to the pressure, Arab radio—Radio Cairo and Radio Damascus—and the Soviet news agency Tass were reporting that the Israelis had initiated attacks on Egypt and the Syrian army, and the reaction in Washington seemed to indicate a belief that Israel was indeed the aggressor.

Sharon was ordered to report to Southern Command headquarters, which he found in considerable disarray. Everyone had assumed that they would have at least forty-eight hours' notice of any attack and they were stunned by this swift double-pronged onslaught. For the first time since 1948, the enemy had seized the initiative. To make matters worse, there was some tension between the officers of the Southern Command. Sharon had no respect for his successor, General Shmuel Gonen, whose dislike of Sharon was certainly mutual. In any case, the canal was two hundred miles away from headquarters and it was necessary for the reserves to get there as soon as possible.

Sharon talked to Gonen on the phone and urged him to leave Beersheba immediately for the Sinai, but Gonen made it clear that he was not about to take advice from Sharon. Things were not starting well. Since many military vehicles were not ready, soldiers drove any kind of truck or van they could find to get to the front. Sharon himself drove a small civilian pickup truck commandeered from a heating company. It was, he said, a "true people's army," with tanks and army trucks mixed with cars and buses. Sharon arrived in Bir Gafgafa, the command center for the Sinai, where things were in a state of great confusion. Gonen, who had moved forward from

Beersheba to a command post twenty-five miles east of the canal, did not answer Sharon's phone calls.[4]

There were sixteen Bar-Lev Line strongholds—called *maozim*—along the canal. These, the first targets of the Egyptian attack, were small outposts strung out along the edge of the canal about five miles apart, each staffed by between twenty and thirty men. For years Sharon had argued against this static defense line, and now events were proving him right. The maozim could not perform their function as lookouts with the men driven from observation posts under what Martin van Creveld calls "one of the heaviest artillery bombardments in modern history."[5] The maozim desperately signalled for help, but, to Sharon's disgust, Gonen sent tanks, not in large forces, but piecemeal, along recognized routes where the Egyptians were ready for them. Tanks were not stationed between the strongholds to support them as they should have been. In addition to everything else, intense antiaircraft fire prevented the Israeli Air Force from getting information to send back to the command post. The Egyptians, who had been expected to run away, instead destroyed two-thirds of the tanks and all of the maozim except one, called Budapest. This last held out under violent attack and, according to Dayan, prevented the Egyptian advance along the northern axis of the Sinai, forcing them to retreat to an area near Port Said.

Dayan pointed out that the maozim were not set up to withstand a massive attack. Each had underground bunkers, but the firing positions and the communication trenches were above ground and were exposed to direct tank fire and artillery shelling. Dayan noted also that the forts were underequipped and the men had not had refresher training in more than two years.[6] If anything, this underscored Sharon's argument that the whole idea of what he called "a static defense" was a very poor one. He had heatedly objected to the Bar-Lev Line at General Headquarters four years earlier.

In the afternoon of October 7, Elazar, Gonen, General Avraham Adan (called "Bren") and Yitzhak Rabin met together with Sharon, who arrived late because of a delayed helicopter pickup, convinced that Gonen had intentionally caused the delay. Sharon told Gonen that what was needed was a concentrated attack by at least two divisions, and that Israeli forces should cross the canal in the Kantara area. The response was firm: plans were already in place and no changes were possible. Adan would attack in the north and go south, parallel with the canal but staying two miles away from it because of the Egyptian force, and Sharon would prepare at dawn to move southeast to northwest and eventually link up with Adan, so that the two forces together could cross the canal. But Sharon was to do nothing the next morning until he received the go-ahead. Adan would try to relieve the maozim somehow—even though he had to stay two miles from the canal.[7]

Sharon was not happy about these instructions, but he complied with them. Consequently, on Monday morning, October 8, his division began to proceed southward, with 200 tanks, trucks and other equipment. From the Kantara area, Adan, with a fraction of the artillery and air support he needed, was moving south swiftly, mostly because he encountered few Egyptians since he was farther away from the canal than he realized. He arrived in good time at Chamutal, halfway down the canal, where he was supposed to link up with Sharon. But he found the last of Sharon's forces there because Sharon had been instructed by Gonen, for no discernible reason, to move on farther south. Conflicting orders began to come from Southern Command. Sharon was told first to attack and then told not to attack, but to wait for Adan's attack to develop. But Adan, who was expected to move from north to south parallel to the canal, passed Sharon's forces to the rear, seven or eight miles from the canal, and then, at about 9:45 am, Adan turned west and engaged the Egyptians.

Sharon watched this development with dismay, convinced that there was no way that Adan could succeed. After about an hour, Sharon received an order to move back ten miles and then go seventy miles to the south and cross the canal to capture Egyptian bridges near Suez. The Southern Command announced that Adan had smashed the Egyptian Second Army and now Sharon could go on to smash the Third Army. Sharon did not want to leave the high ground he was occupying, and which he was convinced he had to hold if there was to be a successful assault on the canal. He believed that he could not reach the bridges, that the bridges would probably not be intact if he did reach them, and that if they were intact and he was able to get to them, they would collapse under the weight of Israeli tanks since they had been built to hold the much lighter Soviet tanks.

He called Gonen to try to get him to countermand the order to evacuate his position, and a heated argument ensued, which Sharon lost. Irritated, he obeyed orders up to a point: he did leave a unit holding two hilltops on either side of a road leading to the canal. Then he left with most of his force, and after covering fifty miles in under four hours, he was intercepted by a Southern Command officer who arrived by helicopter to tell him that Adan had suffered heavy losses and had not been able to cross the canal, and that the Egyptians were attacking along the entire length of the canal and were swarming into the area that Sharon had just left. So Sharon was now ordered to return to that area as quickly as possible.

Sharon describes himself as being numb with rage. "On this absolutely crucial day of battle," he says, his division "had spent their time driving around the desert like idiots." He swung north and returned to the positions he had just abandoned. The two hilltops were still in Israeli hands, but the rest of the area, which had been clear, was now under Egyptian control. The result was heavy losses for Sharon's division and a nasty tank battle that went on for hours. October 8 was a terrible day, a day of confusion and waste.[8]

Sharon made clear to Dayan his frustration and anger. Dayan realized that serious mistakes had been made, and he decided that Gonen was not capable of handling the situation. He suggested to Elazar that either Sharon or Bar-Lev should take over the Southern Command. Elazar decided that the commander would be his close friend Chaim Bar-Lev, now minister of trade and industry, and Golda Meir gave this decision her blessing. Gonen would remain, but as a virtual figurehead under Bar-Lev's orders. This decision infuriated Sharon further; he had strong feelings about Bar-Lev, who had been the judge in Sharon's aborted trial in 1955, and whose rulings had, in Sharon's view, exacerbated the procedure. But apart from that, Sharon had deeply disagreed with Bar-Lev's decision in 1968 to erect the chain of fixed fortifications, the *maozim*, along the canal—a decision which was now proving to have been a grave mistake.

Sharon's frustration was matched by an equally high level of disarray in the upper levels of command, w(Albany, NY) *Times Union* ho had expected to sweep the enemy away with a wave of the hand, so to speak. They now gave orders for a holding operation, the last thing that suited Sharon, who always believed in attacking the enemy from the rear. He sent out a reconnaissance battalion that met no Egyptians, and pushed across the canal plain without incident, without firing a shot, to an area north of the Great Bitter Lake. Sharon knew that he had found an open seam between the Egyptian Second Army in the north and its Third Army in the south. But when he called Gonen to tell him that his forces were near the canal and wanted to prepare for a crossing, he was told coldly to pull back and hold his position until further orders.

In fact, the IDF was concentrating on the war in the Golan Heights, where the Syrians were well-equipped and on the morning of October 9 were relentlessly pushing the 7th Armored Brigade back, while they landed commandos in the Israeli rear. The situation was desperate. Suddenly the Syrians retreated, for reasons that

have never been made clear, and the Israelis were able to pull themselves together and mount a successful counterattack.

While this was going on in the north, Sharon waited in his defensive position for four days, from October 10 to 14. Since all his
instincts told him to attack, he watched in agony as the Egyptians
brought in tanks and infantry and laid mines. His phone calls to
Dayan and others in command evoked no response. Then on Sunday, October 14, shortly after dawn, the Egyptians mounted a full-
scale attack with a thousand tanks. Sharon used tanks in response,
while he evaded Egyptian artillery, and the same thing went on in
the north under General Adan. "By late afternoon," Van Creveld
says, "Adan's and Sharon's men were looking over a sight as unbelievable as it was welcome. The entire plain at their feet was dotted
by hundreds of 'bonfires,' with Egyptian tank losses alone number-
ing around 250." The Israelis claimed the loss of only six tanks.[9]

This was a major victory, even though the enemy still faced them
behind bridgeheads with hundreds of tanks and sophisticated weaponry. Nevertheless this battle, together with successes against the
Syrians, roused General Headquarters to unleash Sharon and Adan
to cross the canal. On the night of October 15, Sharon sent his
forces into the seam he had discovered between the two Egyptian
armies, and the canal was crossed by paratroopers silently on rubber boats, unnoticed by the Egyptians. On October 16, a battalion
of tanks on motorized rafts followed the paratroopers and attacked
Egyptian antiaircraft missiles. The Egyptians responded with heavy
artillery fire at Sharon's men along the canal, while the Israelis used
antitank weapons to probe for Egyptian infantry hidden in dense
vegetation near the canal.

The Egyptian antiaircraft defenses were decimated on the ground
by artillery and tanks, so the Egyptian air force was sent up to fight
a losing battle against the IAF. The Egyptian Third Army was isolated, and Sharon was sixty miles from Cairo, close upon Ismailia.

At this point, on October 21, the UN Security Council called for a cease-fire. The Russians wanted to rescue Sadat from a potential disaster, and the United States, in the person of Secretary of State Henry Kissinger, was willing to work with Brezhnev in this matter, to help defuse the tension between the two superpowers who had supported opposite sides in this conflict. In addition, America was trying to end an Arab oil embargo.

Sharon himself had been involved in various bitter arguments about tactics with Gonen, Bar-Lev and David Elazar, who came with Moshe Dayan to visit the field. In the end, it was only Dayan who stayed in the field with Sharon and it was Dayan who had to hold luncheon discussions with Kissinger about the cease-fire. Dayan came away with the feeling that the American administration "would not hesitate to disassociate" itself from Israel "if forced to choose between aid to Israel . . . and reaching agreement with the Arabs, even at [Israel's] expense." In addition, Dayan understood that the United States feared that "a continuation of the war would lead to the radicalization of the Arab world, to the fall of moderate governments, and their replacement by extremist regimes." And as if that were not bad enough, there was the possibility that if "the Arab armies were utterly routed, the Soviet Union was likely to take extreme measures to save her allies from collapse."[10]

In February and April, 1974, peace agreements were signed. The IDF withdrew to a line twenty miles east of the canal. The Egyptians opened the canal again and agreed to resettle the towns along it; this would act as a deterrent to further aggression on their part. The Israelis were able to retain strategically important posts in the Golan. But this was not a victory to be wholeheartedly celebrated.

17

POLITICS

———

THE YOM KIPPUR WAR fiasco left the Israeli public in a state of shock. The loss of lives—there had been 2600 casualties—was traumatic, as was the realization that the ruling Labor Party had completely misjudged the capabilities of the enemy, who proved to be both daring and clever. The elections, originally scheduled for October 30, 1973, had been postponed to December 31. At the end of October, the opposition leaders asked Sharon to come back and resume his post as campaign manager. However, he did not want to leave his soldiers so soon after the war and stayed at the front with his division for the next three months. He was distraught over the way the war had been fought, he did not trust the cease-fire and he believed that the nation had lost its sense of direction. He felt that Israel was besieged and that he himself was isolated because he was the only prominent military figure who was not a member of the Labor Party—was, indeed, committed to the opposition party, the Likud, a coalition which he himself had helped to create.

He bitterly resented Labor's postwar position that it was the only peace party. He was angry, too, that the Americans had not used the Israeli withdrawal from the canal as a bargaining chip to prevent further oil crises and price rises. Kissinger, he felt, had left a thousand possibilities unexplored. He made his rage and frustration clear to the press, attacking not only Kissinger and his plan for an Arab-Israeli peace conference in Geneva, but also the Labor government and the IDF for their blunders—in particular for the delays and uncertainties he had encountered before he crossed the canal.

When he left his command, he printed and distributed to his soldiers, without Elazar's prior approval, what he called his final "order of the day," in which he said that it was his division's crossing of the canal that had been the turning point of the war and that had resulted in the victory: "We must remember that our victory in the Yom Kippur War was the greatest of all other victories. If, despite the blunders and the mistakes, despite the failures and obstructions, despite the loss of control and authority, we nevertheless achieved our victory, we must therefore recognize that this was the greatest victory the IDF has ever known."[1]

He praised the soldiers' courage, devotion and self-sacrifice, and ended with the promise that he was leaving them "to fight on another front," to fight with all his strength to prevent future wars, but that if they had to come back and resume their fight, he would be with them.[2] These words enraged Labor, as they were meant to do.

The Israeli public made clear at the polls in December that they shared much of Sharon's disillusionment. Sharon was one of thirty-nine opposition candidates in the Likud coalition elected to the Knesset. His last day with the army was January 20, 1974. He left with mixed feelings: finding it difficult to tear himself away from a way of life that offered "friendship . . . mutual dependence and . . . mutual support."[3]

In Geneva, an Egyptian-Israeli Disengagement of Forces Agreement was signed on January 18, 1974. Israeli troops would withdraw from the west bank and establish a line ten to fifteen miles from the canal, a UN-patrolled two-to-four mile buffer zone would be established, and Egypt would hold a six-mile-deep strip along the east bank of the canal, but with a sharply limited military presence. Egypt agreed to open the canal to Israeli goods, but not Israeli ships, and to rebuild the canal-side cities of Suez and Ismailia, acts that would limit the Egyptians' ability to initiate wars in the future. Kissinger's negotiations with Syria were more difficult, since the Syrians refused to meet directly with the Israelis, and held back lists of POWs. Sporadic warfare broke out, and Kissinger traveled back and forth between Damascus and Jerusalem. Finally an agreement of disengagement between Israel and Syria was signed in May, 1974: Israel evacuated the Syrian lands captured in the recent war, but kept most of the territory conquered in 1967, including the Golan Heights, except for a token Syrian strip. A UN one-to-five-mile buffer zone was created between Syria and Israel.

Soon after Sharon's last "order of the day" was published, he appeared at a major Likud rally in Tel Aviv's municipal square, now called Rabin Square, to protest the signing of the Geneva agreement. He attacked the government fiercely and the crowd responded with wild enthusiasm, crying "Arik, King of Israel!" Sharon was amazed at this spontaneous outpouring of support. "Emotionally it had been a powerful experience, a graphic demonstration that in my own right I had the ability to attract support from a large number of people. Here was a new dimension of politics, one I had gotten no taste of during the long weeks when we had hammered out the Likud coalition around tables at the various party headquarters."[4] For the first time he tasted the heady flavor of political power.

Because of the controversial "last order of the day," the speech at the Likud rally, and an interview published in *Harper's Magazine*, David Elazar canceled Sharon's commission as a division commander. The IDF issued an announcement:

> The order of the day published by Major General Sharon as well as the comments attributed to him by *Harper's Magazine* are an affront to the other commanders and units and are a

direct attack on his comrades-in-arms and to the fraternal spirit among soldiers. Despite this violation of good order and of military discipline, the Chief of Staff has decided not to institute military proceedings against Sharon following his release from active reserve duty and the cancellation of his commission as a division commander.[5]

Sharon, whose accusations of IDF blunders were certainly not unfounded, saw David Elazar as an ally of Bar-Lev and the Labor Party and considered that this judgment reflected concern that Sharon had become a political threat. And, in fact, the elections, held on December 31, 1973, made it clear that the voters wanted change. Labor put up the leaders who had presided over the Yom Kippur War. Dayan points out that there were many more young voters on the rolls than ever before, but above all there was public disillusionment with the way the war had been waged, the number of casualties, and the policies that had preceded the war. The upshot was that Labor lost seven seats in the Knesset, and the Likud went from twenty-nine to thirty-nine seats out of 120. Sharon was appointed to a seat on the Committee on Foreign and Security Affairs and became head of the subcommittee on the Defense Budget.

But it was apparent almost from the first that Sharon was not ready for life as a member of the Knesset. He tried to shut out the "nerve-wracking buzz of politicians," avoiding the Knesset cafeteria where politicking and lobbying were incessant. He spent a lot of time walking the halls with another newly elected member, Avraham Yoffe, an old friend who had also been a general in the IDF, and who also disliked "the continual smiling and talking and backslapping." He took "regular refuge" in a small room that he shared with another old friend, Sheikh Hamad Abu Robeiah, a Bedouin Labor member. They discussed mutual agricultural interests, subjects they found more congenial than politics.[6]

Sharon was alienated not only by the political atmosphere in the Knesset, but by the leadership of his own party as well. Menachem Begin and the others did not, he felt, give his suggestions the respect they deserved; they treated him with a kind of polite indulgence. When in December 1974, Rabin, now prime minister, appointed him commander of a reserve armored force, the government, under Labor pressure, passed a regulation prohibiting MKs from holding high-level field command positions. This was aimed squarely at Sharon, but in actual fact he welcomed it, because it gave him a perfect excute to resign from the Knesset, which he did in that same month of December. This was ultimately to lead to his resignation from the Knesset.

18

POST-WAR TURBULENCE

AFTER THE ELECTIONS, CRITICISM of the conduct of the war did not abate; on the contrary, there were increasing calls for an official inquiry. "The storm winds," Dayan said, "continued to howl around us."[1] The government, in turmoil with resignations offered and rescinded, was finally forced to agree to an investigation. In November, 1973, a five-member commission was appointed, headed by Dr Shimon Agranat, President of the Israeli Supreme Court. The other members were a second Supreme Court justice, the state comptroller and two former chiefs of staff. Dr Agranat had been born in Louisville, Kentucky, and received his degree from the University of Chicago Law School. The commission's mandate extended from pre-war events to the first three days of the Yom Kippur War itself.

The commission's first report, published on April 1, 1974, was a scathing indictment of the IDF for its lack of preparation. Major General Eliyahu Zeira, chief of Military Intelligence, was summarily removed from his post, along with three of his subordinates, including the chief intelligence officer of Southern Command. Major General Gonen was suspended from active duty. The most severe criticism was leveled at David Elazar: "the chief of staff," the commission announced, "bears direct responsibility for what happened on the eve of the war, both with regard to the assessment of the situation and the preparedness of the IDF." Their recommendation was that "the term of office of Lt. Gen. David Elazar as chief of staff be terminated."[2]

As for Moshe Dayan, the commission found that "by standards of reasonable behavior . . . the minister [of defense] was not required to issue orders for precautionary measures additional to or different from those proposed to him by the General Staff in accordance with joint assessment and consultation between the Chief of Staff and the Chief of Intelligence."[3] Nevertheless, criticism within the Labor Party, public fury and press attacks put both Dayan and Golda Meir under pressure and a few days later, on April 11, 1974, Mrs Meir announced her resignation. She was replaced in June by Yitzhak Rabin, who had spent the last six years as Israel's ambassador to Washington, and who now formed a new cabinet without Dayan. David Elazar died soon after his forced resignation. The Yom Kippur War government had ended in disgrace.

While all this was going on, the country was facing a resurgence of terrorism from the growing concentration of Palestinians in Lebanon. On the morning of April 11, 1974, the day of Mrs Meir's resignation, Radio Damascus announced that a "suicide squad" from the Popular Front for the Liberation of Palestine had broken into the northern Israeli town of Kiryat Shmonah and taken over a school. The announcement included a warning that any attempt to enter the school would endanger the lives of the students. Hostages were to be held until imprisoned colleagues of the hostage-takers were released.

In fact, when the announcement was broadcast, the three terrorists were already dead. They had indeed entered the school that morning, but found it empty, because the children were away on a field trip. The men then entered a neighboring apartment building, and went from apartment to apartment, throwing hand grenades and shooting the occupants with automatic weapons, without any attempt at hostage-taking, and finally barricaded themselves in a room on the top floor. Israeli security forces arrived and pinned down the intruders in a gun battle until a special unit was able to burst into the barricaded room and kill the three. Sixteen civilians had been murdered, including eight children, and two soldiers lost their lives in the exchange of fire.

In the light of recent events, Dayan's descriptions of the terrorists are worth noting: their bodies were riddled with bullets, he says, "but their faces unmarked. They seemed young, properly shaved, hair neatly cut and if I had met them in the street, they would have aroused no special curiosity on my part." He added that he did not know "whether they valued their lives dearly, but they had certainly shown no concern for the lives of Jewish women and children." The bland neatness of those terrorists cannot help but bring to mind the carefully neutral appearance of the men who destroyed the World Trade Center on September 11, 2001.

One month later, on May 15, there was another attack. Three terrorists broke into a house in the town of Maalot, like Kiryat Shmonah in Northern Galilee, and murdered the entire family. The night before, these men had attacked a truck taking some Arab women home to their village from the late shift at a textile plant north of Haifa, killed one of the women, and wounded ten others, including the bus driver. After they had murdered the family in Maalot, they broke into the schoolhouse where one hundred children and four teachers, who had been on a field trip in Galilee, were spending the night.

One teacher and a couple of children were released to deliver letters outlining the terrorists' demands, which they repeated through a loudspeaker they had with them. The Israelis were given a 6 pm deadline to release twenty convicted terrorists and fly them to Damascus. When Radio Damascus announced their arrival, the children would be freed; otherwise the building, with the children, would be blown up.

Dayan and Elazar, who were still in the cabinet, flew to Maalot, where the school was already surrounded by paratroopers. The cabinet had decided to agree to the exchange of prisoners, but not to leave the children with the terrorists. A stalemate ensued, and when

the six o'clock deadline approached, the soldiers were given permission to break into the school. Dayan went in after the troops.
The scene, he said, "was shattering, the floor covered in blood and
dozens of wounded children huddled against the walls." Before the
three were shot, they had murdered sixteen children, and wounded
sixty-eight.

Dayan found a good deal of fault with the operation: it should
have been carried out earlier in the day when the terrorists were not
as tense as they became as the deadline approached; the phospho-
rous grenade used by the paratroopers was inappropriate because
while they waited for the smoke to clear so that they could attack,
the terrorists had time to massacre the children, and, finally, Dayan
disapproved of the government's agreement to the terrorists' demands.[4]

In June, when Yitzhak Rabin took over as prime minister, Shimon
Peres was appointed to replace Moshe Dayan as defense minister.
Menachem Begin, the Likud leader, proposed that Sharon replace
David Elazar as chief of staff, but even though Sharon had supported Rabin, the Rabin government appointed Mordechai "Motta"
Gur to that post. Peres and Gur were opposed to Sharon having any
role in the IDF; they believed he would be a disruptive element, that
he would upset "the harmony of the army." Sharon responded that
this argument was "a rusty old weapon that has been used against
me in the past." He said he could hardly believe that someone who
had always been called upon to perform the most difficult missions,
and usually successfully, would be accused of destroying the harmony of the army. In any case, he said, "the army is not a harmony
club. The army is for fighting!"[5]

But it soon became apparent that, in order to reform the IDF it
would be necessary to include the help of key veteran officers. In
December, 1974, Sharon, with Rabin's support, received an appointment as commander of a reserve armored force. Labor, however,
argued against the appointment, saying that no one should be al-

lowed to hold a command post and a Knesset seat at the same time. This argument was codified into a law. There were reserve staff officers in the Knesset, but since Sharon was the only one appointed to a field command, he considered the rule an "Anti-Sharon Regulation." In a way, he welcomed it, because it led him to resolve a conflict in his own mind; after "arguing fruitlessly with the Likud for eleven months," he was, he says, "growing more and more depressed about the MK life I was leading." Now he had been handed a way out. In December, 1974, he resigned from the Knesset, telling the Likud that he had been forced to do it by the "arbitrary and anti-democratic decision of the government."[6]

Undoubtedly, he wanted to remain in the army because he had grave doubts about the military abilities of Mordechai Gur and Shimon Peres. But he also wanted badly to become chief of staff after Gur retired. He wanted action, and it was also part of his nature to want control. He had not been able to control elements of his own party in the Knesset; many of them had turned against him.

Now once back in the army, he devised a plan for troop deployment along the cease-fire lines. This was approved by the Southern Commander, Major General Adan, without having been submitted to Chief of Staff Gur. When the latter came from Tel Aviv and examined the proposal, he rejected it summarily, ordering Adan and Sharon to implement a different plan that had been developed by the General Staff. An argument ensued, which was of course won by the chief of staff. The next day, in the course of briefing three division commanders of his corps, Sharon pointed to a map on the wall that detailed Gur's plan, and said, "See the General Staff's plan? Only an idiot could produce a plan like that!"

He took down the map and replaced it with one detailing his own plan. This did not go down well with the staff officers, one of whom rebuked him, telling him that he couldn't call the chief of staff an idiot in front of his soldiers who might be summoned to serve under him in a war. This kind of behavior, the officer pointed out, could only demoralize the men and he felt it his duty to report it to Adan, which he did. Adan ordered Sharon to stop the briefings and return to Tel Aviv. When the briefings resumed, they dealt with Gur's plan.[7]

19

GROUND CONTROL

———

By 1975, WITH THE RATE of inflation rising in Israel, the government devalued the Israeli pound by forty-three percent. Sharon, who had bought his 800-acre farm with a loan linked to the dollar, found himself facing bankruptcy. He decided that his only hope lay in exporting, and went to work with his crew of Jews and Arabs, driving tractors, packing boxes, tending citrus and watermelon fields, sharing meals provided by Lily and the Sharon's cook. He says that he enjoyed this work, and was especially proud of the fact that Jews and Arabs worked together on his farm, and that some foremen were Jews and some were Arabs. He also enjoyed spending time with Lily, who was building a rock garden, and with his two sons, Omri, ten, and Gilad, eight, who liked to race their horses around the farm. But despite all this, he was not a man who wanted to remain out of the public eye. He maintained his reserve command and his intense interest in Israeli preparedness and its dependence on the United States.

In June, 1975, Rabin appointed Sharon his special advisor, a position that Sharon was to hold until February, 1976. Rabin was motivated partly by his lack of confidence in Shimon Peres; the prime minister did not feel he could rely on his defense minister's judgment and he wanted to be able to monitor the defense establishment with his own team. Sharon liked Rabin because he was not an ideologue, despite his lifelong membership in the Labor Party. The two men had always gotten along well, and had many points of agreement. In addition, Sharon hoped that if he worked with Rabin, he might one day realize his ambition of being named chief of staff. It did not bother him that Rabin represented a political party in opposition to his own.[1]

Peres's biographer says that when news of this appointment was reported in the press, both Peres and Motta Gur were shocked, because it was completely without precedent. In the past, prime ministers had been advised on defense matters only by the minister of defense and the chief of staff. To assuage Peres and Gur, Rabin agreed that Sharon would not attend General Staff meetings and that he would be called only advisor, and not national security advisor. A few days earlier, he and Sharon had agreed that the cabinet would be told this in order to avoid an uproar, although Sharon's contract stipulated that he would accompany Rabin to all political and military forums. But despite Rabin's hedging, the appointment did not go down well. It deepened the rift between Peres and Rabin, and angered many Labor people who resented giving a Likud member unprecedented responsibility.

This resentment did not ebb away; if anything it grew over the summer of 1975. On August 7, Rabin, Peres and Gur planned a tour of IDF camps. When Peres discovered that Rabin had invited Sharon to join them, he called the prime minister immediately. "You told me," he said, "that Sharon would not deal with defense matters."

When Rabin replied that Sharon was not dealing with military matters, Peres asked, "So why is he coming along?"

"He's coming because I'm coming," Rabin said.

Peres told him that Rabin had to consider the prestige of the chief of staff. Rabin, irritated, replied that he was aware of that, but he intended to bring along whomever he chose. "If that's the case," Peres said, "and if the person you want to bring is Arik, Arik cannot be subordinate to the chief of staff in his [emergency appointment as commander of the southern front]."

"I don't agree," Rabin said.

Peres, very angry, said that it was his right as a member of the cabinet to ask the opinion of the minister of justice on this matter. Rabin replied that if Peres was going to appeal this question, then by all means the visit should be canceled.

"Fine," Peres said. "We'll cancel the visit."[2]

Clearly, despite the nation's having to exist under conditions of continuing peril on the Lebanon border, cabinet members remained concerned about protecting their own turf, apparently to the exclusion of other considerations. Nevertheless, under Rabin things began to improve. The agreements with Egypt and Syria provided a breathing space for the IDF to rebuild its forces. Sharon himself was able to institute changes as Rabin's advisor, even though because of cabinet hostility, his influence in key defense issues was limited. The Ministry of Defense, for instance, improved its budgeting procedures as a result of Sharon's pressure. Perhaps more important for what lay ahead, he was exposed to national issues at the right hand of the prime minister. He traveled extensively both in and outside Israel. Inside the country he spent a good deal of time in the West Bank, familiarizing himself with the area and outlining proposals for settlements that he believed would be necessary for Israel's security.

Outside Israel, he was able to attend important conferences. It was while with Rabin that he met Henry Kissinger for the first time. The American Secretary of State, he says, looked at him "and growled jovially, 'I hear you are the most dangerous man in the Middle East.'" Sharon, thinking of Kissinger's role in the Yom Kippur cease-fire and its aftermath, "growled back, 'No, Mr Kissinger, I'm not the most dangerous man in the Middle East. *You* are the most dangerous man in the Middle East.'"[3]

In early December, 1975, a group of members of Gush Emunim, a fanatically nationalist movement, evaded IDF roadblocks, appropriated land near the ancient site of Sebastia in the West Bank, and attempted to establish a new settlement called Elon Moreh. The government decided to shut it down and thousands of Gush Emunim supporters flocked to the site to stage a protest. Sharon acted as an intermediary in this dispute, negotiating a compromise in which the government would allow these settlers to build their community on a nearby army base.[4] That was a success for him, but on another occasion, when Syrian forces had entered Lebanon and taken over the city of Jezin, Sharon took the position that Israel should attack. The Rabin government had established a demarcation line for military action, and Jezin was on the line. Gur disagreed with Sharon, maintaining that an ultimatum would force the Syrians to withdraw, and this was in fact what happened. To Gur, this was proof that Sharon was too belligerent. To Sharon, the presence of Syrian forces in Lebanon was a danger signal for the future.[5]

After eight months, Sharon resigned because he had no real power, and because he was convinced that Rabin would never challenge Gur and Peres to secure a permanent high-ranking army appointment for him.

20

PARACHUTING FROM SHLOMZION

———

SHARON NOW HAD THE opportunity to devote all his energy to his farm and family, the life he often said was so attractive to him. But in fact he could not bear to be on the sidelines. He began to give speeches and news conferences, to attack the Rabin government and offer opinions about relations with the US, the Soviets and the Palestinians, among other things. Clearly, he wanted to get back into politics. He had quarrelled with the Liberal faction of the Likud and in fact with the entire Likud, which he had unsuccessfully tried to unify, with himself as its leader. But Menachem Begin was the Likud's choice as party head. So Sharon decided to form a separate party, which he called Shlomzion, Peace for Zion.

The response to Sharon's announcement of the formation of this party was rewarding; he had the power to motivate some very prominent people, apart from his army friends. There was a per-ceived need to change the political climate of the country. More than three years after the shock of the Yom Kippur War, Labor poli-cies seemed stagnant. The party was not attuned to demographic and sociological changes: interests of younger voters and the Shephardim—Jews of Asian and African origin. Consequently, the popularity of the Likud was rising. Begin's campaign chairman was General Ezer Weizman, former chief of the IAF, popularly known as "founder of the world's best air force." In January, 1977, in his keynote speech to the Likud convention, Begin suggested trading land for peace with Egypt. This idea was well received by the war-weary Israeli public.

Sharon opened a small Shlomzion office in Tel Aviv. He called for the removal of the Jordanian monarchy and the establishment of a Palestinian state in Jordan, with the cooperation of Palestinian spokesmen. He told the press, that "there is no advantage to the person who steadfastly maintains the same position over the years just for the sake of consistency. Changing circumstances require changing opinions."[1] He attacked the Likud as well as Labor, saying that he would under no circumstances return to the Likud, even if his own party did not succeed, and he would not abandon that party if it won only a few seats in the Knesset. His goal was in fact to win eight seats.

His appeal was moderate, and he was open to compromise with others, even with many whose views were far left of center. Three weeks after the formation of Shlomzion, Yigael Yadin, a professor of archeology and former IDF commander, formed his own party, the Democratic Movement for Change, which appealed to the same disaffected voters as Shlomzion. This presented a real threat to Sharon, who approached Yadin with the idea of a merger, including an offer to accept the DMC platform. But the new party members refused to have anything to do with Sharon, who withdrew in anger, and turned next to the Independent Liberal Party. This was a dovish party, but it was old and established and had a strong organization.

Sharon surprised everyone by sending Amos Kenan to negotiate with the Independent Liberals. Kenan was a well-known journalist who strongly advocated Palestinian rights, but who said that as a friend of Sharon's, he believed that Sharon could bring about necessary change in the country. With Kenan, Sharon agreed to Palestinian self-rule in the West Bank, if all security arrangements were left in Israeli hands. This is strikingly similar to the position he took in

October, 2001. At that time, in 1977, Sharon also wanted to meet with Yassir Arafat but not one of his senior aides. A meeting in Paris was tentatively scheduled, but at the last minute the PLO cancelled.[2]

In spite of all this, the Independent Liberals decided that they had little or nothing to gain from an association with Sharon, and the party leader, Moshe Kol, told Sharon that any attempt to change their minds would be futile. Sharon had started his party at a time when people were looking for a new political force, when the Labor Party was losing stature and the Likud had not been able to fill the consequent gap. Sharon had charisma and a background that commanded respect, and his party's platform was designed for wide-range appeal. All these things should have ensured its success, but after the initial surge of popularity, Sharon's supporters began to fall away.

According to Uzi Benziman, much of the fault lay with Sharon himself: Benziman says that he treated the party as a personal cult, demanding complete loyalty and refusing to consider differing opinions. Lily also presented a problem, choosing favorites and working for the dismissal of those whose personalities she found incompatible. The atmosphere at party headquarters became irritable and edgy, a situation that grew worse as money began to dry up. In response, Sharon gave up hope for a left or center coalition, and reverted to right-wing nationalism, calling for expansion of Jewish settlements on the West Bank and warning of the possibility of war. He toured the northern border, met with Major Saad Haddad, leader of the Christian Lebanese Militia, which was trained and financed by Israel, and declared that "Lebanon's war was Israel's war."

He called also for tighter government control of the IDF, a twenty percent cut in the defense budget and the establishment of a National Security Council. But Shlomzion continued to lose momentum. Finally, two months before the election, when polls indicated that Sharon would be lucky to win even one Knesset seat, he approached Menachem Begin, who was recuperating from a minor heart ailment, about the possibility of Shlomzion being admitted to the Likud coalition.[3]

Begin, the head of the Likud, had been born in Brest Litovsk in 1913 and became a passionate Zionist in his teens. In 1943, he came to Palestine as a member of the Free Polish Army, and after the war, was part of the Irgun Tsvai Leumi. He had been a virtual outcast, hunted by the British and denounced by fellow Zionists. When Israel achieved statehood, Begin became the leader of the opposition party Herut. In 1965, when Begin's Herut merged with the Liberal Party, it was the basis for the future formation of the Likud coalition. Begin was a fierce nationalist who had resigned from Mrs Meir's National Unity cabinet in 1970 to protest the possible ceding of some occupied territory. He had also opposed all separation-of-forces agreements with Egypt and Syria, accusing the government of weakness. He had been deeply emotionally scarred by Polish anti-Semitism and by the Holocaust.

Begin liked Sharon, and responded favorably to the admission of Shlomzion to Likud. However, Simcha Ehrlich, the Liberal Party leader in the Likud, was adamantly opposed to Sharon, but could not reach Yitzhak Shamir, the Likud's organization chief, before the deadline for parties to submit their lists of candidates to the Knesset committee on elections. Consequently Shlomzion appeared on the ballot as an independent party. The election was a significant victory for the Likud, which won forty-three seats in the 120-seat Knesset. Labor's twenty-nine years of power had ended and Menachem Begin was the new prime minister. Shlomzion won two seats, one of which was taken by Sharon.[4]

Sharon had worked tirelessly in every aspect of the campaign, overcoming his dislike of politicking. He had at least one bizarre experience while he was in the US trying to raise money on the east coast. A wealthy Californian contacted him, saying he wanted to give him a contribution and arrange a fund-raising party for him in

San Francisco with other potential contributors. Sharon rearranged his schedule, flew across the country and arrived at the San Francisco hotel to find a dinner in progress that seemed to have been organized for a cause other than his own. After dinner he gave what he hoped was a rousing speech and his host encouraged the guests to contribute. He handed Sharon an envelope, saying he himself was going to set an example. No one followed his example, however, and after the dinner Sharon discovered that the host had neglected to book a room for him. Fortunately, a husband and wife whom he had known in Israel were at the dinner and invited him to spend the night with them. When he was alone, he opened his envelope and found a check for twenty-five dollars.[5]

He spent the last weeks of the campaign warning of danger to the country's security from Egyptian cease-fire violations and a volatile situation in Lebanon, and even sought support from the nationalist group Gush Emunim, which refused to help him. He was not happy with the performance of Shlomzion, and at dawn after election day, when it was clear that Likud had triumphed, he called Begin to congratulate him. Begin assured him that he belonged in the Likud, and that he must write a conciliatory letter to the Liberal leader Simcha Ehrlich, whom he had attacked toward the end of the campaign. Sharon promptly wrote the letter and sent it that morning. He did not grovel, but he praised Likud's victory and offered to join his two seats to their forty-three.

Begin pressured Ehrlich to accept Sharon's offer, and it was agreed that Shlomzion would be absorbed into the Herut Party in the Likud. Some Shlomzion members were upset that their party was losing its individuality. Sharon responded to them impatiently, and it was understood that his political future had to lie with the Likud. Begin wanted Sharon in his cabinet and originally planned to make him defense minister to replace Shimon Peres. But the Liberals objected to this, and the post went to Ezer Weizman, while Sharon became minister of agriculture, and was also assigned chairmanship of the cabinet committee on new settlements. Raful Eytan, who had been a battalion commander under Sharon, replaced Mordechai Gur as chief of staff.[6]

Under Israel's system of parliamentary democracy, the government needed the support of at least sixty-one of the 120 Knesset members to survive. Begin brought in the National Religious Party with twelve seats and Agudat Yisrael, the ultra-Orthodox religious party, with four. Both these parties had been aligned with Labor. Before he took office, Begin, interviewed about his plans, replied that what was urgently needed was a foreign affairs minister, a kind of public relations expert, who could communicate with foreign populations as well as foreign governments. Four days after the election, Begin offered the post to Moshe Dayan, who accepted, enraging the Labor people.

They were further enraged when they discovered that Dayan had been quietly negotiating with Begin even before the elections. The public, however, was happy to see the return of its old war hero, complete with famous black eye patch. "Dayan," Chaim Herzog commented, "almost gleefully abandoned his party in its hour of defeat, to face violent accusations of political prostitution. He later made quite a convincing case for his belief that he could move Begin toward peace negotiations with Egypt and possibly other Arab states. Depending on one's point of view, he was either treacherous or extremely brave and imaginative. In the final analysis, the was a major force in bringing about the peace agreement with Egypt."[7]

Two months after the elections, Begin presented his new cabinet to the Knesset. He had appointed thirteen ministers, including Sharon, who took his oath of office with his wife, two sons and his eighty-year-old mother looking on. It was an emotional moment for the family: Sharon thought of his father, "an agronomist, a farmer, a pioneer in his field," who would have been overwhelmed to see his son named minister of agriculture.[8] It was also an optimistic moment for Sharon: agriculture was an important policy area in Israel because it covered strategic regions. It had been a major concern in practical Zionism in Sharon's youth, of course, and later the land became a major element in defense.

But apart from that, Sharon knew that in the past, three ministers of agriculture, including Dayan, had become defense ministers.

21

THE SETTLEMENTS

———

WHEN GOLDA MEIR'S LABOR government was in power, Jewish settlement of the occupied territories had been basically strategic, and decisions about it were made by the cabinet. When Yitzhak Rabin took over, he found himself facing a settlement movement driven by the fanatical Gush Emunim, backed by the Mafdal, the National Religious Party, a religious right wing core in the Knesset, dedicated to the idea that Jews must settle the entire expanse of the Holy Land. Rabin tried to stop these people, but because his coalition included Mafdal, he had to tread carefully.

When Begin's Likud came to power in May, 1977, Begin too had to depend on Mafdal for his majority. He himself was not religious, but, unlike Rabin, accepted the belief that the entire country should be settled by Jews. He supported the Gush Emunim settlements, and, with Sharon as minister of agriculture, set about building not only farm settlements, but whole towns. And with government support and low prices, the settlers were no longer limited to Orthodox fanatics. This policy also involved harassment of the Arab population to encourage them to emigrate, and an elaborate licensing system to discourage them from returning. Martin van Creveld says, "By world standards, [Israeli] rule may not have been of the harshest; never were hostages taken, or terrorists executed by formal court order, or entire villages demolished (as the French did in the Algerian war). Still, from the point of view of those affected it was bad enough."[1]

Sharon had been interested in settlements in the West Bank at least from the time he had been Rabin's advisor: the Labor government had built twenty-five settlements, and two more were under construction when the Likud took over. Now that he was minister of agriculture, the settlements were Sharon's responsibility. On September 29, 1977, forty days after he was appointed, he presented what he called the Sharon Plan to the cabinet for new settlements throughout the West Bank, which he, like many other Israelis, referred to as Judea and Samaria. This plan differed from the Labor Party's, which involved a "frontier settlement" policy along the pre-1967 border, known as the Green Line, based on security reasons without emotional connotations.[2]

The Green Line, Sharon said, no longer applied, because there were a number of Arab towns and villages on the Israeli side, and close by on the West Bank side as well, so that people could hardly remember where the Green Line had been. On the rocky hills overlooking "the coastal plain" he wanted to build "a line of urban, industrial settlements" for strategic purposes, to protect the plain. This area, he was careful to say, was not populated, because it was unfit for agriculture.

In addition to the abandonment of the Green Line and the seizure and buildup of the West Bank mountain ridges—known as Crown Lands during the British Mandate—Sharon turned his attention to Jerusalem. Since the 1840s, Jews had comprised the city's largest ethnic population, but after Israel revived Jerusalem in 1967, West Bank Arabs began to move there, to take advantage of jobs, schools, and health and social services. Over ten years, the Arab population grew from 65,000 to 130,000. Sharon stressed to the cabinet the importance of maintaining Jerusalem as a Jewish city, and to do that he proposed ringing the Arab neighborhoods with a "horseshoe" of Jewish settlements that would eventually include about a million people, and secure Jerusalem "as the capital of the Jewish people."[3]

On the same day that Sharon submitted this proposal, it was announced that Tekoa, a new settlement, had been established east of Bethlehem. A few days later, on October 2, the cabinet approved Sharon's plan, evoking a strong negative response from the Carter administration in the US. On October 4, 1977, in an address to the UN General Assembly, Carter emphasized Palestinian "legitimate rights." But settlements, both religious and secular, continued to spring up in the West Bank. On October 30, Mevo Dotan was founded by secular Jews who sought to build up the northeastern portion of the West Bank, and two days later Beit El, a religious settlement, was created on the hills close to the Arab town of Ramallah, with the stated aim of "settl[ing] the land of Israel and [basing] it on the power of Torah and Zionism."[4]

Sharon had always led a secular life, but he said that he had an emotional attachment to the religious settlers, and that his interest in the settlements went beyond security considerations. Those considerations could change with time, he thought, but what would remain constant was the historical justification for settlement of the ancient land. In 1998, he told a journalist, "The cave of Machpela—what other nation had a memorial almost 4000 years old, the burial place of our nation's patriarchs and matriarchs, Abraham and Sarah, Isaac and Rebecca, Jacob and Leah? We go to the United States and see the Jefferson Memorial and the Lincoln Memorial, and millions of people come and look with excitement at a 200-year-old site. We look at sites thousands of years old. It is empowering and inspires a feeling of historic entitlement."[5]

In a radio interview on May 31, 1996, he talked about his feelings for the religious movement. He had had strong bonds for years, he said, with the Orthodox sector, not out of political but out of personal considerations. "That I am first and foremost a Jew, and that the thing that most interests me is the Jewish people—what will happen to us in thirty years, and in 300 years, and in 3000 years." He was fascinated by his meetings with prominent Israeli

Torah scholars, and he was sorry that the secular sector did not really know the Orthodox, who had interesting opinions on politics and security, on immigration and emigration, and even on drugs and crime, from "the background of their desire to deepen the Jewish aspect of our society." They are perceived, he said, as making demands, as asking for religious legislation, but all they really demand is "that we carefully guard the integrity of the Land of Israel." Of course, he added, they would like to see more teaching of the Bible, of Jewish history, "to deepen our connection with the Land and our Jewish identity."[6]

Not everyone accepts Sharon's claim to a personal, emotional involvement with these settlements. Uzi Benziman believes that his "support of the settlements, and in particular of extreme fanatical groups such as Gush Emunim, was opportunistic in nature." At the same time, Benziman, apparently contradicting himself, says that "beyond the fact that they served his own political ambitions, [Sharon] saw these religious settlers as the true pioneers of the 1970s and '80s . . . The aura of pride that radiated from him when he was encircled by the singing and dancing settlers could not be mistaken."[7] But Benziman sees support for his argument of political opportunism in Sharon's "willingness to limit all new settlements to a mere military presence on the West Bank in talks with Yigael Yadin in 1977 and his avid support of the new settlements since the formation of the Begin government."[8] Benziman finds opportunistic motivation behind Sharon's willingness to compromise on the settlements when he became involved with the prospect of peace with Egypt, a conclusion that raises questions about Benziman's own objectivity.

What does seem apparent from all this, perhaps, is the futility of attempting to simplify the motivations of a complex, impassioned and controlling man, who is capable of compromising his positions when he has a participatory role in crucial decision-making.

22

ATTEMPTS AT PEACE WITH EGYPT

———

ON SATURDAY EVENING, NOVEMBER 19, 1977, Anwar Sadat arrived in Israel to meet with Menachem Begin. This important breakthrough visit was the culmination of five months of negotiations so secret that only Begin and Dayan on the Israeli side knew about them. The visit came as a complete surprise to Begin's cabinet. The train had been set in motion with Jimmy Carter's election in November, 1976. What Carter wanted was an Israeli-Palestinian settlement based on United Nations Security Council Resolution 242 of November, 1967, the basis for all peace discussions in the Middle East after that time. The resolution embodied a compromise with the Soviet Union, which had demanded an official condemnation of Israel and an Israeli withdrawal to the June 4 borders. The final resolution called for a trade of land for "a just and lasting peace." Israel was required to withdraw from "territories" occupied in June, 1967, in return for which the Arabs had to put an end to their hostilities and recognize "the sovereignty, territorial integrity and political independence of every state in the area and their right to live in peace within secure and recognized boundaries." The resolution called also for "freedom of navigation through international waterways" and the need to solve the refugee problem.[1]

Both Henry Kissinger—until Nixon's downfall—and Carter in his first months, had been dealing with relatively cooperative Israeli Labor governments. But after June, 1977, Carter and his Secretary of State Cyrus Vance had to negotiate with Begin and the right-wing Likud coalition. Relations got off to a rocky start when Begin told Vance in Jerusalem that America's readiness to deal with the PLO was reminiscent of Neville Chamberlain's attempts to appease Hitler, a comparison Sharon was to resurrect in the fall of 2001, enraging the Bush administration.[2] In any case, Begin showed no willingness to grant territorial concessions, although at the same time he was initiating his secret dialogue with the Egyptians.

He flew to Bucharest in August to request that Nicolae Ceausescu, the Romanian dictator, tell Sadat that the Israelis wanted a meeting with him. On September 4 Dayan, in a wig, moustache and dark glasses, flew to Morocco twice, the first time to get King Hassan to arrange a meeting, and the second time to meet with Hassan Tuhami, the Egyptian deputy prime minister.[3] There were many points of serious disagreement, but also distinct possibilities for compromise. Dayan broke his promise of secrecy to the Egyptians by going to Washington on September 19 to tell the Carter people about the Morocco meeting, and the Egyptian foreign minister, Ismail Fahmy, followed suit two days later. Carter told Fahmy that the domestic political situation would not allow him to put strong pressure on Israel. He had encountered a considerable negative response from the American Jewish community and from politicians in Israel.

Because he could not rely on the Americans, Sadat made the decision to negotiate directly with the Israelis. He was motivated by the realization that these wars were wrecking the Egyptian economy and that Israel possessed the military advantage as well as the frightening possibility of nuclear weapons. On November 9, in a speech to the Egyptian National Assembly, Sadat announced that he would go to the ends of the earth to prevent one more Egyptian soldier from being wounded and was even willing to go and talk to the Knesset. Time, he said, was of the essence. Possibly because no one thought he was serious, he received warm applause, even from Arafat who was present.[4]

In Israel, his remarks were received with surprise, skepticism and distrust, until November 18, 1977, when Begin gave his military and intelligence chiefs the complete background of the secret negotiations. The reaction in the Arab capitals was predictably negative: there were massive demonstrations and in Syria, Assad, declaring a day of mourning, draped public areas in black flags. On November 22, after Sadat's visit, Arafat and Assad sent out a joint statement of condemnation of the visit and called on the Egyptian people to resist Sadat's peace overture. In response, Sadat shut down the PLO offices in Cairo along with its radio transmitters.[5]

When Sadat landed in Israel, his enthusiastic reception at the airport included an Israeli band playing both the Zionist anthem "Hatikvah" and the Egyptian national anthem. Begin's entourage included Golda Meir, whom Sadat greeted good-naturedly as "the old lady," and Sharon, the general who had crossed the canal during the most recent war and had moved on Cairo. Sharon says that as they shook hands, Sadat remarked, "I tried to catch you at the canal," and Sharon responded, "Now you have a chance to catch me as a friend."[6]

The following morning, Sunday, November 20, Begin told the cabinet that he believed that Sadat sincerely wanted a genuine peace. Sharon proposed what Benziman calls "a dramatic show of friendship toward Egypt by opening up the border at the northern Sinai town of El Arish to any Egyptian wishing to visit Israel." Moshe Dayan, however, explained that Sadat had not come to Israel for a small gesture like that, and would be embarrassed by any special show of gratitude from the Israelis, which would also open him up to accusations by the Arab nations of making a separate deal with Israel.[7]

Later on that Sunday, Sadat delivered his speech to the Knesset, in his native Arabic, also one of Israel's official languages. He said that he had not come to Jerusalem only for a separate Egyptian-Israeli peace agreement that would "terminate the state of belligerency at this stage, and put off the entire problem to a subsequent stage." This was "not the radical solution that would steer us to permanent peace." But, he went on, he had come to end the state of belligerency in the region and to seek a true peace based on ending Israeli occupation of all Arab territories seized in 1967, and giving the Palestinian people the right to establish their own state.[8]

The visit itself certainly created some good will in Israel, but clearly little agreement. Begin was willing to give up almost the entire Sinai, but he was not willing to go beyond a limited measure of autonomy, under Israeli military control, for Arabs in the West Bank—referred to habitually by the Likud as Judea and Samaria—and the retention of Jewish settlements there. No Arab states backed Sadat: Syria, Iraq, Libya and the PLO declared an economic and diplomatic boycott of Egypt, although Saudi Arabia and Jordan chose to remain neutral, for the time at least. Many talks ensued between Israel and Egypt, but nothing was achieved.

Carter entered the picture at a point when Sadat was beginning to lose hope and to talk about resigning. Although the American president did not want to cause domestic uproar, he invited Sadat to Washington, and later declared that Israeli settlements in the territories were an illegal impediment to peace and that Resolution 242 applied to all territories, not just the Sinai. Sharon did not help matters in March, 1978, when he sent bulldozers in to prepare an area in the northeast section of the West Bank for settlements. When Ezer Weizman, who was in Washington at the time, learned about this, he phoned Begin and threatened to resign immediately if these bulldozers were not removed. The Liberals in the Likud also talked about resignation. Begin responded in April, by taking the right to approve the establishment of new settlements from the cabinet committee on settlements and giving it to the committee on defense. Sharon was very angry, but Begin had no intention of being intimidated into risking his coalition.[9]

This did not mean that Sharon gave up his settlement plans; Benziman says he worked on settlements whenever the peace discussions seemed to fail, "and he stealthily formed new settlements without government approval by establishing satellites near existing settlements and presenting them as mere expansions of existing ones."[10]

For their part, the Americans did not foresee that Sadat's thinking would change, partly as a result of a series of attacks by Palestinian terrorists against Egyptian, as well as Israeli and Western, targets. Sadat turned fiercely against the PLO, calling them "pygmies and hired killers," and even telling Ezer Weizman privately that he no longer believed that there should be a Palestinian state.[11]

Finally, by the summer of 1978, it became apparent to the Americans that the Sinai was the key to a peace settlement. Sadat wanted it, and Begin was willing to give it up. A very vocal and widespread peace movement, called Peace Now, had sprung up in Israel, making a strong impression on Begin. Consequently, Carter was optimistic as he initiated talks with Sadat and Begin at Camp David on September 5. Sharon had wanted to attend these talks, but many leaders in the Likud did not want him there. Begin kept in touch with him by phone, however, reporting to him because he did not want Sharon to work against the negotiations. And this was wise: by the twelfth day of the peace talks, only one difficult question remained: the existence of Israeli settlements in the northern Sinai. Weizman asked his military attache, Avraham Tamir, a former comrade of Sharon's, to phone Sharon and ask him to concede the settlements for the sake of peace. Sharon thought about it briefly, and then told Tamir to tell Begin that he would make this concession if it were the only sticking point left. Tamir implored Sharon to phone Begin himself and Sharon agreed to do it. "A few hours later," Benziman writes, "as the Israeli mission met for a review of their position, Begin informed those present that he had just spoken to his minister of agriculture and that Sharon had recommended that making the concession was preferable to ending the talks at an impasse over the fate of the settlements."[12]

As we have seen, Uzi Benziman finds Sharon's about-face opportunistic, citing the "ease and alacrity" with which Sharon opted for peace as proof "that his position on the settlements had not been based on either emotional or ideological grounds."[13] Sharon himself says that he "felt strongly that we had to try the experiment of peace with Egypt . . . after thirty years of existing in a state of war, the question of whether we could make peace with an Arab state and then live in peace with them was historic."[14] Certainly it cannot be denied that Sharon had a strong sense of history. But it should also be noted that in crucial matters he believed in presenting a strong front to the international community, downplaying concerns he expressed domestically.

In any case, after two weeks of emotional explosions and retreats and advances, the exhausted participants signed agreements: Israel would withdraw from the Sinai and in return Egypt would grant diplomatic recognition and establish normal relations with the Jewish state, dropping all boycotts; Israeli ships and aircraft would pass freely through Egyptian air and waterways, and arrangements were made for the patrol and control of border regions, involving demilitarization, international forces and warning stations. Within three months, the parties would execute a peace treaty based on UN Resolution 242, which Begin had at first refused to recognize. Although reference was made to an Arab "self-governing authority," and some resolution of the refugee problem, these matters and many others were not dealt with explicitly.

The great majority of Israelis approved these agreements and in the Knesset only nineteen of the 120 members voted against it, while seventeen abstained. The Egyptian people and press in the main seemed relieved to see the possibility of peace after almost thirty years of war and tension, but the Islamic fundamentalists, parties of the left, students and many government officials were furious at Sadat, as were the Palestinians and most of the Arab League. As months passed, the pressure on Sadat became severe, and he reneged on many of the commitments he had signed.

As the peace process deteriorated, the Israelis continued the settlement policy. Begin had given Sharon permission to bolster airfields in the Sinai and also to expand settlements there. Sharon called this "setting facts in the ground," in the belief that building new settlements would force Egypt to accept "facts" or give Israel a better bargaining position. According to Chaim Herzog, by the end of 1977, Sharon had created a minor crisis by telling Israel Radio that there was a government plan to build twenty new settlements in the Sinai, four of them immediately. Sharon later denied that he had done this, but Herzog called him "A superb general but a politician with an insatiable desire for power and attention" who had "dropped a bomb—with the fuse lit—right in Begin's lap."[15] Sharon was also continuing to build new Israeli settlements in the West Bank. Begin and Dayan both supported him, but Defense Minister Ezer Weizman held the view that "Sharon had lost sight of the distinction between his own personal good and the good of the state."[16]

In the winter of 1978, President Carter decided, after consulting with Zbigniew Brzezinski, the head of the US National Security Council and Secretary of State Cyrus Vance, that the peace process would be reinvigorated if he invited Begin and Sadat separately to the White House for further talks. But on March 11, just before Begin was scheduled to leave for Washington, PLO radicals from Lebanon landed on the Israeli coast. After killing Gail Rubin, an American Jewish photographer who had been taking pictures of wildlife, the terrorists hijacked a bus with passengers just north of Tel Aviv, and forced the driver to drive south toward the city. When the bus was stopped by Israeli roadblocks, the infiltrators began to shoot, killing thirty-five people and wounding close to one hundred.

Begin immediately postponed his trip to Washington, and four days later retaliated with Operation Litani, named after the river ten miles from the Lebanon border. Israeli jets bombed southern Lebanon, systematically destroying PLO installations, and followed with an invasion on the ground, attacking PLO bases in full force, and wiping them out. In a few days, the campaign ended with Israeli troops occupying a ten-kilometer strip along the border. Carter and the UN demanded Israel's immediate withdrawal, but the Israelis asked for a "guarantee" that the PLO would not infiltrate again. The Lebanese ambassador to the UN, who was strongly opposed to the PLO presence in his country, expressed the wish that Israeli troops would remain there and "take care of business." Finally, three months later, on June 13, the troops pulled out and were essentially replaced by UN forces.

Both the revolution in Iran and the approaching American election helped to push Sadat toward signing the peace treaty; the former posited a fundamentalist threat to the region, and the latter held the prospect of a new president who might have less sympathy for the Egyptian side. Above all, Sadat wanted to retrieve the Sinai. Carter flew to Cairo on March 7, 1979, and received a gratifying reception. He was enthusiastically applauded when he addressed the parliament and when he toured antique sites and visited Alexandria. But when he arrived in Israel on March 13, he ran into problems over control of Gaza and the question of Egypt supplying Israel annually with 2.5 million gallons of oil to make up for the loss of Sinai oil. Begin tried Carter's patience and Sharon did not help when he declared that Jordan was Palestine and that within twenty years there would be one million Jews in the West Bank, which should be part of Israel.[17] After the intervention of Dayan and Weizman, who threatened to resign, a compromise was reached: Israel agreed to give up the oil demand in return for control of Gaza and an early exchange of ambassadors.

On March 21, after a heated two-day debate, the Knesset voted ninety-five to eighteen in favor of the treaty. The Israeli cabinet had approved the treaty with two dissenters. One of them was Ariel Sharon, but in the Knesset, his was one of the ninety-five votes for approval.

23

THE ROAD TO PEACE

———

AT TWO O'CLOCK IN THE afternoon on March 26, 1979, in a tent on
the White House lawn, Begin and Sadat signed the peace treaty in
an atmosphere of good will and friendship. Ezer Weizman and his
son were present; Weizman had consistently gotten on better with
Sadat than the hard-line Begin. By the terms of the treaty, Israel was
to withdraw completely from the Sinai, where UN personnel would
be stationed; boycotts and other discriminatory practices were to
be abolished; Israeli ships were to have free passage through the
Suez Canal, the Straits of Tiran and the Gulf of Aqaba with flyover
rights as well; armed forces were strictly limited on both sides; normal economic relations were to be established, along with an exchange of ambassadors. Despite Sadat's promise to sell Sinai oil to
Israel at market prices, the United States guaranteed Israel's oil supplies for fifteen years. Begin had actually gained the most from this
treaty; he had made peace with Egypt and pleased the United States
without having had to agree to withdraw from the West Bank or
Gaza. On December 10, 1979, Begin received the Nobel Peace Prize.

Sadat had so enraged the Arab states that all of them except
Oman and Sudan broke off relations with Cairo; Egypt's membership in the Arab League was suspended; the league headquarters
was moved to Tunis, and oil exports to Egypt were cut off, as were
all money grants and loans. Sadat did not believe that this situation
would endure, and time proved him right, although he did not live

to see it. Ten years later, the league headquarters was back in Egypt, and diplomatic relations with all the states had resumed. Sadat had also believed that the Arab states would follow his lead in involving themselves in a peace process with Israel, and to some extent this did happen.

The Jewish settlers in the Sinai were appalled at the prospect of vacating their homes, and, backed by Gush Emunim, put up stiff physical resistance. The government, while bulldozing their settlements, tried to assuage their anger by offering to compensate them financially. A hard-core group of settlers occupied the evacuated town of Yamit and for a week in late April, 1982, a battle ensued between fifteen hundred squatters with rocks and clubs, and twenty thousand IDF soldiers using water cannon. The soldiers won, with no casualties on either side, and Yamit was bulldozed to the ground. Apart from snags like this, implementation of the treaty went more smoothly than most observers had expected. There were diplomatic exchanges and commercial treaties, and the Sinai stayed demilitarized, but Benny Morris points out that the Egyptians hewed to the letter, rather than to the spirit of the agreement. Egypt imported almost nothing from Israel and exported only the oil it had agreed to supply, and while thousands of Israeli tourists visited Egypt—at risk from terrorists there—Cairo prevented Egyptians from visiting Israel. In addition, there was continual anti-Israeli propaganda and incitement from the Egyptian media.[1]

Difficulties arose between Begin and Sadat on the question of self-rule for Gaza, the West Bank and east Jerusalem. In June, 1979, both Dayan and Weizman withdrew from the negotiating team and a few months later resigned from Begin's cabinet in disagreement with what they considered the prime minister's recalcitrant position on autonomy for the occupied territories. In the absence of any sincere effort by Israel or Egypt, along with the exclusion of the PLO and rejection by Jordan, the autonomy talks had collapsed by the end of 1979.

On April 10, 1979, one month after the treaty was signed, Palestinian militants detonated a bomb in Tel Aviv's Carmel Market, killing three people and injuring thirty-two. Six days later, terrorists entered the Brussels airport and threw hand grenades at passengers waiting to board an El Al flight to Israel. El Al security acted quickly and was able to prevent a massacre. Terror against Israel intensified after the signing of the treaty, while West Bank settlements multiplied. More than a decade would pass before Israeli and Palestinian leaders would hold direct talks with each other. Shimon Peres commented: "The great breakthrough in the agreement with Egypt consisted in the fact that this was our first treaty with an Arab country. But the peace with Egypt was also the easiest. The Sinai is not the Holy Land, the historic homeland of the Jewish people. The Sinai, moreover, is virtually empty. Once it is demilitarized by agreement, the question of sovereignty over it becomes less important. The other fronts, I always realized, would be tougher to resolve."[2]

In the summer and autumn of 1979, new settlements were set up in the West Bank and more were planned for the Gaza Strip. This settlement policy, which provoked protest rallies in Tel Aviv, helped to soothe right wing irritation with the withdrawal from the Sinai. In the June, 1981, election, Labor as well as the Likud supported the treaty, so Begin had a strong mandate to continue the withdrawal when Likud won forty-eight seats to Labor's forty-seven. When Dayan resigned in October, 1979, the Foreign Ministry had gone to Yitzhak Shamir, who opposed the peace treaty. And on Weizman's resignation at about the same time, Begin himself acted as interim defense minister, much to the open annoyance of Sharon, who had made clear his own desire to take charge of Defense. Begin had told the press facetiously that he wasn't going to appoint Sharon to that post, because he was afraid that his first act would be to surround the government buildings with tanks.

Now with Likud winning its second election, and establishing itself as a viable political party, Sharon was valuable to Begin, who liked him in spite of his often prickly presence in the cabinet. The bombing of the nuclear reactor in Iraq won popular approval for Likud, and it was Sharon who had convinced Begin to approve that action against Baghdad. The cabinet had known for some time that Iraq was working on an atomic bomb, but most members were not ready to take the drastic step of attempting to destroy the reactor. In May of 1981, Shimon Peres wrote to Begin, "I add my voice, and it is not mine alone, to those who tell you not to act, certainly not under the present timing and circumstances."[3] Ezer Weizman, who was no longer in the cabinet, appealed to Sharon, when they encountered each other at a funeral, to give up the idea of this dangerous operation. He, like others, pointed to the balancing power of atomic weapons in America and Russia, and the preventive factor of mutually assured destruction.

But Sharon could not be moved from his position that the situation in an area as unstable and volatile as the Middle East, with leaders like Saddam Hussein, Hafez al-Assad and Muammar Quaddafi, could not be compared to the great powers' considerations of caution and logic. Apart from anything else, Sharon says, "we would always have to be aware and afraid of the fact that our enemies might make a catastrophic mistake in their evaluations."[4] Begin agreed with this. It was decided to attack on a Sunday when foreign technicians would be away from the reactor site. Accordingly, on June 7, 1981, at four o'clock in the afternoon, F-15 and F-16 planes took off for Iraq and accomplished their mission within two hours.

The timing of this raid must certainly have had an effect on the Likud's victory in the elections which took place on June 30, and led to Sharon's appointment as Begin's defense minister.

24

HOT FARM

———

PROMPTED BY PUBLIC COMPLAINTS that some ministers had invested in private enterprises, the Likud government in August, 1977, set up an ad hoc committee, headed by Judge Shlomo Asher, to investigate conflicts of interest. The finance minister owned a small optical factory; the minister of trade and industry had a large dairy company and Sharon's was one of the largest privately owned farms in the country. The committee decided unanimously that Sharon's ownership of the farm, considering that he was at the same time minister of agriculture, constituted a clear case of conflict of interest.

The committee ruled that the control of any conflicting enterprise should be transferred to a non-relative if possible or a relative who was not a spouse or a minor and who had been working in the business for one full year before the minister took office. At first Sharon tried to lease the farm. When this proved unsuccessful, he hired two attorneys to manage the operation with Lily, but since she was his wife, the Asher committee vetoed this idea as a transparent attempt to evade the ruling. Finally he leased the farm to a close friend and cut himself and his family off from economic involvement with the enterprise.[1]

A year and a half later, the government appointed another committee, the Kanat committee, to see that the Asher committee rulings had been implemented. The Kanat committee concluded that many of Sharon's decisions as minister of agriculture inevitably affected his farm. They were not casting aspersions on his integrity, they said, but they had to consider public reaction. It was impossible to scrutinize every decision of the minister for personal motives. They decided to set up a permanent three-member independent review board to examine cases like Sharon's and allow for reasonable deviations from the law, if any. Sharon protested that the fact that he owned a farm had not influenced him: "All the decisions that I have made were based upon principle even if they worked to my disadvantage."[2]

But the farm caused other controversies. The government was, of course, responsible for the personal security of its leaders, and, unlike most of his colleagues, Sharon, a famous general and prominent politician, lived on that large property isolated in the Negev desert. In the fall of 1978, the security forces decided that Sharon's farm needed a special, very expensive, security fence, and submitted a request for this to the Finance Ministry. The minister, Simcha Ehrlich, who was not fond of Sharon, forwarded the request to the Attorney General, and this referral sparked talk and the implication from Sharon's political opponents that the request was inappropriate.

Sharon, never hesitant to respond to criticism, notified Begin that he was declining extra security measures for his farm. He wrote to Ehrlich, saying, "A few days ago, you presented me with several letters concerning the installation of a security mechanism in my home. Here are my comments on this matter:

> A) I have never approached any security sources or any other sources about the installation of security devices in my home. Security personnel approached me, since they probably thought it was an important issue.
> B) I would like to make clear that I do not have and have never had guards or bodyguards, in my home. I also do not get any security assistance from the IDF, although many neighboring farms do. Personal security and bodyguards have led [in

this country] to a form of kickbacks and personal gratification. And this government [Likud] has even surpassed the former
[Labor] in this regard.

C) I instructed my office to immediately stop the process of
installation of the recommended special security in my farm,
since I wish to end this relentless digging into my affairs. As for
the devices that have already been installed, I ask that you require me to pay for them, or dismantle them.

D) For many years I have had the great privilege of ensur-
ing the safety of others. Today I consider it a great privilege to
safeguard my home and family myself. Let those who enjoy
government perks, deserved or undeserved, do as they like. I
decline.[3]

Simcha Ehrlich replied, "Our security services initiated steps for
your safety. Consequently, the comptroller of the Ministry of Agriculture submitted a request to the head comptroller for financial
approval for this. The head comptroller, with no malice intended,
asked for my personal attention in this matter. I in turn went to the
Attorney General for guidance in light of the sensitivity of this issue. I was told to consult with the prime minister. The prime minister and I believed that you should be informed of the matter and so
we presented you with the letters and documents involved. I am in
complete agreement with your opinion."[4]

Sycamore Farm was a precious place to Sharon, where he could
relax out of the public eye and enjoy his supportive family. Benziman, not in the main a sympathetic biographer, says Sharon "was a
perfect host who charmed his guests with reminiscences and stories
of his past exploits in the army. As he sat with his guests after a
good meal, smoking his cigar, one could not but be impressed with
his warm good humor. [He] never enjoyed the large receptions that
typified public life, where he seemed lost and uncomfortable." Lily,
at home, enjoyed gardening, art and music but, Benziman says, also

came across as "a woman who jealously guarded her prerogatives as a minister's wife."

Benziman says that guests were surprised by this "family environment" and were led to wonder whether "the violent and aggressive nature they had come to know was merely a thorny exterior on a soft and warm-hearted man" and whether "the picture of the nasty irascible politician" was "the result of journalistic hyperbole," or, on the other hand, did the very support he received in the guarded sanctuary of his home and family enable him "to quarrel with everyone else"? Benziman comes to no conclusion about this.[5]

During Sharon's term as minister of agriculture from 1977 to 1981, he was concerned mainly with settlements in the territories, for ideological reasons. He took control of the Land Commission, to the dismay of the minister of housing, and installed his former IDF artillery commander, a Likud sympathizer, as commissioner. But Sharon also replaced most of the top staff in the ministry with Labor people. In 1980, the Likud government established, mostly in the West Bank and Gaza, thirty-eight new settlements, the largest number of new settlements in any one year of Begin's regime.

Sharon also set up Agridev, an agency that transported Israeli agricultural technology abroad. Agridev constructed irrigation systems in countries in Africa, Asia and Latin America. After the peace with Egypt, Agridev established the first pressure-irrigation system for vegetables in the Nile Delta and the arid Nuarya region with Israeli and Egyptian co-financing. And in the Nubaseed area, where Egypt's western desert begins, Agridev set up a deciduous plantation to produce apples, peaches and nectarines.

In January of 1981, Sharon was asked by the Egyptian minister of agriculture to set up a model irrigation system and a vineyard on a farm owned by President Sadat, where irrigation had been performed by yoked oxen walking in circles to release water from buckets into ditches. Although the planting season had almost ended, the Israelis shipped two truckloads of equipment to Sadat's farm, and in less than two weeks, Sadat had a newly planted vineyard and a modern irrigation system.

Five months later, on October 6, Anwar Sadat was assassinated in Cairo by Muslim fundamentalists, while viewing a military parade commemorating the eighth anniversary of the October War. Years later, Sharon told Uri Dan that if Sadat had not been murdered, Israeli-Egyptian agricultural cooperation would have led to potential markets like the Persian Gulf Emirates and Saudi Arabia, countries that imported massive quantities of food. He said he thought that "Israeli-Egyptian co-operation . . . could possibly pave the way for further peace treaties with other Arab nations. When you have such common economic interests even in the face of political unrest, both sides have a solid interest in keeping the peace intact."[6]

25

LEBANON

———

BEFORE THE 1981 ELECTIONS, on April 30, Sharon told a reporter, "Lebanon, in large part, has effectively been annexed by Syria; the world remains silent in the face of the massacre of the Lebanese Christians by the Muslims; and a large part of the country is ruled by terrorists who have converted it into the center for world terrorism operated by the Soviets."

Lebanon had not been involved in the 1967 war. But beginning in 1968, the PLO had taken over Lebanese refugee camps, launching attacks from them against Israel, and the IDF had retaliated with air strikes and commando raids. In 1970 and 1971, Jordan's fierce actions against the Palestinians drove them out of that country to take sanctuary in Lebanon. Arafat set up headquarters in Beirut, and Southern Lebanon and all the refugee camps became a base for various terrorist groups, including not only the PLO, but Black September and German and Japanese gangs acting against international targets. The Lebanese government, plagued by Christian-Muslim discord, could or would do nothing to rid itself of an element that drew intermittent Israeli strikes against its border population.

In the early '70s, the situation got much worse, as attacks and counterattacks spread and many civilians were killed. Through the use of mines, barbed-wire electronic fences, patrols and sophisticated surveillance systems, the Israelis gained some control over these incursions which were further hampered by the outbreak in April,

1975, of civil war in Lebanon between Christians and Muslims. Christians attacked refugee camps, massacred the inhabitants and fought in the south with Israeli help. On May 31, 1976, the Syrians' invasion of Lebanon was at least tacitly accepted by Israel, the United States, the Lebanese Christians and even some Muslims. The Israelis hoped and believed that the Syrians would destroy the PLO, but in fact the PLO actually consolidated its power in the country, setting up its own state to replace vanished Lebanese services.

Attacks on northern Israel resumed in earnest over the next five years; the most egregious occurred on March 11, 1978, when a PLO group from Lebanon landed on the coast near Haifa, hijacked a tour bus and murdered thirty-nine people, including women and children. This, as we have seen, sparked Begin's Operation Litani four days later, a concentrated Israeli attack on PLO strongholds in Lebanese camps, villages and mountain hideouts. International protests were muted, even from the Syrians. The actual operation lasted about a week, but led to the establishment of a six-mile wide security zone inside Lebanon's borders. In addition, the UN sent a six-thousand-troop force to oversee the area and keep PLO attackers out of it.

Nevertheless, over the next three years, sporadic warfare continued between the IDF and the PLO. Israel began to work closely with the Lebanese Christians, especially the main Christian party, the Maronite Phalange, to train militia and supply them with arms and money. The leader of the Phalange was its founder, Pierre Gemayel, with whom Israel had had relations of some kind for over three decades in the hope of establishing a Christian state in Lebanon. In 1976, the Israelis were impressed with Pierre's son Bashir Gemayel, who had taken command of the Phalange militia and was asking for help against the Muslims. Begin, when he took office in 1977, liked the idea of helping these Christians, especially when the Syrians sent in an occupation army that not only tolerated the PLO, but began to brutally murder Christian civilians. Gemayel had provoked the Syrians in the hope of winning Israeli sympathy, and this worked, perhaps too well, because many innocent villagers and inhabitants of east Beirut were killed. Gemayel himself decimated rival Christian militia factions to create a unified force.

Sharon found Bashir Gemayel to be "young, talented and ambitious," and his "pursuit of power . . . something more than simple warlord politics. [He] regarded the Lebanese Christian community as an entity that could best survive by first unifying itself and then looking beyond the essentially hostile Muslim political world that surrounded it." Bashir, he said, was "eager to deepen and specify the long-term relationship the Maronites had maintained with Israel."[1]

According to Uzi Benziman, by January, 1982, Sharon had had the General Staff work out Operation Big Pines, a four-fold plan: "to remove Israeli settlements in the northern Galilee from the range of terrorist shelling; to crush the terrorists in Beirut, militarily and politically; to set up a legitimate government in Lebanon which would sign a peace treaty with Israel"; and "to insure the evacuation of Syrian troops from the Beirut area." Plans for attacks on Lebanon had been developed earlier by Chief of Staff Raful Eytan, while Begin was also acting as minister of defense.[2]

This four-fold plan had begun to be developed against a background of ever-increasing violence that had been suspended in the summer of 1981 when US Special Ambassador Philip Habib was able to negotiate a cease-fire, much to the displeasure of the Israelis, who saw this as an opportunity for the PLO to build and sustain its military presence in southern Lebanon. Begin's cabinet was already frustrated by its inability to protect residents of the Galilee from PLO rocket attacks, which had completely disrupted normal life there. Now they saw the US in effect recognizing the PLO as a state by negotiating with them and forcing Israel to negotiate with them. The Israelis were overwhelmed by the desire to recoup what they considered a massive and humiliating defeat, and between August,

1981, and June, 1982, Begin and Sharon looked for a way to initiate strong offensive action to drive the PLO from Lebanon. This even though the Habib-negotiated cease-fire had brought calm to the border for the first time since 1968. Sharon's position was that this cease-fire was allowing the PLO time to build its arsenal for future attacks.

What Sharon wanted was not only to destroy the PLO and perhaps encourage Palestinians to overthrow the king in Jordan, but also to help the Gemayels establish a Christian majority in Lebanon and drive the Syrian army from that country. He and Chief of Staff Raful Eytan pointed to various PLO incursions as evidence that action against Lebanon was necessary. But Begin's cabinet, led by Interior Minister Yosef Burg, were not eager to embark on a war of this kind without what they considered sufficient provocation, and their doubts were reinforced by leaders of the northern settlements, who felt that the unprecedented border peace should not be disturbed.

There was also the situation with the Americans. In December, 1981, Sharon met with Philip Habib and assured him that if Israel attacked Lebanon, the Syrians would not get involved. This was certainly not what Chief of Israeli Intelligence Yehoshua Saguy told his General Staff in May, 1982. He foresaw a response by the Syrians, a lack of support from the Phalange, and expressed the opinion that it would be much more difficult for the IDF to get out of Lebanon than to enter it. Begin sent Saguy to Washington to confer with Secretary of State Alexander Haig, who was insistent that the incidents of terrorism enumerated by the Israelis—many of which had been perpetrated by terrorist organizations other than the PLO—did not constitute adequate provocation for a full-scale attack on Lebanon.

On May 19, 1982, Sharon went to Washington himself to meet with Haig, who this time gave the impression that he would not object to a quick operation. On May 20, Haig wrote to Begin urging "absolute restraint" in the matter of any offensive. He followed this by telling the Israeli ambassador on May 29 that the US would support a twenty-five-mile invasion by the IDF. These confused messages nevertheless made it clear that possible American support would not go beyond the twenty-five-mile incursion.

The final impetus for the invasion occurred in London on the night of June 3, 1982, when Abu Nidal terrorists shot and severely wounded Shlomo Argov, the Israeli ambassador to the Court of St James. It is probable that Abu Nidal wanted to precipitate an Israeli attack on the PLO, which issued a statement disclaiming responsibility for the shooting. In any case, the Israeli cabinet convened the next day without Sharon, who was in Rumania with Lily on a visit to her birthplace. Despite the PLO statement, the cabinet gave Eytan permission to bomb two targets in Beirut—a PLO ammunition concentration in the sports stadium and a terrorist training camp, both of which supposedly did not contain civilians—and additional PLO targets in southern Lebanon. The PLO responded by shelling settlements in the Galilee.

On Saturday, June 5, the cabinet, including Sharon, who had returned hurriedly from Rumania, met secretly at Begin's home, where Begin urged a massive attack on Lebanon, to destroy the PLO. The majority of the cabinet members agreed with Begin: a few, like Yosef Burg, balked at the idea of a ground attack. The cabinet were told that the purpose of the attack was to establish a twenty-five-mile buffer zone north of the Israeli-Lebanon border and to demolish both the PLO military presence and the terrorist presence in Lebanon, and that the entire operation would last no longer than forty-eight hours. Reaching Beirut itself, they were told, was not a major goal. "Beirut," Sharon told them, "is out of the picture." The IDF would try to get the Syrians to remove the terrorists from the Bekaa Valley, and would work on that if they refused. The matter was left there. The cabinet—with the exception of Yosef Burg, Simcha Ehrlich and Yitzhak Berman—agreed that the IDF's goals were to stop terrorist fire on the settlements from Lebanon, not to attack the Syrians unless they attacked first, and to try to achieve peace with an independent Lebanon.

Apparently, of these cabinet members only Begin and Sharon knew that the IDF that day had already entered Lebanon with tanks, artillery and mortars and that an amphibious unit was ready to land inside Lebanon far beyond the avowed twenty-five-mile limit. At this same meeting, the opposition members of the Knesset— among them Shimon Peres, Yitzhak Rabin and Chaim Bar-Lev— were called in and told by Sharon and Shamir that the operation was intended to create the twenty-five-mile buffer zone and would last no more than twelve to twenty-four hours. The operation that Begin called Operation Peace for Galilee[3] had begun on June 4 with IAF bombing; ground troops went into Lebanon before noon on June 6. Late that afternoon, commandos attacked the Beaufort Crusader Castle and finally captured it after a night-long battle. Begin helicoptered there on June 7 and announced on Israeli TV that no commandos had been lost. This was not true: six soldiers had been killed and several wounded. Sharon was to be accused of misinforming the prime minister about this, and indeed about many facets of the Lebanon operation.

Operation Peace involved four independent divisions, an amphibious brigade, a two-division corp and a reserve corps. The whole, twice as large as the 1973 force that had stopped the Egyptian army, was commanded by Major General Amir Drori. Eytan kept a close watch on the action, and Sharon acted, says Martin van Creveld, "as a kind of super chief of staff." Van Creveld says also that the force was too huge for the arena: since Lebanon is mountainous and has good highways only along the coast, "fuel convoys could not get through, the wounded could not be evacuated, and commanders who went forward to observe got caught in traffic jams and were unable to return to headquarters."[4]

It was difficult and time-consuming to sort out the guerrillas from the civilian population, and difficult to decide what to do with the several thousand prisoners who were sorted out: since the PLO was not a state, an argument could be made that these men were not POWs, but they were wearing uniforms and had been captured on foreign soil, so it could also be argued that they were not criminals. "This," Van Creveld says, "is as good a sign as any that something was very, very wrong with this war." The prisoners were put into detainee camps.[5]

Basically, the IDF was hampered by many factors, including the terrain and an apparent desire to avoid civilian casualties that prevented the wide use of helicopters and heavy artillery fire. The Palestinians escaped into Syrian lines, and the two became indistinguishable. On June 8, Begin told the Knesset that the government was "not interested in a war with Syria" and called upon Assad to refrain from hostile action. Secretary Haig and Philip Habib both accepted this position, and so informed Damascus. There is certainly reason to believe that Sharon and Begin considered the Syrians to be a target, and deliberately misinformed the Americans and Assad. On June 8, the day that Begin was disavowing any intentions against Syria, the IDF attacked a Syrian unit stationed around the town of Jezzine, the Syrians responded and Syria had been drawn into the fight. On June 9, Sharon received permission from the cabinet to destroy Syrian missile bases in Lebanon to protect the IDF. The ministers did not want to engage the Syrians, but they had no idea of the scope and intensity of the fighting; some of them thought that if the missiles were destroyed, the Syrians would be discouraged from attacking on the ground. Others feared that if the missiles were not removed, the IDF forces would be annihilated. What Sharon wanted was to get the Syrians out of the Bekaa Valley. He thought that with the Syrians out of Beirut, the PLO also would be dislodged, and Bashir Gemayel would be elected president of Lebanon and sign a peace treaty with Israel.

On June 9, there was an absolute victory for the Israeli Air

Force, which had studied Syrian air capabilities for over a year by overflying the area, and which consequently shot down nearly 100 Syrian fighter planes, losing only one IAF plane in the battle. The Syrian antiaircraft system and one-fifth of its air force were destroyed. Benny Morris calls the two-hour attack on Syria's missiles "an historic event in modern warfare . . . the first time a Western air force successfully tackled and annihilated a complex, sophisticated Soviet-built SAM network." How this was accomplished is still an Israeli military secret.[6] There were glitches: on June 10, the IAF, attempting to provide close support, accidentally demolished an entire Israeli armored battalion.

Although air power could do little to help the ground troops by bombing and strafing because of the terrain and the guerrilla nature of the war, the IDF performed well against the Syrians, who were defeated at Jezzine, but who later, in a difficult terrain, were able to hold up the Israeli advance to the Beirut-Damascus highway for sixty hours, until June 11, when a cease-fire demanded by Reagan on June 10, went into effect. There was real fear that there would be a full-scale Israeli-Syrian war, and the Soviets might be drawn into it. The Syrians were the main concern: the PLO lacked military intelligence and organization, and many of its soldiers tended to run away, although various independent units fought valiantly.

At their June 10 meeting, the cabinet, already somewhat upset by the unexpected length of the war—there is still a question about whether they were informed about the number of casualties—were further upset by what they considered Reagan's ultimatum coming on the heels of their colossal anti-missile victory. Sharon had argued that he would need several hours to "clear the Syrians back to the twenty-five-mile line," but on June 11 the cabinet accepted the cease-fire, an acceptance that many military men and tacticians were later to say had saved the Syrian army from complete defeat. On June 11, the cease-fire went into effect, but only very briefly. Sharon told the press, "We have no cease-fire with the terrorists. We did not decide on a cease-fire and did not sign a cease-fire agreement with them."[7] Thus the cease-fire was broken, with each side blaming the other, and hostilities resumed. Martin van Creveld believes that with the resumption of hostilities "the only prospect was a war of attrition which the IDF was doomed to lose."[8]

The IDF reached the Beirut-Damascus highway at a high casualty cost, and, without the sanction of the cabinet, entered the Beirut suburbs and began a heavy bombardment of the city. The destruction that ensued in what Benny Morris calls "a bloody nine-week siege,"[9] outraged many Israelis, civilian and military, and much of the West. Inevitably, there was the loss of innocent life from the bombing and the shortages of food, electricity and water. The Lebanese Christians were happy to assist in actions against the hated Syrians and PLO, while Arab leaders in other countries did nothing to help the Beirut Muslims, and were, in addition, far from willing to take in the PLO; they did not trust Arafat and they considered both him and his fighters to be unstable and unpredictable. So Arafat remained in Beirut and the cabinet turned a deaf ear to Sharon's pleas for a major offensive, which Eytan told them could be completed in three days.

Begin was extremely disturbed over the casualty rate and the threat to his coalition if the offensive were to be permitted. In addition, elements in the army itself were vocal in their strong opposition to Sharon's plan. Nearly two hundred reservists chose prison over service in this war, and others undoubtedly found less dramatic ways to avoid service. And even though, as Martin van Creveld points out, "victory was never in doubt, the IDF dominated the sky, and ground troops overran the PLO like a steamroller . . . conditions were relatively good, the weather perfect," from June to August there were six hundred cases of soldiers suffering from what was vaguely called "battle shock," a kind of reaction to stress.[10]

One commander, Colonel Eli Geva, strongly objected to the assault on Beirut, arguing with the IDF officers, with Sharon, and with Begin, that Christian rule could not be imposed on Lebanon, that a war with Syria could result from all this, and that in any case the political gains would not be worth the loss of human life, both military and civilian. Geva finally refused to lead the ground assault because of the high probability of civilian casualties, resigned his command and requested that he be retained in his unit as a common soldier. This request was denied, and Geva was discharged from the army.[11]

When Operation Peace for Galilee began, ninety-three percent of the Israeli public approved of it in varying degrees. Within a month, the approval rate had dropped to sixty-six percent. What upset Israelis was the perception that this was not a defensive action, but what they called "a war of choice," a thing that they considered out of character for their country, which had always reacted to aggression, but had never initiated it. Then too, the enemy this time was a weak one, basically one capable only of harassment, so people began to feel that the game was not worth the candle, so to speak.

But Sharon intensified the campaign against Beirut, even using car bombs as a terror tactic, and giving the strong impression—which has been denied—that he was trying to kill Arafat and the other PLO leaders. Finally, by August first, Arafat accepted the fact that he could not remain in Lebanon. The Americans had created an evacuation plan endorsed by most Arab states, and accepted by the Israeli cabinet on July 11. Sharon, however, continued his massive air assault, either unconvinced or unwilling to believe that the PLO would actually leave Lebanon. Cabinet members were angry about these actions, which had provoked a strong rebuke from President Reagan. Sharon's request to mount a ground offensive in central Beirut was firmly denied, and Begin was extremely short with him in that cabinet meeting.

Sharon's harsh methods dislodged the PLO, and on August 21,

their eleven-day evacuation began under the supervision of a multinational force—Arafat to set up headquarters in Tunisia, many of his men to spread themselves throughout the Middle East and the Syrians to retreat to the Bekaa Valley.

On August 23, the Lebanese parliament, under Israeli pressure and with the help of Israeli bribes, elected Bashir Gemayel president of the country. He was to be inaugurated on September 23. He stated clearly that he wanted to raze the refugee camps around Beirut and send the Palestinians to Syria, while Sharon's desire was to see them moved to Jordan, to create their Palestinian state there. The Syrians were now the deadly enemy of Israel, and of Gemayel. On September 14, a Syrian agent activated a powerful bomb in the apartment above Phalange headquarters in east Beirut, killing Gemayel and several others, including women who had gathered to hear him lecture.

Sharon at once requested and received permission to enter west Beirut, to prevent what he foresaw as a takeover of the city by Lebanese Muslims and a clandestine guerrilla PLO force that he believed still lurked in the area. Begin told Eytan that the Israeli occupation was necessary to prevent the Phalange from avenging Gemayel's murder, and this was certainly an accepted possibility because Sharon himself knew, and had told the Mossad, the Israeli foreign secret service, that the Christians had already killed more than a thousand Muslim civilians over the summer. Nevertheless, Sharon later said after the assassination, that the Phalange were calm, moderate and in control.

Now it was necessary to screen the terrorists from the genuine refugees in the camps. The Lebanese army was approached and refused the request, but the Phalangists agreed to take on the job, since they knew the language and the country. By September 16, the IDF had occupied west Beirut and the Phalangists were getting ready to enter the camps. At that same time, Eytan explicitly told two

American envoys that the Phalange were bent on revenge and could not be stopped. And indeed a few minutes later, after coordinating with the Israeli commanders at the scene, the Phalangists entered the Sabra and Shatilla camps, described by Van Creveld as "dense areas of concrete houses, some several stories tall, and a mass of narrow, winding alleys connected by underground shelters and surrounded by a wall."[12] Having entered on the evening of September 16, they commenced a massacre that lasted until the morning of September 18. Hundreds of unarmed civilians, including women and children, were murdered.

The IDF, which kept its distance, provided illumination with mortar rounds for the Phalangists, whom they had warned to single out terrorists only, and to avoid atrocities. Reports of the killings began, inevitably, to trickle into headquarters, but nothing was done, and, in fact, a second group of Phalangists were allowed into the camps on the afternoon of September 17. Finally, when firm reports of the atrocities were received, an IDF officer ordered the Phalangists to leave the camps. Some lingered and continued the killing. At last they left, and journalists and IDF officers entered the area to find frightful evidence of what had happened. When Sharon received calls about this from Raful Eytan and others, he briefly "considered" launching a formal military investigation, but rejected the idea because, he says, he "did not want to do anything that might give the impression I was trying to take cover for myself behind the army." He soon came to realize that "that decision was a serious mistake."[13]

26

AFTER THE MASSACRE

———

WHEN THE MASSACRE AT Sabra-Shatilla became public knowledge, the world recoiled in revulsion. The Phalange denied responsibility, a bold tactic that convinced nobody, although the PLO and the Muslims appeared to accept the denial, probably because they wanted to remain on good terms with Amin Gemayel, who was about to be appointed president by the Lebanese parliament. The Israeli cabinet at first put out the story that an unidentified Lebanese unit had entered the camps "at a point far from the IDF position." But nobody believed this, either.

Gemayel's administration announced that fifteen women and twenty children were among the 460 casualties. Israeli intelligence put the death toll at seven to eight hundred. (In his autobiography, Sharon repeats the Lebanese government figures and adds, "Israeli Intelligence figures were somewhat higher." But he does not give these Israeli figures.)[1] The Israeli public was outraged and this anger extended to the military where several hundred reservists had already chosen to go to prison rather than to take part in the war. On September 25, about 400,000 people demonstrated against the government in Tel Aviv square, demanding a full official investigation. The Israeli public now condemned the entire Lebanese undertaking.

Begin was forced to act. On September 28, the cabinet created a three-man investigating commission, headed by Yitzhak Kahan, the president of the Supreme Court, with Supreme Court Justice

Aharon Barak and retired Major General Yona Efrat. On February 8, 1983, the commission issued its report, finding that the Phalange had committed the massacre, and that although no IDF soldiers had taken part in it, the IDF was indirectly responsible for it. There was no evidence that the Israelis had known it would happen or had conspired to allow it, but the commission held that they should have known it would happen and should have acted to prevent it.

Both Begin and Shamir were rebuked by the commission, Shamir because he had done nothing when he received the first reports of the murders on September 17. The heaviest censure was aimed at Sharon, who was found to have been "indirectly responsible" for the massacre; the commission recommended that he resign or that the prime minister remove him from office. Chief of Staff Eytan was also found to have been negligent, but since his term of office was almost up, no demand for his dismissal was made. In addition to Sharon, the commission ordered the dismissal of the director of military intelligence, Yehoshua Saguy, and the suspension, for at least three years, of the officer in command, Amos Yaron. Saguy became a Likud MK five years later, and Yaron was promoted and made military attache to Washington.

Sharon implies in his autobiography that much of the furor over the killings was politically motivated: "Buses from the kibbutzim all over the country arrived to feed demonstrations and marches as Labor orchestrated an outpouring of rage." He had, he says, "very bad feelings about the outcome" as the Kahan Commission began its investigation because "a cry for blood" was in the air. "For many," he says, "the killings were a real moral shock—even though everyone knew that in past years both Palestinians and Arab Christians had committed far more terrible slaughters on each other. Many others saw the political opportunity and grabbed at it with both hands." He implies that people were looking for a scapegoat, and that the two Supreme Court Justices were biased against him. They gave him "intense and unfriendly looks" when he encountered them in public. He told Begin that the government must be strong and "keep the ministers focused on the rock-bottom issue—the innocence of the Israeli government and its military." Begin's response was that that would be "a very hard situation."[2]

Sharon was eventually called to testify before the commission. In his defense he argued that Eytan had told him on the night of September 17 that "Phalangists had 'gone too far,' but . . . that the operation had been terminated and the Phalangist force had been ordered to withdraw." No one, he insisted, had foreseen the danger, and none of the IDF or government officers who had been told about the plan to send the Christians into the camps had raised any objections.[3]

Begin received an advance copy of the Kahan Commission report on February 7, 1983. He gave Sharon short shrift on the phone, refusing to discuss the findings with him. As a result, Sharon had more "bad feelings," this time "about the kind of support I could expect from the prime minister."[4] He was called to a cabinet meeting on February 10, 1983, but had trouble getting there because of a large demonstration by peace activists in the road before his farm; he describes them as being "in a state of mad rage." He encountered another demonstration when he arrived in Jerusalem—or rather two demonstrations: one by his supporters who reached out "a thousand hands" to shake his, and another by marchers calling him a murderer.[5]

"If you accept the conclusions of the Kahan Commission," he told the nervous cabinet, "you will be branding the mark of Cain on the foreheads of the Jewish people and the State of Israel with your own hands." Nevertheless, the cabinet voted against Sharon sixteen to one. He accuses them of wearing expressions of "jealousy and anger" at the shouts of "Arik! Arik" that penetrated the closed windows of the cabinet room. He was forced to submit his resignation, with strong feelings of bitterness against Begin, who he believes betrayed him, handing him over "to the mob."[6]

Nowhere in Sharon's discussions of this crisis does one detect a note of self-reproach or sorrow for the innocent victims who were mercilessly hunted down for over forty hours in mid-September, 1982.One might consider, however, that his perspective on this tragedy had become distorted after years of what he believed to be unjust accusations against himself and his family.

In May and June, 2002, on the 20th anniversary of the Lebanon war, *Yediot Aharonoth* ran two interviews with central figures in that conflict. The first, on May 31, was with Amir Drori who, as head of the Northern Command, had led his forces into Lebanon. "Raful [Eytan] told us to go into Beirut," he said, "and we conquered it in thirty hours, but we received an order not to attack . . . Sabra and Shatilla." He believed that the decision had been made to avoid casualties of IDF soldiers.

"The Phalangists," he said, "went into the camps with 150 people. According to our estimates, there were 2000 terrorists in those camps. What concerned me was not that the Phalangists would commit a massacre, but that we would have to go in there and rescue them. Because they were outnumbered."

Asked about Sharon, General Drori said he did not have excessive regard for him, but he had learned from him what it meant to persevere, "to accomplish what you set out to do. If you can't get in the door, then you go through the window. If you can't go through the window, you find a hole." On the other hand, he said Sharon was like a farmer who "milked and milked and milked, and then knocked over the bucket."

The second interview was with Antoine Lachad, who had been military governor of Beirut and commander of the Christian Southern Lebanese army for sixteen years. When the IDF had pulled out in 2000, he had gone to Israel with them. General Lachad told the *Yediot Aharonoth* reporter that he had hoped that Sharon would kill Arafat, so that "Lebanon would calm down, but I know he gave his word to the Americans." He asked Sharon, he said, why he had not gone on from Beirut to Damascus, and why he had not killed Arafat. "He looked at me coldly and said, 'Ask the Americans. It all depended on them.'"

Hobeika, he said, had sent his people into Sabra and Shatilla. Asked how he knew this for a fact, Lachad said, "Listen to me now—something that has never been made public. In September, 1982, immediately after the massacre, when I was the military governor in Beirut, Hobeika's men came to me straight from the camps, the victims' blood all over their clothes. They told me everything—a minute-by-minute account. I know one hundred percent that neither Sharon not anyone from the IDF was involved. But legally Sharon bears responsibility because he knew that Hobeika was a bad person, and he shouldn't have let him in."

27

A TIME OF TRIAL

Sharon resigned the defense post on February 14, and was replaced by Likud's Moshe Arens, an aviation engineer with no military experience. Sharon himself remained in the cabinet as minister without portfolio. But he had not heard the last of Sabra and Shatilla. In its February 21, 1983, issue, under the heading "Cover Stories: The Verdict is Guilty," *Time* magazine ran an article on the Kahan Commission report that said, in part:

> One section of the report, known as Appendix B, was not published at all, mainly for security reasons . . . TIME has learned that it . . . contains further details about Sharon's visit to the Gemayel family on the day after Bashir Gemayel's assassination. Sharon reportedly told the Gemayels that the Israeli army would be moving into West Beirut, and that he expected the Christian forces to go into the Palestinian refugee camps. Sharon also reportedly discussed with the Gemayels the need for the Phalangists to take revenge for the assassination of Bashir, but the details of the conversation are not known.[1]

This story—that in the secret Appendix B the commission had found that Sharon had encouraged the Phalange to avenge Bashir's assassination—was picked up by newspapers everywhere, and received front-page coverage in Israel. Begin and Sharon both pro-

tested the story and demanded an apology, but the reaction from
Time's Jerusalem bureau chief in a cable to New York was: "We
must really have struck a nerve. Cheers."

On February 28, 1983, Sharon filed a libel suit against *Time* in
Israel. His next move was to sue the magazine in New York. He was
advised by many lawyers not to institute libel proceedings in the
United States because of the heavy burden of proof that falls on the
plaintiff. Nevertheless, Sharon persisted and eventually his case was
taken *pro bono* by Milton S. Gould, a partner in the New York
intellectual properties law firm of Shea and Gould. On June 22,
1983, Sharon filed suit in New York, asking fifty million dollars in
damages. At his deposition, Sharon said that his lawyer had set that
figure so "people will take it seriously."[2]

The trial, with *Time* represented by Thomas D. Barr, a partner
in Cravath, Swaine and Moore, began on November 13, 1984. The
paragraph in question had been written by William Smith, based on
a telex report from Harry Kelly, the Jerusalem bureau chief, which
report in turn was based on information from a reporter named
David Halevy who claimed that he had based *his* report on information from "a confidential source." On December 6, 1982, Halevy
had telexed *Time* a story headlined "Green Light for Revenge?" in
which he reported that he had learned from "a highly reliable source"
who had access to official documents—Appendix B—that "notes"
of Sharon's conversation with the Gemayels had been "newly discovered" and that from these notes it appeared that Sharon had
given the Gemayels the "feeling" that he understood "their need for
revenge."

Thus, as Renata Adler puts it, "The entire edifice of *Time* in this
case was poised upon a single reporter claiming to have access to
unnamed sources, who in turn had access to official documents,
which would remain forever secret and which supported *Time*'s
paragraph—or did not."[3]

Sharon had read Appendix B and insisted that *Time*'s report of its content was untrue. The truth was, according to Renata Adler, that the Kahan Report had made mention in a footnote to Appendix B that Sharon had paid a "condolence call" on the Gemayels and nothing more. In August, Judge Abraham Sofaer requested that the Attorney General of Israel grant the court access to relevant documents and other information from Appendix B relating to Sharon's meetings with Phalangists from September 14-16, 1982. It was believed by everyone, including Sharon, that the Israeli government would not cooperate because Appendix B was top-secret, and because Sharon had so many enemies at home. It did indeed prove difficult to get a response from the Israelis. On Christmas Day, 1985, with the case about to go to the jury, the judge, joined by attorneys for both sides, once again made a strong, and this time successful, appeal to the Israelis for access to Appendix B. Finally, on January 9, 1986, the classified evidence arrived from Israel, and in accordance with his agreement with that government Judge Sofaer cleared the courtroom while it was being discussed, to the considerable annoyance of the press.

On January 14, the jury received the charge, and was asked first, whether the paragraph in question was defamatory and if so, was the defamation aggravated by its attribution to Appendix B; second, whether the paragraph was proven false by "clear and convincing evidence," and third, was the paragraph published with "actual malice," with "knowledge that it was false," or with "reckless disregard" of its truth or falsity, or with "serious doubt" of its truth?

On January 16, the jury answered the first question: yes, the paragraph was defamatory and yes, the defamation had been aggravated by its attribution to Appendix B. As *Time* issued a press release explaining that the jury had made a mistake, the jurors resumed their deliberations, and returned on January 18 with the verdict that the plaintiff had proved clearly and convincingly that *Time's* paragraph was false.

Finally, after more deliberations, the jury returned its verdict on the third question of "actual malice": whether the "plaintiff proved by clear and convincing evidence that a person or persons at Time Incorporated responsible for either reporting, writing, editing, or publishing the paragraph at issue did so with actual malice in that he, she or they knew, at the time of publishing any statement that we have found was false or defamatory, that the defamatory statement was false or had serious doubts as to its truth." To that question the jury's answer was no, the plaintiff had not proved "actual malice" by clear and convincing evidence.

This answer to the third question obviated the possibility of damages, which Sharon had said he did not care about anyway. But the jury had received permission from the judge to add this statement to their verdict: "We found that certain *Time* employees, particularly correspondent David Halevy, acted negligently and carelessly in reporting and verifying the information which ultimately found its way into the published paragraph of interest in this case." Despite this statement and the jury's findings for Sharon on the first two parts of the charge, *Time* claimed that it had won the case.

In Tel Aviv, Sharon says, "where libel does not depend on proving maliciousness along with lying and defaming, the court handed down an immediate judgement against the magazine."[4]

28

LEBANON CONTINUED

IN LEBANON IN MAY, 1983, a peace agreement was signed with Amin Gemayel. Sharon pointed to it with pride, but it was an exercise in futility. The Lebanese government disavowed it a year later: they could not endanger their relationships, commercial and otherwise, with other Arab states by signing a separate peace with Israel, and to add to their problems they were soon faced with a civil war between Muslim sects, Christians and Palestinians. The Israelis, as an occupying force, were frequently caught in the crossfire. In September, 1983, mounting casualties, American pressure and growing disaffection in Israel, forced Moshe Arens to call the IDF out of Beirut into central Lebanon. In that same month, Menachem Begin resigned. He was ill, crippled from a fall, and the death of his wife was the final blow. Yitzhak Shamir took over as prime minister.

In central Lebanon, the IDF established a new line running from the mouth of the Awoli River to Mount Dov on the Syrian border, covering 1200 square miles, with a population of more than 500,000 people. This new line, mountainous and wooded, provided a perfect terrain for guerrilla attacks, which the IDF was ill-equipped to deal with. A reported 650 of its soldiers had been killed, and 3000 wounded in this Lebanese venture.

Negotiations for peace were held while American marines entered Beirut to support the Lebanese government. The Israelis wanted security assurances and the withdrawal of the Syrian army, while Syria, which occupied half of Lebanon, was opposed to any agreements with Israel, and the more so because Assad was not included in the negotiations. The Syrians filled the void left by the Israeli withdrawal, and began a battle against Gemayel, the Americans, the IDF and the PLO, whom they drove from Tripoli and its environs. Attacks on the Americans steadily escalated: five marines were injured by a grenade in March, 1983; in April a Shiite suicide bomber destroyed the American Embassy, killing seventeen Americans and fifty-six others; and on October 23, 1983, 241 Americans were killed by a truck-bomb that blew up the marine barracks in Beirut. Fifty-nine French soldiers were killed that same morning by a truck-bomb attack on their compound. The French were there mainly to protect Palestinians.

The Shiite attackers, with the help of Iran which had established training camps in the Syrian-held Bekaa Valley, had formed themselves into the Party of God, the Hezbollah, dedicated to turning Lebanon into a fundamentalist Muslim state. Both the Iranian and Syrian governments gave full support to the Hezbollah. The Americans responded to the attack on the marine barracks by pulling out of Lebanon, and Gemayel's government fell apart and was replaced by one dominated by Syria.

The Israeli occupation engendered a virtual war, no longer against the PLO, but against the Hezbollah, with the IDF being attacked by gunmen, ambushes, mines, booby traps, and above all by suicide bombers, and responding with arrests, torture, infiltration and assassination. The Syrians too sent in suicide bombers, some of them young women.

The Likud, whose leader Yitzhak Shamir became prime minister in October, 1983, lost popularity because of this endless bloodletting; Labor, under Shimon Peres, advocated a quick withdrawal from southern Lebanon. Before the July, 1984, elections, Sharon lost the Likud primary with forty-two percent of the vote to Shamir's fifty-six percent. Sharon says he was overjoyed to receive that percentage, considering everything that had happened.[1] In the election, held on July 23, 1984, Labor won forty-four seats and Likud forty-one. This was so close that the Knesset was paralyzed, and the only answer was a National Unity Government, with Peres serving as prime minister from 1984 to 1986, and Shamir from '86 to '88. It was arranged that under Peres, Shamir would serve both as deputy prime minister and foreign minister. Yitzhak Rabin became minister of defense, a post he was to hold through both premierships, and Peres offered Sharon the Ministry of Trade and Industry, which he accepted.

Peres and Rabin implemented a unilateral withdrawal to the three-to-six-mile security zone with Lebanon. It was true that because of the Israeli incursion into Lebanon, the PLO suffered a devastating blow, losing men and materiel and its base in Lebanon; finally having been evacuated by a multinational force to establish its headquarters in Tunis. The Syrian air force had been decimated. Hundreds of lives were lost. Syria was rearmed by the Soviets and took control of Lebanon, ending the civil conflict and effectively marginalizing the Christians, and the PLO was replaced by the dangerous, fanatical Hezbollah and Shiite factions.

29

THE FIRST INTIFADA[1]

———

ARAB ANGER SMOLDERED IN the West Bank and the Gaza Strip under the Israeli occupation, with its constant, often harsh, surveillance, interrogation and detention. There was also the constant threat of even more severe Israeli action. Under the National Unity Government, the settlement population almost doubled. Israeli hardliners, and some moderates, talked openly about the possibility of Arab displacement. Sharon, who everybody knew was dedicated to the idea that Jordan should be the Palestinian state, moved in December, 1987, into an apartment in the Old City Muslim quarter of Jerusalem, an act that further fanned the flames of rebellion.

Added to this was an economic downturn, and the obvious fact that the IDF had lost its aura of invincibility because it had not been able to cope with the guerrilla warfare in Lebanon, or with terrorist attacks on civilians. Hostile incidents against the occupiers began to multiply, as some Israeli settlers committed terrorist acts of their own. Palestinian rage grew along with the influence of Muslim fundamentalism. All of this anger and resentment exploded on December 8, 1987, when an Israeli tank transporter ran into some vans, killing four Gaza residents and wounding six others. Demonstrations at the funerals turned into riots that spread as thousands burned tires and attacked Israelis with rocks, axes, Molotov cocktails and other homemade weapons.

This uprising was spontaneous and had not been planned or directed by any organized group.[2] But by the time that Arafat's Fatah group had realized what was happening and attempted to take control of the situation in January, a web of various "committees" had developed in villages and camps across the territories to direct the intifada—literally, a "shaking off"[3]—eventually with funds contributed by the PLO from Tunis. The fundamentalist militant organization Hamas made its appearance during this uprising and by mid-1988 had become an important faction, with the goal of destroying Israel in a holy war, opposing any attempts at peace, and converting Arab nations to Muslim fundamentalism so that they would join the conflict.

Hamas and the Islamic Jihad were responsible for some terrorist attacks, but for the most part the PLO put its emphasis on civil disobedience and boycotts. Sharon's voice was often raised against Arab villagers, even when, as in an April 6, 1988, incident, Jewish settlers inadvertently provoked Arab hostility. Sharon called for the razing of villages and mass deportation. But the Shamir government was aware that extreme measures would not be acceptable to world opinion, nor indeed, to a portion of the Israeli public. In January, 1988, Defense Minister Rabin took the position that negotiation and a political settlement were the answers and not military action. But at the same time the territories were flooded with troops, curfews were imposed, rubber and plastic bullets were introduced, and Rabin ordered the troops "to break bones"[4] to quell riots.

All these measures had a brutalizing effect on the IDF, engendering even greater hatred among the Arab population, and upsetting Israelis who had seen their country as an enlightened democracy. Sharon was later to remark, "The difference between the Six-Day War and subsequent ones is that IDF commanders and their decisions were trusted." There were many cases of abuse by the IDF—soldiers were tried and in the main given light sentences—and morale was hurt, leading many young men to abandon the idea of a military career.[5]

When Shamir returned from Washington with a plan to support Palestinian elections in the territories, the result was an unpleasant scene at a Likud Central Committee convention on February 12, 1990. Sharon angrily resigned from the government, and Shamir left the building after his microphone was disconnected by a Sharon ally. Soon after this, Sharon, in an interview, attacked Defense Minister Rabin for failing to stop the intifada. When he was reminded of his own failure in Lebanon, Sharon said, "Indeed I paid a heavy price for Lebanon for not foreseeing that the Christians would massacre the Muslims. But Rabin should pay for his failure to handle the intifada. Whenever he is asked about it, Rabin answers, 'And what about Lebanon?' Assuming Lebanon was a failure, one does not explain the other. Let Rabin explain his colossal mess." Asked under what conditions he would rejoin the government, he replied, "I am not prepared to go back to a Shamir-led government. My mission is to contest this government." Nevertheless, he did return to the government and was appointed minister of construction and housing.[6]

The intifada, which was to end officially in September 1993 with the Oslo peace agreement, began to die down in late October, 1991, when a Middle East peace conference met in Madrid. Terrorism continued after Madrid, and was accelerated by Hamas and the Islamic Jihad in the summer of 1992, when the Labor Party victory was holding out the prospect of peace, Arafat was beginning to show signs of moderating his attitude toward the existence of Israel, and the Arabs had lost their most powerful supporter with the collapse of the Soviet Union. Obviously these radical fundamentalist groups increased their terrorist activities to provoke the Israelis into harsh repression that would antagonize the Arab population further and gain world sympathy for their cause.

30

PEACE CONFERENCES & TERROR

———

IN MARCH, 1990, THE Labor Party, in a dispute over peace strategies, withdrew from the National Unity Government, leaving Shamir's right-wing Likud administration in charge. In 1991 Sharon, who remained in the cabinet as housing minister, started 1300 new residential units in the territories, buoyed by the massive influx of Russian immigrants. This did not bode well for peace initiatives. The Palestinians were exhausted, demoralized by their inability to shake off Israeli control of the West Bank and Gaza and by their economic woes. There were also tensions between the fundamentalist and secular activists.

Arafat exacerbated his difficulties when he chose the wrong side in the Gulf war. Saddam Hussein's invasion of Kuwait on August 2, 1990, led to Operation Desert Storm. For five weeks, beginning on January 16, 1991, Iraq was heavily bombed, and eventually invaded, by a coalition put together by the United States that included France, Britain, Egypt, Saudi Arabia and Syria under the auspices of the UN. Saddam attacked Tel Aviv with thirty-nine Scud missiles, hoping that the Israelis would retaliate, and thus turn the Arab states against the coalition. There was a good deal of damage, a few people were killed and many injured. But the Shamir government exercised restraint as it had been asked to do by the Americans, and did not respond; Washington rewarded them with the deployment of some Patriot antiaircraft missiles that proved to be basically useless against the Scuds.

Arafat and Jordan openly sided with Saddam. As the Scuds hit Tel Aviv, Palestinians stood on their rooftops and cheered, motivated by hatred not only of Israel and the United States, but also of the reactionary governments of Kuwait and Saudi Arabia. By the end of February, with Iraq's infrastructure in ruins, the war had ended. Arafat had made a considerable mistake; the PLO lost the support of the Gulf states and the Western governments. The US took advantage of this to press for an international peace conference. Arafat, having no leverage, had to agree, and Shamir, also disliking the idea, was forced to go along or lose American loan guarantees for ten billion dollars to resettle the Soviet immigrants. Pressure was also exerted on Shamir by the agreement of Syria, Jordan and Egypt to the conference, which was held in Madrid in the fall of 1991 and co-chaired by President George H.W. Bush and Russian President Mikhail Gorbachev. Benjamin Netanyahu was a senior member of the Israeli delegation. In the event, this meeting was noteworthy only for existing at all. The atmosphere was not conducive to an agreement, especially when Yitzhak Shamir launched a verbal attack on Syria as a terrorist state. This evoked a strong Syrian response.

In the June, 1992 general elections, the Likud suffered a defeat, winning only thirty-two seats out of 120. Labor, with forty-four seats, formed a coalition with the twelve-seat left-wing Meretz Party and the ultra-Orthodox Shas Party. Sharon was of course out of the cabinet, as Yitzhak Rabin became prime minister and also acting minister of defense. Without enthusiasm, Rabin appointed Shimon Peres, with whom he was never on good terms, to the foreign minister post. Labor, like the Likud, was opposed to Palestinian statehood. When Peres suggested some kind of contact with the PLO, Rabin, intensely disliking Arafat, vetoed the idea, pointing to a six-year-old Israeli law banning all such contacts. But the prime minister was aware that, with Russian support gone, and Arab states threatened by fundamentalist extremists, an opportunity had arisen to resolve what was unquestionably a stalemate.

In January, 1993, the Knesset repealed the law banning contacts between Israel and the PLO. Rabin was aware that secret Israeli-PLO talks, concerning Israeli withdrawal from Gaza and the development of Palestinian autonomy, had been going on in Oslo for at least a month through back channels. He made no attempt to stop these talks, although neither he nor Peres was enthusiastic about them. Rabin had no love for Palestinians, and had supported Sharon's actions in Lebanon, in disagreement with many of his Labor colleagues. He stood with Sharon when the IDF besieged Beirut and in fact told him to "tighten the siege." He did object, however, to Sharon's continuation of the war to achieve political ends. He did not see, he said, "any constraints on the use of military force by the state of Israel" for state security and to "guarantee national political survival," but he believed it was "a fundamental error" in trying to use "military might to achieve the total imposition of our political will over an Arab state or a group of Arab states."

Although he was certainly capable of moderating his positions, Rabin did not hesitate to use military force for security reasons when he cracked down hard on terrorism in the West Bank, where 1600 militants were arrested after eight Israeli soldiers and policemen were killed in December, 1992. He ordered the expulsion of over 400 Hamas and Islamic Jihad members to Lebanon, much to the annoyance of the Lebanese government, which refused to admit them. For a year, these men existed in tents on a hill between the Israeli security zone and the Lebanese southern border. But terrorist attacks continued in Jerusalem and Tel Aviv and in the security zone, leading to a massive attack on Hezbollah bases in southern Lebanon in July, 1993, and the consequent demolition of many villages. The hope was that Assad would be forced by this attack to control the Hezbollah, which, although damaged, rained rockets and mortars on northern Israel, turning communities there into ghost towns.

Although secret peace talks were still being held in Oslo, the threat of another full-scale invasion of Lebanon was very real. The Clinton administration, alarmed, sent Secretary of State Warren Christopher to Damascus and Jerusalem to try to effect a cease-fire, and his efforts were successful at the end of July, when the shooting stopped. Both sides agreed to stop shelling each other's territory, although Hezbollah was not barred from attacks on the IDF and the South Lebanese Army in the security zone.

By the end of August, the Oslo agreement, finally official and with American backing, was submitted to the cabinet, which accepted it, ignoring objections by Chief of Staff Ehud Barak. Under the terms of the agreement, called the Declaration of Principles, the PLO was granted mutual recognition which it had long demanded; this meant that Israel would recognize the PLO "as the representative of the Palestinian people" for purposes of negotiation. In turn, the PLO recognized the right of Israel to exist as a state "in peace and security" and renounced terrorist activities and all acts of violence.

To be negotiated was the establishment of an interim Palestinian Authority in the West Bank and Gaza Strip, leading to a permanent authority after no more than five years. This interim authority would be administered during those five years by a council chosen democratically in free elections, in which Palestinians living in Jerusalem would participate. Authority in the region over taxes, education, health and welfare and police services would gradually be transferred from Israeli to Palestinian control. And in no later than three years, discussions would begin concerning "permanent status," involving Jerusalem, settlements, refugees and other thorny problems. Finally, the IDF would within four months of the signing of the declaration, withdraw from the Gaza Strip and Jericho, turning these territories and control of all services over to the PLO.

The reaction abroad to this agreement was ecstatic: a new day, it was believed, had dawned, in which the threat of armed conflict or even nuclear war in the area had been dissipated, in which Palestinians would prosper and Israelis would settle down to normal lives. In addition, it was believed that Arab states would now cease their hostility toward Israel, and Iran and Iraq would be isolated from the rest of Islam. "What had justly been called the world's most intractable problem," *Time* magazine enthused, "suddenly looked solvable."[1] This was the beginning of the process that would lead to Rabin, Peres and Arafat being awarded the Nobel Peace Prize in 1994.

The announcement in September, 1993, of the secret peace accord took the right wing by surprise and this, according to its leaders, prevented an effective unified response. The Likud, heavily in debt and almost bankrupt, had split into factions, although it had been hoped that the election of Benjamin Netanyahu as its head earlier in the year would unite party members. A leader of the settlers, who, like the rabbinical establishment, were uniformly opposed to the accords, commented that there was no strategy of the right "because the right is not one camp. The whole political establishment of the right is in disarray." Netanyahu was at odds with former foreign minister David Levy whose base was Sephardic Jews; Sharon, Benjamin Begin and Raful Eytan each had his own power base.

Netanyahu accused Rabin of establishing a "Palestinian terrorist state," saying that the agreement would lead to "renewed conflict, renewed tension and war," and even to rocket attacks on Tel Aviv. Sharon said that Arafat was a war criminal with more Jewish blood on his hands than anyone since Adolf Hitler. He called Rabin a traitor who was behaving like a Nazi, and announced that if the Likud was returned to power, it would not honor this agreement.[2] The wisdom of such a threat had been debated among Likud leaders, along with the question of encouraging civil disobedience. Sharon's rhetoric infuriated Benjamin Begin and other Likud moderates, who could not countenance an attack like this upon a legitimate Israeli government, and who wanted a peaceful parliamentary opposition.

Support for the pact among the Israeli public grew despite the Likud's warnings, and despite the fact that Arafat was held in low esteem—even heads of the Labor Party were reluctant to associate with the PLO leader. Rabin did not originally plan to be part of the signing ceremony on the White House lawn; he was going to send Peres to represent the government. But when he was notified that Arafat was heading the Palestinian delegation, he felt he had to be there, too. A "senior Israeli government official" made it clear to the press that Rabin did not look forward to shaking hands with Arafat. "For many Israelis, even Labor Party voters, it's unbearable," the official said.

Arafat was criticized by his own people in Fatah and by other Arabs because he had agreed to allow the settlements to remain, the IDF to continue in control of most of the West Bank, the Gaza Strip and the Jordanian and Egyptian borders, and the question of east Jerusalem to be taken up later. Nevertheless, although the majority of Palestinians in the territories approved of the agreement, Hamas and the Islamic Jihad attempted to derail it with a renewed series of terrorist attacks and suicide bombings. Arafat made no attempt to rein them in. As a result, the talks were constantly interrupted and delayed, and not just by the actions of Arab militants: on February 25, 1994, a settler named Baruch Goldstein went on a rampage at a mosque in Hebron, killing twenty-nine worshippers and wounding scores more before he was beaten to death by bystanders. The talks were suspended for a month in the subsequent uproar. Many of these Jewish settlers were as much opposed to a peace agreement as the Arab militants, because they feared the uprooting of their settlements.

The agreement on the Gaza Strip and Jericho was finally signed in Cairo on May 4, 1994. Arafat set up his capital in Gaza two months later, instituting an authoritarian regime. He soon ran into all sorts of problems, mostly economic, which engendered considerable unrest in the population of the areas under his control, and sympathy for the terrorist organizations. Arafat's response was to attempt to placate both Israelis and the Palestinian public by arresting these militants and then releasing them after a respectable period. The result, according to Benny Morris, was that "the 1994–96 period was the heyday of the suicide bombers."[3] When Arafat took control of the territory, Hamas and the Islamic Jihad shifted their attacks from outlying districts to Israeli cities, setting off car bombs and using suicide bombers to kill people in restaurants, bus stations, and places where soldiers gathered at weekends.

The Israeli Right held demonstrations, blaming Rabin and Peres for this situation. The Rabin government itself abrogated some of the agreement (known as Oslo I) by expanding settlements and construction in and around east Jerusalem, and holding prisoners it had promised to release. Nevertheless, Oslo II, the main interim agreement, was signed in Washington on September 28, 1995, by Rabin, Peres and Arafat. This promised three Israeli withdrawals: from zone A, which was under Palestinian control; from zone B, which was under Israeli military control in cooperation with the PA, and from zone C which was under sole Israeli control, all withdrawals to be completed by October, 1997. Oslo II also provided for elections in the territories, division of Palestinian police and IDF control, treatment of prisoners and collaborators. The final status agreement on Jerusalem, refugees, the settlements and water rights was to be completed by October, 1999, when the occupation would have ended.

In early winter of 1995, the Palestinian Authority took control of the West Bank towns of Jenin, Qalquilya, Tulkarm, Nablus, Ramallah and Bethlehem. Hebron was set to be turned over to the PA in March, but this was postponed because of another series of suicide bombings. Arafat and his Fatah supporters easily won the elections when they were held in January, 1996.

The signing of Oslo II did not end the enmity of Arab states toward Israel, but it did lead to the signing of a peace treaty between Israel and Jordan on October 26, 1994, even though the Jordanians were wary of any rapprochement between Israel and the PLO. Rabin and King Hussein developed good rapport, and President Clinton sweetened the pot by, among other things, waiving Jordan's seven hundred million dollar debt to the US. The signing of this treaty was certainly a positive action, but it was not a massive concession because King Hussein had long wanted peace with Israel.

31

CHALLENGES, 1994 & 1995

———

SHARON CONTINUED HIS CAMPAIGN against the peace accords through-out 1994. In January he went on a fund-raising mission for the settlements to ten cities in the United States and Canada, seeking money for settlers in the West Bank and Gaza. Though a poll showed that ninety percent of American Jews were in favor of the agreements, Sharon was warmly welcomed in the main. At a synogogue in Seattle, he received two standing ovations from about 350 people, somewhat to his surprise. He called the settlers "soldiers" in the last line of defense against the Palestinians; he had been taught never "to leave wounded soldiers behind," he said, and the people in the settlements needed money for ambulances, hospitals and kindergartens. His appeal garnered envelopes filled with contributions, although one donor commented that she would have liked to hear him talk less about what he was against, and more about what he was for. She wanted to hear "alternatives" for peace. "We all want peace," she said.[1]

In Skokie, Illinois, addressing a responsive audience of 1400, he was asked if he agreed with the assassinated extremist leader Meir Kahane that all Arabs should be expelled from Gaza, the West Bank and from Israel as well. He quickly disagreed with this, eliciting applause along with a few boos. "We have to realize there is a certain situation we have there in Israel," he said.[2]

In May, he announced his intention to lead "a rescue mission to save the Land of Israel and the Jewish people," by forming a broad right-wing coalition that would oust Rabin in the 1996 elections. This declaration caused Benjamin Netanyahu, head of Likud, to call Sharon "a permanent subversive" who should "leave Likud." Netanyahu had maintained that a united right could defeat Labor, and he considered that Sharon was trying to cause a split in the party. "[He] has undermined both Begin and Shamir," he said, "and now he is undermining me. He spreads the seeds of a split." Yitzhak Shamir agreed, saying that Sharon should find more useful things to do than undermine the national interest. Benjamin Begin observed that Sharon was as likely to become prime minister as he was to become a world tennis champion.[3] Not one Likud leader or MK uttered support for Sharon.[4]

A newspaper poll at the time showed Rabin with thirty-six percent of the electorate, Netanyahu with nineteen percent, and Sharon and Eytan with twelve and eleven percent respectively, more or less a tie. The Israeli election system was to change in the next election: the prime minister was no longer to be chosen by the majority party in the Knesset, but was to be elected directly and had to win fifty percent of the popular vote.

In June, Sharon, called "the maverick Israeli rightwinger," said in a radio interview that he was sorry that the Israelis had not assassinated Arafat during the 1982 invasion of Beirut. Plans to kill him, Sharon said, had had to be dropped because of pressure from the United States to allow the PLO leader and his men to withdraw from Lebanon. "Because of this, we could not hit him," Sharon said. "All Israeli governments, from the left [to] what is called the right, made great efforts to hit this person, who is a war criminal in every respect. I am sorry we did not succeed."[5]

The English *Guardian* pointed out that Sharon was not the only Israeli leader who admitted that the intelligence service Mossad had come close to killing Arafat; in their book *Every Spy a Prince*, Dan Raviv and Yossi Melman had written that an Israeli sniper had Arafat "in his sights during the PLO evacuation of Beirut, but that it was considered politically unwise to kill him."[6]

Sharon made his position clear on the Cairo agreement in an article in the *Jerusalem Post*: "For no apparent reason, the weak Jewish government of a strong, victorious nation surrendered unconditionally to the Palestine terrorist organization." The Rabin government, he said, had "set up a terrorist Palestinian state," and had unfortunately given up the "settlement-security" plan, which was needed to protect Israel; a strong military was not enough.

In February, 1995, Sharon came to Washington to lobby for the settlements and against the Oslo accords, and to repeat his accusations that "Arafat is a murderer, a war criminal." He had come, he told reporters, not as a Likud member but "as an Israeli citizen" who wanted to explain that the contribution to peace of the 140,000 settlers in the territories was "very, very important." He said that while he was not asking Congress to cut off funding to the Palestinian Authority, he wanted to make clear that the PA was failing as a peace partner, and that Israeli government officials—referring indirectly to Foreign Minister Shimon Peres—were making a big mistake appealing to the world for funds for the PA. There should not be foreign investment in corrupt Palestinian areas, he said.[7]

In March, in another article in the *Jerusalem Post*, he complained bitterly that the government had not addressed the problem of the Palestinian refugees, which he called "a grave political-security threat," a "sword of Damocles dangling over our heads" and a real "peace ambush." He said that since 1967 he had been asking that "a resolution of the refugee issue be made a precondition of the Arab states' participation in the peace process." Any country that wanted to play a role in the peace process should, he said, try to solve the refugee problem "within its existing borders." The government, in an act of irresponsible folly, neglected to include a clause in the peace treaty with Jordan dealing with settling the refugees "in their present homes."

The Israeli government, he said, was talking deceitfully about "1967 displaced persons," but the bulk of these people were actually "1948 refugees" who had left their homes during Israel's War of Independence to settle in the Palestinian territories, moved to Jordan during the Six-Day War, and eventually scattered to other Arab countries, which refused to absorb them, keeping them in camps. He contrasted that with Israel's absorption of close to a million Jews who were forced to leave Arab countries after 1948 without their property. The number of Arab refugees was estimated by the Palestinian Authority at a million, and by the Rabin government at "only a few hundred thousand." But even if the lower number were true, which Sharon clearly did not believe, he did believe that the return of these people would precipitate a crisis when they came back and had to face for the first time the reality that Jews had taken over cities and fields where they had once lived and worked.[8]

In another article in July, Sharon inveighed against the possibility of a peace with Syria that would involve giving up the Golan Heights, and accepting Syrian refusal to rein in the Hezbollah. He was particularly angered by the Labor position that "only a political solution will end terrorism." Both Labor and the US administration would, he wrote, heighten their chances for reelection if a peace treaty was signed with Syria. "No country in the world," he wrote, "would conceive of any political agreement being a guarantee of security." And as he was to do over five years later, to the outrage of the Bush administration, he invoked the memory of Munich: "When France and Britain signed a pact with Hitler in Munich on the eve of World War II, it was the last time anyone heard that 'peace is security.' No sane government anywhere has since repeated it."[9]

In October, he announced that if the Likud won the elections in 1996, he would not only recommend that present agreements with the PLO be breached, but that Yassir Arafat be captured and brought to Jerusalem to stand trial as a war criminal.[10]

ASSASSINATION

ON NOVEMBER 4, 1995, Labor and the left-wing Meretz Party joined with the organization Peace Now—formed in 1978 to pressure the Begin government to sign the pact with Egypt—to hold a massive rally in Kings of Israel Square in Tel Aviv. About one hundred thousand people turned out to rally in support of Rabin and Peres and their efforts for peace. When the demonstration ended, Rabin walked to a parking area, and began to enter his car. At that moment, a twenty-seven-year-old man with a gun lunged between Rabin's bodyguards and fired three shots, two of which hit the prime minister in the back. He was rushed to Ichilov Hospital, where he died a few minutes later.

The assassin, who was immediately captured, was Yigal Amir, the son of Yemeni Orthodox parents and a law student at Bar-Ilan religious university, who readily admitted that he had planned for some time to kill Rabin to stop the peace process. In words that unhappily echoed some of Sharon's more inflammatory rhetoric, he compared the Labor government to the Nazis and said he had "acted to save the Jewish people."

As Shimon Peres worked to put together an interim government, Sharon called on him to consult with the "mainstream opposition" in an attempt to find a consensus on moves for peace. Polls indicated that the public supported Rabin and Peres and that Labor would win in the 1996 elections. Netanyahu's popularity dropped after the assassination, and Sharon became a candidate for prime minister. But on November 17, Sharon, whose statements many reporters considered a weathervane for the future direction of the right wing, moderated his tone. When asked by members of the Foreign Press Association, during a tour of settlements by bus, whether the Likud intended to reverse the peace process, he replied, "Things that have been done already, I think it will be very, very hard to change . . . but many things have not been done yet. We are going to be in the middle of the process."[1] During the settlement tour, followed by army jeeps and armed security guards, Sharon was in surprisingly good spirits, considering that Israeli troops were moving out of six West Bank cities, an action that he had repeatedly called suicidal. In Peduel, a settlement on the West Bank that he had helped to plan, he pointed to new homes and roads being built, and told the press that business was going on as usual there.[2]

In accord with Oslo II, Israel was to hand over six Arab cities to the Palestinian Authority by the end of 1995, and to evacuate parts of Hebron in spring of 1996. Sharon told the journalists that he was warning Arafat that if the PA harbored terrorists in those cities, the IDF would enter and round the terrorists up. He added that the Israelis would not attack Arafat's police, and would leave the cities after the roundup. The conclusion drawn by the *Jerusalem Post* was that Sharon had signalled that a Likud government "could accept at least the initial implementation of Oslo II if the PLO honored the deal as well."[3]

The *Boston Globe* reported that Sharon's plan would differ from the Labor plan in that "[n]o further authority would be handed over to the Palestinians, and Israel would maintain the right of preemptive action and hot pursuit in Palestinian-controlled cities." This would end the possibility of any real autonomy or statehood for the Palestinians, but would attract the centrist Israeli vote because it would leave the settlements intact, and keep strategic control in the hands of the IDF while giving limited autonomy to the PA. Sharon, the *Globe* commented, had always been a maverick, both a hardliner and a pragmatist. He was often called an opportunist, but he had a strong following on the right, and he was certainly aware that Netanyahu was down in the polls. As he led the journalists through the settlement, Sharon commented that he had had many meetings with Rabin and had warm feelings toward him. And although he accused Peres of trying to push through withdrawal from the West Bank while the public were still in shock from Rabin's murder, he intended, he said, to sit down with Labor leaders and try to come to an agreement with them about the future of the West Bank.

Nevertheless, he made clear that his position on the settlements was not open to negotiation. At Beit Arieh, a hilltop settlement, he said that the high ground was essential to the protection of the Israeli heartland on the coastal plain. From this vantage point, he said, two-thirds of Israel's population could be seen, "like it was in the palm of your hand. This area cannot be, and will never be, under Palestinian control." Pointing to the main runway at Ben-Gurion International Airport, which could be seen in the distant haze, he remarked, "Imagine if a terrorist with a shoulder-fired surface-to-air missile shoots at an airliner with 400 to 500 people on board." This could not happen, he said, if Israeli troops remained in the area. "If this country elects a new government," he said, "it means it wants a new plan."[4]

Early in December, a month after the assassination, Sharon accused the Peres administration of instituting an unjustified crackdown on settlement activists, religious students and rabbis—people connected in some way with the assassin Yigal Amir. Amir's brother Haggai and friend Dror Adani were arrested and eventually convicted of conspiracy, and others in his circle were questioned, but no one else was tried. Sharon said that the administration's behavior was "very dangerous . . . if somebody says a word, his neighbors are complaining and the police come and take him—it's beyond what was in the Iron Curtain." But he granted that the investigation seemed to be petering out and had not reached the "degree" of a "pogrom."[5]

Much of this rhetoric could be discounted as simply political, but Sharon was also reacting to allegations about his command during the war with Egypt in 1956. These accusations had first surfaced in August of 1995 when General Arye Biro asserted without remorse in the newspaper *Maariv* that when his paratroop company in Raful Eytan's Battalion 890, part of Sharon's Parachute Brigade, landed in the Sinai east of Mitla Pass on October 29, 1956, his forces took forty-nine Egyptian civilian workers prisoner, and killed them two days later when the paratroopers moved out.[6]

This account was confirmed by Danni Wolf, a colonel in the reserves who had been one of Biro's soldiers in the Sinai. "Theoretically," he told *Maariv*, "it was possible to leave them there with a little water and food, but the truth is that we didn't have enough water even for ourselves." He said he was not looking for excuses, but "really, any way you look at it, there was nothing to do with these workers." He said that Eytan had given the order. In addition, Biro and another colonel, Shaul Ziv, said that the force had killed fifty-six civilians in a crowded truck on the road to Ras Sudar. After the war, the United Nations had documented a third incident in which chained prisoners were massacred under Eytan's command. No one had said that Sharon was aware of these atrocities, and neither he nor Eytan commented on these stories.[7]

Also in August there were allegations that 300 Egyptian prisoners of war had been killed in the 1967 war, when Rabin was chief of staff. Rabin did not exactly condemn the 1967 allegations, but said that "[i]n the army's early years . . . it was characterized by birth pains of an army that did not yet have battle norms, behavior, discipline. In those years there were exceptions alongside hard combat with poor equipment." As to the 1956 episodes, to which he had no connection, he said, "I condemn them and the acts to which they relate." But "[e]xceptional cases do not reflect the norm."[8]

Now, in the first week of December, Peres announced that he was going to appoint a general in the Israeli reserves to head an inquiry into the alleged 1956 killings. Sharon was forced to comment on this: the allegations, he said, were made against a battalion in his brigade, but did not in any way reflect on him personally. He went on to say that if these killings were to be investigated, then Egypt should investigate the killing and mutilation of Israeli prisoners. "We found our wounded with no fingers, no sex organs, no nose and no ears," Sharon said. He himself was wounded twice in battle, in a hopeless situation, he went on, and what gave him the strength to get out was the knowledge of what the Egyptians did to the wounded. In 1956, the troops had been dropped in an isolated zone 150 miles from any other unit, he said, and had been under non-stop attack. He ended saying, "I do not think it's good to go back."[9]

Later in December, he announced that he was withdrawing his candidacy for prime minister, and called for all his supporters to unite behind Benjamin Netanyahu. This did not come as a surprise to the Likud; Sharon had stopped attacking Netanyahu more than a year earlier. Now he said it was essential for the Likud to be united when the country found itself in what he described as "one of the most dangerous situations it has ever been in," and of which he was not sure the population was fully aware.

He made the point that energy should not be wasted on "internecine battles." But Netanyahu was still facing challenges on the right from Raful Eytan and David Levy, the head of the Gesher faction. On December 21, Netanyahu predicted that all indications were that Peres would call early elections, and this prediction turned out to be true.[10]

33

POLITICAL SHIFT 1996

———

IN OCTOBER, 1995, THE leader of the Islamic Jihad, Fathi Shkaki, was assassinated by the Mossad and in January, 1996, Yahya Ayash, the Hamas bomber chief, was killed by Israeli operatives. These killings were in retaliation for years of bombings and the deaths and wounding of hundreds of Israelis. As could be expected, Hamas plotted revenge. Unimpeded by Arafat, who saluted "all the martyrs, with Ayash at their head," Hamas took its revenge in the form of suicide bombers, one of whom killed twenty-five and wounded more than fifty blowing himself up on a crowded bus; another exploded a few minutes later at a busy corner. The government had closed the territories in early February, because of warnings of attacks, but on February 23, two days before the bus bombing, Peres had opened them again. Other attacks followed in the next few weeks: suicide bombings on crowded streets, and a Hezbollah ambush of Israeli soldiers.

The effect on public confidence in the administration was devastating. Angry crowds demonstrated in the streets, demanding Peres's departure, even though Arafat's police finally moved to arrest some militant leaders and kill others in skirmishes. Arafat also deleted clauses from the Palestinian charter that called for the destruction of Israel, but this did not assuage Likud rage, because he did not issue a new charter.

With Peres responding with bombing of Hezbollah centers in Lebanon and a blockade of the Lebanon coast, the situation swiftly deteriorated into a war, and the IDF accidentally shelled a UN refugee encampment, with great loss of civilian life. As a result, in the face of Arab fury and international pressure, Peres lowered his level of attack and a cease-fire of sorts went into effect on April 27. But the public blamed Peres for all the disasters, and Israeli Arabs, convinced that the attacks on the refugees were intentional, believed that there was no difference between Peres and Netanyahu, and decided not to vote at all.

Thus when elections were held on May 29, Netanyahu's right-wing/religious coalition won sixty-one of the 120 Knesset seats. Netanyahu made it clear that his coalition would oppose a Palestinian state, the "right of return" of Palestinian exiles to Israel, or any change in the status of Jerusalem and the Golan, and would continue to develop settlements. (Rabin and Peres had both banned new settlements and had limited the expansion of existing settlements except for those near Jerusalem.) In early July, Yigal Amir, Rabin's assassin, in the course of an appeal to the Israeli Supreme Court for a moderation of his sentence, said that Netanyahu's election proved that the murder had "opened the eyes" of the public to the dangers of Labor policy. Amir's lawyers argued that their client could not be held accountable for his actions, but Amir contradicted them, saying that he had known exactly what he was doing and was happy that Rabin was dead.[1]

Despite the fact that Sharon had declared solidarity with Netanyahu months earlier, and had mobilized religious and ultra-orthodox parties to support the Likud candidate, the new prime minister snubbed him when he set up his government in June. Sharon had expected a prestigious post in the new cabinet, but Netanyahu offered him the Ministry of Construction and Housing, a position Sharon had held in Shamir's cabinet. Sharon, disappointed, declined the offer, but changed his mind a few hours later. Netanyahu, having just closed a deal with one of the ultra-orthodox parties, told Sharon his acceptance had come too late; the office was no longer available.

Sharon, insulted, withdrew to his farm, and Netanyahu presented his cabinet for confirmation to the Knesset. But Netanyahu's foreign minister, David Levy, backed by some other of Sharon's friends, threatened during live television coverage of a Knesset meeting, to resign unless Sharon was given a cabinet post. Netanyahu, about to leave for Washington for important talks with President Clinton and to embark on an American public relations campaign, had to drop everything and deal with this dangerous political embarrassment. He created a Ministry of National Infrastructure by annexing several departments and on July 8, 1996, Sharon was given that senior cabinet position.[2]

Palestinians were alarmed at this appointment, since Sharon now would have control over land management, rural development, water, roads and energy. They feared Sharon and Netanyahu would incorporate the still-occupied territories into Israel and that Sharon would put an economic squeeze on Arafat's areas to force the Palestinians to emigrate to Jordan, a goal the new minister had sought for years. The Lebanese, too, were uneasy as they remembered what had happened to their country in 1982 when Sharon was defense minister. In general the Arab world did not trust Sharon, whom they considered unpredictable and headstrong.

Netanyahu also may well have remembered that in 1990 Sharon and Levy together gave Shamir trouble to the point that the Israeli press called the two men "handcuffers," because they held Shamir back from making concessions for the Bush administration's peace efforts. However, Netanyahu and Sharon were in agreement on increasing the number of settlements in the West Bank and Netanyahu shared Sharon's hard line on the Golan, a Palestinian state, the "right of return" of the Arab refugees and control of Jerusalem.

In the first months of Netanyahu's term, there were no further Israeli troop withdrawals and little serious negotiation. On September 4, Netanyahu met briefly with Arafat, and the two men, without enthusiasm, shook hands. This grudging encounter sparked a bitter division in the Likud, to the point where Netanyahu had to confront his critics at a party central committee meeting the next day. Half of his audience rose and cheered him, and the other half remained seated and loudly booed him. One woman stood, but holding an open umbrella, a reference to Neville Chamberlain's concessions to Hitler at Munich in 1938. Netanyahu was accused of giving in to international pressure. Benjamin Begin said that the meeting with Arafat was "a severe defeat," and that Netanyahu had betrayed the Likud platform. Sharon warned the prime minister that governments could be replaced, unlike Jewish holy sites in the West Bank and Jerusalem, and reminded the audience of Arafat's history as a terrorist, getting strong applause when he said, "A people that wants to live, does not forget."

On television, before the committee meeting, Netanyahu had threatened to fire any members of his cabinet who argued against his policies. Now he reminded them that he was the first Israeli prime minister elected by direct popular vote, rather than by vote of the Knesset. "There is only one prime minister," he said, and some of the audience responded by shouting Sharon's name. Netanyahu elicited enthusiastic cheers when he said, "There will be no Palestinian state." But many people maintained that he had betrayed them because he had told them he would never meet Arafat or sign agreements with the PLO. Others granted that he had had to meet Arafat because he had had to honor the bad agreement that he had inherited from Labor, but he had met with him too soon, and without first getting favorable commitments. They feared further concessions. Feelings were so strong that after the meeting party members almost came to blows.[3]

Some commentators suggested that this meeting might herald the breakup of Likud, but Begin and Sharon both retained their cabinet seats, and protests died down. Netanyahu, having been pressured by Jordan, Egypt, and of course the United States, to meet Arafat, made it clear at every opportunity that there would be no

Palestinian state, that the Jewish settlements were there for good, and that he would never compromise on Jerusalem.[4]

On September 24, Netanyahu took a step that the Rabin government had avoided: he completed work on a tunnel running along the edge of the hill, in the Muslim Quarter of the Old City of Jerusalem, called the Temple Mount by Jews, and Haram al-Sharif, or Noble Sanctuary, by Muslims. Two mosques, al-Aqsa and the Dome of the Rock, sit there, and it is the site of the Jewish Temple destroyed by the Romans in 70 C.E. The Western Wall running along one side of the hill is the last remnant of the Temple. The tunnel, 300 yards long and five feet wide, was carved out of the rock more than 2000 years ago to serve as part of an aqueduct channeling water to the Temple Mount. It had been discovered by a British explorer in the mid-nineteenth century, but for more than one hundred years, it remained under the earth, filled with mud and water. In 1987 the Israeli Ministry for Religious Affairs began to excavate it to create a pedestrian walkway leading to the Via Dolorosa. It was not completed because of Muslim objections, until Netanyahu personally ordered the last few feet of wall to be broken through during the night to create a new exit with a gray iron door welded into place.

Immediately there were accusations that the Israelis were seeking to destroy the foundations of the al-Aqsa Mosque and the Dome of the Rock, and to strengthen Israel's control over Jerusalem. The Arab League issued a statement condemning the action as "a clear attack on Islamic holy sites," and Arafat denounced it as a "big crime" and ordered a commercial strike in east Jerusalem and protest marches in the West Bank and Gaza Strip. The street combat which ensued, beginning on September 25 and lasting for four days, was the worst since Israel had conquered the Gaza Strip nearly twenty-nine years before. Soldiers and police fought stone throwers in east Jerusalem, the police fired rubber bullets to disperse the crowd, and soldiers chased and beat some protesters. Outside Ramallah, uniformed Palestinian security forces backed the stone throwers with assault rifles, setting off gunfire exchanges that lasted for days and extended to West Bank cities and a couple of Israeli settlements. There were riots and tire burnings in the West Bank towns of Hebron, Ramallah, Nablus and Bethlehem. In Gaza City 5000 Palestinian high school students burned an Israeli flag and chanted, "Death to the criminal Netanyahu."

The Likud mayor of Jerusalem, Ehud Olmert, accused Arafat of incitement and protested that the passage, which actually skirted the Mount, posed no structural danger to the two mosques. The former mayor, Teddy Kollek, saying that Netanyahu had made a mistake, pointed out that the previous government had repeatedly delayed opening the tunnel, because of concern over the possibility of the violence which had now occurred. "They did it during a tense period," Kollek said in a radio interview, "and increased the tension we have in Jerusalem anyhow. It's simply not smart."[5]

In a cabinet meeting that lasted into the wee hours on the third day of violence, Sharon and Raful Eytan demanded that troops and tanks be sent to crush the Palestinian security forces, and in fact the fighting ebbed only when the IDF sent tanks and helicopter gunships into the outskirts of West Bank cities and threatened to invade them if Arafat's men continued to fire their assault rifles. In three days, seventy Palestinians died and hundreds sustained injuries, while fifteen IDF soldiers had been killed and more than thirty were wounded. The Americans, drawn into the situation, asked Netanyahu to close the tunnel, and his own security advisors, including his minister of defense, along with the majority of Israeli voters, thought opening it had been a bad idea. But Netanyahu refused to close the tunnel. Pressure was so heavy that he had to cut short a European tour to meet with Arafat in Washington.

This was only the beginning of three months of negotiation, involving Secretary of State Warren Christopher and his aide Dennis Ross, as well as Israelis and Palestinians. Netanyahu was caught

between his deep disinclination to abide by agreements with the
Palestinians to pull out of Hebron, the last major town in the West
Bank still controlled by Israel, and pressure by the Clinton administration and the Europeans to honor the agreements. He would not
commit himself to a target date for withdrawal from Hebron, while
Arafat demanded firm commitments for withdrawal from disputed
territories in the West Bank within a year.

Toward the end of November, Sharon addressed an audience of
right-wing politicians and settlers on the subject of Hebron. The
situation was dangerous, he said, and Israel must protect the 500
Jewish settlers and seminary students living in the city of 130,000
Palestinians, once Israeli troops withdraw. They must, he said, de-
ploy troops in a smaller area of downtown Hebron than originally
planned, but they must retain full control of that area by building a
wall around it to keep Palestinians out. He made it clear that he had
been cut out of discussions of Hebron among Netanyahu's inner
circle, who had refused even to consider his plan. Clearly he recognized the necessity to give up most of Hebron, but he also said that
the autonomy agreements with the Palestinians reached by the Rabin
government were "grave and dangerous" and Netanyahu should
not hesitate to break them. He could not understand, he said, why
he was not allowed to lay a water pipe for Jewish settlements through
the Jordan Valley because Palestinians could veto it. "Who would
have imagined," he asked, "that the Israeli government would have
given away rights over water?"[6]

In January, 1997, King Hussein met with Arafat and Netanyahu
in Gaza and Israel, and helped to work out an agreement for an
Israeli withdrawal from most of Hebron, leaving safeguards for two
Jewish settlements, and a target date of mid-1998 for further withdrawals, among other things. Netanyahu had to work hard to convince right-wing and religious party members of his cabinet to endorse these agreements, and in the end seven members voted against
them. Benjamin Begin resigned as science minister, and Sharon voted

against the agreement, but remained in his post. The Palestinian extremists objected also. The withdrawal from Hebron was implemented on January 17. Several suicide bombing attacks by Hamas in 1997 underscored the extremist objections and gave Netanyahu reason to delay further withdrawals.

A few days later, Sharon issued a call for a national unity government, something he had been advocating for some months. He had been holding regular meetings on the subject with Labor's Shimon Peres, to the irritation of Netanyahu's supporters, who attributed his remarks to pique at being shut out of the Hebron discussions. Sharon had said on television that "a broad coalition could prevent a situation in which essentially one man decides. It doesn't matter who the man is. It's nothing personal." No side, he said, would be able to attain all of its objectives, but he implied that the government could more strongly resist Arab demands if it had broader support.

He went on to hope that he could play a more important role in coming negotiations; he had been left out of policy decisions so far, he said, and he believed that if he had been "part of the team" he could have helped work out far better arrangements to help protect the Jews in Hebron. He also expressed dismay that "a section of Israeli public opinion" had celebrated the pullback from Hebron; this was a "masochistic and sick" reaction to "an event that should inspire sorrow in Jewish hearts, regardless" of political affiliations.[7]

A spokesman for Netanyahu said that there was no need for a broad coalition. But Netanyahu was not as secure as he perhaps thought. He had certainly blundered by alienating Sharon, who had campaigned hard for him only to be snubbed as a cabinet choice and then left out of the Hebron deliberations. Obviously, Netanyahu considered Sharon a liability: Labor had tried to frighten voters during the campaign by saying that "Bibi"—Netanyahu's nickname—was very much like Sharon. And Sharon was not the only cabinet member alienated: Netanyahu had also initially snubbed the finance minister, Dan Meridor, and had long been on bad terms with Foreign Minister David Levy, who finally resigned in January, 1998. There were other blunders. In April, 1997, Netanyahu found himself being investigated for corruption charges after having appointed as state's attorney, Ronnie Bar On, an allegedly unqualified Jerusalem lawyer. The appointment was short-lived, but cabinet members did not rise to Netanyahu's defense. Then in September, a Mossad attack in Amman on the life of Hamas Political Secretary Khaled Mashaal failed miserably, causing great embarrassment to the Israeli government.

34

JUGGLING FOR POWER

———

IN JUNE 1997, NETANYAHU, who had narrowly survived a no-confidence vote in the Knesset, felt it would be wise to offer Sharon the key post of finance minister, vacated by Dan Meridor, who had resigned that month, saying that he had lost all faith in the prime minister. Netanyahu needed to win Sharon's crucial support to prop up his fracturing coalition, and needed too, perhaps an interesting announcement to divert press attention from an embarrassing TV episode in which his wife Sara made disparaging remarks about Limor Livnat, the only female minister, and about Shimon Peres's wife Sonia, saying that the former had a romantic interest in her, Sara's, husband, and that the latter was "an uneducated woman who washes dishes and plays cards."[1]

Sharon declared on Israel Radio that he had made it clear to the prime minister that if he accepted the finance minister post, he had also to be included in the small inner cabinet. This mini-cabinet dealt with security and politics, and only the prime minister, the foreign minister, David Levy, and the minister of defense, Yitzhak Mordechai, were members. Sharon's position on security issues caused Levy and Mordechai to oppose his appointment and his admission to the so-called kitchen cabinet. Sharon was firmly on record as opposing the Oslo II agreement, saying that it called for "withdrawals" and that "redeployment" was simply a convenient euphemism. He was willing to yield only a quarter of the West Bank in the interim period, remarking that "we may have to make certain modi-

fications in Oslo." And there were his reputation as "Mr Settlement" and his references to Arafat as a war criminal.

As infrastructure minister, Sharon had been very busy: he had
proposed annexing large areas of the West Bank to maintain Israeli
control over water rights, after accusing the PA of deliberately pol-
luting Israel's water sources and their own as well; he had begun
negotiations on joint infrastructure projects with Jordan, including
water transfer and the construction of railway links with that country; and he had gone to Russia early in June to discuss regular purchases of Russian natural gas and coal as well as other infrastructure projects.

In addition, he had been involved with protests by the Jewish
National Fund, the Jewish Agency, and representatives of the Arab
community, against the government-approved Ronen Committee
report, issued in April, 1997, that recommended, among other things,
transferring lands from state control to private ownership, in order
to expand the supply of real estate and to lower prices. Farmers'
groups had given the report a cautious acceptance. Sharon promised that he would negotiate the terms of the report, which he said
had been approved only in principle, and that details were still open
to discussion. The report called for the banning of foreign ownership of state lands, defining foreigners as those not eligible to live in
Israel under the Law of Return. Sharon warned that Palestinians
and other Arabs were attempting to purchase land in Israel through
Israeli lawyers and the setting up of straw companies. Against the
objection, raised by MK Avraham Poraz, that Jews were splitting
the land among themselves and ignoring its previous ownership by
Arabs, Sharon replied that he did not want to discuss the past, but
to look ahead, and to work closely and fairly with Arab leaders. "I
don't distinguish between Arabs and Jews," he said. "They are all
Israeli citizens."

Poraz argued that in a democracy such purchases could not be
prevented, and that it was "a false fear to say that Arabs will buy

land here. After all, despite the fears, the Saudis haven't done it yet." And he asked, "What happens if a company like GM wants to buy some land here and then build a factory on it? Are we going to say, 'I'm sorry, but you're not Jewish?'" Sharon refused to talk about these details publicly, but invited Poraz to a private discussion of them.

Obviously, Sharon's actions as minister of infrastructure were not apt to soften liberal opinion of him; liberals and moderates were horrified at the possibility of his new appointment. Despite his arguments against banning of foreign ownership, Avraham Poraz said that Sharon's support of the Ronen Report was his only positive act: as agriculture minister he had given too much support to farmers; when he ran Industry and Trade, he had opposed free competition in the economy, and when he was in charge of Housing, he had ignored the needs of the central area, and, Poraz went on, "built houses in the Galilee and Negev that no one wanted." Labor and Coalition politicians suggested the names of other candidates, as they expressed fears that Sharon was incapable of handling the budget properly. David Harris in the *Jerusalem Post* underscored this fear by pointing out that Sharon had a "fiscally derelict past," supporting farm subsidies when he was minister of agriculture, favoring exporters and voting against an important austerity program in 1985 when he was minister of industry and trade, and, most egregiously, as minister of housing, overspending his budget by building thousands of unsaleable housing units in towns where there was little employment for immigrants. Avraham Poraz recalled that as trade minister, Sharon had demanded that European cutlery manufacturers inscribe the country of origin on their products in Hebrew, a cumbersome process that no manufacturer would undertake.[2]

Patrick Cockburn, in London's left-leaning *Independent*, recalling the Sabra and Shatilla massacres and Sharon's "masterminding" of the Lebanon invasion in 1982, wrote that Sharon's promotion would move the Israeli cabinet "even further to the right" and was a source of worry to the Palestinian leadership and to the Americans, because as finance minister, he would be able to divert funds to settlers in the occupied settlements for expansion. Cockburn mentioned also heavy-handed Likud attempts to tarnish the name of Ehud Barak, who had just been elected Labor leader.[3] The English *Guardian* characterized Sharon as the "corpulent former defense minister and the prime mover of the 1982 Lebanon war" and commented that his "elevation" had "aptly been described as a red rag to an Arab bull" and "should be opposed by anyone who hopes to revive the fading dream of a just peace in the region."[4] The *Daily Telegraph* called Sharon "a darling of the Jewish settler movement in the occupied territories" who was "seen by critics as a dangerous 'adventurer.'"[5] Foreign Minister Levy and Defense Minister Mordechai were moderates who believed that Sharon would try to scuttle serious peace talks with the PA. Levy had helped secure a cabinet post for Sharon the previous year, but now he refused to meet with Netanyahu to discuss Sharon's promotion and was demanding that the kitchen cabinet be disbanded altogether. The prime minister's coalition was in disarray. Reuters noted that Netanyahu had "lurched from crisis to crisis" in the year since he took power, and hopes for peace had "crumbled over his expansion of Jewish settlement." Some MKs talked about creating an alternative leadership around Dan Meridor, who, according to the *Boston Globe*, had been "pushed aside [from Finance] for being seen as insufficiently loyal."[6]

The former director of the Treasury defended Sharon against some of these criticisms, saying that he was a good administrator who heeded the policy recommendations of the bureaucracies he headed. And some political analysts saw Sharon's appointment as a clever move on Netanyahu's part. Although Sharon was undoubtedly a hard-liner, they said, he was "the ultimate pragmatist" who could bring the party right wing into line behind the peace process, which had been stalled under Netanyahu. And probably to underscore this possibility, it was leaked that earlier in June, Sharon had met secretly with Arafat's deputy Mahmoud Abbas.

Abdul Wahab Dawarshe, an Arab Democratic Party member of the Knesset, arranged the secret meeting with Mahmoud Abbas, known as Abu Mazen, at Sharon's farm in the Negev. Dawarshe, a native of Nazareth, had come to believe that the man whom Arabs called "the Butcher of Beirut," and whom he himself had long avoided, could help to bring the extreme right wing to a peace settlement. Negotiations had been at a standstill for more than three months. "Weak leaders," Dawarshe said, "even if they are good people like Shimon Peres, are not able to lead their people. Only strong leaders have the credibility, and I believe that only Sharon has the ability to lead the right wing to compromises. Now that Netanyahu is not trusted and is so unpopular, he cannot do these things and Sharon can." Dawarshe told the *Christian Science Monitor* that Sharon "thinks it's terrible that things are going so wrong in the peace process and that there will be another war. He told me he wants to contribute with Abu Mazen to make peace for the Palestinian children and the Israeli children."[7]

Ephraim Sneh, a Labor MK, met at the end of June with Arafat, who told him that Sharon's meeting with Dawarshe was intended to revive peace initiatives, and had been coordinated with him. This despite the fact that Sharon had called the PLO a terrorist organization, and Arafat a war criminal. Sneh got the impression that the PA leader believed that Sharon's motive for the meeting with Abbas was to gain entrance to the inner cabinet. Sharon did not reveal any new policies, but the session was polite, and apparently as a result, Arafat ordered enhanced cooperation between Palestinian and Israeli security forces. This meeting, which engendered dismay in extremist factions of the Likud and among most settlers, was interpreted by the press as a watershed event, symbolizing recognition of the PLO by the Likud right wing, and Sharon's acknowledgement of the momentum of the Oslo agreements.

Prospects for peace were not helped when Jewish extremists, apparently trying to foment a war, distributed leaflets in Hebron showing the Prophet Mohammed as a pig wearing a Palestinian headscarf and writing the Koran. Riots were the immediate result, and Netanyahu hurried to denounce the leaflets and disassociate the government from them. Arafat, whose popularity had declined, said that the situation "was on the edge of an abyss," while Sharon told *Maariv* that only he could make peace with the Palestinians.

On the first of July, Netanyahu had a "reconciliation" meeting with David Levy to discuss Levy's conditions for remaining in the fractured cabinet. Yitzhak Mordechai did not want the kitchen cabinet abolished, but he announced through a spokesman that he would accept any decision Netanyahu made about that. Levy was very clear about his distrust of the prime minister, but he denied having expressed opposition to Sharon's pending appointment. However, he said that there should not be a mini-cabinet; it evoked "suspicion among the cabinet ministers."[8]

On July 7, after three weeks of indecision and in-fighting, Netanyahu bowed to moderate pressure, and appointed Yaacov Neeman, a former Justice minister and director-general of the Treasury, to the Finance post. Neeman was Netanyahu's personal lawyer and had lost his justice ministry when he was indicted on charges of suborning perjury in a criminal case. When Neeman was acquitted in June, the prime minister had promised to return him to government. Netanyahu also abolished the kitchen cabinet.

Sharon publicly put on a happy face, chuckling when reporters asked him whether he was angry about losing the appointment. "Oh, really," he said, "I think you must be joking." Watching this performance, one of Sharon's closest aides commented that the General "always laughs in times of crisis."[9] People who knew Sharon expected that he would attempt to wreak vengeance on Netanyahu. He is going to move against the prime minister," a Labor MK said. "The only question is when."[10]

Sharon cancelled a scheduled meeting with Netanyahu and could not be reached by the prime minister's aides for two days. Finally a meeting was set up for July 9 at noon. But Netanyahu had notified the press, and Sharon arrived to find television cameras and microphones. He had no desire to be part of what he considered a Netanyahu "business as usual" charade. He refused to listen to the prime minister's explanation of the Neeman appointment, or Netanyahu's security survey, and abruptly left the room. Later he told reporters that his relationship with Netanyahu was "perfectly correct" and that they would continue to work together amicably.[11]

Netanyahu, for his part, told a TV interviewer that he had never intended to offer the Finance post to Sharon, and had in fact offered it only after Neeman had turned it down. But then Neeman had changed his mind the night before the appointment was to be announced, and Netanyahu said that he "felt a moral obligation" to give him the position.[12] Only a few days after he had officially dissolved the kitchen cabinet, the prime minister met with Mordechai and Levy, its only two cabinet members, to discuss security matters. Sharon, who was not invited, commented to the press while on a tour of upper Nazareth, that the way cabinet decisions were being made was "not acceptable or proper," since many of the ministers did not have the experience and knowledge to make these decisions. The Hebron agreement, he said, was an example of a poor government decision. He did not rule out the possibility that he would challenge Netanyahu in the next elections, but he emphasized that the government should complete its term.[13]

Netanyahu's office said that Sharon was not invited to the meeting because the day before he had left the room without listening to the prime minister's security survey.[14] Netanyahu himself told the press that he would continue to try to consult with Sharon, who

Sharon's house in Kfar Malal, where he grew up. It is now owned by his son Omri and is occupied by tenants.(Ron Zetouni 4/23/02)

RIGHT: *During the Six-Day War, Sharon (right) confers with General Yeshayahu Gavish and field commanders in the Sinai. (6/9/67)*

BELOW: *Sharon (left) with Menachen Begin and General Avraham Yoffe after the Six-Day War. (Moshe Milner 6/13/67)*

ABOVE: *Sharon (center), with Gen Chaim Bar-Lev (to his right) and Gen Yeshayahu Gavish (to his left), arrives by helicopter in the Negev. (David Rubinger 6/1/67)*

Sharon (far left) with Lt Col Shlomo Lahat (2nd from left), Prime Minister Levi Eshkol (3rd from left), Defense Minister Moshe Dayan (with eye patch) and Gen Chaim Bar-Lev (far right) visit Army camps on the West Bank. (Ilan Bruner 9/20/67)

ABOVE: *Sharon (left) tours the Egyptian border and Suez Canal with David Ben-Gurion (2nd from right) and Chief of Staff Chaim Bar-Lev (far right) on Jan 27, 1971.*

Gaza Mayor Rushad A'Shaver launches Finger Pier Gaza Port, flanked on his left by Shimon Peres and Sharon. (Moshe Milner 1/13/72)

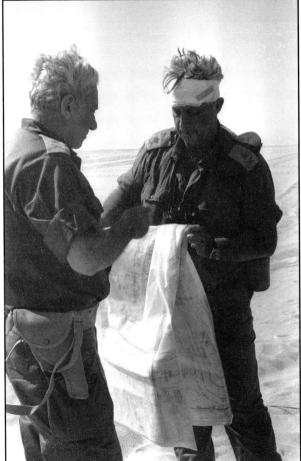

ABOVE: *Sharon (2nd from right) and Gen Shmuel Gonen (right) of the Southern Command confer with officers during the Yom Kippur War. (Shlomo Arad 10/10/73)*

LEFT: *Chaim Bar-Lev (left) and Sharon consult a map during the Yom Kippur War. (Yossi Greenberg 10/17/73)*

RIGHT: *Sharon when he was advisor to Yitzhak Rabin. (Moshe Milner 11/30/75)*

BELOW: *Prime Minister Golda Meir (center) and Gen Sharon (left) visit the Southern Command in the Sinai during the Yom Kippur War. (Yehuda Tzion 10/29/73)*

ABOVE: *Prime Minister Yitzhak Rabin (2nd from left) on the way to a Golan Heights army base with Shimon Peres right and Sharon far right. (Yaacov Saar 12/11/75)*

Prime Minister Yitzhak Rabin (far right) with military aide Ephraim Poran (to his right) and advisor Ariel Sharon in the Sinai. (Moshe Milner 2/19/76)

ABOVE: *Sharon, minister of agriculture, with Att'y Gen Aharon Barak in Jerusalem. (Yaacov Saar 8/9/77)*

Prime Minister Menachem Begin and Agriculture Minister Sharon in the Prime Minister's office. (Yaacov Saar 8/9/77)

LEFT TO RIGHT: *Cabinet session with Aharon Barak, Shmuel Katz, Ezer Weizman, Manachem Begin, Simcha Ehrlich, Yosef Burg, Sharon, Ephraim Evron and (walking in rear) Moshe Dayan. (Yaacov Saar 8/9/77)*

ABOVE: *Newly appointed Defense Minister Sharon reviews honor guard in Tel Aviv, with Chief of Staff Raful Eytan to his right. (Dalia Yankovitz 8/6/81)*

Defense Minister Sharon greets Sadat in Alexandria. (Chanania Herman 8/25/81)

ABOVE: *Defense Minister Sharon and Lily, with their son Gilad, tour the Suez Canal. (Moshe Milner 1/19/82)*

Pres Ronald Reagan (right) flanked by Secretary of State Alexander Haig, Vice President Bush and Defense Secretary Caspar Weinberger meets an Israeli delegation in Washington, consisting of Prime Minister Menachem Begin (left center), Foreign Minister Yitzhak Shamir (to his right), Defense Minister Sharon (to right) and advisors. (Yaacov Saar 9/9/81)

ABOVE: *Sharon and Lily visit the graves of fallen soldiers on Mount Herzl on Memorial Day. (Yitzhak Harari 4/27/82)*

Sharon and Lily attend a parade and air show at an IAF base. (Baruch Rimon 7/15/82)

LEFT: *Lebanese Elie Hubeika. (Courtesy Library of Congress Country Studies)*

BELOW: *US Special Envoy Philip Habib strolls through Sycamore Farm with Sharon. (Yossi Roth 9/24/82)*

ABOVE: *Outgoing Defense Minister Sharon congratulates incoming Minister Moshe Arens in the Knesset. (Photo by Nati Harnik 3/2/83)*

Cabinet members Sharon (left), Raful Eitan and Ezer Weizman during a break after the opening address in the 11th Knesset in Jerusalem. (Chanania Herman 8/13/84)

ABOVE: *Sharon in June, 1985, in the Knesset when he was minister of industry and trade. (Nati Harnick 5/6/85)*

Sharon plays with his boxer on the farm. (Yossi Roth 3/3/84)

Lily and Sharon during the Herut Party convention in Tel Aviv. (Nati Harnick 10/13/86)

retained his position as minister of infrastructure, on important matters. Netanyahu wanted to make peace with Sharon to tamp down the danger of a Likud revolt against the government spearheaded by Meridor and Begin, neither of whom could possibly be won over. After some initial difficulty in getting together, for which each blamed the other, Netanyahu and Sharon met for ninety minutes on July 16 in what was described as "a good atmosphere." Netanyahu, with Neeman's approval, gave Sharon responsibility for free trade zones, and promised to include him in all meetings of the mini-cabinet, which had met twice without Sharon and after the prime minister had supposedly abolished it.[15]

A few days later, Sharon met with Peres to discuss a coalition that would roll back parts of the 1992 electoral reform law and enable sixty-one members, a majority of the Knesset, to bring down the prime minister without having to dissolve the Knesset and hold new elections. The 1992 law required new general elections after a majority no-confidence vote, and a vote of eighty members to remove the prime minister without dissolution of the Knesset. Netanyahu, not unexpectedly, was against this. "I greatly value Sharon," he told the Likud. "I also know that his efforts were made, for sure, with a positive intention."

"The last thing I want is a different government," Sharon said. He lobbied heavily for his proposal, but the bill, which many people saw as motivated by a desire for vengeance on Sharon's part, had little chance of success.[16]

35

LITIGATION AGAIN

———

NINETEEN NINETY-SEVEN WAS NOT a very good year for Sharon. In 1993, he had filed suit against *Haaretz* and reporter (and Sharon biographer) Uzi Benziman because of an article by Benziman that *Haaretz* had run in May, 1991, claiming that Menachem Begin knew that Sharon had deliberately deceived him about his plans to invade Beirut. The trial was held in February, 1997. Among the witnesses for the defense was Begin's son Benjamin, who testified that his father had indeed been astonished and angry to learn that Sharon had always intended to invade Beirut. Then there was the testimony of Major General Avigdor Ben-Gal, a hero in the 1973 war, called by the *Haaretz* lawyers because in 1987 he had stated publicly that Sharon had implemented "a clandestine plan" during the Lebanon war, hiding it from the cabinet.

To the horror of the defense team, on the stand Ben-Gal testified that what he had said fifteen years earlier was "rubbish; it was nonsense," and that he had made the false accusations because he was angry with Sharon for forcing him out of the army. "Sharon did not mislead Begin," Ben-Gal said. "On the contrary, he coordinated and confirmed his plans with the premier before the war even started. All of us who said anything else are guilty of an evil. I want to use this opportunity to set the matter straight."

Outraged *Haaretz* lawyers asked the district court to recall Ben-Gal to the stand, saying that they had discovered that several weeks before the trial, Ben-Gal had gone to Russia with Sharon because he had a business interest in a proposed natural gas deal.[1] The court refused this request, but on November 4, issued a ruling in favor of *Haaretz*, upholding its charge that Sharon had lied to Begin and his cabinet. Sharon called a press conference at his office and said that the district court had made "a grave mistake, perhaps one of the most serious a court can make." He would not, he said, abandon the issue, even if he had to fight for another twenty years. He had no intention, he announced, of resigning from the government or retiring from political life, and he saw himself as a candidate for minister of defense in the future. He would appeal to the Supreme Court. "Over the years," he said, "I have been the victim of intentional and unceasing incitement, incitement which stops at no means or lying," he said.[2]

Arabic News.Com, in reporting on this press conference, commented that as a result of the loss of this libel suit, Sharon's chances of gaining any senior post in the Likud were slim; as were his chances before the Supreme Court. In that case, the analyst wrote, his political career was almost certainly at an end. Opposition to him from Likud members like Benjamin Begin and his "up and down" relationship with Netanyahu had weakened him. "He might still be called a bulldozer ['the human bulldozer,' a title he had earned in the past], but [one] without an engine. Or a paper tiger who threatens nobody."[3]

Not content with its victory, *Haaretz* in early 1998 accused Sharon of bribing Ben-Gal into retracting his earlier statements, and asked for an official investigation into the general's testimony. A secret police investigation was undertaken and dismissed later in the year by the state attorney, who found insufficient evidence for any charges.

On February 19, 2002, the Israeli Supreme Court rejected Sharon's appeal against the lower court decision, but ruled that the district court should not have upheld Benziman's claim. Although the three justices agreed that Benziman had made the allegations in good faith and so was not guilty of libel, they refused to consider whether the allegations were true, declaring that "the determination of 'historical truth,' to the extent there is such a thing, is a matter for historians, not the court, and the more the courts refrain from dealing with such matters, the better it will be. The determination of historical truth is, to a large degree, a matter of assessment which may differ from one historian to another and from one time to another." This decision enabled lawyers for both sides to claim victory.[4]

36

LOOSE CANNON

———

IN MARCH, 1998, SHARON, still serving as infrastructure minister, went to Amman to help repair relations with Jordan that had been strained by the Mossad's bungled attempt to assassinate Hamas leader Khaled Mashaal the previous September, and to secure the release of the two Mossad agents who had tried to poison Mashaal. Sharon met with King Hussein for ninety minutes, for an hour of that with the king alone, and announced that relations were rapidly improving, and that there was now agreement to press ahead with a number of cooperative projects, including improved supply of Israeli water to Jordan, and the construction of a canal to pump water from the Gulf of Eilat to the Dead Sea to generate electricity.[1]

Unfortunately, when he returned home on March 14 in the course of his televised report on his mission to Jordan, he said that he had told the Jordanians, "You should know that we will liquidate Mashaal. I can tell you that we won't do it on your soil." This remark caused an immediate negative reaction from both Jordan and Egypt, the Egyptian foreign minister accusing Israel of state terrorism. This at a time when Robin Cook, the British Foreign Secretary, had just arrived in Cairo to begin three days of an attempt to launch peace talks. The Jordanian government lodged an official protest through the Israeli ambassador, telling him that Jordan would not accept aggression against any Jordanian citizen, in or out of the country, and that the threat was "irresponsible, ill-timed and rude." A Hamas leader in Gaza threatened retaliation if Mashaal were attacked.[2]

A week later Sharon apologized to Jordan for his remark in a letter to Crown Prince Hassan, King Hussein's brother and heir. A Jordanian official said that Jordan was satisfied with the apology: "Mr Sharon said his statement had been misunderstood and that he did not mean to threaten the sovereignty of Jordan, its integrity and its people. We are content with that."[3]

By spring of 1998, it had become obvious that Israel, which had been in Lebanon for twenty years, was losing the battle with Hezbollah gunmen, and needed to extricate itself from the situation. Incidents occurred almost daily, and a record number of thirty-nine Israelis had been killed in Lebanon in 1997. Since the creation of the nine-mile so-called "security zone" in 1985, 200 Israeli soldiers had been killed fighting guerrillas. Netanyahu and his defense minister, Yitzhak Mordechai, declared a readiness to accept UN Security Council Resolution 425, passed in 1978, which called for a unilateral Israeli retreat to the international border, but only if Lebanon guaranteed that the Lebanese army would move into southern Lebanon to prevent Hezbollah attacks on northern Israel. Such a guarantee would of course need the backing of Syrian President Hafez Assad, who kept 35,000 troops in Lebanon, and who wanted any pullback linked to an agreement on the Golan Heights taken by Israel in the 1967 war. Lebanon, after discussions with Syria, refused to negotiate security arrangements, saying that Israel had to withdraw unconditionally. A Hezbollah leader said that Lebanon should not give Israel guarantees, and that Israel had accepted Resolution 425 "as a result of blows by the Islamic resistance." He added in an interview that the Lebanese army would be responsible for security if the Israelis left, and "we will not intervene."[4]

The majority of the Israeli cabinet, eleven to seven, accepted the Netanyahu-Mordechai plan. Sharon offered an alternative plan, which was to withdraw in stages, after warning Lebanon that any guerrilla attacks would prompt massive Israeli retaliation against Beirut. "I propose a redeployment after a warning," he said, "setting very clear rules, withdrawing from a portion of the area, allowing the Lebanese to enter, announcing in advance what we're about to do." He stressed that he accepted UN Resolution 425, but not with any connection to the Golan Heights. "It is inconceivable," he said, "that life in Lebanon should proceed as usual while we spill our blood on the soil." Mordechai rejected Sharon's plan, saying that it would put northern Israel in danger, and that he objected to any proposal that would aggravate the situation on the ground if a vacuum were created by IDF withdrawal. Sharon responded that it would certainly be better if an agreement could be reached, but obviously he did not think this would happen. Rather ironically, this opinion was held also by some strong Labor supporters of unilateral withdrawal, one of whom, Yossi Beilin, said, "If the [Mordechai] plan means leaving Lebanon only on condition of an agreement with Lebanon and Syria, regretfully it will not happen."[5]

The Lebanon plan was not the only challenge Sharon issued to Netanyahu in 1998. In May, he refused to accompany the prime minister to Washington for talks on troop withdrawals from the West Bank, even though Sharon was already in the United States at the time. Netanyahu was under great pressure from the United States because he had failed to comply with Oslo II: he had not implemented either of the two required withdrawals from West Bank areas, had released no prisoners, and had not given the PA air and sea access in Gaza. For his part, Arafat had not changed his covenant calling for the destruction of Israel, and had not cracked down on terrorists. Now Secretary of State Madeleine Albright was pressuring Netanyahu to agree to withdrawal from thirteen percent of the West Bank, while Sharon insisted that giving up more than nine percent of the land would threaten Israel's security. He issued a statement from New York, saying that he didn't see any reason to meet with the Secretary of State before the Israeli cabinet voted on the pullback. To do so, he said, would be to mislead her.[6]

Netanyahu was in a bind, pressured on the one hand to accept the thirteen percent not only by the Americans, Jordan and Egypt, but by his defense minister Yitzhak Mordechai, while the right wing put pressure on him to make no concessions. Arafat threatened to declare a Palestinian state in one year, when the Oslo accords were due to expire, a step that could lead to war. By September, since Netanyahu had given the Clinton administration sufficient reason to believe that he was going to accept the thirteen percent withdrawal, he and Arafat were invited to come to Washington to engage in negotiations. At the end of September, right-wing members of the Likud coalition, upset by reports from America that indicated a deal was in the works, announced that they were going to embark on a campaign to oust Netanyahu if he accepted the thirteen percent figure. About sixty-four members of the 120-seat Knesset signed a petition calling for early elections. On September 28, extreme right-wing groups published a "Map of Calamity" in the *Jerusalem Post*, showing what would happen to various settlements if the thirteen percent withdrawal was implemented. Printed with the map was a warning to the prime minister: "If it becomes a fact . . . then we promise to topple you, and not to reelect you to a second term."

To tamp down this rising danger, Netanyahu let it be known that he was considering offering the foreign minister post, which he himself had been filling since the resignation of David Levy, to Ariel Sharon. In the London *Times*, Christopher Walker commented that despite his hawkish reputation, Sharon was "respected by many Arabs as a man of his word who is able to deliver." They remembered, Walker said, that in 1979, to ensure the peace pact with Egypt, Sharon had supervised the forcible evacuation of 8000 Israeli settlers from a Sinai outpost, and had demolished their homes. In addition, Sharon was "much more powerful than his portfolio would indicate, and he has already held secret talks with Palestinian officials."[7]

The prospect of this appointment caused a considerable stir in the press. It was noted that on October 1, Sharon and Netanyahu were observed dining with their wives at a Chinese restaurant in Tel Aviv, apparently having a serious discussion. It was recalled that a year earlier, Sharon had reacted to Netanyahu's decision to withdraw Israeli troops from eighty percent of Hebron by calling the prime minister "a dangerous man for the state of Israel" and adding, "I do not believe a word that leaves that man's mouth."[8] On October 9, Sharon was asked in a television interview whether he would vote for an agreement with the Palestinians. His reply was that as always he was against a thirteen-percent withdrawal. As for shaking Arafat's hand at the Washington summit, he responded that his stance had not changed on that either. The interviewer asked whether the title of foreign minister would give Sharon "rehabilitation and legitimacy" after the Sabra and Shatilla massacre; Sharon's response was angry: "I do not need anyone to give me legitimacy."[9]

THE WYE CONFERENCE: 1998

———

THE NEXT DAY, A WEEK before the Washington summit, Netanyahu named Sharon to the foreign minister post. On Israeli television that night, Sharon repeated his conviction that nine percent and not thirteen, should be the limit. On the Palestinian side, the reaction was somewhat mixed. Arafat's aide Saeb Erekat commented that Sharon had "shed more Palestinian blood than any other Israeli," and his promotion was "a very bad omen" for peace negotiations.[1] This may have been for domestic consumption, because an unnamed Arafat aide said that "Sharon's appointment means that a resolution of the . . . conflict is imminent because he will give the agreement legitimacy on the Israeli side." Arafat commented only that it was up to the Israelis to decide on appointments.[2] It was generally agreed in the press that Sharon had been quietly talking with Palestinian negotiators for a year, and that they respected him, but distrusted Netanyahu.

Ehud Barak, the Labor Party head, said that Sharon's appointment was "a recipe for a continued stalemate in the peace talks and an escalation of clashes with the Palestinians."[3] It was suggested that Labor oppose the appointment, but the new election law had repealed the requirement for a Knesset vote on cabinet appointments. Sharon himself muddied the waters by telling the cabinet that if they had any reservations about Netanyahu's position, they should speak up before any deals were signed. "Shackle our hands and our legs now," he said, "and tell us what your parameters are.

You won't have another opportunity later." Natan Sharansky, minister for industry and trade, immediately asked for a special meeting of the security cabinet to discuss negotiating points and perhaps vote on them, but Netanyahu refused that suggestion as well as Yitzhak Mordechai's and Sharansky's request that the trip to Washington be postponed.[4] Netanyahu was asked on television, "When . . . the new foreign minister . . . calls on the ministers to shackle you and tie your hands and feet, who will actually believe that Israel is coming to make peace at the summit in good faith?" Netanyahu, obviously uncomfortable, talked around the question, and, pressed further, finally said, "There is no need to shackle or handcuff us."[5]

The sticking points to be ironed out at the meeting, in addition to the thirteen percent withdrawal, were the demand for a PA crackdown on Hamas and other terrorists; a suspension of Jewish settlement activity; an elimination of the Palestinian charter calling for the destruction of Israel; safe passage between Gaza and the West Bank; the release by Israel of 3500 Palestinian prisoners; and the handing over to Israel of thirty accused terrorists; the question of Jerusalem and the so-called Right of Return of Palestinian refugees.

Netanyahu arrived in Maryland on October 15, 1998, for the opening of talks at the secluded Wye River Plantation on the shores of Chesapeake Bay seventy miles from Washington. Sharon flew from Israel to Minnesota to visit King Hussein, who had been undergoing chemotherapy at the Mayo Clinic since July. This was an emotional and dramatic meeting. It signalled Hussein's acceptance of Sharon's new role in the government, and Sharon's respect for an honored Arab leader, but it was also a heartfelt encounter between two old friends. "There is no other leader in the Middle East," Sharon said of the king, "with so much experience and so many years in office . . . He is in good shape, high spirits and has demonstrated courage, which he is known for."[6] The king was to lose his battle against cancer less than four months later, on February 7, 1999.

From Minnesota, Sharon flew to New York where he spent the Sabbath, and then arrived at Wye on October 18, two days into the conference which had begun on the Thursday; some thought his late arrival had been deliberately timed so that he could avoid greeting Arafat at the outset. Still, it was believed by many that he would be pressured into a handshake at Wye. According to reports, Sharon strode confidently into the room, introduced by Netanyahu as "General Sharon." Arafat straightened up and saluted, but Sharon ignored him, shaking hands first with Clinton and then with Mahmoud Abbas, Arafat's deputy, and Ahmed Qurei, speaker of the Palestinian Legislative Council. Sharon was seated directly across from Arafat, but he avoided looking at him while he talked animatedly to everyone else at the table about Palestinian concerns. A Sharon aide said there was no way Sharon would shake hands with Arafat, but that would have no effect on his engaging in serious negotiations. The two matters, the aide said, were "unrelated." Nevertheless, the Americans worried that Sharon would harden Israeli attitudes against compromise; they asked Mordechai to postpone his departure so that he could act as a leavening influence. The Palestinians insisted that Arafat was not upset by Sharon's behavior. "Sharon was responsible for the killing in cold blood of about six thousand Palestinian families in Lebanon," one source said, "but we're here to negotiate and not to flex our muscles."[7]

Although the press was excluded from Wye, it was leaked that things were not going well; President Clinton had to intervene three times in four days, and an announcement was made that the talks, which had been scheduled to end with a signing ceremony at the White House on Monday morning, would be extended for an unexpected fifth day. The Israelis wanted specific commitments on fighting terrorism, and they wanted fewer Palestinian police and the confiscation of unlicensed weapons.[8]

The Americans, who, in addition to Secretary of State Albright, included National Security Advisor Samuel Berger and CIA Director George Tenet, attempted to draft compromise agreements under which the Palestinians themselves would arrest and imprison accused terrorists while the CIA would judge whether the Israeli accusations against them were justified. There were rumors of shouting matches between Netanyahu and Arafat, not least over the Israeli's insistence on calling the West Bank "Judea and Samaria."[9] The situation was not helped by a Palestinian grenade attack on civilians in Israel during the talks. "The issues are difficult," Clinton said. "The distrust is deep. The going has been tough." Pressure was also applied by King Hussein, who flew to his home in Maryland from Minnesota, and by Egyptian President Hosni Mubarak.[10]

On October 23, 1998, ending more than a year and a half of tension and nine days of negotiations, the Wye River Memorandum was signed in the East Room of the White House by Netanyahu and Arafat, with King Hussein present despite his severe illness. At the last minute, Netanyahu tried to tie his agreement to the release of Jonathan Pollard, who was in an American prison because he had spied for Israel, but the prime minister backed off when Clinton called the demand ridiculous, adding, however, that he would take another look at the case. Netanyahu agreed to give the PA full or partial control of forty percent of the West Bank in three stages over three months, and to reduce zone C from seventy-two percent of the land to fifty-nine percent, transferring forty-one percent to zones A and B.

Arafat agreed to a "work plan" to combat terrorism in cooperation with the CIA, and to round up an open number of people on Israeli terrorist lists. He agreed further to convene a broad assembly of PA delegates to review the 1968 PA National Charter with a view to eliminating those clauses inimical to the peace process. There were also agreements on the safe passage routes between Gaza and the West Bank and a Gaza seaport. And it was agreed that continuous negotiations were to be held to reach a "permanent status" settlement by May 4, 1999, the original date set by the Oslo accords.[11]

That Israeli withdrawals were contingent upon the PA carrying out their commitments would seem in retrospect to offer reason to doubt the importance of the entire undertaking, and this was in fact what Netanyahu told the right wing at the time to justify his signing. Nevertheless many of them expressed dismay over the agreement, and it was widely expected that Sharon would refuse to sign it, even though he joined Netanyahu at Wye. His office issued a statement that the foreign minister noted the "considerable achievements in the agreement" but "everything naturally depends on the implementation." Rehavam Zeevi said Netanyahu had trampled on Israel's "self-respect. We got nothing at Wye, we only gave. . . . We will release terrorists and they will get an airport, a seaport . . ." There was talk among the extreme right and the settlers of calling for new elections. It had not been forgotten that when Netanyahu had agreed to withdraw troops from most of Hebron in January, 1997, he had become the first right-wing leader to give up Biblical land. Raful Eytan, the agriculture minister, announced two days after the signing that he had "absolutely no faith in the deal," which had been made necessary because "Arafat failed to live up to what he was supposed to do under the original Oslo accords. We need to talk now about amending the Palestinian Charter, collecting illegal arms and shrinking the PA's police because Arafat cheated from the beginning." Many in the Palestinian Legislative Council expressed distrust of Netanyahu and doubts that he would live up to his end of the agreement.[12]

It was reported that nervousness about the anger of the settlers and Jewish extremists caused security to be increased around Netanyahu, Sharon, Mordechai and Natan Sharansky; Netanyahu was flown from Ben-Gurion Airport to Jerusalem by helicopter to avoid protesters along the highway between Tel Aviv and Jerusalem.[13] Extremists called the Wye Memorandum an "act of treason," but after being accused of using the kind of language that had led to the assassination of Rabin, they called it an "act of surrender." Since they detected no groundswell of national rage to back them up, they decided to respond politically to the accords.

The response from the left was approving, but often cool. Ehud Barak, the chairman of the Labor Party, said that he was glad a deal had been reached, but he could not say that he was excited about it: "This is far from what we need to make peace and this government is totally incapable of making peace. Only a Labor government can bring real peace to Israel." Labor would vote for the agreement, he said, but at the same time work hard to advance the elections; Labor would win, "and then Israel will have peace." Shimon Peres called Wye a victory for the Oslo accords, which many people had said were dead. He was happy that an agreement had been reached, but he warned about problems ahead. When opinion polls showed overwhelming public approval of the peace accords, some Likud cabinet members began to temper their attitudes. The communications minister said, "From what we hear of the deal it is not completely without its achievements. There are some improvements on what we had before. . . . The test will be how much reciprocity there really is here."

Yossi Beilin said that Netanyahu had "meandered" into the peace "unintentionally," while Yossi Sarid said that the same thing could have been achieved long ago "with less destruction of good will with the Palestinians and needless acrimony with the Americans."[14]

Sharon, in a TV interview, said, "We participated in very tough negotiations, perhaps the most difficult ever. In the circumstances . . . I believe we achieved the best results possible. We reduced the dangers. There is no comparison between what Labor was ready to accept or the early US proposal and what we managed to achieve. I expressed my opinion that the scope of the withdrawal is broad and dangerous. That was my position before and that is still my position, but the agreement in general is the best that could have been achieved under the existing circumstances." They had achieved, he said, things that had never been achieved before, "including the annulment of the Palestinian charter . . . [and] a reduction in the size of the Palestinian security forces," something Labor had never demanded. "[The agreement] calls for the imprisonment of terrorists under supervision and, perhaps most important, it contains a detailed working plan to fight the terrorist organizations."

Asked whether he had changed his opinion that Arafat was a war criminal and a terrorist leader, he said he had not, but he preferred to talk about substantive issues. The interviewer pointed out that Sharon had refused to shake Arafat's hand, although he had talked with him, reached an agreement, and had honored him by standing when he finished his speech. "I rose in his honor because the ceremony was at the White House," Sharon said. "The entire audience stood up and so did I—there is such a thing as protocol. But I did not applaud. I did the minimum necessary." He went on to say that a Palestinian state would present a problem. "The danger . . . is that a [Palestinian] state could sign a treaty with Iran or Iraq." The government, he said, "decided to achieve peace. In my opinion, we have to make every effort to achieve peace, but it must be a peace that gives security to Israel and its citizens everywhere and that is what we have achieved."[15]

Some members of the Likud were disturbed by the fact that Israel had not been given access to the secret US-Palestinian security appendix to the Wye accord, so Netanyahu could not present it to his cabinet. In order to assuage the Israelis' distrust of Arafat, the CIA director, George Tenet, had offered at Wye to have his agents monitor the PA anti-terrorist efforts. This, according to Steve Posner, was an idea Arafat readily accepted because he had had a good experience with the CIA in the early 1980s when Secretary of State George Shultz arranged to make Robert Ames, CIA Beirut station chief, a key Mideast advisor to the National Security Council.

Ames, a sympathetic spokesman for the PLO, spoke fluent Arabic and had been rewarded for his distinctive service in Yemen, Kuwait and Iran by a rapid rise through the CIA ranks. While the

PLO was pinned in Beirut by Sharon in 1982, Ames was holding secret meetings with Arafat, his deputy Abu Jihad and Hassan Salameh, whom Steve Posner identifies as the "mastermind" behind the massacre of Israeli athletes at the Munich Olympics. Ames helped to formulate Reagan's Mideast peace plan calling for "the peaceful and orderly transfer of authority from Israel to the Palestinian inhabitants of the West Bank and Gaza," and showed Arafat a copy of the plan. It was never implemented, but the Israelis complained that it gave Arafat legitimacy and new life at a time when they thought they were crushing him once and for all. They denounced Ames as an advocate for the PLO. Ironically, he was killed in 1983 when Lebanese Muslim terrorists blew up the American Embassy in Beirut. In any case, the US brokered a deal that allowed the PLO to find refuge in Tunis where Arafat set up headquarters, and where he was nearly killed in 1985 by Israeli pilots guided by satellite photos secretly conveyed to them by Jonathan Pollard, the spy whose release Netanyahu failed to win at Wye.[16]

38

AFTER WYE

———

IN MID-NOVEMBER, THE KNESSET overwhelmingly endorsed the Wye agreement. But it was Labor and moderates who carried the day. Most of the Likud coalition either abstained or voted no, although at the end of October, a large gathering of Likud central committee members had given Netanyahu a raucously friendly reception, cheering him when he said that he had brought back "tremendous achievements from Wye" and "If the Palestinians give, they will get. If they won't give, they won't get." He had announced the creation of a new leadership team, consisting of himself, his defense minister Yitzhak Mordechai and Sharon, who also gave a rousing and well-received speech. The *Jerusalem Post* found Mordechai simply boring. Despite this successful meeting, Israel TV reported that many government officials were saying that Netanyahu's political life now depended on Sharon's support.[1]

But before the Knesset vote on November 17, the atmosphere had been poisoned for a week or so by unpleasant words from all sides. On the Sunday before the vote, Arafat gave a speech, broadcast on radio, threatening a new intifada if Palestinians were blocked access to holy Muslim sites in Jerusalem. "Those who are far and near must understand," he said, "that our guns are ready. We will take them up if they try to stop us from praying in Jerusalem." Netanyahu, already fending off attack from his own core supporters because of Wye, phoned Arafat to ask him about his remarks, but also responded in kind in a Knesset debate: "I don't intend to carry out any redeployment under these conditions, not even the first, until this is rectified publicly and unequivocally." Israel had already missed the November 16 deadline for a troop pullback from the first two percent of the West Bank. "As for Jerusalem," Netanyahu added, "I have old news for our Palestinian neighbors. Jerusalem was, is and will be the capital of the state of Israel."[2]

Attempts were made to pour some oil on these troubled waters. Saeb Erekat, a senior PA negotiator, responded to Netanyahu that "President Arafat has always and will always say that the strategic choice is the peace process." Arafat announced that he was "still committed to the peace process," and David Bar-Illan, an aide to Netanyahu, remarked, "At the beginning, it's almost to be expected that there will be all these bumps." Netanyahu followed his Knesset address by saying the withdrawal would be carried out within a few days, if the Palestinians began acting "within the spirit of the accord."[3]

Sharon, on the other hand, certainly made matters worse when, on the same Sunday as Arafat's intifada threat, he said in a speech to a right-wing political group, "Everyone should take action, should run, should grab more hills. We'll expand the area. Whatever is seized will be ours. Whatever isn't seized will end up in their hands."[4] This was an unexpected exhortation from the foreign minister who publicly supported the Wye agreement that he had helped to negotiate. Even before Sharon made his comments, settlers had begun at night to set up mobile homes and pitch tents illegally on several hilltops in the disputed territories before being evicted by the IDF in the morning. Now Sharon certainly appeared to be encouraging them in this illegal activity, to seize land before the Wye agreement could be activated.

Palestinian radio reported that in a meeting in the presidential office in Gaza, Arafat told Secretary of Commerce William Daley that he considered Sharon's remarks to be a violation of the Wye accord. Since he had not mentioned specific hilltops, nor made clear whether these were inside or outside existing settlements, Sharon was able to try to tamp down the uproar he had created by explaining that he was only talking about "hills that dominate the existing settlements," within current settlement boundaries, and that he was trying to decrease future tensions, not exacerbate them.[5]

A few days later, while the settlers were still seizing hilltops, Sharon met in Jerusalem with Abu Mazen, Arafat's deputy, to discuss a "final status" or permanent peace accord. The points under discussion included the settlements, the "right of return" of Palestinian refugees, and the status of Jerusalem. The idea of these talks had been initiated in 1996 by Yitzhak Rabin and Shimon Peres; only one meeting had been held before Netanyahu had taken over. Now this second talk would appear to indicate a sincere desire for peace on the part of the Israeli government. But David Horovitz pointed out that these actions had to be weighed in light of the fact that Netanyahu could not afford to alienate the settlers, whose support had been crucial for him.[6]

After that meeting, Sharon went to Jordan with Trade and Industry Minister Natan Sharansky to sign an economic agreement and discuss a water desalination project. Sharon's official reception was pleasant, since both King Hussein, who was still recuperating from cancer treatments in the United States, and his brother Crown Prince Hassan had friendly feelings toward him. "We welcomed Mr Sharon in his first visit since the signing of the Wye Memo," the prince announced in English. But Israeli TV reported that the Jordanian press did not welcome Sharon. They began to ask him about the release of Palestinian prisoners. Sharon replied, "We will not release people with blood on their hands." This answer evoked questions and comments about Sharon's responsibility for the massacre at Sabra and Shatilla. "It was a very grave incident," Sharon said, "in which Christian Arabs seriously harmed Muslim Arabs. None of us was involved in it."[7]

The journalists were not disposed to accept this response. One newspaper commented that not only Sharon's hands, but his entire body, was covered in blood, and he should not have been allowed to come to Jordan at all.[8]

Israeli TV observed that peace with Jordan had taken one step forward and one step back. But Sharansky told Israel radio that ties with Jordan had improved, that the talks had been positive, and that as far as the final status arrangements with the PA were concerned, it was "no secret that Jordan would prefer not to have a strong Palestinian state in its neighborhood. No wonder, therefore that Crown Prince Hassan was particularly interested in hearing Minister Sharon's ideas on the permanent status arrangement." A Palestinian delegation was going to visit Jordan shortly to discuss the same issues.[9]

Jordanian radio underscored Sharansky's evaluation. "The meeting was very constructive," and a joint statement expressed "the hope that the Wye agreement would bolster regional cooperation in the interests of Jordan, Israel and the Palestinians." The aim was to have a continuing dialogue to help bolster "relations in the interest of all peoples of the region."[10]

But the region was a long way from constructive dialogue, although Israel began to comply with the Wye accord, withdrawing on November 20 from two percent of the West Bank, mostly around Jenin. After that the airport in Gaza was opened, and 250 of the promised 750 Palestinian prisoners were released. The Palestinians complained that the majority of these were common criminals and only one hundred were militants, but the Israelis responded that Wye was not specific on this point. On December 14, the clauses in the Palestinian charter calling for the destruction of Israel were nullified by an assembly of Palestinian delegates attended by President Clinton, the first American president to set foot on Palestinian soil.[11]

39

FAILING COALITION, FAILING PEACE

———

THE PALESTINIAN DEMAND FOR the release of more political prisoners led to street violence involving Israeli soldiers and Palestinians. Secretary of State Madeleine Albright, in a joint press conference with Sharon, said that the pullback on the West Bank had to go forward on the Wye timetable. "We think that Wye is very carefully written," she said, "and we want to see both sides carry out what they need to do." But Sharon told her that the second stage of withdrawal, due on December 18, could not be implemented. He also warned that if the PA declared a state in May of 1999, Israel would immediately annex parts of the West Bank. During separate meetings with Albright and Dennis Ross, the US Mideast special envoy, Sharon said that Israel wanted to implement the withdrawal, but gross Palestinian violations had made it impossible: "circumstances are such that nothing can now be done to make the government take a different path."[1]

In actual fact, Netanyahu was under tremendous pressure from the right wing to cancel the redeployments. They threatened to bring down the government if the Wye accord was honored, while the moderates, including Mordechai, threatened a no-confidence vote if the government did not honor the Wye accord. Netanyahu was trying hard to save his government. When David Levy angrily took his party out of the Likud coalition, the prime minister tried to win him back by offering him the finance minister position, pulling the rug, so to speak, out from under Yaakov Neeman. Levy refused this, and Netanyahu reassured Neeman that his job was safe; Levy could only come back as minister of national infrastructure.

Most of his cabinet wanted him to form a national unity coalition, but Netanyahu said that Labor had not supported him on any issue, "not even our opposition to the release of terrorist murderers, not even our fight against the unilateral declaration of a Palestinian state with Jerusalem as its capital. While the PA engaged in the most venemous incitement, we hear the Labor party chairman [Ehud Barak] expressing understanding for the Arab position and castigating the government of Israel." At the same time, Netanyahu rejected what he called "any attempt at blackmail" by the far right; his sympathies and instincts lay with them nevertheless.[2]

Sharon carried Netanyahu's message, of the refusal to implement Wye, to the Clinton administration in Washington and to Kofi Annan in New York in the first weeks of December. In New York he spoke to a gathering of American Jewish leaders, telling them that the Palestinians needed to change their covenant by a formal vote and "not by dancing, shouting, applauding, but by raising hands." The Palestinian National Council should be revived, he said, to vote on the covenant. "They signed it," he said, referring to the Wye agreement, "now they have to do it."[3]

When he got back to Jerusalem, he told a Likud gathering that the government now believed that things had reached the point where early elections were preferable to the impossible task of holding the coalition together.[4] The prime minister had a two-vote majority in the Knesset, but the extreme right in his coalition had turned against him because of the withdrawals. On December 21, the Knesset voted eighty-one to thirty to dissolve the government and hold early elections, Netanyahu voting with the majority.

On December 27, Sharon stated clearly that he had no intention of running for prime minister in the coming elections, which were set for May, 1999, and urged the Likud to support Netanyahu. "We must close ranks," he said, "around the man who was elected to head the movement because there is simply no other choice in a democracy."[5] But a few days later, he said he would not rule out the possibility of entering the race "under exceptional circumstances."[6] Rumors were spreading that since polls showed Netanyahu ten points behind Labor's Ehud Barak, Sharon was thinking of starting a new party and had talked to Dan Meridor and Benjamin Begin who had both defected from the Likud and were running separately for prime minister, about joining it. Sharon denied this, and in any case, if there were such a conspiracy, it never got anywhere.

40

FOREIGN AFFAIRS

—

In January, 1999, Sharon traveled to the US, France, Germany and Russia. In New York he met with US special envoy Dennis Ross, having been snubbed by Madeleine Albright, who was reportedly upset over Israel's failure to implement the Wye accords. In their three-hour meeting, Ross complained that the Israelis were blaming the Palestinian Authority for preventing the implementation of the Wye accord. Sharon said that Israel was committed to the agreement, but that Palestinians were not fulfilling their own commitments. Adding injury to insult, when Sharon got home, he was not only forced to discuss the snub, but he was docked a day's pay by the Knesset Ethics Committee for absenteeism. He protested that he was busy with matters of state and meetings of the security cabinet, but the committee pointed out that he had missed twenty-five out of thirty-eight sessions, not counting the six absences ministers were permitted.[1]

In connection with the Albright snub, Sharon said that the US held the position that the Palestinians had kept most of their commitments, while Israel had not. He had no intention, he said, of "paying a price for a meeting" with Albright. He rejected the suggestion that there was a "crisis" in US-Israeli relations, saying that relations with the US were better than they had ever been before. "It is sad for both sides that there was not a meeting," he went on, but Israel did not have to prove anything. "I do not know any other country in the world that would transfer parts of its homeland for peace." These statements did not prevent Labor's Yossi Sarid from telling Sharon that "the whole world is running away from you."[2]

In Paris, Sharon met with Foreign Minister Hubert Vedrine, and dismissed another snub, this time by President Jacques Chirac and other officials, saying again that "the Israeli government was not prepared to sacrifice the country's vital interests in exchange for meetings." He managed to create something of a stir when asked in an interview with Le Monde whether he could contemplate the idea of a Palestinian state, he replied, "Autonomy will lead to a Palestinian state."[3] This remark caused Shimon Peres to tell the Israeli press that Sharon's position was now close to his. Sharon protested that there were major differences between their positions. "He [Peres] speaks enthusiastically about a Palestinian state, while I speak of a limited sovereignty," he said, "One should not use the term 'state' in the usual concept that one uses when talking of states." He took a further slap at Peres, saying that "[u]nfortunately . . . it sounds to me like he is representing the Palestinians, whereas I am representing the Jewish state."[4]

In his Le Monde interview, Sharon said that if the PA unilaterally declared a state on May 4, Israel would annex all the territories still under its control. "There is no question of our trying to recover Gaza, Nablus or Jenin," he said. "But all the rest that is in our hands today will remain so."[5]

Addressing the French Institute for Foreign Relations, he outlined his plans for two buffer zones that he believed would have to exist on either side of the West Bank, and said that Israel would continue to control security over air space and seaports in a new Palestinian state. One buffer zone would be in the thinly populated Jordan Rift Valley between the West Bank and Jordan, and the other along the old cease-fire line that was Israel's border before the June, 1967 Six-Day War. "For us," he said, "a real independent Palestinian state is a real danger. Therefore, what they call a state would be within the limits and conditions they would have to accept if they got what they called a Palestinian state. There will be limitations of weapons, there will be limitations of alliances with other countries, and Israel will have the right to fly over this area." And there would be no open borders between the two states. In a testy exchange with Arab journalists based in Paris, Sharon lectured them "to advise the Palestinians not to waste time but to begin negotiating with us."[6]

In Germany, after talks with Foreign Minister Joschka Fischer, he told reporters that Israel had implemented "the first phase of the Wye accord" and was ready to negotiate with Syria and Lebanon. But he warned Arafat against a unilateral announcement of the establishment of a Palestinian state. Fischer, seeming to endorse Sharon's stance, said there should be a mutually agreed implementation of the Wye accord.

In Moscow, Sharon received a full reception from Prime Minister Yevgeny Primakov, members of his cabinet, the chairman of the Duma and the mayor of Moscow. Foreign Minister Igor Ivanov said that they felt sure that the visit would further relations between the peoples of Russia and Israel, and that these discussions would promote cooperation in matters of "international stability and security."[7]

Primakov, a former foreign minister who spoke Arabic, told Sharon that Russia intended to play a more active role in the Middle East "in questions relating to Israeli-Palestinian reconciliation and will make further efforts to encourage negotiations." Sharon said in a press interview that he welcomed Russia's renewed interest in the region, because Russia, despite its present problems, remained a superpower with enormous potential. When he was asked why relations between the two countries were not warmer, he replied, "There are problems that are hampering the process." The first of these, he said, was the help Russia was giving Iran "to create ballistic missile delivery systems and develop its nuclear potential." Moscow protested that it was simply building a nuclear power plant in Iran with nothing military in view.[8]

Sharon implied that Primakov was willing to play "a significant role" in interceding for Israel with hostile states, and that the
Russian prime minister recognized the danger of international terrorism from extremist Islamic groups. He emphasized that although
Primakov did not agree with him on everything, there was a good
chance that relations with Russia were going to be "completely different" from the way they had been in the past. The reason, he said,
was that "Russia's attitude to Jews" had changed fundamentally
and all the officials with whom he spoke "sharply and emphatically
condemned anti-Semitism." He believed that the Russian leadership accepted the Israeli position "that any unilateral proclamation
of statehood" would violate the agreements.[9]

Not unconnected with his relations with the Russians was his
position on the situation in Kosovo. When two liberal MKs proposed freezing ties with Yugoslavia and recalling the ambassador
from Belgrade in response to news of the massacre of forty-five ethnic Albanians in that province, Sharon said that Israel was observ-
ing all international sanctions imposed on Yugoslavia, was monitoring events in Kosovo with the rest of the international community, and had officially protested the massacre to the Yugoslav ambassador. At the same time, he said, Israel supported "the territorial
sovereignty of Yugoslavia," would offer humanitarian aid to victims and hoped the rights of the Albanians in Kosovo would be
ensured.[10]

Toward the end of January, Netanyahu named Moshe Arens as
defense minister, replacing Yitzhak Mordechai. Sharon received this
news by telling the press that he himself had been offered the defense post, and had turned it down, because he was happy with his
two ministries, Foreign and Infrastructure. An aide to Netanyahu
said that Sharon's name had come up in discussions, but no formal
offer had been made. It was bruited abroad that it was doubtful
that Sharon could be given the Defense post because he had been
forced out of that position in 1983 by the Kahan Commission re-

port. Sharon showed little enthusiasm for Arens, and no sympathy for Mordechai whose dismissal he supported. When he was reminded that he had made disparaging comments about Arens in the past, Sharon said reporters should forget about the past; he was thinking about the future.[11]

He had his hands full, in fact, fending off dissatisfaction in the international community with Israel's compliance with the Wye accord. In mid-January, the United Nations—with the support of members of the European Union—adopted a resolution calling for a conference of the signatories to the 1949 Fourth Geneva Convention to be convened on July 15 to consider measures to enforce the convention "in the occupied Palestinian territory, including Jerusalem." In a meeting at his Negev farm with an EU envoy, Sharon responded, as he habitually did, that it was the Palestinians who were not living up to their commitments and that "Israel would not accept dictates from any party on issues relating to its security." But he asked the envoy, Miguel Moratinos, who was going to Damascus, to carry the message that Israel was ready to reopen peace talks with Syria on the matter of the Golan Heights, which Israel had occupied in the 1967 war.[12] Earlier in that week, the Knesset passed the Golan Law, requiring the agreement of sixty members of the 120-seat parliament to any proposal to give up any part of Israeli territory, and mandating, after the May elections, a national referendum, in addition to the Knesset majority, to approve any decision to give up land.

A meeting in Washington with Israel, the Palestinians and the Americans, scheduled for February, was abruptly vetoed by Sharon, who told Edward Walker, the American ambassador, that there was no point in a meeting like that until the Palestinians fulfilled their commitments under the Wye agreement. Arafat, however, was going to be in Washington anyway, for a meeting with President Clinton in which he was expected to ask for a statement that Israel was not honoring the accord, while the Palestinians had done their part.

Netanyahu and Sharon sent aides to Washington to undermine the meeting by charging that the Palestinians had released thirty Islamic militants in violation of the accord, but Israeli radio reported that a top Palestinian security agent had provided US officials with evidence that these Israeli allegations were false.

41

THE END OF AN ERA

In THE FIRST WEEK OF February, 1999, King Hussein died, having lost his long battle with cancer. His funeral was an important international event. But even before the funeral Netanyahu and Sharon paid a good will visit to Crown Prince Abdullah, Hussein's son, whom Hussein had named his successor on January 25, two weeks before his death, in place of the king's brother Hassan. Asked whether Abdullah had invited the Israelis to come, Sharon would say only, "We do not spend day in and day out dealing with honor games," thus giving the impression that he and Netanyahu had invited themselves. What was important, Sharon said, was the real issue of cooperation between Israel and Jordan, and the Israeli desire to strengthen that cooperation.[1] It was certainly remembered in Israel that King Hussein had attended Yitzhak Rabin's funeral in 1995 and had outraged hostile Arab nations by his heartfelt tribute to the assassinated Israeli leader. Yassir Arafat had not attended.

Hussein's funeral was remarkable for the wide disparity between the political figures who attended. It was the first time that Hafez al-Assad of Syria, who had often differed with Hussein, shared an event with an Israeli leader, even though the Jordanians made sure that Assad and Netanyahu did not encounter each other. Bill Clinton did speak with Assad, as well as with Boris Yeltsin and the leaders of friendly Gulf states, but he kept away from the Iraqi delegation. There were signs of thawed relationships. Muammar Quaddafi sent his son, and the presence of the Kuwaiti prime minister showed that the emirate had forgiven Jordan for King Hussein's support of Saddam Hussein during the Gulf war.[2]

The atmosphere of good will enveloped Ezer Weizman, the Israeli president, who shook hands in the palace chambers with Nayef Hawatmeh, the Syrian-based leader of the radical Democratic Front for the Liberation of Palestine. This was the group that in 1974 had invaded a school in Maalot in a hostage operation in which more than twenty schoolchildren were killed. This incident of the handshake—in a region where handshakes or refusal of them represent matters of principle—underlined the chasm that existed between Netanyahu's government and his doveish opponents. Before the day was out, Netanyahu and Sharon denounced Weizman's action. "I think we should talk to those who want us on earth rather than buried beneath it," Netanyahu observed.

"True," Weizman responded, "Hawatmeh murdered, but he was willing to extend to me a hand and to speak with me. It is not a pleasure to speak with him. But through him it is possible to arrive at all kinds of things." An aide to Weizman, who had greeted Hawatmeh in Arabic and brought up the topic of peace with Syria and Lebanon, said that an Israeli Arab aide to Arafat had offered to introduce Weizman to Hawatmeh, who had extended his hand. Hawatmeh denied this on Israeli radio, saying that it was Weizman who made the advances to him and first held out his hand.

Netanyahu said he had instantly recognized Hawatmeh from the days when the prime minister had served in an army unit that fought against the militants. "They wanted to murder Jews then, and today he remains committed to the murder of Jews," Netanyahu said. "With such a person I don't shake hands."

Weizman responded angrily that this was an era of peacemaking; Arafat was now Israel's partner in a peace agreement. "What was Arafat, an angel?" he asked. "A dove of peace? He murdered and did all sorts of things. Yet he reached a point where he decided for the good of people he needed to make peace. Yitzhak Rabin shook his hand. I'm for shaking the hand of every person who is willing to shake my hand." He was completely at peace with himself, he said, and he agreed with Vladimir Jabotinsky who had said that he was "ready to meet Satan if it would help the Jewish people."

Commenting on this flap, Deborah Sontag noted in the *New York Times* that when Netanyahu had signed the peace agreement in October, experts had said that there were now fewer differences between Likud and Labor, and that both camps supported the peace effort. But "the debate over the handshake revealed profoundly different attitudes toward peacemaking among those who may seem to agree on paper." She thought it "also pointed up a potential for absurdity in Israeli political machismo."[3]

42

POLITICS 1999

———

In February, as the May elections drew near, Sharon's lawyer announced that the police were investigating his client on suspicion of bribery in Sharon's 1997 libel suit against the newspaper *Haaretz*. At the time of this announcement Sharon was in New York, where his wife Lily was receiving urgent treatment at Sloan-Kettering Cancer Center. *Haaretz* had won the suit, but it was on appeal to the Israeli Supreme Court and *Haaretz* was alleging that Sharon had bribed General Avigdor Ben-Gal to recant his charge, made twelve years earlier in a lecture at Tel Aviv University, that Sharon had deceived Menachem Begin and his cabinet about his intentions in Lebanon. The basis of the bribery investigation was that two weeks before his 1997 testimony, Ben-Gal, chairman of Israel Aircraft Industries, had accompanied Sharon to Russia to explore a deal on importing natural gas. Yossi Sarid, chairman of the leftist Meretz Party, had joined *Haaretz* in urging an investigation. It was strange, Sarid said, that Ben-Gal had not bothered to exonerate Sharon earlier, and had changed his story only after going to Russia with him and expecting a share of the natural gas deal.[1]

There were immediate accusations from the right that this was a politically motivated investigation. The Police Inspector General protested that the probe had been launched seven months earlier before anyone knew that there would be early elections. Uri Dan pointed out in the *New York Post* that the ultra-liberal *Haaretz* was known to hate Netanyahu and Sharon and that *Haaretz* was probably worried by the fact that Sharon's appeal included an affidavit from the Reagan Secretary of State Alexander Haig saying that at Sadat's funeral in October, 1981, Begin told him that Israel was planning military action in Lebanon, that he had no other choice if Arafat threatened Israel. "Specifically," Haig said, "Begin advised me that a large scale force would advance from the Israeli border to the southern suburbs of Beirut." Before the appeal could be heard, *Haaretz* filed its complaint with the police.[2]

Sharon's attorney Yaacov Weinroth said in a radio interview that a declaration had been taken from Ben-Gal on August 28, 1996, long before the trip to Russia, in which he said that it was clear that Begin "was aware of the possibility and even desired that the coming war would bring the IDF to Beirut in order to root out the terrorists from there." Weinroth also said, and Netanyahu confirmed, that the prime minister had suggested that Sharon take Ben-Gal with him to Russia because of his positions both on the board of directors of Israel Aircraft Industries and as director of Tahal, a water research and development company.[3]

At the end of February, with the election only three months away, Sharon was able to announce some good news. For five months the Israelis had been holding talks with the European Union in an attempt to gain participation in its research and development program, worth about fifteen billion US dollars over the next four years. Several EU members had objected in the past to Israel's inclusion because of its peace policies. But now the Council of Ministers of the EU voted fifteen to fourteen to allow Israel to participate in the program, set to begin in March. Sharon commented that this vote demonstrated confidence in Israeli scientific and technological abilities and agreement with Israel's position that research and development should not be politicized. Annual costs for Israel were to be about forty-five million US dollars, but Israeli companies and research institutions would be allowed to participate in various European research programs.[4]

At the beginning of March, Ehud Barak announced that if he won the May 17 elections, he would bring Israeli troops home from Lebanon within a year. More than 900 Israeli soldiers had died in Lebanon in the seventeen years that Israel had been there, with seven deaths in the so-called "buffer zone" in 1999 alone, and there was considerable frustration in Israel with the endless conflict. When Barak made his announcement, the IDF had just begun an intensive military campaign against Hezbollah guerrillas in south Lebanon after two roadside bombs killed an Israeli general, two soldiers and a journalist.

Barak's announcement, which put Lebanon at the heart of the campaign, caught his opposition by surprise. Sharon responded with a proposal that the May elections be postponed and a national "emergency" unity government formed, for a limited time, to work together to solve the Lebanon and Palestinian problems. It was in the national interest, he said, to present a united front in these two areas because bitter policy disagreements were weakening the country. Netanyahu at first agreed with this, and, signalling a change in policy, said he would now consider an unconditional withdrawal from Lebanon, commenting, "Barak's plan, that is if he really has one, should be presented before the minister of defense, myself and other security officials." But he added that he suspected it was "an election gimmick."[5]

David Horovitz commented that if they were asked, most Israelis would probably have accepted the logic of Sharon's plan. But Netanyahu shortly changed his mind and said that the elections would be held as scheduled on May 17 and that if he were reelected, he would be able to work out a solution in Lebanon and deal with the Palestinian situation without sharing power with the opposition. Labor too rejected Sharon's proposal as a gimmick, saying that it proved "that even Sharon realizes Netanyahu is a failure, and is incapable of managing the affairs of the state." Barak said that if he won, he would try to set up a unity government, although probably not including Netanyahu. President Ezer Weizman also rejected Sharon's idea, saying that with the election campaign under way, it was too late to create a unity government.[6]

In response to a letter to the Israeli Foreign Ministry, in which the EU called Jerusalem a separate entity, a *"corpus separatum,"* Sharon touched on another key issue in a speech in Jerusalem to foreign ambassadors at the King David Hotel. He said, "Resolution 181, which speaks about Jerusalem not being part of Israel, is null and void. We have a very wide national consensus about this issue."[7] He was referring to a 1947 UN resolution calling for Jerusalem to be internationalized, and to the objection of the majority of Israelis to granting Palestinians any official rights in the city. The UN considered east Jerusalem to be occupied territory. "It is very hard to imagine," he said, reminiscing about his days as a platoon commander in the 1948 war, probably to emphasize that for fifty years the city had been the nation's capital, "that after all those years we again have to struggle for Jerusalem." He considered that the UN resolution, which in any case had been rejected by the Arabs, had been rendered doubly irrelevant by Israel's military.

According to David Horovitz, the European diplomats were "decidedly under-whelmed by Mr Sharon's performance. One characterized it as a 'non-event,'" since the fact that the envoys had come from Tel Aviv to Jerusalem for this session demonstrated the EU's recognition of Israel's control of west Jerusalem, although Theodor Wallau, the ambassador to Israel from Germany, which held the EU presidency, maintained that the EU would be guided by the UN resolution. However, Mr Wallau stressed that the EU was not seeking a confrontation on the issue and was hopeful that it could be peacefully negotiated. Everyone was aware that politics were involved here. The Likud was claiming that it was best equipped to withstand international pressure on Israel, making the point that when he was head of the Labor Party in 1996, Shimon Peres was willing to allow the city to be divided between Jews and Arabs.

Barak, however, had made clear that he was not open to any compromise on the question of Jerusalem.[8]

The letter from the EU had been prompted by Sharon's action in notifying all embassies in Israel that a meeting of foreign ambassadors under PA auspices could not be held in Orient House, the gated building in east Jerusalem that Palestinians wished to use as their foreign ministry, a place where they could meet with visiting notables. Sharon said that such a meeting "would contravene all the agreements and would stand in total opposition to the government's position that Jerusalem is a united city, the capital of the Jewish people for 3000 years and Israel's eternal capital." He warned everyone concerned that the meeting could not be held. He said this issue had been raised by "broad Palestinian activity" in Europe to lay the groundwork for Jerusalem to become the capital of the Palestinian state.[9]

Ambassador Wallau objected strongly to this injunction, but in any case the Palestinians ignored it and convened a meeting at Orient House with about ten consuls-general and a good many journalists. Among the diplomats were representatives of Germany, France, Britain, Italy, Spain, Sweden and other EU nations, and Canada and Australia. The US Consul-General John Herbst did not attend. Netanyahu at first shrugged off the meeting as a thirty-year-old, meaningless standard procedure and then later punished the three Palestinians involved in the meeting—Ziad Abu Zayad, Hanan Ashrawi and Faisal Husseini, who hosted the affair—by revoking their special travel permits. His office issued a threat that "if the PA continues with such provocations and blatant breaking of the law in Jerusalem, our capital, Israel will respond with the utmost severity."[10]

He was undoubtedly irritated that the meeting gave his opponents an opening for attack. Ehud Barak said that "while Netanyahu talks endlessly about closing Orient House, he doesn't take real action. This is a government of gimmicks, full of troubles, that chooses to cry about bygones while Orient House is holding a party." The Center Party candidate charged that "Orient House is as much a Palestinian Foreign Ministry as ever." Husseini told the press that the meeting was routine, had nothing to do with the Israeli elections and that "there will be two capitals in Jerusalem, one in east Jerusalem that will be the capital of Palestine, and one in west Jerusalem that will be the capital of Israel."[11]

Sharon was decidedly on the defensive in an Israeli TV interview when Imanuel Rosen, one of the two interviewers, said to him that on "the main issue, the question of Jerusalem," which Sharon himself had brought to the fore, it was "one of two things: either you said you had closed down Orient House and now it turns out that you didn't, or you became obsessed yesterday with a trivial event, an unimportant meeting of consuls, and made a big deal out of it to make headlines in the election campaign." Sharon protested that the election had nothing to do with it; the Netanyahu government's position on Orient House represented a complete change from the previous administration. To which Rosen responded that the previous government had "put an end to the meetings of prime ministers, foreign ministers and ambassadors at Orient House." Sharon said that on the contrary, there had been about eighty meetings of these dignitaries at Orient House under the previous administration. Oshrat Kotler, the other interviewer, asked, "But the same is happening today, so what is the difference, really?"

Sharon, clearly backed into a corner, said it was not happening: "[T]he meeting yesterday was like other meetings consuls have been holding in east Jerusalem for thirty years, and there is nothing new about that." The logical next question, which Kotler asked, was, "So why revoke the VIP card of Hanan Ashrawi, Ziad Abu Zayad and others? Why punish them if it was such a routine event?" Sharon was forced to fall back on bombast about the steadfast position of the government.[12]

Through the Orient House flap, Netanyahu and Sharon had called attention to the Jerusalem issue at a time when the Clinton administration was about to decide whether to implement a 1995 US requirement that the embassy be moved from Tel Aviv to Jerusalem. This decision was due by the end of May, and it seemed all but certain that the law would be waived and the embassy would remain where it was. This would signal that the Americans, like the European community, did not recognize Israel's claim that Jerusalem was its capital.

It was already obvious that Ehud Barak was the Clinton administration's choice in the upcoming election. In 1996, Clinton had supported Shimon Peres; this time his administration snubbed Netanyahu and Sharon. David Weinberg in the *Jerusalem Post* made the point that Al Gore had declined to meet the prime minister at the Davos economic summit, and that Assistant Secretary of State for Near East Affairs Martin Indyk avoided Israel when he toured Syria, Jordan, Morocco and Turkey. Madeleine Albright, as we have seen, snubbed Sharon in Washington. Weinberg wrote that Clinton met with Yassir Arafat three times after Wye, two of these times alone, and that there were leaks from Washington about Israeli-Chinese arms deals and about a possible suspension of aid to Israel. In mid-March, Dennis Ross complained about the settlements, and US Army Staff College officials were ordered not to tour the territories. In the second week of April, Albright met with Sharon in her office in Washington and accused Israel of making peace difficult by expanding Jewish settlements on the West Bank. James Rubin, the State Department spokesman, said the department was "particularly concerned" about these settlements, which "in many cases [were] expanding to distant hilltops."[13]

To make relations with the United States even worse, Sharon expressed doubts about the NATO actions against the Serbs in Kosovo, despite the fact that Netanyahu supported those actions and the US was leading the attacks. Israel sent a plane to Albania loaded with medical supplies, winter clothes and other humanitarian aid; at the airport, Sharon told the Israeli delegation that the airlift was Israel's "moral responsibility as Jews," but the Kosovo crisis could be solved only by negotiation. Barak, on the other hand, told the Yugoslav ambassador that Serb actions in Kosovo appeared to be "the systematic murder of innocent people."[14] Netanyahu specifically disassociated himself from Sharon's comments on the situation. The foreign minister was voicing his private views, the prime minister's office announced, and the government of Israel fully supported "NATO's actions to bring about a speedy conclusion to the tragedy in the Balkans."[15]

There was a great deal of speculation about the reasons for Sharon's position on Kosovo. For one thing, Sharon had shown a strong inclination to woo the Russians, and in mid-April made his third visit to Moscow in two months, going directly there from Washington, where Madeleine Albright, who had put off an invitation to him for several months, made clear her displeasure over his pro-Russian conduct, and Martin Indyk was reported to have suggested that Sharon's refusal to condemn the Serbs stemmed from a desire to curry favor with the half million Russian immigrant voters in the coming election. (Sharon had in fact told William Safire, "Two thirds of the Russian Israelis are for Bibi [Netanyahu's nickname] now. If I can get that up to over seventy percent, that's it." And Russian Prime Minister Yevgeny Primakov said that if he were an Israeli, he would vote for Netanyahu.)[16] Indyk also reportedly expressed doubts that Sharon was acting against Netanyahu's wishes.[17]

Sharon said his main purpose in going to Moscow was to stop Russia from helping Iran to develop long-range missiles.[18] As for the Serbs, there was speculation that Sharon was reflecting what David Horovitz called "a certain historical sympathy for the Serbs, who had opposed the Nazis during the second World War."[19] And in New York, Sharon expressed fears that if Kosovo won independence, it could become part of "a greater Albania that will turn into a center of Islamic terrorism in Europe." He was for "every people's right of self-expression and the freedom to decide their own way of life," he said, but "if a big bloc of Islamic states develops in this region, it could serve as a base for extreme Islamic terror—a seed of that is already on the ground—this could lead to instability in Europe and elsewhere."[20] There were rumors that Sharon also believed that an independent Kosovo might set a disturbing precedent that could lead to an independent Arab state in Palestine.[21] He shared this belief with the Russians, who feared that precedent could result in NATO's defense of one of its breakaway republics. Russia's foreign ministry "registered satisfaction" with Sharon's comments.[22]

Netanyahu, announcing that Israel would take in one hundred Kosovo refugees, commented that Sharon's remarks dealt with "the future workings of Kosovo" that did not involve Israel, and did not reflect current Israeli policy, which fully supported NATO activities. The prime minister was careful to point out that Sharon had been among the first to "initiate the policy" of help for the refugees "and supporting NATO's efforts to end the tragedy."[23] The Israelis had held rallies and fund-raising drives to help the Kosovo refugees, had sent six planeloads of food, tents and other goods to the region and had set up a hundred-bed hospital in Macedonia with seventy medical aid workers.[24]

Nevertheless, Sharon's echo of the Serb position caused a firestorm of criticism. A US official said, "Israel has been less than supportive of NATO's policy. Yet when we bombed Iraq, the Israeli government could not get enough of it." The US ambassador, Edwin Walker, pointed out that the US had supported Israel throughout its history, even sometimes against American interests. He did not mention Sharon, but thanked Netanyahu for his support. It was important, he added, "that a country like Israel not be seen as unconcerned with issues such as ethnic cleansing . . . It's a bad message to the rest of the world. This is an issue of real principle."[25]

Ehud Barak called on Netanyahu to take responsibility for Sharon's "outrageous statements" about Kosovo. Yitzhak Mordechai, who was running on the Center Party ticket, said that as defense minister, he had turned down a number of invitations to visit Russia because of Russian aid to Iran. "The budding romance between Netanyahu, Sharon and Russia greatly harms our strategic alliance with the US, which is involved in an effort to halt—at our request—the transfer of technology to Iran." The government should "stop mumbling and trying to win favor with the Russians, and instead stand up behind the actions of the US and NATO."[26]

Sharon's response was that his contacts with Russia were "viewed positively in the US," and that Israel's policy was to pressure Russia "to stop the technology leakage to Iran on the one hand, and work to strengthen Russia's economic situation—and thus its stability—on the other."[27] Opposition party members did not buy any of this. "I never heard of a foreign minister speaking on his own behalf on a diplomatic matter," said Labor MK Shlomo Ben-Ami. "What is he, the foreign minister of himself and his farm? . . . Netanyahu . . . is responsible for this." A Center Party representative, Uri Savir, called Israeli lack of support for the US in war "a diplomatic scandal without precedent." The Meretz Party leader, Yossi Sarid, said, "If there is a wrong side, you can bet that Sharon will back it, and if there is an incorrect and damaging position, you can bet that Sharon will adopt it." He added that only a country without foreign interests could afford to have a foreign minister like Sharon.[28]

The far right stood behind, if not in front of, Sharon; Rehavam Zeevi warned that the NATO mission was "a dangerous precedent of wild intervention in the sovereign territory of a country to help an ethnic minority demanding to secede from it. Such a thing could happen to us in one variation or another." Another MK, Tamar Gozansky, said that NATO was playing "a cynical game with the fate of the Albanians which is not solving anything, but only worsening the problem." The US, she said, was not risking the lives of its soldiers; the only victims were Serbs and Albanians.[29]

As May 17 drew near, campaign accusations and counter-accusations intensified. Netanyahu said that Barak would give away half of Jerusalem, and all of the West Bank and the Golan Heights, and trigger increased terrorism. Barak attacked Netanyahu's character, economic failures and neglect of the peace process, while promising to disentangle Israel from the Lebanon debacle within a year. The Netanyahu administration were well aware of the public's disenchantment with the Israeli presence in Lebanon: Sharon for a long time had been proposing a withdrawal from the buffer zone. Now in mid-April it was reported in *Haaretz* that he wanted the IDF to pull out before election day, and that he had asked the Russians to pressure Syria for a guarantee that Hezbollah and others would not attack northern Israel during and after the pullout, in return for which Israel would reopen talks with Syria about the Golan.[30]

Sharon, returning from Russia, vehemently denied this report, calling it "a lie from beginning to end." The subject had not come up in Moscow, he said. The *Haaretz* reporter, Zeev Schiff, remarked, "A day doesn't go by when the foreign minister isn't denying one thing or another." And in fact, a week earlier, the defense minister, Moshe Arens, had announced a reduction in the number of troops in Lebanon, while the IDF chief of staff insisted that this reduction did not presage any "revolutionary change in the army's operations" because a unilateral withdrawal from Lebanon would pose an "unreasonable risk."[31]

Sharon took time from the campaign to talk at the Vatican with the Pope and other church officials about a dispute in the Israeli-Arab town of Nazareth between Christians and Muslims over Muslim plans to build a mosque on land next to the Church of the Annunciation. Muslims had already erected a temporary mosque on the site, which the Christians wanted to use for a plaza for the couple million pilgrims expected in the future. There had already been street fights over this problem. Sharon invited the Pope to visit Israel and Jerusalem during the 2000 millennium celebrations, and took this opportunity to repeat his standard speech that Jerusalem had been the capital of the Jewish people for 3000 years and the capital of Israel for fifty-one years "and for all times." He used maps to explain the need for security zones in the West Bank, and reiterated his threats against the Palestinians if they declared statehood. These protestations would later prove to have fallen upon deaf ears.[32]

While Sharon was busily traveling the world, the police were interviewing Netanyahu as part of their investigation of the Ben-Gal matter, and on April 29, two-and-a-half weeks before the election, it was leaked that they were recommending bringing charges against Sharon for bribery, witness tampering and obstruction of justice. Netanyahu, who was polling eight percent behind Barak, hinted that there were political motives behind the leaks, and Sharon said that he was "surprised" by the leaks and that he wanted the investigation to be finished before the elections.[33]

43

END OF THE CAMPAIGN

———

THE SECOND WEEK IN MAY, 1999, Sharon went to New York to celebrate the fiftieth anniversary of Israel's membership in the UN by presenting the organization with a fourth-century stone lintel, engraved with a menorah, an olive branch and a ram's horn, that had been in a Roman-era Galilee synogogue. In a brief ceremony, Sharon said that the lintel represented "the uninterrupted Jewish existence for thousands of years in the Land of Israel, the promised land." UN Secretary-General Kofi Annan said, "Just as this lintel has found a home, so too does Israel have a home at the United Nations. I know that at times it may not have seemed like a home, but I think we can agree that today a new climate has taken hold in relations between Israel and the United Nations." He said he had no doubt that Israel and the UN would continue to work as partners in the Middle East and beyond.[1]

Sharon did not say anything about Israel's difficult past relations with the UN which in 1975 had passed a resolution equating Zionism with racism. Nor did he mention the General Assembly's recent unprecedented vote to convene a conference on July 15 to discuss the charge that Israel's settlement activity had violated the Geneva Convention. The *Jerusalem Post* pointed out that he did not hint at Israel's belief that the world body was inherently biased against it, or at its complaint that the UN had failed to close some "antiquated" committees like the one on "the inalienable rights of the Palestinians" that had come into being at the height of the Arab-Israeli conflict.[2]

On May 4, the day that the Palestinians had hoped to declare their independence, Sharon reaffirmed his stand on the settlements, saying that counter to opposition from the Americans and Palestinians, 20,000 more settlers would live in the West Bank by the end of 1999. To a charge by the US State Department that Netanyahu's government had broken a pledge not to expand the settlements beyond the built-up areas, Sharon responded that Israel was honoring an agreement not to build new settlements in the territories, but he admitted that some construction was continuing on land that did not adjoin existing settlements. He defended the takeover of hilltops, arguing that holding the high ground was essential for security in isolated areas. "Democratic countries," he said, should be "careful not to interfere" in Israeli elections. In the main, Palestinians bore their disappointment stoically, although there were some pro-statehood demonstrations.[3]

A week before the elections, Netanyahu, ignoring predictions of slowing economic growth—tax receipts and exports were down from the previous year, and unemployment was up—and over the objections of his finance minister, pushed through new spending plans for roads and subsidized housing for Israelis in east Jerusalem. His Labor opponents called these plans "election bribery" and there were detailed leaks to the press of acrimonious cabinet exchanges. It was reported that Sharon accused finance officials of objecting to the new spending for political reasons. Netanyahu commented, "Finance ministers never want to give out money—that's usual."[4]

Despite the Likud's best efforts, Ehud Barak, whose Labor party was now called One Israel, won the election by twelve points: fifty-six percent to forty-four percent. In the Knesset, the picture was not as clear: both the Likud and Labor lost seats, Labor dropping from thirty-four to twenty-six, and Likud from thirty-two to nineteen. This presented Barak with the problem of building a coalition. He had a choice of a coalition with the Likud or one with three religious parties—two ultra-orthodox and one orthodox—if he could not work out an agreement with the Likud.

Netanyahu conceded early on the basis of exit polls, and announced that he was resigning both as head of the party, and from the Knesset, and giving up politics, although he would remain in place until July when Barak would put his government together. In his concession speech, Netanyahu specifically thanked two people: his wife and Ariel Sharon, who, he said, had not hesitated to stand by him through the most difficult times.[5] Sharon was chosen to lead the Likud at least until the next party primaries, which were to be held three months to a year later. It was thought by many that at seventy-one, he was too old to hold the job permanently.[6]

There ensued weeks of negotiation between Barak's One Israel and the Likud. There were gaps between them on the questions of the control of the West Bank and negotiations on the Golan with Syria. There were also questions of cabinet posts. Barak had great difficulty controlling left-wing elements like the Meretz Party, which balked, first at working with the ultra-orthodox Sephardic Shas Party and then at working with the Likud too. Sharon struggled to keep his own people in line because he wanted a unity government and had been offered the finance post by Barak. Sarah Honig in the *Jerusalem Post* called the process "Barak's strange roller coaster ride" because of the ups and downs and twists of the various negotiations.[7]

In late June, the lame duck Netanyahu administration struck out at Lebanon in retaliation for attacks on northern Israel. In an attempt to ease tensions, the French Foreign Ministry sent two envoys to the region, and immediately got off on the wrong foot by announcing that the diplomats would visit "Tel Aviv and Gaza, Palestine." The situation was not helped by the fact that the men were carrying a letter from French President Jacques Chirac to Barak, who had not yet assumed office, and not to Sharon, who was still foreign minister. Barak, apparently at Sharon's urging, refused to meet with the envoys, who then asked to meet with other senior foreign ministry officials. Sharon refused to meet with them, and sent a letter to Chirac protesting what he called a one-sided and unbalanced reaction to the Israeli air strikes against Lebanon. The envoys met with lower-level Israeli officials.[8]

By June 29, the forty-day roller coaster ride came to an end when Sharon announced that negotiations had broken down because Barak would not rule out withdrawal from the Golan Heights and refused to guarantee continued Jewish construction in Jerusalem. Both Barak and Sharon were attacked because of the failure of the negotiations: Barak was accused of squandering the good will of the election by taking so long to form a cabinet, and Sharon was accused by Likud members of allowing Barak to use him as a pawn to lure Shas into his coalition.[9]

In July, Ehud Barak took office, promising to "strengthen Israel's security by putting an end to one hundred years of conflict in the Middle East." He arranged meetings with President Clinton, King Abdullah of Jordan and Hosni Mubarak of Egypt, offered his hand to Hafez Assad of Syria, spoke on the phone to Arafat, and vowed he would work with the Palestinian leader to "finish the job" of the Wye accord withdrawals and "put an end to the suffering of the Palestinian people."[10]

44

PARTY LEADER

———

ON JULY 6, BARAK PRESENTED the Knesset with his new seven-party government, with Labor, Meretz and Shas as its main constituents. Peace advocates in the main were relieved that Barak's coalition cabinet did not include the Likud. They were pleased also by the appointment as foreign minister of David Levy, who had been born in Morocco and had broken with Netanyahu before the elections because of disagreements over the peace process. There were cavils from both sides: there were no Arabs and only one woman in the cabinet, and several prominent members of the One Israel party had been left out or given relatively minor posts.

Before the end of July, Sharon began to campaign to make permanent his position as Likud leader, for which he was being challenged by Jerusalem Mayor Ehud Olmert and MK Meir Sheetrit. He found time to attack Barak for what he considered the prime minister's palliative approach to Arafat, his lack of a demand for "reciprocity" from the Palestinian leader, and his statement that he would consider the release of Palestinian prisoners. A candidate for Likud head had to get forty percent of the vote in order to win in the first round of the election to be held on September 2. Sharon was considerably ahead in polls of Likud membership, which was unofficially tallied as fifteen to seventeen thousand.[1]

In early August, Netanyahu refused to endorse Sharon for the leadership post in a rather embarrassing moment. Expecting an endorsement, Sharon had invited the press to cover a meeting he had arranged with the former prime minister at the Sheraton Plaza Hotel in Jerusalem. But all Netanyahu would say was, "I approve of the fact that Ariel Sharon is in a central position and will continue to operate in a central role for the good of the security of the State of Israel." When he was asked whether that meant that he backed Sharon's candidacy, he did not answer. Sharon's campaign chairman Ruby Rivlin said that Sharon had made a tactical error "to some extent" because "his entire tactic is based on strengthening himself with Bibi's supporters." Netanyahu's followers, he said, were behind Sharon because he was the only one of the three candidates who promised another leadership election in two years.[2]

Toward the end of the month, the campaign intensified, with Olmert making an unprecedentedly bitter attack on Sharon in a news conference, and Sharon forced to apologize for the behavior of his son Omri and his party general director Uri Shani, who told a journalist that Likud voters were a bunch of wild Indians who were impressed by Sharon's Cadillac. Senior Likud members demanded Shani's resignation, and Sharon's workers complained that Omri and Shani had no history within the Likud and were getting a free ride. Sharon said it was clear that the two, who said they had just been joking, had made a mistake.[3]

On September 2, Sharon won the election for party leader with a landslide: fifty-three percent of the vote to Olmert's twenty-four percent, and Sheetrit's twenty-two. Sharon got almost twice as many votes in Jerusalem as Olmert, the mayor. The turnout, only thirty-five percent, was low. Both Olmert and Sheetrit congratulated Sharon, but Sheetrit said that the big winner was Barak, because the Likud was torn by internal dissension that would undoubtedly get worse in the future. Yitzhak Shamir, who had supported Olmert, agreed that there would be a lot of infighting; he did not know, he said, how Sharon would handle the party.[4]

There was a widespread belief that Sharon was simply paving the way for Netanyahu to return in the 2003 elections. Netanyahu himself, who voted in Jerusalem with his wife, refused to answer questions from the press. "I'm on vacation," he said. "I came to vote, not to give interviews. I'm currently on vacation from interviews as well." Bystanders chanted, "He'll be back! He'll be back!" Sharon told reporters that he didn't know what Netanyahu's plans were; he had never spoken to him about them. "I am not preparing the ground for anyone," he said; he was preparing the Likud for victory in the next elections.[5]

Sheetrit said that he had never seen Ariel Sharon give up his seat for anyone in the past and he didn't expect him to do it in the future. Olmert also dismissed the speculations about Netanyahu's return, saying, "It is always those who don't run who are most popular."[6]

45

IMMUTABLE POSITIONS

———

ON SEPTEMBER 4, 1999, BARAK and Arafat signed the Sharm al-Sheikh agreement with Madeleine Albright, President Mubarak and King Abdullah II of Jordan as witnesses. This accord provided for limited withdrawals from West Bank areas in September and November, 1999, and January, 2000; for the releases, in September and October, of a total of 350 Palestinian prisoners; for the construction of a seaport in Gaza; for a safe route from Gaza to the West Bank, and for negotiations for the framework of a final peace settlement encompassing the difficult questions of settlements, Palestinian refugees, borders and Jerusalem, to be completed by February 13, 2000. For his part, Arafat agreed to cooperate with Israeli agencies to fight terrorism.[1]

Sharon addressed the full Knesset during a vote on the accord. Constantly interrupted by heckling, he called the agreement "grave and sloppy, a chimera." The Palestinians, he said, had no clear-cut commitments to fight against the terrorist infrastructure as they had in the Wye accord; in this new agreement, they were "merely required to make an effort and provide a report." He drew other contrasts between Sharm al-Sheikh and Wye: the inclusion in Wye of a role for the CIA, the reduction of Palestinian forces, surrender of illegal weapons, a ban on incitement to terror—all absent from Sharm al-Sheikh. He complained also about lack of security arrangements in the safe route and the Gaza seaport, and, most vociferously, about the reactivation of the committee on displaced per-

sons, which he warned would "open the road to endless bloodshed," since the Palestinian official in charge of refugees had predicted that it would now be possible to return nearly a million people
to Israel.[2]

Sharon met with the leaders of all the opposition parties to plan
working together to fight Barak's security and social agenda. Of
most concern to them was keeping the Golan out of Syrian control,
but they wanted also to ensure financial aid and military protection
to the West Bank settlements.[3] Sharon also tried to take propaganda
advantage of an Arab League threat to boycott the Disney Company because in the Israeli exhibit at Disney's Florida Epcot Center,
Jerusalem was designated as Israel's capital. He called on President
Clinton to thwart the boycott, saying that this threat demonstrated
that Arabs still hated Israel and was one in "a long series of systematic campaigns in the US, the UN and the world press to delegitimize
Israel and its rightful claim to its 3000-year old capital, Jerusalem."[4]

In the middle of October, Barak succeeded in getting militant
settlers to leave twelve of the forty-two illegal outposts in the West
Bank seized when Sharon had encouraged them to "seize every hilltop" in the face of the Wye accord implementation. The prime minister promised to resettle them in safe areas that would eventually
become part of Israel. Housing Minister Yitzhak Levy said that this
resettlement agreement proved that the remaining thirty outposts
were legal. On the other hand, Moshe Arens, Netanyahu's defense
minister, said he had never approved any of the forty-two outposts
when he was in office.[5]

Sharon announced that if Barak would set down and announce
to the world certain "red lines" or immutable positions before the
Palestinians, the US and others press for further concessions, he
would bring the Likud into Barak's coalition. These lines would
include the right to Jerusalem as the nation's capital "with no political status for anyone else," control of Jewish holy sites and mountain aquifiers, and a permanent eastern twenty-kilometer-wide se-

curity zone along the west bank of the Jordan River. There must also be a security zone along the Green Line and control of the main routes to the Jordan Valley.[6] Foreign Minister David Levy said in the Knesset that the government was setting policy lines just as Arafat set his positions in Oslo, and that these were a "united Jerusalem, blocks of settlements . . . under Israeli sovereignty, no return to the 1967 borders, and no foreign army west of the Jordan River. . . . No Israeli government," he said, "would uproot all the settlements."[7]

In November, Sharon revealed that earlier in the year, with the knowledge of only a few people in Netanyahu's cabinet, he had held secret "indirect" talks with Damascus to see how the Syrians would react to an Israeli withdrawal from Lebanon. The talks failed, he said, because the Syrians would not approve a withdrawal without linking it to a surrender of the Golan Heights. Barak, who was in Paris, voiced optimism that there would be peace between Israel and Syria.[8] Despite Sharon's ability to attract press attention, the *Jerusalem Post* reported that a growing number of Likud MKs were becoming disillusioned with his leadership and believed that only Netanyahu could return them to power. Polls indicated that the party would do even worse in an impending election than it had just done in the last one. "There's no fool like an old fool," one party worker said bluntly. "Everyone knows Sharon is unelectable apart from Sharon himself." Another said that Sharon was out of touch not only with the party but with the day-to-day concerns of the people, since he had always been a soldier and a politician, never an ordinary citizen, and years of media attacks had hurt his image badly.[9]

Ruby Rivlin and others said that Netanyahu would come back if he was welcomed without opposition; otherwise he would run independently. Netanyahu himself issued a statement that he was taking time out from politics and had no political plans, a comment that several of his associates found amusing since, they said, he was busy with meetings and discussions. Sharon said that the last attempt to circumvent the Likud, the setting up of the Center Party, was a complete failure. But anyone who wanted to post a challenge for the leadership was certainly entitled to do so, he said; he himself was committed to facing a runoff for the leadership in two years. Some thought that though Netanyahu was the best candidate, even he would not be able to guarantee victory. "This is the toughest leadership crisis since the Likud's creation," one said.[10]

Some of the disaffected Likud members tried to talk Sharon into running for the presidency if, as was expected, Ezer Weizman were to resign. They said Sharon would be the strongest candidate for the post, but admitted that this would be the best way to remove Sharon from leadership of the party and avoid a bruising struggle for leadership in two years. "This is our golden opportunity," a Likud MK told the *Jerusalem Post.* Sharon, distracted by his wife's illness, was not available for comment, but his office said he intended to continue as Likud head, and to challenge Barak for the premiership when the time came.[11]

Possibly reflecting this attitude, Barak, who had agreed when he took office to hold periodic briefing meetings with Sharon, had set but postponed several meetings with him, showing signs of being "dismissive" toward the Likud leader. But tensions over the budget had grown and some coalition parties were becoming restive, so at the end of November, Barak and Sharon spent two hours alone in Barak's office talking mostly about Iraq and Iran and international terror.[12] Despite this meeting, Sharon and all political leaders were caught off guard on December 8 when Clinton announced that Barak would meet with the Syrian foreign minister in Washington the following week. Madeleine Albright and Dennis Ross had held talks in Damascus in September, and Assad had shown every sign of respecting Barak and believing that peace was possible, and Barak had returned the compliment, saying that Assad had built "a strong, independent, self-confident Syria . . . important for stability in the Middle East."[13]

The Left was delighted. "This is a government that was born to make history," Yossi Sarid of the Meretz Party said. The Tel Aviv stock market rebounded, and Labor erupted in cheers.[14] Barak noted that Netanyahu had failed in his pursuit of peace with Syria, but that he himself had succeeded because he delivered on land-for-peace concessions to the Palestinians. "Today we are able to conduct a dialogue," Barak said. Members of the coalition were not uniformly pleased. Natan Sharansky, the interior minister, said that "if the purpose of the negotiations were to hand over the Golan Heights to one of the darkest and most repressive regimes in the world in exchange for a warning station on Mount Hermon within a few months, then I am opposed." The National Religious Party said it would leave the government if Barak ceded the Golan.[15] As could be expected, the Likud response was decidedly negative. Sharon said the Barak plan was a capitulation both to Assad and to Clinton. "American internal interests don't have a thing to do with vital Israeli interests," he said. "This is a big victory for Syria."[16]

In a poll, forty-seven percent of Israelis were "greatly opposed" to a peace with Syria if it involved withdrawal from the Golan Heights and only twenty-three percent were "greatly" or "somewhat" in favor of such an agreement.[17] Sharon kept up a drumfire of objection to any deal with Assad, giving speeches and writing articles for the *Jerusalem Post* and the *New York Times*.[18]

When Barak met with the Syrian Foreign Minister Farouk al-Shara in Washington in the middle of December, and again in West Virginia in the second week of January, al-Shara was remote and unbending. Clinton stepped in, and Barak apparently agreed to a withdrawal to most of the 1967 borders, but the Syrians wanted a firm commitment, in writing, to the borders as of June 4, 1967, and a return to the waterlines along the northeastern shore of the Sea of Galilee. Clinton, who Sharon warned would "make every effort" to mediate Israeli-Syrian peace talks, met Assad in Geneva in late March and was unpleasantly surprised by the Syrian's intransigence, not only in the matter of the waterlines, but in his attitude toward Israel in general. Barak declared the Galilee issue a deal-breaker and the talks were suspended.

By February, 2000, things were not going well for Barak. In addition to the breakdown of Syrian negotiations, Israelis were enraged by Hezbollah attacks in South Lebanon, and by the increasing volume of anti-Jewish propaganda coming out of Arab capitals. In addition, the Vatican had greeted Arafat with warmth, there was increased unemployment, and a scandal over One Israel campaign funding. The Likud sponsored a no-confidence motion which failed, but significantly members of the Shas Party voted against the government, signalling a weakness in the coalition.[19]

46

LILY

——

AT SEVEN IN THE MORNING on March 25, 2000, in a Tel Aviv hospital, Lily Sharon succumbed to lung cancer, at the age of sixty-three. She had been in and out of the hospital since January 18, and had spent much of the previous year being treated at Sloan-Kettering Cancer Center in New York, where Sharon had often joined her, citing his absence from the Knesset as being for "personal reasons."[1] He had also sought help from doctors in Boston and Los Angeles. The media had not detailed her US visits, both at Sharon's request and out of consideration for the family. Sharon and their two sons, Omri and Gilad, were with her when she died. She left two grandchildren, Rotem and Danya: she did not live to see Gilad's twin sons.

Lily had immigrated from Rumania to Israel with her parents and three sisters. When she was eighteen, she was subject to compulsory conscription into the IDF. Her Orthodox parents objected to this, but when she told them that her request for a dismissal had been denied—which wasn't true—they dropped their objection. Her father was an ordained rabbi, but his principles were relatively flexible; her mother was more unbending. In any case, Lily joined the paratrooper unit, where Sharon was her commanding officer. Her ambition was to be an artist, and when she left the service, she studied at the Avni Art Academy in Tel Aviv, and also produced drawings of wanted criminatls for the police force.

She and Sharon had been married since 1963, one year after his first wife, Lily's sister Margalit, had been killed in a car accident.

She had been by his side during most of his tempestuous life after Margalit's death, sharing the heartbreak of Gur's loss, the Shlomzion fiasco, the humiliation of the aftermath of the Lebanese war, and the tension of the 1984 libel trial in New York. She was already very ill when their home had caught fire the previous December, but only joked, "Now everyone will know we have a warm house."

Although she was joking, it was true that the atmosphere in the house was warm, reflecting the relationship between Sharon and Lily, who filled the house with flowers and music. The flowers she brought in from the large gardens she tended, and she herself played the piano and flute, and offered help to many young musicians. She and Sharon shared a love of music, and she also shared his interest in politics. He always read his speeches and articles to her, and accepted her comments and criticism. She was not just a listener, Sharon said later, but a participant "behind the scenes." She chose to sit in the audience at political events, rather than beside him, and her presence there bucked him up considerably. Their marriage, he said in a later interview, was deeply satisfying, their happiest moments spent at home through the years, talking, laughing and listening to music. Sharing music was one of the losses he found most painful, even months later. Even though he was very close to his sons and daughter-in-law, his life lacked "a certain tenderness, a certain warmth." Their most intimate moments, he told a sympathetic listener, were "intoxicating."[2]

During the year of her battle against cancer, she was very stoical, trying, Sharon remembered, in every way to comfort him. She would always be dressed carefully, her hair and makeup done, facing each day with a kind of inner strength. If she tried to talk to Sharon about what might happen in the future, he would cut her off, telling her that she must not think negatively, that she would beat the disease, that she would recover. He discovered later that she had finally called their driver, Gilbert, and told him that "Arik" had not been to a store for forty years, had no idea how to shop, and that he would not let her talk if she tried to help him plan for a future without her. She told Gilbert, "I am asking you to take care of him because pretty soon I am not going to be around, and Arik doesn't know how to take care of himself."

She refused sedatives because she wanted to stay as alert and lucid as possible. But the day before she died, she told the doctors to do with her what they wished, and she asked her friends not to visit her anymore. "And," Sharon recalled, "the next day she died."[3]

She was buried on the farm in the north Negev desert that they had lived in for the past twenty-seven years. Her funeral was attended by about twenty thousand people. About fifteen hundred others, including Barak and Netanyahu, came to the farm to pay condolences every day of the seven-day *shiva* mourning period. Sharon delivered the eulogy, saying, "Until today I never acted without you. From now on it will be without you. It will not be easy. But I will continue to go on the path in which both of us believed."[4]

Despite these words, many wondered whether Sharon, at seventy-two, would be capable of mounting the challenge to Barak's leadership that he had committed himself to. But March polls showed that if national elections were to be held then, the split between Barak and Netanyahu would be a virtual tie. And this despite the fact that the police were calling for prosecution of Netanyahu on charges of fraud. The polls on that issue showed forty-six percent in favor of the police investigation, and forty-four percent convinced that the investigation had been political. In any case, there was no question that Barak was vulnerable.

All doubts about Sharon's commitment had to vanish when on April 16, three weeks after Lily's death, he called for early elections in six to twelve months and announced his intention to run for prime minister. "I and the Likud," he said, "do not want to participate in the government. We want to overturn the government."[5]

Barak rejected the call for early elections.

47

FAMILY MATTERS

———

EVERY MORNING, SHARON WAS driven to Lily's grave, on the hill covered with poppies above Sycamore Farm. He would stand there for a few minutes before getting back into his armored Cadillac and going on to resume the campaign. At the end of January he had moved back into the farmhouse which Lily had redesigned after it had burned down about a year earlier. They had lost all their family photographs in the fire, but friends sent him pictures they had taken of him and Lily, so they had those. She had made changes to their bedroom, but after her death, Sharon hired an architect and asked him to recreate the old bedroom where the boys would jump into bed with their parents, even when the two of them were grown, after their army service. He was going to live there with his younger son Gilad and his wife Inbal, their son Rotem and newborn twin boys. Both Gilad and Sharon's elder son Omri were involved in the campaign, although the plan was for Omri to stay in politics, while Gilad would work on the ranch.

Omri, 36, never married, has a four-year-old daughter named Danya. He went to law school, but did not graduate because, he said, he still had to "complete some research and a seminar." He likes the good life. Every Friday during the campaign he was to be seen at a popular cafe in Tel Aviv, sometimes joined by Uri Shani, the Likud manager, but always with a group of young friends, most of whom belonged to the Left. A reporter noted that Omri flirted constantly with the waitresses and cafe customers, and "focused closely" on a ring piercing the navel of one of his female friends. "Ever since the start of the campaign," he said, "it's not adrenalin that's been flowing in my blood, but testosterone, and it works very well with the girls." Devoted to his father, whom he considered had been demonized, Omri was working on an advertising campaign to repair his image. "You cannot imagine how difficult it is to market this kind of thing," he said.[1] By January, 2001, there was no political journalist who did not have Omri's cell phone number.

Gilad, 34, was only three when Gur was killed and had grown up at the farm in the shadow of that tragedy. "Gur's death was always around them," said a friend of the family. "Arik was able to talk about him only in the past few years, but Lily always talked about him. She felt toward Gur as if he were her own son."[2]

When they were still quite young, Omri and Gilad worked the farm. Their father was often away in the military, but Omri said that made them more independent. "After school we would work on the farm and it was a wonderful childhood. Our parents told us that if we wanted horses and dogs, we had to feed them. We had to get up early in order to do morning chores. Father made us breakfast, usually oatmeal. We felt we were special. When we rode horses into the countryside with him, Father would explain things, like why one side of a hill is green while the other side is bare. He gave us the feeling that there is order in nature, and in life." Omri remembered that a week before the start of the Yom Kippur War, the family went on a trip to the Sinai and drove down to have a picnic lunch at the Suez Canal. "Gilad forgot his baseball jacket there. During the war we joked that if Father went past the canal, he shouldn't forget to pick up the jacket."[3]

Sharon tried to be a friend to his sons, but he was also a protective father. Lily once said that when the boys were Scouts and went on camping trips, "he would often volunteer to go along as the supervising parent. He not only went on the trip, but he guarded the area at night. He didn't trust anyone else to do it."[4]

Gilad went to the regional kibbutz public school, where his main interest was in history. Lily often said, "I can be proud of raising two independent sons, that each one has his own personality and they do not have the 'son of' complex." But one of Gilad's teachers recalled, "At the start of every class, when I took attendance, Gilad always asked me to call him only by his first name. Somehow he seemed to want to separate himself from his father's famous last name." When, short and skinny, he entered the seventh grade in 1979, he had difficulty at first in being accepted by the other children. A classmate remembered, "Gilad found his place among a group of five kids that stayed together everywhere they went. They were popular, but slightly more individualistic than the others."

Most of the students, coming from kibbutzes in the area, leaned Left. "But," the classmate recalled, "with all that he was never afraid to express his opinions. The kids criticized Gilad and his father, but he would never give in. Even when he saw, during the war in Lebanon, that in the schoolyard someone had written the word "Murderer" about his father. And when the anti-war people would put up signs everywhere against the war in Lebanon." Another student, who had had run-ins with Gilad, said that despite name-calling and heated arguments, "the fact that he was Sharon's son did not make a big difference, perhaps only when a chopper would land near their ranch and we knew that Gilad's father had come home."

His classmates liked to visit Sycamore Farm. "There were some real attractions there," one said. "His father was a different person inside that house, softer. Once I sat down with Gilad's brother Omri and we were reading an article about Sharon in *Playboy* magazine. Gilad looked at us and said, 'It's a serious magazine, they have interesting content.'" The friend went on, "On the shelf above the fireplace, there were cigar boxes. When we came over to see Gilad, his father would offer us a cigar. But not only that. His father would also make us sandwiches for school. Once Arik gave me a jar of homemade hot peppers to give to the food buyer on my kibbutz."

Another childhood friend still remembered the sandwiches. "Our kibbutz was pretty poor, and the only sandwiches we knew were rye bread with a simple spread and a vegetable. Gilad always had a big sandwich, loaded with good food, smoked turkey and mustard. At one point he began to bring two sandwiches to school, one for himself and the other for his friends. I think it was part of his integration, so he could be one of the guys."

But after the war in Lebanon, the area residents ostracized the Sharon family. One resident said, "Naturally it affected the family deeply. They were rejected. Nobody spoke to them. They felt bad." Nevertheless, Omri said, it made them stronger. "During the 1981 election campaign, Gilad and I wore Likud T-shirts, and the others wore their political shirts. We were never conformists. So they demonstrated and we demonstrated on the other side. Afterward we would all go out together. Maybe we were not part of the political consensus, but we were part of the social circle."[5]

When Gilad was seventeen, he would take his father's official Volvo every few weeks and drive his friends to Tel Aviv, where they preferred quiet pubs to noisy dance clubs. In the summer, they liked to sit around a fire on the beach. A friend remembered Gilad hosting parties at the ranch: "Gilad himself was never showy, he didn't dance. Once he invited us all to a pool party at his ranch. I could never forget it. We were all so impressed, because inside the pool there were lights under the water. It was like a rich people's party."

During his service with the IDF, Gilad was a paratrooper and became an officer in a top secret unit. He also worked as an instructor at a training school for officers. Sharon once commented that he thought it was "natural" that his boys would choose to serve in combat units and avoid desk jobs. "Just as it is natural that they have a connection to the earth of this country, so it became natural that they joined the paratroopers. They did what they had to do. We never butted in." Gilad's tie to the soil was strong. When he was released from army duty, he went back to the ranch for three years and then began agriculture studies at the Weizmann Institute. On weekends he came home to help on the farm, and moved back there after he received his master's degree in agricultural economics. Omri started law school at about that same time. Both sons built homes on the ranch. The family also owns an apartment in Tel Aviv.

Gilad married Inbal, a design student, when he was twenty-eight and she was a few years younger. He told his parents that he was going to get married, but did not invite them or anyone else, except Omri, to the ceremony at the rabbinical court. Afterward he phoned his parents and said, "Mission accomplished." Sharon commented, "That was how they wanted to get married. Without parents. I know Omri will do the same thing when he gets married. I was just like them. When I married for the first time, my parents were busy on the farm and didn't come. When I married Lily, I did have a wedding, a small military ceremony."

A close friend of Lily's said, "Inbal had been Gilad's girlfriend since she was seventeen. She practically grew up at their house. She was at the ranch every weekend. You could say that Arik and Lily practically raised her. She's very compatible with the family and when Lily got sick, Inbal took care of her with exceptional devotion. You don't even see things like that between mothers and daughters." Lily's death brought the family even closer together. Omri once said, "In our house there is a real home, and when it's necessary we all unite." Lily's friend added, "The boys' friends always visit. Arik is always surrounded by them. Sometimes they sleep at the ranch. Very few families are that close. The kids actually want to be close to their parents, and make decisions together." The farm, another friend said, "was built as a safe haven, not as a business. The dream was that the children would be with them. And that is how it was."[6]

48

LEBANON & POLITICS

———

DURING APRIL AND MAY, the IDF began to prepare for a unilateral pullout from Lebanon. Early in May, Sharon met with Barak for two hours and complained to the press afterward that he had not received "a single answer" to any of his questions and "after a gap of six months from the previous meeting," had learned nothing that he did not already know from the media. He said he told Barak that the government's planned methods of withdrawal from Lebanon would result in terrorists chasing the IDF to the border because the government was not making clear to the Syrians and Lebanese that they would pay a heavy price if they did not stop terrorist activity. He believed that, although early elections had been rejected by Barak, the government could well collapse under pressures from the coalition; the country was going downhill every day, "from Arab civilian unrest to rising unemployment."[1]

Sharon was concerned about protection of the South Lebanon Army in an IDF pullout. They had been allies of Israel for twenty-five years, and he was afraid that they would be slaughtered by the Hezbollah if they were left behind. The IDF, he maintained, had lost its deterrent power during "a long period of restraint." "Real deterrence," he said, "cannot be created other than through a thorough and continuous operation." What he advocated was hurting Syrian and Lebanese interests in Lebanon by means of thorough, systematic and serious strikes on Lebanese infrastructure. He wanted the government to set "a clear price" that the "Syrians and Lebanese would have to pay if they did not put an end to terrorist activity; the "price" included "power stations, oil refineries, highways and bridges."[2]

Barak, too, was of course concerned about the safety of SLA members: his plan was that hundreds of them, with their families, would move across the border into Israel, and he had negotiated the acceptance of all the others by various countries. But on May 21, before he could activate these arrangements, the SLA, set upon by hundreds of Lebanese civilians who poured unexpectedly into the security zone, retreated in disarray rather than fire upon these non-combatants. The IDF chose not to employ heavy counterattack weaponry, and the SLA melted before the onslaught from the civilians, belatedly joined by the Hezbollah. During the night of May 23, Israeli troops performed a carefully protected pullout, without casualties, because the Hezbollah too had been taken by surprise and did not have time to organize effective assaults against them.

Over 6000 SLA fighters, South Lebanese officials and their families crossed into Israel, while the Hezbollah and their associates set up rocket and mortar emplacements in the border zone. Fifteen hundred SLA men were arrested by the Hezbollah and tried en masse, but their sentences were light. Barak had achieved the pullout he had promised, but it had been so hasty that it looked embarrassingly like a rout. Sharon did not hesitate to pounce on this. He was relieved, he said, that there had been no IDF casualties, and he called the evacuation efficient and prudent. But, he wrote, he felt ashamed at the sight of southern Lebanese fleeing to the border, without their possessions, humiliated, frightened, and with a "sense of betrayal . . . victims of our hasty withdrawal." If, he went on, Israel "had created the necessary deterrent conditions ahead of time, we could have prevented the total disintegration of the SLA."[3]

He predicted that the Hezbollah would soon attack from the border and, for reasons known only to himself, warned a day later that peace could bring a "flood" of "hundreds of thousands of Arabs" taking over the parks and beaches and clogging the roads.

When, as could be expected, he was accused of racism, he responded that he was simply pointing out a logistical problem that could arise from neighboring Arab countries. He was not talking about Israel's one million Arabs, he said, adding "There is no basis to any attempt to present this as something against Arabs or against peace."[4]

The Syrians, like everybody else, were taken by surprise at the swift and, on the whole, successful evacuation of Israeli forces from Lebanon. Assad, who had worked against the Israelis for thirty years, had hoped to use the evacuation issue to bargain for the Golan Heights. That was now obviously out of the question. This, like the Arab defeats in 1967 and 1973 and the collapse of the Soviet Union, was a bitter blow to Assad. On June 10, 2000, he died suddenly of a heart attack at the age of sixty-nine. He was succeeded by his thirty-four-year-old son Bashir Assad who reaffirmed his father's position on the Golan Heights.

Sharon said that he thought Assad's death might help Israel get better peace terms than Barak had tried to get, since "Barak altogether gave up everything." But at the same time Sharon said it made no difference whether Bashir or someone else ruled Syria: "It doesn't make a difference if it's that man or another man—we speak about a regime." He said he saw no threat of war with Syria: "Israel is militarily a strong country and I think they got all the warnings and they understand that Israel doesn't have any intention whatsoever to see any hostile activities." Reacting to Barak's May announcement that he was considering a peace deal that might cede twenty percent of occupied land to the Palestinians, Sharon said that any decision to remove scattered Jewish settlements, where more than 170,000 Jews lived among more than two million Palestinians, would be a major mistake that would rip Israel apart. These West Bank settlements, he said, were entirely different from settlements in the Sinai, which a Likud government, with Sharon's assent, had uprooted in 1979 as part of a peace treaty with Egypt.[5]

On July 9, the seventeen-seat Shas Party, complaining about

Barak's "dangerous territorial concessions," and angry that the Meretz Party had blocked their request for twelve-and-a-half million in aid for their religious schools, quit the coalition, leaving Barak with fifty-one seats, less than a majority in the 120-seat Knesset. Barak said he was willing to negotiate the money, but Sharon promised Shas that Likud would find the funding for them if they left the government. On July 10, on the eve of Barak's departure for Washington, the prime minister survived a no-confidence vote by seven votes, with seven legislators abstaining and seven absent. David Horovitz said that five members of the ultra-Orthodox United Torah Judaism Party abstained in order to punish Sharon for opposing a bill to exempt from military service ultra-Orthodox men who studied Jewish texts full time. Those five votes might have made a difference if they had gone against Barak: "the dramatic splintering of [his] support might have accelerated into total meltdown," preventing him from making it as he did to the summit, "battered but still in power."[6]

Sharon declared himself pleased, saying that although the Likud had failed to muster sixty-one votes, the Barak government was on the verge of collapse.[7] Barak, relieved but irritated, said that the vote was "childish," and that he had two million voters with him, "citizens who want peace, who want to give change a chance, and hope for a different Israel at peace with its neighbors." He promised the Knesset that he would remain with his red lines: Jerusalem united under Israel; no return to the pre-June, 1967 borders; no foreign army west of the Jordan River; protection of settlers in the West Bank, and no responsibility for Palestinian refugees. Sharon called on him not to make any commitments because he had no Knesset majority and no popular support.[8] But a newspaper poll showed that a majority, fifty-two to forty-five percent, backed his Washington trip, and his mandate to make concessions to the Palestinians.[9] Another poll showed that Netanyahu would defeat Barak if the election were held at that time.[10]

CAMP DAVID

———

ON JULY 11, BARAK AND Arafat met at Camp David, with President Clinton and Madeleine Albright as mediators. David Levy, Barak's foreign minister, had refused to accompany him, unconvinced that a final peace agreement was possible, and six other cabinet ministers had deserted the prime minister on the eve of the summit. Hanan Ashrawi, the Palestinian spokeswoman, took a hard line, telling reporters in Washington that Arafat intended to raise "unfinished business" from the Wye accords. "Previous agreements have not been implemented," she said, referring to the turning over of West Bank land and the release of prisoners. "There has been no accountability or enforcement."[1]

Nevertheless, the atmosphere at the outset was warm. TV cameras picked up some friendly jollity at the door to the cabin, where Barak and Arafat put on an "Alphonse-Gaston" show, each refusing to precede the other, and Barak gave Arafat a playful hug before they entered the lodge.[2] But the situation went downhill from there, as the discussions dragged on for more than two weeks, until July 26. During that time, there was considerable upheaval in Israel and the West Bank, with fistfights breaking out between settlers and Palestinians in Hebron, Israeli buses stoned and set on fire in a refugee camp, and right-wing demonstrations against the peace talks in Tel Aviv and Jerusalem. Things were not helped by a media blackout, so that rumors abounded. Sharon proclaimed after a week that Barak had broken all his promises; Foreign Minister Levy, who had

spoken with the prime minister, declared untrue a Palestinian report that "progress had been made" and said that gaps between the
two sides had "not narrowed at all" and the negotiations were "in
crisis." Clinton himself said that there had been "some progress,"
but that success was not certain.[3]

After a week, with sessions going nearly around the clock for
the third night in a row, Clinton postponed a scheduled trip to Japan so that he could stay on for one more day. But at the end of that
day, agreement was so far away that an announcement was made
that the talks had ended. According to Uri Dan, this was because
one hour before Clinton was to leave, Arafat gave him a letter stating, "I, as the representative of Arabs, Muslims and Christians, will
not accept any devaluated sovereignty over Jerusalem. Even if a
Palestinian state is established on 100 percent of Palestinian lands,
with Jerusalem in our hands, I will not confirm that the temple is
buried under Temple Mount."[4] But a few hours later, the talks were
on again, and Clinton left, with Madeleine Albright taking his place.
"Nobody wanted to give up," the president said. King Abdullah II
of Jordan met near Amman with Ezer Weizman, the former president of Israel, to discuss ways to resolve the conflicts, and later the
king phoned Arafat.[5]

After his three-day trip to Japan, Clinton returned, to resume
all-night sessions. Word leaked that Barak offered the PA chairman
double the forty percent of the West Bank already conceded by Israel, autonomy in Arab neighborhoods of Jerusalem and the return
of tens of thousands of Palestinian refugees. Arafat was holding out
for statehood with east Jerusalem as the capital, control of virtually
all of the West Bank, and recognition of the right of return of all
refugees. "We all want peace," Sharon told Israel Radio, "but not
the horrible peace of Barak that I am sorry to say could lead to
war."[6] The newspaper *Haaretz*, however, maintained that "Barak
should be congratulated for his readiness to smash the taboo on
negotiations over Jerusalem." A liberal analyst, Meron Benvenisti,

wrote in *Haaretz* that Barak's willingness to discuss Jerusalem meant that "division of the city" was "an act from which there can be no return."[7]

In the end, Arafat insisted on Palestinian control of the Old City which contained the Temple Mount with the two mosques, the Dome of the Rock and the al-Aqsa Mosque, where Mohammed was believed to have ascended to heaven, rejecting Clinton's compromise suggestion that the Old City be divided between Israel and the Palestinians, with control of the Temple Mount split among the UN Security Council, Morocco and the Palestinians. There was disagreement also over the "right of return," with Barak offering to absorb several thousand refugees over ten years, and to pay compensation for lost property—an offer unacceptable to Arafat, who wanted a right of return of millions of people. Barak was willing to give up eighty-four to ninety percent of the West Bank and almost all of the Gaza Strip, but Arafat wanted all the West Bank and all of Gaza. The talks collapsed for good, and Barak returned home, exhausted, still hoping for an agreement and in deep political trouble, with a minority of forty-two in the Knesset, and only two of his original seven partners remaining in his coalition.

These had been the most generous Israeli offers ever made. Arafat declared that they were unacceptable because Israel would continue to rule the Jordan Valley and the area around east Jerusalem, reducing Palestinian land to the level of cantons. Both Barak and the Americans were surprised and angry at Arafat's rejection of Barak's unprecedented concessions. David Levy resigned on August 2 (another blow to Barak's prestige), and the new foreign minister, Shlomo Ben-Ami, formerly internal security minister, offered the Palestinians ninety to ninety-five percent of the West Bank and a proposal that the Temple Mount be placed under control of the UN Security Council. This offer too was rejected by Arafat.[8]

On July 31, Barak survived two no-confidence motions in the Knesset. The Likud motions on the Camp David talks failed, after three hours of raucous debate with shouted interruptions and insults, to garner the sixty-one votes needed to bring down the government. The votes were fifty to fifty with eight abstentions, including David Levy, and twelve members who simply cast no votes. After this wan victory, Barak suffered a surprising defeat when Shimon Peres, his heavily favored candidate for the presidency, lost to Moshe Katsav, a relatively obscure and colorless Iranian-born Likud member. Peres, who had been prime minister three times and had won the Nobel Peace Prize with Arafat, had been considered a shoo-in by all political analysts and journalists. After the defeat, he wandered the chamber, pale with shock. This was the first time a Likud candidate had been elected president, and Katsav's victory reflected the growing power of Sephardic, Middle Eastern, Jews as opposed to the European Ashkenazi establishment. It was considered a big win for Sharon.

Barak now had to try and piece together a coalition; fortunately for him, the Knesset was about to close down for a three-month recess the following night, giving him some time to rebuild a base. A political radio analyst called Barak "a prime minister without a government" and cited the no-confidence vote as "the worst day for Barak since he was elected." The Likud member Limor Livnat shouted at Barak, "You write a letter to Clinton stating that suddenly it had become clear to you that the Palestinians are not partners to the talks and they are not negotiating in good faith. For this we should say, 'Good morning, Elijah.' Finally you have discovered what we have known for a long time."[9]

Barak mounted the podium and said, "I appeal to each and every one of you and ask you to rise above petty politics." He defended his actions, saying that they had strengthened Israel's standing and removed it from international isolation.[10] The next day, he blamed the Likud for refusing to help put together a national government. Sharon, he said, had rejected his overtures. Sharon denied that this had happened: "This is a pathetic attempt to save his collapsing government." He said that the Likud demanded "peace with a united, undivided Jerusalem under our exclusive sovereignty," and would never join a government that divided Jerusalem.[11] So elections were the only alternative. He told the press, "All the rights of the land are Jewish rights. There is no sharing of Jerusalem."[12] Before his two-hour interview with foreign reporters, Sharon took a moment to praise Shimon Peres, who was not, he said, a "loser," but would be remembered because he had been involved "in every field of life here." What had happened to him was not personal, but political, a reflection of deep disappointment and concern with Barak's actions: "I know what Shimon Peres has done for this country."[13]

The *Boston Globe* noted that some of Sharon's remarks seemed to indicate a shift on the settlement issue, reflecting how much the peace process had changed Israeli politics. He who had supported aggressive construction of settlements in the West Bank, creating a crucial roadblock to the peace process, and who, as Netanyahu's foreign minister, had offered to cede "not an inch more" than nine percent of the territory to PA control, was now "vaguely hinting at flexibility" by saying that "in peace, concessions are made. We are ready to make concessions. But not to the degree that Barak has done." Barak had, of course, offered withdrawal from ninety-seven percent of the West Bank. For the rest, Sharon admitted he was "not at all religious," but did not reply directly to the comment that control of Jewish shrines in Jerusalem was not considered vital by the secular Zionist founders of Israel. He said, "The Temple Mount is the holiest place of the Jewish people, and don't think for a minute we will give up sovereignty there."[14]

He announced the formation of the Jerusalem Coalition, fifty-eight parliament members from major right-wing and religious parties, including Likud, Shas, the Russian immigrant party and the National Religious Party.[15]

International press interest in Sharon's remarks reflected his return to the political spotlight. The *Globe* quoted *Haaretz* columnist
Yoel Marcus: "Only the person who built the time bomb called the
settlements really knows how to dismantle it without us all explod-
ing." But it quoted also commentator Zeev Schiff: "Sharon has made
his comeback already. It was a tough climb. He wants to climb even
higher, but I have my doubts. We would need a real crisis for people
to want to turn to Sharon."[16]

BARAK AT BAY

———

YOSSI SARID, THE MERETZ Party leader, said on August 2 that Barak had ninety days, while the Knesset was in summer recess, to "make a heroic attempt" to complete peace negotiations, and to set up early elections. President Clinton had not given up hope for peace: "If they want it," he said, "they can get it." He put the onus for the revival of the talks on Arafat, who had rejected a compromise on Jerusalem. Barak, Clinton said, was ready to try again. The Vatican, as it had since 1967, called for Jerusalem, or at least its holy sites, to be put under international supervision, an alternative not acceptable to either side. Madeleine Albright commented that "the complication here is [how to handle the fact that] Jerusalem is holy to three religions," and "[a]t Camp David, certainly the issue of internationalization was not the solution."[1]

In 1947, the United Nations partition plan had called for Jerusalem to be under international control. But after the 1948 war, a "Green Line" of barbed wire and sand bags was set up to separate the Israeli west from the Jordanian east. Jews were not allowed to enter the Old City. In 1967, Israel captured east Jerusalem, along with other Jordanian territory, but most foreign embassies, including the American embassy, were in Tel Aviv because Israel's claim to east Jerusalem was not recognized internationally. The Israelis insisted that since they controlled the holy sites, "freedom of access and worship" were never greater. Palestinians countered that when travel from the West Bank or from Gaza was denied on security grounds, freedom of worship was inhibited.[2]

David Levy said on August 3 that he was resigning as foreign minister because Barak's concessions at Camp David would have led to a division of the Old City, with Jews having to go through a walkway to get to the Western Wall. Levy was also clearly annoyed that Barak had used his Internal Security Minister Ben-Ami to conduct negotiations with the Palestinians, rather than using Levy himself. He said that he had given Barak a deadline to make "an honest effort" to form a national unity government, and since the prime minister had not met that deadline, he, Levy, was quitting the cabinet and going to vote in the Knesset for preliminary readings on dissolving parliament and calling for early elections. He followed through on these statements. The two Knesset members of Levy's Gesher Party, which represented Sephardic Jews, bolted Barak's coalition. The number of ministers in Barak's cabinet dropped to twelve from a high of twenty-three; his representation in the Knesset was forty members, one-third of the 120 seats.[3] A few days later, Levy met with Sharon to discuss the possibility of Gesher joining the Likud coalition.[4]

Arafat, meanwhile, made a tour of the Arab world, where his actions at Camp David were widely admired. In Algeria, he said it was time to bring the Russians in as mediators, a step to which Washington was adamantly opposed. Arafat said that the negotiations "were not a total failure" and that he was awaiting results of "attempts underway by the Americans, Europeans and Russians." Earlier, in Saudia Arabia, he said that if negotiations were not complete by September 13, he would issue a unilateral declaration of Palestinian statehood, although if an Arab summit asked him to, he would postpone that act. Clinton said he took this deadline seriously. Most analysts believed that if Arafat made this unilateral declaration at any time, there would be war between the IDF and the Palestinian police.[5]

David Horovitz, a strong proponent of peace, commented that Arafat was fortunate that Barak had survived the no-confidence

motions because that gave the Palestinian leader "a second chance
. . . to moderate his positions." Horovitz said that although Israelis,
with the exception of those on the far left, believed that Arafat had
encouraged street violence against Israeli soldiers, and had not done
enough to prevent suicide bombings over the past seven years, or to
educate his people for a permanent compromise with Israel—despite this, fifty-six percent of Israelis had rejected Natanyahu and
chosen Barak, who had made clear his willingness to compromise
on Jerusalem, to pay "a painful price." Now Arafat had returned
from the summit insisting publicly that all of Jerusalem would be
Palestinian and that he would declare statehood on September 13,
while implying privately that he would be assassinated if he com-
promised on Jerusalem, which was a "pan-Arab issue," or on the
right of return. Barak, Horovitz said, had violated his "red line"
against dividing Jerusalem and had returned home empty-handed.
If his government had fallen, and Netanyahu or Sharon had taken
his place, Arafat, at seventy-one, could have "waved goodbye" to
an independent Palestinian state. Horovitz did not believe that Arafat,
who had infuriated the Americans, would have a third chance to
resolve the conflict.[6]

In early August, a newspaper poll reported that fifty-six percent
of Israelis found Barak "not credible," and that if the election were
held that day, the tally would be forty-three percent for Barak and
thirty-nine percent for Netanyahu. Against Sharon, the prime minister would gain a point to forty-three percent, while Sharon would
garner thirty-nine percent of the vote. Fifty-six percent of Israelis
were against the establishment of a Palestinian state on ninety-five
percent of the West Bank and Gaza, with its capital in east Jerusalem, while forty-one percent were in favor of this Barak formula.[7]
Uri Dan reported that Abu Ala, also known as Ahmed Qurei, a
powerful PLO figure, told the Palestinian Council in Ramallah that
Clinton created "a great evil for the Palestinian people and the Palestinian cause" by blaming Arafat for the failure of the summit.

Saeb Erekat said that Clinton was "completely" on Israel's side, but that the Palestinians had "succeeded in breaking the Israeli taboo. They are ready to negotiate even Temple Mount."[8]

Netanyahu's followers began to canvass support for him for a challenge to Sharon as Likud leader. Sharon himself recognized that Netanyahu would "definitely be a problem"; he could hardly think otherwise since Netanyahu consistently beat him in private Likud opinion polls, and was closing the gap with Barak. After the Camp David summit had started, Netanyahu had called the two major Israeli television channels to his house to make a flag-flanked "dramatic personal announcement" in which he talked of the need for reconciliation and unity and warned that if Jerusalem were divided, it would be "the beginning of the collapse of our nation and people." Netanyahu's main problem was that he and his wife were under investigation for illegally keeping 700 gifts during his term of office, and receiving more than $100,000 in service fees from a private building contractor who wanted to gain political favors. The attorney general was considering whether to prosecute him for bribery, theft and obstruction of justice.[9]

By late August, Barak's situation was becoming desperate. He announced that when the Knesset reconvened in October, he would try to win passage of a constitution, something that had never been done because of religious and Arab-rights issues. He said that he would also "raise the flag of a civil society," legalizing civil marriage, improving women's rights, abolishing the Ministry of Religious Affairs and ending military exemptions for ultra-Orthodox Jews and Israeli Arabs. He would discontinue government subsidies to ultra-Orthodox schools if they did not add secular subjects—mathematics, English, science and civics—to their curricula of Talmud, Bible and other Jewish studies. He was also taking into consideration the question of El Al flights and bus service on the Sabbath.[10]

Barak must have been hoping to attract new supporters, since he would inevitably alienate the religious parties. But the country was stunned by this new agenda, and even Barak's One Israel party greeted the initiative with little enthusiasm. Shimon Peres pointed out that this strategy would alienate the Shas Party, which controlled seventeen crucial Knesset seats, and prevent it backing any imminent peace agreement, and that this agenda seemed to reflect Barak's pessimism about chances for peace.[11] Many political analysts agreed with Peres; others thought the agenda was intended to be a signal to Arafat that time was running out, or to scare Shas into cooperation with One Israel. There was one school of thought that held it was a cynical move, since Barak could never get that program through the Knesset, and another that believed that Israelis craved peace so much and were so fed up with the power of the ultra-Orthodox, that they would empower Barak once more.[12]

Barak then said that if the peace talks failed—and he would "not make peace at any price or by any date"[13]—he planned to invite the opposition to join him in a national unity government, with Sharon as foreign minister. He said his "admiration" for Sharon was "not a secret."[14] The Meretz Party, which quit the cabinet but not the coalition in late June, did not share this admiration: its leader Yossi Sarid had refused to shake Sharon's hand because of the Sabra and Shatilla massacre in Lebanon, and the party members said they would not sit with Sharon. Many other liberal leaders refused to accept the failure of the peace process. The One Israel justice minister Yossi Beilin said that a national unity government would announce to the world that Israel was not committed to peace.[15] In any case, Sharon rejected the invitation, saying that he disagreed with every component of the Camp David deal, and considered the proposal to reduce religious power to be an untenable political "stunt." He called for early elections.[16]

At the end of August, Netanyahu and Sharon held a meeting on neutral ground in the offices of an advertising executive. Sharon sat at the head of the table, emphasizing his position as leader of the opposition. Netanyahu announced that he and Sharon saw "eye-to-eye on the [perilous] situation in which Israel finds itself."[17] "Bibi" was awaiting the attorney general's decision, and if he was exonerated, even his enemies in the Likud had to concede that Netanyahu could probably win seventy to eighty percent of the 2,700 votes of the party's central committee.[18]

Shortly before the September 13 deadline for the declaration of an independent state, the Palestinian Central Council announced a decision to postpone the declaration for some weeks, to allow more time for negotiation with the Israelis. Experts on Palestinian politics believed that Arafat was "developing some negative attitudes" toward Clinton, whose term was running out, and preferred to deal with someone else after the president left office. It was thought that Arafat had no intention of compromising on east Jerusalem, and probably not on withdrawal to the June, 1967, borders, since he had to palliate Arab extremists who really wanted all of Palestine, including Israel. Since he had offered to guarantee unlimited access to the Western Wall, Arafat could not understand why he could not be granted legal sovereignty over the Temple Mount, which was already under practical Palestinian control.[19]

Barak did not have enough political strength left to reach an agreement with Arafat. Even Yitzhak Rabin's widow Leah said that her husband had to be spinning in his grave over Barak's concessions on Jerusalem.[20] Barak himself believed that an agreement with Arafat could save his government, but Arafat was said to think that a right-wing government like Netanyahu's, would generate more international sympathy for the Palestinian cause. Barak wanted a unity government. He sent his communications minister, Binyamin Ben-Eliezer, to dine with Sharon at the Negev farm; Sharon described the evening as a family social event, and nothing more. It was thought that Sharon would not take kindly to the fact that Barak did not come in person but sent a deputy, and in any case at that time Sharon

could not alienate his allies, right-wing and religious, by dealing
politically with One Israel.[21]

51

AL-AQSA INTIFADA

───

THE ANNOUNCEMENT THAT SHARON intended to visit the Temple Mount on September 28, twenty-four hours before the start of Rosh Hashonah, engendered criticism and warnings from Palestinian officials, who called it a provocation that would lead to violence. The Palestinian Legislative Council called the visit a "flagrant aggression against the holy places and disregard for the feelings of the Palestinian people and the Arab and Islamic nations" that "would create an explosive situation in the holy city." The Palestinian Ministry of Information called on citizens to be present at the al-Aqsa Mosque "to defend it should Sharon and his gang try to defile it or encroach on it."[1] The Fatah youth organization and the head of the Waqf, the Muslim board of trustees that administered the Temple Mount mosques, announced that they would use "any means" to prevent the visit, which had been cleared with Barak.[2] Israel had taken over the area in the 1967 war, but Moshe Dayan, who was chief of staff at the time, had given Muslim authorities control of the mosque sites to demonstrate religious tolerance, even though under the Jordanians, Jews had been denied access to the Western Wall, the holiest site in Judaism.

Although street fighting had already broken out, the Israeli police and security services did not recommend against the visit, saying that they did not foresee a problem, and anyway Knesset members could not be prevented from visiting the Temple Mount. This despite the fact that in 1990 false rumors that Jewish extremists were going to rebuild the temple started a riot in which seventeen Palestinians were killed and 140 wounded by Israeli police, and in 1996 the opening of the archaeological tunnel outside the Mount had resulted in eighty deaths, most of them Palestinians. "Every citizen and tourist has the right to visit the Temple Mount," Justice Minister Yossi Beilin said. He added that if Sharon went, he would see that Israel was not the sovereign power there, and that the Waqf was running things.[3]

On September 28, on the eve of Rosh Hashonah, Sharon paid his visit to the tree-shaded mosque compound, strolling about happily for nearly half an hour, accompanied by six Likud members, while a thousand Israeli policemen in full riot gear were deployed about the site. He made no attempt to enter the mosques or to approach them.[4] He was interested, he said, in inspecting construction near Solomon's Stables, medieval underground vaults where the Waqf had built a new mosque. In the event, he was not able to visit Solomon's Stables. As he left, he was followed by three irate Arab MKs, who waved their fists and shouted, "This is Palestine! It belongs to us!" In the street below, Sharon supporters responded, "This is Jewish land! Get out!"[5] Sharon's motive for this seems to have been connected to a desire to denigrate Barak's peace initiative. It should be pointed out that in 1987 Sharon had leased a house in the Muslim quarter of the Old City after an Arab family had been evicted for non-payment of rent. That had been called a provocation by Palestinians and by Israeli liberals, including Teddy Kollek, then the mayor of Jerusalem. Now since Lily's death Sharon had been spending more time in this house, which sported a twenty-foot Israeli flag and a ten-foot steel menorah with plastic-encased lights.[6]

Moments after Sharon and his retinue left the site, dozens of youths, some students with school bags, shouting "God is great!" and "Murderer out!" in Arabic, began to throw rocks, bottles, chairs and trash cans at the police, who fired rubber bullets, tear gas and live ammunition at them and clubbed them to force them out of the streets. Some of the debris rained down on shocked Jews praying at the Western Wall just below the Temple Mount. Four Palestinians were killed and at least 207 wounded, and twenty-five policemen, including the Israeli police chief, were injured, along with four paramedics. Sharon denied that he was trying to provoke anyone. "We came here today with a message of peace," he said, adding that the Palestinian reaction made him wonder about future coexistence.[7]

On September 29, a Friday, as an al-Aqsa imam urged Muslims to defend the mosque, rioting erupted again and spread throughout Jerusalem: figures varied, but five Palestinians were reported killed, and more than 200 injured; forty-four police officers, fifteen Israeli civilians and five German tourists were hurt. In the rioting crowds were two top PA officials, Faisal Husseini, Arafat's Jerusalem representative, Tawfiq Tirawi, a senior PA intelligence officer in civilian clothes and Marwan Barghouti, head of Arafat's Fatah movement, which had announced it had intended to disrupt Sharon's visit.[8]

On Saturday the uproar spread through the West Bank and Gaza with clashes between Israeli troops and young Palestinians, while PA leaders called on radio and television for jihad and a general strike. Yassir Arafat condemned Sharon's visit as "a serious step against the Islamic holy places" and called on "the Arab and Islamic world to move immediately to stop these aggressions and Israeli practices against holy Jerusalem." When he was asked what he wanted the Arab world to do, Arafat replied, "They should move quickly." He called too on the United States to dissuade Israel from "provocative behavior."[9]

Ehud Barak in his turn phoned Arafat and urged him to act to prevent more bloodshed. He said that he made it clear "that Israel cannot tolerate these kinds of attacks" and that the government expected "the Palestinian Authority to work with all its resources against the terrorist elements within the Palestinian areas and within the Palestinian Authority itself."[10] In an interview with the *Jerusalem Post*, Barak said that an agreement that ended the conflict would include Jerusalem as two capitals side by side: Jerusalem the capital of Israel, and next to it the capital of Palestine, called Al Quds.[11]

Sharon called this suggestion "a major historical mistake" and vowed to use "every democratic means" to resist the division of Jerusalem.[12] A Palestinian source said that Barak had discussed the Al Quds idea with Arafat earlier, and that Barak was repeating what the Palestinians had been "telling the Israelis for a long time," that once there was an agreement on sharing Jerusalem, the whole world would recognize the city as Israel's capital, and would recognize Israel's borders, and relations would be normalized between Israel and the Arab states. There had also, Palestinian officials said, been a discussion of a suggestion by the US and Egypt to place the Temple Mount under the temporary supervision of the UN Security Council and the three Arab members of the Jerusalem committee.[13]

The Voice of Palestine radio in Ramallah quoted the speaker of the Palestinian Legislative Council, who said that Sharon's "provocative visit . . . defiled" the Temple Mount and was "a clear and flagrant expression of the Israeli schemes against Al-Haram al-Sharif [the Temple Mount], Jerusalem and the entire Palestine question." The Palestinian information minister said he could not rule out the possibility that Likud and Barak's coalition had planned the visit in order to obstruct the peace negotiations, and that Sharon was "a symbol of racism, massacres and bloodshed."[14] From Beirut, Hezbollah called for "resistance and jihad" against the "sheer barbarity . . . tantamount to a declaration of war" of "the violation of the sanctity of al-Aqsa Mosque by terrorist Ariel Sharon, the butcher of Sabra and Shatilla massacres, amid tight security measures by Zionist occupation soldiers."[15]

Israeli police said they believed the rioting had been planned, since Palestinians had emerged from the mosques carrying stones.[16] But a new intifada had clearly begun. Israeli Arabs joined in the uprising, as they had not done in the first intifada, attacking cars, setting fire to gas stations and banks, while shooting and bombing by PA militiamen and police became widespread. There was some feeling among Israelis and the international press that Barak had neglected to address the very real grievances of Israeli Arabs, who had given him ninety-five percent of their vote in 1999. He had no Arabs in his coalition. And in the West Bank and Gaza, Barak had approved the enlargement of settlements.

On the same day that Sharon made his visit to the Temple Mount, Attorney General Elyakim Rubenstein issued his decision on the accusations against Netanyahu and his wife: he had decided against prosecution because of insufficient evidence. Although Rubenstein also said that the Netanyahus had had an improper relationship with a contractor who had been alleged to have done more than $100,000 worth of free work for them, his decision not to prosecute was bad news for both Barak and Sharon. Netanyahu was returning to Israel from the United States, where he had been living and working as a business consultant.[17]

Sharon, as could be expected, was widely criticized for his visit. Arafat, who had suffered a public relations defeat after he refused Barak's peace offer, was now regaining international sympathy. But Sharon was characteristically unrepentant: he wrote a letter to Madeleine Albright saying that State Department disapproval of his action was "totally unacceptable," that Jerusalem and the Temple Mount were "under full Israeli sovereignty" and that neither he, "nor any Israeli citizen," needed "to seek permission from the Palestinian Authority, or from any foreign entity, to visit there."[18]

In fact, there was no prohibition against Jews going to the Temple Mount. Reuven Rivlin, who had been with Sharon there, said he went to the Western Wall and the Temple Mount before every holiday, adding, "It really burns me that Israeli Arabs can enter the site freely, but Israeli MKs need a thousand policemen to safeguard their visit."[19] Uri Dan quoted Sharon saying, "The Jews in Israel and all over the world should know that if this kind of security is needed to protect a legitimate visit by Israeli parliamentarians, just imagine how many troops will have to be deployed if, God forbid, Mr Barak hands over east Jerusalem to Arafat."[20] This observation raises the possibility that the visit to the Temple Mount was intended to denigrate Barak's stand on two capitals.

By October 9, at least eighty-three people were dead, mostly Palestinians, and America had abstained from a UN Security Council vote condemning the "excessive use of force" against the Palestinians. After three days of negotiations, the US succeeded in removing an explicit condemnation of Israeli security forces. All the other fourteen Security Council members voted for the resolution. Richard Holbrooke, the American ambassador to the UN, decried the resolution, but said that he had been personally instructed by the president to abstain, because a US veto would have destroyed all Arab confidence in the US as a fair mediator. Saying that he had literally been up day and night because of the violence, President Clinton phoned Barak and Arafat several times trying to "get things calmed down" and get them back on the peace track for a summit in Egypt, an idea that Hosni Mubarak rejected. The president was fearful that this situation could spread to other countries and lead to a regional war: there were massive anti-Israel protests in Jordan, Egypt, Sudan and even Morocco, which had had quiet relations with Israel. The Jordanian parliament had demanded that diplomatic relations with Israel be broken off, a demand rejected by King Abdullah who had, however, postponed the arrival of Jordan's new ambassador in Tel Aviv.[21]

Barak threatened stronger action and an end to peace talks if the violence did not end; Arafat, calling the Israeli attacks "criminal," made no public appeal for calm; Kofi Annan and the British and Russian foreign ministers visited both Barak and Arafat; in Jerusalem Arabs threw rocks at Israeli motorists, closing the main road; in Tel Aviv the mayor asked citizens to stay indoors after hundreds of Jews burned tires, smashed Arab cars, and shouted "Death to the Arabs!"[22] The London *Daily Telegraph* gave its view of the situation: "Mr Arafat is manipulating religious sentiment for political ends—to consolidate his support at home, rally the sympathies of the Arab and wider Muslim world, and shake up western diplomacy after the stalemate at Camp David. Likewise, Mr Sharon's visit to the Haram al-Sharif was about politics, not religion. By visiting the area with a train of 1000 policemen to protect him, he was making a statement that Israel should not give up its sovereignty over the Temple Mount."[23]

Rage escalated: the televised death in his father's arms of a twelve-year-old Palestinian boy cowering from crossfire on a street corner in Gaza, upset viewers worldwide. (In March, 2002, a documentary on German television channel ARD found that the boy, Mohammed a-Dura, was most likely shot dead by Palestinian gunmen firing at Israeli troops.)[24] Then on October 12 a Palestinian mob broke into a Ramallah police station and beat to death two Israeli reserve soldiers who had driven into Ramallah by mistake and been detained by the police. Both bodies were dragged through the streets and set on fire. A third body was found later, charred beyond recognition. Television, despite PA attempts at censorship, showed one of the killers displaying his bloody hands to the delighted mob. Barak, whose popularity had hit an all-time low, struck back with what he called a "limited, symbolic" response with advance warning so that targeted areas could be evacuated. Israeli tanks, battleships and helicopters surrounded the Palestinian areas; a security headquarters in Gaza and the Ramallah police station were demolished by rockets and a television station was strafed. Arafat called the air strikes a "declaration of war," while Sharon called them insufficient.[25]

Jerusalem turned into a ghost town with riot police and soldiers everywhere. Because Muslims under the age of forty-five were now barred from entering the Temple Mount area, hundreds of them gathered to worship at the Damascus gate outside the walls of the Old City. Barak said that Arafat no longer seemed to be a partner for peace.[26] A Jewish shrine, Joseph's Tomb, had been attacked in

Nablus, Torah scrolls had been destroyed and a rabbi murdered; in Jericho the ancient synagogue had been set afire; rocks were thrown down from the Temple Mount on Jewish worshippers at the Western Wall below. But Barak was most upset when Arafat released up to ninety Hamas and Islamic Jihad activists from his jails in Gaza, among them a man blamed for the death of sixty Israelis in suicide bombings, and another thought to have made a bomb that killed twenty-two Israelis in 1995. In addition, Hamas representatives were participating in Palestine Authority cabinet meetings.[27]

Off the record, White House officials let it be known that the president and Mrs Albright felt betrayed by Arafat's failure to try to stop the riots. They believed with some bitterness that they had turned him from a pariah to a respected international figure: since the 1993 rapprochement with Rabin, Arafat had been in the Oval Office a dozen times. But it had been difficult to get the Palestinian leader to the Camp David negotiations the previous July, and when he did come, the White House said he had behaved in a cold and noncommittal manner, and was particularly difficult on the Jerusalem issue. Now they were beginning to believe that he had lost control, if he had ever had it. Outside observers pointed out that the Americans had not solicited the opinions of Arab leaders before Camp David, and these had advised Arafat not to compromise on Jerusalem.[28]

Barak, who had no majority in the parliament, wanted to set up an "emergency unity coalition" with Sharon and some other parties; he did not include the ultra-right-wing or Israeli Arab parties. To avoid being voted out of office, the prime minister needed to bolster his coalition when the Knesset reconvened at the end of October. Sharon did not in the end agree to join this coalition, since he probably had no intention of helping Barak's political survival, but the Israeli left wing was horrified that Sharon, the architect of the Lebanon war, would be offered a cabinet post by the man whom they had considered Yitzhak Rabin's heir. (Arafat too protested the overture to Sharon. His spokesman Saeb Erekat said on TV, "Barak has to choose between negotiations with the Palestinians or the inclusion of Ariel Sharon in his government.")[29] Apart from this, the Left was depressed and disillusioned for a myriad of reasons: they had believed that the 1993 Oslo accords had marked the beginning of an inevitable peace process, and they had rejoiced in new relations with the Palestinians, and with the acceptance by their fellow citizens of the idea of an independent Palestinian state, after thirty years of often angry rejection.

But with Sharon's visit to the Temple Mount, their dreams were punctured. At first they blamed him for his provocative act. But as they watched the violence spread and heard the Palestinian rhetoric, they began to think back to the Camp David meetings in July, and to conclude that Barak had gone the limit, endangering his own career by his willingness to compromise, and that Arafat had simply rejected him and moved back to a militant position. The Left had insisted that the PA chairman was sincere and would stay the course of peace; now they felt humiliated. Amos Oz, the Israeli novelist, one of the strongest supporters of the peace process, said he blamed the Palestinian leadership. Arafat, he commented bitterly, perhaps preferred to be Che Guevara and not Fidel Castro. "If he becomes the leader of Palestine, he'll be the leader of a rough Third World country and have to deal with sewage in Hebron, drugs in Gaza, and the corruption in his own government." In the liberal newspaper *Haaretz*, Lily Galilee said, "It is one thing to be thought of as a liberal, and even a traitor. It is an entirely different matter to be considered a fool whom reality has slapped in the face."[30]

But Peace Now still maintained that the Jewish settlements were the main obstacle to peace, angering the Palestinians and presenting a security burden to Israel. Arafat insisted that Barak's concessions simply consisted of small non-contiguous packets of land that did not constitute a real state—a position contested by Clinton's envoy Dennis Ross, who maintained that the proposed area was contiguous, and did not consist of "cantons."[31] The Left feared that Barak would be gone and Sharon, or even Netanyahu, would take his place. The only possibility for optimism for them was the fact that it was the Likud's Begin who had made peace with Egypt by returning the Sinai, that the right-wing Nixon had gone to China, and that Sharon had evacuated Jewish settlements in the Sinai, and, when he became Netanyahu's foreign minister, had dropped his opposition to negotiations. So Sharon might be the only one who could hand over east Jerusalem and remove the settlers, a solution that the Left saw as inevitable.

Another cause for concern was the condition of the Israeli military. Charles Heyman, the editor of *Jane's World Armies*, was quoted in the London *Daily Telegraph* as saying that the recent "unsophisticated attempts at riot control" demonstrated that the Israeli army was not what it had been; the reservists being called up were "just shooting into the crowd." The best and the brightest were no longer choosing the army as a career, the springboard for men like Dayan, Sharon and Barak, but industry. Since few liberals chose an army career, the army had developed a right-wing cast, and thus, apart from tension between the IDF and the liberal Ehud Barak, there was "the potential for greater violence in any internal security operations against Palestinians."[32]

On October 15, after three weeks of violence, with about a hundred people dead, mostly Palestinians and Israeli Arabs, and thousands wounded, Arafat agreed to an emergency summit meeting with Barak and Clinton at Sharm al-Sheikh on the Red Sea in Egypt, brokered by Kofi Annan, Hosni Mubarak and King Abdullah, as well as Clinton, who had spent the preceding week working the phones to ask Mideast leaders to help solve what he called "one of the greatest tragedies of our time and one of the very hardest problems to solve," adding, "Every step forward has been marked with pain."[33] Hamas condemned the summit, and Iraq and other hardline Muslim states criticized Arafat for cooperating. Jewish settlers in their turn denounced Barak for meeting Arafat while the violence went on. The Likud said that Barak should limit the talks to immediate arrangements for a cease-fire.

The ability of Arafat to stop the violence was coming into question. Sheik Hassan Nasrallah, a leader of the Shiite Muslim Hezbollah, which had its own flag and was working closely with Iran, urged his audience at a rally to stab Israelis: "If you don't have bullets, who among you doesn't have knives? Hide the knife, and when he comes close to the enemy, let him stab him. Let the stab be fatal." His message was repeatedly broadcast on radio and on the independent satellite Arab television station al-Jazeera. It was believed that young members of Arafat's Fatah organization were becoming disillusioned with the chairman and had formed Tanzim, their own faction with close ties to Hamas and Hezbollah.[34]

Across the Mideast, Arab response to the announcement of the Sharm al-Sheikh summit was decidedly negative. In Baghdad, Tehran, Cairo and Tunis, thousands marched through the streets, burned Israeli and US flags, shouted "Death to Israel!" and offered to fight with the Palestinians. In Tunis, 3000 people held a peaceful demonstration against Sharon. In Tehran, the crowd chanted, "Israel will be annihilated and Palestine shall be liberated." They also chanted slogans against Arafat, accusing him of selling out to Israel.[35] Robin Wright wrote about "visible anger" in the normally tranquil streets of Morocco, Bahrain, Oman, the United Arab Emirates, Kuwait, Saudi Arabia, Syria, Jordan, Yemen and other states where "the current crisis offers a pretext to vent grievances otherwise banned at home." These demonstrations were particularly notable in Morocco, a moderate state that had good, if discreet, relations with Israel, and Kuwait, which was firmly pro-Western. Half a million people called for a jihad in Rabat, and in Casablanca police were forced to use tear gas on demonstrators.[36] In the Gaza Strip and the West Bank, violence increased as demonstrators urged Arafat not to bend to US and Israeli pressure to call off the intifada. Hundreds of

Fatah supporters, many of them armed, held a rally in Gaza City announcing "the creation of military cells to continue the uprising and strike the Zionist occupation wherever it may be."[37]

At the two-day Sharm al-Sheikh summit meeting, a truce was agreed upon, but nothing was signed, and there was no handshake between Arafat and Barak. It was arranged that a committee would be set up to look into the intifada and seek resolutions to the problems. Barak himself was not sanguine about the summit's accomplishments. "From our point of view," he said, "we achieved our goal, but it remains to be seen to what extent it will be implemented." His security advisor said, "We will wait and see what happens tonight and tomorrow. In the light of this, Israel may have to reconsider."[38] Sharon issued a statement saying that he took "a severe view of Barak's agreement to continue the Camp David process from the point where it left off as if nothing happened." That Camp David "process" involved Barak's offer of a Palestinian state in more than ninety percent of the West Bank and Gaza Strip. Although sixty-two percent of Israelis favored a national unity government, Sharon said there was "no possibility for unity as long as the prime minister is not willing to disassociate himself from the Camp David principles." He viewed also as "very grave" Israel's agreement to the investigating committee, and its failure to demand the dismantling of the Tanzim faction and the imprisonment of freed Hamas militants.[39] Barak, a government official said, "is now in a miserable situation."[40]

Arafat too seemed to have gained nothing from the summit. He returned to Gaza without fanfare, in an aura of defeat. His office issued a statement, but he would not put his name on it. All he said was that "the most important thing" was "implementation of the accord, which we want to be to the letter."[41] Marwan Barghouti, leader of Arafat's Fatah group, said that at the summit "they failed to read the genuine message of the intifada because the Palestinian people cannot live with the occupation. . . . The current intifada will continue and perhaps even intensify. I personally don't want it to stop." But he would continue it, he said, "in peaceful ways. Most of the violence isn't on our side, but on Israel's side. Fact: 100 Palestinians dead and thousands injured. We have paid, and are paying, a heavy price."[42]

But perhaps Arafat had not failed completely. Over the objections of the United States, the UN General Assembly convened an emergency session and passed a resolution condemning Israel's "excessive use of force" against Palestinian civilians. It specifically put the onus for the uprising, and more than 100 Arab deaths, on Sharon's "provocative" visit to the Temple Mount. The US and Israel voted against the motion, and Britain and Germany abstained. And a special session of the UN Commission on Human Rights was meeting in Geneva to discuss a resolution accusing Israel of "crimes against humanity." The commission noted that a third of the people killed since Sharon's visit were children; it listed violations of UN conventions and called for investigation by representatives of seven UN human rights departments.[43]

Immediately after Sharm al-Sheikh, on October 21–22, the leaders of the twenty-one states of the Arab League held an emergency summit at Cairo, their first in four years. The attempt was to endorse the peace process and at the same time make clear a sense of outrage at Israeli behavior and give strong support to Arafat, who was present, and who made an impassioned speech saying that Sharon's visit had been deliberately planned with the Israeli government to escalate the tensions in the area, and add a dangerous religious dimension to them. The summit endorsed the "right of return" of Palestinian refugees, Palestinian control of east Jerusalem, an international war crimes tribunal to try Israeli perpetrators of atrocities, and the establishment of a new billion-dollar fund to ease the plight of Palestinians, to which Saudi Arabia promised to donate twenty-five million.

The Libyan delegation walked out after the first session, saying that they believed the group's pronouncements would be "toothless." Saddam Hussein, invited for the first time since Iraq invaded Kuwait in 1990, sent a long message, the point of which was: "Holy war is the only way to free Palestine." The president of Yemen said that normalizing relations with Israel "has weakened us." He was saying, he said, "Yes to holy war, yes to donations, yes to sending weapons" to the Palestinians. "But," he added mysteriously, "we are not calling for war." King Abdullah called for a freeze on diplomatic relations to punish Israel, and Egypt did in fact withdraw its ambassador, while Jordan did not send a new one to Tel Aviv. Those with partial diplomatic relations with Israel, including Tunisia and Morocco, broke them off. Iran, not a member of the Arab League, called for holy war against Israel, donated an ambulance and other humanitarian aid to the Palestinians and transported some wounded by air to hospitals for urgent care.[44]

Marwan Barghouti of the Fatah, reflecting the response of the Palestinian streets, said that the summit results did not do justice to the nearly 200 people who had died, and the more than 3000 who had been injured. He was disappointed that Jordan and Egypt did not take concrete action against Israel.

On October 22, Barak, still attempting to placate the Likud in order to form a national unity government and stave off early elections, condemned the "language of threats" that had come from the Arab summit, and announced that Israel was breaking off all peace negotiations as long as violence continued. He did not discuss this "time out" with his cabinet before announcing it, and Planning Minister Shimon Peres, Justice Minister Yossi Beilin and Foreign Minister Shlomo Ben-Ami made clear their opposition to it.[45] Arafat responded angrily that "our people are continuing on the road to Jerusalem, capital of the independent Palestinian state," and Barak could "go to hell."[46]

The Egyptian foreign minister Amr Moussa was quoted in a leading Lebanese newspaper as saying, "The peace process in its present form is over. No Arab or Palestinian leaders will agree to return to the negotiating table according to the previous rules. The Arabs should now give first priority to help the Palestinians in opposing the Israeli occupation. The Arab world should determine a new and final framework for a solution according to the Arab perception." A Tanzim leader in the West Bank said that when Barak "chose" to form a coalition with Sharon, "he killed the peace process." The intifada, he went on, would continue until "independence—until we liberate east Jerusalem and get rid of the settlers." All four Arab parties in the Knesset agreed that Barak "had shot the peace process" and Sharon's inclusion in the government would be "a death certificate to peace."[47] The Arab MKs said they would vote against the budget, even if it included an aid package for the Arab sector, because they would not sell out the peace process.

Not only Barak's One Israel party, Labor and the Arab MKs were against Sharon, but White House officials, while intimating that Arafat had made no effort to rein in the violence, said privately that they did not want to do or say anything that would help Sharon politically, because they believed that his inclusion in the coalition would end all chance of resuming peace talks. Clinton said that Barak was "getting the worst of both worlds." The same day that the president said this, the US House of Representatives passed a nonbinding resolution, 365 to thirty, condemning Arafat and other Palestinian leaders for "encouraging the violence and doing so little for so long to stop it, resulting in the senseless loss of life."[48]

Arafat called his government to Gaza for continuous meetings. His hope, it was said, was that doves in the Labor Party would rebel against Barak's attempt to join with Sharon. Rumors that there were plans for Israel to separate itself from the Palestinians alarmed the settlers, who put out a statement: "The people who have awakened from an imaginary peace will not agree to give Arafat a prize for violence in the form of transferring Jews out of their homes." Barak phoned both Russian President Vladimir Putin and British Prime Minister Tony Blair, while Foreign Minister Ben-Ami contacted various European counterparts, in attempts to get foreign pressure put on Arafat to cease the violence and act in accordance with the Sharm al-Sheikh agreement. Ben-Ami said plaintively, "I turn to Israeli Arabs. Does anybody think that there is a sane person in this country, this government, who wants to harm the sacredness of Islam, who wants to harm al-Aqsa? We have had sovereignty over the Temple Mount for thirty years and we have never changed the status quo. Under our sovereignty, the biggest mosque in the Middle East has been constructed."[49]

In return for joining a national unity government, Sharon demanded veto power on diplomatic and security policies, top cabinet jobs for Likud MKs and that elections be called within six months if Labor violated any paragraph of the coalition agreement. Barak had offered Sharon a voice in deciding the security cabinet agenda, but not early elections and other things; now he delayed responding to Sharon's demands. Labor stalwarts passed a resolution calling for continuing peace efforts, "a fundamental part of the Labor Party ideology and platform," although they also called on Arafat to act to stop the violence.[50] The prime minister, desperate for Sharon's cooperation but unwilling to alienate his own base where there was talk about replacing him as a candidate in the next elections, vowed not to abandon Oslo and Camp David, although he knew that Sharon could not join him unless he did abandon those agreements.[51]

It was not only the Likud that objected to the Oslo agreements. In the US, the Association of State Green Parties passed a resolution condemning the use of force against Palestinians. Tom Sevigny, the co-chair of its steering committee said, "It's significant that the very mechanism for achieving peace, the Oslo Process, has ignored international law, which is the only equitable basis for resolving ethnic conflict. Instead, Oslo has been subject to inherent biases that are antithetical to international law. It privileges Israeli goals and needs at the expense of inalienable Palestinian rights to self-determination, political and economic freedom and return of refugees."[52]

Meanwhile Benjamin Netanyahu waited in the wings, ready to challenge Sharon for the leadership of Likud. His poll numbers were good; he had forty-nine percent to Barak's twenty-five. He had alienated many in the Likud with his secret maneuverings, but an official said, "Forget what he was like when he was prime minister. The people now see Barak who does not communicate, who keeps changing his mind, who is arrogant and got us into this war with the Palestinians. They think Netanyahu can rescue them from this mess." One of Barak's cabinet ministers said, "Unfortunately, I know who our next prime minister is." Projecting the image of a strong leader, Netanyahu said he was not talking about "tax reforms or public transportation," he was talking about deciding between a policy "based on continuous diplomatic concessions or [one] based on rebuilding Israel's deterrent power and strength."[53]

But the "mess" involved more than deterrence and strength; at the end of October, the economy was in bad shape, both in Israel and the West Bank. Tourism had fallen by fifty percent, causing a billion-dollar loss in foreign currency, the loss of thousands of jobs and a drop in the value of the shekel; olives rotted on the trees and construction stopped because Palestinian laborers were not allowed into the country. The Palestinian economy was losing about ten million dollars a day; the unemployment rate in the territories, which had been about thirteen percent before the intifada, had gone up to forty-five percent in Gaza and around thirty-one percent in the West Bank. Maher Masri, PA minister of trade and economy, said that the Israeli blockade was keeping 120,000 Palestinians from their jobs inside Israel, stopping imports from reaching the territories, and strangling economic activity. He warned that if Israel kept up its "economic siege" much longer, "it is a call for more violence in the land." The billion dollars that the Arabs had pledged at their Cairo summit had not yet been received. In Gaza, Arafat told reporters that the uprising would continue until "a boy or a girl raises the Palestinian flag above Al Quds [Jerusalem], the capital of our Palestinian state."[54]

Sharon expressed no regrets for his visit to the Temple Mount. In October, in his first important address since the uprising began, he told a gathering of some 4000 cheering, shouting, evangelical Christians that although "the land of Israel" was sacred to Jews, Christians and Muslims, "it was promised by God only to the Jews," and that Jerusalem would remain "the undivided capital of Israel forever," as the Bible said.[55] In early November, he spoke to the Foreign Press Association, saying that the Palestinians had taken advantage of his visit to the Temple Mount, where he had gone "from time to time," to implement their plans for violence after Camp David, and that if he hadn't gone, "they would have found another excuse." He said that before he went, he had cleared the visit with the police and the security service and that Ben-Ami, the foreign minister, had discussed it with Jibril Rajoub, the PA security head, who had given the go-ahead, a statement that Rajoub denied. Sharon repeated his defense later in the month to a group in New York, where he also said that Barak was taking a dangerous conciliatory approach to the Palestinians and that there was a "gray area between peace at any price and war."[56]

On November 19, 2000, after seven weeks of bloodshed leaving 230 dead and 8000 injured, Peter Beaumont, the London *Observer* foreign affairs editor, published an in-depth piece on the al-Aqsa intifada, based on interviews with Western diplomats and senior military, intelligence and political figures on both sides of the conflict. Beaumont's month-long investigation led him to the conclusion that the uprising was not really a reaction to Sharon's visit to the Temple Mount, that the genuine anger and disillusionment of Palestinians was being "cynically manipulated for political ends." He cited a conversation with a Hamas leader who responded to a question about Palestinian deaths by saying with a smile, "This is all a play. The intifada is a game. The violence and deaths are part of the negotiations for the peace process. But no one is going to tell that to the parents of the children and young men who have died." Beaumont stood at a flashpoint in Ramallah and other places, and noted that the "boys come and throw stones, get shot, get bored and drift away. It is then that an older man comes and encourages them back to the barricades." Hussein al-Sheikh, the Fatah commander in Ramallah, told Beaumont that it was the Israelis who decided to go to war because they were looking for an excuse to annex territory. Barak, he said, was pushing the Palestinians into war while he talked peace.

On the Israeli side, the soldiers fired back even if the rocks did not land near them. The senior Israeli military intelligence officer on the spot said that his people had first heard about plans for an uprising the previous November a year earlier, from warnings in the Palestinian press that there would be a disaster unless Barak reached a settlement with them. The Israelis calculated that with the millennium celebrations and the Pope's visit, nothing would happen until at least March, 2001, but it was on May 15, 2000, the national holiday celebrating the creation of the Jewish state, that Israeli intelligence saw "explicit signs of preparations" for an autumn uprising: military exercises by PA security forces, weapon smuggling, and in the summer "dozens of training camps for the stone-throwers." The Israelis told Beaumont that when the Camp David talks collapsed at the end of July, the "crisis began in earnest." Arafat did not issue the explicit order to start the planned uprising then, but his leading lieutenants gave inflammatory statements to the Palestinian press during the month of August.

Western diplomats told Beaumont that they knew in May that Palestinians were sick of the Israelis, the peace process, and the PA itself, and that Arafat had a billion-dollar war chest, but they thought it was encouraging that Barak and Arafat were still talking. One diplomat said that the international diplomatic community believed that the reaction to Sharon's visit in September had caught Arafat by surprise. The Israeli intelligence officer agreed with that, saying that Intelligence believed Arafat had planned his uprising for the middle of November and adjusted his timetable when Sharon visited the Mount.[57]

This cynical view of the source of the intifada was born out in April, 2001, when Edward Walker, the US Assistant Secretary of State for Near East Affairs, told the House International Relations Subcommittee on the Middle East and South Asia that "a reasonable person could assume" that the Palestinians had planned the violence well before Sharon made his visit in September. Walker was referring apparently to remarks made by Imad Falouji, Arafat's communications minister, who told a PLO rally that the intifada "had been planned since Chairman Yassir Arafat's return from Camp David, when he turned the tables in the face of the former US president and rejected the American conditions."

Sharon, Walker said, had taken specific steps to ease the Palestinians' economic difficulties and seemed willing to act further if the violence stopped, but "[i]n contrast, we've seen absolutely no response from Arafat to our urgings to him to now bring the violence to a stop. He has made no statements that would indicate he even wants to see it stopped. In fact, he has called for the continuation of the intifada. He has not given any orders, secret or otherwise, to his forces which would bring some measure of control of the situation. His forces are prepared to do what he wants them to do. So we're perplexed."[58]

POLITICAL MANEUVERS

———

ON NOVEMBER 22, IN DOWNTOWN Jerusalem, 100,000 people protested Barak's policy of restraint. Sharon told the rally that Oslo was dead, and that Arafat was a "skillful enemy, whom we must fight." He addressed the settlers in the crowd, telling them that they were "a paradigm of the spirit of volunteerism in the country," and that they were needed "in these hard days when the whole country had become a front."[1]

A couple of days later, Israel closed down ten joint-security compounds in the West Bank and Gaza Strip, ousting hundreds of Palestinians from them after a bomb exploded in one of them, killing an Israeli officer and wounding several others, and after Palestinian officers rushed away from one moments before a mortar was lobbed into it. These joint compounds had been set up in Israeli territory in the mid-'90s to provide points of contact where problems could be resolved. One of the Palestinian officers protested that this meant "cutting the last ties between us and the Israelis."[2]

At the end of the month Barak surprised everyone by agreeing to hold elections as early as the following spring. "I'm not blind," he said, to heckling and boos in the Knesset, "and I can see that the Knesset wants elections. So I say to you, you want to have elections? I'm ready to have elections—general elections for the Knesset and the prime minister with the date determined in coordination and consultation among the parties."[3] The Knesset voted seventy-five to one for new elections, with twenty-nine abstentions—all that was left of Barak's support in the parliament. Even the ten Israeli Arab MKs defected from Barak, angered because he had tried to forge a coalition with Sharon, and because of Palestinian casualties in the intifada. One of them admitted that a Likud prime minister would be worse than Barak, but added that at least Netanyahu didn't kill thirteen Israeli Arab citizens or bomb Arab villages. Netanyahu was leading Barak by twenty points in the polls, and it was widely believed that he would challenge and unseat Sharon, who led Barak by ten points, as the Likud candidate for prime minister.[4]

Barak, Israel's most-decorated war hero and a brilliant military strategist, had won by a landslide in May, 1999, and taken office on July 6 of that year. He had campaigned on a peace platform, promising to resolve the Palestinian and Syrian conflicts, curb the influence of the religious parties, and withdraw troops from Lebanon. He did pull out from Lebanon, although in a more hectic way than he had planned. He lost his parliamentary majority before he left for Camp David, was left with a minority government of thirty members, and was seen as isolated, incompetent and arrogant. It was widely believed that Barak's fate lay in Arafat's hands. But one Israeli official said, "Barak, for a while, turned the tables on the Palestinians and won back international support. Arafat might not be crying if Netanyahu was elected again." And indeed Netanyahu's policies had alienated secular Jews and President Clinton. Saeb Erekat said, "We can wait for a better deal. So what if they try to threaten us with the prospect of Likud returning to power? We dealt with Netanyahu. We dealt with Barak. What's the difference?" The time would eventually come, he said, when the Israelis were really ready for peace.[5]

Hamas spokesmen made their conviction clear that Labor and Likud policies were indistinguishable from each other, but that they preferred Netanyahu because Barak was likely to receive broad international support. One officer was quoted as saying, "Labor ruins us and receives a Nobel Prize for it, while the Likud ruins us and

is denounced and internationally isolated." In general, the PLO and
the PA agreed with this position. The General Secretary of the PA
cabinet said, "Barak's fall is one of the outstanding accomplishments of the intifada."[6]

Robert Fisk pointed out in the British *Independent* that in 1982,
despite the suffering of the Lebanese, Arafat had decided to pursue
his unwinnable fight against the powerful Israeli army. In the end,
he was escorted out of Beirut by US warships, leaving up to 800
Palestinian civilians to be slaughtered in the Sabra and Shatilla camps,
a massacre for which the blame fell on Ariel Sharon, who was
branded a war criminal by the Arab world. In that sense Arafat
won, and now, Fisk wrote, he "understands the endgame. Let the
Israelis attack and kill the Palestinians. The world will understand."[7]

On December 9, to the surprise of everyone, including the Clinton
administration, Barak announced that he was resigning and would
run in new elections in sixty days. This move effectively barred
Netanyahu from running, since according to the law, only sitting
members of the Knesset could run against a prime minister who
resigned. Cynics said that Barak had planned this so that he could
run against Sharon, a far weaker candidate than Netanyahu, although polls predicted defeat for the entire peace camp.[8] Netanyahu
announced his candidacy hours after Barak's announcement, saying he would try to persuade the Knesset to dissolve itself, so that he
could legally run in an election for both prime minister and parliament.[9] A little more than a week later, Netanyahu issued an ultimatum, saying that he would not run for Likud leader unless parliament dissolved.[10] On December 19, hours after the Knesset rejected
a bill for dissolution, sixty-eight to forty-eight, Netanyahu did in
fact pull out of the race for both Likud head and prime minister.
The Likud then announced it was cancelling its primaries and rally-
ing behind Sharon.[11]

On December 21, Shimon Peres entered the race for the
premiership, believing that in a three-man race Barak would finish

last and be eliminated in the first round, and that Peres would be a stronger candidate than the prime minister because he alone could seal a peace agreement with the Palestinians. Polls showed that he was ahead of Barak, although both were behind Sharon. Peres sought the endorsement of the ten-MK Meretz Party, since under the law, he needed the nomination of a party with at least ten MKs. But Meretz declined to endorse him for fear of splitting the peace vote. Peres then withdrew his candidacy.[12]

53

CLINTON'S LAST TRY

———

MEANWHILE, CLINTON, WHOSE PRESIDENCY was ending in January, 2001, continued to work on peace proposals, and in mid-December, Israeli and Palestinian delegates gathered at Bolling Air Force Base in southeast Washington to discuss the peace process with Dennis Ross. Arafat's delegation lacked two senior negotiators who had refused to go, a reflection of internal PA opposition to the talks. In addition, Sharon announced that he would not honor any peace agreement Barak signed with the Palestinians.[1] In New York, the Palestinians worked for more than a month to get a UN observer force of 2000 deployed in the West Bank and Gaza, but were defeated in the Security Council on December 18, when the US, Russia, Britain, France, the Netherlands, Canada and Argentina abstained, arguing that this move could endanger peace negotiations. The Palestinians were supported by China, Bangladesh, Ukraine, Jamaica, Malaysia, Mali, Namibia and Tunisia.[2]

On December 23, after five days of negotiations, the Israelis and Palestinians met briefly with Clinton at the White House, where he presented his proposals to them before they left Washington to report back to their respective leaders. The proposals, which were not put into writing, were described as a series of options. Among them was the proposal that Israel give up sovereignty over the Temple Mount and the Old City while retaining control of the Western Wall and the area under the Mount, and that the Palestinians drop their demand for a right of return of nearly four million refugees to Is-

324

rael, although several thousand would be allowed to return to Israel to reunite families. Israel would have been required to turn over about ninety-five percent of the West Bank and all of the Gaza Strip to the Palestinians for an independent state, along with some territory in the Negev, presumably adjoining the Gaza Strip, to compensate for West Bank territory held for the settlements, most of which would have been evacuated. The Palestinian state would be demilitarized, and an international force would secure the borders between the West Bank and Jordan. If the two sides agreed to negotiate these proposals, Clinton hoped for a three-way summit by the end of December.[3]

Arafat's immediate response was that he was being offered "much less" than at Camp David; he and his spokesman Saeb Erekat mentioned numerous obstacles and the vagueness of many points on Jerusalem, the refugees and the territories. One Palestinian negotiator accused the Israelis of "verbal trickery" in trying to hang on to the area under the Temple Mount. Fatah leader Marwan Barghouti said the proposals, "full of land mines," were an improvement over Camp David, but only because of the intifada. "So," he said, "if we continue the intifada, we can get more. We should not be rushing."[4] At that point, there had been 350 deaths, most of them Palestinian.

Sharon, far ahead of Barak in the polls, said that Barak was trying to hold a "fire sale" of Israeli assets, auctioning off the country to get a hurried agreement. Sharon said that these were not "genuine peace negotiations," and that Jerusalem belonged to the entire Jewish people, who were "guardians of the walls" placed in their hands "as a deposit for generations." Barak responded that these concessions were "tearing him apart," but that if an agreement was not reached, there could be "an all-out war in the Middle East" and Israel could be isolated internationally. Any agreement he reached would have had to be approved by the Knesset, and he had no majority there. Limor Livnat of the Likud argued that "a caretaker prime minister" had no right to negotiate crucial matters, asking whether Ehud Barak could "tie the hands of the nation and the state of Israel for generations to come closing a deal on issues which have been the very soul of Judaism and Zionism for thousands of years?" Prominent rabbis and members of the Shas Party demanded that not "one inch" of the Temple Mount be ceded; settlers, especially in Gaza, swore they would build bunkers and fight to the death for their homes, and in any case Sharon had said that if elected he would not honor any accords signed by Barak. Netanyahu weighed in on TV, saying that major concessions were "irresponsible" and Palestinian expectations must be reined in.[5]

Nevertheless, at the end of December, the Israelis officially accepted these proposals "with reservations" as the basis for a settlement, this despite the fact that although there was overwhelming Israeli support for a peace process, fifty-seven percent of Israelis said they would not accept these proposals.[6] Barak's position was not helped by an increase in guerrilla attacks on soldiers and settlers in the West Bank. Arafat asked for clarification and made no commitment one way or the other, although the PLO Executive Committee implied that the proposals would be rejected. The Palestinian newspaper *Al Ayyam* said that chiefly objectionable were the proposals that Israel would retain rights to the earth beneath the Temple Mount, and that Israel would have a corridor running in effect from Jerusalem to the Dead Sea and a twenty-year lease for land in Hebron with a militant settler presence.[7]

Arafat's negotiators asked for clarification on twenty-six points, one being whether the Palestinian state would be contiguous, or whether it would be cut by roads leading to settlements. Another was whether the neighborhoods of east Jerusalem would be linked under Palestinian sovereignty. The English *Guardian* agreed that Clinton's proposals did not spell out "the shape of the land pockets on the West Bank which Israel would hand back, the width of the security corridors which it would keep and the nature of the international peace force which was to move into the Jordan valley when the Israeli army left." There was also the consideration mentioned in the *New York Times*, that Arafat could not act without weighing the reaction to him of extremist groups and refugees in Gaza and the West Bank, especially if he gave up the "right of return."[8]

Palestinians were arguing whether it would be wise to come to an agreement while Clinton and Barak were still in charge, or to wait until February 6 to see if Sharon won. Hani Masri, a PA spokesman, wrote that saving Barak should not be a Palestinian goal, and, in fact, if Sharon won and cracked down on the uprising in the territories, "Israel will quickly become isolated internationally and divided internally. This will make his government more willing to make concessions than Barak or any other leader of the left or peace camp." Some Palestinians counseled holding off a decision because they believed that George W. Bush, about to assume the presidency, would be more sympathetic to them than Clinton.[9]

Others disagreed, noting that Bush might not be as involved as Clinton, that Sharon would never accept a Palestinian state, and that Arafat had a history of pushing too far and losing his advantage. This had happened in the 1970s in Jordan and in the 1980s in Lebanon, when he alienated his hosts by striving for power against them and was tossed out of those countries. Edward Luttwak, a senior fellow at the Center for Strategic and International Studies in Washington, said Arafat "has never recognized that any ascending power in a world of others must reach a culminating point where there is only loss and eventual defeat."[10] Said Aburish, a Palestinian writer living in London, noted that Arafat was energized by tense situations, which also served as a distraction from his corrupt and repressive regime. "He's not a man actually accustomed to actually managing anything," Aburish said of Arafat. "He's not a statesman, he's a trapeze artist. He doesn't know how to commit himself and stay the course."[11]

Hanan Ashrawi, a spokeswoman for the Palestinian Legislative Council, had no hesitation in telling the *Independent* that it would be "irresponsible" for Arafat to accept the Clinton proposals, which were not "remotely acceptable," falling short of the expectations of the Palestinian people and United Nations resolutions. Asked about time running out for Clinton and Barak, she said she was "more concerned about the substance than ticking clocks." Barak, she said, "made an unacceptable offer. Sharon will make an unacceptable offer. We don't think Barak was the saviour of peace. Barak built more settlements, imposed a cruel closure on our towns and villages, and killed more Palestinians than ever before. That has left us with nothing to fear from the Likud. We are not succumbing to panic politics." The *Independent*, apparently disagreeing, commented that if Sharon were elected, the recent bloodshed would "look like a dress rehearsal."[12]

Polls indicated that fifty-six percent of Israelis considered the Clinton proposals to be unworkable, and only thirty-eight percent approved of them. Support for Barak was running about thirty percent to Sharon's fifty-three percent. Despite all this, members of Barak's cabinet approved Clinton's proposals reluctantly, while at least two of them said they would never agree to the division of Jerusalem. "My main mission," Barak told them, "is to keep to a minimum the number of military cemeteries." Angry talk escalated among the right wing. One Knesset member, Rehaavam Zeevi, called Barak insane, and explained that he was "protecting him by saying he has gone mad, because if he has not lost his mind, he has committed treason. The punishment for a traitor according to Israeli law is death."[13]

This was the way much of the right wing had talked about Yitzhak Rabin after he signed the Oslo accords in 1993 and before he was assassinated. Netanyahu had been criticized for standing silently by at demonstrations when Rabin was called a traitor. Now Sharon was quick to say that Barak was not a traitor and "using extremist words like 'traitor' is absolutely forbidden. There are essential differences and sharp contrasts between our world views,

but it is forbidden to let ourselves be drawn into hotheaded recrimi-
nations." He said that he was interested in a national unity government with Barak, but did not cease to accuse the prime minister of
selling out Israeli interests "in an election ploy designed to bypass
democracy and the Knesset."[14]

Barak's campaign did not hesitate to fire back, saying that "[t]he
pursuit of peace is a matter of survival and not an election ploy,"
and "It would be better for Ariel Sharon, before he preaches morality to the prime minister, to remember who jeopardized his job for
peace, and who was willing to crawl into Barak's government in
order to keep his job and stop Netanyahu."[15] Rhetoric became heated
as December wound down, with a One Israel MK and former diplomat, Colette Avital, saying that Sharon had an international image as a war criminal like Slobodan Milosevic, that he was blamed
abroad for igniting the intifada by his visit to the Temple Mount,
that in France he was still called the butcher of Sabra and Shatilla,
that the "peace" he would bring would be "the peace of the grave,"
and that he was loathed by eighty percent of the Jewish community
abroad, including liberals and leaders of federations.[16] Justice Minister Yossi Beilin called Sharon "the ugly Israeli . . . all that is wicked
in our society, with his cynicism and the unnecessary wars he brought
us into . . . a dangerous man with a sheep's mask" responsible for
the deaths of more than 1000 soldiers in the Lebanon war.[17]

MK Benny Alon responded to Beilin's attack by saying that this
damaged the country because it "delegitimized in the eyes of the
world the man who will be the democratic choice of the Israeli voters." Sharon had hired Arthur Finkelstein, the right-wing American
political public relations expert, to direct campaign strategy, and to
paint Sharon as a moderate peacemaker with important experience,
who had a staged settlement plan for the peace process. To bolster
this impression, Sharon announced that he would like to appoint
an Arab minister to his cabinet. The response of Sharon's defenders
in Israel to strong attacks from the left was relatively mild—Alon

talked about Barak's "nice baby face" and "politically correct" appearance, but complained about his "improper" remarks.[18]

Not so restrained were Sharon supporters in the US. Eric Fettmann complained bitterly in the *New York Post* that Barak had sent "a dangerous message" to Arafat that there were no red lines that he could not and would not cross. Sharon, Fettmann said, was "vilified and demonized" as "the butcher of Beirut," the "architect" of the "disastrous" Lebanon war, reviled by most Palestinians. The previous week, Wolfgang Thierse, president of the German Bundestag, had told the *Jerusalem Post* that "in Germany, we are very concerned about Sharon, and the consequences of what may happen if he takes power." Fettmann contrasted these comments with profiles of Arafat, where there was no mention of his being "'reviled by most Israelis and supporters of Israel,' having been the 'architect' of such bloody episodes as the massacre of schoolchildren at Maalot, the murder of Jewish athletes at Munich, the kidnapping and killing of American diplomats in Sudan and the brutal death of Leon Klinghoffer aboard the *Achille Lauro*—as well as dozens of other such episodes." Sharon, Fettmann concluded, believed in "the politics of realism."[19]

Wolfgang Thierse's comments about Sharon caused considerable diplomatic uproar and headlines in the German press. Zalman Shoval, who had been Israeli ambassador to the United States, and who was designated as a spokesman to try to salvage Sharon's image abroad, said that "in principle" it was not acceptable "for a foreign politician to interfere in the democratic process of another, friendly, country." He said of Thierse that having grown up "under the anti-democratic circumstances of Communist East Germany," perhaps he was unfamiliar with these "principles"; Shoval also took pains to remind the Bundestag president of another painful period in German history: "I think it must be agreed that the Jewish people, in its homeland, in the light of the terrible experiences through the ages, but especially during the Nazi period, have every right to make its own decisions affecting its national goals, its security—and perhaps its very survival."[20]

A Syrian editorial said that claims by "Zionist extremists headed by war criminal Ariel Sharon" that "the Jews have historic rights in Palestine and Jerusalem" were false; that Jews "have no relationship with the ancient Hebrews" and that "[t]he alleged kingdom of David lasted for a short time and was established on the edges of Palestine and not in the Palestinian territories they are now occupying by force and terrorism." Both Sharon and Barak, the editorial said, were criminals who should be referred to international tribunals for punishment, and the United States had allowed Israel to become "a state out of control similar to the Hitlerite Nazis."[21]

On December 28, on the occasion of the Id el-Fitr holiday and the end of Ramadan, Sharon for the first time sent a goodwill message to Arafat, expressing wishes for "a permanent peace between Israelis and Palestinians, so our two peoples can live in the region in peace, security and economic prosperity." Sharon's office said that the letter was not specifically addressed to the chairman and copies had been sent to King Abdullah, Hosni Mubarak and other Arab leaders. A PA official said that the Palestinians did not attach much importance to the message.[22]

At the end of December, the intifada death toll was 322 Palestinians and forty-one Israelis, and the violence was escalating as Barak's support was eroding. Fifty-six percent said that they did not want the prime minister to make a deal before the election, fifty-one percent said they would not support the Clinton proposals, and fifty-five percent doubted that a peace agreement would end the conflict. *Maariv's* political analyst said that the public did not believe or trust Barak or support his actions, and "the details of President Clinton's bridging proposals have seriously hardened the public's attitude to a permanent-status agreement."[23]

54

ON THE CAMPAIGN TRAIL

———

By early February, the polls were in Sharon's favor. He campaigned hard, and was very organized. Everywhere he went he took with him a spiral-bound notebook with lined pages. Every page was headed by a date, and each day he wrote his message for that day in a round, clear, legible hand. On the 31st of January, for instance, he reminded himself to stress his themes of "peace, unity and security" in every speech and every interview; to criticize Peres for not making a strong defense when Arafat attacked the IDF chief at the World Economic Conference in Davos; to transmit a sense of optimism over the hundred years of Zionist accomplishment; to deny that he would hand plum appointments to Omri and Likud manager Uri Shani; and to emphasize that he would discuss political nominations only after the election had been won.

Nobody, Sharon said, was telling him what to say. Each day he himself decided what messages he wanted to convey and wrote them in his notebook, a habit he had had for years: "at every meeting, at every conference, I write in my notebook what I say. Not what the others say, only what I say." But his advisors had important input. Every day, mostly in the early morning, he met with his planning staff, including Omri and Gilad, sometimes in Tel Aviv, sometimes at the farm. A key person was Yakov Maor, whose job it was to try to work with Sharon to deliver clear, catchy messages. Maor accompanied the candidate everywhere, listened to him and tried to see how his words were coming across to the public. "You don't understand how frustrating it is," Maor said. "Sharon does not know how to express himself simply. Most of the time he sounds unclear and gauche, or monotonously repetitive."[1]

An example of this occurred one evening when Sharon met with supporters from kibbutzes and moshavs in the Golan and the Jordan Valley. He was supposed to tell them that if Israel gave up the Jordan Valley and the Palestinians took over the Jordanian monarchy, the Palestinian state would expand from Iraq to the outskirts of Tel Aviv. But he jumbled his words so that nobody knew what he was talking about, and the speech certainly made no headlines. Maor was carrying a final draft of Sharon's victory speech in his briefcase. All he needed was Sharon's okay. But Sharon told him that the battle was not over, and there could not be a victory speech. Then he went on to say that in the speech that couldn't exist, he intended to call for unity in order to reach peace and security. "Have I mentioned unity?" he asked, and burst into laughter.[2]

He said in an interview that he watched the reporters who were following him to see if they were listening. "Usually I say 'Peace, Security and Unity,'" he said. "When I notice that you're not paying attention, I change the order and confuse you."[3]

The Sharon campaign set about wooing the business community and got tens of thousands of shekels from insurance companies and various wealthy individuals. Many of them had previously contributed to Barak, and they may have hedged their bets by also giving to Barak in this election as well. One Saturday night a party was set up for Sharon in a Tel Aviv suburb at a posh villa owned by David Federman, head of Elite, a food conglomerate. More than eighty prominent business people were invited, and Federman told Sharon that he had decided to vote for him, but that his wife Irit, who was supporting Barak, needed to be convinced. The atmosphere was very friendly to Sharon. As could be expected from a food magnate, the delicacies were impressive: tiny sandwiches with foie gras, sushi and ginger, teriyaki chicken, tuna specialties, roast beef, and good wine. When Sharon was offered a tray, he told the server to take it away, but not too far.

As anyone who has seen Sharon would assume, he is fond of good food. When his planning staff came to the ranch during the campaign, they were served lavish breakfasts: various smoked fishes; a cheese tray with Camembert, Brie, Mozarella, Swiss; breads, rice cakes, crackers; freshly squeezed orange juice from the citrus groves; omelets, thinly chopped vegetable salad; fruit plates, and—Sharon's special favorite—sardines from Thailand. He was the only one who ate the sardines, which he offered to everyone.

During one television interview, asked for the twentieth time about his relations with the White House and his talks with George Bush and Condoleezza Rice, he said flippantly, "I have to admit, it was hard for me to concentrate during my meeting with Rice, she has very beautiful legs." To which the interviewer responded, "I'm certain you wouldn't have had the same problem with Madeleine Albright."[4]

Asked in another interview about Lily, he said that it hurt him that she had not lived to see the new twins. But she had established a strong friendship with the children and Gilad's wife Inbal and now the boys were "not just sons, but friends and partners." He smiled when he talked about Lily because there were many good memories. But, he added, "a person is allowed to cry and needs to cry sometimes." He cried sometimes, he said.

The reporter asked him whether if he won, he thought he could find the "vindication" he was seeking to erase "memories of Lebanon and the destruction of Yamit." This was a question he was asked often, and it did not sit well with him. He did not need to be "legitimized," he said. "I am proud of all that I have done. Wars, building the land, settlements, immigration absorption, and crossing the canal." As for Lebanon, "It was a war of survival that was not less important than any other war."

The one thing he apologized for was the destruction of Yamit. He had already said he was sorry for that, he told the reporter. "It was a mistake. . . . Yes, we did try to exchange part of the Negev in order to keep Yamit, but the Egyptians did not agree."[5]

55

ELECTION 2001:

"ONLY SHARON CAN BRING PEACE"

———

TOWARD THE MIDDLE OF JANUARY, rumors began to spread that
One Israel wanted to replace Barak with Shimon Peres. Peres denied these rumors, although activists on his behalf, calling themselves Israel Now, had begun demonstrating, collecting petitions and
distributing T-shirts and bumper stickers reading "Peres for Prime
Minister." Three newspaper polls indicated that Peres would beat
Sharon by a percentage less than the margin of error.[1] Peres said in
a television interview that he had not asked the activists to start, so
he did not see the need to ask them to stop, but when ten Labor
MKs asked him in a letter to repudiate these actions, he complied,
urging his supporters to work for Barak.[2] But relations between the
two men were reportedly far from warm. On January 18, Peres
referred to Barak as the Left's "representative," not as its leader. At
the same time, there was a change in the polls, indicating that Sharon
would defeat Peres as well as Barak.[3] On January 22, the chair-
woman of Israel Now announced that they had decided to drop
their campaign for Peres and concentrate on working against Sharon.
The organization had not been able to gain open support from any
public figures, and had been much criticized for running an adver-
tisement that showed a mother grieving over a grave and that asked
Barak what he would say to the woman if Sharon won.[4]

Sharon, who was greeted by his enthusiastic supporters with
cries of "Arik, King of Israel!" laid out his "diplomatic plan," un-

der which all 140 settlements would remain, and Israel would keep control of a united Jerusalem, the Golan Heights, eastern and western security zones, and the roads connecting the Jordan Valley with the coastal plain. If the Palestinians agreed to these points, Israel would begin to ease security strictures and consider concessions. The plan, Sharon said, would lead to cooperation in working toward the establishment of a Palestinian state. Barak aired a TV commercial in which he said that if peace were to be achieved, more than ninety percent of the West Bank would have to be ceded to the Palestinians. Eighty percent of the settlers would remain in Israeli-controlled "blocks" while some settlements would be evacuated, and Israel would retain control of the Western Wall, the Temple Mount and the Mount of Olives, while a "special arrangement" would be made for the Old City. If there was no deal within a year, Barak said, Israel would start a two-year unilateral process of separating itself from the Palestinians.[5]

Arafat proposed more talks be held in Taba, an Egyptian Red Sea resort. While Barak was mulling this proposal, a bullet-ridden body was discovered in a shallow grave in Ramallah; this was sixteen-year-old Ofir Rahum, who had been lured from his home in Ramallah by what he thought was an Internet romance with an American tourist in Jerusalem. He met the girl there and was somehow persuaded to go with her to Ramallah, where he was murdered in the street by gunmen who pulled up alongside the couple in a van, shot him and fled with the body. The woman was apparently a Palestinian; a twenty-five-year-old freelance journalist from east Jerusalem who was arrested by undercover Israeli agents in her parents' home in a West Bank village. A senior Israeli army officer said, "It seems he was having a virtual romance. It was a trap." He noted that Rahum was one of about two dozen Israeli civilians, most of them West Bank or Gaza settlers, killed since the uprising began.[6]

The killing received extensive press coverage in Israel and, in an unusual step, was condemned by the Palestinian Authority, although the head of police investigation in Ramallah said that the motive for the murder was probably criminal and not political. Barak, calling the killing "a heinous act, devoid of humanity," immediately postponed a special cabinet meeting called to decide on the Taba talks, commenting that it was "difficult to hold serious talks in an atmosphere of such violence." Sharon said that "negotiations conducted under the threat of terrorism weaken Israel."[7]

Terrorism also affected the Palestinian Authority in those weeks. An obscure group called the al-Aqsa Martyrs Brigade announced that it was responsible for the assassination of Hisham Mekki, a senior official of Palestinian television, and a close associate of Arafat's. The group said it killed Mekki because he was corrupt. To some Palestinian officials, this was a disturbing sign of the breakdown of law and order in the area. Hanan Ashrawi commented that it was "vital, in this time of crisis, to put our house in order. If government institutions and officials do not apply the rule of law and due process, then this will become a natural outcome where people start settling scores and taking the law into their own hands."[8] The *Financial Times* printed a report from "a Palestinian source" that the murder had been "authorized at a high level because 'Mekki skimmed off more money than he was allowed.'"[9]

In an interview with the *New Yorker* magazine in November 2000, before he became a candidate, Sharon had called Arafat a murderer, a liar, and Israel's bitter enemy with whom it was impossible to make peace. He also said that Arabs face Mecca, not Jerusalem, when they pray. As Barak's people used this against him in the campaign, and Israeli Arabs expressed outrage, Sharon gave an interview to the same reporter in mid-January, moderating his language considerably, speaking of hopes for a peaceful solution to the conflict. Asked about the interviews, he responded, "I think we all know who Arafat is . . . I will sit with Yassir Arafat because he is the chairman of the Palestinian Authority, but on condition that there is quiet and security."[10]

To offset the November interview, and also knowing that leaders in moderate Arab countries like Jordan, Egypt and Morocco dreaded the effect his election would have on their populations, Sharon gave an interview to the popular daily *Yediot Aharonoth*, saying he wanted to talk about his "demonization." He said he was "known, after all, as someone who eats Arabs for breakfast. This is baseless." He protested that he had never mistreated prisoners, that he had always respected their dignity and that he was "not in favor of waging war with the Arab world."[11] Behind the scenes, David Horovitz reported, Sharon had dispatched "a close aide" to various Arab capitals, to reassure leaders that he would seek compromise and not confrontation. A large number of Israeli Arabs had made it clear that they would vote for neither Barak or Sharon, in effect boycotting the election. In a basically temperate article in the *Jerusalem Post*, Evelyn Gordon took the somewhat unusual position of agreeing that Sharon had been "demonized." It was understandable, she said, that Arabs, the West and the Israeli Left despised him; she was surprised that many right wingers also supported him without enthusiasm, and this was, she thought, because the Left had successfully attacked him, redefining his "many achievements as failures."[12]

His success in fighting Arab terrorism was, she said, "virtually unmatched." In Gaza in 1971, he had reduced the number of attacks from thirty-six in June to one in December. And even leftists had to admit that he had virtually saved the country from defeat by Egypt in the Yom Kippur War, but they countered that by pointing to his failure in Lebanon, where, she said, Israel had achieved less than he wanted and paid a higher price than he expected. But that campaign "did significantly improve the lives of Israel's northern residents," whose suffering before 1982 under incessant shelling and terrorism from the PLO in Lebanon, it had become fashionable to forget. It had been unacceptable to allow the PLO to continue killing civilians.[13]

And on economic affairs, it was constantly pointed out that as housing minister, from 1990 to 1992, Sharon had wasted billions. It was true, she said, that he had committed the government to buying many unsold houses, but this guarantee of government support was to convince contractors to build houses for the flood of Russian immigrants who would otherwise have been sleeping in the streets, and as a result within a decade these million immigrants were successfully absorbed. She granted his mistakes; no one could deny that the Sabra and Shatilla massacre reflected, at best, poor judgment on his part. But, she concluded, "despite such occasional failures, on balance, Israel has benefited from Sharon's long career of public service."[14]

On January 20, Bill Clinton's term officially ended, and he wrote letters to the Israelis and Palestinians, bidding them farewell and urging them to sacrifice for peace. Nothing will be accomplished by violence, he told the Palestinians, and to the Israelis he said that violence demonstrated that the quest for peace had not gone far enough. Both sides, he said, were "closer today than ever before to ending their 100-year-long struggle for peace and normalcy." He told the Palestinians that he supported their right to self-determination "on their own land" and that courage was not only—or mainly—measured by struggle, but "in the ability to seize historic opportunities." In this last comment was the only hint of frustration with Arafat, whom US officials believed was about to throw away his only chance for peace and an independent state.[15]

On January 21, negotiations began in Taba, although several members of Barak's cabinet said that it was not "proper, ethical or right" to hold talks so close to the election, because the peace process would be tainted by politics. The Palestinians were upset by a cabinet vote that laid down three firm positions: 1) that Israel would never allow the "right of return"; 2) that Barak would not sign any paper giving away sovereignty over the Temple Mount; and 3) that eighty percent of the settlers in the West Bank and Gaza would remain in settlement blocks under Israeli control. These positions, the Palestinians said, would doom the talks, which were set to last for as long as ten days.[16]

On January 23, Barak recalled his emissaries from Taba in response to the killing of two Israelis in the West Bank. The men, who owned restaurants near Tel Aviv, had been shopping for produce in the town of Tulkarm. When they stopped for lunch, several masked men pulled them from the restaurant, took them to a nearby village, shot them in the head and dumped their bodies in a ditch. Hamas claimed responsibility for the attack. Barak said no contacts with the Palestinians would be conducted for the present. But Deputy Defense Minister Ephraim Sneh said that the talks had to resume, especially now that there was "a glimmer of hope" and that terrorists should not be allowed to thwart the process. And, indeed, Barak decided to resume the peace talks after the funerals of the two men.[17]

Sharon called on Barak to cancel the negotiations because of the violence. "With the terrible incitement in the Palestinian media," he said, "you can't expect peace." But in a Council on Foreign Relations forum, he said he had lived among Arabs since he was a child and hoped to live with them in peace, remarking, "As a Jew, I know it is not easy to be a Palestinian. We have to take steps to make the Palestinians' lives easier," including making it easier for civilians to work. A Palestinian state was being created in "Judea and Samaria," he said. "We are the only nation in the world ready to give up our cradle, part of our history, to reach peace."[18] In response to the Barak campaign's repeated reference to Sharon's role in the Lebanon War, Sharon said, "What happened in Lebanon, which we didn't have any connection to or anything, was that Christian Arabs killed Muslim Arabs, and because of the hysterical atmosphere created in the country, I was forced to step down."[19]

The Bush administration made a tentative step into the picture, with Secretary of State Colin Powell speaking for the first time to Arafat and twice in one week to Barak. Bush himself phoned the leaders of Saudi Arabia, Egypt and Jordan.[20] Powell, however, disbanded Dennis Ross's operation, melding it into the Mideast section of the State Department.[21] Sharon said that he welcomed US help as "a mediator, an honest broker," in resolving Israeli-Palestinian differences, but in the end it had to be up to the two sides to work out their peace terms themselves.[22] Hanan Ashrawi commented that Palestinians would find Bush preferable to Clinton, who had an "exclusively Israeli point of view." She predicted that Bush would not be "involved directly in the micromanagement of the negotiations" and there would be no "peace team that has its own pro-Israeli agenda."[23]

Henry Kissinger told the *Jerusalem Post* that the US had to welcome Sharon as the leader of Israel if he was elected, despite apprehension that this would damage relations with Arab allies. In early December, in a *Washington Post* op-ed piece, Kissinger had laid out peace settlement ideas, the basics of which Sharon picked up. Kissinger said that the focus on a final peace should be dropped in favor of "principles of coexistence," that an interim solution should be put in place, because the sides were not ready for a final settlement. There should, he wrote, not be a return to the 1967 borders because that would not provide adequate protection against guerrilla warfare. Sharon said that Oslo "was empty of any content,"[24] and that Kissinger had advised "that the only way to reach peace is by going slowly, gradually, step by step, and implementing something . . . similar to non-belligerency, and only when we see the benefit, and a relationship . . . develop[s], will we be able to reach a permanent peace."[25] Kissinger said he could see how Sharon had derived his ideas from the op-ed piece, but that Sharon's plan went a little further than his. Kissinger had also written that Palestinian territory should be contiguous, the Israelis should significantly reduce their checkpoints, and that the settlement policy—much of which was Sharon's—should be reviewed.[26]

The talks at Taba resumed at five in the evening on January 25, after a two-day suspension because of the murders in Tulkarm. Two hours later, the negotiators received news that an Israeli motorist had been shot dead north of Jerusalem. The Israelis left the meeting and phoned Barak, who told them to continue despite the "despicable" occurrence. (That night two Palestinians were killed in Gaza by Israeli troops who said they were trying to enter a Jewish settlement.)[27] On January 27, the talks concluded, with a joint statement that the "ambience" had been unprecedentedly positive and that "substantial progress" had been made, but there was no time to complete a "final status" arrangement before the February 6 elections. In fact, no progress had been made, although Barak was so eager to produce an agreement shortly before the election that Arafat may well have missed a last historic opportunity to achieve statehood.[28]

Sharon's comment on Taba was that "Ehud Barak is endangering the state of Israel to obtain a piece of paper to help him in the election," and that he himself would honor and respect any agreement ratified by a majority of sixty-one Knesset members. Barak's campaign responded that "[t]he hysterical response of the Sharon team proves that their shallow campaign cannot come up with a real alternative." Arafat, who had sent a representative to meet with Sharon's advisors in Vienna, commented that he was convinced that Sharon would not be able to achieve peace. Saeb Erekat carried this idea further, saying that Sharon's election would lead to an all-out war. Sharon's consistent response was that he would willingly continue negotiations once the violence stopped. Fighting was already going on, he said, thanks to Barak's policies.[29]

On January 28, the day after the conclusion of the Taba talks, both Arafat and Peres addressed the World Economic Forum in Davos, Switzerland. Peres talked about the need for the two sides to work together to achieve the inevitable goal of peace. Arafat said Israel "is waging and has waged for the past four months a savage and barbaric war as well as a blatant and fascist military aggression against our Palestinian people," and was attempting to destroy them by starving them and using uranium-tipped shells against them. Peres, taken aback, said, "I must admit that I came prepared for a wedding, not a divorce." He pulled himself together enough to say that Israel had never initiated attacks, but had responded in self-defense. "None of us," he said, "would like to see a single Palestinian suffer." He urged Arafat to work for peace, and added, "Let us restrain our voices and see the horizon."[30]

As a result of this unfortunate incident, which ended when the two men shook hands and received a standing ovation from the audience, Barak, whose hopes for an accord before the election had gone glimmering, announced that he was breaking off any further "political contacts" with Arafat, whom he accused of attacking the army and unleashing a barrage of lies against Israel. He was still committed to peace efforts, he said, but "[i]f, God forbid, it becomes clear that it's not possible, then we will fight." The Israeli army denied using depleted uranium on their weapons. After he met with Kofi Annan in Switzerland, Arafat said he had had no intention of denigrating the peace process; all he wanted to do was focus on the suffering of Palestinians. "We strive to achieve a comprehensive, just and lasting peace," he told the press. "We don't want a breakdown of the peace process."[31]

Arafat stayed with the latter conciliatory position in a rare interview in English on Israeli TV on January 30, in which he said that progress had been made at Taba, "not all what we are looking for, not all what you are looking for, but it was a step forward." Most importantly, he said, "we are insisting to continue." Responding to a question about Sharon's proposal that the PA be given forty-two percent of the territories, he said that was not what Sharon had said at Wye River in 1997. "You can ask Clinton," he said. "Land for peace . . . What you have done in south Lebanon, what you have done in Sinai," referring to complete withdrawal. He exhibited warm friendliness to the interviewer, smiling at him and even putting his hand on his arm at one point. He said he understood and respected the devotion of Jews to the Western Wall since he had been fascinated to watch them praying there when he was a child. Asked about the election, he said he would not interfere "in the Israeli business. I respect completely what you are doing. It is your election and I haven't the right to affect it." As for Sharon, who had called him a murderer and refused to shake his hand, he said he would respect and deal with whomever the Israelis elected.[32]

Hosni Mubarak, interviewed on the same station, also said he was neutral in the election, but he mentioned Sharon's visit to the Temple Mount, as well as the Sabra and Shatilla massacres, and added that he had not seen Sharon since 1982 and had no connection with him, as he had with Barak. There would be no peace, he said, unless the Temple Mount was placed under Arab control, and unless the entire Golan was turned over to Syria. He said he would talk to Sharon if it benefited "stability in the region," but he would not contact him "just for the sake of contacts." He reminded the interviewer that Egypt had a peace treaty with Israel, and asked, "Do I have to speak with Mr Sharon? If he needs something and comes to me he is welcome. But if he needs nothing, let him stay where he is." Sharon's response was, "I wasn't planning to call him. He has nothing to worry about."[33]

At a meeting in the West Bank, the Fatah leadership called for an escalation of the intifada, since Israel had not yet agreed to the right of return, or Palestinian sovereignty over east Jerusalem and the Temple Mount. Hussein Sheikh said that "nothing new" had come out of the Taba talks, which were "just a waste of time, an Israeli election ploy" and that Fatah had no desire to help Barak, who had "killed over 400 Palestinians in four months." He said that no one had asked Fatah to stop the intifada or slow it down, although a senior Palestinian security official had admitted that an escalation would push Israelis to vote for Sharon, and that the people did not understand "the political implications." It was reported that Arafat wanted Barak to win, but that he wanted the intifada to escalate if Sharon won, on the premise that escalation would cause Israelis to bring down a Sharon government. Hathem Abdul Qadder, a Fatah leader and member of the Palestinian Legislative Council, said Sharon's election would hurt all Israelis because it would trigger an escalation of violence. Some Fatah leaders argued frankly that a Sharon victory would be useful to them, since the world would hold Israel responsible for the escalation.[34]

The US investment house of Merrill Lynch, reacting to concerns that "an election victory by Ariel Sharon could damage sentiment towards the market," downgraded Israel's rating from "neutral" to "underweight." A Merrill Lynch publication said that "while a near-term Nasdaq bounce and lower interest rates are positives, we are bothered by the potential for politics to depress market sentiments." Egypt, however, was upgraded from neutral to overweight, with the explanation that "while this may seem perverse, given the concerns over Sharon, this market is already near its all-time low."[35]

56

VICTORY

———

ON FEBRUARY 6, 2001, SHARON became Israel's eleventh prime minister, the sixth in the past ten years, winning 62.5 percent of the vote to Barak's 37.5. Voter turnout was about sixty-one percent, the lowest in Israeli history, but this was the first election for prime minister only. In 1999, voter turnout had been 78.7 percent, but that had been an election for both the Knesset and the premiership. Fewer than twenty-five percent of Arabs voted, as opposed to more than seventy percent in 1999, although it was later posited that even if seventy-five percent of Arabs had voted ninety-five percent for Barak, Sharon would still have won by twelve or thirteen percent. In Arab communities there were no campaign posters, and polling places were virtually deserted. Some people cast blank ballots, even though they knew that would help elect Sharon. There were few overt protests, beyond some loudspeaker vans urging a boycott of the election and one incident of youths throwing rocks at polling places. An MK spokesman for the Arab Movement for Renewal said that a message had been sent to the Labor Party: "Every time the Left wants to put up a candidate . . . they will have to take us into account, otherwise we will not take them into account."[1]

This vote for Sharon did not reflect a rejection of peace: according to a poll taken by Tel Aviv University's Steinmetz Center, sixty-eight percent of the public believed that to reach peace, Israel should be "less conciliatory" with the Palestinians, and by a margin of fifty-three to twenty-seven percent, the Israelis believed that Sharon could "advance the peace process . . . while protecting the State of Israel's vital interests" more ably than Barak. The *Jerusalem Post* commented that if the Israeli people had "learned anything in the past four months and the past seven years, it is that the Right's vision of a peace without Palestinian self-determination and the Left's vision of peace based on satisfying Palestinian demands are both fundamentally flawed." Narrow governments that did not reconcile these two viewpoints were doomed to failure, politically and practically.[2]

Michael Freund, in the same newspaper, said that the voters had repudiated both Barak's character and his concessions. Barak, Freund said, had "repeatedly staked out red lines, only to cross them weeks or even days later." He had promised to preserve a united Jerusalem, but at Taba he had come close to dividing the city and giving up control over the Temple Mount; although he had vowed that he would not negotiate when violence went on, he had continued the talks at Taba after several terrorist incidents. And despite his willingness to return to the Green Line, he had been unable to achieve an accord. He "zigzagged endlessly, retreating from yesterday's commitments in the face of today's pressures." The majority of Israelis, Freund concluded, preferred "Sharon's red lines to Barak's Green Line."[3]

On election night, Barak resigned from politics and from the Knesset, saying that time would vindicate his actions. Sharon, after first paying respects to Lily, gave a highly conciliatory victory speech, calling for a unity government and calling upon "our Palestinian neighbors to abandon the path of violence and return to the path of dialogue and solving the conflicts between us by peaceful means."[4] In neighboring Arab countries, the press on the whole greeted his victory with cries of rage and warnings of waves of bloodshed. Hosni Mubarak said that Egypt would wait and see what Sharon, who was "famous for a policy of suppression and for the Sabra and Shatilla," would do. His foreign minister added, "We will wait, but not for long . . ." The Syrian government newspaper commented that "[t]he victory of the bloody terrorist and war criminal Sharon . . . amount[s] to an official declaration of war," and in Lebanon Palestinian refugees burned Sharon in swastika-hung effigy. The Jordanian foreign minister said his country would judge the Israeli government in terms of its commitment to the peace process, and warned against "premature judgments" of Sharon. The Iraqis would not discuss "a Zionist regime" but only "a Palestinian state." The United Arab Emirates *Al Ittihad* newspaper headline read, "The Butcher Sharon, Israel's Prime Minister." It is interesting to note that General Pervez Musharraf of Pakistan commented that "Sharon might be the only person who could take decisions leading to peace in the Middle East."[5]

The response in Europe was mixed. The European Union expressed the hope that Sharon would continue the peace dialogue, a hope echoed by leaders in Denmark, Sweden and Finland, while the latter two said it was important to judge Sharon by his future actions and not by earlier remarks. The Norwegian foreign minister was less optimistic, saying that if Sharon followed through on his campaign statements, there was "good reason to fear what can happen. Judging from what he has said, it is a policy that Norway cannot support." British Prime Minister Tony Blair congratulated Sharon in a five-minute phone call and offered help in reaching a peace agreement. His foreign secretary Robin Cook said he was looking forward to working with Sharon. John Howard, the Australian prime minister, also congratulated Sharon, while remarking in a radio interview that he thought it was "a great tragedy that the Palestinians didn't take advantage of the peace offer that Barak made, because it is a very fraught tragic situation and I think he displayed very great courage in going as far as he did." The Japanese foreign minister called to congratulate Sharon and expressed hopes that he would work for a just and lasting negotiated peace, building on past negotiations.[6]

President George W. Bush and Secretary of State Colin Powell
both telephoned Sharon shortly after his victory and both said they
had spoken to leaders in Jordan, Saudi Arabia, Syria and Egypt,
telling them to let the new government get settled and help quiet the
region. Powell counseled restraint, and said he would visit the region later in the month.[7] In his victory speech, Sharon acknowledged Bush's call, saying that the president, after reminding him
that they had traveled together through the West Bank in 1998,
said, "No one would have believed then that I would be president
and you would be prime minister."[8] Bush spoke also to Barak, praising him for a valiant fight. Powell made it clear that the Bush administration would not follow in Clinton's footsteps by embroiling
itself directly in the peace process, which he now referred to as
"Middle East peace negotiations." It was believed that the Bush
people did not want to be perceived as pro-Israel because of their
desire to build an Arab coalition against Saddam Hussein. Bush
phoned Mubarak and vowed to consult frequently with him while
Sharon was prime minister.[9]

Thomas Friedman's comment in an op-ed piece in the *New York
Times* was that the Oslo "test" was over, and that the Israelis had
elected Sharon because, unlike with Barak, they knew exactly who
he was, and because seven years of Oslo had taught them exactly
who Yassir Arafat was.[10] The *Times* itself editorialized that Sharon's
campaign promises did not offer a realistic formula for long-term
peace, although like Nixon in China, his hard-line credentials could
give him latitude "to try more creative approaches to the Palestinians." The *Washington Post* confined itself to sadness over the eclipse
of Barak, who despite his bungling of major decisions, had broken
Israeli political taboos and provided a sketch of a peace achievable
"if and when the Palestinian leadership matures." The *Wall Street
Journal* considered Sharon's election—along with George W.
Bush's—"a unique opportunity to get Middle East policy back on a
more rational footing."[11]

Sharon took the position that Israel would honor only written and ratified documents, like the 1998 Wye River and the 1999 Sharm al-Sheikh agreements. Barak supported this position, saying that Sharon's administration was under no obligation to recognize any of the discussions held with Palestinians during Barak's term of office. The defeated candidate wrote to President Bush that his government had made every effort to end the conflict, but had failed because the other side would not compromise. Thus, nothing that was discussed at Camp David or at Taba was "legally or politically binding" because the guiding principle was "nothing is agreed until everything is agreed." Even Bill Clinton, Barak said, had held that his proposals would not be valid after he left office.[12]

Palestinian and Arab leaders objected to this premise. Saeb Erekat said on Palestinian TV that great progress had been made during Barak's term and that the PA would not accept suggestions that negotiations start "from point zero." The Egyptians echoed that "agreements and understandings" reached in past talks "should be the basis for future negotiations." But Alan Baker, the Israeli Foreign Ministry's legal advisor, said that all that had come out of Camp David or Taba was a general commitment to continue the talks, and that neither conference had produced any document spelling out specifics. Baker reminded the Egyptians that in March, 1979, Sadat had made a commitment that Egypt would send a resident ambassador to Israel within one month after Israel withdrew from the Sinai, and that Egypt had withdrawn its ambassador in November, 2000, and thus had not honored that commitment.[13]

President Bush phoned Arafat and asked him to allow Sharon time to build his government and develop a peace process, while his administration made it clear that they would not repeat Clinton's involvement in the area. A State Department spokesman said that the offers discussed by Clinton with Barak and Arafat were "no longer United States proposals." Condoleezza Rice, the National

Security Advisor, said, "We shouldn't think of American involvement for the sake of American involvement."[14]

When he was planning his inauguration speech, Sharon was advised to begin by paying tribute to Lily, but he put off mentioning her until the end of his remarks because, he explained later, if he had spoken her name at the beginning, he would not have been able to continue. In this moment of victory, he thought about the alternation of joy and tragedy which seemed to punctuate his entire life. When he returned home as a paratroop commander, his happiness was dampened by his father's illness; when his first son Gur was born, the euphoria was marred by his father's death; after the triumphant end of the Six-Day War, Gur was killed in a tragic accident; and now he was elected prime minister, but deprived of the one person whose joy in this accompishment he most wanted to share.[15]

POST-ELECTION

———

THE LAW GAVE SHARON FORTY-FIVE DAYS from the election to form a coalition; until he did, Barak remained as caretaker. If Sharon failed to bring together his government on time or if his budget was not approved by a clear majority by March 31, new elections would have been called. Sharon needed a national unity government because Likud had only nineteen seats in the seventeen-party, 120-seat Knesset inherited from the Barak administration. As gunfire was exchanged in Ramallah, Hebron and the Gaza Strip, Sharon offered Barak the post of defense minister and asked Shimon Peres to take on the Foreign Ministry. Peres declared he was open to this offer, while the prospect of an alliance with Likud revealed deep and ugly divisions within Labor. Peres joined with Barak in affirming the Likud decision to consider that the Camp David and Taba talks were nullified. Several Labor stalwarts were enraged. At a party meeting, Yossi Beilin, a leading peace advocate, shouted at Peres, "You are a man of peace, a man of truth! Don't give him [Sharon] legitimacy around the world!" Some Leftists expressed fears that if there were a national unity government, it would be evident that there were no big differences between Labor and Likud.[1]

A feud between Barak and Peres became evident when Peres was named to head the team discussing national unity with Sharon. Barak unexpectedly said he was going to co-chair the talks with Peres, and then changed his mind and said he alone would conduct the talks and decide what portfolios Labor would receive. The Meretz party urged Barak not to join with Sharon and attacked Peres for being willing to do that after trying to run as a Meretz candidate for prime minister. His behavior, a Meretz MK said, justified their refusal to endorse him. Peres retorted on TV that if he had been a candidate, he would have beaten Sharon.[2]

The new prime minister pledged to appoint an Arab minister to his new cabinet. One Arab MK called this a public relations exercise, without substance. Others felt differently and a new forum of Israeli Arabs, Druse and Bedouin was set up to promote non-Jewish interests. Ghassan Khatib, a Palestinian political scientist, said it was "too early to see things clearly." He doubted the Palestinian leadership had a long-range strategy, but he predicted—correctly, as it happened—that there would be an immediate escalation of low-level violence in the occupied territories, along with an attempt to keep the peace process alive and paint Sharon as intransigent. The Palestinian leadership, according to David Rudge, had underestimated the depth of disillusionment with Barak and were also surprised that all Barak's concessions had been taken off the table. They rejected the Israeli view that Palestinian violence and refusal of Barak's concessions had helped to elect Sharon. Arafat, they said, could have risked a rebellion if he had accepted the proposals. Mustafa Barghouti, a Ramallah activist, said that the only way to deal with Sharon was to forge new links with the Israeli "peace camp" to undercut him.[3]

After the election, there was an exchange of letters between Sharon and Arafat, leading to a "congenial" phone call from Arafat in which he congratulated Sharon on the birth of twin grandsons. The primary reason for the call was apparently the economic pressure being felt by the Palestinians. Arafat said that for the past few months Israel had not transferred sales tax money to the PA and he was having trouble paying salaries. In addition, closure of Palestinian cities was preventing people from getting to work. Sharon's response was that he was willing to take immediate steps to ameliorate the situation, but that depended upon the PA moving against political violence. There was also the fact that suspects arrested by the PA in the January murder of two Israeli restaurateurs in Tulkarm had recently been released in Ramallah. The conversation, a source close to Arafat said, ended on a note of "good feeling." Other Palestinian sources said that the authority was on the verge of collapse because of lack of money. There was also the problem of armed groups and individuals spinning out of control and assassinating suspected collaborators and others. One security official said that the PA needed a continuation of peace talks to make credible a demand for a cessation of violence. But many other PA officials believed that an escalation of the intifada was their only hope. If Sharon would not pick up from where the Barak negotiations left off, one source said, "We will bring him down like we brought Barak and Netanyahu down before him."[4]

Sharon had not yet taken office, but violence escalated nevertheless. Massoud Ayad, a senior officer of Arafat's elite bodyguard unit, was killed in the Gaza Strip by Israeli missiles fired at his car from two attack helicopters, as part of Israel's assassination policy. The IDF said Ayad was setting up a branch of Hezbollah in the Strip.[5] Then a day later, on February 14, a Palestinian bus driver rammed his vehicle into a crowd at a bus stop at Azor outside Tel Aviv during the morning rush hour, injuring twenty and killing eight: four female and three male Israeli soldiers, aged between eighteen and twenty-one, and a thirty-year-old civilian woman. The driver, Gazan Khalil Abu-Olbeh, 35, a father of five from Gaza, had just dropped off fifty Palestinian workers at jobs in Israel. He attempted to escape with his bus into Gaza, but was pursued on the highway by police and crashed into a truck when they shot and wounded him. This was the heaviest death toll inside Israel in four years. Eyewitnesses said that the bus had suddenly accelerated toward them, leaving "body parts, heads split open, guts spilled . . . blood everywhere . . ." Infuriated residents of the suburb shouting "Death to the Arabs!" had to be restrained by police from attacking a construction site where Palestinians were employed. Some young men accused the police of "working for the leftists."[6]

Abu-Olbeh had a work permit that had been renewed just two weeks before after an intensive security screening. Hamas had claimed responsibility for his act. Abu-Olbeh's family said he had no connection with any extremist organization, but had become disconsolate because of border closings that limited his ability to work, and angry at the violent Israeli response to the intifada. In reaction to the bus attack, Barak sealed off the West Bank and Gaza, and closed off the airport in Gaza which had just been reopened to allow around 7000 Muslims to fly to Mecca.[7]

Arafat, who was visiting Jordan and Turkey, at first blamed the tragedy on "Israel's military escalation, which has a direct effect on the feelings of all the Palestinian people." A little while later, he dismissed it as "a road accident."[8] Toward evening, after what was reported as a furious phone call from Colin Powell, Arafat's planning minister Nabil Shaath condemned the act.[9] Not so Ghassan Khatib, director of the Jerusalem Media and Communications Center, who said, "During these times, Palestinians welcome any harm to Israelis, especially soldiers and settlers. Even if there was going to be an earthquake in Tel Aviv, Palestinians would be happy."[10] The next day, Arafat accused Israel of using "depleted uranium" and "poisonous gases," and Palestinian TV showed alleged victims of these attacks writhing in agony. The Israel military denied these allegations and Israeli politicians asked Arafat to call for a cessation of violence and to stop what they called "anti-Israel incitement" on television.[11]

Also in the second week of February, about fifty Palestinian gunmen inside the Khan Yunis refugee camp in the southern Gaza Strip fought a six-hour battle with Israeli soldiers in an attempt, they said, to stop the Israelis from bulldozing farmland. After an Israeli motorist was killed in an ambush in the West Bank, Fatah, the main faction of Arafat's PLO, issued leaflets threatening to bring down "the criminal Sharon and all his settlements," and to kill any Israeli journalist who entered Bethlehem. The PA information minister called "[t]hreats of this nature . . . unacceptable," saying that the PA would "not allow anything to interfere with journalists working in our area." Fatah also announced that it would continue shooting at Gilo, a Jewish suburb of Jerusalem that had been annexed as a result of the 1967 war, and that was claimed by the Palestinians for their independent state.[12]

On February 16, Barak announced that he was willing to accept the post of defense minister in Sharon's coalition government. After almost three hours of talks with Sharon, Barak's office issued a written statement that the two had "agreed to establish a national unity government . . . conditional upon the completion of the policy guidelines and coalition agreements."[13] This reversal of his announcement on February 6 that he was going to retire from politics was opposed by his close allies and advisors and brought renewed accusations that he was "zigzagging," along with threats of challenges to his leadership of Labor.[14] Four days later, on February 20, Barak reversed himself again, announcing that he would not join Sharon's government, that he was resigning as head of the Labor Party and leaving the Knesset. In his resignation letter, Barak said that Sharon's preference for the identity of the defense minister to remain open "seriously harmed the trust between us and does not allow me to accept the position."[15] He was apparently referring to hints from Sharon's people that because of Labor's all-too-evident disillusionment with Barak, the post of defense minister might be offered instead to Shimon Peres. Many Labor members had been saying that they were willing to join the unity government, but not with Barak, whose communications minister Binyamin Ben-Eliezer, one of his closest aides, had told him, "You've lost your public and media credibility. If you are defense minister, the Right will also bury you. Whatever decision you make, people will say you've failed."[16]

Sharon expressed sorrow that Barak had felt "compelled to resign," and went on to say that he had known Barak "for many years, as a soldier and then in political life. As a man I really feel pained that it had to come to this." He made clear that he still wanted to form a government with Labor. A spokesman commented, "We cannot fight terrorism and reach peace with a narrow government. In such a difficult hour we really need a broad base."[17] Some senior Labor leaders—Yossi Beilin, Barak's justice minister, and Shlomo Ben-Ami, his foreign minister, in particular—were adamantly opposed to the unity government, and accused cooperative politicians like Peres of "cheap opportunism" and "total moral bankruptcy."[18]

"Why the hell does Labor need to be there?" Beilin asked. "To be a fourth of the government? To carry out the extremist policies of the Right and legitimize the biggest extremists in our society? It's beyond me."[19] It was generally accepted that Labor had suffered a trauma in the past weeks. Eitan Haber, a staunch Labor supporter, went so far as to write in *Yediot Aharonoth* that the party was on its deathbed, that it had "lost its ideological value," had said or done little "in the social arena in the past few years" and had become "a hornet's nest, a group whose most noticeable achievement" was "sharpening and drawing its knives."[20]

Shimon Peres was unanimously elected temporary head of the Labor Party, the day after he commented that he would prefer the foreign to the defense portfolio that Sharon had offered him. Peres explained that he and his party were interested in diplomatic initiatives rather than defensive reactions. There were lines, he said, that could not be crossed for Labor in a Sharon government: Israel, he said, had to work with the PA, and the IDF should not be sent into Palestinian-controlled A territory in response to increases in violence.[21] On February 26, after a raucously emotional six-hour central committee meeting in a Tel Aviv movie theater, amidst boos, catcalls and shouts of "Traitor!" Labor voted to form a government with Sharon. Outside three ambulances waited while the police struggled to separate scuffling demonstrators.[22]

Peres gave an impassioned pro-unity speech in which he said that Labor could influence the government to continue peace talks with the Palestinians. The consequent majority in favor of unity was larger than would have been supposed from the fierceness of the opposition. David Horovitz pointed out that what lay behind Labor's ideological crisis was Barak's failure to establish a real peace agreement with Arafat. The split in the party was between those who believed that Barak had come close to an accord and that one could still be reached, and those who had lost all faith in Arafat.[23] It was obvious at the central committee convention that the doves had lost not only the majority of the voters, but were alienated also from the majority of their own party. At one point in the evening Yossi Beilin, complaining that Sharon would not negotiate under fire, was interrupted by shouts of "Sharon's right!"[24]

In any case, Sharon could now look forward to being sworn into office within a few weeks. The next important item on his agenda was a visit from Colin Powell, who made a four-day tour through the Middle East and Europe, arriving in Jerusalem from Cairo on February 25. At a press conference after the meeting, Powell called on both sides to control their passions, while agreeing with Sharon that it was not the time to renew negotiations since Sharon had not yet formed his government or prepared proposals for peace discussions. He said that "the relationship between the United States and Israel is unbreakable and has been so for many years. America's commitment to the security of Israel is rock-solid and will remain so under the Bush administration." Sharon said that he would not negotiate with Arafat "under the pressure of terror and violence. We will conduct negotiations when the hostile acts stop."[25]

Powell moved on in the afternoon for a two-hour meeting in Ramallah with Arafat, to whom he presented a message from Sharon asking Arafat to publish "an unequivocal declaration to his people to stop the violence and incitement and to renew Israeli-Palestinian security coordination, in return for the lifting of economic sanctions."[26] During that press conference, Arafat said he remained committed to the peace process and that Barak's proposals could not be "erased" by Sharon.[27] Palestinian feeling toward Powell was hardly friendly, especially since the US and Britain had carried out air strikes against Iraq ten days earlier. PA police had increased security in Ramallah and closed most roads. The West Bank Fatah had called for a general strike to protest Powell's visit but demonstrations did not erupt until Powell had left the city, although people in the streets held up large posters of Saddam Hussein as Powell's motorcade sped by.[28] A Palestinian source said that the shooting of two Israelis by Tanzim militants near Ramallah "was the Palestinians' answer to Powell's arrogant demand that both sides do more to end the violence."[29]

In the Gaza Strip, more than 2000 people filled the streets, poured gasoline on US and Israeli flags and a picture of Powell and set them on fire, while shouting at Powell to go home. Shopkeepers in the West Bank closed their stores early, in response to warnings by Hamas and other militant groups.[30] In what the *Wall Street Journal* called "unusually frank comments to reporters," Powell later said that Sharon struck him as thoughtful and reflective and ready to push for peace, and that Arafat was "more obstinate."[31]

A day or two earlier, the Bush administration had called on Israel to turn over about 54 million in tax money owed to the Palestinian Authority, money that was allegedly desperately needed by Arafat's government to meet February and March payrolls. A State Department official called the practice of withholding payments because of Palestinian-Israeli clashes, "primarily punitive."[32] A few days after Powell's visit, the US State Department, in its annual report on human rights practices—a report mandated by federal law and compiled from reports from international American embassy staff—accused Israel of "numerous serious human-rights abuses," including the use of "excessive force" against Israeli Arabs and Palestinians and callous treatment of Palestinian prisoners, mostly since the onset of the intifada in late September, 2000. In the 1999 report, Israel had been praised for its human-rights record, but the 2000 report lumped Israel with states like North Korea, China and Cuba, the world's worst violators of human rights. The Palestinian Authority was also singled out for a worsened human-rights record, with "very poor" prison conditions and lack of due process.[33]

58

BUILDING A COALITION

———

ON MARCH 7, 2001, SHARON WAS SWORN in as Israel's eleventh prime minister, heading a national unity government of seven parties, the largest coalition in Israeli history with twenty-six cabinet ministers and fourteen deputy ministers. Hours earlier the Knesset voted 72 to 37 to abandon the direct election of prime ministers in which voters had cast one ballot for prime minister and another for members of parliament elected by party slates under a system of proportional representation. Direct election had been in force for five years. Two prime ministers—Netanyahu in 1996 and Barak in 1999—had been elected under that system, and both had had to resign early when they lost the support of numerous small parties in the Knesset. Both Likud and Labor had supported restoring the earlier parliamentary system in which legislators choose the prime minister, and which would favor the two big parties. Under the previous law Israelis could split their tickets, and small parties—many of them single-issue—proliferated, and were able to put pressure on the big parties. Now these would have to merge to survive. One problem remaining was that the threshold for winning seats in the Knesset was only 1.5 percent of the votes cast, and attempts to raise this threshold to two percent had failed. Nevertheless, this electoral reform made it difficult for Netanyahu to take the Likud leadership from Sharon and run for prime minister, since Netanyahu had been out of the Knesset since 1998.[1]

Sharon's coalition was so large that the table in his office had to be extended and an extra row of seats was added to the government benches in the Knesset. Shimon Peres was appointed foreign minister; Benjamin Ben-Eliezer was named defense minister and he in turn appointed Dalia Rabin-Pelossof, Yitzhak Rabin's daughter, as his deputy minister of defense. Rehavam Zeevi, a retired general who headed the far-right National Union faction, was appointed minister of tourism. Zeevi, who would speak only Hebrew to visitors even though he was fluent in English, and who advocated "transferring" all Arabs to Jordan, was to be assassinated in October.[2]

Saleh Tarif, a Druze, appointed minister without portfolio to fill one of Labor's eight seats, was the first Israeli Arab to serve in a cabinet. The nation's 100,000 Druze, who years earlier had forged a "blood pact" with Israel and are consequently perceived as loyal to the state, serve in the Israeli military, unlike other Israeli Arabs, who constitute about twenty percent of the population. Tarif, in eight years of army service in which he reached the rank of major, fought against Arabs both in Lebanon and the West Bank as a paratrooper and then a tank commander. Other Arab MKs were not happy with Tarif's acceptance of a cabinet post under Sharon, seeing him as an appeaser or worse. But Tarif had worked hard for Arab rights in his ten years in the Knesset, not hesitating to criticize Labor policy. At the close of the Labor meeting in which he was chosen as minister, Tarif refused to join in the customary singing of the national anthem, saying: "I just can't sing [it]. It's not natural." He said that he believed that Sharon would initiate a new peace process with the Palestinians, but that if that process was damaged, he would resign from the cabinet.[3] Unfortunately at the end of January, 2002, Tarif was forced to resign because of an imminent indictment on corruption charges. He was suspected of having paid $5000 to a senior Interior Ministry official on behalf of a Palestinian businessman who was trying to become an Israeli citizen. Tarif emphatically denied these charges.[4]

In late February, before he was sworn in, Sharon was asked by leaders of women's groups to discuss appointing more women to the cabinet and other senior positions. He replied that he would have women in his cabinet, that he supported the idea of women in senior positions, but that he could not give numbers until coalition negotiations were completed.[5] In the event, there were five women in his cabinet: Dalia Itzik, minister of industry and trade; Limor Livnat, minister of education; Tzippi Livni, minister without portfolio; Naomi Blumenthal, deputy minister of national infrastructure, and Dalia Rabin-Pelossof, deputy minister of defense. Dalia Itzik had been in Barak's cabinet and Limor Livnat in Netanyahu's. Livni and Blumenthal were Likud; Rabin-Pelossof, center-Left, was accused by the Left of betraying her father's legacy for a purely "decorative" position. She was the first woman to achieve such a high rank in the Defense Ministry.[6]

This coalition was so mixed, with peace advocates like Peres and Dalia Rabin, and hardliners like Zeevi, Limor Livnat and Avigdor Lieberman, that analysts could not tell what direction Sharon would take. Gone were Oslo champions Yossi Beilin and Uri Savir. The Likud itself controlled only nineteen seats in the Knesset, while Labor controlled twenty-three. Sharon apologized at a Likud faction meeting for having to leave so many members out of the government, and called for unity. There were some complaints: Meir Sheetrit, who was made justice minister, said that he had wanted the Education post given to Limor Livnat. Yossi Sarid, who had been Barak's education minister, said that Sheetrit should have had that job instead of Livnat, whom he feared would "brainwash the nation's youth with nationalism and racism." The Knesset approved the coalition 72–21, with some absences, but no abstentions.[7]

In his opening address to the Knesset, Sharon urged Arafat's PA to "choose the path of peace and reconciliation" and pledged that if it "honor[ed] its commitment to fight against terrorism," it would find "a genuine partner" in his government. He promised to "open a new page" in relations with Israeli Arabs, but restated his commitment to retain control of Jerusalem, the Golan and the Jordan Valley.[8]

Ephraim Inbar, a prominent political scientist, commented that it was "definitely not a picnic having so many politicians in one government." But Sharon began, apparently determined, the *Irish Times* commented "to reshape public discourse in a country where debate is nearly always impassioned and courtesy a sometimes secondary issue." Sharon ordered his twenty-five politicians to be punctual, to keep comments to a minimum during meetings and never to "shout down" colleagues. Sharon's first cabinet meeting was also the first ever to begin on time.[9]

As Sharon settled into his office, he received an invitation from the White House to visit President Bush on March 20, and a letter from Yassir Arafat congratulating him on his election and calling for a revival of negotiations. Three days earlier Arafat had vowed publicly that the five-month-old intifada would continue "until we raise the Palestinian flag on the wall of Jerusalem," and that the Israelis were to blame for the "dangerous military escalation." One of his cabinet ministers, Imad Falouji, said that the Palestinians had planned the intifada after Arafat rejected the peace proposals at Camp David the previous summer.[10] The Palestinian mufti, Sheikh Ekrima Sabri, said at the same time that Palestinians would keep on with the "blessed intifada" despite the sacrifices they were forced to make. A Hamas leader in Gaza, taking responsibility for a bomb attack in Netanya which killed three Israelis and wounded more than ninety, said Hamas had suicide bombers "lined up" to "greet" the Sharon government. He said it was permissible to attack Israelis inside Israel. "In wartime, you need to use all effective weapons against your enemies. We do not have airplanes, we do not have tanks, we do not have support from outside, like the Israelis have the support of the Americans." So, he said, it was legitimate to re-taliate "in any place, at any time," because no one was trying to deter the Israelis or to convince them to withdraw.[11]

Marwan Barghouti, the leader of Arafat's Fatah faction, said that the situation would deteriorate under Sharon who would un-dertake more "aggressive attacks against the Palestinians." Sharon had to understand, he said, that the occupation was dead "and the only thing he can do is to decide the moment of the funeral." In Damascus, Syrian media printed extracts from Sharon's Knesset speech, but omitted his call for peace with Syria and Lebanon. An official Syrian newspaper editorialized that "a dangerous Israeli threat . . . is directed against our very existence as Arabs" and that Israel was threatening to expand its "war of atrocities" against Pal-estinians "into a regional war." Knowledgeable Syrian sources said that Sharon had let Syria know through a European Union envoy that he was ready for secret peace talks, but that this offer had been definitely rejected.[12]

The press was much interested in contrasting Sharon the hawk and Peres the dove, now that both men, in their seventies, were in the cabinet together. Their rhetoric was very different: Sharon in-sisted on reciprocal action from the Palestinians, who, he said, would never "get something for nothing," while Peres held that "[i]f people are starving and unemployed, all the reciprocity will be in vain." Then, too, Sharon and his closest advisors had ruled out direct talks with the PA until ten days passed without violence, but Peres wanted to meet with Arafat as soon as possible.[13]

Deborah Sontag pointed out, however, that the two men had more in common than at first met the eye. They were both gradual-ists who aimed for interim arrangements. Peres said that Sharon "accepts my ideas, but disagrees with my timeline." And they both faulted Ehud Barak on his handling of the peace process, although their criticism reflected a split in their attitudes. Sharon disliked Barak's failure to follow through on ultimatums, and Peres criticized his failure to keep promises to turn over some Arab villages to the PA, although Peres said also that Barak had carried his concessions too far.[14] This disagreement over the former prime minister's policies existed despite warm words between Barak and Sharon when Sharon took formal possession of the prime minister's office: Sharon regretting that Barak had not joined his coalition and declaring that he would not hesitate to seek counsel from Barak when the occasion arose, and Barak praising his successor as a proven leader who "embodied the unbending spirit of the State of Israel."[15]

BLOCKADE

———

ON MARCH 11, LESS THAN a week after he took office, Sharon inaugurated what was believed to be a new policy of putting pressure on areas seen as breeding places of terrorism, by digging a trench, 150 yards long, around Ramallah, a business center and unofficial PA headquarters under full PA control, to isolate it from about thirty surrounding villages, at some of which concrete barriers and checkpoints were set up. Sharon denied that this was a new policy, saying that it was actually implemented only to stop a car bombing in Jerusalem. Defense Minister Ben-Eliezer also denied that this was a new policy, saying that "blockades were not born yesterday," a reference to the fact that Barak had also instituted blockades. Peres too said that this policy was not initiated by Sharon, but by Barak.[1]

The army tore up a seven-mile stretch of road between Ramallah and Bir Zeit, the site of Bir Zeit University, a road which had been completed the year before at a cost of four million dollars, some of which had been borrowed from the World Bank, with the remainder coming from South Korea and OPEC. The road was used not only by the university's 5000 students, but by 200,000 village residents who traveled on it back and forth to hospitals, businesses and cultural centers in Ramallah. March 13 was supposed to be registration day for spring semester at the university. Using rubber bullets, tear gas and stun grenades, troops battled youthful stone throwers and hundreds of protesters attempting to open the road at one of the villages with a bulldozer. One Palestinian was killed and at least forty were injured.

An army roadblock was set up near the Kalandia refugee camp south of Ramallah to check identification papers of Palestinians on their way to Jerusalem. This caused considerable traffic backup and extended a twenty-minute trip to about two hours. The Bir Zeit students had not been involved in this second intifada unlike their leadership role in 1987. Now they were planning a protest march from Ramallah. Hannah Nasir, the president of the university, said that this closure was "going to energize everyone. It is a rape of the land and it's only going to cause more trouble for the army."[2]

The week before, the army had dug a ten-mile-long trench around Jericho and had also blockaded Jenin in the north West Bank. Spokesmen for the army said the blockades were necessary to curtail terrorist activity. Raanan Gissin, a Sharon advisor, said the army had acted in "self-defense," because the Ramallah area had "seen a marked increase in terrorist activity" from "a large concentration of Tanzim and members of security forces" and was the base for Marwan Barghouti, the Fatah leader.[3]

These closures badly hurt the Palestinian economy and evoked considerable negative comment, even within the Israeli military. PA unemployment quadrupled and the poverty rate shot up. Colin Powell commented that this economic pressure and consequent hardships did nothing to alleviate security dangers, and critics noted that education and the transportation of the sick and wounded were being disrupted. Peres said the digging of the trenches should be reexamined to see if they painfully disturbed "daily life in the territories." Sharon's response was that he wanted to ease the hardships of the Palestinians, but that first there had to be a cessation of violence, and that Arafat could accomplish that if he wanted to.[4]

In the opinion of some analysts, Sharon's policy was aimed at disrupting normal life in the territories in the hope of disillusioning moderate Arabs with their leaders while at the same time avoiding the international condemnation that a military escalation would engender. Many analysts pointed out that this policy could have the opposite effect and harden anti-Israel feelings.[5] Sharon's plan seemed to be a sort of replay of his fight against terrorism years earlier, in which the territory was divided into small parcels, each of which was tightly controlled by the army. A Palestinian source said that if this was to be Sharon's policy, the people would not take it for long; there would be an "explosion." Barghouti said the intifada would continue and that Sharon, "the certified Israeli war criminal," was behaving as expected.[6]

The European Union was not happy with Israel. Hubert Vedrine, the French foreign minister, in a paper on the Middle East sent to EU governments in February, said that the EU "should make the US recognize that it is legitimate for Europe to take its own approach to peace."[7] The danger to Israel was the possible suspension of all or part of an association agreement between the EU and Israel that had been ratified in 2000 when Barak had taken over from Netanyahu. This agreement included cooperation in several key areas and trade preferences worth millions of dollars a year. Britain and Germany were unlikely to go along with so drastic a measure, but Spain and Greece would probably accept France's lead. A lesser threat was the possibility of suspension of cooperation with Israel in talks on science, technology and agriculture. The EU also urged Sharon to remit the $57 million in tax revenues it was withholding from the PA. Chris Patten, EU commissioner for external relations, said that the "siege," which had cost the Palestinian economy more than a billion and a half dollars, was causing mass unemployment which in the end would lead to more violence. Washington, too, told the Israelis that if the PA collapsed, it would hurt prospects for peace.[8]

Sharon responded by opening two roads to Ramallah. The PA information minister, Yassir Abed Rabbo, commented that these were cosmetic changes, intended to deceive the world into believing that the closure had ended. In response to the question of the tax revenues, brought up in a meeting with an EU delegation that included Chris Patten and Anna Lindh, the Swedish foreign minister and EU president, Sharon said that it was "immoral" to ask Israel to transfer money that the PA would use to pay salaries to security forces engaging in terrorist acts. He responded to the call for a lifting of economic pressure by saying the Palestinian economic crisis had been caused by the PA choosing to use violence and terror, walking out on negotiations and breaching agreements.[9] After meetings with Sharon and Peres, Anna Lindh said that Europe would work to bring about renewed negotiations and help the Palestinians economically. She said she thought there was "a strong will from both sides."[10]

On the eve of Sharon's departure for Washington, Sheikh Ahmed Yassin, the Hamas leader, vowed "bigger, better and greater" bomb attacks against Israel. During an Islamic Jihad rally in Gaza City, young Palestinian boys acted out a suicide bombing, one boy dressed in white lying down in a coffin covered with an Israeli flag while another ignited a firecracker to simulate a bomb blast. There were other protest marches and rallies in several West Bank cities after what had seemed to be a waning of popular support for the intifada; these renewed demonstrations were thought to be a reaction to the Ramallah blockade.[11] At the same time, Suzanne Goldenberg wrote in the English *Observer*, there were calls from some prominent Palestinians for a non-violent protest movement coupled with pressure on Arafat to purge the PA of corrupt and incompetent elements; to, as *al Quds* newspaper put it, get his house in order and heed the call for democracy and human rights.[12]

Marwan Barghouti said that Sharon's policies had pushed more and more people into taking part in the intifada, and "at the same time, more people are talking about repairing and fixing what is going on in Palestinian society." At a funeral in Ramallah, activists called for a ban on street demonstrations by masked men firing automatic weapons in the air, and participants at a town meeting called for renewed communication with Jewish peace advocates who could influence the Israeli government. "In nearby El-Bireh and in Beit Jala, a suburb of Bethlehem," Goldenberg wrote, "widespread anger at the gunmen whose nightly pot shots at Jewish settlements have provoked devastating reprisals from the Israeli army forced Fatah commanders to order a new ban on the use of firearms in populous areas." No one complained about stone-throwing; that was seen as "a symbolic form of protest" against Israeli soldiers and settlers. But Barghouti said that "civil and peaceful forms of struggle" were going to supplant guns and bombs to give the world "a far better impression of the Palestinian people."[13]

In his two days in Washington, Sharon had separate, closed-door meetings with President Bush, Colin Powell, Defense Secretary Donald Rumsfeld, National Security Advisor Condoleezza Rice, CIA chief George Tenet, and met also with Dick Gephardt and the leadership of the House Democratic Caucus. He gave a major address to 2,200 supporters of the America Israel Public Affairs Committee (AIPAC), the most influential US pro-Israel lobby, at that organization's annual Salute-to-Congress dinner at the Hilton Washington; present also were more than forty senators and 100 congressmen, Bush administration members and diplomats. "I bring you greetings from Jerusalem, the eternal capital of the Jewish people," he began, and was immediately interrupted by a standing ovation. Some in the audience may have recalled that earlier in the month Colin Powell had committed a diplomatic faux pas when he called Jerusalem "the capital of Israel" in testimony before a congressional committee, a remark for which he was forced to apologize to several Arab governments.[14]

At one point Sharon departed from his prepared text to remark with a smile, "I always thought it's good to be prime minister. It's also hard." He went on to condemn terrorism, and to single out

Iraq, Iran and Syria as presenting serious threats to Israel's security. He said he believed that Israel could reach an agreement with the Palestinians, and he would make every effort to reach that agreement. But he did not fail to make clear his feeling about Arafat, saying that "Yassir Arafat and the Palestinian Authority are returning to the belief they can defeat Israel by means of armed struggle. They feel that violence will produce further Israeli concessions. Arafat is willing to destabilize the entire Middle East, including moderate Arab regimes, in order to achieve his goals."[15]

Security was very tight and across the street from the hotel members of the Council on American-Islamic relations and other Muslim groups protested, while a smaller group of Israel supporters filled the street directly in front of the hotel. One guest, who did not give his name, said, "He's back to square one. There's a lot of pessimism. It's almost like two petulant children who have to be separated." He paused with a sigh and added, "The problem is the violence." But the response from the audience was positive. Martin Indyk, the US ambassador to Israel, remarked, "The prime minister comes here with an overwhelming mandate of the people. There's a lot of business that can be done with him." AIPAC board member Ron Lauder said he thought Sharon had done a superb job in creating the unity government that he had said he wanted: "For the first time, Left and Right are speaking as one, and that means Israel is standing firm." Henry Waxman, Democratic Representative from California commented, "Whether it's Republican or Democrat, Labor or Likud, the relationship between Israel and the United States transcends parties."[16] This was borne out by Henry Hyde, the Illinois Republican chairman of the House International Relations Committee, who told the AIPAC: "Ties between the United States and Israel have never been stronger . . . Republicans and Democrats, members of the executive branch and Congress alike share a commitment to Israel's peace and security."[17]

In their closed meeting, Colin Powell urged Sharon to ease the pressure on the Palestinians. Sharon replied that he had eased some trade and travel restrictions but he saw no lessening of violence, no response from the other side. In fact, an Israeli settler, the father of six, had been killed in a drive-by shooting shortly after Sharon left for Washington, causing the IDF to blockade Bethlehem again only days after it had been opened for trade and travel. Sharon refused US requests to pay the PA the $50 million owed in taxes and custom duties. "I know it is their money," he said, "but they'll use it to pay people who are shooting at us."[18] Despite Colin Powell's urging, Sharon also would not agree to direct talks with the PA unless violence ceased. Despite these differences—tagged a "discussion among allies" by a State Department official—Powell told AIPAC that US support for Israel remained "rock solid . . . an unconditional bond that is both deep and wide, one based on history, on interests, on values and on principle."[19] The audience received him warmly, but there was an interesting moment when he referred to "the famous handshake" between Arafat and Rabin on the White House lawn in 1993. What was obviously expected to be a sure applause generator was met with cold silence. The "handshake" had led to the Oslo accords; it was obvious that this audience in the main agreed with Sharon that the accords were dead.[20]

Powell made it clear that Bush policy toward the Middle East differed significantly from Clinton policy when he said, "Turning to the United States or other outside parties to pressure one or another party, or to impose a settlement, is not the answer."[21] This was a firm denial of Palestinian requests, widely supported by the UN membership, for an international force to monitor the situation in the West Bank and Gaza Strip. Powell did express sympathy for the Palestinians, noting that the Israeli blockade had made a "shambles" of the PA economy, with skyrocketing unemployment. But he also told the AIPAC that "leaders have a responsibility to denounce violence, strip it of its legitimacy, stop it."[22]

Sharon could reasonably consider his visit to Washington a success, especially when it was contrasted with a visit he had made ten years earlier when he was minister of housing. Members of the first Bush administration refused to have formal contact with him, Secretary of Defense Caspar Weinberger criticized him for Israel's actions in Lebanon, and James Baker, who was Secretary of State at the time, later wrote in his memoirs that he considered Sharon an "obstacle to peace."[23] Now the prime minister was honored on the Pentagon lawn by a nineteen-gun salute and a fifteen-minute color guard ceremony. There was also his reception by high-ranking administration officials and members of Congress. He undoubtedly took satisfaction from the knowledge that Yassir Arafat was no longer welcome in Washington, although Mubarak and King Abdullah had been invited to the White House, and that Powell had nowhere mentioned a "peace process"—a favorite phrase of the Clinton administration—and had done away with the office held by Dennis Ross. Under Clinton, Arafat had received many invitations to the White House. An administration foreign policy official told the New York Daily News, "That's Clinton . . . here we start with allies first. Israel is an ally. The Palestinian Authority is not on the same level as some of our allies from that region." No one, the source said, had talked about bringing Arafat to Washington. It was not "imminent."[24]

This visit had been presented as a "get acquainted" meeting for Sharon, and the atmosphere was friendly and informal in a joint press conference with President Bush, who recalled his first meeting with Sharon in 1998 when Bush visited Israel with several other governors. Sharon, then a minister in Netanyahu's cabinet, had been the tour guide for a helicopter ride over the West Bank. Bush said he had been impressed by Sharon's "marvelous sense of history," and added, "Mr Prime Minister, you didn't think you were going to be the prime minister, and you probably darn sure didn't think I was going to be the president." Sitting beside Bush in the Oval Office,

Sharon told the press that he had been assured that the president accepted the Israeli premise that there should be no negotiations until the violence ended.[25]

Sharon's reception caused dismay in Gaza and the West Bank. Hanan Ashrawi said she was "worried about this emerging love fest, as though the United States is suffering collective amnesia about Sharon's previous crimes."[26] Arafat, who was visiting Qatar, said the Israelis were brutal aggressors, and called upon the Arab world to "confront" that aggression, presumably by a trade boycott of Israel and a breaking of Jordanian and Egyptian ties to that country. PA spokesmen in Gaza angrily refuted Sharon's charge that Arafat's Force 17 Presidential Guard had been involved in terrorist attacks, and rejected Sharon's plan for "interim agreements" that would create a Palestinian state on fifty percent of the West Bank, with Jerusalem and the refugee question set aside for the present.[27] The Palestinians were further upset a few days later when the *Washington Post* reported that the US, believing that the two sides should deal directly with each other, had ended the CIA's role as a broker between the Israeli and PA security services. PA officials had asked that the CIA continue to exchange intelligence information and "help curb terrorism." Bush's comment that Jerusalem's fate should be determined by the "concerned parties," also did not sit well in Amman, where members of the Jordanian parliament angrily called for a boycott of US products.[28]

From Washington, Sharon went to New York to meet for over an hour with United Nations Secretary-General Kofi Annan, who asked for an easing of economic restrictions on the PA and for Sharon's cooperation with George Mitchell's three-member commission appointed by Clinton to investigate the causes of the infitada. Sharon said that he intended to meet with them shortly, although he was opposed to the idea behind the committee, because, as he had told Barak, he considered it "an historic error to agree to the establishment of a committee" that would bring Israel before a kind of international tribunal. On the question of building and expanding the settlement Har Homa, Sharon's rationale was that Har Homa had been necessary to prevent Bethlehem from merging with east Jerusalem, which would lead to a border dispute, but that there was "nothing new" going on there, and that he had publicly stated that there would be no new settlements.[29]

Sharon raised the issue of the failure of UN forces and the Lebanese army to control Hezbollah activity on the southern Lebanese border. Annan showed the prime minister a letter he had recently sent to Bashir Assad telling him that Israel had fulfilled its obligations in complying with UN Resolution 425 and that Lebanon should respect the border. Sharon touched on Syrian efforts to get a Security Council seat, saying that he had no desire to interfere with UN arrangements, but that he had to point out that Syria was in actuality occupying Lebanon and turning it into a center of international terrorism. When Annan brought up Israel's failure to transfer tax money to the PA, Sharon replied, as he had to Powell, that Israel would not transfer money that would go to hostile groups like Arafat's Force 17 Presidential Guard. He "would be happy," he said, if the Arab countries made financial contributions to ease the conditions in the territories. As he had made clear at the White House, Sharon was unequivocal in his opposition to the sending of any UN observers or police to the West Bank and Gaza Strip.[30]

In Manhattan, Sharon was the guest of honor at a private reception given by New York Rabbi Shmuley Boteach and the psychic Uri Geller, who was famous for being able to bend spoons with his mental concentration. The pop star Michael Jackson, an acquaintance of Boteach's, dropped in at the reception and exchanged a few words with Sharon, telling him that he was "a big fan of Israel." Sharon, who was known to favor classical music, was asked whether he knew who Jackson was, and whether he would even recognize him on the street. Sharon answered, "Sure, what do you think, that I'm not familiar with the modern music scene?" He said later that he knew Geller had entered the room when the fork he was eating pasta with "went crooked."[31]

On his return to Israel, Sharon declared his visit to the US a success, saying that he had found agreement with Israel's stance on "regional threats" and sympathy for its "right to defend the lives of its citizens." The Americans, he said, recognized Israel "as a partner to develop defensive and deterrent systems to the growing threat of ballistic missiles." A cloud over his homecoming appeared in questions from the press about several incidents that had occurred during his absence: mortar shelling of West Bank settlements and inside the Green Line from the Gaza Strip. The IDF said these incidents had crossed the red line. What did Sharon intend to do about it? He said he could not be expected to stand there and tell the press what was going to happen in the next few days. But he had told the Americans that first, he was going to implement a "two-phased arrangement": to ease restrictions on the civilian population whose "only concern is to put bread on the table and bring up their children," and second, to take action against terrorists and their supporters "while making an effort not to escalate the situation."[32]

60

DARK TUNNEL

———

ONE RESULT OF THE WASHINGTON visit was a dust-up with Egypt over American aid. In 2001, US military aid to Egypt was $1.3 billion, and to Israel just under $2 billion, plus economic aid of $695 million and $840 million respectively. Israeli Army radio reported that at a closed-door meeting with congressional leaders, Sharon had urged that American aid to Egypt be halted because Egypt was playing a "negative role" in the peace talks. Hosni Mubarak immediately responded that Egypt would consider such an action a "hostile" one that would cause his country to change its attitude toward Sharon. The Egyptian foreign minister, Amr Moussa—who was preparing to leave for Washington to prepare for Mubarak's visit—said that US policy toward Israel should change and that he did not trust Israeli politicians. About Sharon's call for a lessening of violence in the territories, he said that the "entire Arab world" would never accept "Sharon's logic," and "nobody from our side will advise them to do it." Not surprisingly, he did not see "any light at the end of the tunnel" in the present conflict.[1]

A few days later, Mubarak announced that he had been assured that Sharon had not attempted to end US aid to Egypt and he believed that reports to that effect were "untrue."[2] This flap occurred on the eve of the first Arab League summit in a decade in Amman, where twenty-two heads of state and their representatives were to gather. The Israeli envoy, Zvi Mazel, asked Egypt to help calm the PA and other Arab hardliners, because the situation

was "really explosive." Egyptian officials said that the "thesis of
security before negotiating" was not "practical, pragmatic or logical," but a "cover-up for a new policy they want to impose on everyone." Arab leaders, shortly before the summit, promised to give
the PA $40 million a month, although they had released only $60
million of the $1 billion they had promised four months earlier at
their Cairo meeting. The $40 million, they said, was to go directly
to the PA; they had sent the $60 million to the Islamic Development
Fund for disbursement because they did not want to release money
to the PA without what the Middle East News Online called "sufficient monitoring mechanisms." In any case, a PA official said that
because of the intifada their losses were $3.25 billion and "it's go-
ing to get worse before it gets better." Arafat's aides said they would
believe the promise of Arab League money when they saw the first
check. Saddam Hussein, who was seeking to garner support for
repeal of the sanctions against him and to overcome the animus of
Kuwait and Saudi Arabia, sent $10,000 to each bereaved Palestin-
ian family and $500 to each family with members injured in the
intifada.[3]

The meeting, called the Summit of Accord and Agreement, was
completely dominated by the Palestinian situation. If they could agree
on nothing else, the leaders could condemn Israel and offer Arafat
moral support. President Bashir Assad of Syria called the Israelis
"more racist than the Nazis," referred to Sharon as "a man of massacres, a killer and a man who hates Arabs" and attacked Arab
moderates who wanted to give Sharon a chance. The Israelis, he
said, were insecure, because they knew they were living on "Arab
land." This speech surprised many foreign diplomats who were sympathetic to the Palestinian cause and had thought that Assad was
going to take his country down a more democratic road; one Western envoy said it was the sort of rhetoric that proved to Israelis that
"the Arabs really want to destroy Israel." In 1993, Syria had bro-

ken with the Palestinians over the signing of the Oslo accords, but
the intifada and Sharon's election had brought about an apparent
reconciliation. One Lebanese political analyst said that Assad wanted
to make sure that Arafat did not back away from the "right of return" or compromise on Jerusalem.[4]

After Assad's speech, Arafat said that the Israelis had used "illegal weapons" against the Palestinians, but that he wanted to resume peace talks; he condemned terrorist acts in general, without
mentioning two bombings that had occurred in Jerusalem the day
before. Kofi Annan, who was present as an observer, said that "the
international community and the Arab world have every right to
criticize Israel for its continued occupation of Palestinian and Syrian territory and for its excessively harsh response to the intifada."
He went on to ask the Arabs to acknowledge Israel's right "to exist
in safety" and to work for a negotiated settlement of differences, a
sentiment entirely lost on the Syrian and Iraqi delegations.[5]

On March 26, before the summit, the situation had escalated
when about five o'clock in the afternoon, a sniper killed a ten-month-
old girl named Shalhevet Pass in her stroller outside her family home
in a fortified Jewish enclave near the center of Hebron below Abu
Sneinah, a PA community on a 500-foot-high bluff from which gunmen fired down into Jewish neighborhoods. The baby's father and
brother were wounded. Almost immediately, Israeli soldiers attacked
Abu Sneinah with tank shells and machine guns, terrorizing families. In the family of Saadi Eddin Miteb, 39, a former PLO colonel
who fought in Beirut in 1982, three children under the age of seven
became so hysterical with fear that they had to be medically tran-
quillized.[6] Later that evening enraged settlers stormed the Palestinian marketplace, set fires and had to be forcibly restrained by Israeli
troops from invading Abu Sneinah, whose residents were advised
to evacuate their homes for their own safety. A blockade of Hebron,
where about 500 Jewish families lived near the town's main market,

was announced. Sharon's spokesman Raanan Gissen said that the Palestinians were trying to provoke tightened blockades in order to gain sympathy from the West, where the blockades had been decried. He said that snipers were "not gun-toting youth," but part of "professional security forces" under Arafat's control; he promised retaliation. Arafat himself told the Arab summit on March 27 that Palestinians were victims of Israeli "state terrorism" and urged the Arabs to defend them against "violent and terrorist occupation."[7] Defense Minister Benjamin Ben-Eliezer told the settlers, who were demanding that the army take over the hills around Hebron, to calm themselves. "The cruel murder of Shalhevet Pass is a hard blow," he said, "but we cannot lower ourselves to the level of her murderers." The Palestinians did not comment directly on the baby's death.[8]

But the settlers did not calm down; they had to be forcibly restrained from attempting to vandalize Palestinian property. In the ensuing struggle, at least one policeman was injured and seven settlers were arrested. Yossi Sarid, the leftist Meretz Party leader, calling on Sharon to evacuate the settlers from Hebron, said, "People that bite the hand that protects them, the hand of police officers and soldiers, cannot be considered balanced or normal people."[9] The settlers, none of whom were reported injured, blamed the clashes on "excessive force displayed by the special police unit in Hebron." Eddin Miteb, the Abu Sneinah resident, believed the uprising was futile against Israeli power, but that talks with Sharon would also be useless. He said he wanted negotiations, but the majority of Palestinians did not, "and so it will continue until something changes . . ." The settlers as a group had a different view. "Just one thing will help now," a rabbi said. "A big war . . . we have to fight back."[10]

The next day two bombs exploded in Jerusalem, slightly injuring about thirty people. The Islamic Jihad took responsibility for the first, a car bomb that went off in the early morning in an industrial area. Six hours later a suicide bomber blew himself up as he stepped off a bus at a busy intersection. He was the only fatality, which was a relief to the populace, but coming after the killing of Shalhevet Pass—whose parents said they would not bury her until the army occupied Abu Sneinah—these bombings ignited considerable public anger and impatience. As he had in Washington, Sharon accused Yassir Arafat of being the "one man responsible" for the violence, of directing his presidential guard to carry out violent acts.[11] Members of Sharon's coalition clamored for action. Gidon Ezra, the deputy minister of public security, said that Sharon was talking tougher than Barak, but that was the only difference between them. Other right-wing politicians complained that Sharon had not reacted and was not serious about protecting citizens.[12] Sharon was in a difficult position. He did not want to be provoked into a military action that would serve Palestinian interests by reinventing his image as a "warmonger," but at the same time he could not afford to look like Ehud Barak, whom the Arabs—and the Israeli Right— perceived as being full of sound and fury, and little else. He could not even do certain militant things that Barak had done, for fear of calling up shades of Sabra and Shatilla.

State Department spokesman Richard Boucher condemned the infant's death and the bombings, saying, "We look to the Palestinian Authority to do all it can to fight terrorism. It can do such things like preempting attacks, arresting people who are responsible and bringing them to justice." The State Department had made a practice of calling on both sides to reduce violence; this specific reference seemed to indicate American impatience with the PA.[13] Palestinian militia leaders said there was by no means any plan to eliminate the gunmen but there was evidence that PA leaders were trying to project a more acceptable image of the intifada, staging peaceful protests by middle-class businessmen and intellectuals.[14] Marwan Barghouti told *Haaretz* that the uprising had "evolved" to reflect grassroots, non-violent participation, and that its name would be changed from the National Islamic Leadership of the Intifada to the Popular Committee of the Intifada.[15]

Both sides stumbled in the last week of March. The Israelis apparently mistakenly lobbed stun grenades at a peaceful women's demonstration and slightly injured Hanan Ashrawi, while Arafat shut down the offices of al-Jazeera, the Qatar-based television station widely watched in the Arab world, because he found one of their commercials offensive. Three days later, after Hanan Ashrawi argued that this denial of free speech could backfire, Arafat relented and the station reopened.

As PA leaders were intent on demonstrating that the intifada was not basically a military enterprise, possibly because it appeared to be less of a grassroots movement than the first five-year intifada which had begun in 1987, there was evidence that questions were being raised, although quietly, by some Palestinians: academics and even clerics and government officials. Some objected only to the militants basing themselves in residential neighborhoods. A construction worker's nine-year-old son was killed while he played in his bedroom by Israeli gunfire aimed at snipers in a nearby building, and the apartment of the heartbroken family was consequently filled with officials and militants bearing plaques and wreaths in honor of the "martyred" child. The distraught father told the press he now hated the Israelis; when his teenage daughter began to blame the Palestinian gunmen, he anxiously told her to hush.[16]

The chairman of the political science department at Bir Zeit University, Saleh Abdel Jawad, was the first influential Palestinian to condemn the use of guns during popular demonstrations and in attacks on soldiers and settlers, as "fruitless . . . suicidal," giving the Israelis an excuse to "direct far greater firepower at us." He said the day would come "when the Israelis shoot without waiting for the Palestinian guns to fire first." Many Palestinians disagreed with Abdel Jawad, arguing that the intifada had forced the Israelis to offer more at Taba than they had at Camp David, and had aroused the sympathy of the Arab world. But about 375 Palestinians had been killed and thousands wounded in five months and the United Nations estimated that the intifada was costing the Palestinian economy $11 million a day. In addition, tight and punitive Israeli security was making travel limited and uncomfortable. A journalist, Daoud Kuttab, wrote a column saying that some intellectuals and businessmen were asking if there was a "point of diminishing returns." For the first time, Kuttab wrote, hard questions were being posed about where "all this" was leading, whether Clinton's proposals should have been accepted, and whether there was any valid reason to bring back the militant rhetoric of the '70s and '80s. Some Palestinians were asking, he said, "Are we entering into a dark tunnel without an end in sight?"[17]

In a sort of echo to this, the English *Guardian* ran a headline: "Six months of intifada: the timeline to nowhere."[18]

61

DAYS OF RAGE

———

ON MARCH 28, HOURS AFTER the close of the Arab summit in Amman, Israel launched helicopter missile strikes against bases and training camps of Arafat's Force 17 bodyguard in Ramallah and the Gaza Strip, in retaliation for a wave of bombings that week inside Israel. It was the first time in four months that airborne attacks were mounted within PA territory, and the first big offensive since Sharon had become prime minister three weeks earlier. Artillery and rockets killed at least two people, injured more than twenty, and damaged Arafat's house and helicopter landing pad in Gaza City, where Palestinian gunmen returned fire with submachine guns. Arafat was in Jordan at the time. Missiles were also fired into the Palestinian Broadcasting Authority headquarters in Ramallah, which the Israelis had accused of incitement. As rumors spread that Israel was invading the city, the streets were filled with excited youths with guns and the sound of horns blaring on careening cars. Western diplomats said it was easier to target Force 17 than to hit Hamas and Islamic Jihad, which had taken responsibility for the bombings. Hanan Ashrawi accused Sharon of trying to make a scapegoat of Arafat.[1]

Early that morning, a suicide bomber killed himself and two Israeli teenagers who were waiting for an armored school bus near the Palestinian city of Qalqilya. Another student was critically injured and a second was wounded in the eye by nails packed inside the bomb. This was the third successful bombing in two days; several other bombs had been found and neutralized before they could explode. Anger inside Israel was at the boiling point. Even leftists had turned against Arafat. Yossi Sarid addressed him from the Knesset, saying that perhaps he should "spend less time flitting from one country to another, and sit in Gaza and in Ramallah and begin to make order because this anarchy is creating a tragedy for your people as well as ours." The suspicion was arising, Sarid said, that Arafat was more interested in "armed and violent struggle" than in achieving a Palestinian state. Shimon Peres commented, "We do not want to see blood, not our own, not Palestinian. But the last two days were simply horrific and crossed every possible border of restraint and patience. Arafat must rectify his mistakes."[2]

In Hebron, the settlers continued to set fire to cars and property belonging to Palestinians. The dead baby's family still refused to bury her until the government invaded Abu Sneinah, rejecting a phone call from Sharon, who asked that the child be buried for humanitarian reasons. One settler stabbed an Israeli soldier who was trying to stop him from entering the Palestinian neighborhood. Sharon, who had surprised even his critics by refusing to be rushed into a response, had apparently waited until the Arab summit ended before acting under mounting pressure. Two-thirds of the Israeli public polled supported tougher military action against the Palestinians. Polls showed further that if there were elections then, the Likud would win about forty Knesset seats, a great improvement over the nineteen seats it currently held. Defense Minister Benjamin Ben-Eliezer said that "[a]s long as the terrorism continues, everything as of now is kosher." However, the Ramallah and Gaza attacks did not satisfy the far right-wing leaders, who called them "theater." At Jewish settlements in the West Bank, militant rabbis called for Sharon's downfall.[3]

Arafat returned from Jordan two days later to pray at the ruins of Force 17 headquarters in Ramallah, after which he pledged to continue the uprising "until we raise the Palestinian flag over every mosque and church and on the walls of Jerusalem."[4] This comment did not go down well with President Bush, who called a press conference a few hours later and said he was sending a signal to the Palestinians to "Stop the violence." He urged Arafat to speak out "loud and clear" against bloodshed, to arrest perpetrators and to help Israeli security forces prevent terrorist attacks. He also told the Israelis to ease up on border checkpoints and road closings that were making Palestinians' lives miserable. Shortly after the press conference, Colin Powell phoned Arafat and urged him to call, in both Arabic and English, for an end to the intifada. Palestinian leaders said Israel's "barbaric aggression" had been encouraged by the United States veto on March 28 of a Security Council proposal to send unarmed UN observers to monitor Israeli actions in the West Bank and Gaza. It was the first veto by the US in four years.[5]

Daniel Williams of the *Washington Post* commented that Arafat's defiant stance was reflected in talk in Ramallah of a three-pronged assault: street demonstrations and attacks on settlers and soldiers in the West Bank, along with terrorist activity inside Israel itself. Fatah members said that they were forced to target settlers and soldiers by Israel's "hard-line attitude." But one Fatah member complained that Hamas bombings served only to harden Israeli resolve and had a negative effect on world opinion. Some civic groups in Ramallah protested stone-throwing, and shooting from within the city by Fatah gunmen during marches, because it caused the Israelis to counterattack. Williams said that after seven months of intifada, fewer and fewer people were joining street protests, to the dismay of organizers who wanted to emphasize a grassroots uprising rather than an armed struggle. Mustafa Barghouti said, "It is all the people against occupation forces."[6]

But the intifada did not appear to be losing strength on Land Day, a "day of rage" in commemoration of a 1976 protest in which six Israeli Arabs were killed. Tens of thousands of Palestinians marched across the West Bank and Gaza on March 30, burned Israeli and US flags and effigies of Sharon.[7] In one march led by thirty Fatah gunmen firing into the air, the crowd chanted. "Sharon, wait, Fatah is going to open your grave in Gaza." In Ramallah, hundreds of people threw stones at troops who fired rubber bullets and live rounds at them, killing a twenty-one-year-old Palestinian. Three Palestinians were killed by troops in Nablus, and in Hebron Israeli tanks shelled gunmen who were firing at the Jewish enclave. Arafat said the Palestinian deaths were caused by Israel's "horrible crimes," and that the uprising would continue.[8]

In the Hebron enclave, the spot where Shalhevet Pass was shot to death was marked by a lighted candle, an elegy for her was affixed to the stone wall of her house, and neighbors, who hung her glossy photo around their necks, swore revenge. Six days after her death—a very long time for religious Jews, who bury their dead immediately—a funeral was held for Shalhevet Pass, possibly in response to pleas from Sharon and Chief Rabbi Meir Lau. Relatives carried the baby, wrapped in a blue velvet shroud, leading a procession of mourners past tanks and sandbags to the cemetery. Her father, who had been wounded by one of the bullets that killed her, was in a wheelchair. Palestinian houses along the route were shuttered; the Israelis had imposed a curfew for the day. But some settlers threw stones at the houses and at one point young settlers and Palestinians threw rocks at each other. After the funeral, Israeli soldiers had to restrain some settlers from running into a Muslim cemetery and others from attacking Abu Sneinah. Although the nation mourned, only one senior official, a cabinet minister from the ultra-orthodox Shas Party, attended the funeral. Sharon had probably been advised not to come for security reasons.[9]

To add to his headaches, Sharon's government had to settle a strike of municipal workers in Tel Aviv, Jerusalem and Haifa. When 120,000 workers walked off the job, garbage piled up and parking violations were ignored. The head of the Union of Local Authorities said that the Finance Ministry would bear the responsibility for any

casualties if terrorist bombs were hidden in piles of trash accumu-
lating in city streets. The Chief Rabbi had called on the local authorities to settle the strike, which he said "may be justified, but it is
inconceivable that it should, God forbid, cause tragedy." The strike
was settled when the cities and their mayors agreed to Finance Ministry terms.[10] Then there was the threat from Netanyahu, who had
appointed a chief of staff and political advisors, was meeting around
the clock with Likud Central Committee members and showing up
at their family parties. An aide to Sharon commented, "We have no
problem with the fact that Bibi is meeting with committee members, because we don't think these meetings will bring Bibi back to
power or hurt Arik . . . We do not feel that we are in the midst of a
war between camps. Arik's job now is to run the country, and at the
same time he is strengthening his position in the Likud."[11]

Sharon, under increasing pressure to live up to his soubriquet as
"the Iron Fist," fired dozens of rockets at four Force 17 bases in the
Gaza Strip in the first week of April, after a ten-month-old boy was
badly injured by mortar fire in Atzmona, a heavily guarded settlement in the southern Gaza Strip. Hezbollah-Palestine claimed responsibility, but the army said it believed the mortar rounds had
been lobbed from the nearby refugee camp of Rafah by Arafat's
guard.[12] In a separate incident, four Israeli helicopter gunships
launched a rocket attack on Mohammed Abdelal, 29, killing him in
his pickup truck at Rafah. Abdelal was reported to be an important
member of Al Quds Brigade, the military wing of Islamic Jihad,
whom the IDF accused of killing an Israeli soldier in 1994, of helping plan a suicide bombing that killed more than twenty Israelis and
of planting two bombs in Gaza the previous February. Thousands
of Palestinian mourners followed Abdelal's body through the streets,
crying out for revenge. Israeli officials had confirmed a policy of
assassination of members of terrorist squads, and according to the
London *Independent*, at least twenty Palestinians had been assassinated in the seven months since the intifada had started.[13]

In a meeting at the White House, President Bush urged Hosni Mubarak to use his influence to encourage Arafat to end the violence.[14] Mubarak, who was Arafat's closest advisor outside his immediate circle, said that the Americans were mistaken about Arafat's ability to put an end to the unrest: "They will not listen to him." He was not defending Arafat, he said, but years of growing anger could not be quelled by a declaration.[15] Condoleezza Rice was reported to have told the Egyptian foreign minister that Egypt had not done enough to rein in the Palestinians, that it should be explained to Arafat that the situation could cause a regional conflict. At the White House, Mubarak mentioned a "non-paper" or informal Egyptian-Jordanian solution, that called for Israel to cease military and economic action against the territories, to withdraw to positions it held before the September intifada, and to transfer PA funds it was holding. This proposal, drawn up with the Palestinians, had been rejected by both Sharon and Peres.[16]

The *Chicago Sun-Times* commented that Mubarak was ambivalent, that Egypt had a history of working against a general war, but also against a comprehensive peace. Egypt had, after all, recalled its ambassador after the Camp David summit while Barak, the prime minister most cooperative with the Palestinians, was still in office. And Mubarak was boycotting Sharon.[17] This was particularly noticeable when Yassir Arafat phoned Sharon ostensibly to extend good wishes on the Passover celebration—as he had done on February 6 to congratulate the prime minister-elect—while Mubarak made a point of phoning only Peres with holiday greetings. In this conversation, less than a week after he had told Bush that Arafat could not control the uprising in the territories, Mubarak told Peres that he would try to persuade Arafat to lessen the violence there.[18]

There were sporadic discussions. Israel Radio reported that in the Passover telephone talk, Sharon told Arafat he would ease restrictions on the Palestinian population, but not on militants, and that Palestinians were not exercising the option to come and work in Israel. In early April Peres met in Athens with Saeb Erekat and Nabil Shaath, the PA planning minister, to discuss cease-fire arrangements, the first open contacts between senior officials since Sharon became prime minister. Right-wing politicians expressed fears that in these talks, set up by Colin Powell, Peres was secretly "plotting peace."[19]

Sharon himself came under heavy right-wing criticism for sending his son Omri to meet secretly with Arafat in Ramallah despite the "no negotiations under fire" pledge. He defended this action by saying that Omri had given Arafat an unequivocal message to halt the violence. He pledged to work against "internationalization" of the conflict and any solution that impinged on Israel's "sovereignty and independence." He also took care to praise the "heroism . . . in difficult conditions" of the settlers who, especially in Hebron, were demanding unilateral military action.[20] The Israeli press reported that a senior Israeli official had met recently with Mahmoud Abbas, secretary of the PLO executive committee, but Abbas denied this, although he said that there were constant Israeli-Palestinian contacts. He said that the Jordanian-Egyptian "non-paper," already rejected by the Israelis, was being "discussed" with the Americans and Europeans.[21] A British attempt at a peace initiative by Lord Levy, Tony Blair's special envoy, failed when Sharon refused Levy's offer to carry a constructive message to Arafat, and Arafat insisted that any talks would have to follow the Camp David guidelines.

In the first week of April, Iyad Hardan, 25, a member of Islamic Jihad who had been released from his West Bank prison cell to make a phone call, was killed when the public telephone he was using exploded. Israel had used booby-trapped telephones to kill its enemies for more than twenty years; the most celebrated was the assassination in 1996 of Yihya Ayyash, a Hamas explosives expert, killed when his mobile phone exploded. But the PA did not immediately blame the Israelis for Hardan's death. Instead Arafat's police spokesman tersely announced that "[h]e went to make a phone call and the telephone exploded and killed him." Speculation arose at once that this killing was the result of an attempt by Arafat to control militant elements who had claimed responsibility for attacks on Israelis since the intifada began seven months earlier.[22] A more clear-cut Palestinian-on-Palestinian murder occurred shortly afterward when three masked gunmen fired fourteen bullets into Mamoun Freij, a thirty-seven-year-old suspected collaborator, as he sat in his shop in Tulkarm. Freij had lived in the north Israeli city of Hadera for some years after he received Israeli citizenship for cooperating during the first intifada, and had been living in Tulkarm for three years. Responsibility for this killing was claimed by a group connected to Arafat's Fatah movement, that issued a leaflet announcing: "The killing of this spy is a message to all the spies that we will punish them." Since September, two Palestinian informers had been tried and executed in the West Bank and Gaza Strip, and in April several others were on PA death row.[23]

These incidents occurred about the same time as what diplomats described as a "fiasco that could have started a war," when Israeli troops exchanged fire at Erez on the Gaza border with Arafat's security officials whose three-car convoy was returning from top-level security talks with Israelis and CIA. The Palestinians accused the Israelis of a plot to assassinate the security chiefs, while the Israelis said that the first two shots had been fired at border guards from the lead car of the convoy or from a nearby field. Brigadier Ron Kitrey, an IDF spokesman, said the whole thing was a "terrible mistake," and added, "There is no way our troops would have opened fire without provocation on people whom we could have arrested or attacked at any time on the drive each way with their meetings with our own generals. We are trying to work with these people, not kill them." The Palestinians demanded an apology. Sharon expressed regret over the incident in a letter to Colin Powell, but refused to apologize. He also maintained that these talks had not been actual "negotiations," but merely discussions paving the way for real talks later. Some commentators assumed that he was saying this to deflect right-wing outrage at any possibility that he was negotiating under fire, and that this was an encouraging sign of his flexibility.[24]

Less encouraging was his interest in expanding the settlements, and in allowing non-Muslims to visit the Temple Mount compound, which had been closed to visitors since the uprising in September. Hamas had called upon Muslims to take any steps necessary to prevent visits to the compound by Jews, and the police had barred such visits. During Passover a Jewish group wishing to pray on the Temple Mount, a holy site for them, had been turned away by the police, a decision that was upheld by the Israeli Supreme Court.[25] In mid-April, shortly after Sharon held an "initial discussion" with senior security officials of the possibility of readmission of tourists and Israeli visitors to the compound, dozens of Israeli police had to enter the compound to rescue beleaguered fellow officers in a small police station there, under attack by Palestinian stone-throwers after Muslim prayers. Two policemen were injured, and the attackers left without being forced. It was the first time a large number of police had entered the compound since the September riots. They did not enter the mosques.[26]

STRIKES & COUNTER-STRIKES

———

SIXTY PERCENT OF THE Palestinian-controlled Gaza Strip, a sandy coastal area about twenty-five miles long and only four miles wide in some places, is home to more than one million Palestinians, most of them still housed in camps set up after the 1948 war. Seven thousand Jewish settlers live on the remaining forty percent of the narrow strip of land.

Beginning in the second week of April, 2001, Sharon embarked on a series of invasions of Gaza, to put an end to mortar and gunfire attacks on Israeli settlements. In the first incursion, tanks and bulldozers entered the Khan Yunis refugee camp, destroying and damaging about two dozen houses and an olive grove. Calls for resistance from mosque loudspeakers brought hundreds of gunmen into the streets, and a four-hour battle ensued, in which two Palestinians were killed and twenty-five were injured. About 160,000 people lived in Khan Yunis, which abuts the Gush Katif Jewish settlements. Uzi Landau, the public security minister, said the attack would be followed by "a policy of hitting at them all the time, everywhere, and not necessarily just where the mortars are." He said the objective was to make the PA "begin to pay such a heavy price that in the course of time it will become unbearable."[1]

On April 16, the Israeli Air Force destroyed a Syrian radar station in eastern Lebanon, killing three Syrian soldiers and wounding six, in retaliation for a Hezbollah attack on Shebaa Farms, a disputed piece of land called Har Dov by the Israelis, where the Lebanese, Syrian and Israeli borders meet. An Israeli soldier was killed. It was the first Israeli attack on a Syrian target since April, 1996. There was a considerable outcry from Arab leaders over the attack on the radar station, but within Israel there was a surprising consensus in favor of the action, with the exception of Arab MKs. Labor's Defense Minister Ben-Eliezer said that the "rules of the game in Lebanon" had changed from an Israeli "policy of restraint," and Syria, with its military presence in Lebanon of 30,000 troops, was being held responsible for the actions of Hezbollah. Shimon Peres voted against the action when it was presented to the cabinet, but publicly defended it when it was an accomplished fact. Even Labor's Yossi Beilin, who had defended Arafat on Israeli television, said that since Israel had strictly adhered to the UN-determined border with Lebanon, it was fully justified in retaliating for Hezbollah attacks. Syria, he said, "must pay the price if Israel is hurt." One Arab MK, Mohammed Barakeh, of the Communist Hadash party, said that Sharon, like Slobodan Milosevic, should be tried for "crimes against humanity." Another, Abdulmalik Dehamshe, calling the strike an act of terrorism, sent a telegram of condolence to Bashir Assad.[2]

Later that night of April 16, Israel launched a ground, sea and air offensive on the Gaza Strip, capturing Palestinian territory, after several mortar bombs from buildings in the Gaza village of Beit Hanoun hit the Israeli town of Sderot, a couple of miles from the Strip. Less than twenty-four hours later, after Colin Powell called the occupation "excessive and disproportionate," the troops were withdrawn. The incursion, the first reoccupation of land there since Gaza was turned over to the PA in 1994, cut the territory into three sections, halted north-south traffic and sealed off all border crossings, including one with Egypt. Hamas claimed responsibility for the mortar attack, but the Israelis blamed Arafat's security forces, and destroyed buildings used by them. This action followed repeated warnings to Arafat to stop the violence. A wave of more than 100 mortar shells had rained down on Israeli towns and settlements in the preceding two weeks, and the latest mortars had landed less than three miles from Sharon's farm in the southern Israel desert.[3] The day after Powell's rebuke, State Department spokesman Richard Boucher said, "We haven't seen on the Palestinian side the kind of calls for an end to violence to stop the shootings."[4] But Powell's "excessive and disproportionate" remark was taken as a sign that the Bush administration did not wish to be seen by Arabs and other governments as blindly pro-Israel.

Arafat denounced the operation as an "unforgivable crime" and said his people would not "kneel before gangs."[5] Hosni Mubarak blamed Sharon, as did the governments of Britain, France, Russia and the United States, through their ambassadors to Israel. Hours after the Israelis withdrew, Palestinians launched more missiles at Jewish settlements.[6] A six-hour battle took place that night between Palestinian gunmen and Israeli troops on the outskirts of Bethlehem. Israeli critics attacked Sharon for giving in to what they saw as American pressure, since the operation commander, Brigadier-General Yair Naveh, had told reporters that his troops would remain in Palestinian territory for "days, weeks or months." When the army responded that the commander "had exceeded his authority," Israeli politicians on both left and right and many in the IDF, accused Sharon of trying to use General Naveh to cover his own cave-in to the Americans. Labor and Social Affairs Minister Shlomo Benizri publicly criticized Sharon for not informing the security cabinet in advance of his plans to enter Gaza, and for allowing the impression to be given that the IDF and the politicians had "hung the general out to dry." Sharon responded by telling the security cabinet that he would notify them by phone before he made any significant military or diplomatic actions.[7]

In Washington, Gary Ackerman of New York, the top Democrat on the House subcommittee on the Middle East, calling Powell's remarks "very unfortunate," said they gave "a moral equivalence to somebody being attacked and somebody responding to an attack. They are not moral equivalents."[8] Powell had tempered his rebuke by adding that the Israeli operation in Gaza had followed "provocative Palestinian mortar attacks." Ten hours after they withdrew, the Israelis reentered the Gaza Strip with a tank and two bulldozers and demolished a police station near Gaza International Airport in the south.

Sharon, in an interview with the French newspaper *Le Figaro,* said that foreign criticism of the raids was encouraging Palestinian violence, and repeated that Arafat could once more become a partner for peace only when he ended the terror. It was not, Sharon said, up to Israelis to decide who should lead the Palestinians, "but how can you have as a partner someone who is trying to kill you?" He said he had no intention of returning to Gaza, but it would be a mistake for Palestinians to think that "these terrorists, these assassins" were safe in Area A. "The first duty of a state," he declared, "is to ensure the security of its citizens. When it comes to Jews, the criteria suddenly seem to be different. People never stop asking them what right they have to defend their lives." Mubarak told *Der Spiegel* that Sharon was a trouble-maker who was "only interested in violence" and "forc[ing] the Palestinians to follow his line." But he added that if "talks really turned to war, the Americans would get involved and prevent an all-out war from happening."[9]

Mubarak's reluctance to entertain war talk was not echoed at a two-day Arab conference in Tehran called the International Conference for Support of the Intifada. The Iranians had responded angrily to reports that, in his meeting in Washington, Sharon had told George Bush and Condoleezza Rice that, in addition to training and funding Hezbollah fighters, Iran had shipped, from Tehran to Beirut via Damascus, long-range rockets capable of reaching central Israel, rocket-propelled grenades, Katyusha rocket launchers and light antitank weapons. The Hezbollah Secretary-General refused to confirm or deny Sharon's statement, but Iran issued an official denial. The Iranian news agency reported that President Mohammed

Khatami had praised the Syrian people and government for their fight against Israel, saying that cooperation among Iran, Syria and Lebanon had been crucial to the victory of Hezbollah in southern Lebanon.[10]

The Tehran conference was attended by the heads of all major Islamic groups: Hezbollah, Hamas, the Islamic Jihad, the Popular Front for the Liberation of Palestine, as well as militants operating internationally. Yassir Arafat was present, arriving after paying his first visit to Bashir Assad in Damascus. Arafat had been persona non grata in Tehran because of his talk of peace, but Iranian intelligence had recently decided that he had "resumed the path of the people" by launching the intifada, and he was therefore invited to the conference, where the goal set was to seek "ways to establish an independent Palestinian state from the Jordan River to the Mediterranean Sea." The opening speeches called for a holy war, for attacks by a united Islamic army to strike "terror and fear" in Israel, and warned that Sharon planned to reoccupy parts of southern Lebanon. Iran's supreme leader Ayatollah Ali Khameni spoke, supporting an intensification of the intifada. The US State Department commented that Khameni's "deplorable and outrageous" comments provided evidence of Iran's support for terrorism. Further, Washington said the Tehran gathering was "no garden party" and warned that a soon-to-be-released State Department report on terrorism would note Iranian "relations and overtures" to Hezbollah and Hamas. The Iranians responded that Iran would continue its "moral and humanitarian support" for Hezbollah and the PA, for which US approval was not needed, and condemned Washington for its support of "Israeli terrorism."[11]

Representative Jim Kolbe, an Arizona Republican, chairman of the House subcommittee on foreign operations and head of a bipartisan US congressional delegation to the region, met with Sharon, Peres and Ben-Eliezer, and then with Arafat before going on to Jordan and Egypt. Kolbe said that Sharon had rejected a suggestion by

Arafat that diplomatic negotiations begin without preconditions and that he and Sharon make a joint television appeal for peace. Sharon responded that he wanted to see "actions and not declarations," and officials in his office told Kolbe that Arafat made these suggestions so that he would look constructive enough to be invited to the White House. Even though Arafat, who had made "a terrible mistake" in rejecting Barak's offer, was now "fairly desperate to get back to the peace table," Kolbe was "not terribly optimistic" about any breakthrough for peace, since both sides were "talking past each other" and were "not on the same wavelength."[12]

Sharon told *Maariv* that he was willing to recognize a demilitarized, limited Palestinian state on up to forty-two percent of the West Bank and seventy percent of the Gaza Strip, as a long-term interim solution to the conflict. Barak, he said, had made a "horrible mistake" by offering virtually all of the West Bank and Gaza Strip as well as east Jerusalem. Sharon's offer was rejected by the Palestinians and by the Egyptian Foreign Minister Amr Moussa. Dr Nabil Shaath, a Palestinian minister and negotiator, called the plan "nonsense" that would only help "destroy the peace process." He said also that the "US position is bad. It is worse than that of any previous US administration," and he hoped that Europe would play a role and help the Palestinians.[13]

Although Sharon had said repeatedly that he would not negotiate until the violence ended, his son Omri had at least two secret meetings with Arafat. Since Lily's death, Sharon had come to rely heavily on Omri, described as "a giant of a man," a businessman who had been a naval commando and had gone to law school. Sharon had told *Haaretz* that without Omri he would not have become prime minister: "Many years ago he told me that if I wanted to be in politics, I must not see things in black and white. He had an extraordinary influence." Omri's two meetings seemed to have helped to ease distrust between the two sides. Mohammed Rashid, Arafat's economic advisor, said that in the short time he had known Omri, "he has elicited great trust from me and other senior officials. He knows how to build good relations with Chairman Arafat." Palestinians said that Omri was the first person they called at the end of March when fire was exchanged between Israeli soldiers and the three-car convoy of Palestinian security chiefs. They said Omri was very different from his father, whom they characterized as "a man from another age."[14]

Israeli politicians on both sides of the spectrum objected fiercely to Omri's contacts with the Palestinians. The far right was angry because they felt the contacts to be a violation of Sharon's pledge not to negotiate under fire. The left accused Sharon of nepotism, a failing common in Arab governments. The attorney general, Elyakim Rubenstein, gave an explicit opinion that the prime minister's office could not employ the prime minister's son, and could not send him on official business. When it was discovered that Omri had had his second meeting with Arafat after Rubenstein's opinion, the Meretz party threatened to petition the Supreme Court to put an end to Omri's missions. Yossi Sarid, the Meretz leader, said using Omri was an "improper phenomenon" unacceptable in democratic countries, and that it put the status of the attorney general at risk.[15] In the first week of May, Israel's High Court of Justice instructed Sharon that he could not send his son to meet with Arafat unless he received permission from the attorney general, because civil service regulations barred the prime minister from appointing a member of his family to carry out assignments like that except in "exceptional" circumstances. Rubenstein issued a statement that Sharon could send Omri "only in special and concrete circumstances and specific occasions in which genuine life and death situations justified the specific use of the son of the prime minister, rather than anyone else, to convey the message." He added that he would consult a security official before he decided whether to authorize using Omri Sharon. Sharon's lawyer accepted the decision, while making it very clear that his client disagreed with it.[16]

63

ACTIONS & NO DECISIONS

———

THE FIRST ISRAELI REACTION TO the news that a joint Egyptian-Jordanian peace proposal was to be presented to Sharon was a negative one. The day before Jordanian Foreign Minister Abdul al-Khatib was to arrive in the West Bank with the proposal, Israeli sources described the initiative as a plan "hatched" by Arafat and former Justice Minister Yossi Beilin that would be rejected outright "because it set out a timetable for the attainment of a final agreement." The proposal was based on the Sharm al-Sheikh discussions between Arafat and Barak with Clinton and called for both sides to end violence and negotiations on the basis of UN resolutions 242 and 338, which Sharon had repeatedly said he did not recognize as the basis for a peace settlement.[1] The Egyptians had told a London-based Arab newspaper that the return of the Egyptian ambassador to Tel Aviv was contingent on the Israeli acceptance of this proposal, the main points of which were, in addition to a pledge to implement the Sharm al-Sheikh negotiations and a mutual announcement by both sides of an end to all forms of violence, a) withdrawal of Israeli forces and lifting of all blockades from Palestinian towns; b) continuations of the Taba discussions and other negotiations, including with Syria; and c) a freezing of settlements and a stop to all other provocations of the Palestinian people.[2]

Despite Israel's initial negative reaction, Shimon Peres responded to the formal presentation of the Egyptian-Jordanian proposal by saying that Israel appreciated the effort and would "seriously consider" it.[3] Hopes were lifted when Defense Minister Ben-Eliezer described the proposal as "worthy of examination."[4] The Belgian foreign minister, Louis Michel, carried alternative drafts of the plan back and forth between Israeli and Palestinian leaders. Hopes rose higher when Arafat said, after meeting with Michel, that "the Palestinian people are opposed to killing innocent civilians on both sides, Palestinians and Israelis."[5] One diplomatic source said that Sharon and Peres were careful not to hold in-depth discussions of the proposals with Khatib, because they did not want to be accused of "negotiating under fire."[6] There was no way, however, that they could prevent the right wing from making that very accusation.

Sharon specifically objected to four points in the proposals: one was the clause calling for a freeze on settlements; second was a clause barring the use of "weapons banned under international law," since Israel denied ever using such weapons in the intifada clashes. Thirdly, Israel would not recognize any verbal agreements reached by Barak at Camp David or Taba, and fourthly, Israel demanded a detailed list of "confidence-building" steps the Palestinians had to take, like arresting terrorists and collecting illegal weapons. Sharon objected, too, to the time limit of six months to complete a comprehensive peace treaty.[7] Peres went to Cairo to submit the Israeli response to the proposal informally to Hosni Mubarak. After the meeting, Mubarak announced that a cease-fire deal had been reached and talks would resume four weeks after the deal took effect. But Peres denied that a deal had been reached; there had only, he said, been a discussion.[8]

Sharon reiterated his position that Israel would not resume negotiations unless there was "a complete halt to terrorism in all its forms." Ahmed Qurei, speaker for the Palestinian Legislative Council, said that the Palestinians had accepted the Egyptian-Jordanian plan, and called on the US to pressure Israel to accept it as well.[9] But Marwan Barghouti, the Fatah leader, denounced the plan as a waste of time and criticized Khatib's visit, as well as Peres's, saying that

Khatib should not have come, and that "no Arab capital should welcome any member" of the Israeli government.[10] Hamas warned that "black days" were coming for "the Zionists. Sharon will wish his mother had never given birth to him."[11]

Right-wing politicians insisted that negotiations with the Palestinians could only be successful after full-scale war, a massive unlimited IDF strike into Area A, accompanied by an international public relations campaign explaining that Israel was fighting for survival. Avigdor Lieberman decried Peres's trip to Cairo, demanded that Sharon hit the Palestinians harder and called Arafat "the twin of Osama bin Laden, but cleverer." He said the government was "grovelling" to Mubarak as previous administrations had done. "Egypt," he said, "cannot be part of the peace process when it has not returned its ambassador and all our diplomatic contacts with them take place in Egypt."[12] Sharon, in turn, accused Yossi Beilin of acting behind his back to run "the Palestinian lobby in Washington." Beilin's spokesman scoffed: "Sharon's posturing doesn't scare us. Sharon's and Peres's about-face on the Egyptian-Jordanian initiative shows there are fruits to our efforts." Yossi Sarid, the Meretz leader, happened to be meeting with Arafat when Mubarak announced the cease-fire agreement. He said the Palestinians were taken completely by surprise, because they believed the cease-fire would only happen after the Israelis agreed to a freeze on the settlements.[13]

In the midst of this, suicide bombings and gun battles continued, as did secret meetings between Palestinian and Israeli security officials. The Israeli press reported that Ahmed Qurei had met with Peres; Qurei denied this, but Palestinian sources confirmed that secret meetings were being held. Bassam Abu Sharif, an Arafat advisor, said that the PA was convinced that Sharon was using newspaper interviews and military escalation to prepare the ground for a rejection of the Egyptian-Jordanian proposal, and that he was holding the security meetings to mislead the Americans while he worked to sabotage the results. But other Palestinian sources said they believed that Sharon, like Arafat, was genuinely looking for a way to end the violence, since nothing was being achieved by it. Mohammed Dahlan, the Gaza security head, said the security meetings were useless. He had boycotted these meetings after the shootings at the Erez border crossings when he had been in the three-car convoy—shootings he believed were an "ambush" ordered by Sharon. The Palestinian security services were no longer able to fight terrorism, he said, because they had been weakened by Israeli attacks, but the PA would take immediate action against terror once Israel withdrew to its pre-intifada positions. Asked by Israel Radio about a Hamas bombmaker, Mohammed Deif, Dahlan responded that Deif was "no longer" in his custody.[14]

Hassan Asfur, a senior Palestinian official, told a London-based Arab newspaper that these security meetings were orchestrated by the Israelis to give the world the impression that they wanted peace, while they were attacking PA security agencies and residential areas. Asfur singled out Shimon Peres for harsh criticism, saying that it was he who spread exaggerated reports about contacts and meetings. Asfur did not deny that these had occurred—there had been one three days earlier between Peres and Saeb Erekat—but, Asfur said, these contacts, made at Peres's request, led to nothing because Peres had no influence over anything and was exaggerating the importance of the contacts to prove that he was influential, although Sharon had bypassed him by using Omri to contact Arafat. Asfur claimed that Peres was trying to counter a "fierce campaign" against him inside the Labor Party, where he hoped to be elected to the leadership. He had become temporary leader when Barak was defeated. Peres told Israel Radio, "I am holding secret contacts with the Palestinians to put out the fire. Once these contacts produce any result, I will announce it. We cannot end the violence through using force only. Dialogue is also required . . . We should achieve a breakthrough. This is possible, although it is difficult . . . In the past, I managed to emerge from many difficult situations."[15]

The question that had emerged for Israeli security officials was whether Arafat was in full control of the seven-month-old intifada and would be able to end it if he wanted to. The army, relying on military intelligence, believed that Arafat was in control and was manipulating the level of violence. But the Shin Bet, the domestic security arm, agreed with King Abdullah of Jordan who told a German magazine that Arafat was "no longer in control after the events of the last months, but remains a symbol for the Palestinians." Shin Bet was convinced that the intifada was being directed by the commanders of the PA security services and the Tanzim, the activist Fatah faction. The Palestinians rejected this opinion. Arafat advisor Abu Sharif commented, "If Arafat wanted to call off the intifada, he could do it in one hour—no more. But why should he? We are acting in self-defense."[16]

Those who agreed with Abu Sharif argued that mortar firing was drastically reduced after Arafat issued an order to that effect, and there had been many pauses in attacks when Arafat saw fit to call them for diplomatic reasons. But these had usually been followed by car or suicide bombings carried out by members of Hamas or Islamic Jihad, many of whom had been jailed by Arafat but whom he had released when the intifada began. Sharon's government blamed Arafat directly for terrorist activities, saying that his Palestinian Authority controlled the mortar-producing factories in Gaza, that it was up to Arafat to round up the militants and that he was pretending to be weak so that Israel would reward him for calling off the intifada.[17]

But a senior Shin Bet official disagreed, saying that even before the intifada there were signs that the Tanzim were "increasingly organized in independent fiefdoms" and that Arafat could not control them. "He is waiting for someone else to do it for him. He is waiting for something from God." Alan Philps of the *Daily Telegraph* pointed out that Arafat had 40,000 armed men in his security forces, enough to rein in the Tanzim. But this action would endanger Arafat's position: he would be seen as a traitor if he turned on the fighters after 400 Palestinians had lost their lives in the struggle, and that could lead to a civil war. A member of the Palestinian opposition said, "The rage of the people is directed against Israel. If the clashes stopped, it would be directed against the men of dubious morality who run the Palestinian Authority. You cannot order a fire where to burn."[18]

The effect of this intifada on both sides was destructive, but it was particularly devastating to the Palestinian economy, at which it seemed the Israelis had aimed a coordinated onslaught, even before Sharon took office. In early 2000, "Palestine's oil" was what Arafat had called tourism to PA Christian sites, especially in Bethlehem, but by the spring of 2001 his trade minister was saying that "the tourist sector is dead on its feet." Tanks and helicopter gun-ships had frightened away foreign investors by systematically pounding hotels, office blocks and other commercial enterprises in Ramallah, the PA commercial capital, forcing formerly prosperous businessmen to lay off employees. Farms had provided healthy income, with good sales inside Israel, but now the IDF had destroyed olive and orange groves, anything that could provide cover for militants. One heartbroken farmer in Gaza said it was true that mortars had been launched from his fields against an Israeli settlement, "but there's nothing I can do to stop that and now I'm a ruined man." It was estimated that unemployment in the West Bank was about thirty-five percent, with half of Gaza's adult population out of work. The expensive new airport in Gaza was a white elephant, and bombardments of Gaza City had wrecked the economic activity—hotels, shops, small businesses—that had sprung up when Arafat set up his headquarters there. Travel restrictions prevented thousands of workers from leaving PA territory for work in Israel. Palestinian officials estimated overall losses at one billion dollars and growing.[19]

In 1998, outside Jericho, a Biblical town on the Jordanian border, Austrian entrepreneurs had opened the Oasis Casino, in which the PA held a $60 million interest. Since it was the only casino in either Israel or the territories, it was wildly successful, with busloads of Israelis coming to gamble. A luxury hotel opened, along with a fish restaurant, and more than 2000 people found jobs at the Oasis. But when the intifada began in September, 2000, there were gun and tank battles near the casino; the front windows were shattered, and the Oasis closed down, taking the hotel and restaurant businesses with it. When it was suggested that the casino reopen, the Palestinians objected, saying not just Jericho, but all their villages closed off by IDF checkpoints should be reopened. Sharon said security demanded the restrictions: "We are not saying, "Don't kill us, and we will open a casino for you." Nur al-Din, a dealer, commented, "We would welcome the Israelis back—they love to gamble." He was sure they would be "one hundred percent safe if they returned."[20]

All over the West Bank and Gaza Strip, roads were blocked by concrete and earthen barriers manned by Israeli soldiers. Yellow Israeli license plates allowed relatively easy access between settlements, but green Palestinian Authority plates were a different story. Before the intifada, a Palestinian cellphone dealer could drive from his home in Hebron to Jerusalem in no more than forty-five minutes; now seven months later, it was a three-hour trip involving five taxicabs and two long walks. His business, he said, had fallen off seventy-five percent. A journey from Hebron to Nablus that used to take two-and-a-half hours now could run as long as five to seven hours. Going from Hebron to Ramallah through Jerusalem used to take about an hour; it now involved an eight-hour trip, crammed with as many as eight people in a taxi, on a twisting route that had to bypass Jerusalem. The purpose of the closures, according to Sharon's advisor Dore Gold, was to "reduce . . . chances of a major terrorist attack in the heart of Israeli cities, especially at sensitive times." In principle, he said, Israel "would like to alleviate the economic burden on the Palestinians" but "as long as the Palestinian

Authority refuses to assume the responsibility it has been given in respect to internal security, Israel has no choice."[21]

April 25, 2001, Israel's Memorial Day and fifty-third Independence Day, was not a joyful occasion. Seven months of intifada had cost seventy-four Israeli lives: women, children, settlers, Israeli residents and thirty-one soldiers and other members of the security forces, blown up, shot by snipers, attacked by mobs, run over. Four hundred Palestinians were dead, most of them killed by Israeli security forces. As a normal way of life, Israelis now kept away from crowded places as much as possible, avoiding malls and buses. An Independence Day poll showed that only twenty-three percent of citizens believed that there could be real peace between Israel and Palestinians and other Arab nations during the next fifty years. The left-wing peace camp was demoralized. Oz Almog, a sociologist, said, "We don't have any more right and left. We've all become right." Sharon told Israel Radio, "We all want peace, but I am not so pretentious as to think we can have absolute peace. I think we should strive for a long-term, interim cease-fire."[22] He was aware that Barak had been heavily criticized for trying to reach a final agreement too quickly with Arafat.

64

MITCHELL "COTTON CANDY"

———

IN EARLY MAY, TWO WEEKS before its formal publication, basic premises of the report of the five-member Sharm al-Sheikh Factfinding Committee, appointed by then-President Clinton and chaired by George Mitchell, were leaked to the press. The commission had been established in September, 2000, during the summit attended by Clinton, Arafat and Barak. The report did not place blame on either side for the start of the intifada; although they found Sharon's visit to the Temple Mount to be "badly timed" and ill-considered, the committee rejected Palestinian claims that the visit had set off the uprising. At the same time, the committee also rejected Israeli claims that the PA had deliberately planned the violence after peace talks broke down the previous July. It did find that Israel had responded to the rioting with "excessive force": the IDF, with its large number of very young enlistees, was poorly disciplined and not sufficiently controlled by senior officers. The committee members—besides Senator Mitchell—were ex-Senator Warren Rudman, ex-President of Turkey Sulyman Demirel, Norway Foreign Minister Thorbjorn Jagland and Javier Solana, the EU High Representative for Common Foreign and Security Policy. They demanded that Israel lift its blockade of PA territories, pay tax revenues withheld from the PA, stop demolishing homes in the PA area, and allow the return to their jobs of the 140,000 Palestinians who had been employed in Israel before the intifada began.[1]

Perhaps most importantly, the 32-page document called for an immediate freeze on all settlement building, even "natural growth," in the territories. The committee endorsed the opinion of former Secretary of State James Baker that there was no "bigger obstacle to peace than the settlement activity."[2] The *Financial Times* called this "a victory for the Palestinians," which placed "the onus on Israel to change its policy." In April, Sharon had announced plans to build 700 homes in the settlements and had asked for extra funding for the settlers.[3]

On the Palestinian side, the report rejected PA demands for an international force to police the territories, and condemned the shooting by gunmen at Israelis from towns and villages, a practice that had caused many civilian deaths by provoking Israeli reprisals. The committee found "very troubling" the "lack of control exercised by the Palestinian Authority over its own security personnel and armed elements affiliated with the PA leadership." Arafat, the report said, should take "concrete action" to make clear that "terrorism is reprehensible and unacceptable and that the PA will make a 100 percent effort to prevent terrorist operations and to punish perpetrators," by arresting and jailing them.[4]

Israel accepted the basic guidelines of the report, but Sharon said that the committee should have blamed the PA for the wave of violence. He said it was clear, even from comments made by PA spokesmen, that the intifada was "the result of a strategic decision taken by the Palestinian Authority immediately after the Camp David summit." Peres, on the other hand, found the report "reasonable and balanced" because it exonerated Sharon from the accusation that he had deliberately provoked the violence; it called for "confidence-building measures" from both sides during a cooling-off period, and it ruled out forcing either side to accept agreements. Sharon found unacceptable, as was to be expected, the report's call for a cessation of building in the settlements, but he expressed satisfaction with the rejection of the PA demand for international observers and the call for the PA to act forcefully against terrorism.[5]

Palestinian officials, too, accepted the report, particularly praising its insistence on a settlement freeze: PA Minister Yassir Abbed Rabbo said the PA accepted the report on the causes of the intifada "inasmuch as they point directly to Israel's continued occupation of Palestinian land." But privately they were disappointed that they seemed to be asked to end the intifada without any guarantees that the settlements would be frozen. The Fatah leader Marwan Barghouti said the report was "not balanced enough" and was "useless" as a basis for a cease-fire agreement because it "did not demand the full withdrawal of Israeli forces from the West Bank, Gaza and east Jerusalem," and thus would not "achieve anything on the ground." Arafat suggested that the two sides hold a summit to discuss the report, but the Israelis said that the PA must first call a halt to the violence.[6]

On May 8, at his news conference in the banquet room of the King David Hotel in west Jerusalem, his first with foreign reporters since he had taken office two months earlier, Sharon challenged the Western and UN position that the settlements were illegal because they were built on land that Israel had held in military occupation since 1967. It was not "occupied territory," he said, "but disputed territory." His grandfather "was facing Arab terror, my father, my sons, as reserve officers, face it. I know families who have been facing Arab terror—five, six generations." As a former general who had been wounded and lost friends in warfare, he said, he was committed to peace and understood it better than "all those politicians who speak of peace." All the seventy-five newsmen were "young people, and do not always have time to bother yourself with facts from the past. But who occupied what? Let's put the facts straight." Then he launched into a history lesson about occupation: Egypt occupied Gaza and Iraq, and Jordan occupied the West Bank. When a reporter asked him why Jordan's rule of the West Bank was "occupation," while Israel's control of the territory was not, Sharon simply smiled at him and did not answer. He apologized for his thickly accented English, explaining that when he was growing up on his father's farm there was no time to study languages while he was milking cows and driving tractors. But he repeated a favorite phrase: "I say what I mean and I mean what I say." As an aside, he mentioned that he still lived on a farm, Sycamore Ranch, in the Negev, and invited the foreign reporters to visit him there: "We are short of labor."[7]

He said that he had accepted the idea of freezing new settlements, as demanded by the Labor Party, in order to form a unity government. But the "natural growth" of existing settlements could not be contained. He would not stop building settlements to "reward" the Palestinians for stopping the uprising: "My dear friend, we do not have to pay in order not to get killed. It's very simple. We will not pay protection money." He went on to argue against the settlement freeze. "Let's assume a family is going to have a baby. It happens. They have to leave the place where they were born? What should they do? Abortion? What, there should be three generations in two small rooms?"[8]

As if to underscore his point, later that day he visited the hilltop settlement of Maale Adumim, a suburb of Jerusalem with 25,000 residents, where he was warmly welcomed. He told the settlement schoolchildren who greeted him waving flags, "You not only live in the prettiest place, you live in a place of the highest importance to the security and future of the state of Israel." Peace Now activists questioned Sharon's position on the settlements, saying that nearly 7000 new housing units were being built in the existing settlements, and an additional 3000 were vacant at that time. Thus, Peace Now said, there were 10,000 units that could meet the demands of growing families for the next four years.[9]

A senior Israeli Foreign Ministry official told the *Washington Post* that the two sides were caught in a cycle that was certainly going to get much worse, pointing out that the Israelis had just captured a fishing boat carrying anti-aircraft missiles and fifty short-range rockets to be smuggled into the Gaza Strip. Obviously, he said, the antiaircraft missiles were "the next logical step. What do you expect them to do if we send helicopters to rocket them? . . . What we have to look forward to is each side testing the other's ability to suffer."[10]

The Dutch foreign minister Jozias van Aartsen told the *Jerusalem Post* that there was a "strong international alliance of support" for the Mitchell Committee report, which he found "wise and balanced." The problem, he felt, was Sharon's precondition of a cessation of violence before "confidence-building measures"—but not a settlement freeze—could take place. The Dutch government, Van Aartsen said, endorsed a settlement freeze, "including natural growth." After meeting with Sharon, he realized that implementing this freeze would be "difficult," but the Mitchell report was "the only game in town." Van Aartsen had also met with Arafat in Gaza: "In strong words, I appealed to him to put an end to terror. I said that what is in his reach, he should do. He assured me that he would do that." When the *Post* reporter questioned the value of these assurances while the violence raged on, Van Aartsen replied, "I think it is important at this stage for him to give assurances. I think there is the possibility—that's the overriding issue at this stage—the possibility to resume talks if he can assure the Israeli government that he will do everything within his responsibility and ability to end the violence." He added that he did not believe that Arafat had complete control of the violence. "He doesn't have all the Palestinians on a string."[11] Van Aartsen was one of fifteen foreign ministers comprising the EU General Affairs Council scheduled to meet in Brussels and expected wholeheartedly to endorse the Mitchell report, inasmuch as Mitchell Committee members Javier Solana and Thorbjorn Jagland were members of the council.

The editorial reaction of the *Jerusalem Post* was a strong defense of the settlement policy. The report did not, the paper said, claim that the settlement activity violated the Oslo agreements themselves, but rather the "spirit of Oslo." But Rabin had told the Knesset that Oslo did not commit Israel to "the uprooting of any settlement in the framework of the interim agreement, nor to a freeze of construction and natural growth." Joel Singer, the legal advisor to the Foreign Ministry who had been central to the drafting of the Oslo agreement, was quoted as saying that Oslo not only permitted "natural growth," but the building of new settlements. Israeli governments since Oslo had unilaterally agreed not to establish new settlements, but had never agreed to halt "natural growth." Netanyahu had agreed to restrict building to the municipal boundaries of existing settlements and that, the paper held, Sharon would be wise to do after a cease-fire took place. But a freeze on settlements at that point would be a "reward" to the PA for violence.[12] In a later editorial the *Post* referred to the "atmosphere of movement surrounding the release of the report" as "Mitchell's cotton candy"—something that looked substantial, but had little substance. Even if a freeze were to go into place, the editorial held, the violence would not end: "The settlement issue is just a convenient place for the Palestinians to hang their hat, because it is the issue on which Israel and the US are most seriously divided." What was needed was "the military defeat of the Palestinian offensive, followed by negotiations that would take into account the bitter lessons of the past eight months."[14]

The State Department was dismayed to learn that Sharon was expected to recommend an allocation of $375 million to the settlements for "security needs." Sharon lowered the allocation to $150 million, but a State Department official said that the US position, stated many times, was unchanged: "Settlement activity continues to be provocative and inflames an already volatile situation." Sharon had ordered officials to begin planning three new settlements in the dunes area of the Western Negev in southern Israel to prevent the area being turned over to the PA, a possibility that Barak had discussed with the Palestinians. Since the 1967 war, Israel had built more than 140 settlements in the West Bank and Gaza Strip. Peres supported a compromise by which no new land would be appropriated for settlements, but construction for "natural growth" would be allowed. Labor MKs were upset that they could not give their opinions on these matters, because Peres had asked them not to attack government policies.[14]

Colin Powell's first reaction to the Mitchell report was that it was "very fine," but the State Department would not comment further until the final report was released. Unfortunately at this time a four-month-old Palestinian baby, Iman Hejjo, was killed by IDF tank fire in the Khan Yunis refugee camp in the Gaza Strip. Her nineteen-year-old mother, her grandmother, and three other children were wounded in the attack, which was in retaliation for the firing of mortar shells at two Jewish settlements in Gaza. Sharon said that he was sorry for the baby's death, and that "children and babies should not be involved in this terrible war that we would like one day to finish." Peres too expressed "deep sorrow" over the baby's death. The army expressed regrets and called on the PA leadership to prevent attacks from inside populated civilian areas so that innocent civilians would not be hurt.[15]

This tragedy was followed by the brutal killing of two Israeli teenagers who were found battered to death in an ancient cave near the West Bank settlement of Teqoa. The two boys, thirteen and fourteen years old, had skipped school to explore ruins in the area. They were so badly mauled that the families had difficulty identifying them. The police were able to conclude that there had been three assailants, because the murderers had wiped their bloody hands on the walls of the cave. The army's preliminary investigation indicated that the killers were not an organized cell but had simply stumbled on the boys by accident. The thirteen-year-old, Kobi Mandell, was a US citizen whose family had immigrated from Silver Springs, Maryland, seven years earlier.[16] Colin Powell angrily denounced the killings as "an outrageous act against humanity." He told Congress that Sharon was "a man who does want peace" but did not want to reopen negotiations until the violence stopped. Yassir Arafat, who, Powell said, was "anxious to get the peace process started again," had "considerable authority" over attackers of Israel but did "not have control over every rock thrower" although he had a "powerful voice." He had been urging Arafat, he said, "to speak out."[17]

The Yesha Council, an umbrella group representing 200,000 settlers in the territories, stated that it was "fed up with the condolences from successive Israeli governments," and demanded that Arafat's Palestinian Authority be defined as a terrorist organization and overthrown. Arafat did not condemn the killings when he was asked about them. He mentioned a three-month-old infant who had been injured when troops opened fire on a refugee camp in Gaza.[18] Yossi Beilin said that the Mitchell report should be used as a basis for dialogue, and diplomacy should be used instead of military measures.[19]

The fishing boat seized by the navy had been headed to the Gaza Strip from Lebanon, loaded with Katyusha rockets, anti-aircraft missiles, rocket-propelled grenades and land mines.[20] When two Romanian farm workers repairing a security fence on the Gaza border were killed by a roadside bomb, the Israelis retaliated by striking Arafat's Gaza City installations with rockets.[21] The defense minister, Benjamin Ben-Eliezer, said that "in principle" he had approved any entry by troops into Palestinian Area A if it was necessary for security purposes.[22] While all this was going on, Sharon instructed the police and security forces to find a way to open the Temple Mount for Jewish visitors and tourists. The police were nervous about actions that could be taken by radical Jews; some of the security people were apprehensive that banning visits to the mount would heighten the possibility of such actions.[23]

The situation deteriorated drastically when a twenty-one-year-old suicide bomber, a grocery store clerk, blew himself up at the entrance to a crowded shopping mall in Netanya, killing five Israelis and wounding more than one hundred.[24] Sharon called an emergency cabinet meeting. Then, placing the blame directly on Arafat, although Hamas claimed responsibility for the attack, he responded by sending F-16 fighters to fire missiles at Palestinian security headquarters in the West Bank and the Gaza Strip, hitting Nablus, Gaza City and Tulkarm. This was the first Israeli use of fighter jets since the 1967 war. In addition, helicopter gunships blew up a building of Arafat's elite Force 17 bodyguards.[25] This action generated a good deal of hostile comment, both in Israel and outside it. One Israeli military analyst called it "a gross diplomatic-strategic error"; another complained that Sharon might be "playing into [Arafat's] hands by bringing closer the international intervention he wants to see here." The use of F-16s was condemned by four Israeli dailies, and left-wing Israelis increased their references to Sharon's involvement in Lebanon in 1982. Interestingly, in the light of what was to happen in the future, one *Haaretz* columnist, Doron Rosenblum, asked sarcastically, "What would happen after a terror attack in which, God forbid, twenty people were killed? An atomic bomb on Ramallah?"[26]

Sharon responded, "We will do what it takes and use everything at our disposal to protect the citizens of Israel. The Americans understand that we cannot take any more." After the terrorism was stopped, he said, his country would work to enter negotiations aimed at reaching a political settlement.[27] Vice President Dick Cheney, asked about the F-16s, commented, "I think they should stop. Both sides should stop and think about where they're headed here and recognize that down this road lies disaster."[28] This was taken by the *Fi-*

nancial Times to be a "strong condemnation" of Sharon's action just as the Mitchell report was to be formally released.[29] But asked on "Meet the Press" whether the US would try to force Israel to ground the F-16s, Cheney replied, "It's a very delicate situation."[30]

Netanyahu rushed to Sharon's defense, saying, "We have to put all our differences aside and join together because now we are in a battle." He compared Israel's response to British attacks on German cities in World War II, which hurt civilians even though they were intended specifically for the enemy.[31] Netanyahu also defended Sharon against criticism by ex-President Bill Clinton, who remarked to reporters after speaking to a private conference in Vienna that Sharon had provoked the intifada by visiting the Temple Mount the previous fall. Netanyahu said that it was Arafat's policy and not Sharon's visit that had caused the intifada, and that he was sorry that "Clinton couldn't understand what even the Mitchell Committee understood" about the causes of the uprising. Clinton had added that Arafat need not have responded with violence, but he said also that Sharon could become a "security problem" for Israel, that the Middle East conflict was more dangerous than other crises because of the low standard of living of the Palestinian people, and that he believed that Arafat would be able to control radical Palestinian groups "for some time."[32]

65

"A VERY DELICATE SITUATION"

———

A US OFFICIAL TOLD THE press that there was "little enthusiasm" in the Bush administration for the Mitchell Committee recommendation for a blanket freeze on settlements, although US policy felt that "additional settlement activity" was unhelpful because it undermined confidence. The concern, the official said, was "about grabbing hilltops, not building in these settlement blocks." Sharon's "underlying premise that violence shouldn't be rewarded is something that resonates with President Bush."[1]

George W. Bush and Sharon had first met in 1998, when Bush visited Israel with a group of governors. Sharon, who was foreign minister at the time, gave him a helicopter tour of the country, and the two hit it off from the start. Bush, a born-again Christian, described this visit as "an incredible experience." The Texas governor had had little foreign affairs experience and this trip was seen as part of a way to build up his credentials as a credible presidential candidate. The trip's organizers had, in advance, attempted repeatedly to set up a meeting with Arafat or at least another prominent Palestinian leader, but each attempt received nothing but claims of scheduling conflicts. To make matters worse, when Bush and his retinue landed, they became involved in a confrontation with local journalists who demanded to know why the governor was snubbing Arafat and the Palestinians, but who were not in a mood to accept explanations. As president, Bush pointedly did not invite Arafat to the White House, and in 2001 rejected an attempt to arrange for an informal handshake with him on the floor of the United Nations General Assembly.[2]

Sharon, on the other hand, was welcome at the White House, and at his first meeting there with Bush in March, 2001, he told the president that Palestinians involved in terrorist attacks would have to be "removed" from society, but that he would make every effort to avoid disrupting the stability of the region. Bush's response, according to an onlooker, was, "You don't need to elaborate." His attitude was in strong contrast to his father's. The first President Bush had had a great deal of trouble with the right-wing premier Yitzhak Shamir, who had certainly done his best to disrupt the Madrid peace conference. In 1991, George H.W. Bush had blocked a ten billion dollar loan guarantee designated for the relocation of Russian Jews to Israel because he believed the prime minister was expanding the settlements in the territories. The resulting uproar stemming from American Jewish organizations prompted the president to characterize himself as "one lonely little guy" being attacked by the powerful pro-Israel lobby.[3]

Colin Powell commented, "If there was any solution that I could come up with, any conference or meeting that could be held right away that might move us in such a direction, I would leap at it." Nevertheless, the escalating violence pushed the administration into filling the post of peace envoy, which Powell had said only a week earlier was not a "full-time job."[4] Dennis Ross, who was Bill Clinton's peace envoy, called on George Bush to involve himself in the conflict to give Arafat a proposal to "respond" to, since Arafat would never "initiate" but would only "respond," and to provide Sharon with "an initiative that did not reward Palestinian violence."[5] After endorsing the Mitchell report, Powell appointed as peace envoy William Burns, who had been ambassador to Jordan and was awaiting confirmation as assistant secretary of state for the Near East.[6] Powell made it clear that this appointment did not mean that the Bush administration would emulate in any way what they considered Clinton's excessive immersion in the Middle East conflict, his "photo-op diplomacy."[7]

At a meeting in Brussels of the EU-Israel association council, Sweden, the holder of the European Union presidency, voiced strong disapproval of Sharon, calling upon him to end "extra-judicial killing" of Palestinians, to reopen the borders of the territories and to pay Arafat the revenue owed to him. The EU was Israel's biggest trade market, taking nearly a third of Israeli exports.[8] At an emergency meeting of the Arab League in Cairo, Arab foreign ministers urged their countries to sever "all Arab political communication with Israel," the airstrikes being the immediate reason. Sharon's spokesman Raanan Gissin called this action "self-defeating," asking, "If they do sever relations with Israel, then what? Who are they going to talk to, each other?" He said they were giving Arafat "a prize for violence."[9] Mubarak's foreign minister said the Arab League resolution would not affect Egypt's ties with Israel, that the embassies would "continue working normally."[10] But Mubarak condemned Israel for using warplanes "against people who use only stones or even mortar guns," and accused Sharon of trying to undermine the Egyptian-Jordanian peace initiative.[11]

One exceptional Arab state was Mauritania, whose foreign minister honored a months-old commitment to visit Israel despite the Arab League resolution, and met with Sharon, Peres and Moshe Katsav, the Israeli president. In a joint press conference with Peres, the minister, Dah Ould Abdi, said that he had come because his was "an independent, tolerant and open country in favor of peace and who stick to our word." He said that it was "time to end the cycle of death in which innocent people were caught on both sides, and return to the negotiating table." Despite coming from a poor, underpopulated country, Abdi received a royal reception from the Israelis, while an Arab MK demanded that the Arab League revoke Mauritania's membership. One Israeli diplomat said that Mauritania wanted good relations with Israel, not solely because Israel was helping to build a cancer hospital in Mauritania, but because the country needed help to improve its image in the light of charges by human rights organizations that ethnic Moors there were enslaving thousands of blacks. Earlier, in another episode with an Arab state, Qatar's foreign minister announced that he had invited Sharon and Arafat to come to the Qatari capital of Doha to negotiate. Sharon did not respond, and Arafat told a news conference that "this invitation does not exist."[12]

Vladimir Putin phoned Sharon and urged him to take all measures to stop the violence in the Palestinian territories. Sharon told the Russian president that Peres, who was due in Moscow the next day, would provide "a realistic picture of what was happening in the Middle East." In Moscow, Peres defended the action as only a response to Palestinian "acts of cruelty and aggression against Israelis." He said he was "disappointed" by the Arab League resolution and "surprised" that the league "has never said a word about the terrorising and murder of women and children" in Israel. "Russia's input into the peace process at this stage," he said, "could be highly significant."[13]

On May 22, in an unexpected "first step" in response to US calls for an end to violence, the Israeli Defense Ministry announced in English that troops had been ordered to open fire only when their lives were endangered and that a "cease-fire" was otherwise in effect. This followed a televised press conference in which Sharon, speaking only Hebrew, said that Israel saw the Mitchell report as a "positive basis that can enable both sides to end the cycle of violence and return to the negotiating table" and that "[i]f the Palestinians accept the proposal to stop firing, we will stop the firing immediately." He addressed the Palestinians: "Peace will only be achieved through talks. Stop the violence and accept us as a serious and responsible partner for reaching peace." He pointed out that the report called for a "significant cooling-off period" between the ending of violence and a resumption of talks, and called on Egypt and

Lebanon to help restore calm to the region, and to Syria and Lebanon to start working for peace.

Sharon tried to ameliorate his refusal to agree to a freeze on settlements by offering the cloudily phrased assertion that within the guidelines of the national unity government—which called only for construction to meet the settlers' ongoing needs, and no construction of new settlements—it was possible to find a way to "allay the fears of the Palestinians of creating facts on the ground that would predetermine the negotiations." The Mitchell report had determined, he said, that there was no connection between the settlements and a cease-fire. Asked about expropriation of land, he replied, "We definitely see that there is no need to expropriate land for settlements' needs. The settlements were established on state land, and there is enough land there." However, land would be expropriated for bypass roads if there were security needs for them.[14]

Palestinian officials accused Sharon of "trying to play games" with the Mitchell report by saying he accepted it and then not implementing all its recommendations, including a total freeze of all settlement activities. A spokesman for Arafat said, "It seems that Sharon wants to propose a new proposal, instead of the Mitchell report."[15] The Palestinian Authority issued an official statement: "The Palestinian leadership considers Sharon's attempt to deal in a selective manner with the report and with the Arab peace initiative to be part of an overall bid to find excuses for further aggression against the Palestinian people." Jibril Rajoub, the West Bank security chief, said, "I can't understand this term 'cease-fire.' We are not in a war between the two of us. There is a unilateral war, unilateral attacks by the Israelis against the Palestinian people. I think, as a professional security person, that ninety percent of the Israeli measures on the ground have nothing to do with assuring security to the Israelis. They are humiliating Palestinians. Therefore I think that Uncle Sam should ask Israel, which is attacking the Palestinian people, to stop its attacks."[16]

On May 20, Rajoub had been slightly wounded and his house in Ramallah badly damaged by Israeli tank fire. This was surprising, since Rajoub was considered to be an ally of the United States, one of the more moderate Palestinian leaders, and his Preventive Security Force had not been a prominent presence in the eight-month uprising. In fact, earlier in that same day a group of Israeli journalists had been guests in his house. The IDF said the shelling had occurred during an exchange of fire between Palestinian gunmen and soldiers guarding a nearby settlement; Defense Minister Ben-Eliezer said the troops had not been trying to hit Rajoub, who himself, while calling the attack "a clear message to the international community that the Israeli government is insisting to use state terror against the Palestinian people," remarked, "I don't think that this is an assassination attempt on my life."[17] Almost a year later, in the midst of extensive military incursions into Area A, Israeli forces surrounded and attacked the Preventive Security Force compound in Bethlehem, where several hundred Palestinian militants, many of whom were on Israel's wanted list, had taken shelter. Rajoub was not in the compound, but, apparently as a result of his relationship with the CIA, the US brokered the surrender of about 200 of the militants to the IDF. The compound was left a virtual wreck, with scorched and battered buildings and every window shattered.

GOOD COP BAD COP

———

ON MAY 23, PRESIDENT BUSH phoned Sharon and praised his decision to announce a cease-fire, something that had to be put into effect before the "confidence-building measures" recommended by the Mitchell Commission would be feasible. The president said he would "welcome a similar statement from the Palestinians."[1] But the Israel Defense Ministry was not happy with the manner in which Sharon had made his cease-fire announcement. It was generally agreed that he had not made his point clear, so that Defense Minister Ben-Eliezer had to spell out that the IDF had indeed halted preemptive actions. Further, the impact abroad was muted because Sharon had not spoken in English. One government official called the organization of Sharon's press conference "amateurish." But Sam Lehman-Wilzig, the head of the communications department at Bar-Ilan University, said that Ben-Eliezer announced the immediate cease-fire after the press conference because Sharon wanted to avoid having to clarify details to the media. "Sharon does not really trust the media," Professor Lehman-Wilzig said. "He prefers to present the important news without the media present so he does not have to answer the difficult questions." In this case, the difficult questions concerned the settlements and how long the cease-fire would last.[2]

Labor Party leaders seized on the fuzziness of Sharon's language to question his commitment to the Mitchell report. It was left to Shimon Peres to tell the Labor Party bureau, "I am saying this clear and simple as a spokesman for the government. We accept the

Mitchell report completely. Don't believe any old wives tales and don't allow anyone to tell you any different. It's the other side that hasn't accepted it." Peres charged that the Palestinians had planted eleven bombs in shopping malls since the second intifada had begun, and that he himself had worked constantly, holding dialogues to negotiate a cease-fire. "When the Palestinians told me that they thought Sharon's cease-fire was a public relations trick," he said, "I told them they should try the same trick." Two former Labor ministers, Haim Ramon and Avraham Shochat, who had come to the Labor Party bureau primed to attack Peres for not completely accepting the report, were somewhat at a loss, but rallied to complain about Sharon with a slap at Peres. One said he wanted to hear an endorsement of the report "from Sharon himself, not from a minor minister."[3]

Peres expressed some exasperation with leftists who accused him and other Labor politicians of sacrificing their beliefs to remain in the coalition; if Labor had not been in the government, he said, the Mitchell report would have been rejected. He commented on the fact that Peace Now had held a rally outside his house the night before: "They seem to forget that the reason we are in a government of the Right is we lost big. I never asked to become a minority." He argued that the settlement clause in the Mitchell report should not be a point of contention because it was part of the series of confidence-building measures that would come only after the cease-fire and cooling-off period. To satisfy that clause, Israel would agree not to build new settlements and not to expropriate land for "natural growth." A former Labor secretary, Nisim Zvili, backed Peres against the leftists, saying, "None of you protested against the Barak government when he built thousands of apartments in the settlements and now you are demanding a freeze?"[4]

Despite their differing political faiths, Peres and Sharon appeared able to work together. In the first week of May, some reports in the press created a tempest in a teapot. In the US for a week, Peres gave a speech at the Washington Institute for Near East Policy, in which he said, according to Barry Schweid of the Associated Press, that "[s]ome dissident groups and some forces under Arafat participate in the killings without the knowledge of Arafat." An aide to Sharon commented that if Peres had said that, it was "not okay." An Israel Radio commentator called the remark a "scandal" and quoted "senior diplomatic sources" as saying that "damage" had been done. Netanyahu agreed that it was a scandal, prompting Sharon's office to issue a statement that "the present attacks are the result of a strategic decision of Arafat," and that Arafat's organizations, like Fatah, as well as others—Hamas, Islamic Jihad and Hezbollah— "understand that they have a 'green light' for continuation of attacks against Israel."[5]

What Peres had actually said, in reply to a question about why the violence persisted, was: "I'm not sure I have a good explanation, partly because of dissident groups, and partly because the forces under Arafat are not disciplined. They themselves participate, some of them, in the shooting and killing occasionally without the permission of Arafat." Barry Schweid told the *Jerusalem Post* that his story was "taken out of context." It was true that Peres had referred to Arafat as a "partner" who had been elected, "and even if he commits mistakes, we know that partners can commit mistakes. Even we can commit mistakes. We don't demonize the Palestinians. We demonize terror." But he said also that "the Palestinians must show a capacity for central control and discipline and performance. Otherwise they will pay, in my judgment and in the eyes of world public opinion, a very heavy price."[6] When all this was explained to Sharon's office, it issued another statement saying that the subject was closed. Peres commented that it was "unacceptable that they tried to make a scandal out of such a ridiculous thing. They wanted to make it seem as if there was a rift between the prime minister and me." Asked to clarify his opinion of Arafat's level of responsibility, he said, "By definition he is fully responsible to prevent attacks.

That's the Oslo agreement. And why should I release him from that?"
He elaborated: "I mean, we are a democracy and we don't get orders every morning which words to use." He protested that neither
he nor the prime minister wanted to see "the government winding
up in fire and blood. We may differ on the methods, but we do not
differ on the destination."[7]

While Peres was seeking the middle ground in Washington,
Sharon was attempting to maintain his core support among the restless militant settlers, leading to an article in the *Los Angeles Times*
about Israel's "two faces" headlined "Good Cop, Bad Cop." In that
week, a settler from Ofra in the West Bank was killed in a roadside
ambush three months after his father had been shot down in the
same way; forty Israeli schoolchildren had narrowly escaped injury
or death when a bomb exploded near their bullet-proof bus, and
five teenagers were hurt by mortars fired at their Gaza settlement.
During a condolence call on the family at Ofra, Sharon was asked
by the widow, "Where is the old Arik?" Sharon responded, "Believe me, this is the same Arik." New tactics, he said, would be used
against the Palestinians: "There are things we will tell the public
about, there are things we will deny, and there are things that will
remain hidden forever." He told settlers that the Jordan Valley would
"remain forever in Israeli hands" and would not be subject to negotiation. "The army," he said later, "has absolute freedom of action.
All restrictions have been lifted. The army has very broad freedom
of action, beyond any imagination. There are no restrictions."[8]

These statements were criticized by both the Right and the Left.
The comment about denials and mysteries, especially, was characterized by Yossi Sarid, the Meretz leader, as "one of the stupidest
remarks" ever uttered by an Israeli prime minister because it would
open the country to all sorts of accusations. The Likud's Gideon
Ezra, deputy public security minister, who had earlier said that a
cease-fire might make matters worse by giving the Palestinians the
opportunity to rearm, agreed with Sarid: "These remarks in my

opinion would have been better left unsaid." The mayor of Haifa, Amram Mitzna, who had been a senior army officer during the first intifada, said, "The army can win. But the price it would have to exact is unacceptable for a democratic state. We are not Syria. We can send in F-15 jets, Merkava tanks and so on and so on. The physical means exist. But there are things that a state, like the State of Israel, which also has to get up every morning and look at itself in the mirror, cannot do."⁹

As these comments and the encounter between Peres and the two Labor ministers demonstrate, the fact that there was a national unity government did not mean that Israeli politicians were willing to unify behind it. There was the admittedly extreme example of former Labor MK Yossi Beilin—a key architect of the Oslo accords and, as Barak's justice minister, a top negotiator at Camp David and Taba—who had gone in April to meet with Arafat in Ramallah at Arafat's invitation, and returned to defend Arafat on Israeli television. Beilin had left the Knesset to become justice minister in the Barak administration, but remained a member of the Labor party. In his television interview, Beilin said that Arafat could not be expected to order an end to the violence, since such an order from him would not be honored by the Palestinians. Asked about the current intifada, Beilin said that it had been caused by Sharon's visit to the Temple Mount, and that Barak should not have reported to the Mitchell Commission that Palestinians were to blame. Beilin dismissed as false PA Communications Minister Imad Falouji's boast that the PA had prepared the uprising before Sharon made his visit; Falouji, Beilin said, had made the claim because as a former member of Hamas he wanted to embarrass the PA. Beilin called on all Labor Party members of the Sharon cabinet to strongly criticize the Sharon government, and to support the resumption of full negotiations with the Palestinians despite the violence, which might abate as progress was made in the talks. Further, the Jordanian-Egyptian proposal should, he said, be accepted as it stood. Sources in Sharon's office said that Beilin had helped to draw up that proposal.[10]

Shlomo Ben-Ami, a Labor Party member who had been Barak's foreign minister and one of the chief negotiators at Camp David and Taba, said that he agreed with Sharon that Beilin's "independent diplomatic initiatives" were undermining the government's efforts to get the Palestinians to stop the violence before there could be "any return to the negotiating table. Sharon had implied that Beilin was lobbying the White House to invite Arafat there. Ben-Ami said that Beilin's actions not only created false impressions among the Palestinians, but were undemocratic. Those whose views had been defeated democratically, Ben-Ami told Israel Radio, should not "continue to hold discussions that bypass the elected government. I think it is wrong in terms of democratic culture, and wrong in and of itself." He himself, he said, had not joined the Sharon government "because the path, of which I was one of the leaders, was defeated, and I accepted the results."[11]

Ben-Ami did not believe that Arafat was capable of reaching a conclusive agreement with Israel: "I'm not saying he doesn't want that, I'm saying that it is impossible to reach it with him." The discussions should not be with the Palestinians, but "within Israeli society to pave the way" for the implementation of Clinton's Camp David proposals. Ben-Ami strongly condemned Sharon's plans to increase state funding for the settlements, saying the move was "mistaken not only diplomatically, but also socially," and the money should be invested instead in development of towns in the south of Israel or on its northern border.[12]

At the opposite extreme from Beilin was Avigdor Lieberman, the national infrastructure minister and leader of the right-wing Yisrael Betenu party, who called for the army to invade Area A and in forty-eight hours "[c]ompletely destroy their military infrastructure, all their police buildings, warehouses, security facilities" and "not leave a stone standing. Disassemble everything. Two days and we're out." Sharon's office responded that Lieberman's proposal was "unacceptable."[13] The Netanyahu camp, meanwhile, pointed to the "peace coalition," formed when Yossi Beilin and several Labor Party MKs joined with Peace Now activists, as proof that Sharon was working with only part of Labor and could not have a mandate for his policies. The more Labor moved to the left, Yisrael Katz, Netanyahu's campaign chairman, said in early May, the less likely it was that Sharon's government could survive, and this leftward movement was imminent. The Labor whip Effi Oshaya, who enforced coalition discipline on his party, said there was no objection to holding opinions that differed from government policy, but Labor MKs could not demonstrate against the government or vote against it: "The MKs in Labor owe their seat to the party, and therefore they are obligated to the policy of the party, which decided overwhelmingly to join a national-unity government. As partners in the coalition, we must support the government's policies."[14]

Peace Now chairman Tzali Reshef said that the formation of the peace coalition meant that the Left, which was going to "wake up and return to the streets," had recovered from its "big shock" at "the painful loss of Ehud Barak" and now people had overcome their doubts about Arafat and realized that there was no alternative to "a diplomatic solution with the Palestinian Authority." Reshef, like Katz, made these remarks in early May, 2001. By late May, Sharon had accepted the Mitchell report but rejected the freezing of settlements, and Arafat had said he would accept the report if Israel accepted all of it. In a newspaper poll, sixty-one percent of Israelis said they would support a freeze in return for the end of Palestinian violence. But Sharon's right-wing core threatened to quit his coalition if he yielded on this point, and that would mean the end of his government.[15]

But the Left itself was not unified. Dalia Rabin-Pelessof, Yitzhak Rabin's daughter, had chosen to stand for the Knesset from the small new Center Party rather than from Labor, and when Sharon won, had accepted the post of deputy defense minister, becoming the first woman to hold a senior post in the defense establishment. She defended her action, which was heavily criticized by Labor members, including her mother Leah, saying that she wanted "to balance the right wing" and that she would try to keep to her principles, and fight for her father's legacy. She said she was not to the right of her father, who was "no peacenik," and who had fought terror. Yitzhak Rabin, she said, "had no illusions about Arafat" while respecting his "manipulative ability" and "cleverness," and Arafat trusted Rabin. She supported the campaign, in which at that time more than twenty Palestinian extremists had been killed by Israeli security forces, as Israel's only option.[16]

By the latter part of May, attitudes had hardened to the point that the security establishment was considering the possibility that the Palestinian Authority might collapse, and Yassir Arafat be exiled once more to Tunisia. Dalia Rabin-Pelessof said that some members of the defense organization believed that it would be "better for Israel" if Arafat were to be replaced by younger, "more pragmatic" leaders, although she added that she did not know anything about "specific discussions" for replacing Arafat.[17] Retired Brigadier General Effie Fein Eitam called Arafat "the poor man's Saddam Hussein," and said that Israel had to dismantle the Palestinian Authority, as the US had tried to do with Saddam's government in Iraq. "We are not speaking of killing Arafat," Eitam said, "but of removing him." Shlomo Avineri, a political scientist at the Hebrew University of Jerusalem, said that "Israel has often tried in the past to get another leadership. To imagine that there will be another leadership that will be more amenable to what Israel wants is an illusion."[18]

Yossi Sarid, the opposition leader, infuriated at suggestions that Arafat be removed, called it "a twisted idea, a delusional idea" that brought to mind "Ariel Sharon's 'New Order' in Lebanon."[19] "The

New Order" was of course Adolph Hitler's phrase for his ethnic-cleansed state. Apart from the demonization of Sharon, Sarid's rhetoric seemed to reflect the level of frustration on the far left with the growing feeling in the country that negotiating with the Palestinian Authority was an exercise in futility.

67

"HOW MUCH LONGER?"

———

AT 10:40 PM ON THURSDAY evening, May 24, a three-story building collapsed in a Jerusalem suburb during a wedding celebration with 700 guests and employees present, causing the worst civil disaster in Israel's fifty-three-year history. An amateur photographer was videotaping the festivities when suddenly the dancers vanished as the floor collapsed beneath them and they plunged to their death while people left standing on the edge of the abyss screamed in horror. The top floor had given way and caved onto the floors beneath, and then two walls on opposite sides collapsed into the crater on top of the guests struggling inside it. At least twenty-six people, ranging in age from three to eighty, were killed, four hundred injured and thirty to sixty missing at first count. Rescuers received permission from the chief rabbi to work through the Sabbath, from Friday sunset to Saturday sunset and through the Shavuot holiday upcoming on the following Monday, digging for survivors under the debris. Unfortunately the only bodies recovered were four dug out on Friday morning. A criminal investigation began immediately, and nine people were arrested: the four owners of the hall, the building and renovation contractors, the building engineer and the person who designed the floor supports for the hall.[1]

Sharon, after expressing his condolences and the nation's gratitude to the men and women—soldiers and reserve officers—who had sifted through the rubble for forty hours, announced that there would be a commission of inquiry and that he would seek compensation for the victims. Expressions of sympathy and offers of help came in from George Bush on behalf of the American people, and from the Palestinian National Authority through a spokesman who said the PA department of civil defense had been instructed to offer help in rescue operations.[2] On the afternoon of May 25, two Palestinians drove a car loaded with explosives into a crowded bus in Hadera, a town on the coast. The men blew themselves up and injured about sixty-three Israelis, most of them bus passengers, none of them seriously. Earlier in the day, a member of Hamas tried to drive a truck full of explosives into a fortified Israeli army post in the Gaza Strip; the soldiers fired on the truck and it blew up, killing the occupant who had left behind a videotape announcing his intention to kill Israelis.[3]

Despite these events, Sharon did not retaliate, and, after visiting the site of the wedding hall collapse, repeated his call for a cease-fire and urged Arafat to do the same.[4] He seemed to reserve his anger for the ineptitude and possible corruption that had led to the tragedy, and, at the start of a Knesset debate on the building collapse, said that "Israel has an unusual array of talents in all fields of life that are drowned in a sea of amateurism and often boorishness . . . Every day we pay a terrible, unnecessary price of blood because of sloppiness, brash overconfidence, arrogance and superficiality." He said the state commission of inquiry would try to go beyond the wedding hall incident and put it in a wider context of unacceptable social behavior "which must be rooted out by education on the one hand and severe penalties on the other," to bring about a "change in our lives." Yossi Sarid commented that the disaster was caused by "greed and corruption" and the country's devoting so much of its energy and resources to conflicts with its neighbors.[5] Sharon's response was, "Let us stop and take ourselves in hand." These remarks gave rise to an editorial in the newspaper *Yediot Aharonoth* disputing "the intuitive conclusion that we are especially negligent, and corrupt to the point of rottenness."[6]

Sharon defended his declaration of a unilateral cease-fire against criticism from the right, saying that he had a responsibility to accept the Mitchell report: "The campaign is not only for security. We must fight in the complicated diplomatic campaign and succeed in it." He was interrupted and even prevented from speaking for several minutes by heckling from hard-right MKs who demanded to know "how much longer" it would be before Israel took revenge for the attacks. He responded that he knew that "blood is boiling," but, he said, raising his voice and pounding the lectern with his fist, no one should keep asking "'How much longer?'. . . Whoever asks every single day, 'How much longer?' will lose. I repeat, he who asks 'How much longer?' will lose." Sometimes it was necessary, he went on, to "know how to endure over time, as we have done in the past." At this point he praised the settlers for their "perseverance" and sent them his "warm regards," probably because settlers were among the most vociferous critics of his cease-fire. Yossi Sarid commented that when Sharon was opposition leader, he had asked "How much longer?" after every terrorist attack.[7]

At the end of May, William Burns, President Bush's new Mideast emissary, met separately with both Sharon and Arafat, urging a continuation of restraint on Sharon and asking Arafat to "do everything possible" to stop the terrorism attacks.[8] This was especially difficult because there had just been two new car bombings in the heart of west Jerusalem: the first exploded just after midnight on Saturday in the Russian Compound area, a strip of nightclubs frequented by young people; the second, packed with six mortar shells, nails and bullets, detonated nine hours later about a block away near Jaffa Street, an area that would normally have been busy, but that was not as crowded as usual because of the upcoming Shavuot holiday on Monday. In the first explosion no one was hurt; in the second two people suffered minor injuries from flying glass shards. The Popular Front for the Liberation of Palestine claimed responsibility for the first attack, and the Islamic Jihad, claiming responsibility for the second, issued a statement that "[m]ore car bombs and martyrs are on their way."[9] Angry crowds gathered at the bomb sites, demanding that Sharon strike back. "It is very difficult to continue to be restrained," said Ehud Olmert, the right-wing mayor of Jerusalem. "We cannot allow our capital to be put under siege. We cannot go on like this."[10]

Burns had been US ambassador to Jordan, and was awaiting confirmation as Assistant Secretary of State for Near Eastern affairs. His visit marked a first tentative effort at involvement in this situation by the Bush administration which had given every indication that it would stay out of it. Sharon said he would continue Israel's "unilateral cease-fire" and not initiate military action for the moment, and his spokesman Raanan Gissin said, "We are giving Yassir Arafat additional time to comply with the Mitchell report and stop the violence."[11] Burns praised his restraint, but Sharon was said to have told him that "this 'letting it pass' stage can't continue forever." His office issued a statement that "Israel continues to show restraint, but is nearing the limits of its patience, since our utmost commitment is to protect the lives of our citizens." While Arafat was demanding a freeze on settlement activity as a condition for a truce, Sharon said that he did not want to "reward violence" by promising Arafat anything in return for a cease-fire.[12] The director of public security in Gaza said in a news release that Israel had violated its cease-fire more than ninety times, shooting Palestinians and repeatedly invading their territory. Hosni Mubarak, in an interview with an Egyptian state-owned daily, called Sharon's cease-fire a "deception of international public opinion," maintaining that Israel was still shelling PA land and infrastructure.[13]

Whatever Israel was doing, it was not enough for the far right, and it was much too much for the far left. Benjamin Netanyahu caused a considerable commotion by telling a Likud forum at the end of May that Sharon should increase military action to cause the collapse of the Palestinian Authority. Sharon responded to this in a speech to a meeting of the Likud secretariat, throughout which he was heckled consistently by Aaron Greenstein, a member of the secretariat who had been a Sharon supporter but had switched his allegiance to Netanyahu. By continuing the cease-fire, Greenstein shouted, Sharon was letting his people die in order to appease the Americans. "No one has a monopoly on tragedies," Sharon told Greenstein. "I have seen tragedy with my own eyes, and I personally had to tell widows of their husbands' deaths. Neither you nor anyone else can lecture me on tragedy." In a reference to Netanyahu, he told Greenstein, "I know you're serving someone with what you say."[14]

He said he would continue with the cease-fire as the first stage in implementing the Mitchell report and as part of his commitment to the national unity government. "Some people," he said, in another reference to Netanyahu, "thought forming a national unity government was not a good idea, and that the government would not last long, but despite what certain people said, the government is working well and will continue to work well until November, 2003." He had no claims, he said, "against people who attack me, but this situation is really complicated. We need to act carefully. My blood boils too. The responsibility is on my shoulders and not on anyone else's."[15]

Netanyahu's office responded that the former prime minister had not criticized Sharon: "He merely offered his assistance. He did not address the question of the cease-fire because it is clear from the words of the prime minister that it will end shortly." What Netanyahu was addressing, his office said, was "the need after the cease-fire ends to deal with the war of attrition at a new stage of decisive action against the Palestinian Authority."[16] The settlers expressed themselves with less caution: they fought with soldiers and staged sit-ins at sites where there had been terrorist killings; a few hundred settlers demonstrated outside Sharon's house in Jerusalem, where the mayor of Efrat announced the roads would be patrolled by armed civilians. "We gave you our complete faith," he said, addressing Sharon, "but it's not blind faith . . ." Other settlers announced plans for large-scale demonstrations, blocking of highway intersections and prayer vigils at the Western Wall. The police investigated shootings, stonings of cars and beatings of Palestinians by enraged settlers.[17]

On the left, the level of rage was equally high. In the June 1, 2001, *Jerusalem Post*, Jonathan Rosenblum discussed the political posture of those Israelis who maintained an adamant confidence in Arafat's good will. Gideon Sapir was mentioned, a writer who had advised Palestinians to use kamikaze tactics against settlements and army bases, but not malls on Sapir's side of the Green Line. There was Uri Avneri's Peace Now/ Peace Bloc (Gush/Shalom) website, which carried caricatures of Israeli soldiers killing Arab children and traced "settler genocide" against Palestinians back to the Old Testament. Avneri, who called Barak a "peace criminal," and his wife Rachel had received the Alternative Peace Prize. There was Yossi Sarid, who advised Arafat not to accept a cease-fire without an absolute freeze on settlements which, according to Rosenblum, included for Arafat at least a dozen Jerusalem neighborhoods.

There were fewer of these voices in Israel than there had been, Rosenblum said, but these voices were making themselves heard abroad where they were being welcomed by elements with anti-Israel agendas. In the US, Yossi Beilin had repeated his accusations that Sharon's visit to the Temple Mount had triggered the intifada, and his criticism of Barak for reporting to the Mitchell Commission that the violence was planned by Arafat. Shulamit Aloni, minister of education in the Barak cabinet, and recipient of an Israel Prize for her work in human rights, in an interview with the French *Le Monde* only days after the two Israeli soldiers were murdered in Ramallah, placed the guilt for war crimes in the intifada on Israel alone. In Rome, *Haaretz* columnist Gideon Levy was accused by Ofer Bavly, a spokesman for the Israeli Embassy there, of "slandering" Israel in a panel discussion with a Palestinian human-rights activist.

Rosenblum sought to find psychological reasons for these attitudes. "Those who placed messianic hopes in Oslo," he wrote, "are suffering from post-traumatic stress syndrome in the wake of the renewed intifada . . . following Barak's extraordinarily generous proposals at Camp David . . ." He believed that "at some level" Beilin knew that Sharon had not caused the intifada, because as Barak's justice minister, Beilin had had access to army intelligence reports predicting as early as June that Arafat intended to "initiate mass violence in the territories that might well spiral out of control." And then there was Imad Falouji's telling a symposium of Arab journalists in Gaza that Arafat had begun preparations for the intifada immediately after Camp David. Rosenblum quoted Beilin's remark that "he could not go on living in a world in which peace is impossible," and concluded that Beilin and all those who shared his hopes for Oslo, had "to preserve the possibility of peace, and therefore of life itself" at all costs.[18]

THE DOLPHINARIUM

——

ON JUNE 1, 2002, WHILE Israeli police stood by, security restrictions were lifted and tens of thousands of Palestinians waving Palestinian and Hezbollah flags were allowed to march through east Jerusalem to accompany the body of Faisal Husseini, a senior PA official, to burial in the al-Aqsa Mosque. Husseini, the leader of the campaign to claim Jerusalem as the Palestinian capital, had died in Kuwait at sixty of asthma and a heart attack.[1] Yassir Arafat called Husseini a martyr and blamed Israel for his death.[2]

At about eleven o'clock that night, a Palestinian terrorist blew himself up at the entrance to a seaside dance club in Tel Aviv—The Dolphinarium—popular with young Russian immigrants who were lined up outside waiting to enter the club, which was holding a "girls-get-in-free" night. At midnight victims were still lying on stretchers covered with white plastic, and the pavement and windshields of parked cars were streaked with blood. Eighteen teenagers had been killed and about ninety injured, fifteen of them critically, and two more died in the next hours, bringing the death total to twenty. Most of the dead were aged fourteen to eighteen; only two were older than nineteen. Club owners said that an hour later, more than 1000 people would have been waiting in the lines.[3]

This came as pressure from the Right was mounting on Sharon to end his eleven-day "unilateral cease-fire." President Bush issued a statement deploring the attack and called "upon Chairman Arafat to condemn this act and to call for an immediate cease-fire. There is no justification for senseless attacks against innocent civilians."[4] Arafat had no immediate response, but sometime later a spokesman, who refused to give his name, said that Arafat condemned the attack and called for "all sides to show self-restraint," and for "an end to the military escalation and siege and all forms of violence and a return to the negotiations in order to achieve a just and comprehensive peace."[5] Some media reported that no one had claimed responsibility for the attack; other papers reported that the Islamic Jihad had claimed responsibility and threatened that more were on the way. It was agreed that, hours before at a rally in the Gaza Strip, Abdallah al-Shami, an Islamic Jihad leader, had sworn to ignore Sharon's calls for a cease-fire and continue the bombings. "Go to hell, Sharon," he said to his followers, "you and your state, and your settlers."[6]

Two days later, Hamas claimed responsibility. The suicide bomber was identified as a twenty-two-year-old man who had moved from Jordan to the West Bank two years earlier. His father said he knew of no link between his son and Hamas, but added, "I am very happy and proud of what my son did and I hope all men of Palestine and Jordan would do the same."[7]

Sharon called off a planned trip to Europe and convened an emergency cabinet meeting, a rare event on a Sabbath morning. The meeting lasted seven hours. Foreign leaders strongly condemned the attack, but urged the Israeli government not to cease seeking a peaceful solution to the conflict. The French and Australian prime ministers, the Russian Foreign Ministry, the German chancellor and all fifteen members of the European Union deplored the disaster, and asked fervently for "patience and calm."[8] Outside the Defense Ministry where the cabinet had met, about 200 Israelis held a peace demonstration. But others flooded the streets of Tel Aviv, setting cars on fire and throwing chunks of paving stones for hours at worshippers besieged in a mosque—some of whom emerged briefly to throw stones back—and breaking windows of an Arab-owned bakery. There were scattered scuffles with police, several of whom were injured before they managed to rescue the Arabs in an armored vehicle.[9]

Thousands of Palestinians fled Ramallah, fearing it would be the main target of a retaliatory Israeli strike. The PA ordered its employees to evacuate their offices, and told the citizens of Nablus to remain indoors. Israeli officials did not order airstrikes and artillery bombardments, but announced that they held Arafat personally responsible for the bombing and barred him from using the Gaza airport. Since they had closed all border crossings, blocking all movement into and out of all Palestinian cities and towns, Arafat could not return to his Gaza headquarters. All Palestinians, including the 120,000 who worked in Israel, were barred not only from entering Israel, but also from going from PA territory to Jordan and Egypt. The reactions from individuals in the Israeli and Palestinian streets were predictable. One Meretz voter, an electronics engineer, said, "I want revenge. I want 500 Palestinians killed, that's what I want. Maybe 5000."[10] A Ramallah blacksmith said, "There are no innocent people among those who were killed. This is the only language that Sharon understands."[11]

In Sharon's first speech after the bombing, he said, "This is certainly not a simple situation. We need to see the whole picture. Restraint," he added, "is a show of strength."[12] Arafat said he was ready to do "whatever is necessary" for an immediate and unconditional cease-fire in a joint effort with Israel, and appealed for American help to calm the situation, a statement Israel Radio dismissed as "hypocritical condemnation."[13] It was reported that Arafat ordered his security services to implement a cease-fire without delay, although the IDF said that gunmen were still shooting at Israeli settlements in the West Bank. PA TV and radio announced cease-fire steps to end the intifada, and began patrolling danger spots to monitor the situation. A senior PA official said that the authority would arrest anyone shooting at Jewish settlements or at Israel, but only if Israel withdrew its tanks and stopped "provoking the Palestinian people."[14]

Edward Luttwak, in the London *Sunday Telegraph* commented, "Mr Arafat is not an elected leader who must satisfy the desire of his people for decent conditions of life. He is after his own personal victory. As he sees it, he toppled the last Israeli prime minister, Ehud Barak, by spurning his peace offer, and he now means to topple Mr Sharon by spurning his cease-fire."[15]

Yediot Aharonoth reported that fifty-three percent of Israelis polled did not want Sharon to continue the unilateral cease-fire.[16] A cabinet meeting called by Sharon to discuss Arafat's cease-fire call was reportedly a stormy one, with what Israel Radio called "verbal exchanges between the ministers stemming from the differences between the reactions to the terrorist attack in Tel Aviv and previous terrorist attacks." Sharon told the cabinet that military intelligence believed Arafat's declaration was "tactical in nature," prompted by fear of Israeli retaliation and in response to international pressure. Defense Minister Benjamin Ben-Eliezer, a cabinet moderate, said that the government should wait and see whether Arafat would really follow through by ordering the shooting to stop, halting incitement, arresting Hamas and Islamic Jihad activists, and foiling terrorist attacks.[17]

The London *Times* reported that Arafat had called the cease-fire after "a heated exchange" in Ramallah with Joschka Fischer, the German foreign minister, who threatened a cut-off of aid to the PA if the Palestinians did not declare a truce. Fischer had happened to jog past the Dolphinarium a few hours before the bomb exploded.[18] The Europeans were particularly upset that this atrocity had occurred upon the heels of Arafat's return from Europe, where he had been given a sympathetic hearing, and after Israel had borne ten days of violence without retaliating, and had demonstrated good will by allowing the enormous funeral procession for Faisal Husseini in Jerusalem. The Americans were already disappointed with Arafat's response to the Mitchell report, and annoyed that while they were trying to meet with him, he was traveling all over Europe, attempting, they thought, to avoid them.[19]

Western diplomats said that Fischer had drafted the statement which Arafat read aloud at a news conference: "We exerted, and we will now continue to exert, our utmost efforts to stop the bloodshed of our people and of the Israeli people and to do all that is needed to achieve an immediate and unconditional cease-fire."[20] Arafat said that he repeated his "condemnation of this tragic operation against civilians and of all operations that result in the killing of civilians." Representatives of fourteen Palestinian "factions"—Hamas and Islamic Jihad and twelve factions of the PLO, including Arafat's Al-Fatah movement—met in Gaza on June 3 and issued a statement: "Our people have a right to defend themselves against aggression, occupation and settlements and pursue the popular intifada as a legitimate means against the continuing occupation of our land and to achieve our national rights."[21] They did not mention Arafat's promise of a cease-fire, which Colin Powell called "a very important statement." Powell did not issue the usual call on Israel to exercise restraint, saying instead that Israelis "reserve the option to retaliate, but I think they are trying to see this situation not get any worse."[22]

STRAINED RESTRAINT

———

A FEW DAYS AFTER THE DISCO bombing, Sharon and Netanyahu engaged in a shouting match at a Likud meeting filmed by the foreign press. Sharon was accused of endangering the lives of his people for public relations purposes by exercising restraint, which showed weakness and not strength, and of continuing Barak's mistakes by "zigzagging" as Barak had done. "I am glad there are those who want to share the responsibility," Sharon said, apparently referring to Netanyahu, "but it's on my shoulders and it's going to stay that way for quite some time. Criticism usually comes from the opposition, but I have no way of preventing it. It doesn't make me happy, but it's natural. Even if I don't receive any help from you, I will continue to fulfil my responsibilities."[1]

There was some discussion in government circles of the idea, floated during Barak's term, of fencing off the West Bank, a move that would involve unilateral withdrawal from isolated Jewish settlements. The border between Israel and the West Bank was the 1948 cease-fire line. The towns of Qalqiliya and Tulkarm, from which two suicide bombers had come, lay along the border. Gissin, calling this idea impractical, said, "It's a very long and winding border. You would have to build 1000 kilometers [600 miles] of fences. There are however some places where fencing and certain obstacles can make it more difficult to infiltrate."[2]

Sharon's refusal to retaliate for the Dolphinarium atrocity aroused a good deal of speculation in the light of his reputation as a

Likud "fist." Some analysts thought that he had deliberately encouraged Netanyahu's people to attack him in front of cameras of the foreign press so that the world would know that he was under political pressure to attack, so that he could justify his "significant" response later on. Tracy Wilkinson of the *Los Angeles Times* wrote about the possible reasons for Sharon's restraint, but said that "in the end . . . this may simply be the lull before the massive firestorm" because there was a widespread belief that Sharon was "too old a tiger to change his stripes and that his greatest wish remained the collapse of the Palestinian Authority and the fall of Arafat."[3] This image was underlined when, in an interview on Russian TV, he called Arafat a "murderer and a pathological liar" who did not behave like "a head of state," but like "a head of terrorists and murderers."[4] At the same time, Sharon's office announced that it had given the PA the names of some 300 terrorists whom it wanted arrested, members of Arafat's Fatah faction, and of Hamas and Islamic Jihad, in Jericho, Ramallah and Tulkarm. Hamas announced that it intended to ignore Arafat's call for a cease-fire.[5]

George Bush said that enough progress had been made on the cease-fire so that he could send George Tenet, the head of the Central Intelligence Agency, to the area for security talks about how to make sure the cease-fire continued. Israel eased economic and travel restrictions to let Palestinians return from Egypt and Jordan and allow delivery of gasoline and other raw materials to the territories. These concessions were greeted with rage by the settlers, who demonstrated in the streets by the thousands, and by Rehavam Zeevi, the hard-line tourism minister, who compared the Sharon government to the Vichy regime in France, which had collaborated with the Nazis. Israeli officials were increasingly critical of Arafat. Sharon's spokesman Raanan Gissin asked, "What cease-fire? We are ceasing, they are firing."[6]

But David Ivry, the Israeli ambassador to the US and former head of the IAF, said that his government was engaged in a "limited conflict" and there was a limit to using power, because it was understood that "[y]ou cannot achieve peace by military force." The policy of restraint, he said, did not come from American pressure, but from an Israeli unity government based on compromise among cabinet officers with divergent political views. He told the press that the Iranians were shipping weapons through Syria to be used by Hezbollah and Islamic Jihad guerrillas in Lebanon, and smuggled from Lebanon, possibly through Egypt, to Palestinian fighters for attacks on Israel. Ivry added that Egyptian officials said they were "unaware" of weapons smuggling over their borders.[7]

In an interview with the *Financial Times*, Arafat, then seventy-one years old, said that he would not accept the watered-down version of the settlement freeze that Sharon wanted; in 1995, he had, he said, reached an understanding with Yitzhak Rabin that all construction and government funding of settlements would cease, and he wanted that agreement to stand. He wanted also an accord that dealt with the occupied land, the fate of the settlements, and the status of the three-and-a-half million refugees. But Arafat also said that it was wrong to believe, as many Palestinians did, that it would be impossible to reach an agreement with Sharon. "Do you forget," he asked, "that Sharon implemented the decision to dismantle settlements in the Sinai and that he was involved in the Wye River accords?" He dismissed the notion that there was a personal feud between Sharon and himself, and insisted that "[t]he intifada gave the Arab nation a historic legacy and a human legacy in defense of Islam and Christianity's holy sites and in the search for a comprehensive, lasting and just peace."[8]

George Tenet met with both Sharon and Arafat. After the meeting in Tel Aviv, Sharon told reporters that he had given Tenet a list to give Arafat of names of Palestinians wanted for terrorist activities by the Israelis. The CIA reportedly told Sharon that Fatah fighters should be left off the list because Fatah was Arafat's power base and he could not be expected to arrest them. In any case, Nabil

Shaath, the Palestinian minister for International Cooperation, said that the PA had no intention of honoring the Israeli request. "The PA is not going to act as Israel's policeman," he said.[9] (When the European Union got Shaath and Shimon Peres in the same room together in Luxembourg, the two men refused to shake hands.)[10] An Islamist leader in Ramallah, who demanded anonymity, warned Jibril Rajoub, the head of the Palestinian Preventive Security Agency, against arrests of Hamas, Fatah and Islamic Jihad members, saying it would be "a colossal scandal to see Jibril's men start arresting the freedom fighters who defended our women and children against the barbaric Zionist rampage" and that if Rajoub "did such a thing, he would be ejected by the people and worse."[11]

On June 11, Israel Radio reported that a senior IDF intelligence officer said that Arafat had recently prevented several serious terror attacks inside Israel and had detained several terrorists. But overall, the official said, Palestinian action against terrorists was "superficial." Arafat, he said, believed that if the national unity government were to fall, it would "make it easier to internationalize the conflict." The official said that the Iranians had never been as deeply involved in terrorist activities in south Lebanon as they now were with the Hezbollah, and that "this was a most dangerous process over the long run."[12]

Talks between the two sides initiated by Tenet did not go well, degenerating at times into loud arguments over settlements, blockades, withdrawal and terrorist attacks. The Israelis were showing strong signs of complete disenchantment with Arafat. David Horovitz reported that Defense Minister Ben-Eliezer said that Arafat had "'finished his historical role' and that Israel would have to wait in its bid to make peace for a new generation of more 'pragmatic' leaders. However, he said that did not mean Israel intended to topple Mr Arafat." But others did talk about toppling him. Israeli political scientist Barry Rubin said that Israel now felt there was "no more incentive in preserving Arafat and his administration . . . What we're talking about is a series of political and military measures that would force his collapse." He added that it might be enough simply to frighten Arafat into acting against the terrorists without actually bringing him down. There had always been a strong concern among Israeli officials that without Arafat the territories would degenerate into total anarchy.[13] But Netanyahu wrote in the *Jerusalem Post* that "any means necessary" must be employed to stop terrorist attacks "even if that entails the end of the Palestinian Authority."[14] This was the first time a major Israeli leader had implied a desire for Arafat's ouster. In the Knesset, Dan Meridor assailed Sharon for calling Arafat a liar and a murderer, saying this was no way to talk about someone you were going to negotiate with.[15]

Abdullah Hourani, a Palestinian academic in Gaza, said it would be more dangerous for Israel if Arafat stepped aside than if he stayed on. "Chaos on your border is always worse than belligerency," Hourani said, and advised Arafat to "threaten to dissolve his own administration if he doesn't get what he wants. Nothing could be worse for Israel."[16]

Despite all this, on June 12, both Israelis and Palestinians accepted the Tenet plan, details of which had not been made public, but which required Israel to pull its troops back to pre-intifada positions and end the blockade of Palestinian towns, and the Palestinians to enforce a cessation of violence, cooperate with Israel on security, arrest Hamas and Islamic Jihad terrorists, collect illegal weapons, and cease incitement in the media. After a six-week "cooling-off" period, the Mitchell report "confidence-building measures" would kick in, including a settlement freeze and resumption of negotiations. Arafat objected strongly to a clause in the plan calling for buffer zones between Israeli and Palestinian lines in the West Bank and Gaza, but since Israel had announced its acceptance earlier, he did not want to be isolated in his refusal to cooperate.[17]

While Tenet was meeting with Arafat in Ramallah, hundreds, led by Fatah Tanzim official Marwan Barghouti, marched in the streets there, chanting that the intifada would continue. Barghouti announced that they had come to tell Tenet, "who came to save Sharon, 'get out of here.' We tell Arafat to reject bowing to Tenet and to reject Tenet's proposals. Our resistance will continue until occupation ends."[18] In Gaza, Abdel-Aziz Rantissi, a Hamas leader, said that Arafat had only signed the deal because of pressure from the US and the EU and that Arafat—whom Middle East Online called "comatose"[19]—would probably not arrest Hamas members or enforce the truce for long. "I do not think that the Palestinian Authority will stand against the will of the people," Rantissi said on the Hamas website.[20] Abed Rabbo said "the Palestinian side" had not signed the Tenet document and would sign it only when the "whole package" was agreed to, foremost being a halt to all settlement activities.[21]

Sharon said he couldn't say he was "enthusiastic about the plan, but on the whole we can work and move forward."[22] He was particularly uneasy about parts of the plan that held Arafat accountable only for violence carried on from areas under his control, and said Israel reserved the right to carry out "deterrent defensive operations."[23] Jibril Rajoub, the Palestinian security chief, considered a moderate by the CIA, told Palestine Radio that "we took the expression 'arrest of Hamas members' out of our lexicon long ago."[24] Later, Nabil Amr, a PA cabinet minister, said his people were ready to accept the Tenet plan "in principle," while Raanan Gissin said Israel was accepting it "as is."[25]

The settlers in the West Bank and the Gaza Strip said that Sharon's agreement to the plan meant "the abandonment of Jewish residents to Arafat's terrorists, and the continuation of the spilling of Jewish blood," especially since the cease-fire had been rejected by Hamas, Fatah Tanzim and Islamic Jihad. The settlers said they would take over every army post vacated by Israeli soldiers.[26] The Likud secretariat, responding to the settlers, attacked Sharon for agreeing to the plan, saying that he was making decisions with Labor and ignoring his own party. Passions were enflamed when a five-month-old baby boy died when he was hit by a rock thrown by Palestinians through the windshield of his parents' car as they drove near the settlement of Shiloh. At a demonstration outside Sharon's office, the baby's father, Benny Shoham, urged Sharon to hit back at the PA for his son's death. Sharon, who had earlier attended the baby's funeral, came out to talk to the demonstrators and told them to "stand firm" and that Israel would lose if its people pressed for harsh military action every day.[27]

The right wing was angry also because the government made no move against Azmi Bishara, an Israeli Arab MK, who, in a speech in Syria on the first anniversary of the death of Hafez Assad, said that Sharon was giving Arabs a choice between "accepting Israel's dictates or full-scale war," and that the "third alternative, the path of resistance," had to be "enlarged." Bishara defended himself saying that he had been trying to "prevent war," but Attorney General Elyakim Rubenstein noted that Syria was "formally at war with Israel" and that Bishara had attended the ceremonies with the Hezbollah leader Sheikh Hassan Nasrallah and other enemies of Israel. However, Rubenstein said it would be hard to indict Bishara because it would be difficult to prove that his remarks were "close to certain" to provoke violence, and Justice Minister Meir Sheetrit of the Likud counseled against "a political trial" that would give Bishara the status of "a tortured saint." Other prominent Israeli Arabs did not rush to Bishara's defense.[28]

Netanyahu publicly criticized Sharon's policy of restraint, saying it would only encourage terror, and remarked privately that the prime minister was a "prisoner" of the Labor Party. His spokeswoman said that Netanyahu believed that "the current Knesset does not reflect the will of the people" because there had not been general elections after Barak resigned. However, Sharon was leading Netanyahu in the polls.[29]

SABRA & SHATILLA AGAIN:
BELGIUM & THE BBC

ISRAELIS ACROSS THE POLITICAL spectrum were enraged when, on June 17, 2001, the BBC ran a Panorama documentary entitled "The Accused," giving the strong impression that Sharon should be indicted for his purported role in the Sabra and Shatilla massacres. Three prominent experts in international law were quoted in the documentary: Morris Draper, the US envoy to the Middle East at the time of the massacres; Richard Falk, a professor of international law at Princeton, who was vice chairman of an international commission that investigated Israel's invasion of Lebanon, and Richard Goldstone, a South African judge who was chief prosecutor of the UN war crimes tribunals from 1994 to 1996. Mr Draper made the emphatic point in "The Accused" that Sharon should have expected the bloodbath unless he was "appallingly ignorant . . . I mean, I suppose if you came down from the moon that day, you might not predict it." Professor Falk said there was no question in his mind that Sharon was "indictable for the kind of knowledge that he either had or should have had."[1]

Judge Goldstone's comments were more problematic. He was asked in the documentary, "I understand that as a judge in a South African court, you don't want to get into labelling people in other countries as 'war criminals,' but in your assessment of command responsibility, isn't it reasonable to say that if responsibility goes all

the way to the top, to the person who gave the orders, that poten-
tially makes Ariel Sharon a war criminal?"

Goldstone replied, "Well, it depends very much on the facts,
but if the person who gave the command knows, or should know,
on the facts available to him or her that there's a situation where
innocent civilians are going to be injured or killed, then that person
is as responsible—in fact, in my book more responsible, even—than
the people who carry out the orders."[2]

After the program was aired, the judge told *Jerusalem Post* Radio that he had agreed to talk to the BBC "as an expert on the law
in general, on command responsibility, but I said I would not in any
way comment on any liability, criminal or civil, of Ariel Sharon and
I didn't do so. I haven't yet seen the program, but if it comes across
that way it's incorrect . . . I certainly didn't comment on the responsibility of Sharon."[3] The day after the program was aired, the London *Independent* reported that Judge Goldstone had "suggested"
that Sharon "should be tried for war crimes in connection with the
1982 massacre of Palestinian civilians in Lebanon. . . ." and em-
broidered further on the facts by adding that "Judge Goldstone said
it was regrettable that no criminal prosecution had been brought."[4]

Israelis pointed out that on the question of who "the person
who gave the orders" was, and what the orders were, no move had
been made to prosecute the Phalangists who led the attack on the
camps, including Elie Hobeika, a cabinet minister in Lebanon. The
BBC said its website had been "inundated" by responses, and after
a few days announced it had stopped posting them.[5]

Sharon refused to comment, but the Israeli Foreign Ministry
condemned the documentary as "distorted, unfair and intentionally
hostile," and threatened some unspecified action against the BBC
news bureau in Jerusalem. Raanan Gissin said "there's anti-Semitism,
there's deception, there's malice—all put in one show with a sinister
intent." Gideon Meir, director-general for public affairs for the For-

eign Ministry, called the program a journalistic "crime" and added that the anti-Israel union of lawyers in Cairo had just announced that they too would publicly try Sharon as a war criminal. "I simply don't understand how a serious station like the BBC can place itself on the same level," Meir said. "It is beyond my understanding."[6]

The *Wall Street Journal* editorialized: "For years, Mr Sharon's political opponents, in Israel and abroad, along with a host of Arab leaders, have exploited Sabra and Shatilla to score moral points against Israel—even as Syria made an ally of Elie Hobeika, the Phalangist personally responsible for carrying out the massacres. Now the BBC has piled on with its smartly made documentary, which in tone and thrust, and through the omission of such details as the findings of the New York court, re-indicts Mr Sharon for the crimes of which he has already been cleared. This is viewer manipulation and politicized journalism at its worst."[7] In fact, before the program was aired, the Israelis had reminded the BBC in London that in 1985, when Sharon sued *Time* for libel, a federal jury in Manhattan had faulted *Time* for careless and negligent reporting and *Time* had been forced to retract part of its story.[8]

The Italian newspaper *La Stampa* complained that it was "worrying and frightening" that media power "should be brought to bear on the Middle East crisis by putting out a political lie instead of factual reality." The documentary, *La Stampa* went on, "brought no new evidence, no previously unheard-of documents. It omitted to mention the *Time* case and took no trouble to find out why, for example, Hobeika, the leader of the militias that invaded the camp, was subsequently a minister in Lebanon for eight years, and no one has ever pressed evidence against him . . ." It was "common knowledge" that "Sharon has been the man they all love to hate, or rather whose image they have loved to hate, since the day he took office. It is reassuring to say 'Sharon, the hawk', it is like an old tune that everyone knows, like 'Volare.' Who cares about his policies?"[9]

All the Israeli interviewees declared that they had been misled by the BBC team who asked them to record their memories of the massacre, but did not tell them that Sharon was the object of the documentary. Even Sharon's Israeli critics questioned the BBC's motives. Zeev Schiff, a *Haaretz* correspondent who had been among the first to break the massacre story said, "Very nice, but what's new?"[10] Calev Ben-David of the *Jerusalem Post* said that the BBC had finally brought him to issue a defense of Sharon, who he thought should have been disqualified by the Kahan Commission report from "ever again holding public office"—although he felt now that Sharon was doing a good job as prime minister.[11]

Why, Ben-David asked, should Sharon have been singled out as a war criminal, when Arafat had not; nor had Mubarak, whose "brutal suppression of Muslim extremists" violated human rights standards; nor had the government of Russia for the war on Chechnya; nor China for Tiananmen Square and rights suppressions "at home and in Tibet"; nor Jacques Chirac, who brutally suppressed riots on Fiji and contaminated "the entire southwest Pacific ocean with atomic bomb testing"; nor Ronald Reagan whose CIA had killed "innocent civilians in Central America," nor Margaret Thatcher for the Falklands War and "excesses in the struggle against Irish nationalists. And why not Nelson Mandela for killings by the African National Congress extremists and by his wife Winnie, or Bill Clinton, Tony Blair and NATO leadership for deaths of Serbian civilians during the war in Kosovo? Not, Ben-David said, that war crimes should not be prosecuted, as in the case of Slobodan Milosevic or Augusto Pinochet, and not that there might not be a case against Sharon—but, he asked, why single him out from all the others?[12]

His conclusion was that the BBC's coverage of the Middle East had "simply lost all credibility." He pointed to a BBC documentary produced and hosted by hard-line Palestinian polemicist Edward Said, or the embarrassing revelation that "its Arabic Service correspondent Faid Abu Shimalla had told a Hamas gathering in Gaza that journalists and media organizations are 'waging the campaign shoulder-to-shoulder together with the Palestinian people.'" The reasons for all this, Ben-David said, apart from an ancient imperial bias toward Arabs, were the growing size of Britain's Muslim population and the necessity for the BBC to maintain its Arabic Service in Arab countries.[13]

The BBC denied that it was anti-Semitic and defended the documentary by saying that since Sharon had been elected in March and there was a new international focus on war crimes prosecution, a fresh look at Sabra and Shatilla was justified. "The debate over war crimes has never been more relevant," said Fergal Keane, the documentary's producer.[14] Two days after the airing, Mark Damazer, BBC deputy head of news, said that the program made clear that Sharon had not been in the camps "wielding guns and knives and killing people." He insisted that Sharon had not been branded a war criminal by "The Accused."[15]

The day after "The Accused" was aired, three lawyers representing twenty-eight Palestinian survivors of the massacre asked a Belgian court to indict Sharon under a 1993 law allowing trials in Belgium for war crimes no matter where they occurred, and whether or not the accusers or the accused were Belgians.[16] The law had been used in June to prosecute and convict four Rwandan Hutus and two Roman Catholic nuns for genocide against the Tutsis in 1994, a verdict that had been hailed by human rights activists. Now, Human Rights Watch in New York called for a criminal investigation of Sharon. One of the Palestinians' lawyers, Michael Verhaeghe, said that since these crimes were "the most serious offenses possible," both in Belgium and internationally, the maximum sentence would be life imprisonment, and according to his "legal analysis," Sharon was "morally responsible . . . In our file there are more than sufficient indications of guilt." Asked how long Sharon would have to serve in jail if he were found guilty, Verhaeghe said that Rwandan war criminals were recently sentenced in Belgium to fifteen years, but they would actually serve five or six years. In a press release, the lawyers noted that Israel had "invoked universal customary law when it tried Eichmann for war crimes."[17] This was actually the second complaint filed against Sharon in Belgium. The first had been filed in Brussels two weeks earlier on June 2, 2001, by an ad hoc committee of Palestinians, Lebanese, Moroccans and Belgian citizens.

On June 30, the Brussels Department of Public Prosecutions found merit in both complaints lodged against Sharon, and Patrick Collignon, the examining judge, then began to try to determine whether to send the case to trial and order Sharon's arrest. The Belgian embassy in Tel Aviv was promptly pelted with stones, although David Horovitz reported that after the BBC furor died down, the war-crimes issue had little public impact. The Belgian ambassador to Israel, Wilfred Geens, said that the perception that his government was acting against the prime minister was "completely wrong. It is Lebanese citizens using a Belgian law to try to get reparations for their suffering in the . . . massacre." But, Geens said, the law, which had engendered many suits against various world leaders in addition to Sharon, had made Belgian diplomacy more difficult.[18] He pointed out that Belgium, through the diamond trade, was Israel's second-largest trading partner after the US, and that there were some 1300 Belgians on the list of Righteous Gentiles at Yad Vashem. Ambassador Geens mentioned also a new factor, "the birth of pro-Islamic, pro-Arab lobbies at work" in the Belgian parliament. He put the number of Muslims in Belgium at around 750,000 and the number of Jews at 80,000.[19]

Sharon suggested that the Belgian prosecutors might look into their own country's atrocities in the Congo. Peres, asked about the matter on Belgian television when he was in Brussels, responded angrily, "You have no right to judge. Where were you, five times, when Israel was in difficult wars against numerous armies? You want to talk to me about the war in 1982, and I am willing to talk about the 1973 war when . . . Sharon displayed great courage, determination and logic—and none of the Belgians stood up and said a good word about us, let alone came to help us. And today you want to be judges? I ask you, who gave you that moral right?" Peres was referring to Belgium's refusal during the 1973 war to allow Holland to send badly needed oil to Israel from the Belgian port of Antwerp.[20]

Sharon was planning a European trip on July 5 and 6, and had planned to visit Belgium, which had assumed the six-month rotating EU presidency on July 1, but after the lodging of the complaint against him, he dropped Brussels from his itinerary.[21] The Belgian foreign minister, Louis Michel, went to Berlin to meet Sharon and in effect to apologize for the legal proceedings. Before the meeting in a hotel, Michel said that "under no circumstances would he support the legal steps launched in Brussels against Ariel Sharon in the matter of the Sabra and Shatilla massacre." He explained that like all democracies, the Belgian government could not interfere with the courts, but that the Belgians were working to amend the law to prevent this type of embarrassment by exempting incumbent heads of state from prosecution, arrest and search. A 1999 amendment to the law had removed immunity from prosecution for incumbent heads of state.[22]

Patrick Collignon, the Belgian judge, had the option of issuing a secret indictment against Sharon so that he could be caught unaware as he pursued his diplomatic business. Chibli Mallet, one of the lawyers representing the Palestinians, said this meant that "[i]f Sharon is in Spain and the indictment is prepared in secret, it's possible that the Spanish authorities will arrest him for extradition to Belgium."[23] Attorney General Rubinstein said that it was ironic that Israel had been the only country to establish a judicial commission to investigate the massacre and that it had applied "administrative rather than criminal sanctions." He agreed with Sharon that the lawsuits were not Sharon's personal issue, and because they were politically motivated, the Justice Ministry was joining with the prime minister's office and the Foreign Ministry to deal with them. The legal team included the prime minister's legal advisor Alon Geller, Sharon's personal lawyer Dov Weissglas, Irit Kohn and counsel in Belgium.[24]

Israeli officials were confronted with another uproar at the end of July when Peres nominated Carmi Gillon to be Israel's ambassador to Denmark. Gillon had been head of Shin Bet, the domestic security agency, until 1996 when he resigned after Rabin's assassination, to become director of a foundation dedicated to working for Israeli-Arab peace—a not-unexpected move, since his doveish views were well-known and as a member of the Left, he had had warm relations with Palestinians and other Arabs. Consequently the ambassadorial nomination received an excellent response. But then, in an interview on Danish television, Gillon admitted that Shin Bet used "moderate physical pressure" on Palestinian detainees. He said that the practice was outlawed by the Israeli Supreme Court in 1999, but that it might have to be reinstated to save lives. "You must understand," he said, "that the method was used only against Islamic fundamentalists who refused to volunteer information, especially on suicide bombers. It was part of fighting terrorism."[25]

These remarks set off a furor in Denmark where the justice minister, Frank Jensen, said in the first flush of outrage that under the terms of the UN anti-torture convention, Gillon could be arrested immediately when he arrived in Copenhagen. B'Tselem, the Israeli human rights organization, had said that under Gillon, Shin Bet had tortured hundreds of detainees, and human rights groups were claiming that even after the Supreme Court decision Palestinian prisoners were being beaten, chained to pipes, doused with freezing and hot water and forced to hold agonizing physical positions. But Jensen had to step back from his threat to arrest Gillon when it was pointed out that as ambassador he would have diplomatic immunity. A spokesman for B'Tselem said, "Carmi Gillon is one of our guys, a sort of labor left-wing person. But even if a person is a peacenik, that does not clean his hands for being involved in torture. This is not something that can be wiped out."[26]

President Moshe Katsav took another view, telling journalists that he found Denmark's reaction "astonishing." To his regret, he said, "Denmark did not protest, as required, when Palestinian terrorists were blowing up crowded shopping centers, discotheques and railway stations in which dozens of civilians were killed, including women and children. I did not hear that Denmark took any international initiative when Palestinian terrorists used stones to smash the skulls of two fourteen-year-old boys, or when two innocent soldiers were brutally lynched."[27] Yehuda Blum, a former Israeli ambassador to the UN and professor of international law, commented, "It is a farcical situation because you have to ask yourself why doesn't anyone raise the question of operatives of the Palestine Liberation Organization who travel around the world." Aeyel Gross, a director of the Association for Civil Rights in Israel, said that the policy of demolition of houses and assassination of suspected terrorists would inevitably create international difficulties because it violated "the fourth Geneva convention on the protection of civilian persons in time of war."[28]

Not only leftist lawmakers and newspapers, but some hard-liners pushed to reverse the nomination, saying that after what he had said, Gillon could not be an effective diplomat. But Peres did not back down. "I can't understand people in Denmark," he said, echoing Moshe Katsav, "who meet Palestinians who were engaged in terror and not meet Israelis who were involved in anti-terror." The Gillon nomination stood.[29]

It was not only Israelis who were at risk of indictments in the Belgian imbroglio. The Kahan Commission in 1983 had named Elie Hobeika, the former head of intelligence for the Lebanese Christian

Maronite Forces or Phalanges, as the man who had personally directed the slaughter of Palestinian refugees in Sabra and Shatilla. He had told the Israelis that there were 2000 Palestinian terrorists hiding in the camps, and was given the green light to go in and get them. They did go in, and in over two days they slaughtered around 1000 men, women and children. The commission said that when Hobeika was asked by a Phalangist colleague over the radio what should be done with the fifty Palestinian women and children in their custody, he answered, "This is the last time you are going to ask me a question like that. You know exactly what to do." His colleague had laughed. But Hobeika was never tried. When the Lebanese civil war ended in 1990, he switched his allegiance from Lebanon to Syria and became, somewhat ironically, minister for the displaced, and then electricity minister; in 1998 he lost that portfolio, and in 2000 he lost his seat in the Lebanese parliament. After the case was filed against Sharon in Brussels, Hobeika, then a Beirut businessman, called a news conference and said he was eager to testify in Belgium to prove his innocence. The killings, he told reporters, had been carried out by "Lebanese and Israelis of all denominations." He said he had documents that would discredit the Kahan Commission findings.[30]

His credibility had been badly dented in 1999 when Robert Hatem, one of his bodyguards nicknamed "Cobra," published a book called From Israel to Damascus: The Painful Road to Blood, Betrayal and Deception, which covered Hobeika's alliance with Israel and his subsequent "sell-out" of the Christian resistance in return for Syrian political patronage. Hatem called Hobeika a war criminal who had been under strict orders not to resort to unnecessary violence, but who had ordered his men to carry out "total extermination, camps to be wiped out."[31] Nevertheless, the lawyers for the Palestinians, one of whom, Chibli Mallat, was a Lebanese whose law firm was located in Beirut, made no attempt to contact Hobeika, concentrating instead on what they called the principle of "command responsibility." On the eighteenth anniversary of the massacres, a number of Arab newspapers carried reports that relatives of the victims blamed Hobeika for the deaths, and complained that he had never been questioned or tried for his involvement. There was suspicion among some analysts that the massacres had been intended to further Syrian interests by increasing the division between the PLO and the Maronites, and allowing Damascus to step in as the only power that could save the country.[32]

In late November, 2001, the Belgian legal panel postponed its ruling on whether Sharon could be prosecuted for war crimes, saying the decision was to come in January, Also in late November, a suit under the same law was brought by about thirty Israelis and Belgians against Yassir Arafat, accusing him of genocide, war crimes and crimes against humanity. In addition to Arafat, the suit included personal claims against Marwan Barghouti, the Tanzim leader, and Palestinian Preventive Security heads Jibril Rajoub and Mohammed Dahlan. The plaintiffs were families or victims of terrorism and included National Religious party head Yitzhak Levy, whose daughter died in a Jerusalem bombing and Yitzhak Pass, the father of ten-month-old Shalhevet Pass, who had been killed by a sniper in Hebron.[33]

In late January, 2002, Elie Hobeika was killed at the age of forty-five in a massive bomb attack on his house in a Beirut suburb. A month later, the International Court of Justice in the Hague ruled that Belgium could not try former and current world leaders for war crimes, because they have diplomatic immunity. Jan Devadder, the legal advisor to the Belgian Foreign Ministry, said that the Hague court's ruling would probably mean that Belgium would drop its case against Sharon. "The Sharon case, in my opinion, is closed," he said.[34]

CHANGE OF IMAGE?

———

BY JUNE, SHARON'S APPROVAL RATING was sixty-two percent in a newspaper poll, seventy percent in a television poll, very high for any Israeli prime minister, and especially after only one hundred days in office, and despite the BBC documentary and the proceedings in Belgium.[1] For three weeks, despite the provocation of the Dolphinarium bombing, he had shown uncharacteristic restraint. People who had not voted for him and had never trusted him expressed pleased surprise. Alona Golan, a TV producer and Labor supporter, said, "He was considered very right-wing and I was concerned he would start a war. He always seemed so aggressive. But during this period he has remained calm and shown restraint. He comes across like a pleasant grandfather." Yael Dayan, a Labor MK, said, "My impression is so far, so good." She said that many Israelis believed that the country had done "more than its duty" when it held a state inquiry after the Sabra and Shatilla massacre. It was not forgotten, she said, and "still worries some people tremendously. But it's not a reason not to have confidence in Sharon now, even if it is a reason to be suspicious about his attitude toward Arabs."[2]

What may have been partly responsible for a softening of the general attitude toward Sharon was that, possibly as a result of the intifada and the failure of the Camp David talks, and certainly because of the suicide bombings, there was a general hardening of the Israeli attitude toward Palestinians. It was noted by a *Haaretz* media critic, Roger Alpher, that newscasts often no longer reported

Palestinian fatalities, but instead sometimes said only that there were "no casualties among our forces."[3] After the Dolphinarium bombing, Israel Radio temporarily banned interviews with Arab MKs. Sharon's "restraint" was praised even though during the cease-fire, he continued his avowed policy of assassination, or what he called "active self-defense" against suspected terrorists. Even Uzi Benziman, certainly no friend to Sharon, limited himself to questioning Sharon's sincerity and motivation, saying that his "long-term intentions" were "hard to discern," but that "on face value" the prime minister wanted "a cease-fire and a cessation of violence that would be a great success." However, it would be the Palestinians, Benziman concluded, who would "decide how Sharon will act."[4]

International opinion too had changed toward Sharon. When he stopped briefly in London on his way to a meeting with President Bush in Washington, Sharon was praised by Prime Minister Tony Blair for his "restraint" in the face of Palestinian attacks. Sharon told Blair he was ready to make compromises for peace, but that Britain and Europe should exert more pressure on the Palestinians to end the violence, and he told the *Washington Post* that Israelis were running out of patience with Arafat, whom he called an "obstacle" to peace.[5] Arafat himself told Israeli journalists in Ramallah: "The time has come to make peace, not to incite." He said he wanted a complete cease-fire, but he could not control areas of the West Bank where the Israelis were in charge of security measures. Around that time in Nablus an al-Aksa Brigade activist long sought by the Israelis had been killed when a public telephone he habitually used exploded, prompting Marwan Barghouti to say, "With this assassination, Sharon has opened the gates of hell for the Israelis."[6] Six Israelis and eight Palestinians had died since the cease-fire had come into effect in the month of June.[7] When it endorsed the cease-fire plan, Israel gave the PA details of eight planned suicide attacks along with the names of twenty-six perpetrators of terrorist attacks whom it wanted arrested. The Tenet plan did not obligate the Palestinians to arrest those responsible for past attacks, and PA officials said they had no intention of doing so, that as long as Israel does not restrain and arrest violent settlers, they saw no reason to arrest Palestinians. In the middle of June the Fatah Central Committee ordered all Fatah members to abide by the cease-fire, but Marwan Barghouti and other local Fatah leaders said they would continue the violence. At a demonstration in Nablus, activists of Fatah, Hamas and Islamic Jihad denounced the Tenet plan and burned US and Israeli flags and a picture of George Tenet.[8]

It was generally acknowledged that Sharon had learned from the experience of preceding Israeli prime ministers, and at the moment had outmaneuvered Arafat on the diplomatic front.[9] His government had even altered its language on the settlement freeze, substituting the phrase "current needs of existing communities" for "natural growth." Defense Minister Benjamin Ben-Eliezer announced the dismantlement of fifteen illegal settlement outposts erected since Sharon took office in February, and the rejection of about one hundred requests for new projects in existing settlements.[10]

Kofi Annan, visiting the area, suggested talks between himself, Peres and Arafat. Peres liked this idea, but Sharon rejected it. The result was a public clash in a cabinet meeting, with Peres telling Sharon that he did not have to take orders from the prime minister.[11] The *Financial Times* was not alone in seeing this as a sign that "[t]he first cracks were developing" in the national unity government,[12] but that did not appear to be the case. Peres and Sharon had dinner together and rumors died down somewhat, although never completely. Sharon said that it was incorrect to assume that his government was in danger of falling, and that he and Peres differed only on later stages of the Mitchell plan that might never be reached.[13] The settlers and other members of the right wing were putting tremendous pressure on Sharon to retaliate for drive-by shootings in the territories for which Fatah claimed responsibility, but he would not budge from his policy of restraint. "To take the people now to war, in my view," he said, "is a mistake of the first order from every perspective."[14] Some on the right blamed Peres for Sharon's policy of restraint, some on the left called him a "sell-out" and a "lapdog" for working with Sharon at all; others praised him for being behind the restraint policy. Peres himself hinted that the Mitchell report would not have been accepted without the presence of Labor in the cabinet.[15] Arafat called the Sharon government "war crazed."[16]

In late June, Sharon made his second visit to the White House in three months. During a joint news conference President Bush said, "The cycle of violence must be broken," and that he was sending Colin Powell to the Middle East to "further advance the peace process." Sharon said that there had to be "complete quiet" for ten days, after which he expected a six-week cooling-off period to be followed by efforts to freeze settlement expansion and by other confidence-building measures. Bush told Sharon that he had "no better friend than the United States." Arafat had yet to be invited to the White House.[17]

In New York, Sharon addressed several hundred guests of the America-Israel Friendship League at a black-tie dinner at the Pierre Hotel. Three companies with considerable investment in Israel were praised at the dinner: AOL Time Warner, IBM and Rupert Murdoch's News Corporation. Murdoch, who co-chaired the dinner with President Bush, said that Israel's greatest strength is "its human capital . . . the potential of its people to better their skills." Murdoch said that News Corporation's NDS, a digital technology company based in Jerusalem, had grown from twenty to 600 employees over the past decade. Lawrence Ricciardi, the senior vice president and general counsel of IBM, said that his company employed 1700 people in Israel, and that "This wedge of land and the huge ideals it represents are very important to IBM." AOL Time Warner vice chairman Kenneth Novack said IBM invested in Israel "because Israel is a great investment." The Bank of Israel reported that foreign investment in Israel had dropped 58.7 percent in the first five months of

2001, to $2.2 billion, compared to $5.3 billion during the first five months of 2000.[18]

Foreign investment was not the only important part of the economy to suffer from the intifada. The Israel Hotel Association reported that since September, 2000, the number of tourists had dropped by fifty-five percent, and as a result, the country was losing $2 billion, and some 60,000 workers were probably going to lose their jobs.[19]

A RISING TIDE

———

As the summer of 2001 wore on, the strains on the so-called cease-fire became more and more apparent. Sharon had to balance the far right and Labor in his cabinet, while there were suicide bombings and daily battles with Palestinian gunmen and rock-throwing teenagers. The IDF bulldozed Palestinian houses built without permits or sheltering snipers, and the government pursued a policy of targeted killings of militant leaders, actions that were roundly condemned by the international community. In addition, there were attacks on Palestinians by Jewish vigilantes, the most outrageous of which ended in the death of a five-month-old baby. Sharon ordered the police and Shin Bet to find these killers, "whoever they are," and deal with them with "an iron hand."[1] His attempts to retain the support of the settlers were not meeting with success as he persisted in his "restraint" policy. Extremists in the settlements mocked him with a display of dummy ducks to dramatize their claim that they were "sitting ducks" for Palestinian terrorists. An extremist Jewish cell, the Committee for Road Safety, which had been outlawed after Rabin's assassination, was believed to have reorganized and to have been responsible for four roadside ambushes of Palestinians in July.[2]

Hard-line ministers in the cabinet, echoing the settlers, demanded an all-out military assault to liquidate Arafat and destroy the Palestinian Authority. Sharon responded, "You're all big heroes with your advice. At the end of the day, the responsibility is mine. This region is not going to war." But the communications minister, Reuven Rivlin, who was close to Sharon, said, "Our patience is coming to an end, and we can't bear every day another casualty. We are sitting on the edge of a volcano, and the volcano could explode any moment now."[3]

Minutes before the opening on July 16 in Jerusalem of the sixteenth Maccabiah Games, an international sporting competition known as "the Jewish Olympics," an Islamic Jihad suicide bomber killed two Israeli soldiers and injured four others near a train station in a Tel Aviv suburb. The army retaliated at once by shelling four West Bank security targets. Before dawn on that same day, two Palestinians who were apparently trying to plant a bomb close to the stadium were killed when the bomb exploded prematurely. Security was extremely tight, with over 1000 policemen patrolling the area: prominent Israeli politicians, including Sharon, attended the games, in which more than 2000 Jewish athletes from forty-three countries competed, and which went ahead as scheduled.[4]

That one of the two Palestinians planting the bomb was a member of Arafat's Fatah organization did not help the situation. Anger against Arafat was mounting in the country, and not just on the right. Ehud Barak called him a "rogue leader and a thug," and compared him to Slobodan Milosevic, Saddam Hussein and, as Sharon had done, to Osama bin Laden, and said that for years the PLO leader had talked "in English about his readiness to make peace and in Arabic about eliminating Israel in stages," and that after Camp David, Arafat "decided that only by turning to violence could he once again create world sympathy." Barak said he would support any moves Sharon took to eliminate the Palestinian Authority, but only as a "very last resort." But he felt that there would not be a peace agreement with Arafat.[5]

Martin Indyk, the American ambassador whose term was ending, criticized the Israelis for their settlement and assassination policies, but reserved his strongest words for the PA chairman who, he said, had not worked to prevent terrorism and worse still, had not "forsworn violence" as he had promised to do in 1993 "as a tool for achieving his objectives." Asked whether he agreed with Sharon that Arafat was "Israel's Osama bin Laden," Indyk said no, Arafat was "the leader of the Palestinian people," and added, "There is nothing that Israel or the United States for that matter, can do about that."[6]

Dennis Ross, who was Clinton's special envoy to the region, said that the peace process had failed because the Americans did not make it clear to Arafat "that if you're committed to negotiating peace, then you don't continue to socialize your public to violence. You don't promote grievance. You don't constantly incite. You don't educate in your school system a process of hatred, as opposed to a process of reconciliation."[7]

The Palestinian Authority had its own position. Hanan Ashrawi, who in addition to serving on Arafat's legislative council, was media commissioner for the Arab League, said in an interview with *Der Spiegel* that Sharon could not develop a peace policy, "because he has never had a peace concept in the first place. When he thinks of 'Palestinian,' he just thinks of oppression." Asked about the ceasefire Sharon demanded before negotiations could begin, Ashrawi replied that this was "absurd . . . the first time in history that an occupied people is asked to protect the occupation army." On attacks on Jewish settlers, she said, "Those who, in violation of the UN decisions and the statutes of international law, are entrenching themselves with dumb violence in occupied Palestinian territory, are criminals. They steal our fields, destroy our harvest and nobody stops them. It is incredible that the world watches passively and contents itself with set phrases like 'not conducive to peace.' As if Israel were justified to ignore the UN resolutions without being punished."[8]

Sharon, she said, had the military power to reoccupy the territories and expel the PA and Arafat, but if he tried to do that, "[t]he Palestinians, all Arabs and the countries of the world would never permit this . . . [I]nternational solidarization . . . would be so com-

ABOVE: *Moledet Party leader Rehavam Zeevi (left) greets Sharon (Maggi Ayalon 11/3/88)*

Sharon and another Likud leader shake hands with the leaders of the Aguda Party across the negotiation table in the Prime Minister's office in Jerusalem. (Maggi Ayalon 11/3/88)

ABOVE: *Aerial view of Sycamore Farm. (Tsvika Israeli 8/27/90)*

Housing Minister Sharon (left) and Lily entertain their guest, Prime Minister Shamir. (Tsvika Israeli 8/27/90)

ABOVE: *Election day at Jabotinsky House: Sharon and Moshe Arens console each other at the disappointing results. (Tsvika Israeli 6/23/92)*

ABOVE: *King Hussein of Jordan greets Minister of Infrastructure Sharon in Akaba. (Gershom Ben Amos 8/13/97)*

ABOVE: *Wye Plantation meeting: Foreign Minister Sharon (right), Natan Sharansky (2nd from right), and Prime Minister Benjamin Netanyahu (2nd from left). (Avi Ohayon 10/18/98)*

Wye Agreement signed in the White House, Palestinian Authority Chairman Yassir Arafat at the podium, President Clinton (left), Sharon (right), Sarah Netanyahu (left of Sharon). (Yaacov Saar 10/23/98)

ABOVE: *Prime Minister Shimon Peres and Palestinian Authority Chairman Yassir Arafat meeting at the Erez checkpoint. (Avi Ohayon 1/24/96)*

Moshe Arens (left) is appointed defense minister by Prime Minister Benjamin Netanyahu as Foreign Minister Sharon looks on. (Gershom Ben Amos 1/26/99)

ABOVE: *Palestinians stoning Israeli security forces near Jerusalem during violent clashes following the opening of the Western Wall tunnel. (Nati Shohat 9/24/96)*

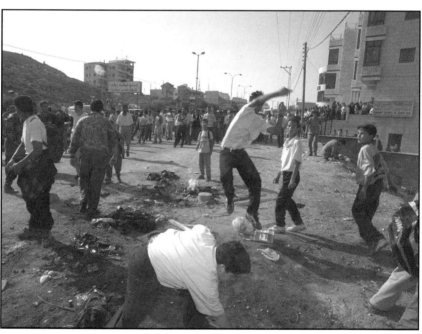

More rioting in reaction to the opening of the Western Wall tunnel. (Nati Shohat 9/24/96)

ABOVE: *Prime Minister Ehud Barak (left) with Palestinian Authority Chairman Yassir Arafat (center) and Mohammad Dahlan at the Erez checkpoint in the Gaza Strip. (Avi Ohayon 7/11/99)*

ABOVE: *Pres Weizman, Prime Minister Barak and Foreign Minister Levy meeting Palestinian Authority Chairman Yassir Arafat during the funeral of King Hassan II of Morocco in Rabat. (Avi Ohayon 7/25/99)*

ABOVE: *Prime Minister Ehud Barak and Arafat sign the Sharm al-Sheikh agreement, behind them (left to right) Gilad Sher, Hosni Mubarak, Madeleine Albright and Saeb Erekat. (Moshe Milner 9/4/99)*

A summit meeting in Oslo, Norway, between (left to right) Prime Minister Barak, US President Bill Clinton and the Chairman of the Palestinian Authority Yassir Arafat. (Avi Ohayon 11/2/99)

ABOVE: *Sharon meets with Vice President Cheney in Washington. (Photo by Yaacov Saar 3/2/01)*

Riots in the territories. A Palestinian demonstrator burning the Israeli flag in Ayosh Junction. (Avi Ohayon 10/24/00)

RIGHT: *IDF soldier
firing tear gas at
Palestinian rioters in
Ayosh Junction near
Ramalla. (Avi Ohayon
10/24/00)*

BELOW: *Deployment of
IDF forces near Gilo,
Jerusalem, in response
to hostile fire from Beit
Jala in the Palestinian
Authority. (Avi
Ohayon 10/29/00)*

ABOVE: *Sharon and son Omri on a plane to Washington. (Yaacov Saar 3/18/01)*

National Security Advisor Condoleezza Rice greets Sharon at Blair House.
(Yaacov Saar 3/19/01)

ABOVE: *Prime Minister Sharon meets with Arab local council chairmen at his office in Jerusalem. (Avi Ohayon 4/17/01)*

Meeting with British Prime Minister Tony Blair in London. (Avi Ohayon 6/24/01)

ABOVE: *In front of his sheep shed at Sycamore Farm in the Negev. (Moshe Milner 8/3/01)*

George W. Bush accepts a picture of himself in a yarmulke at the Western Wall. (Gershom Ben Amos 12/2/01)

Rocket launchers (above) and mines (below) from the captured ship Karine A, *on exhibit in the port of Eilat. (Moshe Milner 1/6/02)*

ABOVE: *IDF anti-terror operation in Balata near Nablus. (Boaz Mesika 3/2/02)*

Sharon shakes hands with Dan Rather near Jenin during Operation Defensive Shield. Uri Dan with camera. (Moshe Milner 4/10/02)

RIGHT: *Former Prime Minister Benjamin Netanyahu meets with Prime Minister Sharon in the latter's office in Tel Aviv. (Moshe Milner 4/18/02)*

BELOW: *Prime Minister Sharon with Chief of Staff Shaul Mofaz in Tel Nof at a memorial ceremony for paratroopers who died in the Yom Kippur War. (Moshe Milner 9/25/01)*

prehensive that the world's big ones, above all the United States and Europe, would have to fear for their long-term interests and would not permit Sharon to engage in such adventures." In reply to a question about whether Arafat had missed "a big opportunity" when he rejected Barak's proposals, she said, "Neither in Camp David, nor later on in Taba in Egypt, was there an offer that a responsible Palestinian could have signed." She said that Sharon's "trial" in Belgium for Sabra and Shatilla was a sign that Israel would eventually feel pressure from the rest of the world.[9]

Arafat was feeling some pressure from within the territories. Marwan Barghouti, the Fatah leader, began a call for a National Unity government to replace the Palestinian Authority. In an interview with Australian television, Barghouti said that this new government should include "other Palestinian factions to be part of the make-up. Like Hamas, Islamic Jihad, Popular Front and Democratic Front and other people who are in the opposition during the last ten years. This is the best time to strengthen the Palestinian unity." Asked whether this was a move to form a unity government to challenge Arafat's leadership, Barghouti said, "No, I think the unity government has to be chaired by Mr Arafat, no question about that. He is the elected president for the Palestinian people."[10]

Arafat had refused to align himself with these extremists, but in early August, 2001, he said he "would react favorably to approaches from all those who may wish to join the current government." His information minister, Yassir Abed Rabbo, told the press in Ramallah that Arafat was going to chair a committee to launch "a national dialogue" with all Palestinian groups. He had come under severe criticism from militants for refusing to denounce the peace process and for surrounding himself with people seen as incompetent or corrupt and "defeatist," as opposed to "honest" Hamas militants. Husam Khader, a Fatah leader in Nablus, said, "We face a serious choice. Either we escalate the struggle against Israel, or we end the lie that we're involved in an uprising." He said he had called on

Arafat "to rebuild Palestinian institutions on the basis of national unity," and warned, "If we don't get rid of the corrupt elements, we're heading for another catastrophe."[11]

There had been clashes between Palestinian gunmen and PA security forces who tried to enforce an order to stop shooting at Israelis. Arafat was in the difficult position of risking civil war if he attempted to crack down on militants. When a Gaza security chief attempted to arrest four militants, hundreds of protesters, including about twenty gunmen, rioted, and it took at least 100 policemen four hours to disperse the mob by shooting over their heads. No one was arrested.[12]

At the end of July, a riot broke out on the Temple Mount when a small ultra-right Jewish group of about forty people, called the Temple Mount Faithful, marked a fast day of mourning for the destruction of the First and Second Temples, by laying a symbolic marble foundation stone for a temple. The Israeli courts had traditionally prevented the group from ascending the mount, and this year, as usual, the Israeli police blocked their way, forcing them to perform their rites in a parking lot outside the walls of the Old City, some 300 yards from the Temple Mount. As soon as the cornerstone, driven on a truck, had reached its destination in the parking lot, the police supervised its immediate return to its resting place near the American consulate in east Jerusalem.[13]

Although it had been clear for days that these people would not get near the compound, Muslims had been called upon by the Islamic Movement, the PA and Arab MKs to "defend" the site with "souls and blood." About 2000 Muslims responded by gathering on the mount and began to hurl rocks and jagged stones at Jews praying below them at the Western Wall. Hundreds of worshippers ran for cover, shielding their heads with plastic chairs, prayer shawls and even prayer books, as they dodged the stones. The police briefly cleared the area before the wall, and stormed the plateau, firing tear gas and stun guns at the rioters and fending off the stones with plastic shields. Within half an hour the stone-throwing stopped, and the Jews were allowed back. However, for about two hours, about 100 young Palestinians continued to throw bottles, bricks, rocks and shoes of the faithful at the policemen, five of whom were taken to the hospital. The police waited for the Waqf or Palestinian security officials to act, and when they did not, hundreds of Israeli policemen re-entered the mount and dispersed the stone-throwers with stun guns. They did not enter the mosques, but arrested twenty-eight young Arabs. About thirty-five Palestinians and fifteen policemen were injured.[14]

Jerusalem police chief Mickey Levy said that people do not understand that the mount is "a volcano waiting to erupt which can set the whole region aflame," and that Arab MKs Ahmed Tibi and Abdul Malik Dahamshe had been on the mount inciting the youths. Dahamshe's fourteen-year-old son had been one of those arrested. "We say it again and again," Dahamshe said, "this is the holy mosque of the Muslims, al-Aqsa is its name. It's not a Jewish temple . . . And Mr Sharon and all the Jewish people have nothing to do here and they should not come here to beat us and kill us inside the al-Aqsa mosque." The Palestinian Authority issued a statement: "As a result of Arab and international efforts, especially those by the US administration and the European Union," the Israeli forces had "lifted their siege."[15]

THE SILENCE OF DEATH

———

ON AUGUST 9, 2001, A twenty-three-year-old Palestinian, explosives packed with nails and shrapnel strapped to his body, blew himself up in the Sbarro pizzeria in Jerusalem at lunchtime when the restaurant was crowded with young families. Six children and thirteen adults were killed instantly, and at least ninety others were injured, about a dozen very seriously. Islamic Jihad quickly claimed responsibility for this attack, the aftermath of which was described by Mark Ellis in the London *Mirror* as a "scene of total devastation. Glass and metal which were part of the shop window lay shattered, drenched in blood. The restaurant was a blackened shell . . ." Ellis quoted a policeman who said, "'Two children were lying there. I can't describe how they looked. There was the smell of gunpowder, blood and death.' And pointing to the scene, he said: 'Do you hear that silence? It's the silence of death.'"[1]

President Bush condemned the bombing and demanded that Arafat arrest and punish those responsible, but both he and Colin Powell urged the Israelis to exercise restraint. The fear was that Sharon would do something draconian and tip the region into all-out war. At the same time, the administration was showing some signs of irritation with Arafat. Richard Boucher, spokesman for the State Department, said, "Chairman Arafat said in Ramallah he would make a maximum effort. We are [still] looking for that effort." Members of both the Senate and the House of Representatives were demanding that Arafat rein in the violence.[2] The situation was not improved when Arafat issued what the *Washington Post* called "a weak statement condemning the bombing and 'all acts that harm civilians,'" followed by a comment from Yassir Abed Rabbo, the PA information minister, that "We believe Sharon alone is responsible for the cycle of violence." Marwan Barghouti expressed the opinion that the bombing was "the only way to end the occupation of Palestinian territories."[3] The London *Times* speculated that Arafat saw divisions widening between the US and the Europeans and between Colin Powell on the one hand and Vice President Cheney and Donald Rumsfeld on the other, and also between elements within Sharon's national unity government; that he expected these divisions to work to his advantage, and that his goal was "to force Israel further and further on to a war footing." He could then have justification to demand "the deployment of an international 'protective' force." This, the *Times* concluded, was "a trap into which European governments must not fall."[4]

An attack had not been unexpected ever since the Israelis had attacked a Hamas office the previous week, killing eight people, including two children. But there was tremendous anger in the country. Hundreds of people gathered at the bomb site, some wearing T-shirts reading "No Arabs means no bombs," and shouting "Death to Arabs and death to leftwingers!" at a handful of peace protesters holding signs saying "Revenge equals continuing the cycle of blood." The general revulsion galvanized support for Sharon, with people saying that whatever he did, they would support him.[5]

After urgent consultation with his cabinet, which split over this decision, Sharon responded to the attack early the next day by sending a large contingent of policemen to surround and seize Orient House, a stone building in east Jerusalem, formerly a hotel, that had served as the Palestinian political headquarters there, a de facto Palestinian Foreign Ministry, and a symbol of the PA claim to east Jerusalem as their future capital. Policemen removed stacks of documents from the building and climbed on the roof to replace the

Palestinian flag with the Israeli Star of David. These actions implied that the Israelis were there to stay, and National Security Minister Uzi Landau announced that this occupation was not temporary. In a further retaliation, in Ramallah Israeli F-16 warplanes destroyed a police building that had been evacuated, and the Israelis seized nine PA buildings in Abu Dis, a suburb of Jerusalem.[6]

President Bush said he was "frustrated" by the situation, and that "Mr Arafat can do a better job. I am deeply concerned that some of the more radical groups are beginning to affect his ability and obviously are as provocative as heck toward the Israelis." But the State Department said that seizing Orient House was a "political escalation" that was undermining confidence in a negotiated settlement.[7] Shimon Peres and other Left politicians also condemned the move, as did Jordan, Egypt and France. The *Daily Telegraph*, taking an opposite view, criticized the seizure of the building as too "measured" a response that "would send a signal of impotence" and that seemed "designed to impress the international media with Israel's restraint rather than to deter future suicide attacks." The *Telegraph* held that "[e]ven the targeted assassination of Hamas terrorists or other Muslim extremists poses no threat to Mr Arafat," who was making "common cause with them" and whose TV station "glorifies suicide bombers as martyrs" while "his associates preach jihad against the Jews from the mosques of Gaza and Jerusalem, and his Arabic propaganda calls for the destruction of Israel." Both Palestinians and Israelis wondered "why Mr Sharon is willing to wound, but afraid to strike," and, the *Telegraph* went on, unless Sharon could persuade Israelis that his government could protect them against suicide-bomb carnage, he "may shortly find himself out on his ear."[8]

Arafat joined much of the international community and the press in calling the Orient House closure an act of aggression, and Hanan Ashrawi led a few dozen protesters in a demonstration at the police barricades outside the building. In the ensuing fracas, a dozen protesters were arrested and eleven Palestinians and one policeman were injured. "We are unarmed, we are civilians and we have the right to go anywhere in Palestine, including Jerusalem," Mrs Ashrawi said. "This is our city and Orient House is our house."[9] Palestinian leaders told a news conference that they would reclaim the building "by any means necessary" and that a violent uprising would occur in the heart of Jerusalem.[10] Although in response to international pressure, the Israeli flag was lowered from the building, Sharon said, "The offices in Orient House will not open again. Ever." He wanted, he said, to strike the Palestinians "in their soft underbelly, in the place that would disturb them the most."[11] Peres told a Labor Party meeting that the government had broken promises to the Palestinians to ease border restrictions on West Bank cities, and this was breeding hatred that was making the conflict worse.[12]

Three days later, a few hours after Sharon had agreed to allow Peres to resume talks with the Palestinians, a young Palestinian entered the Wall Street Cafe near Haifa, asked a waitress, "Do you know what this is?", pulled out a lighter, ignited a fuse and blew himself up. Islamic Jihad took responsibility for the attack, in which there were mostly light injuries to about twenty people. No one was killed except the bomber.[13]

A few days after that, Israeli forces invaded the West Bank city of Jenin for three hours, bulldozing two police stations, and later the Beit Jala area south of Jerusalem, from which Palestinian gunmen had fired shots for five hours at the Jewish neighborhood of Gilo. When they withdrew from Jenin, the Israelis took with them about seventy Palestinians who had been jailed as collaborators by Jenin authorities. The Jenin incursion was roundly condemned internationally, and Arafat's information minister, Yassir Abed Rabbo, thanked Sharon for it, explaining that Israel "has now shown the world that it is an invading army."[14] Yossi Beilin called on Peres to leave the government immediately because in attacking Jenin, Sharon was attacking Peres himself and everything Peres's peace efforts had accomplished over the last ten years. Sharon, Beilin said, was "resorting to the same reprisal operations that he commanded fifty years ago. He is incapable of understanding that the situation has changed since then, and is leading Israel to disaster."[15] Meretz leader Yossi Sarid said, "The Jenin incursion will be added to the long list of worthless maneuvers intended entirely for internal consumption. As long as the government continues using strong-arm tactics without backing them up with significant diplomatic steps, it will only succeed in intensifying the violence."[16] The incursion was criticized on the Right as well, but for different reasons. Herut MK Michael Kleiner said the IDF should have stayed in Jenin, "imposed a curfew, and set up a court to catch terrorists and confiscate weapons. The operation made the same impression as the flight from Lebanon, and raises more doubts as to Israel's deterrent capability."[17]

Peres warned the Knesset Foreign Affairs and Defense Committee that Hamas could take over the Palestinian Authority and "Khomeinize" the area, and that a few of Arafat's organizations were slowly moving toward rapprochement with Hamas.[18] Khalil Shikaki, a Palestinian pollster and political analyst, said that Arafat was in a bad situation, with dwindling popularity and resources. Sharon was no longer treating Arafat as a serious partner as Barak had done, and Palestinians were blaming Arafat and his 40,000-man security forces for their inability to protect the militants, admired as folk heroes, who were being hunted down and killed on Palestinian soil. Husam Khader, a Palestinian legislator, said, "We are being hunted down like rabbits."[19] Arafat's response was to arrest, put on trial and often sentence to death suspected collaborators who supposedly helped Israeli security forces to track down wanted men. Khader said this policy did nothing to reform what he called "the fundamental corruption" of the PA, which he called "woefully inept" both at providing civil services and physically fighting the Israelis. Khader, like Marwan Barghouti, called publicly upon Arafat to purge corrupt ministers and include Hamas and Islamic

Jihad with Fatah in a "national unity" government to conduct armed conflict instead of discussions.[20]

Arafat had indeed promised to meet with the militant organizations and his Palestine National Council had formed a committee to discuss "national dialogue." But the council had also appointed a committee to investigate Khader and his criticisms. Shakaki said that Arafat's promise to consider national unity was not serious, but simply a ploy to drum up support. At the same time, Shakaki was convinced that Arafat would not jail militants, as the Israelis demanded; if he did, "[t]he Israelis will spit in his face, and the Palestinians will call him a traitor." If the Israelis offered Arafat "something tangible" that would "materially change the lives of the Palestinians for the better, that would make it worth it to him to take the risk" of acting against the Islamists.[21]

Hosni Mubarak was sufficiently alarmed by the seizure of Orient House, which seemed to the Egyptians to signal the death of Oslo, to send his main foreign policy advisor, Osama al-Baz, to Washington to talk about starting up diplomacy once again, and immediately creating an international force to oversee a cease-fire as the first step. "It's clear Egypt has to do something," the al-Ahram newspaper said in the middle of August. "The observers are a key element that would be the means by which you could fill the gap between a cease-fire and a resumption of negotiations."[22] Arafat had gone to Cairo earlier in the month to talk to Mubarak about convening a summit, but Mubarak had flatly rejected the idea, without bothering to help Arafat save face: "It's not logical to say every time something happens, 'Let's hold a summit.' What will a summit achieve?"[23]

Mubarak had moderated his tone toward Israel since the middle of July, when he had said, "Frankly speaking, it is clear that there is no solution with Sharon. He is a man who only understands murder, strikes and war. His value is to use power and his nature does not accept peace. To be more frank, I don't see hope with Sharon and his government, which includes extremists. Once again, I say it, the personalities are unbalanced and talking with them is fruitless."[24] In the main, the Israelis shrugged off these remarks as an attempt to palliate the Arab League, which was demanding that Egypt cut off diplomatic relations with Israel, and to deflect criticism for having invited Peres to Egypt. One official said the same people in the Foreign Ministry were saying that Mubarak's message to the US was that if he was "talking like this, then the atmosphere in the region really is bad." Sharon's response was a statement that government policy "is to reach peace agreements with all the Arab countries and the Palestinian Authority."[25] In any case, although Egypt had withdrawn its ambassador from Israel less than two months after the start of the intifada, now in August Osama al-Baz told a pan-Arab newspaper that there was no possibility that Egypt would close its embassy in Tel Aviv. And neither Egypt nor Jordan attended an Arab meeting called to revive the boycott against Israel.[26]

The US rejected Mubarak's request for a group of observers, saying it would not consider such an action without Israel's full agreement and until there had been seven days without violence. Colin Powell said, "Sending international observers at this time, where there is still a conflict underway and the two sides do not agree to the presence of international observers, I don't think is a way to move forward."[27]

DURBAN & MOSCOW

———

In the first week of September, 2001, the United States and Israel withdrew from the United Nations World Conference Against Racism held in Durban, South Africa, in protest at the preparation of a final document that condemned Zionism as "based on racial superiority" and singled out Israel, from all other countries, as a racist, apartheid state, guilty of crimes against humanity. Colin Powell, who had remained in Washington, referred to "hateful language" in the drafts, and said he had instructed his handful of mid-level State Department officials to return home, and California Democratic Representative Tom Lantos, a Holocaust survivor, who had been part of the US contingent, said that "extremist elements" had "hijacked" the conference "for its own purposes," and wrecked it. "The United States from Day One," he said, "approached this conference with the finest of intentions." Shimon Peres called the conference a "farce" and "an unbelievable attempt to smear Israel." Sharon, told of the walkout in advance by Powell in a phone call, said the conference did not deal with the real problems of racism, but instead indulged in a political attempt to incite anger against Israel. He told the *New York Post* that the US-Israeli walkout was "a slap on the face to this bunch of anti-Semites in Durban."[1]

The South African government and UN Secretary-General Kofi Annan called the walkout "unfortunate and unnecessary," with Annan remarking, "In these circumstances, each country should be at the table to discuss. I would have preferred that the US was there."

Reed Brody of Human Rights Watch, said the walkout was a "disappointment for victims of racism everywhere" and accused the US of "using a political smoke screen to avoid dealing with the many very real issues at this conference."[2] Reverend Jesse Jackson, who was at the conference, said he was disappointed that President Bush had allowed the Israeli question to determine American participation.[3] The Palestinian ambassador to South Africa, Salman el Herfi, said the Arab delegations had been "very reasonable" but the US delegation had refused to compromise. "It's sad they didn't leave room for dialogue; they didn't leave room for flexibility," he said.[4] Amr Moussa, Secretary General of the Arab League, said the league had no response: "It is a sovereign decision, whoever wants to come should come; whoever wants to go out should."[5] The PA called the walkout good, because it was a blow to Sharon's government which opposed Mideast peace. At the same time, some Palestinian officials condemned the walkout as an endorsement of Israeli attacks on Palestinians, adding that the real reason the Americans had walked out was to avoid apologizing for slavery and being forced to pay reparations.

The European Union said it would not leave the conference, but that Belgium, holding the rotating EU presidency, disagreed with the drafted resolutions and was trying to put together a totally new text. Mary Robinson, the UN High Commissioner for Human Rights, said, "It is inappropriate to use hurtful language of accusations of a kind of fascism and equating Zionism as racism and even using the word 'genocide' is . . . not only very hurtful, it's alone in a context of a world conference of these approaches. Every country has problems. If we single out one that is using it for political ends."[6] Some groups had hoped to highlight issues such as reparations for slavery, the worldwide plight of refugees and the situation of the untouchables in India, but the Israeli-Arab question had overshadowed all of that.[7]

The Israeli Foreign Ministry drew a direct line between the rhetoric at this conference, which ran from August 31 to September 7, and the fifth bomb attack in Jerusalem in two days when on September 4, a bomber dressed as an Orthodox Jew blew himself up as he was approached by policemen outside two international schools where children were arriving.[8] This attack occurred two blocks from the Sbarro pizzeria, which had been blown up on August 9. The mayor of Jerusalem, Ehud Olmert, said that the bomber had first tried to enter a hospital down the street, but had been blocked by a security guard. The bomb, containing nails, screws and metal shards, injured about twenty people, including the two Israeli border policemen who had noticed the bomber was acting strangely and had come within a few yards of him just as he reached into his backpack and detonated the device. Neither policeman was seriously injured. There was considerable anger against the international community in Israelis of all political persuasions, who felt diplomatically isolated. This surfaced at the scene of the bombing when Javier Solana, EU foreign policy chief, came to survey the damage; at least one bystander shouted at him, "Take your suitcases and get out of here! Why did you come?"[9]

David Horovitz, a peace supporter, said, "The main danger of Durban is that it legitimizes Palestinian aggression against Israel. There are definitely things that Israel should be challenged over, but the bottom line is that we have to defend ourselves."[10] The Labor Party, which was now marginalized, held its leadership elections on the same day as the bombing. The candidates were Avraham Burg, the speaker of the Knesset, and Minister of Defense Benjamin "Fuad" Ben-Eliezer, both of whom promised to maintain Sharon's national unity government, although Burg wanted talks with the Palestinians, and Ben-Eliezer, who had been an army chief, was believed by some to be more right-wing than Sharon. Burg accused both Meretz leader Yossi Sarid and Sharon's son Omri of working against him.

Sarid was quoted as saying that he had no intention of intervening in the primary, because he had not the slightest interest in either Labor candidate. Polls showed that more than half of Labor's members disliked both men and most top party leaders refused to endorse either, although Barak threw his support to Ben-Eliezer.[11]

Fewer than 55,000 Labor Party members cast their vote in the leadership elections, less than half of what David Horovitz called "a pitifully low national membership of 117,000." The result was a near-tie. Burg claimed victory by a margin of about 1000 votes, but Ben-Eliezer accused his opposition of ballot-stuffing and other voting irregularities, especially among Israeli Arabs, including the Druse, who had turned out in relatively high numbers to vote for Burg even though Ben-Eliezer had been born in Iraq and Burg's family had come from Germany. Both men hired lawyers.[12]

Labor in its glory days had won Israel's first eight prime ministerial elections under a system without primaries, where candidates were nominated by a clique of party officials and unanimously approved by the central committee. After the system was democratized, Labor had won only two of the last eight general elections, with Rabin in 1992 and Barak in 1999. Now, clearly because of the collapse of Oslo and the failure of Barak's Camp David negotiations, Labor had, as David Horovitz put it, "reached rock bottom" and its election had "descended into farce."[13] Uzi Baram, who had quit the party earlier in the year in disagreement with its direction, said, "There's no doubt that the collapse of Barak did big damage to the image, policy and attraction of the Labor party. But Israel needs a strong Labor party. We have to produce and create alternatives to the policies of Sharon. The romance between Peres and Sharon cannot continue more than a few months."[14]

On September 3, Sharon arrived in Russia for a three-day working visit to discuss the Middle East situation and trade relations with President Vladimir Putin and Foreign Minister Igor Ivanov, as well as members of the Russian parliament. He brought with him what he called "a very representative delegation of members of the Israeli business community, in order to expand our economic cooperation." Sharon said, "We would like to buy more and sell more."[15] The Russian premier, Mikhail Kasyanov, gave a business lunch for the Israelis, amid announcements that the trade turnover between Russia and Israel had grown substantially and now exceeded the one-billion-dollar volume in 2000. "On the whole," Putin said, "our relations are in a good state."[16] One thing on the agenda was said to be a quiet deal on supplying Israel with Russian natural gas. A feasibility study in 1995 had suggested that Russia's Blue Stream pipeline to Turkey could easily be extended to Israel; Netanyahu had prevented action on this because of a reluctance to rely on Russian goodwill and because he thought he had an alternative in Egyptian gas, although that deal fell through with the outbreak of the al-Aqsa intifada.[17]

One relationship Sharon wanted to discuss with Putin was Russia's with Iran: Moscow had agreed in March to supply Tehran with $7 billion worth of arms over the next several years. The Russians assured Sharon that they would provide only defensive weapons and promised not to send dual-purpose technology that could help Iran develop its nuclear program. Ivanov said that Russia was taking stringent measures for export control and would continue to develop relations with Iran and Iraq without infringing international proliferation agreements. Both Israel and the US were critical of Russia's construction of a 1000 megawatt nuclear power plant in Bushehr, Iran, despite the insistence of both Moscow and Iran that the project had no military purpose.[18]

Putin stressed Russia's commitment to the international fight against terrorism, and, mentioning the Orthodox-disguised suicide bomber who had blown himself up in Jerusalem that day, expressed concern for the safety of the one million Russian-speakers living in Israel. "We are not indifferent to the fate of these people," Putin said. "On the other hand, you know we have traditionally good relations with the Arab world, including the Palestinian Authority. This seems a good basis for Russia to make a substantial contribution to resolving the situation in the region."[19] Sharon agreed that it was important that Russia have good relations with the Arab states because Israel believed "the time will come when it will play a significant role in the negotiating process." He hoped that it would be a positive role: Russia, like Israel, he said in an obvious reference to Russia's problems in Chechnya, "now understands the danger of fundamentalist, extremist Islamic terror, knows it well." Indeed, with the war in Chechnya continuing, it would have been difficult for the Kremlin to criticize Israeli actions against Hamas and Islamic Jihad. Sharon said also that "Israel is ready to accept painful compromises for the sake of . . . peace, but it should be a real, durable and safe peace. . . . I have always been of the opinion that we can live in peace with Arabs."[20] The main obstacle to peace, he maintained, was Arafat, who "only understands the language of pressure."[21] He told the Russian news media that in important international organizations, and specifically in the UN, "[a]n Arab, Muslim international elite is waging a fight against Israel." He said that he and Peres were agreed that Israel would never allow international observers, who permitted "terrorists to hide behind them." With the exceptions of India, Serbia and Singapore, "nonaligned countries" support this Arab elite, he said, and automatically vote against Israeli interests. He said frankly that Russia was one of the countries that habitually voted against Israel.[22] However, analysts commented that Sharon's visit seemed to reflect a more balanced Russian position, a desire to move away from its traditional pro-Arab line.

Sharon said he was grateful to Russia for its key role in World War II, which he said had saved the world and saved those Jews who had managed to stay alive during those war years. Speaking only English and Hebrew, despite his family's Russian roots, Sharon addressed Russian Jews at an elegant reception in Moscow's Maryina Roshcha Jewish Public Center, asking them to help Israel in this "difficult hour" and calling upon them to establish permanent residence in Israel. "One million immigrants from the Soviet Union have already arrived, and their contribution to the development of Israel is extraordinary," he said, and now Israel needed another million, concluding with the remark: "At one time Jews from the Soviet Union asked me for help. Now I am asking you for help."[23]

Shortly after Sharon returned home, a suicide bomber struck on a crowded platform at a train station near the Lebanese border in the northern coastal town of Nahariya, killing three and injuring seventeen others. This was only one incident on a day of widespread violence, but it was noteworthy because for the first time the bomber was an Israeli Arab, a resident of Abu Snaan, a small village in the western Galilee, not even six miles from the station. The man, Mohammed Shaqir Habishi, who did not fit the profile of a suicide bomber, was forty-five years old, and left a family of two wives and six children. Israeli authorities said Habishi was active in the Islamic Movement and Israeli security agents had been hunting him for ten days, after repeatedly asking the Palestinian Authority to arrest him when he collected his explosives in the West Bank city of Jenin from Hamas, which claimed responsibility for the bombing. This was an alarming development, but Israeli Arab leaders and residents of Abu Snaan, all Israeli citizens, insisted that Israeli Arabs were not about to enter upon a terror campaign. Some villagers even suggested that Habishi's family should be expelled from Abu Snaan, and that Habishi should not be buried there. Ahmed Tibi, an Arab MK who was hardly a moderate, said this bombing was "extraordinary" and did not "represent any trend. But definitely yes, Arabs are bitter and angry against the Israeli government and the oppression and aggression against the Palestinians . . . We are talking about the same nation, the same families."[24]

As the Palestinians mounted a string of assaults, Sharon was attacked continually by MKs on both the Left and the Right: the Right maintaining that the best defense was offense, including the reoccupation of the territories and the eviction of Arafat, and the Left demanding the evacuation of the settlements and a return to the negotiating table. One proposed solution was an IDF plan to create buffer zones along sections of the Green Line. These would be closed military zones aimed at preventing infiltration into the country by hostile elements, and involving military tribunals for transgressors. While Sharon was in Russia, blueprints for the buffer zone were announced by the army. This angered Sharon, who thought that the generals, making a decision that should be left to political leaders, had gone too far.[25] Accordingly his military secretary instructed the defense secretary to postpone implementation of the zone plan, saying that the prime minister had no quarrel with the army "thickening" the dividing line, but the inner cabinet wanted further discussion on the question of annexing territories to turn them into closed military zones. Sharon said these closed zones in densely populated areas would cause hardship to innocent Palestinians and would raise serious legal and international issues.[26] This irritated Defense Minister Ben-Eliezer, who said he had given the army permission to implement the moves; he implied in closed forums that the IDF felt that Sharon was "making political capital" at its expense, causing it to lose confidence, and to fear that the prime minister was trying to "destroy" it.[27] On the other hand, a senior IDF source said the buffer plan was "actually unenforceable," entailing "very serious restrictions on the Palestinians," and would "wear out the troops and cause serious damage to Israel's public image. Amnon Lipkin-Shahak, a former IDF chief of staff, said, "If anyone thinks [the buffer zone] will solve the problem of suicide bombers or terror cells trying to get into Israel, they are creating an illusion."[28]

Peres announced that he intended to meet with Arafat to try to stop the escalating violence as Israel responded to Palestinian gunfire and bombings by "targeted strikes" at terrorist leaders. One target that escaped a helicopter missile attack on his car was Raed

Karmi, a member of Fatah's al-Aqsa Martyrs Brigade, who had con-fessed to the murder of the two Israeli restaurateurs in Tulkarm. Karmi escaped with light injuries, but two men traveling with him were killed. David Horovitz wrote that "Karmi's name was one of seven the Israeli government had made public earlier [in the sum-mer]—branding them the key organizers of intifada violence, de-claring that Mr Arafat had refused its repeated requests for their arrest, and intimating it would now attempt to track down and eliminate them." The Palestinians, not unexpectedly, called these assassinations "extra-judicial killings" and the attack on Karmi, "murder in cold blood."[29]

Under these circumstances, and with Sharon saying that Arafat's signature on peace accords was worth "nothing more than a signa-ture on a piece of ice," it did not appear that Peres's peace initiative would get very far. In a telephone interview with the *New York Times*, Sharon said that the PA was "a kingdom of terror" that Arafat had formed "a coalition of terror" against Israel, and that Peres believed that he could influence Arafat "to stop firing. I have doubts about that. But I told him, 'If you can do that, of course it's a good thing to meet.'" He said that ordinary Palestinians were living in a state of siege and he hoped a Peres-Arafat meeting would ease conditions for them. He also called for the establishment of a military buffer zone up to two miles wide between the West Bank and Israel and said he would not stop the expansion of existing settlements: "There are young soldiers coming back from the army," he said. "They want to get married. What are they going to do? They have to get a formal agreement for marriage from Arafat?" Oslo, he said, had failed and "what was left was Arafat's Nobel Prize." Asked whether he supported a grassroots campaign by US Jews to revoke that 1994 Peace Prize, he laughed. "How can one take it? I believe he has to volunteer to give it back."[30]

Despite all this, Sharon gave Peres a "full mandate" to hold talks "to move forward the implementation of the Tenet and Mitchell plans." In Washington, President Bush was under pressure from Saudi Arabia and Egypt to grant Arafat an audience, as he had done twice with Sharon. There was an inclination in the White House to use the projected meeting between Peres and Arafat as an opening for the president to meet with the PA chairman at the United Nations in New York. It was hoped that the Peres-Arafat talk would be the first of a series that would initiate a serious peace process. On September 9, 2001, the *New York Times* reported that Bush and his advisors were planning to watch what happened over the next ten days or so. If the Peres-Arafat discussions went well, the administration would consider changing its approach to the Mideast conflict.[31]

75

DAY OF MOURNING

———

Two days later, on September 11, Arab terrorists killed 3000 people on American soil. Israel declared a day of national mourning, evacuated its embassies and consulates around the world, closed its airspace to foreign planes, put its air force on high alert and beefed up security at already tight checkpoints. Sharon issued a statement of condolence and sympathy, in which he said that "all Israelis stand as one with the American people."[1] The *Boston Globe* reported that in Jerusalem and Ramallah, young Palestinians danced in the streets and handed out candies in celebration. In Jerusalem, Israeli buses and cars were stoned. The *Globe* reporter, Charles Radin, commented on the "remarkable consensus of opinion" among Palestinian "businessmen, laborers and students," who condemned the deaths of civilians, but put the blame for the tragedy squarely on the Americans for their "history of aggression."[2]

Arafat condemned the attacks, offered condolences and expressed "complete shock."[3] A few days later, Colin Powell received Arafat's assent to a meeting "as soon as possible" with Peres, to defuse the tension, which did not abate as IDF tanks and bulldozers shelled buildings and exchanged fire with gunmen in incursions into Jenin and Jericho; their stated purpose "to root out terror." The raid on Jenin, described by Israeli officials as "a nest of terrorism," was apparently prompted by the belief that the Israeli Arab suicide bomber had been fitted out with his explosives in that West Bank city. Shortly before the IDF raid, Hamas had released a video tape of the bomber holding a rifle in one hand and the Koran in the other. Yassir Abed Rabbo, the PA information minister, said, "The Israeli government is hiding behind the dust and tragedy in New York and Washington, D.C., to commit these crimes against our innocent civilians and cities."[4] Sharon was quoted by Israel Radio as telling Powell over the phone, "Everyone has his own bin Laden. Arafat is our bin Laden."[5]

At the same time, the Associated Press said that a freelance cameraman who had videotaped Palestinians celebrating the September 11 attacks had been summoned to a PA office and told that the video must not be aired. Dan Perry, the AP Jerusalem bureau chief, was quoted in USA Today: "At this point, we believe there to be a serious threat to our staff if the video is released."[6] Hanan Ashrawi said the footage distorted the real response to the September 11 attacks, which was "one of grief for the loss of innocent lives."[7] Most West Bank towns were quiet after the World Trade Center attacks, but a rally was held in Nablus in support of the attacks, and journalists there were threatened by Palestinian gunmen to the point where AP footage of the rally was not released because the AP cameraman on the scene felt that releasing it would endanger his life. The New York Times reported that the Foreign Press Association in Jerusalem had lodged an official protest against the PA's "harassment of journalists" and "direct threats made against local videographers by local militia members." PA officials denied that these threats had been made.[8]

On September 15, Agence France-Presse reported that five journalists were briefly detained in Gaza and their equipment was seized by the Palestinian police after they filmed a demonstration by Hamas honoring Mohammed Habishi, the Israeli Arab suicide bomber who had killed three people at the railroad station in Nahariya. In a Gaza Strip refugee camp, about 1500 Palestinians, many of them Hamas supporters, burned Israeli flags and marched carrying a large poster of Osama bin Laden. After the rally, plainclothes PA policemen questioned journalists and confiscated videotape, film and camera equipment. An AP photographer was warned not to publish pictures of the bin Laden poster.[9]

Sharon expressed some concern that an international coalition called for by Bush would include hostile countries like Egypt that would put pressure on the president to force concessions from Israel. "I feel," he said, "there is an attempt to draw distinctions between terror in Israel and terror against the rest of the world." He urged US Jewish leaders to "make it very clear that one cannot draw any distinctions between terror against Israeli citizens and terror against American citizens. There is not good terror and bad terror. Terror is terror, murder is murder." The states that should be targeted by such a coalition for their role in supporting terrorism were, he said, Syria, Iran and "the terrorist organization that is led by Arafat."[10]

Feeling as he did, it was not surprising that Sharon defied a telephoned request from President Bush and, with barely forty-eight hours notice, cancelled a tentatively scheduled meeting between Peres and Arafat, saying that he was not opposed "in principle" to a meeting to discuss a cease-fire and easing of restrictions on Palestinians, but "the timing of a meeting now is a mistake." Arafat, he said, "acts only when he is under pressure and isolated" and a meeting would "encourage him to continue with terror."[11] Terje Roed-Larsen, the UN Middle East envoy, decried the cancellation of the meeting, saying that Arafat and Peres were "the parents of the peace process that was conceived in Oslo" and that meeting might be "the last chance for peace-making after a year of bloodshed."[12] Peres commented, "I do not understand why Yassir Arafat has suddenly become an Osama bin Laden, while the prime minister had earlier given me the green light to meet him." Washington too was not pleased by Sharon's Osama bin Laden talk; the Israelis received signals that they should keep a low profile, as they had during theGulf war. Colin Powell told the Arabic TV network al-Jazeera that he "saw no role for Israel in any military response" to bin Laden's Al Queda network.[13] Israeli officials said they understood the American position: "It's not the most important thing that we should be on the bandstand at the victory parade," Sharon's advisor Zalman Shoval said. "We are not going to force ourselves upon anyone. And our practical role in helping the effort—this is going to be there, with or without being official members of the coalition."[14]

On the Jewish New Year in the middle of September, Arafat said in Arabic that he had ordered his forces to observe a cease-fire and told reporters, "We Palestinians and Israelis have to work together to break the vicious cycle of violence," adding that Israel had the right to live within secure borders.[15] Sharon said he was dubious about Arafat's commitment but that he would allow Peres to hold talks with the chairman and would cease offensive operations if a cease-fire held for forty-eight hours. He sent his son Omri and Peres's senior aide Avi Gil to meet with Arafat and work out what statements would be issued and suspended actions against the Palestinians, ordering troops out of the territories.

Yassir Abed Rabbo called Sharon's call for forty-eight hours of peace "a game" to stall talks. "He will pretend that there was an incident here or there," Rabbo said. "As long as he is the judge, who can guarantee forty-eight hours or forty-eight minutes?" A Hamas spokesman in Ramallah said that his organization had "nothing to do" with Arafat's cease-fire. "We are still under occupation and attack by the Israeli army," he said.[16] Islamic Jihad also rejected the cease-fire. Alan Philps commented in the *Daily Telegraph,* "The Palestinians recognize that the world has changed since the attacks in New York and Washington last week, and that they cannot wage a struggle including suicide bombings inside Israel at a time when President Bush has declared a war on terrorism."[17] Terje Roed-Larsen said he sensed a shift on the Palestinian side, that there was "a strong belief" there "that power is no longer in the barrel of a gun, that power now is based on diplomatic instruments to be used at the negotiating table."[18]

A STRAW IN THE WIND

———

ON SEPTEMBER 12, REPORTER Derek Brown had written in the English *Guardian* that "contrary to the tawdry view which is peddled too often, the Arab and Islamic worlds are not teeming with crazed fanatics seeking holy martyrdom. . . . They feel sullied and threatened by the startling success of Israel in colonizing part of their region and they bitterly resent America's decisive role in that process. That is why they danced in the streets of occupied east Jerusalem . . ." In late September, the *Guardian* ran a front-page article speculating that President Bush had "forced" a cease-fire on Sharon and Arafat and had brought Sharon in particular "to heel" in order to keep Arabs and Muslims in his military coalition. The president, the *Guardian* said, was "taking a tougher line with Israel," and "In an indication of the extent to which patience with Sharon has ended, a senior British Foreign Office source described Mr Sharon as 'the cancer at the center of the Middle East crisis.'"[1]

A Foreign Office spokesman told the *Jerusalem Post* that these remarks "were in no way authorized" by the Foreign Office, which dissociated itself from them. He could not say whether these views were held within the Foreign Office, but he was definite that the *Guardian* had not fabricated the quotation; it had indeed come, he said, "from a senior British Foreign Office source."[2] The response from the Israeli embassy in London may be imagined.

At about this same time, British Foreign Secretary Jack Straw, the first British foreign secretary to visit Iran since the 1979 revolution as part of an effort to build a bridge to Tehran in the war against terrorism, published an article in an Iranian newspaper in which he said that "one of the factors that helps breed terrorism is the anger that many people in this region feel at events over the years in Palestine."[3] This comment infuriated the Israelis: first, because it implied that Israel itself was responsible for terrorist attacks upon it, and secondly, because of two references to "Palestine," an entity the Israelis did not recognize.

Sharon's spokesman Raanan Gissin said the remarks were "despicable" and "ignorant," bordering on anti-Semitism.[4] Ephraim Sneh called the article "an obscenity" and "a stab in the back" which "turns Israel from the victim of terrorism into the accused." Peres said he did not "accept these words" and that Palestinians had turned down two opportunities for a state, in 1947, and again at Camp David, and there was no justification for terror. The Israeli Foreign Ministry Director-General Avi Gill said, "This approach could lead to an escalation of terrorism . . . especially since the remarks were published in Iran, a country that supports terrorism, has an official policy calling for the destruction of Israel, and actively aids terrorist elements."[5] An Israeli diplomat said that Straw's comment, taken with a statement two weeks earlier by Jacques Huntziger, the French ambassador to Israel, differentiating between terror in Israel and terror in the US, reflected "a very disturbing trend in Europe."[6]

Sharon canceled a planned meeting with Straw, who was coming directly from Tehran, because of "scheduling problems,"[7] and Peres canceled a formal banquet in Straw's honor. Straw refused to apologize for his comments, saying that he had made "a statement of the obvious" and that his visit to the region "was always going to be sensitive for some people, but there is a bigger picture which is to build up an international consensus against the terrorist atrocities of 11 September." His aides went further, saying that there was no question of an apology and that it was "very important" to make sure countries like Iran "were on board."[8] At a news conference in

Iran, Straw rejected the description by Dr Kamal Kharrazi, the Iranian foreign minister, of Israel as a "racist Zionist regime." Britain, Straw said, had "consistently opposed violence for political ends committed against the Jewish population across the world, the people of Israel, and violence for political ends committed against Palestinians and others."[9]

This "balanced" approach did little to assuage Israeli anger. Downing Street tried to distance itself from Straw's remarks, saying it habitually referred to "the Palestinian territories" and not to "Palestine," and that there had been no intention to "cause offense in Israel," and neither the foreign secretary nor the government would in future refer to "Palestine."[10] But Tony Blair was forced to intervene personally, placing a fifteen-minute phone call to Sharon, whose aides said that the meetings would go ahead out of goodwill toward Blair, who had consistently supported Israel, and that Sharon would communicate his "anger, outrage and disappointment" directly to Jack Straw.[11] Blair had first heard about this imbroglio when he was phoned by Lord Levy, his special envoy to the Middle East, who was in Israel for Yom Kippur, and who in turn had been awakened by Peres and told that Straw's visit was going to be boycotted. Lord Levy, after talking to Blair, had been able to assure Peres that British policy had not changed, and to set up the phone call between Blair and Sharon.[12]

Blair was reportedly furious that he had not been shown an advance copy of the controversial article; according to the *Sunday Telegraph*, the Foreign Office had ignored normal procedure and failed to send the copy to Downing Street.[13] In addition, the Israel desk at the Foreign Office, which would certainly have raised objections, had not been consulted. A senior diplomatic official said that "any self-respecting enlightened country would have declared Straw persona non grata after his comments. Could you imagine what would have happened had an Israeli minister gone to Britain and justified the IRA by saying that its actions are the result of the British treatment of the Catholics?" Israeli officials were careful to distinguish between Straw, whom they repeatedly described as "inexperienced," and Blair considered by the government and the Foreign Ministry to be a strong friend of Israel.[14]

When he was asked before his meeting with Sharon, if he apologized for his statement, Straw responded that he was looking forward to his meeting with the prime minister. The Foreign Secretary did however have an eighty-minute meeting with Sharon, which seemed to have had a healing effect on the situation so that Straw was granted VIP status for the rest of his visit. Noting the onset of Yom Kippur, he said, "I come in knowledge of the appalling cruelties that men, women and children in Israel have suffered through the cause of terrorism." But as far as an apology went, he said, "I am not going to get involved in any textual analysis. I stand very firmly against terrorism."[15]

Levy's intervention was seen by some as an embarrassment for Straw, since Blair had bypassed the Foreign Office to rely on what the *Daily Telegraph* referred to as "the crony network" when it came to "delicate dealings in the Middle East."[16] On the day after all this, Iran announced it was withdrawing its full support for the war in Afghanistan, leaving the impression that Secretary Straw's mission had failed. The *Telegraph* reported that Downing Street was angry at the Foreign Office's failure to prevent the incident, but believed that it was a "cock-up" rather than a deliberate attempt to press a more pro-Arab policy. "It is probable," an official said, "that the Iran desk was overexcited by the prospect of reopening relations with Tehran and let their enthusiasm run away."[17]

A week or so later, Ben Bradshaw, the junior Foreign Office minister, standing in for Straw at a meeting arranged by the Labour Middle East Council and Trade Union Friends of Palestine, said that Sharon's "constant insistence that there should be no talks until there had been forty-eight hours of absolute quiet plays straight into the hands of those extremists and terrorist groups. In fact, it gives them a veto over the process." Bradshaw went on to maintain that Tony Blair had not apologized to Sharon for Straw's remarks. "The idea that there is some split between the Foreign Office and Number Ten is absolutely wrong," Bradshaw said. "It is used by the Israelis. They play this game with the Americans between the State Department and the White House. It happens all the time. It happens every time. We learn to expect it. There was no apology given whatsoever to the Israeli government or to Mr Sharon following Jack's remarks. There was no retraction of any of those remarks."[18]

The Israeli embassy in London refused comment.

OCTOBER UPROAR

———

BARELY A WEEK AFTER SHIMON Peres and Arafat met and agreed to a reaffirmation of the cease-fire, at least eighteen Palestinians died and more than 200 were wounded in the territories in clashes with troops. More than a dozen Israelis were wounded in Palestinian mortar attacks. There was a car bombing by Islamic Jihad in Jerusalem, but no one was injured. Peres was upset by a cabinet decision to give Arafat just forty-eight more hours to enforce the cease-fire. In an interview with *Yediot Aharonoth*, Peres accused senior army officers, who he said did not understand "Palestinian distress," of undertaking a mud-slinging campaign against him and said that Maj. Gen. Moshe Yaalon, the deputy chief of staff, was plotting to kill Arafat. In Cairo, Arafat more or less agreed, saying that Israeli political and military officials were "deliberately escalating" violence to undermine the cease-fire.[1] This opinion was shared to some extent by the Israeli Left: Yossi Sarid said that Sharon was not committed to the cease-fire: "otherwise it is impossible to explain the especially large number killed and wounded on the Palestinian side."[2]

"Let's say we assassinate [Arafat]," Peres said. "What happens next? With all the criticism of Arafat, he is the Palestinian who recognizes the map on which Jordan and Israel exist. In his place will come Hamas, Islamic Jihad and Hezbollah." Peres distanced himself further from Sharon by disagreeing with the prime minister's often-repeated assertion that Arafat was Israel's bin Laden. "Bin

Laden," Peres said, "has no nation and country. He wouldn't stop at anything. You can't say that about Arafat."[3]

These statements, as was inevitable, drew a harsh response from the Right. Internal Security Minister Uzi Landau told Israel Radio that Peres had hurt Israel badly by agreeing to meet with Arafat and "blurring the distinction between the good guys and the bad guys." He compared the meeting to Peres's opposition to the bombing of the Iraqi nuclear reactor in 1981.[4] Interior Minister Eli Yishai and Labor and Social Affairs Minister Shlomo Benizri called on Sharon to take over policy explanations from Peres, whose views Benizri said did not represent the majority of the government. Rehavam Zeevi, the tourism minister, and Avigdor Lieberman, the national infrastructure minister, announced they were forming an "anti-Peres coalition," but Uzi Landau said he would not join it, and Tzipi Livni, who was in charge of public relations for the prime minister, defended Peres, saying that he and Sharon decided government policy together.[5]

Finally, Sharon called on the ministers to refrain from public criticism of Peres. "Let's learn from the great United States what unity is," he said. "We are in a difficult time and I ask of every minister to respect the opinion of his colleague, even if he doesn't agree with it." At the same time, Sharon phoned Colin Powell to make a personal plea that the US include Hamas, Islamic Jihad and Hezbollah on its list of terrorist groups targeted after the September 11 attack on the World Trade Center.[6]

The *New York Times* reported that the Bush administration had planned that, in the last week of September at the United Nations General Assembly meeting in New York, Colin Powell would give a speech announcing a new Middle East peace initiative with a Palestinian state as a key element, and that Bush would meet Arafat there. But after September 11, the UN gathering had to be canceled because New York's public safety agencies were overburdened.[7] Although the administration badly wanted Arab cooperation in the coalition against terrorism, the Israeli-Palestinian initiative was postponed. Richard Boucher of the State Department said there was no speech scheduled, and no decisions had been made before September 11 on ending the Israeli-Palestinian violence.[8] Dennis Ross said he thought it would be very difficult for the Bush administration to proceed at that time with a new framework for peace, even if they had decided "what to put in it," which he doubted. "The mood of the Israeli and Palestinian public is all wrong for that," he said, "because you have got a situation where neither side thinks he has a partner for peace."[9]

Despite these reports that the US was going to support a Palestinian state, and despite an agreement between Peres and Arafat to make a "maximum effort" to enforce the latest cease-fire, the situation deteriorated in the first week of October. On October 3, two Palestinian gunmen attacked a settlement on the northern edge of the Gaza Strip, killing a young couple and wounding fifteen others, seven of whom were soldiers, before being shot dead by Israeli sharpshooters after a three-hour standoff. The gunmen had cut their way through a flimsy fence; the settlers had asked repeatedly for a stronger, electrified barricade, but the government had refused to spend the money. Hamas claimed responsibility for the attack, saying that "Zionist security" was "soft and weak."[10] Some Palestinian policemen in Gaza called the gunmen heroes, "winners twice over . . . because they are martyrs who will go to paradise. And they have won because they have killed settlers living illegally on our land." But the policemen said they supported the cease-fire and if they had seen the gunmen, they would have arrested them, because they wanted to prove to Sharon that they were doing their best.[11] Israeli tanks shelled PA territory in Gaza south of the settlement, killing six, while Sharon made a speech accusing Arafat of not abiding by the cease-fire. This despite the fact that Arafat condemned the attack and promised "a quick and decisive limit" to breaches of the cease-fire.[12] A Hamas political leader in Gaza said he did not believe there would be large-scale arrests. "I don't think the Palestinian streets will agree," he said, "and the arrest of one or two will have no effect."[13]

Earlier in the day Arafat had responded to Israeli demands by arresting Atef Abayat, a militant leader in Bethlehem, accused of a drive-by killing two weeks earlier. Then on October 4, a Palestinian disguised as an Israeli fired an assault rifle helter-skelter into a crowded bus station in the central town of Afula, killing three and wounding at least thirteen. The next day tanks, helicopter gunships and troops attacked Hebron where for the past few days Palestinian snipers had been firing on Jewish residents and tourists. At least five Palestinians were killed in gun battles and twelve wounded in shelling. Yassir Abed Rabbo, the PA information minister, accused Israel of using any pretext to undermine the cease-fire.[14] The Israelis canceled plans to ease travel restrictions between Palestinian cities in the West Bank and said they might resume targeted killings. A CIA-mediated security meeting between the two sides, scheduled for October 3, was also canceled.

Sharon reacted with anger, telling a Christian group that he had given in to American requests for a meeting between Peres and Arafat, and more killings were his thanks. "The world was happy," Sharon said. "Arafat declared a cease-fire, but the fire did not stop for one minute. The world demanded, they said it would be important if our minister of foreign affairs, Mr Shimon Peres, would meet with Arafat. . . . The pressure stopped. They met. The reaction was terror, and again terror, and again terror."[15] Sharon was upset on several counts. The newspaper *Yediot Aharonoth* had said that "Israel continues to play the fool" by holding discussions with Arafat in the midst of all the violence, and a settlers' council had accused Sharon of breaking his promise to protect the citizens of Israel. His government, they said, "project[ed] confusion" and "a lack of decisiveness in the struggle against terror." Sharon was frustrated also by Washington's unwillingness to include Hamas, Hezbollah, Islamic Jihad and similar groups in their list of terrorist organizations.[16]

The result of all this was that at a late-night news conference called to comment on the apparently accidental shooting-down over the Black Sea of a Russian airliner carrying seventy-six Israelis, Sharon did not stop at condemning the Palestinians, but went on to direct his anger at US policy as well. Washington, he said, was sacrificing Israel to bring Arab states into Bush's anti-terrorism coalition. "Do not," he thundered, "try to appease the Arabs at our expense." Israel, he said, making an unfortunate comparison to Neville Chamberlain's sacrifice of Czechoslovakia in the failed attempt to appease Hitler in 1938, "will not be Czechoslovakia. We will not be able to accept that. Israel will fight terrorism."[17]

This, called by the New York Times "an unusually harsh and public rebuke of Israel's most valued ally,"[18] provoked an equally harsh response from the Bush administration. Ari Fleischer, the White House press secretary, throwing Sharon's "acceptable" comment back at him, said, "The prime minister's comments are unacceptable," and denied that US policy would sacrifice Israel's security.[19] The president's displeasure was communicated officially through the National Security Council and the American embassy in Israel. In Israel, too, Sharon's remarks were roundly criticized, and leaders of Jewish organizations hurried to assure the president that they were behind him, although they too expressed concerns about US relations with Islamic nations hostile to Israel and about the lists of terrorist organizations. On American television, the talk-show host Geraldo Rivera, apparently confusing Chamberlain with Hitler, expressed outrage that Sharon had compared the Americans to Nazis. In Israel, Nahum Barnea, a columnist for Yediot Aharonoth, said, "Mentioning Munich was a gross exaggeration, a mistake, and even Israeli public opinion cannot buy that argument and saw it as hysterical."[20]

Colin Powell said he had spoken to Sharon by phone after the prime minister's outburst and, "I don't think there is anything to that comment. From time to time we have these little cloudbursts. But that doesn't affect the strength of our relationship."[21] Sharon told American and Israeli newspapers that he was sorry his "metaphor" of Czechoslovakia had been misunderstood and he praised Bush for his "courageous decision" to eradicate terrorism.[22] The *New York Times* reported that Sharon expressed regret five times in less than five minutes. An Israeli official said, "Sharon is caught. If he escalates, he angers the Americans. If he starts negotiating, he loses his right wing and maybe his government."[23] Serge Schmemann pointed out in the *New York Times* that Sharon, sitting on "a very fragile coalition of left and right" was "keenly aware that both his predecessors, Ehud Barak and Benjamin Netanyahu, fell from power because they could not keep their coalitions together" and his determination "not to follow suit" required "a keen balancing act, for example, excoriating Mr Arafat at every turn while letting the dovish foreign minister, Shimon Peres, meet with him."[24]

Asher Susser, a professor of Middle Eastern history at Tel Aviv University, commented, "A lot of people are very critical of the way Sharon said what he said. But it was expressive of a real Israeli frustration. We who are on the receiving end of so much terrorism are being left out, while Yassir Arafat and Syria are being courted. There is a certain anxiety that Israel may be pushed aside." Professor Susser, recalling earlier "bumpier periods" of US-Israeli relations, mentioned the cut-off of supplies of American aircraft after Israel destroyed the Iraqi nuclear reactor in the early '80s, and concluded that he was sure "they will smooth this over and there will not be a long-term downturn."[25]

On October 8, Sharon's office issued a statement saying that Israel would offer "all help possible" to the US in the war in Afghanistan, but would not take part in that war. Colin Powell had publicly ruled out any Israeli military role in this conflict, just as the

Americans had asked Israel to remain passive in the Gulf war in order to avoid alienating Arab partners.[26] After an emergency meeting held to assess the risks of attacks on Israel in response to the bombing in Afghanistan, an IDF spokesman said that the general staff was not worried, but would keep on the alert. In Tel Aviv, Israelis, remembering Iraqi missile attacks during the Gulf war, lined up for gas masks.[27]

The Palestinian reaction to the attack on Afghanistan was more ambiguous. A month after the World Trade Center tragedy, PA leaders were unresponsive to press inquiries. One reached by phone told James Bennet of the *New York Times* that he was waiting for an official reaction before responding. Bennet commented that the PA did not want to make the same mistake they made when their support of Saddam Hussein in the Gulf war resulted in the loss of some of their international backing; he quoted Dr Ziad Abu Amr, a political scientist and chairman of the political committee of the Palestinian Legislative Council, who said that "emotions" were with bin Laden, but there would be no gambling on his position, because Palestinians were skeptical of Arab support for their cause.[28]

To add to Sharon's October headaches, on September 30, the state comptroller, Eliezer Goldberg accused him of campaign funding irregularities in the February, 2001 elections in connection with a $1.4 million donation from Annex Research, an overseas company that was apparently set up by one of Sharon's lawyers and run by his son Omri. The comptroller also raised questions about campaign salaries to several of Sharon's friends, including Omri, who refused to cooperate with Goldberg's office. Sharon, the report said, may have broken the law by setting up fictitious companies to transfer funds from abroad to his campaign. It is illegal in Israel for foreigners to make donations to political campaigns.[29]

Several days later, Attorney General Rubinstein ordered police to open a criminal investigation against Sharon and Omri. Sharon responded that Omri alone dealt with money matters and vowed to return any money received illegally, something he had already begun to do. In an August 27 letter to Goldberg, Sharon said he had first learned of the existence of Annex Research when he read a draft of the comptroller's report earlier in the year and he agreed to return about $1 million that the comptroller said had been spent illegally in the campaign for Likud leadership. Sharon's office stated that the prime minister and his son had "full faith in the judicial system and . . . the decision taken was acceptable to them." On November 12, Sharon's office announced that the prime minister had taken out a bank loan to pay the money back. There were rumors that he had taken out a mortgage on Sycamore Ranch.[30]

Goldberg's report held accusations of campaign-funding abuse not only against Sharon but against several other political parties. This was not unusual; since the mid-90s, when a new law—now rescinded—called for the direct election of the prime minister, and expensive primaries began to be held, Israeli politicians had repeatedly been accused of fund-raising irregularities. Goldberg had fined both Likud and Labor for violating campaign laws. Barak's aides had been questioned by police about setting up dummy nonprofit organizations to launder money from foreigners for his 1999 campaign. These questions were similar to those raised about actions by Sharon and Omri, except that the latter were accused of using a corporation rather than an ostensibly nonpartisan nonprofit organization. No charges were filed against Barak, but in October 2001 the investigation was still open.[31]

ZEEVI

———

ON OCTOBER 15, AVIGDOR Lieberman, the infrastructure minister, and Rehavam Zeevi, the tourism minister, resigned from the government; their seven-person National Unity Party became part of the opposition. Zeevi said he had been unhappy for a long time with Peres's influence on the coalition, and with Sharon's endorsement of a Palestinian state, and that the IDF's withdrawal after ten days from two Palestinian neighborhoods in Hebron, had been "the last straw."[1] The IDF Chief of Staff, General Shaul Mofaz, had also expressed opposition to the Hebron withdrawal, but apologized a few days later on the 15th, saying he had not intended to "oppose the decisions of the political echelon."[2] Sharon still had the support of seventy-six of the 120 MKs, and may well have been relieved that he no longer had to deal with two of his most right-wing critics: Lieberman had said that the greatest challenge before the state of Israel was how to "stymie" a new peace initiative by the Bush administration.[3] But Sharon recognized that he still had to worry about retaining his Likud support while avoiding alienating the Americans. "You have caused me great anguish," he said publicly to Lieberman and Zeevi. "But by contrast you have given Arafat great pleasure today. For him this is a dream."[4]

Sharon's outline for a future Palestinian state was tough: Israel would insist on maintaining sovereignty over Jerusalem, security areas in the West Bank and the "external borders" of a demilitarized Palestine, which would not be allowed to sign treaties with nations hostile to Israel. This position was certainly less generous than Barak's, offering no more than the forty percent of territory the PA already controlled, but nevertheless it represented a moderation of Sharon's previous stance.

The situation took an unexpected turn two days later when gunmen shot and killed Zeevi in a hallway outside his room in the Hyatt Hotel in Jerusalem. At about 7:00 am, the minister was just returning from breakfast to his eighth-floor room when he was shot three times in the head and face. His wife found him lying on his back in the corridor in a pool of blood. Sharon immediately called a cabinet meeting. It was past midnight when the cabinet demanded that the Palestinian Authority immediately extradite those behind the attack as well as "other terrorist organizations operating in the Palestinian areas."[5] The coalition government unanimously declared that Arafat was a sponsor of terrorism. Sharon rescinded a loosening of travel curbs he had ordered three days before and virtually sealed off Ramallah, Nablus and Jenin, ordering tanks and armored vehicles into those PA cities, triggering fights which left three Palestinians dead, including a twelve-year-old girl. Tanks rolled to within a half-mile of Arafat's headquarters in Ramallah. Diplomatic relations with the PA were frozen, and Arafat was banned from using the PA airport in the Gaza Strip. "Everything has changed," Sharon told the cabinet. "The situation is different today, and it will not be like it was yesterday."[6]

The Popular Front for the Liberation of Palestine announced that a "special squad" had hunted down Zeevi in revenge for the killing on August 27 of their leader Mustafa Zibri, known as Abu Ali Mustafa, when Israeli helicopters fired two missiles into his offices in Ramallah.[7] Over the year, Israel had killed more than fifty Palestinians, including several bystanders, in these targeted assassinations. Al Jazeera, the Arabic television network, showed a videotape of three men, faces covered by red-and-white head cloths, one of whom said, "The head of the criminal Zeevi will be the first step on the path of tit-for-tat."[8] Lyla Khaled, a PFLP militant, said the group intended to kill more Israeli politicians and that Sharon was at the top of the list. The Palestinians said they had "uncovered" an Israeli plot to kill Arafat; the Israelis said that was nonsense.[9]

Arafat's spokesman Yassir Abed Rabbo expressed regret for Zeevi's murder but said, in answer to the demand that the killers be turned over to Israel, "The answer is no." By agreement, he added, the PA had the right to try anyone arrested in its territory. Palestinian security forces, he said, were searching for those responsible. He said also that Sharon had provoked the attack because of his policy of assassination. "We think he shared the responsibility with those who committed the crime," Rabbo said. The PA announced that it had brought three members of the PFLP in for questioning, but let them go. PA sources announced that the PA remained committed to a truce with Israel, but denied the Israeli assertion that the PA had been given the names of Zeevi's killers and their handlers. In any case, Rabbo said, "We do not receive our orders or directions from Sharon."[10]

There were some cautionary voices. Sari Nusseibeh, a moderate Palestinian who was president of Al Quds University in east Jerusalem, and who had replaced the late Faisal al-Husseini as Palestinian representative there, commented, "It's as if, somehow, history was being determined not by rational choices but by a series of acts perpetrated by people on the fringes, who nevertheless affect the course of events."[11] Nusseibeh, who came from a prominent Jerusalem family and was respected by many Israelis, had called for the demand for the right of return to be dropped, and had criticized the intifada as futile, although he had been active in the first intifada. He had been jailed by the Israelis for three months during the Gulf war, and severely beaten by Palestinian militants in 1987 for meeting with right-wing Israeli politicians. Nusseibeh's moderate words were echoed by Dalia Rabin-Pelossof, a deputy minister, who said, "We must stop, take a deep breath, wait for a day, comprehend the trauma, hold the funeral, and only then think long and hard about where we go from here."[12] Yossi Sarid, as the leader of the opposition, took the opportunity to remind the country that the attempted assassination in 1982 of Israel's ambassador to London, had given Sharon a "pretext" to invade Lebanon.[13]

The Bush administration reacted sharply to Zeevi's killing, calling on the PA to "immediately find and bring to justice those who committed this murder, as well as those who would do harm to efforts to restore an atmosphere of calm and security for Israelis and Palestinians," Bush Communications Director Ari Fleischer said. "It is not enough for the Palestinian Authority to condemn the slaying. Words are not enough. It is time for the Palestinian Authority to take vigorous action against terrorists."[14] This position was echoed by Terje Roed-Larsen, the UN special envoy to the region, generally considered a friend of the Palestinians, who also said, "Words are not enough . . . the test is now," and admonished Arafat that he would have to "arrest the culprits and prove himself capable of leading and controlling his people."[15] Shimon Peres, who was alone among Israeli officials in communicating with Arafat, warned the chairman that if he did not act, "everything will go up in flames."[16]

But this presented a difficult situation for Arafat, who had invited the PFLP to relocate to the West Bank in 2000 as part of his "reconciliation dialogue" with Palestinian factions. There was strong popular support for the militants among his people. The PFLP deputy secretary-general, Abdul Rahim Mallouh, said on Al Jazeera that he was sure that Arafat had "enough political wisdom" not to try to squeeze fellow Palestinians.[17] Hassan Youssef, a Hamas spokesman, said that extradition was "absolutely unacceptable for the Palestinian street" and that Arafat would face a popular rebellion if he handed over the suspects to Israel.[18] And indeed, a few days earlier, crowds of stone-throwers in the Gaza Strip had driven off Palestinian policemen who were trying to arrest a radical Islamic imam from Hamas. In November, when the Palestinian police took

Mahmoud Tawalbi, an Islamic Jihad leader wanted by Israel for recruiting suicide bombers, off a Jenin street and jailed him in Nablus, about 3000 Palestinians surrounded Palestinian Preventive Security headquarters in Jenin, burning cars, hurling grenades and firing guns.

There was considerable anger in the Israeli streets as well. Zeevi's state funeral was attended by thousands and his son, Yiftah-Palmach Zeevi, after addressing the Palestinians as "temporary residents in this land of Canaan," called out to an impassive Sharon for revenge: "Arik, avenge as 'Ghandi' would have avenged your death. And go back to being the leader we once knew."[19] Zeevi's nickname was "Ghandi," despite his twenty-six-year military career and his refusal to countenance compromise with the Palestinians. The reference was to his slender build and some of his behavior as a youth, rather than to his politics.

Zeevi, 75, the father of five and the grandfather of eighteen, was the sixth generation of his family to be born in Jerusalem, and deeply resented Arab statements that Jews had little historical claim to the region. He had been a member of the Palmach and the Haganah, was one of the last of the commanders who had fought in the 1948 war alongside Rabin and Sharon, and from 1964 to 1968 he had headed the Central Command in an area including the West Bank. He had entered politics in 1988, founding Moledet, or Homeland, a small right-wing party that called for the "transfer" of Palestinians out of the West Bank and Gaza Strip to areas east of the Jordan River. His strong feelings led him to stage a hunger strike with two other far-right MKs to protest the 1993 Oslo accords, to compare Arafat to Hitler, and to refer to illegal Palestinian workers in Israel as "lice" and a "cancer spreading within us." He often said that Arafat should be "eliminated" if he did not accept "a one-way ticket to Tunis."[20]

Zeevi was not averse to attracting attention, keeping a caged lion as a mascot in his headquarters near Jerusalem and once modelling a cowboy outfit, including boots and a ten-gallon hat, in newspaper ads for his daughter's upmarket boutique. He was, however, considered to be agreeable, friendly and courteous by both Right and Left, including Arab MKs—despite his public heckling of opponents in parliament—and was respected for his considerable knowledge of the Holy Land, having amassed a huge library of Holy Land history and travel books, and running a small publishing house that brought out facsimiles of rare books. He edited some seventy publications on Israeli history. He had also founded and ran the Tel Aviv Haaretz Museum of archaeological artifacts and other Jewish memorabilia.

Zeevi appeared to court danger, often going into the West Bank without a bodyguard and carrying an Uzi submachine gun. In fact, with his somewhat swaggering demeanor, he refused all security service offers of bodyguards. He lived in a suburb of Tel Aviv, but stayed in Jerusalem when the Knesset was in session. Other MKs stayed in west Jerusalem and were careful to move from time to time. Zeevi, however, insisted on staying only in the Hyatt, which is on the line between east and west Jerusalem. His lack of caution had helped to create an extremely serious situation. According to Tracy Wilkinson in the *Los Angeles Times,* "analysts and diplomats" conjectured that Zeevi's assassination might "prove a turning point toward disaster . . . or toward new actions, especially by the Palestinians, that could ultimately ease tensions."[21] There is no question that the assassination marked a turning point: "As far as I'm concerned," Sharon supposedly told his cabinet, "the era of Arafat is over."[22] Shimon Peres voted in favor of a cabinet statement warning Arafat that if he did not move against his "coalition of terror," Israel would act against the PA.[23] Most significant were the words of Avraham Burg, a former Peace Now leader and Labour Party moderate, who had refused on principle to join Sharon's coalition. "The dead man's blood," Burg said, addressing Arafat, "fills your hands."[24]

Tony Blair phoned Arafat, who was trapped in Gaza by a travel ban, and urged him to act to calm the situation. Colin Powell, concerned that new violence would undermine weak Arab support for the campaign in Afghanistan, put off a major keynote address on the Middle East, phoned Sharon as well as Arafat, and discussed the situation with Jordan's King Abdullah, the Egyptian foreign minister and Javier Solana of the EU. Italy's Prime Minister Silvio Berlusconi asked Sharon to behave with moderation. Hosni Mubarak, caught in something of a bind because of his support for US action against Al Queda, told *Newsweek* that the Israeli-Palestinian conflict was not the reason for bin Laden's attacks on the US. "Osama bin Laden made his explosions and then started talking about the Palestinians," Mubarak said. "He never talked about them before." Mubarak also said that Arafat "has some terrible people around him, like [Marwan] Barghouti," and that Sharon had made promises to him, but had implemented none of them. Saudi Arabia's King Fuad sent a letter to Mubarak warning of the "dangerous situation in Palestine, the continuity of the Israeli aggression on the Palestinian people and the necessity of working to stop such practices so that peace talks could resume."[25]

Israeli tanks and troops pushed into Palestinian territory, tightened roadblocks, fought in the streets of Bethlehem and seven other Palestinian towns, and generally began to conduct what was called the "broadest military campaign" since the Oslo agreement was signed in 1993, despite threats from Labor Party MKs to leave the government, and despite condemnation from the Bush administration who called the incursion "unacceptable," while calling on Arafat to arrest Zeevi's assassins. Arafat responded by arresting two dozen PFLP members and outlawing the PFLP's military arm, an act that infuriated extremist Palestinian groups. Thousands of right-wing Israelis, mostly settlers, held a rally in Jerusalem calling for the expulsion of Arafat and the toppling of his regime.[26]

On November 15, Shimon Peres told the UN General Assembly that his people supported the formation of a Palestinian state, and, although this prompted hard-line cabinet ministers to call for Peres's dismissal, a week later a Gallup poll in the daily *Maariv* bore him out: fifty-nine percent of Israelis said they supported the creation of a state to thirty-six percent who did not support it. Seventy-three percent believed there would be a Palestinian state, regardless of what they thought.[27] A week after that, the *Jerusalem Post* ran the results of another poll which found that sixty-eight percent of the Israeli Jews polled believed that the establishment of a Palestinian state, no matter what its size or strength, would constitute a threat to the State of Israel.[28]

In late November, Sharon received an honorary doctorate from Ben-Gurion University in the Negev as part of a series of events honoring David Ben-Gurion, who had stressed the importance of developing the southern Negev and worked to encourage settlement there. Sharon, whose farm was of course in the Negev, was honored for his work in developing the desert area and for building Israel's security. In his address, Sharon said he loved the Negev, "its open spaces, its wonderful landscapes and the fascinating past embedded in its earth," and would "always return to this place." He said the vision of a "blossoming" Negev was yet to be realized. "The blossoming Negev will be the land of peace. The Negev has always been a bridge between cultures; here Israel and the Arab countries can meet on the shores of the Red Sea, extract the treasures of the Dead Sea, and develop the Mediterranean coastline in Rafiah, Gaza, and Ashkelon.[29]

Although the university faculty senate in the main supported the degree for Sharon, thirty-seven lecturers sent a petition to the president of the university protesting the honor because Sharon was a man who relied on force and had "created a deep controversy" that divided the country. David Newman, chair of the Department of Politics and Government at the university, wrote in the *Jerusalem Post*, "Sharon may be a democratically elected prime minister, he may have contributed a great deal to the country at different times in his checkered history, but his infamous past record, not least during the Lebanon War, for which he was publicly reprimanded by the Kahan Commission, means that he is unworthy to receive such an honor from an institution which should set an example in the promotion of ethical and moral standards."[30]

A group of about thirty students, some members of Young Meretz and some Israeli Arabs, protested outside the university gates on the day of the award, wearing robes and holding signs saying "Sharon is a doctor of assassinations, unemployment and Lebanon." Amir Rosenblitt, a spokesman for the university, said that Yitzhak Rabin had also received an honorary degree and that that honor too had been protested. Sharon, Rosenblitt said, had worked "tirelessly to advance the region and has acted as a true partner of Ben-Gurion University. Sharon has dedicated the best years of his life both in and out of uniform to the Jewish state."[31]

Objections to Sharon were somewhat less mild in parts of the Arab world. On November 17, Abu Dhabi Television, the second most popular Arab TV station, presented the first episode in a series on Sharon called "Terrorism" to be broadcast during Ramadan. In an excerpt broadcast on Israel TV, a character portraying Sharon was shown drinking the blood of Arab children and expressing satisfaction while Israeli soldiers shot Arabs in the back, and a grotesque Orthodox person looked on. In another skit, Dracula was shown biting Sharon and dying himself because Sharon's blood was poisonous.[32]

Peres, calling the show "repulsive," lodged a formal complaint with the UN over the airing of the series. Guy Verhofstadt, the Belgian prime minister, who was in Israel as the head of an EU delegation said the depiction was a "scandal." Ferrero, an Italian firm which advertised its Kinder brand of chocolate on the program, announced it would immediately end its involvement there. Proctor & Gamble, which advertised its Pantene Shampoo on the program, also pulled its ads. "We made a mistake," a P&G spokeswoman said, "and we have taken steps to correct it." The director of Abu Dhabi TV said that Peres seemed to have lost his sense of humor.[33]

79

ZINNI'S DAYS

———

What ensued from the Zeevi assassination were incursions, pull-backs, shelling, shootings on both sides, demonstrations, calls for withdrawals and negotiation from the US and other foreign governments, handshakes between Peres and Arafat, and terrorist attacks on crowded buses. Nevertheless, the Bush administration decided to enter the fray by sending retired Marine Corps General Anthony Zinni as the new US special envoy to the Middle East. On the eve of a five-day visit to the United States, Sharon irritated Peres by appointing Meir Dagan, a counterterrorism expert, to head talks with Zinni, instead of a higher level team headed by Peres himself. The *Jerusalem Post* reported that Peres said, "You are bypassing me and establishing a second Foreign Ministry." He said achieving a cease-fire required an experienced negotiator like himself with a "diplomatic vision." He disagreed too with Sharon's demand that there must be seven days of quiet before negotiations could begin; Sharon had also said, "In the end, we will reach a solution in which there will be a Palestinian state," but this could be reached only through a series of interim arrangements. Peres said he accepted Sharon's directive, because Labor had lost the election, and must remain in the government to encourage a diplomatic solution; he doubted, he said, that Labor would be in power any time in the next six years.[1]

It was not perhaps Peres whom Sharon saw as a threat. Polls showed that Netanyahu had fifty-percent support against Sharon's thirty-five percent. The *Chicago Sun-Times* reported that as Sharon chatted with Israeli journalists in the Knesset cafeteria, one of the reporters said that he sometimes fantasized that an Apache gunship fired a missile through the window of a certain house in east Jerusalem with a huge Israeli flag flying in front of it. After a pause, Sharon said, "I didn't know Netanyahu had a pilot's license."[2]

Zinni arrived in Israel in the last week of November. He, Assistant Secretary of State William Burns, US Ambassador Daniel Kurtzer and Sharon embarked on a four-hour helicopter tour of Israel and the West Bank; before noon two gunmen from the Jenin refugee camp, wearing tracksuits, opened fire, shooting indiscriminately at passers-by with Kalashnikov rifles near the central bus station in the northern Israeli town of Afula, ten miles north of Jenin, killing two and wounding dozens before they were shot dead by police. Islamic Jihad and Fatah told Reuters they had carried out the attack to avenge the death of Mahmoud Abu Hanoud, a Hamas leader who had been killed a few days earlier near Jenin.[3] Fifteen people were hospitalized, five in serious condition. As the helicopter hovered over the chaotic scene, the Americans watched the wounded being evacuated from bloodstained streets. Later that night a Palestinian opened fire on a convoy near Jewish settlements in the Gaza Strip, killing one woman and wounding three others, including a two-year-old girl. Hamas claimed responsibility for the attack, and the PA denounced it. The Islamic Jihad claimed responsibility for a suicide bombing on a bus heading for Tel Aviv in which three Israeli passengers were killed. Big celebrations of the attack in Jenin, the home of the bomber, were quickly shut down by Arafat.[4]

At the end of the day, which in addition to the helicopter tour included briefings with the entire Israeli political and military establishment, Zinni said he had learned a lot. It was "a very valuable day," he said, "a long day but a very valuable day." The killing, he said, pointed out "the importance of gaining a cease-fire and as the prime minister said, the cease-fire is what we need so we can get on to something more comprehensive and more lasting."[5]

But these attacks were the prelude to what the *Independent* called "a twelve-hour blitz of violence."[6] Shortly after 11:30 pm on December 1, Jerusalem was hit by a massive double explosion as two Hamas suicide bombers, standing about thirty yards from each other, blew themselves up simultaneously in the Ben Yehuda shopping promenade, down the street from the Sbarro pizzeria. The blasts were so powerful that they shattered the windows of cars parked a block away. Blood was splattered across store fronts and the ground was strewn with pieces of flesh and metal bolts from the explosives.[7] Ten young Israelis, ranging in age from fourteen to twenty, who were strolling outside coffee bars and sitting at sidewalk cafes, were killed, and about 180 more were taken to the hospital. Half an hour later, as workers were trying to tend to the wounded, a booby-trapped car exploded and burst into flames fifty yards away on the other side of the Jaffa Road. The intention was apparently to hit rescue workers and spectators, but they escaped injury. Nevertheless, the health minister, Nissim Dahan, said there were so many casualties that the hospitals were "almost at the limit of our capacity to take in the wounded."[8]

The Palestinian Authority expressed its "deep anger . . . and pain" and accused the perpetrators of trying to derail the US peace process.[9] The Israelis, President Bush and General Zinni called on Arafat to do more to rein in terrorism; Saeb Erekat said "finger pointing and assigning blame is wrong," and Israel must come back to the negotiating table.[10] Hamas did not immediately claim responsibility, but Abdel Aziz Rantisi, a Hamas leader in the Gaza Strip, said that Hamas would not cease to attack. "We have said several times that we are not going to accept the occupation to remain in our land,"[11] he said. "We are fighting Jewish terrorism, we are fighting the killers and defending our freedom, our stability and our dignity."[12] Zinni said that the groups that had done this were clearly trying to make his mission fail, but they would not succeed. He was committed, he said, "to work for action on the ground and I will be here as long as it takes me."[13] Sharon, on a planned five-day visit to Washington and New York—where he had visited the site of the World Trade Center attack—rescheduled a meeting with Bush, Powell and Condoleezza Rice, so that he could return to Israel. The president, who came back from Camp David a day early for the emergency meeting, did not issue his usual call for restraint.[14]

The next morning another suicide bomber blew himself up on a crowded bus in Haifa, killing fifteen passengers and wounding at least forty-five, two critically. The *Independent*'s Phil Reeves said the bomb "tore the roof back like a sardine tin and buckled the vehicle's steel frame."[15] Haifa for a long time had been a symbol of hope for Arab-Jewish reconciliation, with good relations between the two groups; now members of both groups rushed into the street after the blast, giving water to the wounded and helping them into ambulances. Meir Shetreet, a construction worker, said, "In Haifa, there are no Arabs and Jews. Everyone is the same."[16] Palestinian gunmen in the territories, and in at least six Palestinian refugee camps in Lebanon, celebrated the attack by firing into the air, but some Palestinians said they were tired of the bloodshed. In the *Chicago Sun-Times*, Barry Schweid quoted an engineer in Gaza who said, "The world should help both of us, Israelis and Palestinians, to get out of this pool of blood."[17]

These attacks came at a bad time for Arafat, causing the onus on peace initiatives to shift from Sharon to the PA chairman, whose relevance began to be questioned by Bush administration officials. Bronwen Maddox in the London *Times* suggested that the success of the American offensive in Afghanistan had lessened their worries about keeping Arab countries in the anti-terrorist coalition.[18] Defense Secretary Donald Rumsfeld said, "[Arafat] is not a particularly strong leader. And I don't know that he has good control over the Palestinian situation."[19] Colin Powell said he had "made absolutely clear that these despicable and cowardly actions must be brought to an end through immediate, comprehensive and sustained action by the Palestinian Authority against both the individuals responsible and the infrastructure of those groups that support them."[20] On CNN Powell described the bombings as an attack on Arafat's authority as well as "a terrible attack against innocent Israelis."[21]

Sharon addressed the nation, saying that Arafat was "the greatest obstacle to peace and stability in the Middle East."[22] Israel, he said, would fight on principle against terrorism, but would not declare the PA "a terrorist entity." This angered the new tourism minister, Benny Elon, and the national infrastructure minister Avigdor Lieberman, who had rescinded his resignation from the cabinet after Zeevi's assassination. Before the speech, they threatened to resign if the government did not declare the PA a terrorist entity. The PA called the speech "a declaration of war" while the US announced that Israel had the right to defend itself.[23] Germany, Russia, Switzerland, Italy, the Pope and the EU condemned the attacks, as did Hosni Mubarak. Jack Straw too condemned them, although some in his Foreign Office tended to mitigate Arafat's responsibility for them.[24] French President Jacques Chirac equivocated, saying that "violence always triggers violence," and his foreign minister Hubert Vedrine said that "it would be a fatal error to lay the blame on the Palestinian Authority in order to weaken it or even eliminate it." Syria, another exception, placed the blame squarely on Israel.[25]

Arafat's security forces arrested over 100 suspected Islamic militants, including two Hamas leaders in Gaza, in a sweep derided by the Israelis as a charade designed to prevent Israeli reprisals. Palestinian security officials said, on condition of anonymity, that Sheikh Ahmed Yassin, the spiritual leader of Hamas, had been placed under house arrest and ordered not to speak to reporters. But Yassin's family said that they were not aware of these restrictions. Jibril Rajoub, head of the Palestinian Preventive Security Force, told Israeli Army Radio that these latest attacks ran against Palestinian "national interests" and "part of our mission is to stop some of the people who sent them." At the same time, he said he hoped that "the Israeli nation will understand our message and will understand that its closures and assassinations will not bring them security."[26]

The IDF blockaded towns in the West Bank as the IAF launched heavy air strikes against Palestinian targets. Nine missiles were fired from Apache helicopters at Arafat's Gaza City headquarters; two of his three Russian-made, Egyptian-supplied personal helicopters were destroyed along with the helipad, and the third helicopter was badly damaged. Seventeen Palestinians were wounded in the attack. Arafat, who was in Ramallah for Ramadan, had used these helicopters to travel between the West Bank and Gaza, so, as the army intended, his movements were immediately restricted. He would have had to ask Israel's permission to leave Ramallah. The helicopters were destroyed, the IDF spokesman said, because "they were symbols of his mobility and freedom."[27] Bulldozers plowed up the runways of the PA international airport, which had opened three years before amid great celebrations. The airport had actually been shut down since the intifada began in 2000, but a senior Israeli official said it had now been turned "into a flourishing greenhouse." Saeb Erekat called on Bush to "stop Sharon before it's too late." He added, "We're really going down the drain tonight."[28]

Shortly afterward, F-16s struck Jenin, hitting a police station and the governor's offices. Most of the security facilities, including the jail, had been destroyed earlier. In November, the arrest by Palestinian authorities of an Islamic Jihad commander in Jenin had triggered three days of riots involving more than 2500 people there. Palestinian police admitted that their men hesitated to arrest militants who were considered heroes by the population. Now at the Deheishe refugee camp on the outskirts of Bethlehem, a hostile crowd barred the policemen's way; young men fired in the air to get help and soon the narrow streets were filled with hundreds of people. The police did not make any arrests. In Nablus, about 1000 activists defied the police and marched in memory of the suicide bomber who had destroyed the bus and many of its passengers in Haifa.

Israel had given the PA a list of 100 most wanted men, but few of those were picked up, and the Israelis and Americans both believed that those who were picked up would be allowed to come and go at will, and that on several occasions PA jailers had shown more respect to their Hamas prisoners than to their own supervisors.

On December 4, the cabinet passed, by an eighteen-to-ten majority, the right-wing resolution declaring the PA a "terror-supporting entity" which should be "dealt with accordingly," and labeled as "terrorist groups"[29] Arafat's armed Fatah wing and his Force 17 security units. Labor Party ministers, including Peres, walked out on the meeting rather than vote on the resolution, which Sharon's spokesman Raanan Gissin said in effect prohibited any negotiations with the Palestinians, but could be reversed if Arafat really reined in the terrorists.[30]

There were splits on the issue within Labor. Some ministers accused Peres of using them to extort more power for himself from Sharon, and said that his threats to leave were making a mockery of the party because the public no longer believed them. Raanan Cohen, minister without portfolio, said, "We can't threaten a crisis every day. We need to stop these games and make a decision already." Defense Minister Ben-Eliezer told Peres, "If you want to leave the government, then leave, but do it honorably."[31] Peres put a stop to a showdown between MKs wanting to quit the government and ministers who wanted to stay in it by saying firmly that he had no intention of resigning. Labor Party leaders backed him up, saying that voters would punish Labor for deserting the government during a time of crisis. Political pollster Rafi Smith said that the ministers' reluctance to bolt reflected the fact over the past three months there had been a massive defection from the Labor Party. "Labor is getting the lowest support in all our polls that it's ever gotten," Smith said. In May, 1999, the party received 21.5 percent of the Jewish vote, and Smith's most recent vote showed the party getting ten percent of that vote if elections were held in December.[32]

Peres said he wanted to give Arafat one more chance and speculated that he might meet the PA chairman "by accident" at that month's Nobel Prize ceremonies in Oslo. But the foreign minister might have received a chilly reception in Oslo: as it did every year, the UN General Assembly strongly criticized Israel's policies toward the Palestinians, while ignoring a request by the Israeli ambassador to make a "moral choice" and reject Palestinian terrorism. George Bush's spokesman, Ari Fleischer, on the other hand, said, "Israel is a sovereign country and has a right to defend herself and the president understands that clearly."[33]

THE PRISONER OF RAMALLAH

———

BEFORE THE END OF THE first week of December, Yassir Arafat was trapped in a corner of Ramallah. His office shook as two helicopter gunships blasted a security post at the entrance to his government compound, forcing him to retreat to a bomb shelter. Some of his military had fired automatic weapons at the helicopters, but most of them had stood in shock watching their offices, lodgings and vehicles being reduced to burning ruins. "The Israelis were trying to kill people," one youth said. "They know we live in there as well as work." An Israeli spokesman said, "Of course it's personal, and we hope he gets the message at long last." The Israelis knew that Arafat was at his desk when they attacked because he had been making phone calls to Israelis he considered sympathetic to him, pleading with them to help arrange the truce while he arrested more militants.[1]

Arafat—born Muhammed Abdel-Raouf Arafat al-Qidwa al-Hussein in Cairo in 1929—had always been able to surmount difficulties. He had been driven from the West Bank to Jordan by the Israelis in 1967; driven from Jordan to Lebanon by King Hussein in 1971; driven from Lebanon to Tunis by Sharon in 1982. Despite all this, he had been invited to address the UN General Assembly, had received the Nobel Peace Prize and had returned triumphantly to the West Bank to be elected chairman of the Palestinian Authority in 1996. Now two Israeli tanks were parked three hundred yards away from his office, their gun barrels pointing toward him.

Ramallah residents watched in disbelief as Israeli troops blew up the 100-foot main radio transmission tower of Arafat's Palestinian Broadcasting Corporation, another of his symbols of power. His Voice of Palestine radio had to shift from AM to FM transmission. His bodyguard, Force 17, and his prized Preventive Security police had been hit in Gaza. The loss of his airport there was especially painful: he had traveled the world, even to Vietnam and South Africa, to garner support for his cause, and he had been the foreign leader who had paid the most visits to the Clinton White House. Now it appeared that his traveling days might be over. He was not to be allowed to leave Ramallah to attend a meeting of Arab leaders in Qatar, or even to go to Bethlehem to celebrate midnight mass on Christmas Eve. In fact, he was to remain shut up in his Ramallah compound for five months.

He told his aides that he was convinced that Sharon was going to kill him.[2] But Sharon had given his word to Mubarak and others that he would not kill him, and Arafat did not appear fearful on December 9, when, dressed in olive fatigues and wearing his trademark headscarf draped in the shape of Palestine, he gave press interviews from the compound, formerly an Israeli prison. In his lapel were miniature replicas of Palestinian and American flags, an olive branch and a pin showing the Virgin Mary and infant Jesus. His self-confidence appeared intact when an AP reporter asked him whether he was prepared to handle resistance from the extremists and their increasing number of followers. He smiled and said, "You are speaking with Yassir Arafat. I know how to do it. I know how to do it." He said he had already arrested seventeen key militants out of a list of thirty-three given him by Zinni, and he was pursuing the rest of them.[3]

A few days earlier, in a Friday interview with Israeli television, Arafat had shown signs of irritation with the US. The Bush administration was criticizing his actions against the extremists, and Sharon's linking of Palestinian terrorism with Osama bin Laden's attack on the World Trade Center was reinforced as the mayor of New York Rudolph Giuliani, his successor Michael Bloomberg and New York Governor George Pataki paid a lightning visit to Jerusalem, where Giuliani said, "Freedom and democracy is under attack here and that is exactly what was put under attack in America on September 11."[4] Asked about his response to American pressure, Arafat said, "Dear God, who cares about the Americans?" The Americans, he told Israelis, "are on your side, and they give you everything. Who gave you the airplanes? The Americans. Who gave you the tanks? The Americans." When the interviewer brought up US efforts to bring about a cease-fire, Arafat interrupted him, saying, "Don't talk to me about the Americans." Talking about Sharon, he said, "Your leaders don't stop the incitement against us. You say that I am bin Laden and the Palestinian Authority is the Taliban. Am I bin Laden?"[5]

Questions were arising, not about Arafat's control of terrorism, but about his ability to control it. He called Peres to complain that airstrikes on his security offices were making it impossible for him to carry out arrests of militants. Sharon then granted him a twelve-hour reprieve, one day after the cabinet declared the PA a "terror-supporting entity" and even after the Islamic Jihad orchestrated a suicide bombing during rush hour in the street outside the luxury hotel David's Citadel in downtown Jerusalem. Two ministers were in the hotel at the time, and Mayor Ehud Olmert had left a break-fast meeting there moments before. None of the officials was hurt, but five people were slightly injured by flying glass. The bomber was a forty-five-year-old father of eight. Islamic Jihad said his intention was to attack "Zionist" leaders in the hotel, but "because of special circumstances evaluated by the martyr, he decided to blow himself up outside."[6] On a grisly note, the press reported that the bomber's head was found on the second floor of the hotel.[7]

Sharon's restraint surprised many people. By ignoring calls from the Likud to destroy the PA, he found himself to the left of the majority of Israelis. In a *Yediot Aharonoth* poll, fifty-three percent said that Arafat should be forced out.[8]

There were indications that, far from being bin Laden, Arafat was losing his grip on Palestinian factions. In Gaza, when PA security services tried to block off the house of Sheik Ahmed Yassin, the revered quadriplegic leader of Hamas, boys threw stones, not at Israeli soldiers, but at Arafat's police, who at first threw stones back and beat some of the boys with long wooden batons. When a neighbor called for Yassin's followers to "protect him from the Palestinian Authority," about 1500 men poured into the muddy streets, shouting and shooting at first into the air and then directly at the police, who responded with tear gas, rubber bullets and riot sticks. Finally, after one man was killed and three others wounded, Yassin agreed to house arrest and the police withdrew, stationing themselves a mile away at the entrance to the Hamas stronghold that was Yassin's neighborhood.[9]

In West Bank towns—Qalquilya, Tulkarm, Nablus, Jenin—the Palestinian Authority announced in advance that police were coming to raid the homes of suspected Hamas militants; consequently the police arrived to find that the men had fled. Nevertheless in Nablus, the family of one fugitive cursed the PA whose security officers had ransacked his house and had reported that they found explosives there. The fugitive's mother said the agents' behavior was worse then the Israelis' and that they must have "lost their minds" because "yesterday" they and Hamas had been working together.[10] When Israeli missiles destroyed the security headquarters in Gaza City, killing a policeman and a seventeen-year-old boy and injuring about 150, some twenty seriously, one man whose wife and daughter-in-law were hurt when his house was hit, evinced bitterness. "This is a tragedy," he said. "Maybe Arafat is happy now. Let him and his group be happy, that's what I want."[11]

On Friday, December 8, Palestinian policemen stayed out of sight as more than 1000 Palestinians marched in a funeral procession for a Hamas extremist who had been killed by the police on Wednesday night. Youths threw stones at a truck carrying policemen and at security buildings along the way. One teenager said of the PA, "They are arresting our men. They are killing us."[12] The policemen themselves showed little enthusiasm for Arafat's pledge to "arrest all those who give the occupation an excuse to act against our people." In Ramallah, Michael Zielenziger of the *Seattle Times* spoke to officers who had to sit in their cars to interrogate witnesses and tied prisoners to trees because the police station had been destroyed by Israeli missiles. "Our first priority is to keep the peace and security of the city," said Col. Mohammed Salah, head of the 900-man Ramallah police district. "To stop thieves, protect our people and keep the cars from blocking our roads." He asked rhetorically whether it was his men's responsibility to protect Israeli citizens when "Israelis boast that they have one of the best security forces in the world, and they want us to help them? Besides," he added, "how can you prevent anybody from taking his own life?"[13]

Marwan Barghouti said that all Palestinians supported Arafat, but that there was no reason to arrest members of Hamas and Islamic Jihad. He said that Fatah was "not a terrorist group, and the Hamas and Islamic Jihad, all of them, are part of the Palestine liberation national movement, and they have the right to fight against the Israeli occupation." He would continue to fight with those groups, he said.[14] Barghouti was a wanted man. In late September, the Justice Ministry had officially asked the PA for his extradition to Israel on charges of aiding and attempting murder—including the murder of a Greek monk on a Jerusalem highway—possession of illegal weapons, holding unlicensed military training exercises and activity in illegal organizations. Barghouti had been the head of Fatah's student union at Bir Zeit University during the first intifada and had been deported to Jordan in 1987. The Olso agreement allowed his return in 1994; he was elected secretary-general of the High Committee of Fatah in the West Bank and he was also a member of the PA Legislative Council. The Israelis were aware that the Palestinians would not extradite him; they had not extradited anyone since 1993, but the request singled Barghouti out as a marked man.[15] Now in December he was a fugitive, and soldiers had taken over the three-room apartment in Ramallah where his wife and four children still lived. His popularity had moved from zero to eleven percent in December and the following May, it was to rise to nineteen percent.

Concern was inevitably arising, and not just in Israel, over what would happen if Arafat, for whatever reason, were no longer there. It was conjectured that there could be a long interim of collective leadership. Or worse, civil uproar with local strongmen fighting for control. Labor doves like Shimon Peres feared that the inevitable replacement for Arafat could be Hamas or Hezbollah. Some right-wing ministers, however, refused to be frightened by this prospect. Finance Minister Silvan Shalom said Arafat was a "terrorist in a diplomat's suit," while Hamas was an avowed enemy that could be justifiably attacked. "Between Hamas and Arafat," Shalom said, "I prefer Hamas."[16]

A Basic Law for the autonomous areas had been drafted under which the speaker of the Palestinian Legislative Council would lead the PA for sixty days while new elections were held, but Arafat had never made any attempt to complete it. New elections were supposed to be held in 2000; Arafat made no attempt to arrange for those either. His election in 1996 had been monitored by over 600 international observers, including former President Jimmy Carter. There were more than 700 candidates from a multitude of parties and slates and turnout supposedly was over seventy percent, although questions have been raised about double registration, intimidation and disqualifications. Fatah held internal elections to decide the candidates for each seat, but Arafat discarded the results and created his own official slate. Many of his discarded candidates won seats as independents in the eighty-eight-member Palestinian

National Council. Arafat's opposition at the top of the ticket was Samiha Khalil, a 72-year-old female social worker who surprised the international press by garnering 9.3 percent of the vote. While Reporteurs sans Frontieres recorded "a very strong imbalance" in Palestinian TV coverage, Jimmy Carter hailed the election as "open and fair," although he said on election day that there was no doubt that the Israelis were "doing everything they can to intimidate Palestinians." Former CIA director Jim Woolsey remarked, "Arafat was essentially elected the same way Stalin was, but not nearly as democratically as Hitler, who at least had actual opponents."[17]

"A FACTORY OF LIES":
THE *KARINE A*

———

ON DECEMBER 12 THREE HAMAS gunmen set off bombs underneath a bus in the West Bank and shot passengers as they tried to flee. The bus, which was not armored, exploded about a quarter of a mile away from its destination, an orthodox settlement northwest of Jerusalem. Ten of the forty passengers were killed and about twenty-nine people were wounded, some of whom were rescue workers from the settlement. One terrorist was run over by an army jeep and then shot, and the other two escaped into the hills. A few minutes after that, in Gaza, two Hamas suicide bombers blew themselves up outside an Israeli settlement, wounding four people. The IAF and the IDF began heavy attacks in Gaza and the West Bank even before the Israeli cabinet announced that "Chairman Arafat had made himself irrelevant as far as Israel is concerned."[1]

These actions followed a call by General Zinni for a forty-eight-hour truce. Since the general had arrived in the region on November 26, sixty-three Palestinians and forty-four Israelis had been killed. On December 14, Zinni departed for discussions in Egypt and Jordan, after which he said he intended to return to Washington for his Christmas vacation. Colin Powell made no effort to rebuke Israel for using helicopters, missiles and warplanes against the PA; both he and Bush's spokesman Ari Fleischer put the onus on Arafat to act decisively against terrorist groups.[2] "Now is his time to perform," the president said, and a senior US official said that Powell, on an overseas visit, had asked Berlin, Paris and London to "[k]eep [Arafat's] feet to the fire."³ Zinni, Powell said, would return to the Mideast "when circumstances suggest there is a real reason for him to go back." Zinni's mission had not failed, Powell said. "The parties have failed. Zinni went to help them and they were not ready ... The failure is with the parties in the region—especially, I have to say, on the part of the Palestinians for not getting the violence under control."⁴

Arafat responded in a television address to his people that he was repeating his admonition "that all sorts of armed activities should be stopped and there should be no more attacks, especially the suicide and bombing attacks that we have always condemned," and that he would "arrest all those who planned these attacks." His security chief Jibril Rajoub, who had been considered cooperative by the Israelis and the Americans, said, "We will not surrender to Sharon. We do not want to be Taliban, but at the same time we will not be beaten." The terrorist groups, he said, were a threat to the Palestinian future as well as to Israeli security, but Arafat had not been given time enough to act against them. For Arafat to act, Israel had to end its blockades and military strikes and hold out hope for a return to negotiations. But, PA officials said, on December 16, the PA closed four offices of Hamas and Islamic Jihad in the Gaza Strip.⁵ A US official, on condition of anonymity, said that General Zinni had given Arafat a list of about thirty Palestinian extremists, but that the PA had picked up only about twelve, and few of these had really been arrested.⁶

Not unexpectedly, Hamas, Islamic Jihad and the PFLP rejected Arafat's calls for a cessation of violence. What followed were a series of attacks and reprisals from both sides. For some reason, the Israeli police prevented Sari Nusseibeh, a moderate Palestinian academic, from holding a holiday reception, detaining and interrogating him for two hours. Professor Nusseibeh had once been beaten by Palestinian thugs, possibly because he had said he did not believe in the right of return of refugees to Israel. Moshe Amirav, in the *Jerusalem Post*, suggested that Sharon and Uzi Landau did not want to deal with Nusseibeh because they were afraid that his creative compromise approach might lead to a partition of Jerusalem and the end of the present failed policy of Israeli sovereignty.[7]

At the end of December, after a nearly four-month struggle over the results of the Labor primary, Benjamin Ben-Eliezer, the defense minister, won the leadership over the Speaker, Avraham Burg, in a new election. In the September ballot, Burg had won by one percentage point, but the result was challenged because of a suspiciously large Druze vote for Burg. The rerun election was boycotted by the Druze, who were offended by charges of irregularities in their vote, and this resulted in Ben-Eliezer's victory. Burg, a supporter of Peace Now, called the election an "undemocratic farce."[8] Ben-Eliezer, 65, had been born in Iraq and immigrated to Israel as a teenager in 1949; he had been a military governor of the West Bank and was considered to share Sharon's hawkish views. There was little public interest in this election, and analysts said the main reason was that Labor was nearly irrelevant because of the failure of Camp David and the long intifada, or, going back farther, because of the depressing results of Yitzhak Rabin's Oslo accords. Barry Rubin, a political scientist at a think tank near Tel Aviv, said that a victory for Burg would have doomed the party. "It would have been suicide for Labor to go with the disgraced Left," he said. "The party would have been destroyed."[9]

On January 3, General Zinni returned, planning to spend four days talking to both sides about possible peace negotiations. As a gesture of good will, and because there had been relative calm for the past three weeks, the Israelis pulled their troops and tanks from several West Bank towns and lifted roadblocks, although Sharon still insisted on seven days of complete quiet before talks could begin. But two days after Zinni's arrival, another crisis loomed. On January 5, the Israeli army announced that at dawn on January 3, naval commandos had stormed a weapons-smuggling ship, the *Karine A*, about 300 miles off the Red Sea port of Eilat. The commandos had been backed by combat helicopters, and the crew had surrendered without a fight. Senior Bush administration officials admitted that the US had helped to track the *Karine A*, which was carrying fifty tons of rockets, anti-tank missiles, mortars, mines and sniper rifles from Iran. Israeli army Chief of Staff Shaul Mofaz said the weapons included Katyusha rockets with a twelve-mile range that would be able to reach most areas of Israel from PA territory.

PA officials denied any connection to the ship. Marwan Kanafani, an Arafat spokesman, said that although it was true that Omar Akawi, the ship's captain, was a Fatah member who worked for the PA merchant marine, the weapons were not intended for Palestinians. Kanafani said that Israeli patrols off the coast made it almost impossible to smuggle weapons into Gaza. Akawi said in a TV interview from an Israeli prison that he had been a member of Arafat's Fatah movement since 1976, was now a naval advisor to the PA Transport Ministry, and had been instructed to smuggle the weapons from Iran by a PA official named Adel Awadallah. He said he was told to sail the ship up the Suez Canal and connect near Alexandria with three smaller boats which were going to float the weapons ashore off the Gaza coast in watertight containers that would be picked up by fishermen or divers.

Akawi said he was nervous about getting caught: the Americans, he said, were on the alert in the area of the gulf, the Israelis in the Red Sea and the Egyptians checked everything passing through the canal. He said he was surprised not to be ordered to turn back after Arafat issued an appeal in December for an end to violence against the Israelis. Kanafani said the PA had no record of an Awadallah, whom the Israelis claimed was an arms buyer for Arafat. "The Israelis," Kanafani said, "have a dark history of forcing prisoners into saying something that was not true. We are not in an arms race with Israel." Akawi, whom *Chicago Tribune* reporters said seemed to be at ease and to speak freely, said he had no evidence that Arafat knew about this operation. He thought perhaps the weapons had been donated by Hezbollah.[10]

Sharon, who had personally approved the action to seize the *Karine A*, held a news conference at the ship, where the vast array of weapons covered the entire deck. The Israeli government flew hundreds of diplomats and reporters to the conference at a naval yard in the port of Eilat. Sharon accused both Arafat and Iran of plotting to make the weapons available. "This is the choice of the person heading the Palestinian authority," Sharon said. "Arafat chooses to purchase long-range Katyushas instead of education for the children . . . to purchase mortars instead of investing the money in creating jobs . . . to invest millions of dollars in missiles, mines and rifles, instead of investing them in the welfare of his people."[11] He called Iran the "world center of terror," and said that the fact that the Palestinians and Iran were working together was "a very dangerous development."[12]

Arafat said he was forming "an internal investigative panel" to look into the Israeli charges in the *Karine A* affair. "If anything is revealed—and I personally do not think so—we will not hesitate to being them before a trial."[13] Despite this, Jibril Rajoub, the PA Preventive Security chief, called the incident a "Sharon lie," while other PA spokesmen suggested that Israel was behind the smuggling operation.[14] A few days later Hanan Ashrawi said that the PA had "decided to detain and question people [about] whether this was a private enterprise or . . . an arms trade deal." Three men, the Palestinians said, were detained for questioning: Adel al-Mughrabi, a PA naval officer whom the Israelis called the chief agent for the arms deal, Fuad Shobaki, a financial officer for the PLO military and Fathi al-Razem, deputy commander of the PA naval police. Later it was announced that al-Razem had not been detained, but was being sought, and that the two others were being held "based on information received from international sources."[15]

The Israelis said they did not believe anyone was being detained. Some hours later, the PA revised its statement again, saying that only one man, Fuad Shobaki, had been detained and that the other two, whose arrests had been reported two days before, were not in PA territory and might be living abroad. These revisions did little to help Arafat prove his credibility in this affair. Ahmed Abdel Rahman, secretary-general of the PA cabinet, said, "We didn't lie." He explained that the PA had made "the decision to hold them for interrogation" and that the two men had been suspended from their official duties, and the PA expected to find them.[16]

The White House at first hesitated to accept the PA's participation in the smuggling scheme, and was particularly dismayed at the possibility that Iran, whose cooperation the US wanted in the war against terrorism, might have been involved. The Israelis sent intelligence officers to the US and Europe to back up their accusations, and said they would soon release documents to that effect. Richard Boucher, the State Department spokesman, said that the Israeli allegations were "credible," that US diplomats who had examined many of the weapons were "seriously concerned" by their "quantity and quality," and about "the involvement of Palestinians in this arms shipment." Defense Secretary Donald Rumsfeld added that the Israelis "clearly had very good intelligence that those weapons were going to be used against them and they . . . preempt[ed] that ship from landing and unloading and then providing those weapons to be used against Israel." Boucher said the State Department was "waiting to hear a full explanation of the incident from Chairman Arafat."[17]

A senior Israeli official said that his government had provided evidence to the Bush administration that "all parts of the Iranian government" knew about the operation. Bush officials said they believed "parts of the Iranian government were involved" but US intelligence was trying to assess whether "all parts" participated or whether the operation was conducted only by Revolutionary Guard militants who often worked without the knowledge of President Mohammed Khatami.[18] But Ziad Abu Amr, a PA legislator, said that accusations against Iran were "nonsense. Iran has been set on undermining the Palestinian Authority from the start because it accepts peace with Israel, and they are opposed to the peace process."[19]

On March 24, the *New York Times* stated that American and Israeli intelligence officers had discovered that in a secret meeting in Moscow in May, 2001, while Arafat was visiting President Putin, the PA chairman, through two trusted aides, had personally forged "a new alliance with Iran" that involved "Iranian shipments of heavy weapons and millions of dollars" to Palestinian terrorist groups. The Americans and Israelis said they had concluded, on the basis of Israeli intelligence reports provided to the Bush administration after the ship's interception, that the *Karine A* shipment was part of a broader relationship and not a "rogue operation," but a "direct outgrowth" of the clandestine Moscow meeting.

Yassir Abed Rabbo, the PA minister of information, called this conclusion "a factory of lies" concocted by a colonial power to blame "outsiders," adding that "[t]here has not been a single Iranian here since the fourteenth century." The Iranian government too denied any involvement with the Palestinians. It was true that relations between Arafat and Tehran had been so bad after 1994 that Arafat had been convinced that fundamentalist Iranian leaders had ordered his execution. But American intelligence officers said that they believed that the intifada in 2000 had "stirred the radical juices in Iran." They said that, for instance, Tehran had paid millions of dollars in cash bonuses to Islamic Jihad for each attack against Israel.

Help had also been given to Hezbollah, which had received tens of millions of dollars worth of munitions during its eighteen-year conflict with Israel. "The strategy," a senior American intelligence office said, "is to make the West Bank another Lebanon." Hezbollah and Iranian representatives did not meet, apparently, in

PA territory, but in Syria, Jordan and Lebanon. Jordanian intelligence officials said they had foiled many attacks on Israel by Iran and its agents; the secretary general of Hezbollah, Sayyed Hassan Nasrallah, had, in fact, recently criticized Jordan for blocking weapon-smuggling. The Americans emphasized that Omar Akawi, the captain of the *Karine A,* was an officer in the PA navy living in Libya, that one of the three Palestinian crew members had taken diving lessons in Lebanon paid for by Hezbollah, and that Adel al-Mughrabi, a PA naval officer, had bought the ship and stayed "in radio contact with its crew during its voyage from an island off the coast of Iran where it picked up the weapons to the point in the Red Sea where the ship was seized by Israelis."

According to the *Times,* a Palestinian negotiator said that the deal with Iran angered moderates in PA political circles because of the risks to American relations. Secretary of Defense Donald Rumsfeld and other Bush administration officials argued that relations with Arafat should be cut off, while Colin Powell made the case that such an action would not accomplish anything. In the end, the administration settled for a public rebuke of Arafat.[20]

82

FITS & STARTS

—

IN EARLY FEBRUARY, SHARON WENT to Washington for his fourth visit with President Bush, as attacks and reprisals continued in the West Bank and Gaza Strip. Arafat sat in Ramallah as he had for two months, cheered by strong support from his constituents—thousands rallied for him in Ramallah and throughout the territories—but reportedly seething with rage at his old antagonist's reception by the American president, whom Arafat had never met. The chairman, who had spent much of his time in past years jetting to foreign capitals and rarely spending two nights in the same place, consoled himself by saying that he was the only Arab general ever to have defeated Sharon. One diplomat reported that Arafat, referring to the forced PLO evacuation from Lebanon, said, "I defeated him in Beirut—I defeated him!"[1] Sharon, for his part, spoke bluntly about Arafat in Lebanon. "There was an agreement in Lebanon not to kill Yassir Arafat," Sharon told the newspaper *Maariv*. "Actually I am sorry that we did not kill him."[2] These remarks, described by Richard Boucher as "unhelpful," reinforced a tendency in the press to simplify the present Israeli-Palestinian conflict by presenting it as a reflection of personal hostility between two old antagonists.

Sharon had said that Arafat would not be allowed to leave the compound until he arrested the gunmen who had killed Zeevi on October 17. Arafat called repeatedly for a cease-fire, but made fiery speeches to his supporters about defiance and his own martyrdom. There were rumors that some of his top officials were prevented from trying to replace the chairman only by the support given to him by Arab nations and the European Union. The EU foreign ministers said there should be less emphasis on security and more on politics, and that Arafat should be released.[3] But the American refusal to join that chorus sparked anger in the PA. Jibril Rajoub said of President Bush: "I think he has something deeply in his heart against the Arab world, not just Abu Amar," referring to one of Arafat's soubriquets. At the same time Rajoub blamed the Israel lobby in the US for Bush's position.[4]

Polls were suggesting that Sharon's support was softening. In a *Maariv* poll, his approval rating was forty-eight percent, with thirty-seven percent approving of his handling of security, and only eighteen percent approving of his handling of "socio-economic matters." Fifty-four percent of Israelis agreed with Netanyahu that Arafat should be "toppled" and that the government should act aggressively against the PA. At the same time, a plurality also supported more aggressive moves toward peace. *Yediot Aharonoth* said Sharon found amusing a poll showing that seventy percent of Israelis wanted him to attack the Palestinians, while seventy percent wanted him to give up the West Bank and Gaza. "So," he said, "what should I do?"[5]

Although it was generally agreed that the peace movement had lost its relevance because there seemed to be nobody to make peace with, there were signs that some Israeli resolve was crumbling. On February 1, more than 100 army reservists including combat officers and soldiers—a number which was to grow until it was sharply reversed after the end of March—published their intention to refuse to serve in the West Bank and Gaza because Israel's policies there involved "dominating, expelling, starving and humiliating an entire people." The reservists' declaration in *Haaretz* said, "The price of occupation is the loss of the Israel Defense Forces' semblance of humanity and the corruption of all Israeli society." Chief of Staff Lt. Gen Shaul Mofaz was disturbed enough to say that he suspected "someone" was "organizing a campaign on an ideological basis," and Sharon warned, "It will be the beginning of the end of democracy if soldiers don't carry out the decisions of the elected government."[6]

There was apparently some loss of morale in the more remote settlements in the Jordan Valley, some of which had as few as forty families. According to figures from the Jordan Valley Settlers Council, 680 families, with about 4000 members, were living in the valley before the intifada. By early 2002, religious communities had increased by twenty-five families, but small secular settlements had lost fifty-five families, shrinking by eight percent. One settler, Rafael Ganani, who had helped found the small settlement of Hamra in 1971, discussed with James Bennet of the *New York Times* a recent attack on Hamra by a Palestinian gunman who had cut through a fence, shot an army reservist and broken into a house where he killed a woman and her eleven-year-old daughter before being killed himself. Asked whether it would be necessary to close the settlements to reach peace, Ganani replied, "The honest, painful truth? You have to close everything—and I've lived most of my life here. You have to close the country and get out."[7]

Israeli actions against Palestinian towns escalated when Hamas fired new types of rockets from the Gaza Strip into a kibbutz and a moshav in southern Israel. In retaliation, Israeli warplanes attacked a Force 17 headquarters in Gaza City near Arafat's office there, injuring more than twenty police officers and civilians and damaging buildings in a wide area. Windows were blown out in the offices of Terje Roed-Larsen, the UN coordinator for the Middle East, and two employees were hurt by flying glass. Roed-Larsen, who had been involved in the creation of the Oslo accords, issued a statement: "Israel's security needs will not be met by hitting civilian targets or by destroying the Palestinians' ability to police and maintain order." Israel apologized for the damage. Mr Roed-Larsen then met with members of extremist Palestinian factions, including Hamas, saying he thought it "incredibly important to have a dialogue with all factions of the Palestinian society based on the principle of zero tolerance for terrorism and on the principle of using peaceful means in order to reach an agreement." Bombs, he said, "don't produce peace. They strengthen extremism."[8]

While he was in Washington, Sharon created something of a stir by saying that there would be a Palestinian state some day. A State Department official called this "significant," but most Israelis knew that Sharon's vision of a Palestinian state was not Colin Powell's: Sharon, they believed, saw a state that comprised forty-two percent of the West Bank and Gaza Strip, as opposed to the ninety-eight percent offered by Barak; an undivided Israeli Jerusalem; 250,000 settlers remaining in place; Israeli control of Palestinian borders, airspace, security, and relations with other countries. His foreign policy advisor, Zalman Shoval, said that Sharon did not have a plan, but a "concept" and that Arafat could not be part of that concept.[9]

While Arafat remained in Ramallah, his Palestinian Authority was not delivering basic services to its people. Nobody was picking up garbage, sewage flowed uncontrolled, doctors and teachers were often prevented by Israeli checkpoints from reaching hospitals and schools which, in addition to personnel, lacked crucial supplies and the money to pay for them. Law and order were also breaking down, as a mob stormed a jail in Hebron and freed Islamic militants, and in Jenin another mob broke into a courtroom and, because of a blood feud, executed three men who had just been found guilty of killing a PA security officer. The PA had to rely on Hamas and Islamic Jihad to provide help for the needy. Before the 2000 intifada there had been widespread discontent among Palestinians with corruption and cronyism in Arafat's regime. But now that the chairman was confined to the Ramallah compound, his popularity had gone up, despite signs that the authority was collapsing.

An anonymous Western diplomat said, "The danger is that if the Palestinian Authority's situation deteriorates even more, we will have chaos. I am not sure it is in the interest of anybody to have the authority collapse." The anxiety level increased when word leaked out in the middle of February that Arafat had pulled a gun on Jibril Rajoub during a shouting match over what Arafat saw as Rajoub's negligence in allowing the jail-storming in Hebron. Sources said that Arafat was shaking during the argument and the pistol fell from his hand. PA officials, including Rajoub, denied that this incident had taken place, but a Palestinian think tank analyst said that Arafat was "old, weak and very doubtful. He doesn't trust anyone around him. And now, because of the siege and his age, it all comes together."[10]

What seemed to be coming together was a strong Palestinian emphasis on martyrdom. A depressing and ominous situation arose when Wafa Idris, 28, the first female suicide bomber, blew herself up on the Jaffa Road in Jerusalem, killing an eighty-one-year-old man and wounding many passersby. Two weeks later, by mid-February, Idris, a member of Fatah, had been virtually deified by the Arab press. The head of psychiatry at an Egyptian university was quoted by a London Arabic newspaper as saying, "From Mary's womb issued a child who eliminated oppression, while the body of Wafa became shrapnel that eliminated despair and aroused hope." An Egyptian columnist wrote, "She bore in her belly the fetus of a rare heroism, and gave birth by blowing herself up." Arafat condemned Idris's act, although he continued to praise "martyrs" and huge posters of the woman were pasted up all over Ramallah. A cautionary note was sounded by Sheikh Ahmed Yassin, the spiritual leader of Hamas, who said that under Islamic law women should not act if men were available, but that if a female bomber did go out on a mission for more than a full day, she should be accompanied by a male chaperone.[11]

Nevertheless, as suicide bombers were celebrated like rock stars all over the Arab world, more young people, including girls, blew themselves up in Israel and the West Bank. This celebration was to have an effect that upset many Palestinians when, toward the end of April, three boys, two of them fifteen and one fourteen years old, set out armed with knives and homemade bombs, to attack a heavily fortified settlement near their homes in Gaza City. The younger boy left a note saying he wanted his grave "to be like the grave of Mohammed, not so big. Don't cry for me. Bury me with my brothers the martyrs. And visit my grave if you have time." The three boys were shot dead by Israeli soldiers fifteen yards from the settlement walls. The boys' parents did not accept congratulations on their martyrdom but demanded an investigation to see whether radical groups had recruited these children. Both Hamas and Islamic Jihad denied responsibility and said they would begin a campaign in local mosques urging children not to undertake suicidal attacks.[12]

This tragedy took place about ten days after Arafat's wife, Suha al-Taweel Arafat, said in an interview with a London-based Arabic magazine, that if she had a son "there would be no greater honor" than to sacrifice him for the Palestinian cause. She was quoted as saying that she and her children could not be expected to be "less patriotic and more eager to live" than her countrymen and her husband who was "seeking martyrdom."[13] Mrs Arafat, who lived in Paris, had a daughter and no sons.

Israeli troops made strong incursions into Bethlehem, Ramallah and several Palestinian refugee camps, prompting a public rebuke in the form of a letter to Sharon from UN Secretary General Kofi Annan who, briefed by Terje Roed-Larsen and UN Palestinian Relief Agency head Peter Hansen, noted that the fighting now resembled "all-out conventional warfare" in which "hundreds of innocent noncombatant civilians—men, women and children—have been injured or killed, and many buildings and homes have been damaged or destroyed." The letter contained a brief allusion to "terror," but did not mention Arafat, although on the same day in a speech to the Security Council, Annan, describing Palestinian attacks on Israeli civilians as "morally repugnant," said that "the Palestinians have played their full part in the escalating cycle of violence, counterviolence and revenge."[14] Annan had made the letter public after waiting six days in vain for a response from Sharon, who in the end left the response to the Israeli mission to the UN.

Hopes for a resolution of the crisis flickered fitfully. Arafat announced that he had detained three of Zeevi's assassins, but the Israelis responded only by talking about extradition of them to Israel, something that they were aware Arafat would not accept. General Zinni returned and held more talks on a cease-fire. Vice President Cheney came to Israel as part of his Mideastern tour to sound out support for a US strike at Iraq, and urged that Arafat be allowed to attend an upcoming two-day Arab League summit in Beirut where it was hoped there would be meaningful discussion of a peace initiative floated by Saudi Crown Prince Abdullah that offered "normalization" of relations with Arab nations if Israel agreed to return to its 1967 borders and make other concessions, including the right of return of Palestinian refugees. Cheney said that he would meet with Arafat if the chairman spoke to the Palestinian people in Arabic about ending terrorism and took steps to implement the Tenet plan. Sharon said that Arafat could go to Beirut if the US guaranteed that Israel could bar the chairman from returning to Ramallah if there were more terror attacks during his absence.

In the event, the vice president did not meet with Arafat, and Arafat did not go to Beirut, although he addressed the meeting by television. His was not the only notable absence: about half of the Arab leaders, including Hosni Mubarak and Jordan's King Abdullah, did not show up, and the Saudi intelligence chief had to be taken away after suffering a stroke. The Arab League leaders accepted Crown Prince Abdullah's peace inititative to the Israelis, while at the same time urging the Palestinians to keep fighting. This, coupled with the summit coinciding with a horrendous suicide bombing on the Jewish Passover holiday, caused the *Wall Street Journal* to refer to the meeting's "irrelevance."[15] One notable event was the public embrace bestowed on Saddam Hussein's representative by the Saudi crown prince, in what looked to be the Arab response to Vice President Cheney's attempt to muster support in the region for an American invasion of Iraq. As the summit leaders rode in their limousines to their private jets, Youssef Majdoub, a Palestinian refugee living in a shack in Sabra and Shatilla, commented, "Their talk is just politics." The Lebanese government bans the 400,000 refugees from entering most professions, limits their civil rights, and has refused to allow Majdoub to rebuild the house which was destroyed in the 1982 Israeli invasion.[16]

Sharon, whose disapproval rating in the polls had reached sixty percent, told *Yediot Aharonoth* that he had made a mistake when he promised President Bush that he would not "physically harm" Arafat. "I should have told them, 'I can't keep that commitment,'" he said.[17]

RECONSIDERED STRATEGY:
OPERATION DEFENSIVE SHIELD

—

ON MARCH 27, ABDEL-BASSET Odeh, a twenty-three-year-old member of Hamas wearing a long-haired wig, walked past a security guard at the door of the Park Hotel in the coastal city of Netanya, and began to move through the lobby. When the reception clerk spoke to him, he darted into the dining room where 250 people were attending a seder, a Passover ceremonial dinner, and detonated the bomb he was wearing. Twenty-nine people were killed and 140 injured, twenty seriously. Odeh, who had come from the West Bank city of Tulkarm, six miles east of Netanya, had worked in hotels in Netanya and elsewhere in Israel. His name was on the list of wanted terrorists given several times to the PA by the Israelis.

Odeh was the son of a prosperous vegetable wholesaler, who accepted congratulations on his son's actions from a stream of friends and neighbors in Tulkarm, all of whom believed an Israeli retaliatory attack was inevitable, but none of whom seemed worried about it. Forty Odeh relatives who lived in a connected apartment complex, expected the Israelis to demolish it, but no one made any attempt to leave. "We will stay here in the house, and they can come if they want," said the bomber's father. His brother said, "Everyone is proud of him. There is a war. Yes, he's the one who changed everything." The PA legislative representative from Tulkarm agreed with a smile. "Yes," he said, "everything is changing." What he was thinking about, he said, was who would succeed Arafat if the chairman was expelled or killed.[1]

Hamas stated that this "operation" was "a response to the crimes of the Zionist enemy" and "a message to the summit convening in Lebanon that our Palestinian people's option is resistance and resistance only." Emmanuel Nahshon, the deputy spokesman for the Israeli Foreign Ministry, commented that this attack certainly meant, "if not the death of the mission, at least the Zinni mission cannot continue in the same way."[2] An Israeli official said, "We'll have to reconsider our whole strategy now. We'll have to do something else."[3]

Sharon called an emergency cabinet meeting that lasted for eight hours. The *Chicago Tribune* reporter noted that the 74-year-old Sharon did not look "the least bit tired" as he emerged from the all-night session to comment that Arafat was "the enemy" who headed "a coalition of terrorism" and who must be "isolated." He would, he said, "uproot the whole infrastructure" of terrorism.[4] Even as the cabinet was meeting, Israeli tanks and bulldozers were rolling into Ramallah to ring Arafat's compound and demolish the fence around it. Residents fled the city by the hundreds, expecting a harsh, sustained attack. Most buildings in Arafat's compound were empty, and an ambulance was parked outside it. Arafat said he was now ready to work toward a cease-fire, and his security forces announced that they were starting to arrest Hamas and Islamic Jihad militants in Ramallah, Bethlehem, Hebron and Nablus. Sharon's spokesman Raanan Gissin replied that this was the tenth time Arafat had offered a cease-fire and Israel was "fed up. The only thing that can save him now is action to stop terror. And he understands very well that an action of this magnitude, the Passover massacre, will result in a harsh Israeli reaction."[5] Arafat's aides said that he had come under pressure to agree to a cease-fire from the German foreign minister, from Kofi Annan, and from officials of the EU and the French government, among others. But at a news conference on March 28, he set several conditions that would require protracted

negotiation. The most significant objection to the latest Zinni cease-
fire proposal was that it was not tied directly to discussions that
would lead to an independent Palestinian state.[6]

Dozens of tanks rolled into Qalquilya and entered Bethlehem,
stopping 500 yards from the Church of the Nativity in Manger
Square, where a few hundred Palestinian gunmen and some civilians were holed up, creating a standoff. In Ramallah, Israeli troops
smashed through walls in Arafat's compound while the chairman
appealed in English "to the international community to stop this
aggression against our people, this military aggression, this killing."
He added in Arabic: "Together we will march until one of our children raises the Palestinian flag over the churches and mosques of
Jerusalem."[7] Israeli troops conducted house-to-house searches for
suspected terrorists in Ramallah while another suicide bomber struck
in Haifa, this time blowing up a restaurant owned by Israeli Arabs,
several of whom were killed in the explosion. In Jerusalem, another
female suicide bomber, this one eighteen years old, blew herself up
at the entrance to a supermarket, killing two people and wounding
thirty. In succeeding days, the IDF moved into other West Bank
towns: Beit Jala, Tulkarm, Jenin, Salfit, and into Nablus, the largest
West Bank city, where the attack in the first days was heaviest. Beginning about 10 pm on April 3, tanks surrounded Nablus and advanced in all directions down the main streets and toward refugee
camps around the city. The area echoed with the rattle of helicopters, the steady thunder of tank fire and the crackle of rapid automatic gunfire.

When the tanks first appeared at a considerable distance, teenage boys climbed hilltops to act as lookouts, while members of Fatah,
al-Aqsa and PFLP, faces hidden behind ski masks, Kalashnikovs slung
across their chests, loaded rockets onto cars, and made roadblocks
out of crushed cars and sand-filled garbage bins. Al-Aqsa said they
planned a defense in the center of the city, in the old marketplace, or
souk. They boobytrapped passageways and eaves there, turning the

souk into a tangle of sandbags, trip wires and mines. An al-Aqsa member told a reporter that he was "proud" to say that "the preparations of the armed people of Nablus" were "higher than any other refugee camp. The resistance there will be tougher than any other place in the West Bank."[8] City residents hurried to stock up on bottled water, canned meat and bread because they knew that in other cities the Israelis had enforced strict curfews that made it difficult for people to leave their homes, and in Ramallah there was no water after the main pumping station had been destroyed when troops shelled the PA security compound.

Also on April 3, there was an unpleasant incident when soldiers beat and fired tear gas at several hundred Israeli Arabs, including three Arab MKs, and leftist peace activists who were attempting to block the road from Jerusalem to Ramallah. On March 29, some 600 foreigners arrived in Ramallah to offer themselves, they said, as human shields for the Palestinians. Among them was Jose Bové, a French farm union leader and anti-globalist, who said, "We are going to stay here in Ramallah in particular to provide the Palestinians with protection."[9] More than forty of these activists, some of whom were Jewish, were filmed on television rushing past Israeli armed vehicles into Arafat's offices where they joined the besieged occupants. In a telephone interview from one of the offices, an activist named Claude Leostic remarked, "We thought as long as there were internationals here, there would be no vicious Israeli attack." Leostic was a native of Brest, France, a country with a large Arab population where a considerable amount of pro-Palestinian feeling had led to a series of anti-Semitic attacks. The Israelis responded to this entry into Arafat's offices by banning foreigners, including journalists, from Ramallah. When the French protesters, including Bové, left the compound, they were arrested and deported.[10]

The actions of these Palestinian sympathizers, many of whom came from France and Italy, had been organized by two West Bank groups: the International Solidarity Movement and Grass-Roots

International Protection for the Palestinian People. During the intifada these people had removed roadblocks, planted uprooted trees, demonstrated in front of Israeli tanks and tried to walk through army checkpoints.[11] One group had walked into Bethlehem on March 30. On April 1, another group, marching in Beit Jala after the incursion, had been fired upon by Israeli troops. Six protesters and a Palestinian TV cameraman had been slightly injured by shrapnel; a seventh protester, a woman from Australia, was shot in the abdomen and remained in serious condition after surgery in a Beit Jala hospital.The marchers were taken aback to realize that the troops were using live ammunition.

A State Department spokesman decried "Israeli Defense Force actions that put civilians in harm's way, including the shooting of peaceful demonstrators," and urged the IDF not only to "exercise the utmost restraint and discipline to avoid further harm to civilians," but to "conduct a thorough investigation" so that "incidents like that" would not be repeated. Israeli officials responded that the demonstrators had breached a closed military area. Justice Minister Meir Sheetrit said, "It's a group of people who are causing provocations. A person playing with fire should not yell when they get burned." The IDF spokesman, Colonel Olivier Rafowicz, added, "We believe what you are calling a peace demonstration was a provocation. I'm much more concerned by the dead people in Haifa than people who are wounded because they are looking for an incident."[12]

Crown Prince Abdullah called the IDF actions at Arafat's compound "a savage, despicable act, an inhuman and cruel act." He said he did not think "any human being can accept this at all. Whether he's removed or not, the resistance to occupation will continue. Every Palestinian is a Yassir Arafat." Sharon, he said, was "soaked in blood," and it was he who had rejected the Saudi peace initiative. The crown prince was reflecting, if not anticipating, the reaction of outraged crowds and politicians in half a dozen Arab capitals. The *New York Times* noted the appearance once again of "the two policy tracks that emerged from the Beirut summit meeting; on the one hand an offer of peace and on the other full support for a Palestinian uprising as long as Israeli occupation persisted." [13]

The reaction in Israel to the Saudi offer, or vision, was mixed even before it had been accepted by the Arab nations at the summit. One government spokesman called it a "nonstarter," while another said it was "an important and interesting initiative" that warranted further discussion. Sharon, interviewed by *Yediot Aharonoth*, said, "A return to the 1967 borders will destroy Israel. The entire world is talking about the Saudi plan; everyone enthusiastically recommends endorsing it, and the only one that no one asks is Israel. No one!" [14]

Horrific details piled up of the suffering of Palestinians as a result of the Israeli offensive in the West Bank: wounded bleeding to death because the IDF prevented medical help from reaching them; innocent civilians shot to death crossing the street; curfews preventing people from buying food and medicine; water supplies cut off. Ambulances in Bethlehem could not get past Israeli armored vehicles blocking the narrow streets. In Gaza, Hamas leaders expressed satisfaction with the situation. "Our spirit is high, our mood is good," said Ismail Abu Shanab. The Passover attack that killed twenty-five in Netanya, and the bombing in the Arab-owned Haifa cafe where fifteen died, were, Shanab said, the most successful attacks they had ever made, partly because Hamas was now using weapons-grade explosives instead of home-made fertilizer bombs. "Forty were killed and 200 injured in just two operations," another leader, Mahmoud al-Zahar, told a reporter, with a smile. [15]

On April 4, Israeli forces rolled into Hebron, completing a sweep of major West Bank cities. There was heavy fighting throughout the area, and especially in Jenin, where soldiers were going house to house searching for weapons and wanted militants. The Israelis controlled all of Bethlehem except for the Church of the Nativity. The action had taken eight days; Chief of Staff Shaul Mofaz said the army would need about eight more weeks to complete the operation. But President Bush reversed himself on April 5, and, giving the Israelis just four hours notice, called for an end to the military offensive. He did not mention a specific time frame, but the next day Secretary of State Powell said that the President expected a withdrawal of IDF forces "without delay."[16]

Israel now found itself working against the clock, so to speak, as Sharon said only that he would "make every effort to accelerate" the mission.[17] He did not give the Secretary of State a definite timetable when Powell came to the region in the middle of April and the secretary's meeting with Arafat in Ramallah was equally fruitless. Arafat spoke to Powell for an hour in Arabic, mostly about Israeli actions in the Jenin refugee camp, where the Palestinians were claiming there had been a massacre, and about the standoff at the church in Bethlehem. These two situations became focal points of attention as the Israelis began to wind down their offensive.

REVERSAL OF FORTUNE

———

JENIN WAS A SCENE OF GREAT devastation, much of its center reduced to rubble by bulldozers and booby traps. When the Israelis
ended their two-week operation there, people poured into the area
to dig beneath the ruins for possible survivors or to retrieve the
dead. But tanks and troops continued to surround the city and armored vehicles could still be seen in the streets. Terje Roed-Larsen,
visiting the ruined camp, called the scene "horrifying beyond belief," and added, "Combating terrorism does not give a blank check
to kill civilians." He suggested that people might still be alive, buried among the dead: "You can yourself smell the stench of death all
over the place," he said. "No doubt about it, there are bodies all
over the place." The Israelis were infuriated by his remarks and by
his accusation that they had blocked access to the camp by UN and
humanitarian workers for eleven days. They accused Roed-Larsen
in turn of ignoring the deaths of twenty-three Israeli soldiers who
had been killed in the fierce fighting, and protested that they had
not allowed outsiders into the camp because of the danger of booby
traps left by Palestinian militants.[1] The centrist newspaper *Maariv*
carried a front-page column by its editor in chief describing Roed-
Larsen as "a good friend and an enthusiastic supporter of Yassir
Arafat" who "simply is not capable of distinguishing between good
and evil."[2]

Kofi Annan said he was "deeply disturbed" by reports from
Roed-Larsen and Peter Hansen on Jenin and urged the Security

Council to send a "robust" multinational peacekeeping force to the area to "halt the tragic and terrifying descent into bloodletting." The parties, he said, "left to themselves, cannot resolve their differences." Sharon responded that "Israel cannot accept international forces here." The US was likely to block such a move in the Security Council. A senior UN official said that the call for peacekeepers was "way ahead of what the market will bear right now."[3]

The Israelis agreed to let Kofi Annan send a fact-finding team to Jenin, but added that Roed-Larsen, Hansen and Mary Robinson, the UN high commissioner for human rights, would not be acceptable as fact finders.[4] Amnesty International said its preliminary review of the Jenin situation indicated that "serious breaches of international human rights and humanitarian law were committed, including war crimes." Civilians appeared to have been used as human shields and there was "credible evidence" that medical care and relief assistance had been denied. PA spokesmen said that 500 civilians had been massacred in Jenin and buried in mass graves.

Colin Powell testified before a Senate subcommittee that he had so far seen no evidence of a massacre or mass killings in Jenin. He believed a fact-finding mission was preferable to "the coarse speculation that was out there as to what happened, with terms being tossed around like massacre and mass graves, none of which so far seems to be the case."[5] But the Israelis balked at the mission, objecting to the three appointees—Martti Ahtisaari, an ex-president of Finland, Sadako Ogata, former UN high commissioner for refugees, and Cornelio Sommaruga, head of the International Committee of the Red Cross (ICRC) from 1987 to 1999. When the Israelis complained that no military man was included, Annan added William Nash, a retired US major general.

There was still unease over this mission in Israel. The *New Republic* pointed out that there was a particular objection to Sommaruga, who had worked to prevent Israel's Magen David Adom from being admitted to the ICRC.[6] There was concern, too, that

Annan had spoken of "findings and conclusions," which sounded like more than a gathering of facts, and that he had said the mission would "focus on Jenin to begin with," which gave the impression that the investigation would go beyond Jenin. In the end, Israeli resistance caused Annan to drop the mission, and as journalists, humanitarian workers and others flooded into Jenin the estimates of the number of dead dropped to around fifty, of which about a dozen were probably noncombatants. Soldiers admitted that they had used civilians as shields to protect them from booby traps while they moved house to house. Everywhere, they said, were hundreds of booby traps: "every carton, every box, there was a booby-trapped car." They insisted that no Palestinians used as shields had been killed in that way.[7] The Israelis complained that the refugee camps, under the supervision of the UN, were not supposed to harbor weapons or gunmen among the civilian population.

Arafat attempted to end his isolation in Ramallah by announcing that he had tried the five assassins of Zeevi in his compound and they, along with a man accused of arranging weapons shipments from Iran, had been sentenced to varying prison terms. These men had lived in the basement of the compound for months since they had been arrested by the Palestinians with American help. The Israelis wanted them extradited for trial in Israel, but the Americans pressured them into agreeing to lift the siege on Arafat's headquarters, in return for which the six would be removed to a prison in Jericho under guard by US and British personnel. At the beginning of May, tanks were withdrawn from the area, and President Bush said, "Chairman Arafat is now free to move around and free to lead, and we expect him to do so."[8]

The five-week standoff at the Church of the Nativity was brought to an end when the 123 Palestinian gunmen holed up there finally emerged on May 10, after an agreement was brokered by which thirteen of them, who the Israelis said had "blood on their hands," were flown on a British military plane to the beach resort of Larnaca in Cyprus to await final destinations in Europe, where they were to remain in exile possibly for three to six years. The Cypriots made it clear they were taking the men "as a temporary measure." Twenty-six other gunmen from the church were transferred to the Gaza Strip, where they were released to be welcomed as heroes. The fifteen nations of the EU had vowed to take the thirteen "senior terrorists," but when the moment arrived, they exhibited some reluctance to commit to them. After nearly two weeks of wrangling, Italy and Spain each agreed to take three of the men, Greece and Ireland each accepted two, and Portugal and Belgium one apiece. The thirteenth man, whom Israel considered the most dangerous of the group—Abdullah Daoud, the PA intelligence chief in Bethlehem—remained in Cyprus until a country could be found that was willing to take him.[9]

After Palestinian security officials and civilians left the church to be sent home, Israeli policemen, accompanied by PA officers, went in to force out ten International Solidarity foreigners who had entered the church two weeks earlier. These people were taken to a nearby police station to be held while deportation papers were being prepared for them. With the permission of church officials, IDF explosives experts went in to search for weapons and defuse bombs, if any. Ninety weapons, including M-16s and Kalashnikovs, were collected, as well as ammunition, walkie talkies and knives, and handed over to the Americans. Twenty-five bombs, discovered hidden in cupboards, were defused. The church itself was left in considerable disarray, reeking of urine, with mattresses and blankets lying on the floor, food scraps and bottles tossed on altars and a baptisimal font used as a sort of sink.[10]

Yassir Arafat was indeed free to move around, but there was a question about whether he would "lead." The heightened popularity he had enjoyed when he was imprisoned in Ramallah seemed to fizzle away when he was released, like air from a punctured balloon. He hovered in a borrowed helicopter over the ruins of Jenin and flew away without landing, having apparently been warned that there were hostile elements in the crowd that had gathered there to greet him. There were demands for reform and a new election from Palestinians, Arab nations and the EU. The infrastructure of the Palestinian Authority had been destroyed. The Israelis had found, in the offices they had invaded, documentation that implicated Arafat in suicide bombings, along with evidence that the Saudis and Iraqis had provided financial help to the families of the bombers.

As Arafat's standing plummeted, Sharon enjoyed the highest popularity ratings of any prime minister in Israeli history. Martin Indyk, in mid-March, 2002, wrote about Sharon's "three faces": the general, the politician and the statesman. The politician Indyk saw as torn between the Left and especially the Right, where Benjamin Netanyahu presented a "formidable challenge" to him and was "gaining strength" because of his "unabashed" advocacy of the destruction of the PA and the expulsion of Arafat. Sharon could only outflank Netanyahu, Indyk thought, by adopting his positions. And, indeed, on May 12, Netanyahu won a victory over Sharon when the Central Committee of the Likud voted to reject Palestinian statehood despite Sharon's argument that Israel's diplomatic options should not be limited. It was, however, a Pyrrhic victory for Netanyahu, whose approval ratings in the next weeks sank to thirteen percent while Sharon's soared to well over seventy percent.

On the other hand, Indyk saw the danger of Sharon's losing Labor from his coalition if he went "too far with force" and tried to reoccupy the West Bank and Gaza. With Labor gone, the coalition could collapse, early elections would be called and Sharon could lose the Likud leadership to Netanyahu. Now, at this writing, two months have passed: Sharon used extreme force in the West Bank and maintains a military presence there. He evidently feels his government is secure, since he ejected ministers of two Orthodox parties from his coalition because they tried to vote down his austerity budget. This action, unprecedented in any Israeli administration, increased his popularity.

Sharon's third face, Indyk wrote, is the statesman, "surprised to find himself inhabiting the prime minister's residence at the very end of his controversial career" and aware that "he has been given one last chance to remove the stigma of the ill-fated war in Lebanon from his historical legacy." In this incarnation, Sharon, unlike Sharon the general, has proposed an independent Palestinian state, hints at dismantling the settlements, and recognizes "that Arafat can benefit more than Israel from an escalation that precipitates international intervention." The statesman, Indyk concludes, must "assert himself" over the general and "become receptive to a US initiative that not only aims to stop the terror and violence but also launches a political process."[11]

Certainly it is true that Sharon has changed many of his views from the days when he was a general. But it is questionable whether there is a difference between the statesman and the politician: statesmen too must weigh initiatives and employ tactics. In the two months since Ambassador Indyk wrote his article, many imponderables have become more evident. Arafat obviously did not benefit from the military escalation; on the contrary, his Palestinian Authority is now widely understood to be corrupt and incompetent. In the matter of American support, there is the emergence of a strong pro-Israel faction in the Bush administration, which has caused the president to send many mixed signals to the Mideast. There are also the mixed responses of Arab nations. And any "political process" would surely have to consider the existence of terrorist organizations whose avowed purpose is not the establishment of a Palestinian state sharing borders with Israel, but a Palestinian state supplanting Israel.

In March of 2002, asked in an interview how he would respond to Netanyahu's suggestion that the Israelis "go after" Arafat and disarm the Palestinian Authority, Sharon replied, "There are three-and-a-half million Palestinians. Are we going once again to be re-

sponsible for their education, their health program. . . ?"[12] This was
the response of a realist, whether politician or statesman. Days later,
Sharon did go after Arafat and his intention was certainly to disarm
the Palestinian Authority. This does not necessarily mean that his
earlier response was disingenuous. What it perhaps reflects are complex problems to which no one has yet provided an immediate solution.

NOTES

CHAPTER 1: EARLY YEARS
1. Benziman, 11–12.
2. Shavitt, 13–14. (Portions of this early biography have been incorporated into this present volume.)
3. Sharon, 23.
4. Ibid., 10.
5. Benziman, 16.
6. Sharon, 25–26.
7. *Jerusalem Post*, 15 Feb 2001.
8. *Maariv*, 16 Feb 2001.
9. Ibid.
10. Ibid.
11. Ibid.
12. Benziman, 20.
13. Van Creveld, 17.
14. Morris, 99.
15. Ibid., 130.
16. Ibid., 161–62.
17. Ibid., 164.
18. Sharon, 35.
19. Ibid., 37.
20. Ibid., 37–38.
21. Ibid., 38–39.
22. Gilbert, 164.
23. Tessler, 258–61.
24. Sharon, 44.
25. Oren, *Latrun*, 154.
26. Shavitt, 26.
27. Sharon, 67.
28. Ibid., 71.
29. Shavitt, 28–30.
30. Sharon, 79–82.

CHAPTER 2: FORMATION OF UNIT 101
1. Sharon, 82.
2. Shavitt, 39.
3. Sharon, 83–91.
4. Shavitt, 43.
5. Ibid., 44.
6. Ibid., 52–53.

CHAPTER 3: THE ATTACK ON KIBEYEH
1. Shavitt, 55–63.
2. Sharon, 89–91.

CHAPTER 4: UNIT 101 & THE PARATROOPERS
1. Shavitt, 71.
2. Sharon, 93.
3. Shavitt, 72–75.

CHAPTER 5: THE GIBLI AFFAIR
1. Shavitt, 81–85.
2. Ibid.
3. Sharon, 119.

CHAPTER 6: THE GAZA RAID
1. Shavitt, 96.
2. Van Creveld, 134.
3. Ibid., 134.
4. Sharon, 102.
5. Ibid., 102–8.
6. Avneri, *Sabra*, 50.

CHAPTER 7: KUNTILLA
1. Sharon, 121–22.
2. Ibid., 113–15.
3. Shavitt, 108–12.
4. Van Creveld, 136.
5. Sharon, 119–20.

CHAPTER 8: QALQUILYA
1. Van Creveld, 138.
2. Sharon, 139–40.
3. Shavitt, 129–30.

CHAPTER 9: THE SINAI
CAMPAIGN: MITLA PASS
1. Tessler, 345.
2. Sharon, 133–34.
3. Van Creveld, 143.
4. Ibid., 146.
5. Sharon, 146–53.
6. Van Creveld, 151.

CHAPTER 10: CHANGE OF PACE
1. Sharon, 154–56.
2. Ibid., 156.
3. Ibid., 163.
4. Ibid., 168.
5. Gilbert, 352.
6. Sharon, 168.
7. Ibid., 154–63.

CHAPTER 11: THE SIX-DAY WAR
1. Sharon, 180–83.
2. Van Creveld, 183.
3. Sharon, 199–201.
4. Shavitt, 153.

CHAPTER 12: A NEW REALITY
1. Gilbert, 394.
2. Herzog, 171.
3. Kimche, 254–55.
4. Sharon, 213–14.

5. Ibid., 209.
6. Ibid., 210.
7. Ibid., 215.
8. Ibid., 217.
9. Benziman, 105.

CHAPTER 13: THE WAR OF ATTRITION
1. Herzog, 176–77.
2. Sharon, 219.
3. Hohenberg, 99.
4. Morris, 347.
5. Avneri, *War*, 62.
6. Van Creveld, 211.
7. Gilbert, 407.
8. Sharon, 220.
9. Ibid., 221.
10. Ibid., 222–27.
11. Avneri, *War*, 49.
12. Sharon, 231–32.
13. Elli Lieberman, "Deterrence
    Theory: Success or Failure in Arab-
    Israeli Wars," National Defense
    University, McNair Paper 45, Oct
    1995.
14. Sharon, 228–29.
15. Ibid., 229–30.
16. Morris, 354, 360.
17. Ibid., 362. According to Dr Meir
    Pael, 911 Israelis died on all fronts
    in the War of Attrition.

CHAPTER 14: FIGHTING TERROR
1. Sharon, 240.
2. Ibid., 241.
3. Dayan, 515–17.
4. Morris, 377, 380.
5. Gilbert, 418.
6. Ibid., 417.
7. Van Creveld, 210.

8. Herzog, 156.
9. Sharon, 249.
10. Ibid., 250.
11. Sharon, 250.
12. Ibid., 252.
13. Ibid., 253.
14. Dayan, 486–88.
15. Sharon, 261.
16. Benziman, 117–18.
17. Sharon, 262.

CHAPTER 15: WHOOP'D OUT
1. Sharon, 265.
2. Ibid., 267–68.
3. Ibid., 271.
4. Benziman, 124.
5. Ibid., 123.
6. Sharon, 278–81.
7. Ibid., 286–87.
8. Benziman, 135.

CHAPTER 16: THE YOM KIPPUR WAR
1. Nakdimon, 81.
2. Ibid., 89.
3. Dayan, 564.
4. Sharon, 290–92.
5. Van Creveld, 227.
6. Dayan, 592–94.
7. Sharon, 298–99.
8. Ibid., 303.
9. Van Creveld, 233.
10. Dayan, 654–55.

CHAPTER 17: POLITICS
1. Benziman, 174.
2. Sharon, 339.
3. Ibid., 338.
4. Ibid., 340.
5. Benziman, 177.

6. Sharon, 341.

CHAPTER 18: POST-WAR TURBULENCE
1. Dayan, 736.
2. Sela, 388.
3. Ibid., 743.
4. Ibid.
5. Ibid, 709–20.
6. Benziman, 182.
7. Sharon, 341.
8. Benziman, 183.

CHAPTER 19: GROUND CONTROL
1. Benziman, 184.
2. Golan, 135–36.
3. Sharon, 347.
4. Gilbert, 469–70.
5. Benziman, 185–86.

CHAPTER 20: PARACHUTING FROM SHLOMZION
1. Benziman, 192.
2. Ibid., 193–94.
3. Ibid., 195–96.
4. Sharon, 352–53.
5. Ibid., 300–51.
6. Benziman, 200–1.
7. Herzog, 222–23.
8. Sharon, 354.

CHAPTER 21: THE SETTLEMENTS
1. Van Creveld, 340.
2. Benziman, 206–7.
3. Sharon, 357–59.
4. Gilbert, 486.
5. Interview with Uri Dan in a special supplement to Maariv, 1998.
6. Arutz 7 Radio.
7. Benziman, 218.
8. Ibid., 214.

CHAPTER 22: ATTEMPTS AT
PEACE WITH EGYPT
1. Gilbert, 399–400.
2. Morris, 446.
3. Ibid., 447.
4. Ibid., 449.
5. Ibid., 451, 455.
6. Sharon, 376.
7. Benziman, 204.
8. Morris, 453.
9. Benziman, 211.
10. Ibid.
11. Morris, 460.
12. Benziman, 213.
13. Ibid., 214.
14. Sharon, 396–97.
15. Herzog, 231.
16. Benziman, 209.
17. Morris, 483.

CHAPTER 23: THE ROAD TO PEACE
1. Morris, 491–93.
2. Hohenberg, 210–11.
3. Sharon, 383.
4. Ibid., 381.

CHAPTER 24: HOT FARM
1. Benziman, 227.
2. Avneri, War, 88.
3. Ibid., 90–91.
4. Ibid., 91.
5. Benziman, 227–28.
6. Interview with Uri Dan in a special
supplement to Maariv, 1998.

CHAPTER 25: LEBANON
1. Sharon, 427.
2. Benziman, 231.
3. Morris, 521.

4. Van Creveld, 292.
5. Ibid., 293.
6. Morris, 528.
7. Ibid., 531.
8. Van Creveld, 297.
9. Morris, 533.
10. Van Creveld, 299–301.
11. Ibid., 299.
12. Ibid., 298.
13. Sharon, 508.

CHAPTER 26: AFTER THE MASSACRE
1. Sharon, n507.
2. Sharon, 509, 510, 517.
3. Ibid., 516.
4. Ibid., 518.
5. Ibid., 519–20.
6. Ibid., 521.

CHAPTER 27: A TIME OF TRIAL
Credit for details must go to Renata
Adler's Reckless Disregard.
1. Adler, 8.
2. Ibid., 14.
3. Ibid., 23.
4. Sharon, 528.

CHAPTER 28: LEBANON CONTINUED
1. Sharon, 529.

CHAPTER 29: THE FIRST INTIFADA
1. Discussions in Van Creveld, 335–52;
Morris, 561–610; Gilbert, 525–42.
2. Van Creveld, 342.
3. Ibid., 341.
4. Ibid., 343. See also Gilbert, 526,
for a different reading of the
"breaking bones" admonition.
5. Van Creveld, 355.

6. Avneri, *War*, 381–84. At the Central Committee meeting, Shamir called for an open vote on his policy; Sharon, who had expected a secret ballot, shouted out loaded questions for his own open vote ("Whoever is in favor of stopping terror in Jerusalem, raise your hand"). It was discovered later that Sharon's ally, Uri Shani, had disconnected Shamir's microphone. Shamir then departed the building with several ministers, leaving Sharon, David Levy and Yitzhak Modai in charge of the meeting.

CHAPTER 30: PEACE CONFERENCES & TERROR
1. *Time Europe*, 20 Sep 1993.
2. Morris, 634–35.
3. Ibid., 626.

CHAPTER 31: CHALLENGES, 1994 & 1995
1. *Seattle Times*, 13 Jan 1994.
2. *Washington Post*, 13 Jan 1994.
3. *Los Angeles Times*, 28 May 1994.
4. *Jerusalem Post*, 29 May 1994.
5. *Los Angeles Times*, 28 May 1994.
6. *Guardian* (UK), 7 June 1994.
7. *Jerusalem Post*, 23 Feb 1995.
8. Ibid., 20 Mar 1995.
9. Ibid., 7 July 1995.
10. (London) *Times*, 19 Oct 1995.

CHAPTER 32: ASSASSINATION
1. *Jerusalem Post*, 17 Nov 1995.
2. *Boston Globe*, 17 Nov 1995.
3. *Jerusalem Post*, 17 Nov 1995.
4. *Boston Globe*, 17 Nov 1995.
5. *Washington Times*, 8 Dec 1995.

6. *Los Angeles Times*, 17 Aug 1995.
7. *San Francisco Chronicle,* 17 Aug 1995.
8. *Los Angeles Times*, 17 Aug 1995.
9. *Washington Times*, 12 Aug 1995.
10. *Jerusalem Post*, 22 Dec 1995.

CHAPTER 33: POLITICAL SHIFT 1996
1. *Irish Times* (Dublin), 8 July 1996.
2. *Los Angeles Times*, 14 July 1996.
3. Ibid., 6 Sep 1996.
4. *Irish Times* (Dublin), 7 Sep 1996.
5. CNN Report from Jerrold Kessel, 25 Sep 1996; Nadav Shragai, "The Tunnel," *Haaretz,* 25 Sep 1996; AP, 25 Sep 1996.
6. (Bloomington, IL) *Pantagraph*, 25 Nov 1996.
7. *Jerusalem Post*, 19 Sep 1997.

CHAPTER 34: JUGGLING FOR POWER
1. *Boston Globe*, 27 June 1997.
2. *Jerusalem Post*, 27 June 1997.
3. *Independent* (UK), 25 Jun 1997.
4. *Guardian* (UK), 26 Jun 1997.
5. *Daily Telegraph* (London), 26 Jun 1997.
6. *Boston Globe,* 27 Jun 1997.
7. *Christian Science Monitor,* 3 Jul 1997.
8. *Jerusalem Post*, 1 Jul 1997.
9. *Irish Times* (Dublin), 9 Jul 1997.
10. *Washington Post*, 10 Jul 1997.
11. *Jerusalem Post*, 10 Jul 1997.
12. Ibid.
13. Ibid., 11 Jul 1997.
14. Ibid.
15. Ibid., 16 Jul 1997.
16. Ibid., 22 Sep 1997.

CHAPTER 35: LITIGATION AGAIN
1. Morris, *n*724.
2. *Milwaukee Journal Sentinel*, 5 Nov 1997.
3. *ArabicNews.com*, 6 Nov 1997.
4. *Jerusalem Post*, 20 Feb 2002.

CHAPTER 36: LOOSE CANNON
1. *Jerusalem Post*, 9 Mar 1998.
2. *Guardian* (UK), 16 Mar 1998.
3. *Jerusalem Post*, 22 Mar 1998.
4. *Irish Times* (Dublin), 16 Mar 1998.
5. CNN, Jerrold Kessel with AP and Reuters, 1 Apr 1998.
6. *New York Times*, 13 May 1998.
7. (London) *Times*, 29 Sep 1998.
8. *Seattle Times*, 10 Oct 1998.
9. BBC Monitoring, Israel TV Channel 1, 9 Oct 1998.

CHAPTER 37: THE WYE CONFERENCE: 1998
1. *Los Angeles Times*, 10 Nov 1998.
2. *Tulsa World*, 10 Oct 1998.
3. BBC Monitoring, Voice of Israel Radio.
4. *Jerusalem Post*, 14 Oct 1998. Natan Sharansky was a famous dissenter who had been in prison in Russia and released to immigrate to Israel.
5. BBC Monitoring, Israel Educational TV, 14 Oct 1998.
6. *Jerusalem Post*, 18 Oct 1998.
7. Ibid., 21 Oct 1998.
8. *Irish Times* (Dublin), 19 Oct 1998.
9. Ibid.
10. *New York Times*, 20 Oct 1998.
11. Morris, 646–47.

12. BBC Monitoring, Voice of Israel Radio, 24 Oct 1998.
13. *Jerusalem Post*, 26 Oct 1998.
14. BBC Monitoring, Voice of Israel Radio, 24 Oct 1998.
15. BBC Monitoring, Israel TV Channel 1.
16. *Boston Globe*, 27 Oct 1998.

CHAPTER 38: AFTER WYE
1. *Jerusalem Post*, 29 Oct 1998.
2. *Washington Post*, 17 Nov 1998.
3. Ibid.
4. Ibid.
5. *Irish Times* (Dublin), 17 Nov 1998.
6. Ibid., 19 Nov 1998.
7. BBC Monitoring, Israel TV Channel 2, 23 Nov 1998.
8. Ibid.
9. BBC Monitoring, Newsfile, 23 Nov 1998.
10. Ibid.
11. Morris, 648–49.

CHAPTER 39: FAILING COALITION, FAILING PEACE
1. *Jerusalem Post*, 8 Dec 1998.
2. Ibid., 10 Dec 1998.
3. Ibid., 11 Dec 1998.
4. BBC Monitoring, Israel TV Channel 1, 16 Dec 1998.
5. BBC Monitoring, Voice of Israel Radio, 27 Dec 1998.
6. Xinhua News Agency, 5 Jan 1999.

CHAPTER 40: FOREIGN AFFAIRS
1. *Jerusalem Post*, 14 Jan 1999.
2. Ibid., 13 Jan 1999.
3. Ibid., 14 Jan 1999.
4. Ibid., 15 Jan 1999.

5. Ibid., 14 Jan 1999.
6. Ibid., 15 Jan 1999.
7. Itar-Tass News Wire, 20 Jan 1999.
8. *Jerusalem Post*, 22 Jan 1999.
9. BBC Monitoring, 29 Jan 1999.
10. *Jerusalem Post*, 19 Jan 1999.
11. Ibid., 25 Jan 1999.
12. BBC Monitoring, Newsfile, 29 Jan 1999.

CHAPTER 41: THE END OF AN ERA
1. *Jerusalem Post*, 4 Feb 1999.
2. *Guardian* (UK), 9 Feb 1999.
3. *New York Times*, 10 Feb 1999.

CHAPTER 42: POLITICS 1999
1. *New York Times*, 16 Feb 1999.
2. Ibid., 17 Feb 1999; *New York Post*, 21 Feb 1999.
3. *Jerusalem Post*, 19 Feb 1999.
4. Xinhua News Agency, 22 Feb 1999.
5. *Irish Times* (Dublin), 4 Mar 1999.
6. Ibid.
7. (London) *Times*, 17 Mar 1999.
8. *Irish Times* (Dublin), 17 Mar 1999.
9. *Jerusalem Post*, 19 Mar 1999.
10. Ibid.
11. Ibid.
12. BBC Monitoring, Israel TV Channel 2, 20 Mar 1999.
13. *Jerusalem Post*, 21 Mar 1999.
14. *Irish Times* (Dublin), 3 Apr 1999; Xinhua News Agency, 2 Apr 1999.
15. BBC Monitoring, Voice of Israel Radio, 6 Apr 1999.
16. *Jerusalem Post*, 11 Apr 1999.
17. *Independent* (UK), 13 Apr 1999.
18. Ibid.
19 *Irish Times* (Dublin), 3 Apr 1999.

20. *New York Times*, 7 Apr 1999.
21. *Irish Times* (Dublin), 3 Apr 1999.
22. *Financial Times*, 12 Apr 1999.
23. *Jerusalem Post*, 3 Apr 1999.
24. *New York Times*, 7 Apr 1999.
25. *Jerusalem Post*, 9 Apr 1999.
26. Ibid.
27. Ibid., 11 Apr 1999.
28. Ibid., 8 Apr 1999.
29. Ibid., 15 Apr 1999.
30. *Irish Times* (Dublin), 14 Apr 1999.
31. *Jerusalem Post*, 14 Apr 1999.
32. Ibid., 26 Apr 1999.
33. Ibid., 3 May 1999.

CHAPTER 43: END OF THE CAMPAIGN
1. *Washington Times*, 17 May 1999.
2. *Jerusalem Post*, 12 May 1999.
3. *Milwaukee Journal Sentinel*, 5 May 1999.
4. *New York Times*, 11 May 1999.
5. BBC Monitoring, Israel TV Channel 2, 17 May 1999.
6. *Jerusalem Post*, 19 May 1999.
7. Ibid., 3 Jun 1999.
8. BBC Monitoring, Newsfile, Voice of Israel Radio, *Jerusalem Post*, 28 Jun 1999.
9. *New York Post, Jerusalem Post*, 29 Jun 1999.
10. *Irish Times* (Dublin), 7 Jul 1999.

CHAPTER 44: PARTY LEADER
1. *Jerusalem Post*, 12 Jul 1999.
2. Ibid., 11 Aug 1999.
3. Ibid., 23 Aug 1999.
4. Ibid., 5 Sep 1999.
5. Ibid., 3 Sep 1999.
6. Ibid.

CHAPTER 45: IMMUTABLE POSITIONS
1. Morris, 653.
2. BBC Monitoring, Voice of Israel Radio, 8 Sep 1999.
3. *Jerusalem Post*, 24 Sep 1999.
4. Ibid., 16 Sep 1999.
5. *Independent* (UK), 15 Oct 1999.
6. *Jerusalem Post*, 20 Oct 1999.
7. Ibid., 4 Nov 1999.
8. Ibid., 9 Nov 1999.
9. Ibid., 12 Nov 1999.
10. Ibid.
11. Ibid.
12. Ibid., 1 Dec 1999.
13. *New York Times*, 10 Dec 1999.
14. Ibid.
15. *Jerusalem Post*, 10 Dec 1999.
16. *New York Times*, 10 Dec 1999.
17. Ibid.
18. *Jerusalem Post*, 17 Dec 1999; *New York Times*, 28 Dec 1999.
19. Ibid., 22 Feb 2000.

CHAPTER 46: LILY
1. *Jerusalem Post*, 26 Mar 2000.
2. *Maariv*, 22 Mar 2001.
3. Ibid.
4. *New York Post*, 2 Apr 2000.
5. *Jerusalem Post*, 17 Apr 2000.

CHAPTER 47: FAMILY MATTERS
1. *Yediot Aharonoth*, 2 Feb 2001.
2. *Tel Aviv Magazine*, 12 Jan 2001.
3. Ibid.
4. Ibid.
5. Ibid.
6. Ibid.

CHAPTER 48: LEBANON & POLITICS
1. *Jerusalem Post*, 4 May 2000.
2. BBC Monitoring, Israel TV Channel 1, 6 May 2000.
3. *Wall Street Journal*, 31 May 2000.
4. *Jerusalem Post*, 1 Jun 2000.
5. Middle East News Online, 13 Jun 2000.
6. *Irish Times* (Dublin), 11 Jul 2000.
7. BBC Monitoring, Israel TV Channel 1, 10 Jul 2000.
8. *Jerusalem Post*, 11 Jul 2000.
9. *Irish Times* (Dublin), 11 Jul 2000.
10. *Washington Times*, 12 Jul 2000.

CHAPTER 49: CAMP DAVID
1. *Washington Times*, 12 Jul 2000.
2. Ibid.
3. *Irish Times* (Dublin), 17 Jul 2000.
4. *New York Post*, 6 Aug 2000.
5. *St. Louis Post-Dispatch*, 21 Jul 2000.
6. Ibid.
7. *New York Times*, 21 Jul 2000.
8. Morris, 659.
9. *New York Times*, 1 Aug 2000.
10. Ibid.
11. *Jerusalem Post*, 1 Aug 2000.
12. *Boston Globe*, 2 Aug 2000.
13. *Jerusalem Post*, 2 Aug 2000.
14. *Boston Globe*, 2 Aug 2000.
15. Ibid.
16. Ibid.

CHAPTER 50: BARAK AT BAY
1. *Los Angeles Times*, 2 Aug 2000.
2. *Boston Globe*, 20 Aug 2000.
3. *Jerusalem Post*, 3 Aug 2000.
4. *Irish Times* (Dublin), 9 Aug 2000.

5. *Los Angeles Times*, 2 Aug 2000.
6. *Irish Times* (Dublin), 2 Aug 2000.
7. *New York Post*, 6 Aug 2000.
8. Ibid.
9. *Sunday Telegraph* (London), 6 Aug 2000.
10. *South China Morning Post*, 21 Aug 2000.
11. Ibid.
12. *Los Angeles Times*, 22 Aug 2000.
13. *New York Times*, 24 Aug 2000.
14. *Jerusalem Post*, 25 Aug 2000.
15. Ibid., 27 Aug 2000.
16. *New York Times*, 25 Aug 2000.
17. *Jerusalem Post*, 31 Aug 2000.
18. *Los Angeles Times*, 26 Aug 2000.
19. *New York Times*, 6 Sep 2000.
20. *Los Angeles Times*, 12 Sep 2000.
21. *Jerusalem Post*, 12 Sep 2000.

CHAPTER: 51: AL-AQSA INTIFADA
1. BBC Monitoring, Voice of Palestine Radio, Ramallah, 27 Sep 2000.
2. *Jerusalem Post*, 27 Sep 2000.
3. Ibid.
4. Morris, 660.
5. *Los Angeles Times*, 29 Sep 2000.
6. *Boston Globe*, 2 Aug 2000.
7. *Los Angeles Times*, 29 Sep 2000.
8. Ibid.
9. *Washington Post*, 30 Sep 2000; BBC Monitoring, Voice of Palestine Radio, Ramallah, 28 Sep 2000.
10. (London) *Times*, 30 Sep 2000.
11. *Jerusalem Post*, 29 Sep 2000.
12. Ibid.
13. Ibid.

14. BBC Monitoring, Voice of Palestine Radio, Ramallah, 28 Sep 2000.
15. BBC Monitoring, Manar TV, Beirut, 28 Sep 2000.
16. *Washington Post*, 30 Sep 2000.
17. *St. Louis Post-Dispatch*, 28 Sep 2000.
18. *New York Daily News*, 28 Sep 2000.
19. *Jerusalem Post*, 29 Sep 2000.
20. *New York Post*, 29 Sep 2000.
21. *Independent* (UK), 9 Oct 2000.
22. *USA Today*, 10 Oct 2000.
23. *Daily Telegraph* (London), 10 Oct 2000.
24. *Guardian* (UK), 11 Oct 2000. The documentary evidence was based on the Gaza pathologist's determination that "the bullets that hit the boy were fired from above" and that "Israeli soldiers were stationed in low positions." In any case, the documentary found the boy's death to be accidental. See Ellis Shuman, *Israeli Insider,* 20 Mar 2002.
25. *Palm Beach Post*, 13 Oct 2000.
26. *Cleveland Plain Dealer*, 14 Oct 2000.
27. *Irish Times* (Dublin), 14 Oct 2000.
28. *Guardian* (UK), 13 Oct 2000.
29. *New York Post*, 15 Oct 2000.
30. *Independent* (UK), 13 Oct 2000.
31. Interview with Brit Hume on Fox News, 21 Apr 2000.
32. *Daily Telegraph* (London), 14 Oct 2000.

33. *Washington Post*, 15 Oct 2000.
34. *New York Times*, 15 Oct 2000.
35. *Jerusalem Post*, 17 Oct 2000.
36. *Newsday*, 17 Oct 2000.
37. Middle East News Online, 17 Oct 2000.
38. *Daily Telegraph* (London), 18 Oct 2000.
39. *Jerusalem Post*, 18 Oct 2000.
40. *Financial Times*, 18 Oct 2000.
41. *Daily Telegraph* (London), 18 Oct 2000.
42. Middle East News Online (from *Haaretz*), 19 Oct 2000.
43. *Los Angeles Times*, 19 Oct 2000.
44. Ibid., 22 Oct 2000.
45. (London) *Times*, 24 Oct 2000.
46. Middle East News Online, 23 Oct 2000.
47. *Jerusalem Post*, 25 Oct 2000.
48. *New York Times*, 26 Oct 2000.
49. *Jerusalem Post*, 25 Oct 2000.
50. Ibid., 27 Oct 2000.
51. Ibid.
52. Middle East News Online, 31 Oct 2000.
53. *Financial Times*, 27 Oct 2000.
54. *Los Angeles Times*, 30 Oct 2000.
55. *Jerusalem Post*, 22 Oct 2000; *Christian Century*, 8 Nov 2000.
56. *Jerusalem Post*, 2 Nov 2000.
57. *Observer* (UK), 19 Nov 2000.
58. *Jerusalem Post*, 1 Apr 2001.

CHAPTER 52: POLITICAL MANEUVERS
1. *Jerusalem Post*, 23 Nov 2000.
2. *New York Post*, 24 Nov 2000.
3. *New York Times*, 23 Nov 2000.

4. *Washington Post*, 29 Nov 2000.
5. *Financial Times*, 30 Nov 2000.
6. Middle East News Online, 6 Dec 2000.
7. *Independent* (UK), 14 Oct 2000.
8. *New York Times*, 10 Dec 2000.
9. *Boston Globe*, 11 Dec 2000.
10. *Jerusalem Post*, 17 Dec 2000.
11. *New York Times*, 19 Dec 2000.
12. *Washington Post*, 22 Dec 2000.

CHAPTER 53: CLINTON'S LAST TRY
1. *Los Angeles Times*, 19 Dec 2000.
2. *Washington Times*, 19 Dec 2000.
3. *Pittsburgh Post-Gazette*, 26 Dec 2000.
4. *Los Angeles Times*, 27 Dec 2000.
5. Ibid.
6. *Financial Times*, 27 Dec 2000.
7. *Los Angeles Times*, 28 Dec 2000.
8. *Guardian* (UK), 29 Dec 2000.
9. *Los Angeles Times*, 28 Dec 2000.
10. *Christian Science Monitor*, 29 Dec 2000.
11. Ibid.
12. *Independent* (UK), 31 Dec 2000.
13. *Los Angeles Times*, 28 Dec 2000.
14. *Jerusalem Post*, 28 Dec 2000.
15. Ibid.
16. *Jerusalem Post*, 26 Dec 2000.
17. Ibid., 27 Dec 2000.
18. Ibid.
19. *New York Post*, 28 Dec 2000.
20. *Jerusalem Post*, 28 Dec 2000.
21. BBC Monitoring, Tishrin website, Damascus, 28 Dec 2000.
22. *Jerusalem Post*, 29 Dec 2000.
23. *Independent* (UK), 30 Dec 2000.

CHAPTER 54: ON THE CAMPAIGN TRAIL
1. *Yediot Aharonoth*, 2 Feb 2001.
2. Ibid.
3. Ibid.
4. Ibid.
5. Ibid.

CHAPTER 55: ELECTION 2001: "ONLY SHARON CAN BRING PEACE"
1. *Jerusalem Post*, 14 Jan 2001.
2. Ibid., 15 Jan 2001.
3. Ibid., 19 Jan 2001.
4. Ibid., 23 Jan 2001.
5. Ibid., 19 Jan 2001.
6. *Los Angeles Times*, 20 Jan 2001 & 21 Jan 2001; *Sunday Times* (London), 21 Jan 2001.
7. *Los Angeles Times*, 21 Jan 2001.
8. *Financial Times*, 19 Jan 2001.
9. *Sunday Times* (London), 21 Jan 2001.
10. *Jerusalem Post*, 21 Jan 2001.
11. *Financial Times*, 20 Jan 2001.
12. *Jerusalem Post*, 23 Jan 2001.
13. Ibid.
14. Ibid.
15. *Washington Post*, 20 Jan 2001.
16. *Jerusalem Post*, 22 Jan 2001.
17. *Washington Times*, 24 Jan 2001.
18. Ibid., 25 Jan 2001.
19. *Scotsman* (Edinburgh), 26 Jan 2001.
20. *Washington Times*, 25 Jan 2001.
21. (Baltimore) *Sun*, 27 Jan 2001.
22. *Jerusalem Post*, 25 Jan 2001.
23. *St. Louis Post-Dispatch*, 25 Jan 2001.
24. *Boston Globe*, 25 Jan 2001.

25. *Jerusalem Post*, 25 Jan 2001.
26. Ibid., 26 Jan 2001.
27. *Irish Times* (Dublin), 26 Jan 2001.
28. *Washington Post*, 28 Jan 2001.
29. *Jerusalem Post*, 28 Jan 2001.
30. *New York Times*, 29 Jan 2001.
31. (Bergen County, NJ) *Evening Record*, 30 Jan 2001.
32. *Jerusalem Post*, *New York Times*, 30 Jan 2001.
33. *New York Times*, 30 Jan 2001.
34. *Jerusalem Post*, 31 Jan 2001.
35. Ibid., 29 Jan 2001.

CHAPTER 56: VICTORY
1. *Jerusalem Post*, 7 Feb 2001.
2. Ibid.
3. Ibid.
4. *Denver Post*, 7 Feb 2001.
5. *Jerusalem Post*, 8 Feb 2001.
6. Ibid.
7. Ibid.
8. *New York Times*, 7 Feb 2001.
9. *Jerusalem Post*, 8 Feb 2001.
10. *New York Times*, 8 Feb 2001.
11. Agence France-Presse, 7 Feb 2001.
12. *Jerusalem Post*, 9 Feb 2001.
13. Ibid.
14. *Independent* (UK), 10 Feb 2001.
15. *Maariv*, 22 Mar 2001.

CHAPTER 57: POST-ELECTION
1. *Guardian* (UK), 12 Feb 2001.
2. *Jerusalem Post*, 11 Feb 2001.
3. Ibid., 12 Feb 2001.
4. Ibid., 11 Feb 2001.
5. *Los Angeles Times*, 14 Feb 2001.
6. *Christian Science Monitor*, *Jerusalem Post*, 15 Feb 2001.

7. *Pittsburgh Post-Gazette*, 15 Feb 2001.
8. Ibid.
9. *Irish Times* (Dublin), 15 Feb 2001.
10. *Christian Science Monitor*, 15 Feb 2001.
11. *Irish Times* (Dublin), *Cincinnati Post*, *Jerusalem Post*, 16 Feb 2001.
12. *New York Times*, 13 Feb 2001.
13. *Washington Post*, 16 Feb 2001.
14. *New York Times* & *Irish Times* (Dublin), 16 Feb 2001; *Los Angeles Times*, 15 Feb 2001.
15. *Boston Globe*, 21 Feb 2001.
16. (London) *Times*, 22 Feb 2001.
17. *Jerusalem Post*, 22 Feb 2001.
18. *Los Angeles Times*, 22 Feb 2001.
19. *Jerusalem Post*, 23 Feb 2001.
20. *Los Angeles Times*, 22 Feb 2001.
21. Xinhua New Agency, 24 Feb 2001.
22. *Los Angeles Times*, 27 Feb 2001; *Jerusalem Post*, 26 Feb 2001.
23. *Irish Times* (Dublin), 27 Feb 2001.
24. *Jerusalem Post*, 27 Feb 2001.
25. Ibid., 26 Feb 2001.
26. Ibid.
27. *St. Louis Post-Dispatch*, 26 Feb 2001.
28. *Wall Street Journal*, 26 Feb 2001.
29. *Jerusalem Post*, 26 Feb 2001.
30. Ibid.
31. *Wall Street Journal*, 26 Feb 2001.
32. *Washington Post*, 22 Feb 2001.
33. *Jerusalem Post*, 27 Feb 2001.

CHAPTER 58: BUILDING A COALITION
1. *New York Times*, 8 Mar 2001.
2. *Daily Telegraph* (London), 8 Mar 2001.

3. *Boston Globe*, 8 Mar 2001.
4. Middle East News Online, 31 Aug 2001.
5. *Jerusalem Post*, 23 Feb 2001.
6. *Daily Telegraph* (London), 7 Mar 2001.
7. *Jerusalem Post*, 8 Mar 2001.
8. *Irish Times* (Dublin), 8 Mar 2001.
9 Ibid., 14 Mar 2001.
10. *Jerusalem Post*, 4 Mar 2001. *Al-Ayam*, the PA daily newspaper reported (6 Dec 2000) that Falouji, speaking at a symposium in Gaza, confirmed that the PA had begun to prepare the intifada immediately upon conclusion of the Camp David talks. On March 4, 2001, Lamia Lahoud reported in the *Jerusalem Post* that Falouji told a PLO rally in a South Lebanon refugee camp that the intifada "was not a spontaneous reaction to [Sharon's] September visit to the Temple Mount but was planned after peace talks failed in July."
11. *Jerusalem Post*, 6 Mar 2001.
12. Ibid., 8 Mar 2001.
13. *New York Times*, 9 Mar 2001.
14. Ibid.
15. *Jerusalem Post*, 9 Mar 2001.

CHAPTER 59: BLOCKADE
1. *Jerusalem Post*, 13 Mar 2001.
2. *Los Angeles Times*, 12 Mar 2001.
3. (Baltimore) *Sun*, 12 Mar 2001.
4. Ibid.
5. *Los Angeles Times*, 12 Mar 2001.
6. *Jerusalem Post*, 12 Mar 2001.
7. *Guardian* (UK), 14 Mar 2001.

8. *Financial Times*, 14 Mar 2001.
9. Ibid.
10. *Jerusalem Post*, 14 Mar 2001.
11. *Irish Times* (Dublin), 17 Mar 2001.
12. *Observer* (UK), 18 Mar 2001.
13. Ibid.
14. *Washington Post*, 20 Mar 2001.
15. Ibid.
16. Ibid.
17. *Washington Times*, 20 Mar 2001.
18. Ibid.
19. Ibid.
20. *Los Angeles Times*, 20 Mar 2001.
21. Ibid.
22. *Washington Post*, 20 Mar 2001.
23. Ibid.
24. *New York Daily News*, 22 Mar 2001.
25. *New York Times*, 20 Mar 2001.
26. *San Diego Union-Tribune*, 21 Mar 2001.
27. *Irish Times* (Dublin), 21 Mar 2001.
28. Middle East News Online, 22 Mar 2001.
29. *Jerusalem Post*, 22 Mar 2001.
30. Ibid.
31. *Washington Post*, 23 Mar 2001.
32. BBC Monitoring, Israel TV Channel 1, 22 Mar 2001.

CHAPTER 60: DARK TUNNEL
1. Xinhua New Agency & Middle East News Online, 23 Mar 2001.
2. Xinhua News Agency, 26 Mar 2001.
3. *Los Angeles Times*, 23 Mar 2001.
4. (London) *Times*, 28 Mar 2001.

5. Ibid.
6. *Washington Post*, 2 Apr 2001.
7. *Jerusalem Post*, 28 Mar 2001.
8. *New York Times, Washington Post & Los Angeles Times*, 27 Mar 2001.
9. Xinhua News Agency, 30 Mar 2001.
10. *Jerusalem Post*, 30 Mar 2001.
11. Ibid., 28 Mar 2001.
12. *Newsday*, 28 Mar 2001.
13. *Jerusalem Post*, 28 Mar 2001.
14. *Los Angeles Times*, 27 Mar 2001.
15. *Financial Times*, 27 Mar 2001.
16. Middle East News Online, 27 Mar 2001.
17. Ibid.
18. *Guardian* (UK), 28 Mar 2001.

CHAPTER 61: DAYS OF RAGE
1. *Financial Times*, 29 Mar 2001.
2. *New York Times*, 29 Mar 2001.
3. Ibid.; *Washington Post*, 30 Mar 2001.
4. *Washington Post*, 30 Mar 2001.
5. *Atlanta Journal-Constitution*, 30 Mar 2001.
6. *Washington Post*, 30 Mar 2001.
7. *Chicago Sun-Times*, 1 Apr 2001.
8. *Daily Mail* (London), 31 Mar 2001.
9. *New York Times*, 2 Apr 2001.
10. *Jerusalem Post*, 2 Apr 2001.
11. Ibid., 3 Apr 2001.
12. *Los Angeles Times*, 4 Apt 200.
13. *Independent*, 3 Apr 2001.
14. Middle East News Online, 3 Apr 2001.
15. *Boston Globe*, 4 Apr 2001.
16. *Jerusalem Post*, 6 Apr 2001.

17. *Chicago Sun-Times*, 3 Apr 2001.
18. Middle East News Online, 8 Apr 2001.
19. *New York Times*, 5 Apr 2001.
20. *Jerusalem Post*, 6 Apr 2001.
21. BBC Monitoring, 4 Apr 2001.
22. (London) *Times*, 6 Apr 2001.
23. Middle East News Online, 8 Apr 2001.
24. (London) *Times*, 6 Apr 2001.
25. Middle East News Online, 8 Apr 2001.
26. *St. Louis Post-Dispatch*, 21 Apr 2001.

CHAPTER 62: STRIKES &
COUNTER-STRIKES
1. *Los Angeles Times*, 12 Apr 2001.
2. *Irish Times* (Dublin), 17 Apr 2001.
3. *USA Today*, 18 Apr 2001.
4. (Augusta, GA) *Chronicle*, 19 Apr 2001.
5. Ibid.
6. (London) *Times*, 19 Apr 2001.
7. *Jerusalem Post*, 23 Apr 2001.
8. *USA Today*, 18 Apr 2001.
9. *Jerusalem Post*, 22 Apr 2001.
10. Middle East News Online, 25 Apr 2001.
11. Ibid.
12. *Birmingham Post* (UK), 21 Apr 2001.
13. BBC Monitoring, 14 Apr 2001; *San Diego Union-Tribune*, 14 Apr 2001.
14. *Daily Telegraph* (London), 21 Apr 2001.
15. *Jerusalem Post*, 17 Apr 2001.
16. Ibid., 7 May 2001.

CHAPTER 63: ACTIONS & NO DECISIONS
1. BBC Monitoring, 15 Apr 2001.
2. Ibid., 13 Apr 2001
3. *Jerusalem Post*, 17 Apr 2001.
4. *Irish Times* (Dublin), 24 Apr 2001.
5. *Jerusalem Post*, 24 Apr 2001.
6. Ibid., 17 Apr 2001.
7. *Irish Times* (Dublin), 24 Apr 2001.
8. Ibid., 30 Apr 2001.
9. Xinhua News Agency, 19 Apr 2001.
10. *Jerusalem Post*, 17 Apr 2001.
11. *Irish Times* (Dublin), 24 Apr 2001.
12. BBC Monitoring, 30 Apr 2001.
13. *Irish Times* (Dublin), 30 Apr 2001.
14. *Jerusalem Post*, 16 Apr 2001.
15. BBC Monitoring, Al-Sharq Al-Awsat website, 22 Apr 2001.
16. *Daily Telegraph* (London), 24 Apr 2001.
17. Ibid.
18. Ibid.
19. *Evening Standard* (London), 25 Apr 2001.
20. (Grand Rapids, MI) *Press*, 24 Apr 2001.
21. *Newsday*, 27 Apr 2001.
22. *Washington Post*, 26 Apr 2001.

CHAPTER 64: MITCHELL
"COTTON CANDY"
1. *New York Times*, 6 May 2001.
2. (London) *Times*, 8 May 2001.
3. *Financial Times*, 7 May 2001; (London) *Times*, 8 May 2001.
4. (London) *Times*, 8 May 2001.
5. *Jerusalem Post*, 7 May 2001.
6. Ibid.

7. *New York Times, Boston Globe*, 9 May 2001.

8. *Boston Globe*, 9 May 2001.

9. *New York Times*, 9 May 2001.

10. *Jerusalem Post*, 9 May 2001.

11. Ibid., 10 May 2001.

12. Ibid., 8 May 2001.

13. Ibid., 22 May 2001.

14. *Boston Globe*, 9 May 2001.

15. Xinhua News Agency, 7 May 2001.

16. *Los Angeles Times*, 10 May 2001; (London) *Times*, 10 May 2001.

17. (Vancouver, WA) *Columbian*, 11 May 2001.

18. *Los Angeles Times*, 10 May 2001.

19. *New York Times*, 11 May 2001.

20. *Irish Times* (Dublin), 8 May 2001.

21. *Guardian* (UK), 11 May 2001.

22. *Irish Times* (Dublin), 7 May 2001.

23. BBC Monitoring, Voice of Israel Radio, 7 May 2001.

24. *New York Times*, 19 May 2001.

25. *Los Angeles Times*, 19 May 2001.

26. *Financial Times*, 21 May 2001.

27. *Chicago Sun-Times*, 21 May 2001.

28. *Houston Chronicle*, 21 May 2001.

29. *Financial Times*, 21 May 2001.

30. *New York Times*, 21 May 2001.

31. *Jerusalem Post*, 21 May 2001.

32. Ibid., 18 May 2001.

CHAPTER 65: "A VERY DELICATE SITUATION"

1. *Jerusalem Post*, 18 May 2001.

2. *Houston Chronicle*, 1 Dec 1998.

3. Mary McGrory, *Washington Post*, 1 Oct 1991.

4. *Los Angeles Times*, 22 May 2001.

5. *Newsday*, 22 May 2001.

6. Ibid.

7. *Seattle Times*, 21 May 2001.

8. *Guardian* (UK), 22 May 2001.

9. *Austin American Statesman*, 20 May 2001.

10. *Seattle Times*, 21 May 2001.

11. *Chicago Sun-Times*, 21 May 2001.

12. *Jerusalem Post*, 24 May 2001.

13. BBC Monitoring, Interfax News Agency, Moscow, 20 May 2001.

14. *Financial Times*, 23 May 2001.

15. *Jerusalem Post*, 23 May 2001.

16. *New York Times*, 23 May 2001.

17. *Financial Times*, 23 May 2001.

CHAPTER 66: GOOD COP BAD COP

1. *Washington Times*, 23 May 2001.

2. *Jerusalem Post*, 24 May 2001.

3. Ibid., 25 May 2001.

4. Ibid.

5. *Guardian* (UK), 3 May 2001; *San Diego Union-Tribune*, 2 May 2001; BBC Monitoring, Voice of Israel Radio, 4 May 2001.

6. *Jerusalem Post*, 4 May 2001.

7. *Newsday*, 4 May 2001.

8. *Los Angeles Times*, 4 May 2001.

9. Ibid.

10. Middle East News Online, 12 Apr 2001.

11. *Jerusalem Post*, 4 May 2001.

12. Ibid.

13. BBC Monitoring, Voice of Israel Radio, 4 May 2001; *Financial Times*, 5 May 2001.

14. *Jerusalem Post*, 9 May 2001.

15. Ibid.

16. (London) *Sunday Times*, 6 May 2001.

17. *Jerusalem Post, Los Angeles Times*, 22 May 2001.

18. (Bergen County, NJ) *Record*, 24 May 2001.

19. *Jerusalem Post*, 22 May 2001.

CHAPTER 67: "HOW MUCH LONGER?"

1. Xinhua News Agency, 25 May 2001; *Jerusalem Post*, 27 May 2001.

2. *Jerusalem Post*, 27 May 2001.

3. *Los Angeles Times*, 20 May 2001.

4. Ibid.

5. *Jerusalem Post*, 31 May 2001.

6. *New York Times*, 31 May 2001.

7. *Jerusalem Post*, 31 May 2001.

8. *San Diego Union-Tribune*, 28 May 2001.

9. *Boston Globe* , 28 May 20001.

10. *Los Angeles Times*, 28 May 2001.

11. *Independent* (UK), 28 May 2001.

12. *San Diego Union-Tribune*, 28 May 2001.

13. *Irish Times* (Dublin), 29 May 2001.

14. *Jerusalem Post*, 1 Jun 2001.

15. Ibid.

16. Ibid.

17. Ibid.

18. Jonathan Rosenblum, "Why Israel is Always Wrong," *Jerusalem Post*, 1 Jul 2001.

CHAPTER 68: THE DOLPHINARIUM

1. *San Diego Union-Tribune*, 2 Jun 2001.

2. *Washington Times*, 3 Jun 2001.

3. *San Diego Union-Tribune*, 2 Jun 2001.

4. *Los Angeles Times*, 2 Jun 2001.

5. Ibid.

6. *Boston Globe*, 2 Jun 2001.

7. (London) *Times*, 4 Jun 2001.

8. *Jerusalem Post*, 3 Jun 2001.

9. *Washington Post*, 3 Jun 2001.

10. Ibid.

11. Ibid.

12. Xinhua News Agency, 3 Jun 2001.

13. (London) *Sunday Times*, 3 Jun 2001.

14. Xinhua News Agency, 3 Jun 2001.

15. *Sunday Telegraph* (London), 3 Jun 2001.

16. *Washington Post*, 3 Jun 2001

17. BBC Monitoring, Voice of Israel Radio, 3 Jun 2001.

18. (London) *Times*, 4 Jun 2001.

19. *Jerusalem Post*, 5 Jun 2001.

20. *Washington Post*, 3 Jun 2001.

21. *New York Times*, 4 Jun 2001.

22. *Jerusalem Post*, 4 Jun 2001.

CHAPTER 69: STRAINED RESTRAINT

1. *Jerusalem Post*, 5 Jun 2001.

2. Middle East News Online, 7 Jun 2001.

3. *Los Angeles Times*, 6 Jun 2001.

4. *Washington Times*, 12 Jun 2001.

5. *Jerusalem Post*, 7 Jun 2001.

6. (Bergen County, NJ) *Record*, 7 Jun 2001.

7. Ibid., 8 Jun 2001.

8. *Financial Times*, 8 Jun 2001.

9. Middle East News Online, 8 Jun 2001.

10. (Bergen County, NJ) *Record*, 12 Jun 2001.

11. Middle East News Online, 8 Jun 2001.

12. BBC Monitoring, Voice of Israel Radio, 11 Jun 2001.

13. *Washington Times*, 12 Jun 2001.

14. Ibid.

15. BBC Monitoring, Voice of Israel Radio, 11 Jun 2001.

16. *Washington Times*, 12 Jun 2001.

17. *Los Angeles Times*, 13 Jun 2001.

18. *Washington Times*, 13 Jun 2001.

19. Middle East News Online, 14 Jun 2001.

20. *Washington Times*, 13 Jun 2001.

21. Ibid.

22. Ibid.

23. *Daily Telegraph* (London), 13 Jun 2001.

24. *Los Angeles Times*, 13 Jun 2001.

25. Ibid.

26. *Jerusalem Post*, 14 Jun 2001.

27. (Bergen County, NJ) *Record*, 12 Jun 2001.

28. *Irish Times* (Dublin), 12 Jun 2001.

29. *Jerusalem Post*, 14 Jun 2001.

CHAPTER 70: SABRA & SHATILLA AGAIN: BELGIUM AND THE BBC

1. *Washington Post*, 25 Jun 2001.

2. *Jerusalem Post*, 20 Jun 2001.

3. Ibid.

4. *Independent* (UK), 18 Jun 2001.

5. *Washington Post*, 25 Jun 2001.

6. *Jerusalem Post*, 15 Jun 2001.

7. *Wall Street Journal*, 25 Jun 2001.

8. *Jerusalem Post*, 15 Jun 2001.

9. BBC Monitoring, *La Stampa* website, Turin, 22 Jun 2001.

10. *Washington Post*, 25 Jun 2001; *Jerusalem Post*, 16 Jul 2001.

11. *Jerusalem Post*, 22 Jun 2001.

12. Ibid.

13. Ibid.

14. *Washington Post* Foreign Service, 25 Jun 2001.

15. *Irish Times* (Dublin), 19 Jun 2001.

16. *Financial Times*, 18 Jun 2001.

17. *Jerusalem Post*, 20 Jun 2001.

18. *Irish Times* (Dublin), 17 Jul 2001.

19. *Jerusalem Post,* 13 Jul 2001.

20. Ibid., 15 Jun 2001.

21. BBC Monitoring, *De Standaard* website, Groot-Biggaarden, 27 Jun 2001.

22. BBC Monitoring, Voice of Israel Radio, 5 Jul 2001; *Jerusalem Post*, 6 Jul 2001.

23. *Christian Science Monitor*, 30 Jul 2001.

24. *Jerusalem Post*, 11 Jul 2001.

25. *Washington Post*, 29 Jul 2001.

26. Ibid.

27. *Jerusalem Post*, 27 Jul 2001.

28. *Financial Times*, 27 Jul 2001.

29. *Washington Post*, 29 Jul 2001.

30. Middle East New Online, 20 Jul 2001.

31. *Guardian* (UK), 25 Jan 2002.

32. *Jerusalem Report*, 24 Sep 2001.

33. BBC News, 28 Nov 2001; *Israel Insider*, 28 Nov 2001.

34. *Guardian* (UK), 15 Feb 2002.

CHAPTER 71: CHANGE OF IMAGE?

1. *Jerusalem Post*, 15 Jun 2001.
2. *Christian Science Monitor*, 22 Jun 2001.
3. Ibid.
4. Ibid.
5. *Daily Telegraph* (London), 25 Jun 2001.
6. Ibid.
7. (London) *Times*, 25 Jun 2001.
8. *Washington Times*, 13 Jun 2001.
9. Herb Keinon, *Jerusalem Post*, 15 Jun 2001.
10. Ibid., Janine Zacharia.
11. Middle East News Online; *Irish Times* (Dublin), 18 Jun 2001.
12. *Financial Times*, 18 Jun 2001.
13. *Jerusalem Post*, 19 Jun 2001.
14. *Washington Post* , 19 Jun 2001.
15. *Los Angeles Times*, 19 Jun 2001.
16. Middle East News Online, 18 Jun 2001.
17. *Washington Times*, 27 Jun 2001.
18 *Jerusalem Post*, 27 Jun 2001.
19. Ibid., 4 Jul 2001.

CHAPTER 72: A RISING TIDE

1. BBC Monitoring, Voice of Israel Radio, 23 Jul 2001.
2. *St. Louis Post-Dispatch*, 21 Jul 2001.
3. (Ft. Wayne, IN) *Journal-Gazette*, 13 Jul 2001.
4. *Financial Times, Jerusalem Post, Irish Times* (Dublin), 17 Jul 2001.
5. *USA Today*, 20 Jul 2001.
6. *Irish Times* (Dublin), 5 Jul 2001.
7. Ibid.

8. BBC Monitoring, *Der Spiegel*, Hamburg, 30 Jul 2001.
9. Ibid.
10. Australian DateLine, 8 Aug 2001.
11. *Daily Telegraph* (London), 9 Aug 2001.
12. *Newsday*, 25 Jul 2001.
13. (Baltimore) *Sun*; *New York Times*; *Jerusalem Post*; (London) *Times*, 30 Jul 2001.
14. Ibid.
15. Ibid.

CHAPTER 73: THE SILENCE OF DEATH

1. (London) *Mirror*, 10 Aug 2001.
2. *Los Angeles Times*, 10 Aug 2001.
3. *Washington Post*, 10 Aug 2001.
4. (London) *Times*, 10 Aug 2001.
5. *Daily Telegraph* (London), 10 Aug 2001.
6. (London) *Times* 11 Aug 2001.
7. Ibid.
8. *Daily Telegraph* (London), 11 Aug 2001.
9. *Washington Post*, 12 Aug 2001.
10. (Baltimore) *Sun*, 13 Aug 2001.
11. *Financial Times*, 13 Aug 2001.
12. (Baltimore) *Sun*, 13 Aug 2001.
13. *Los Angeles Times*, 13 Aug 2001.
14. *Irish Times* (Dublin), 14 Aug 2001.
15. *Jerusalem Post*, 15 Aug 2001.
16. Ibid.
17. Ibid.
18. Ibid.
19. *Los Angeles Times*, 12 Aug 2001.
20. Ibid.
21. Ibid.
22. *Financial Times*, 15 Aug 2001.

23. Ibid.

24. BBC Monitoring, MENA News Agency, Cairo, 18 Jul 2001.

25. *Jerusalem Post*, 20 Jul 2001.

26. *Financial Times*, 15 Aug 2001.

27. *Jerusalem Post*, 7 Aug 2001.

CHAPTER 74: DURBAN & MOSCOW

1. *New York Post*, 4 Sep 2001.

2. Ibid.

3. Middle East News Online, 4 Sep 2001.

4. *New York Post*, 4 Sep 2001.

5. Middle East News Online, 4 Sep 2001.

6. Ibid.

7. *Seattle Times*, 5 Sep 2001.

8. *Financial Times*, 5 Sep 2001.

9. *Irish Times* (Dublin), 5 Sep 2001.

10 *Seattle Times*, 5 Sep 2001.

11. *Jerusalem Post*, 3 Sep 2001; *Guardian* (UK), 4 Sep 2001; *Los Angeles Times*, 5 Sep 2001.

12. *Irish Times* (Dublin), 6 Sep 2001.

13. Ibid.

14. *Los Angeles Times*, 5 Sep 2001.

15. *Financial Times*, 5 Sep 2001.

16. Itar-Tass News Wire, 4 Sep 2001.

17. *Los Angeles Times*, 5 Sep 2001.

18. Middle East News Online, 4 Sep 2001.

19. *Financial Times*, 5 Sep 2001.

20. Itar-Tass News wire, 6 Sep 2001.

21. BBC Monitoring, Interfax News Agency, Moscow, 6 Sep 2001.

22. Ibid.

23. Ibid.

24. *Washington Post*, *Guardian* (UK), *Jerusalem Post*, 10 Sep 2001.

25. BBC Monitoring, Israel TV Channels 1 & 2, 5 Sep 2001.

26. BBC Monitoring, 6 Sep 2001.

27. BBC Monitoring, Israel TV Channel 2, 6 Sep 2001.

28. *Daily Telegraph* (London), 7 Sep 2001.

29 *Irish Times* (Dublin), 7 Sep 2001.

30. *Jerusalem Post*, 9 Sep 2001.

31. *New York Times*, 9 Sep 2001.

CHAPTER 75: DAY OF MOURNING

1. *Jerusalem Post*, 12 Sep 2001.

2. *Boston Globe*, 12 Sep 2001.

3. Ibid.

4. *Newsday*, 14 Sep 2001.

5. *USA Today*, 14 Sep 2001.

6. Ibid.

7. *Irish Times* (Dublin), 15 Sep 2001.

8. *New York Times*, 15 Sep 2001.

9. *Washington Post*, 15 Sep 2001.

10. *Jerusalem Post*, 16 Sep 2001.

11. Ibid.

12, *Financial Times*, 15 Sep 2001.

13. *New York Times*, 19 Sep 2001.

14. Ibid.

15. CNN, 19 Sep 2001.

16. *New York Times*, 16 Sep 2001.

17. *Daily Telegraph* (London), 19 Sep 2001.

18. *Guardian* (UK), 19 Sep 2001.

CHAPTER 76: A STRAW IN THE WIND

1. *Jerusalem Post*, 23 Sep 2001.

2. Ibid.

3. *Guardian* (UK), 26 Sep 2001.

4. *Independent* (UK), 25 Sep 2001.

5. *Jerusalem Post*, 25 Sep 2001.

6. Ibid.

7. Ibid.
8. *Evening Standard* (London), 25 Sep 2001.
9. *Liverpool Echo*, 25 Sep 2001.
10. *Guardian* (UK), 26 Sep 2001.
11. Ibid.
12. *Sunday Telegraph* (London), 30 Sep 2001.
13. Ibid.
14. *Jerusalem Post*, 26 Sep 2001.
15. *Guardian* (UK), 26 Sep 2001.
16. *Daily Telegraph* (London), 29 Sep 2001.
17. Ibid., 30 Sep 2001.
18. Ibid., 2 Oct 2001.

CHAPTER 77: OCTOBER UPROAR
1. *Daily Telegraph* (London), 1 Oct 2001.
2. *Irish Times* (Dublin), 2 Oct 2001.
3. Ibid.
4. *Jerusalem Post*, 1 Oct 2001.
5. Ibid.
6. Ibid.
7. *New York Times*, 2 Oct 2001.
8. *Los Angeles Times*, 3 Oct 2001.
9. *New York Times*, 2 Oct 2001.
10. Ibid., 3 Oct 2001.
11. *Independent* (UK), 4 Oct 2001.
12. *New York Times*, 3 Oct 2001.
13. *South China Morning Post*, 4 Oct 2001.
14. Ibid.
15. (Baltimore) *Sun*, 4 Oct 2001.
16. Ibid.
17. *Los Angeles Times*, 5 Oct 2001.
18. *New York Times*, 5 Oct 2001.
19. *Boston Globe*, 6 Oct 2001.
20. *New York Times*, 6 Oct 2001.

21. *Chicago Sun-Times*, 6 Oct 2001.
22. *Los Angeles Times*, 7 Oct 2001.
23. *Washington Post*, 7 Oct 2001.
24. *New York Times*, 6 Oct 2001.
25. *Boston Globe*, 6 Oct 2001.
26. *New York Times*, 19 Sep 2001.
27. Ibid., 8 Oct 2001.
28. Ibid.
29. *Los Angeles Times*, 11 Oct 2001.
30. *Jerusalem Post*, 11 Oct 2001.
31. *Los Angeles Times*, 11 Oct 2001.

CHAPTER 78: ZEEVI
1. *Irish Times* (Dublin), 16 Oct 2001.
2. Xinhua News Agency, 15 Oct 2001.
3. *Irish Times* (Dublin), 16 Oct 2001.
4. *New York Times*, 16 Oct 2001.
5. Ibid., 18 Oct 2001.
6. *Financial Times*, 18 Oct 2001.
7. *New York Times*, 18 Oct 2001.
8. Ibid.
9. *Washington Post*, 19 Oct 2001.
10. *Birmingham Post* (UK), 19 Oct 2001.
11. *Los Angeles Times*, 18 Oct 2001.
12. Ibid.
13. *Jerusalem Post*, 18 Oct 2001.
14. *Washington Post*, 18 Oct 2001.
15. *Los Angeles Times* 18 Oct 2001.
16. Ibid.
17. Ibid.
18. *Washington Post*, 19 Oct 2001.
19. (London) *Times*, 19 Oct 2001.
20. *New York Times*, 18 Oct 2001.
21. *Los Angeles Times*, 18 Oct 2001.
22. *Washington Post*, 19 Oct 2001.
23. *Irish Times* (Dublin), 19 Oct 2001.
24. (London) *Times*, 19 Oct 2001.
25. *Newsweek*, 29 Oct 2001.

26. *Los Angeles Times*, 23 Oct 2001.
27. *Statesman* (India), 24 Nov 2001.
28. *Jerusalem Post*, 30 Nov 2001.
29. Ibid., 22 Nov 2001.
30. Ibid., 21 Nov 2001.
31. Ibid., 22 Nov 2001.
32. BBC Monitoring, 18 Nov 2001.
33. *Jerusalem Post*, 20 Nov 2001.

CHAPTER 79: ZINNI'S DAYS
1. *Jerusalem Post*, 29 Nov 2001.
2. *Chicago Sun-Times*, 30 Nov 2001.
3. *Los Angeles Times*, 28 Nov 2001.
4. (London) *Times*, 30 Nov 2001.
5. (Montreal) *Gazette*, 28 Nov 2001.
6. *Independent* (UK), 3 Dec 2001.
7. *Newsday*, 2 Dec 2001.
8. *Independent* (UK) 2 Dec 2001.
9. *Newsday*, 2 Dec 2001.
10. *Boston Globe*, 2 Dec 2001.
11. *Newsday*, 2 Dec 2001.
12. *Daily Record* (Glasgow), 3 Dec 2001.
13. *Chicago Sun-Times*, 2 Dec 2001.
14. *Christian Science Monitor*, 4 Dec 2001.
15. *Independent* (UK), 3 Dec 2001.
16. *Daily Record* (Glasgow), 3 Dec 2001.
17. *Chicago Sun-Times*, 3 Dec 2001.
18. (London) *Times*, 3 Dec 2001.
19. *New York Times*, 3 Dec 2001.
20. *St. Louis Post-Dispatch*, 2 Dec 2001.
21. *Dallas Morning News*, 6 Dec 2001.
22. *New York Times*, 4 Dec 2001.
23. Ibid.
24. Itar-Tass News Wire, New York, 13 Dec 2001.

25. Middle East News Online, 5 Dec 2001.
26. *Irish Times* (Dublin), 3 Dec 2001.
27. (London) *Times*, 4 Dec 2001.
28. *Los Angeles Times*, 4 Dec 2001.
29. *Jerusalem Post*, 5 Dec 2001.
30. *Evening Standard* (London), 4 Dec 2001.
31. *Jerusalem Post*, 6 Dec 2001.
32. BBC Monitoring, 17 Jan 2002.
33. *Jerusalem Post*, 4 Dec 2001.

CHAPTER 80: THE PRISONER OF RAMALLAH
1. (London) *Times*, 5 Dec 2001.
2. Ibid., 6 Dec 2001.
3. (Memphis, TN) *Commercial Appeal*, 9 Dec 2001.
4. *Irish Times* (Dublin), 10 Dec 2001.
5. *Seattle Times*, 8 Dec 2001.
6. *Los Angeles Times*, 6 Dec 2001.
7. *New York Daily News*, 6 Dec 2001.
8. *Austin American Statesman*, 12 Dec 2001.
9. *Boston Globe*, 7 Dec 2001.
10. Ibid.
11. *Pittsburgh Post-Gazette*, 5 Dec 2001.
12. *Houston Chronicle*, 8 Dec 2001.
13. *Seattle Times*, 20 Dec 2001.
14. *Pittsburgh Post-Gazette*, 5 Dec 2001.
15. *Jerusalem Post*, 24 Sep 2001.
16. *Daily Telegraph* (London), 7 Dec 2001.
17. Joel Mowbray, "Arafat Elected? The Sharon 1996 Vote," *National Review*, April 2002.

CHAPTER 81: "A FACTORY OF LIES":
THE *KARINE A*
1. *New York Times*, 13 Dec 2001.
2. *Washington Times*, 15 Dec 2001.
3. *Newsday*, 15 Dec 2001.
4. *Washington Post*, 17 Dec 2001.
5. *New York Times*, 16 Dec 2001.
6. Ibid., 14 Dec 2001.
7. Moshe Asnevan, "The Myth of Israeli Sovereignty," *Jerusalem Post*, 18 Dec 2001.
8. *Daily Telegraph*, 27 Dec 2001.
9. *Boston Globe*, 30 Dec 2001.
10. *Chicago Tribune*, 8 Jan 2002.
11. *London Times*, 7 Jan 2002.
12. *Chicago Tribune*, 14 Jan 2002.
13. *Jerusalem Post*, 8 Jan 2002.
14. *Irish Times* (Dublin), 9 Jan 2002.
15. *Chicago Tribune*, 13 Jan 2002.
16. *New York Times International*, 12 & 13 Jan 2002.
17. *New York Daily News*, 9 Jan 2002.
18. *Wall Street Journal*, 11 Jan 2002.
19. *Chicago Tribune*, 14 Jan 2002.
20. *New York Times*, 24 Mar 2002.

CHAPTER 82: FITS & STARTS
1. *New York Times*, 4 Feb 2002.
2. *Chicago Tribune*, 2 Feb 2002.
3. *New York Times*, 10 Feb 2002.
4. Ibid., 4 Feb 2002.
5. Ibid., 2 Feb 2002.
6. Ibid.
7. *New York Times*, 8 Feb 2002.
8. Ibid., 11 & 12 Feb 2001.
9. *Chicago Tribune*, 11 Feb 2002.
10. Ibid., 15 Feb 2002.
11. *New York Times*, 11 Feb 2002.
12. Ibid., 25 Apr 2002.

13. Ibid., 15 Apr 2002.
14. Ibid., 19 Mar 2002.
15. *Wall Street Journal*, 28 Mar 2002.
16. Ibid., 29 Mar 2002.
17. Ibid., 27 Mar 2002.

CHAPTER 83: RECONSIDERED STRATEGY
1. *New York Times*, 1 Apr 2002.
2. Ibid., 28 Mar 2002.
3. *Washington Post*, 28 Mar 2002.
4. *Chicago Tribune*, 1 May 2002.
5. *New York Times*, 29 Mar 2002.
6. Ibid.
7. Ibid., 31 Mar 2002.
8. *Chicago Tribune*, 4 Apr 2002.
9. *New York Times*, 29 Mar 2002.
10. Ibid., 3 Apr 2002.
11. Ibid.
12. *Chicago Tribune*, 2 Apr 2002.
13. *New York Times*, 30 Mar 2002.
14. Ibid., 29 Mar 2002.
15. Ibid., 4 Apr 2002.
16. Ibid., 6 Apr 2002.
17. Ibid., 7 Apr 2002.

CHAPTER 84: REVERSAL OF FORTUNE
1. *New York Times*, 19 Apr 2002.
2. Ibid., 20 Apr 2002.
3. Ibid., 19 Apr 2002.
4. Ibid., 21 Apr 2002.
5. Ibid., 25 Apr 2002.
6. *New Republic*, 6 May 2000.
7. *New York Times*, 15 Apr 2002.
8. *Wall Street Journal*, 29 Apr 2002.
9. *Jerusalem Post*, 12 May 2002.
10. Ibid.
11. Martin Indyk, "3 Faces of Sharon: A Man Alone," *Washington Post*, 17 Mar 2002.
12. *Washington Post,* 23 Mar 2002.

WORKS CONSULTED

BOOKS

Adler, Renata. *Reckless Disregard: Westmoreland v CBS et al; Sharon v Time.* New York: Alfred A. Knopf, 1986.

Arian, Asher. *Politics in Israel: The Second Generation,* revised edition. Chatham, NJ: Chatham House Publishers, 1989.

Avneri, Arieh. *War of Attrition.* Tel Aviv: Olive Books of Israel, 1970.

———. *Sabra Commandos.* Tel Aviv: Olive Books of Israel, 1972.

Benziman, Uzi. *Sharon: An Israeli Caesar.* New York: Adama Books, 1983.

Dayan, Moshe. *Story of My Life: An Autobiography.* New York: Warner Books, paperback, 1977.

Elon, Amos. *The Israelis.* London: Weidenfeld and Nicolson, 1971.

———. *The Defeat: The Fall of the Likud Government.* Tel Aviv: Midot Publishing, 1993.

Friedman, Thomas L. *From Beirut to Jerusalem.* New York: Farrar Straus Giroux, 1989.

Gilbert, Martin. *Israel: A History.* New York: William Morrow, 1998.

Golan, Matti. *Shimon Peres, A Biography.* London: Weidenfeld and Nicolson, 1982.

———. *The Secret Conversations of Henry Kissinger.* Chicago: Quadrangle Books, 1976.

Gorenberg, Gershom. *The End of Days: Fundamentalism and the Struggle for the Temple Mount.* New York: The Free Press, 2000.

Halevi, Yossi Klein. *At the Entrance to the Garden of Eden: A Jew's Search for God With Christians and Muslims in the Holy Land.* New York: William Morrow, 2001

Herzog, Chaim. *Living History: A Memoir.* New York: Pantheon Books, 1996.

Hohenberg, John. *Israel at 50: A Journalist's Perspective.* Syracuse: Syracuse University Press, 1998.

Horovitz, David. *A Little Too Close to God: The Thrills and Panic of a Life in Israel.* New York: Alfred A. Knopf, 2000.

Kimke, David. *The Last Option, After Nasser, Arafat and Saddam Hussein: The Quest for Peace in the Middle East*. Tel Aviv: Edanim Publishers (Yediot Aharonoth), 1992.

Leach, Ann Mosley and Mark Tessler. *Israel, Egypt and the Palestinians: From Camp David to Intifada*. Bloomington: Indiana University Press, 1989.

Morris, Benny. *Righteous Victims: A History of the Zionist-Arab Conflict, 1881-2001*. New York: Vintage Books, paperback, 2001.

Nakdimon, Shlomo. *Low Probability: A Narrative of the Dramatic Story Preceding the Yom Kippur War and the Fateful Events Which Followed*. Tel Aviv: Revivim Publishing House, *Yediot Aharonoth* edition, 1982.

Oren, Michael B. *Six days of War: June 1967 and the Making of the Modern Middle East*. New York: Oxford University Press, 2002.

Oren, Ram. *Latrun*. Tel Aviv: Keshet Publishing, 2002.

Peled, Alisa Rubin. *Debating Islam in the Jewish State: The Development of Policy Toward Islamic Institutions in Israel*. Albany: SUNY Press, 2001.

Richards, Alan and John Waterbury. *A Political Economy of the Middle East: State, Class and Economic Development*. Boulder: Westview Press, 1990.

Sela, Avraham. *Political Encyclopedia of the Middle East*. Jerusalem: The Jerusalem Publishing House Ltd, 1999.

Sharon, Ariel with David Chanoff. *Warrior: The Autobiography of Ariel Sharon*. New York: Simon & Schuster, 1989.

Shavitt, Matti. *On the Wings of Eagles: The Story of Ariel Sharon, Commander of the Israeli Paratroopers*. Tel Aviv: Olive Books of Israel, 1970.

Shehadeh, Raja. *Strangers in the House: Coming of Age in Occupied Palestine*. South Royalton, VT: Steerforth Press, 2002.

Smith, Anthony D. *Nationalism in the Twentieth Century*. New York: New York University Press, 1979.

Tessler, Mark. *A History of the Israeli-Palestine Conflict*. Bloomington: Indiana University Press, 1994.

Van Creveld, Martin. *The Sword and the Olive: A Critical History of the Israeli Defense Force*. New York: Public Affairs, 1998.

Viorst, Milton. *In the Shadow of the Prophet*. Boulder: Westview Press, 2001.

Wallach, Janet and John Wallach. *Arafat: In the Eyes of the Beholder*. New York: Carol Publishing, 1990.

NEWSPAPERS, PERIODICALS, ELECTRONIC SOURCES

ABIX (Australian Business Intelligence)
AFP News Agency, Paris (BBC
   Monitoring—BBCM)
Afghan News
Agence France-Presse
Al-Ahram Weekly
(Albany, NY) *Times Union*
Al-Bilad, Amman (BBCME)
Al-Dustur, Amman (BBCME)
Al Jazeera TV, Doha (BBCME)
Al Majd, Amman (BBCM)
Al Manar, Jordan (Middle East News
   Online—MENO)
   (www.middleeastnews.com)
Al Quds Website, Jerusalem (BBCME)
Al-Sharq, Al-Awsat, London (BBCM)
Anatolia News Agency, Ankara
   (BBCME)
ANSA News Agency, Rome (BBC
   Monitoring Middle East—BBCME)
Arutz 7 Radio
Association of State Green Parties
   (MENO)
Atlanta Journal-Constitution
Atlantic Monthly
(Augusta, GA) *Chronicle*
Austin American Statesman
Australian
BADIL—Resource Center for Palestin-
   ian Residency & Refugee Rights
   (www.badil.org/)
(Baltimore) *Sun*
BBC Monitoring
   (www.bbcmonitoring.com)
(Bergen County, NJ) *Evening Record*

Birmingham Post (UK)
(Bloomington, IL) *Pantagraph*
Boston Globe
Buffalo News
Cairo Press Review
   (www.sis.gov.eg/front.htm)
Canadian Jewish Review
Centre for Policy Analysis on Palestine
   (www.palestinecenter.org)
Chicago Sun-Times
Chicago Tribune
China Daily, New York
Christian Century
Christian Science Monitor
Cincinnati Post
Cleveland Plain Dealer
Commentary
Daily Mail (UK)
Daily Record (Glasgow)
Daily Telegraph (UK)
DDP News Agency, Berlin (BBCME)
Debka-Net-Weekly (www.debka.com)
Denver Post
Der Spiegel (Hamburg)
Detroit News
Dissent
Economist
Edmonton Journal (Canada)
Emirates News Agency (MENO)
Evening Standard (UK)
Financial Times
(Ft. Lauderdale) *South Florida
   Sun-Sentinel*
(Ft. Wayne, IN) *Journal-Gazette*
France 2 TV, Paris (BBCM)

Frankfurter Allgemeine
(Gary, IN) *Post-Tribune*
(Glasgow) *Herald*
(Grand Rapids, MI) *Press*
Guardian (UK)
Haaretz
(Harrisburg, PA) *Patriot-News*
Houston Chronicle
IDF Radio, Tel Aviv (BBCM)
Independent (UK)
Indian Express
Interfax News Agency, Moscow
    (BBCME)
International Herald Tribune
Iran News (MENO)
Iranian
Irish Times (Dublin)
Islamic Association for Palestine
    (MENO)
Israel Educational TV
Israel TV, Channel 1
Israel TV, Channel 2
Israeli Government Website
    (www.israel.org./mfa/home.asp)
Israeli Insider
Israeli Parliament Website
    (www.knesset.gov.il/index/html)
Isvestia, Moscow (BBCM former
    Soviet Union)
Itar-Tass News Wire, New York
Jaffee Center for Strategic Studies, Tel
    Aviv University (www.tau.ac.il/jcss)
Jane's Defense
Jerusalem Post
Jordan Times, Amman (MENO)
Journal of Palestine Studies
Knight Ridder/Tribune Business News,
    Washington, DC

Kuwait Times (MENO)
La Stampa
Lebanese Center for Policy Studies
    (www.lcps-lebanon.org/)
Liverpool Echo (UK)
(London) *Times*
(Los Angeles) *Daily News*
Los Angeles Times
Maariv
Manar Television, Beirut (BBCME)
Mauritanian TV, Novakchott
    (BBCME)
(Memphis, TN) *Commercial Appeal*
MENA News Agency, Cairo (BBCM)
Middle East News Online
    (Durham, NC)
*Middle East Review of
    International Affairs*
Milwaukee Journal Sentinel
(Minneapolis) *Star Tribune*
Mirror (UK)
(Montreal) *Gazette*
Nation
National Defense University
    (McNair Paper #45)
National Post
National Review
New Republic
New York Daily News
New York Post
New York Times
Newsday
Newsweek
Observer (UK)
Orlando Sentinel
Palestine National Authority
    (www.pna.org/)

Palestinian News Agency, Wafa
  Website, Gaza (BBCME)
Palestine Society for the Protection
  of Human Rights and the
  Environment (www.lawsociety.org)
Palm Beach Post
Pittsburgh Post-Gazette
(Portland) Oregonian
Radio Free Europe/Radio Liberty
Radio Lebanon, Beirut (BBCM)
Richmond Times-Dispatch
Rompres Website, Bucharest (BBCME)
RTBF Radio 1, Brussels (BBC)
St. Louis Post-Dispatch
St. Petersburg Times
Salon
San Diego Union-Tribune
San Francisco Chronicle
(Santa Ana, CA) Orange County
  Register
Scotsman (UK)
Seattle Times
South China Morning Post,
  Hong Kong
Statesman (India)
Sunday Telegraph (UK)
Sunday Times (UK)
Syria Times (MENO)
Tehran Times (MENO)
Tel Aviv Magazine
Time
Times of India
Tishrin, Damascus (BBCME)
Tulsa World
US News and World Report
US Newswire, Washington, DC
USA Today

University of Texas Middle
  East Archives
  (www.link.lanic.utexas.edu/menic)
(Vancouver, WA) Columbian
Village Voice
Voice of America News (MENO)
Voice of Israel Radio (BBCME)
Voice of the Islamic Republic of Iran,
  Tehran (BBCME)
Voice of Palestine Radio,
  Ramallah (BBCM)
Wall Street Journal
Washington Institute for Near East
  Policy(www.washingtoninstitute.org)
Washington Post
Washington Times
Xinhua News Agency
Yediot Aharonoth
Yemen Times Website, Sanaa (BBCME)

INDEX

———

MAPS

LIST OF MAPS

———

Palestine
Pre-1947 Borders

1

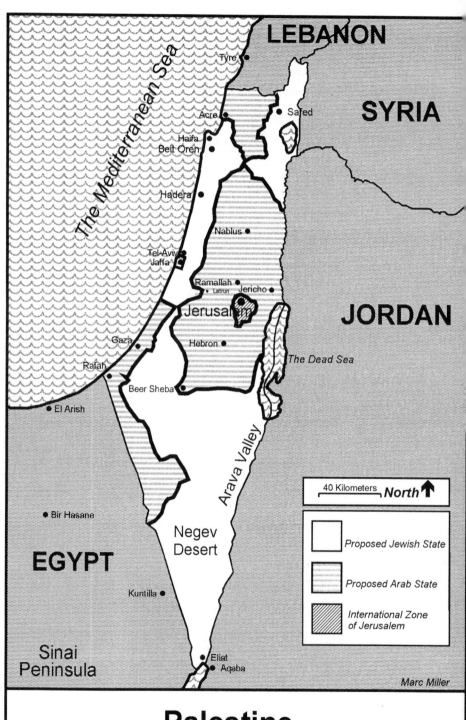

Palestine
United Nations Partition Plan 1947

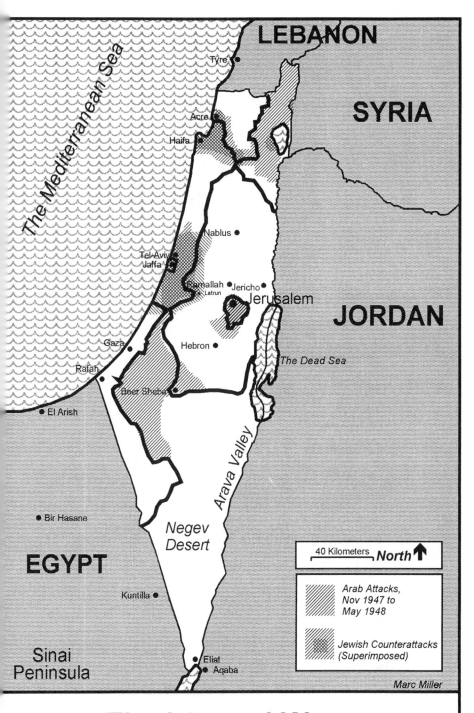

The Internal War
November 1947 to May 1948

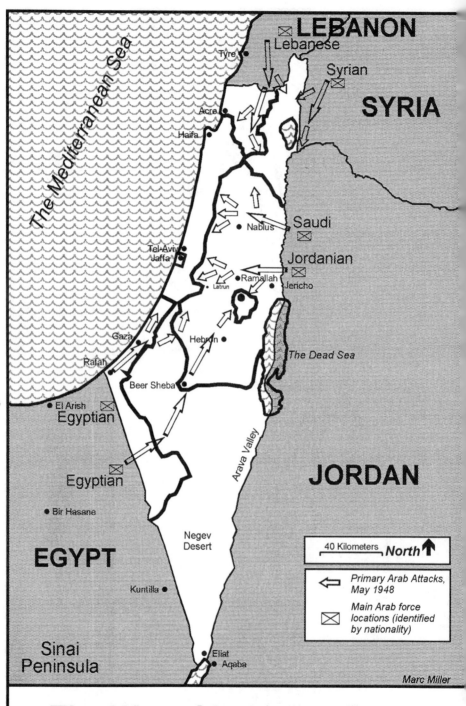

The War of Independence
May and June 1948

4

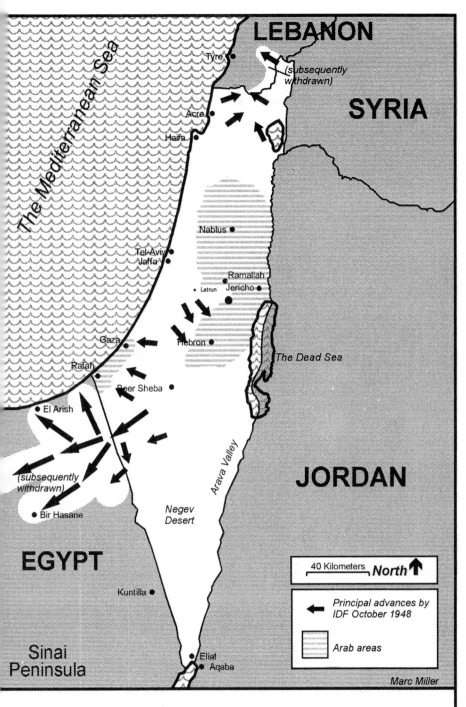

The War of Independence
June to October 1948

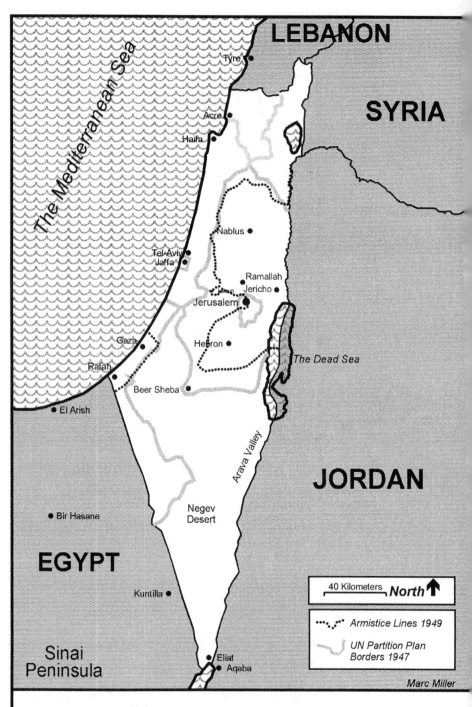

The War of Independence
Armistice Lines 1949

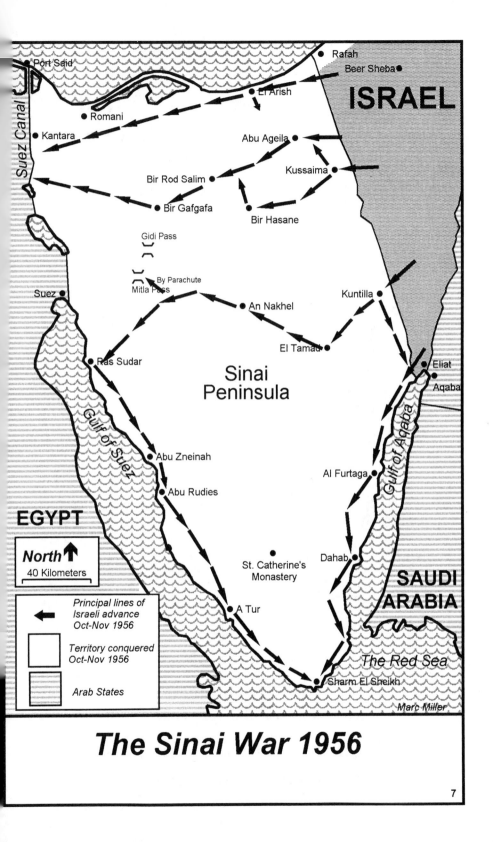

The Sinai War 1956

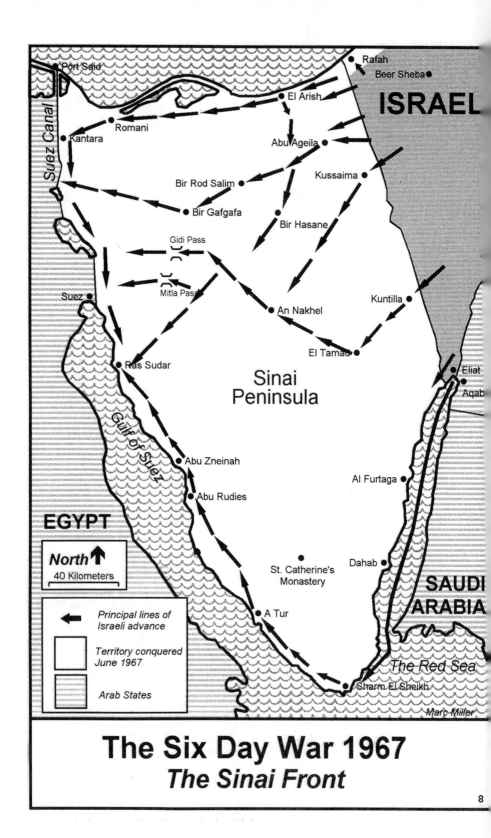

The Six Day War 1967
The Sinai Front

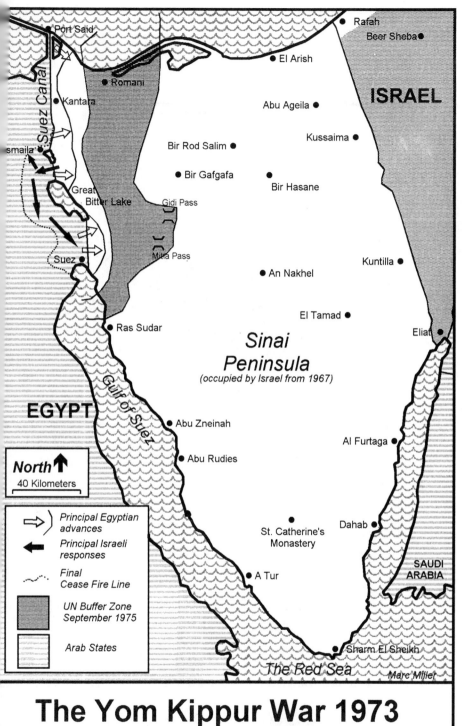

The Yom Kippur War 1973
The Sinai Front

Port Said
Rafah
Beer Sheba
El Arish
Romani
ISRAEL
Kantara
Abu Ageila
Kussaima
Bir Rod Salim
Suez Canal
smaila
Bir Gafgafa
Bir Hasane
Great Bitter Lake
Gidi Pass
Mitla Pass
Kuntilla
An Nakhel
Suez
El Tamad
Eliat
Ras Sudar

Sinai Peninsula
(occupied by Israel from 1967)

Gulf of Suez
EGYPT
Abu Zneinah
Al Furtaga
Abu Rudies

North ↑
40 Kilometers

⇒) *Principal Egyptian advances*
← *Principal Israeli responses*
......·. *Final Cease Fire Line*
■ *UN Buffer Zone September 1975*
□ *Arab States*

Dahab
St. Catherine's Monastery
SAUDI ARABIA
A Tur
Sharm El Sheikh
The Red Sea
Marc Millet

9

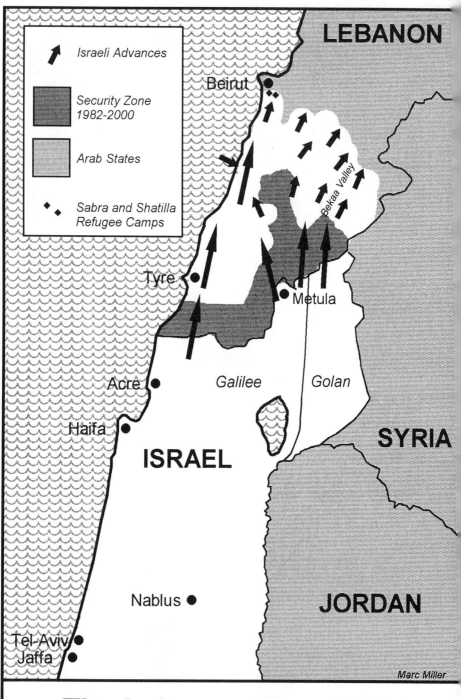

The Lebanon War 1982
IDF Operations

10

Oslo I - Jericho and Gaza
Agreement of May 4, 1994

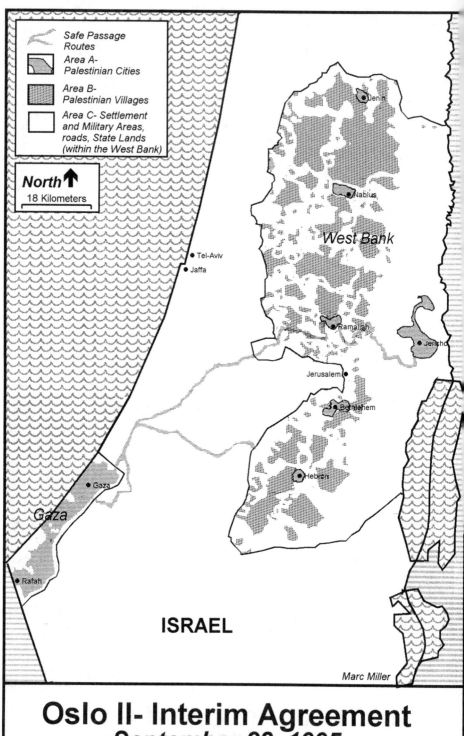

Oslo II- Interim Agreement
September 28, 1995

ACKNOWLEDGMENTS

———

First and foremost, thanks to Sarah Olson for her indispensable contributions to the design and production of this work. Sarah's participation has been invaluable.

Thanks also to Susan Phillips and Stephanie Kitchen for their comprehensive internet research, and to Carolyn Sperry, Joan Andreski and Andrew Yankech for their conscientious proofreading of the manuscript.

Mark Crispin Miller provided invaluable assistance and advice.

The authors are indebted to Josseph Zetouni for the book's concept, intitiative and early content. We should also like to acknowledge the assistance of Pam Berns, Nechama Duek, Nini Fine, Marc Miller, Joshua Neustein, Neta Rotman, Wendy Shafir, Dekel Yarchi, the Zetounis—Noam, Adi, Orit, Yael, Dror, Ron, Leah—and Yael Zilberstein.